EVERYMAN'S LIBRARY

EVERYMAN,
I WILL GO WITH THEE,
AND BE THY GUIDE,
IN THY MOST NEED
TO GO BY THY SIDE

GEORGE HERBERT

*The Complete
English Works*

Edited and introduced by
Ann Pasternak Slater

EVERYMAN'S LIBRARY

*204*

This book is one of 250 volumes in Everyman's Library
which have been distributed to 4500 state schools
throughout the United Kingdom.
The project has been supported by a grant of £4 million
from the Millennium Commission.

The poems of George Herbert first published in Everyman's Library,
1908, re-edited 1974.
New edition © David Campbell Publishers Ltd., 1995
Introduction, Bibliography and Chronology © David Campbell
Publishers Ltd., 1995
Typography by Peter B. Willberg

ISBN 1-85715-204-2

A CIP catalogue record for this book is available from the
British Library

Published by David Campbell Publishers Ltd.,
Gloucester Mansions, 140A Shaftesbury Avenue,
London WC2H 8HD

Distributed by Random House (UK) Ltd.,
20 Vauxhall Bridge Road, London SW1V 2SA

# GEORGE HERBERT

# CONTENTS

# GEORGE HERBERT

# INTRODUCTION

In his *Brief Lives*, the arch-gossip John Aubrey tells us that Herbert married a kinswoman of his, who was 'a handsome *bona roba* and ingeniose'. It is an enigmatic eulogy; the precise implications of Aubrey's favourite adjective, 'ingeniose', have never been definitively determined. Ingenuity is, however, the major key to Herbert's work. It is neatly illustrated by Aubrey's description of the church at Bemerton, where Herbert ended his life as a modest country parson:

In the Chancel are many apt sentences of the Scripture. At his Wife's Seat, *My Life is hid with Christ in God* (he hath verses on this text in his poems). Above, in a little window-blinded, with a Veil (ill painted) *Thou art my hiding place*.[1]

It is typical of Herbert's quiet economy of wit that he should utilize a flaw in the church's architecture, laying a treasure-hunt of significance from the text at his wife's seat to the bricked-up window above it. There are three stages: the text itself ('My life is hid with Christ in God'); a simpler text ('Thou art my hiding place') illustrated by the bricked-up window; and finally the simpler text explained by the picture of a veil for his less literate parishioners. James Joyce had a similar appetite for the apposite, and kept a picture of Cork in a cork frame.

Aubrey's disdain for the clumsily painted veil recurs when he dismisses Bemerton as 'a pitiful little chapel of ease'. It is only mollified by his last words: ' 'Tis an honour to the place, to have had the heavenly and ingeniose contemplation of this good man.' In fact, Bemerton was given a high gloss by Herbert, who both restored its physical structure and conferred intricate meaning on it. The apt biblical quotations painted in its chancel mirror the poetic techniques of Herbert's single major work, the collection of religious poems now commonly known as *The Temple*, which Herbert may well have originally titled, more simply, *The Church*.[2]

*The Church* contains poems which are obviously equivalent

to Bemerton's blind window with its holy gloss – poetic allegories of church architecture like 'The Windows' and 'The Church-floor'. Both illustrate Herbert's skill in matching careful physical observation to appropriate metaphysical connotations. 'The Windows' sets up a contrast between 'brittle, crazy' plain glass, whose light is 'watrish, bleak, and thin', and stained glass. Quite unlike Donne, Herbert leads us gently through the steps of his argument. Man as a preacher of God's word is like plain glass, full of imperfections ('crazy' suggests the distorting flaws in old floated glass), and yet he is allowed the supreme role of being a window onto divine light:

> Lord, how can man preach thy eternal word?
> He is a brittle crazy glass:
> Yet in thy temple thou dost him afford
> This glorious and transcendent place,
> To be a window, through thy grace.

But as the preacher is the deputy of Christ, he is more. He is like stained glass, which has the divine story sealed in it. Just as it wins the congregation over with its richness, so he does, by the dignity of his function:

> But when thou dost anneal in glass thy story,
> Making thy life to shine within
> The holy Preacher's; then the light and glory
> More rev'rend grows, and more doth win:
> Which else shows watrish, bleak, and thin.

The third stanza takes the argument to its final stage. The priest must also practise what he preaches. Herbert clearly identifies his correlatives. Precept is openly equated with the 'doctrine' of the preacher's sermons and the 'colours' of stained glass; his practice is equated with his own 'life' and God's 'light'. If the preacher merely speaks God's word without fulfilling it himself, he is an empty show, like a stained glass window – a meaningless blaze of colour which is quickly gone when the sun's light is clouded over.[3]

> Doctrine and life, colours and light, in one
> When they combine and mingle, bring
> A strong regard and awe: but speech alone

Doth vanish like a flaring thing,
And in the ear, not conscience ring.

In contrast to this beautifully sustained, and intricate association of image and argument, 'The Church-floor' offers a more candidly pedestrian process of emblematization:

Mark you the floor? that square and speckled stone,
Which looks so firm and strong,
Is *Patience*:

And th' other black and grave, wherewith each one
Is checker'd all along,
*Humility*:

There are few Herbert poems which do not repay close scrutiny. After two more stanzas of point-to-point allegory, the next step seems obvious enough:

Hither sometimes Sin steals, and stains
The marble's neat and curious veins.

The moral aphorism underlying the following line also seems self-evident: '. . . But all is cleansed when the marble weeps' – tears of remorse can wash away our sins. Herbert, however, is too good a poet to impose on the physical object a moral message with inappropriate connotations – indeed, impossible properties, like a capacity for tears. How can marble weep, really? Scholarship annotates the line learnedly but unhelpfully, proffering, for instance, the Virgilian analogue: 'Et maestum illacrimat templis ebur, aeraque sudant' ['And the ivory of the temple weeps in mourning, and the bronzes sweat']. Behind both literary images lies an observable phenomenon which Herbert has evoked with the lightest touch. As the members of the congregation crowd into the church their body heat and breath condense on the cold stone, which seems to weep. The image, then, is at once pointed and unforced.

'The Windows' and 'The Church-floor' appear in a little run of poems meditating on church props: 'Church-monuments', 'Church-music', 'Church-lock and key' are the others. A sequence like this alerts us to the arrangement of the whole volume, which is Herbert's own, and shows the same care as his architectural puns at Bemerton. *The Church* begins by creating an ecclesiastical structure. It opens with *The Church-porch*, a section containing a single poem, 'Perirrhanterium', which is the aspergil, the instrument used for sprinkling holy water. It is Herbert's longest and most overtly didactic poem, which unfortunately makes it as off-putting an introduction to Herbert as Bridges feared 'The Wreck of the Deutschland' would be to Hopkins. For seventy-six stanzas the reader is devoutly drenched in friendly but firm moral instruction ('Calmness is great advantage ... Mark what another says ... Scorn no man's love'). Well-washed, he turns from the porch to the threshold and the poem above the threshold, 'Superliminare', which begins:

> Thou, whom the former precepts have
> Sprinkled and taught, how to behave
> Thyself in church; approach, and taste
> The church's mystical repast.

The door is open, the reader enters *The Church* proper, and of course the first things to be seen are the altar, and the cross above it. 'The Altar' is a concrete poem, a mimetopoetic *carmen figuratum*, in the shape of a classic pillar. Its plinth, the last couplet, raises Herbert's recurrent wish for reciprocity between man and Christ:

> O let thy blessed SACRIFICE be mine,
> And sanctify this ALTAR to be thine.

'The Sacrifice', which comes next, duly fulfils this injunction, because in this poem alone Herbert speaks entirely in the voice of the crucified Christ and thus makes Christ's sacrifice his own. The architectural coherence of the sequence continues to be sustained by Herbert from this poem to the next. Its insistent refrain, 'Was ever grief like mine?' is acknowledged in the opening of the next poem, 'The Thanksgiving':

> Oh King of grief! (a title strange, yet true,
>     To thee of all kings only due).

A typical minor link between the two poems is Christ's painful broken line in 'The Sacrifice' which is further marked by a change of refrain:

> But, *O my God, my God!* why leav'st thou me,
> The son, in whom thou dost delight to be?
> *My God, my God*————
> > Never was grief like mine.

The broken line is completed in 'The Thanksgiving':

> *My God, my God, why dost thou part from me?*
> Was such a grief as cannot be.

In 'The Thanksgiving' Herbert meditates on man's inability to respond adequately to the supreme sacrifice of the Crucifixion. He ends with the faltering boast and the despairing cry:

> Then for thy passion—I will do for that—
> Alas, my God, I know not what.

This is immediately picked up by the next poem, 'The Reprisal':

> I have consider'd it, and find
> There is no dealing with thy mighty passion.

*The Church* does not only emulate ecclesiastical architecture. Herbert's abiding theme is that man's soul is God's temple. His poems seek to build such a temple in his readers. They are also confessional. They are counsels of improvement and records of backsliding. This is clear from his dying request (related by Izaak Walton) that the manuscript be sent to his friend, Nicholas Ferrar:

... tell him he shall find in it a picture of the many spiritual conflicts that have passed betwixt God and my soul, before I could subject mine to the will of Jesus my Master; in whose service I have now found perfect freedom; desire him to read it; and then, if he can think it may turn to the advantage of any dejected poor soul, let it be made public; if not, let him burn it ...

The collection ends with the soul emerging from its vicissitudes in a sequence of poems running from 'Death', 'Dooms-day', 'Judgement', 'Heaven' (but, typically for Herbert, not Hell),[4] and finally, heart-catchingly, to his best poem, 'Love (3)'. We need to imagine the soul on its final journey, to feel the full charge of the dirty traveller's diffident arrival:

> Love bade me welcome: yet my soul drew back,
> Guilty of dust and sin.

Heaven is God's love, his welcome to the mystical repast that 'Superliminare' promised. It is symbolized on earth by communion, the meal at which Christ serves and man is the undeserving, beloved guest:

> You must sit down, says Love, and taste my meat:
> So I did sit and eat.

But the volume does not finish here. Even the traditional last word, *FINIS*, which follows the last poem, is not the end. *The Church* closes with the song of the angels at Christ's birth, '*Glory be to God on high, and on earth peace, good will towards men.*' The end of Herbert's sequence evokes a beginning, the beginning of Christianity.

In his biography, Izaak Walton records that Herbert took particular care to teach his parishioners the rationale of the church year and its cycle of festivals, because by them 'the Church keeps an historical and circular commemoration of times as they pass by us'. The circularity of *The Church*'s structure, where Christ's birth at its end points chronologically forward, and formally backwards, to his death at its beginning, is thus characteristic of Herbert. His love of form, evident in the broad design and particular runs of poems within it, is much more complex and various in single poems. The link between form and content is not often as visually mimetic as the mimetopoesis of 'The Altar' and 'Easter wings'. Sometimes it is simply numerical, 'Sunday' being made up of seven-line stanzas, and 'Trinity Sunday' of three three-line stanzas. 'Man' celebrates humankind as the mansion God has built for his own habitation, mirroring this beautiful building in nine six-line stanzas (or 'pretty rooms', as Donne renders the Italian). Each has a different rhyme pattern, so that by the end of the poem nearly every possible permutation has been played out. In this way Herbert builds a poetic equivalent to the text, 'In my father's house are many mansions'

(*John* 14: 2). 'Clasping of hands' intricately alternates 'thine' and 'mine' as its dominant rhyme-words within and across two stanzas. This enacts the reciprocity invoked at the end of 'The Altar' by creating a stanzaic equivalent of the interlaced fingers of man's hand clasped in God's. 'Sin's round' repeats the pattern of Donne's sequence of holy sonnets, 'La Corona' (which he dedicated to his friend, Herbert's mother), and is also comparable to the beautiful run of sonnets 31 to 34 of Daniel's *Delia* (which was published the year before Herbert was born). That is, each stanza begins with the last line of its predecessor, and the poem's last line is also its first, so that its form represents the vicious circle of its title.

'A Wreath' uses this kind of circularity with even greater ingenuity. Like 'The Windows', it is a good example of Herbert's high craftsmanship. Like 'The Windows', too, it is built on a contrast – this time between a plaited wreath, and the plain circlet of a crown, the first being an image of man's crooked mortal path, the second of the straight road to God.

### A Wreath

> A wreathed garland of deserved praise,
> Of praise deserved, unto thee I give,
> I give to thee, who knowest all my ways,
> My crooked winding ways, wherein I live,
> Wherein I die, not live: for life is straight,
> Straight as a line, and ever tends to thee,
> To thee, who art more far above deceit,
> Than deceit seems above simplicity.
> Give me simplicity, that I may live,
> So live and like, that I may know thy ways,
> Know them and practise them: then shall I give
> For this poor wreath, give thee a crown of praise.

The poem is another *carmen figuratum*. Its form mimics both wreath and crown because its rhyme-scheme is circular, the rhyme-words of the first four lines being repeated in reverse order in the last four. More than that, it imitates the different constructions of wreath and crown in its own syntax. Its opening description of the wreath reverses and corrects the
· end of each line at the beginning of the next ('of deserved

praise,/Of praise deserved'; 'unto thee I give,/I give to thee'), just as the twigs of a wreath are bent back and looped forwards. The change comes with the fifth line, 'Wherein I die, not live: for life is straight'. Now Herbert turns to the better alternative of a life directed to God. Instead of reversing themselves the lines repeat straightforwardly in a pattern of cumulative affirmation: a crown, rather than a plaited wreath:

> for life is straight,
> Straight as a line, and ever tends to thee,
> To thee, who art more far above deceit,
> Than deceit seems above simplicity.

'A Wreath' also illustrates a recurrent Herbertian debate between his aesthetic pleasure in complexity, and his moral disapprobation of it. 'Give me simplicity' seems disingenuous in a poem that is quite so ingeniose. Dryden scathingly consigned Herbert to 'some peaceful Province in Acrostic Land', but Herbert was himself well aware of the danger. Many of his poems return to the dilemma, invariably ending, often with regret, in a resolution favouring simplicity. It is evident from the autobiographical retrospects of the two 'Jordan' poems and 'The Forerunners' that Herbert grew out of a predilection for elaborate ornament into an overtly plainer style. His reservations about the interwoven intricacies of 'Clasping of hands' or 'A Wreath' are implicit in his choice of vocabulary which often associates such frippery with profane love poetry:

> The wanton lover in a curious strain
> > Can praise his fairest fair;
> And with quaint metaphors her curled hair
> > Curl o're again.
>
> > > ('Dullness')
>
> Who says that fictions only and false hair
> Become a verse? Is there in truth no beauty?
> Is all good structure in a winding stair?
>
> > > ('Jordan (1)')
>
> Curling with metaphors a plain intention.
>
> > > ('Jordan (2)')

Of course the artistic arrangement of *The Church* obscures the

order of composition, but we can guess that too obviously in-
genious poems may be earlier works – poems like 'Coloss. 3.3.',
which hides a text, acrostic-wise, in the body of the poem.[5] The
conceit hardly seems worth the carriage, though it at least corro-
borates Aubrey's anecdote, and provides an inferior, astrono-
mical version of the dual movement exploited in 'A Wreath':

Coloss. 3.3.
*Our life is hid with Christ in God.*

*My* words and thoughts do both express this notion,
That *Life* hath with the sun a double motion.
The first *Is* straight, and our diurnal friend,
The other *Hid*, and doth obliquely bend.
One life is wrapt *In* flesh, and tends to earth.
The other winds towards *Him*, whose happy birth
Taught me to live here so, *That* still one eye
Should aim and shoot at that which *Is* on high:
Quitting with daily labour all *My* pleasure,
To gain at harvest an eternal *Treasure*.

We might also deduce a chronological development where
poems use the same conceit with progressive subtlety, the
surface of the poem appearing increasingly simple, while the
poetic surprise is better hidden, and correspondingly intensi-
fied. For instance, in 'Heaven', Herbert imitates a popular
sixteenth-century form, the echo poem, such as Philisides sings
in the Second Eclogue of the *Old Arcadia* (published in 1598,
when Herbert was five years old). At its crudest, the echo is
used directly:

O who will show me those delights on high?
*Echo.*          *I.*
Thou Echo, thou art mortal, all men know.
*Echo.*          *No.*

('Heaven')

But the nub of a good echo poem lies in its pointed alteration
of meaning as the rhyme-word is imperfectly repeated – a
technique used bluntly by Sidney:

| *Philisides* | *Echo* |
|---|---|
| Horrible is this blasphemy unto the most holy. | O lie. |

xix

> Tell yet again me the names of these fair formed
> <div style="text-align:center">to do ev'ls.</div>                    Dev'ls.

and candidly by Herbert:

> But are there cares and business with the pleasure?
> <div style="text-align:center">*Echo.*</div>                *Leisure.*
> Light, joy, and leisure; but shall they persever?
> <div style="text-align:center">*Echo.*</div>                *Ever.*

It is easy to see that in 'Paradise' Herbert refines this technique. The first stanza sets up God as the gardener, pruning his human orchard, just as the last word of each line is trimmed back:

> I bless thee, Lord, because I GROW
> Among thy trees, which in a ROW
> To thee both fruit and order OW.

The circularity beloved of Herbert recurs in this poem's last stanza, because the quick of the final rhyme survives the clipping of its progenitor:

> Such sharpness shows the sweetest FREND:
> Such cuttings rather heal than REND:
> And such beginnings touch their END.

'The Pulley' is even more sophisticated.[6] Here Herbert invents a parable in which God pours a glass full of blessings over new-created man, only stopping himself in time when he sees that one last blessing, the blessing of rest, remains. Rest is kept back, lest man forget God in a state of self-sufficient bliss. The final stanza, spoken by God, puns on 'rest' as 'the remainder' of his blessings, and 'repose'. The key word is hidden, in the manner of echo poems (where, for instance, 'ever' lies within 'persever', and 'end' inside 'frend'), in the only place where man will find it:

> Yet let him keep the rest,
> But keep them with repining restlessness:
> Let him be rich and weary, that at least
> If goodness lead him not, yet weariness
> May toss him to my breast.

xx

The point is no longer driven home by the spelling, as in 'Paradise', but lies quietly dormant inside an unpretentious rhyme. Rest resides in God's breast.

In his distaste for decayed literary decoration, Herbert has strong links with Sidney. *Astrophel and Stella* (first published with the *Old Arcadia*) satirizes the clichés of the continental sonneteers – their Ovidian metamorphoses, Pindaric tropes, Petrarchan paradoxes, pastoralism, 'rhymes running in rattling rows' – in opposition to Sidney's own direct spontaneity. There is little difference in stance between his sixth sonnet, for instance, and Herbert's 'Jordan (1)':

> Some one his song in Jove, and Jove's strange tales attires,
> Broider'd with bulls and swans, powdered with golden rain:
> Another humbler wit to shepherd's pipe retires,
> Yet hiding royal blood full oft in rural vein ...
>   I can speak what I feel, and feel as much as they,
>   But think that all the Map of my state I display,
> When trembling voice brings forth that I do Stella love.
>
> (Astrophel and Stella, 6)

> Is it no verse, except enchanted groves
> And sudden arbours shadow coarse-spun lines?
> Must purling streams refresh a lover's loves?
> Must all be veil'd, while he that reads, divines,
>   Catching the sense at two removes?
>
> Shepherds are honest people; let them sing:
> Riddle who list, for me, and pull for Prime:
> I envy no man's nightingale or spring;
> Nor let them punish me with loss of rhyme,
>   Who plainly say, *My God, My King.*
>
> ('Jordan (1)')

The crucial distinction is, of course, the one repeatedly made by Herbert, that his poems celebrate divine rather than profane love. Walton quotes his earliest known sonnet, written at the age of seventeen. It demands 'Doth Poetry/Wear Venus' livery? only serve her turn?/ ... Cannot thy dove/Outstrip their Cupid easily in flight?' 'Love I' repeats the idea with some bitterness:

Who sings thy praise? only a scarf or glove
Doth warm our hands, and make them write of love.

'Dullness' takes the argument further, as Herbert criticizes himself for his inability to use the forms of love poetry for a greater love:

Thou art my loveliness, my life, my light,
Beauty alone to me:
Thy bloody death and undeserv'd, makes thee
Pure red and white.
. . .
Where are my lines then? my approaches? views?
Where are my window songs?
Lovers are still pretending, and ev'n wrongs
Sharpen their Muse:

But I am lost in flesh, whose sugred lies
Still mock me, and grow bold:
Sure thou didst put a mind there, if I could
Find where it lies.

However, Herbert does find a 'mind' – some intellectual substance – in the sweet deceits of erotic verse. He frequently adapts the forms and motifs of profane love poetry to religious ends. The point is made clearly in 'The Forerunners', which is a lament for lost inspiration, freighted with sensuous regret – 'Lovely enchanting language, sugar-cane,/Honey of roses, whither wilt thou fly?' In the course of the poem, though, Herbert comes clean:

Farewell sweet phrases, lovely metaphors.
But will ye leave me thus? when ye before
Of stews and brothels only knew the doors,
Then did I wash you with my tears, and more
Brought you to Church well drest and clad:
My God must have my best, ev'n all I had.

We do find well-washed Magdalenes, transfigured profanities, in Herbert's *Church*. Puttenham, the sixteenth-century literary theorist, said that figures yielding 'an ocular representation' (i.e. the mimetopoesis of *carmina figurata*) were 'fittest for the pretty amourets in Court to entertain their servants and the time withal'.[7] Yet Herbert transfers 'these courtly trifles' to much higher ends in 'The Altar' and 'Easter wings'. Another example of Herbert's transposition of the profane to the sacred is his use of the aubade, or 'window song', traditionally sung at dawn under the beloved's window, calling on her to get up.[8] Herbert plays several variations on this motif in his work. 'The Dawning' is an unremarkable transposition in which the heart is urged to 'awake' and 'arise' from its gloom, with the key words used as refrains in the standard manner. 'Easter' is more interesting. It begins with an exhortation to the heart to sing in praise of the risen Christ. A change of verse-form marks the heart's song, which follows. It is, apparently, a traditional aubade, initially giving no hint of its divine subject. Christ's Resurrection with uncorrupted flesh after three days in the tomb is delicately disguised in a conventional image of the beloved's fragrance:

> I got me flowers to straw thy way;
> I got me boughs off many a tree:
> But thou wast up by break of day,
> And brought'st thy sweets along with thee.

Herbert's criticism of contemporary literary fashions is not confined to genres. It also includes sniping at his greatest compeer. A friend and admirer of Herbert's mother, Donne visited the family and preached her funeral sermon in tears, according to Izaak Walton, who was a witness. For all the modesty of the younger poet, there is something distinctly sharp in Herbert's evocation of Donne's 'The Sun Rising' and 'The Good-Morrow' in two poems, 'The Temper' and 'The Discharge'. Donne begins 'The Sun Rising' on a note of inconsiderate coarseness, grossness even, impertinently chiding the elderly sun for interrupting the lovers ('Busy old fool, unruly Sun,/Why dost thou thus,/Through windows, and through curtains call on us?'), and ends by instructing the sun that, since the lovers encapsulate the world, its task will be done merely by shining on them ('Shine here to us, and thou art every where;/This bed thy centre is, these walls, thy sphere'). The latter image is put more enigmatically in 'The Good-Morrow': 'For love all love of other sights controls,/And makes one little room an everywhere.' Herbert's 'The Temper' echoes both poems in its own last lines where, with greater propriety, divine love has transforming force: 'Thy power and love, my love and trust/Make one place ev'ry where'. More pointedly critical is the opening of 'The Discharge', which echoes the beginning of 'The Sun Rising' in order to attack the vanity of curiosity:

> Busy enquiring heart, what wouldst thou know?
> Why dost thou pry,
> And turn, and leer, and with a licorous eye
> Look high and low;
> And in thy lookings stretch and grow?

It is curious that C. A. Patrides, the editor of both Herbert and Donne, should say that 'Herbert did not once borrow directly from Donne'.[9] Although other echoes are more open to question, these two critical allusions seem distinct. And further echoes cluster round another identifiable, equally bravura passage in Donne's 'Second Anniversary' on the death of Elizabeth Drury. This contains a breath-stopping evocation of the soul's journey through the galaxies to God, described with casual, irresistible know-how. One image is particularly memorable:

> But ere she can consider how she went,
> At once is at, and through the Firmament.
> And as these stars were but so many beads
> Strung on one string, speed undistinguish'd leads
> Her through those Spheres, as through the beads, a string,
> Whose quick succession makes it still one thing.
>
> ('The Second Anniversary', ll.205ff.)

In 'Vanity' Herbert appears to praise the astronomic advances of his time in a stanza evocative both of this image, and Donne's almost impertinent personification of the sun and stars in the 'First Anniversary' (ll.263ff.). Herbert's poem begins:

> The fleet Astronomer can bore,
> And thread the spheres with his quick-piercing mind:
> He views their stations, walks from door to door,
> Surveys, as if he had design'd

> To make a purchase there: he sees their dances,
>> And knoweth long before,
> Both their full-ey'd aspects, and secret glances.

In fact this apparent praise is undermined by the poem's title, 'Vanity'. Herbert takes up a similar position to Donne's since he too is making a mockery of scientific hubris: as Donne says, 'They have impal'd within a Zodiac/The free-born Sun'. But Donne exults in as well as ironizes the insolent scope of Renaissance learning, while Herbert is more sober in his disapprobation:

> Philosophers have measur'd mountains,
> Fathom'd the depths of seas, of states, and kings,
> Walk'd with a staff to heav'n, and traced fountains:
>> But there are two vast, spacious things,
> The which to measure it doth more behove:
> Yet few there are that sound them; Sin and Love.
>> ('The Agony')

Herbert's handbook for *The Country Parson* confirms his condemnation of intellectual vanity: 'Curiosity in prying into high speculative and unprofitable questions is another stumbling block to the holiness of scholars' (ch.ix). In this sense Herbert is the antithesis of Sir Thomas Browne with his self-confessed delight in pursuing abstruse speculation: 'I love to lose my self in a mystery, to pursue my Reason to an *O altitudo!*'[10] Herbert, by contrast, is pragmatic, consciously straightforward, anti-intellectual. He dissociates himself from the contemporary style in sermonizing (well exemplified by Launcelot Andrewes) when he instructs his country parson to avoid elaborate scriptural deconstruction:

The parson's method in handling of a text consists of two parts: first, a plain and evident declaration of the meaning of the text; and secondly, some choice observations drawn out of the whole text as it lies entire and unbroken in the Scripture itself. This he thinks natural, and sweet, and grave. Whereas the other way of crumbling a text into small parts, as, the person speaking or spoken to, the subject and object, and the like, hath neither in it sweetness, nor gravity, nor variety, since the words apart are not Scripture, but a dictionary ...
>> (ch.vii)

The same spirit informs Herbert's poetry. Even though much of it is inward-turned and confessional in origin, the overall thrust of *The Church* is affective and effective – its end is religious persuasion. Herbert's abiding popularity even in our own sceptical age can be attributed to a number of virtues: the artistic wit and ingenuity discussed above, and, paradoxically, the qualities suggested in his image of the good preacher, whose text is plain and evident, natural, sweet and grave.

Herbert's poetics of persuasion are essentially the same as those recommended to the parson in his several roles. *The Country Parson* shows the perceptive common sense of a genuinely gifted educational psychologist, most engagingly so in his advice to the parson teasing sense out of his dullest parishioners:

... the skill consists but in these three points: First, an aim and mark of the whole discourse, whither to drive the answerer, which the questionist must have in his mind before any question be propounded, upon which and to which the questions are to be chained; secondly, a most plain and easy framing the question, even containing, in virtue, the answer also, especially to the more ignorant; thirdly, when the answerer sticks, an illustrating the thing by something else which he knows, making what he knows to serve him in that which he knows not; as, when the parson once demanded, after other questions about man's misery, since man is so miserable, what is to be done? And the answerer could not tell; he asked him again, what he would do if he were in a ditch? This familiar illustration made the answer so plain that he was even ashamed of his ignorance, for he could not but say he would haste out of it as fast as he could. Then he proceeded to ask whether he could get out of the ditch alone, or whether he needed a helper, and who was that helper? This is the skill ...

(ch.xxi)

With characteristic catholicity, Herbert praises 'the singular dexterity of Socrates in this kind', as well as relating his own practice to that of the Bible – 'doubtless the holy Scripture intends as much when it condescends to the naming of a plough, a hatchet, a bushel, leaven'. The sonnet 'Prayer' has a wonderful fourteen-line run of images for prayer, including 'Heaven in ordinary, man well drest'. The two phrases draw out the idea of a meal raised in the poem's first words ('Prayer

xxvi

the Church's banquet') which is rooted in the concept of communion. They suggest a meal at which man tries to dress himself up as smartly as he can to meet God, and God descends to man's ordinary level – a meaning strengthened by the seventeenth-century use of the word 'ordinary' for a fixed-price meal in a tavern. The use of familiar illustrations like the plough, leaven, and the hapless rustic mired in a ditch, are all examples of 'Heaven in ordinary', as are Herbert's ubiquitous parables, fables, and proverbs.

The proverbial is an especially fertile matrix in Herbert's work, as it is in many of his contemporaries. In the popular wisdom of proverbs general truths are concretized and personified in vividly metaphoric and sometimes enigmatic ways. It is not surprising that Herbert should be generally credited with compiling the collection called *Outlandish* (i.e. foreign) *Proverbs*, which amply illustrate their prime appeal, that of homely good sense:

> He that wipes the child's nose, kisseth the mother's cheek.
> Better a snotty child, than his nose wip'd off.
> When children stand quiet, they have done some ill.

and gnomic punch:

> A white wall is the paper of a fool.
> To fine folks a little ill finely wrapt.
> Thorns whiten yet do nothing.

Often the truths are worldly-wise:

> The river past, and God forgotten.
> Living well is the best revenge.
> The back door robs the house.
> A flatterer's throat is an open sepulchre.

Taken literally, proverbs can often appear quasi-surreal. 'Be not a Baker, if your head be of butter' could easily find a place in that great pictorial compendium of proverbs, Pieter Brueghel the Elder's *Netherlandish Proverbs* (1559) which now hangs in the Dahlem Museum in Berlin. In this painting, many outlandish (in every sense) proverbs are bizarrely, because literally, depicted. There is a contradiction in all proverbs –

they are declarative in form, but obscure in content; imperative in form but fugitive in content; 'dark instructions'. The initial impact is often powerfully enigmatic:

> The groundsel speaks not what it heard at the hinges.
> A master of straw eats a servant of steel.
> He that hath one foot in the straw, hath another in the spittle.
> A stone in a well is not lost.

The Aesopian animal fable and the proverb often combine:

> He that comes of a hen must scratch.
> The Wolf must die in its own skin.
> The ignorant hath an Eagle's wings, and an Owl's eyes.
> It is better to be the head of a Lizard, than the tail of a Lion.
> Flies are busiest about lean horses.

Blake's work is shot through with the irrefutable, knotted logic of such proverbs, most overtly, of course, in his own invented collection, *Proverbs of Hell*, with their memorably amoral, flat veracity ('The bird a nest, the spider a web, man friendship'). His 'Auguries of Innocence' is simply an extended proverbial sequence whose arresting strength derives from its dogmatic, sainted-idiot blankness:

> The caterpillar on the leaf
> Repeats to thee thy mother's grief.

One can see a narrative extension of the same concretization of moral and psychological truths in *Songs of Experience* like 'A Poison Tree'.

In Herbert the proverbial can be evoked directly: 'Wouldst thou both eat thy cake and have it?' ('The Size'); 'I took thy sweetened pill' ('Affliction (1)'). Often the worldly proverb is modified to religious ends. 'To burn daylight' is a common Renaissance metaphor of wasted time; in *Romeo and Juliet* Mercutio hurries his friends to the Capulets' ball, saying 'Come, we burn daylight, ho!' The phrase has further literal appositeness because they are all carrying torches, according to the authorial stage direction. Herbert delicately, poignantly alludes to the saying when Christ, who is both Son and sun of man, describes Judas with the priests and elders coming to betray him and take him captive:

# INTRODUCTION

> Arise, arise, they come. Look how they run.
> Alas! What haste they make to be undone!
> How with their lanterns do they seek the sun!
> > Was ever grief like mine?
> > > ('The Sacrifice')

Frequently the proverbial statement seems to be of Herbert's own devising:

> Kneeling ne're spoil'd silk stockings.
> > ('Perirrhanterium')

> God chains the dog till night: wilt loose the chain,
> > And wake thy sorrow?
> > > ('The Discharge')

> Make not thy sport, abuses: for the fly
> That feeds on dung, is coloured thereby.
> > ('Perirrhanterium')

Herbert, unlike Blake, uses the proverbial to make moral ideas immediate and accessible, rather than arcane. Consequently, in the last example, the moral aphorism precedes and explains the characteristically accurate visual image. Similarly, occasional explanations are included in the *Outlandish Proverbs*, like 'Were it not for the bone in the leg, all the world would turn Carpenters (to make them crutches).'

The proverbial bias towards personification and the concrete also underlies Herbert's habitual use of domestic imagery for spiritual states:

> My mirth and edge was lost; a blunted knife
> > Was of more use than I.
> > > ('Affliction (1)')

> Go search this thing,
> Tumble thy breast, and turn thy book.
> > ('The Method')

> And the cream of all my heart
> > I will bring thee.
> > > ('Praise (2)')

For Herbert, there is no impropriety in this low imagery, not even in the yellow dung-fly. He shares with Hopkins the conviction that God sanctifies everything:

> Teach me, my God and King,
> In all things thee to see,
> And what I do in any thing,
> To do it as for thee:
> ...
>
> A servant with this clause
> Makes drudgery divine:
> Who sweeps a room, as for thy laws,
> Makes that and th' action fine.
>
> ('The Elixir')

And here is Hopkins:

When a man is in God's grace and free from mortal sin, then everything he does, so long as there is no sin in it, gives God glory ... To lift up the hands in prayer gives God glory, but a man with a dungfork in his hand, a woman with a slop-pail, give him glory too.[11]

As Herbert says in *The Country Parson*, when the Bible refers to hatchets and ploughs it shows that 'things of ordinary use are not only to serve in the way of drudgery, but to be washed and cleansed and serve for lights even of heavenly truths'. *Heaven in ordinary*. The commonplace is not merely capable of sanctity; it is what can most easily explain the transcendent to us.

Unsurprisingly, Herbert's use of proverbs is enlarged in those poems which tell parables based, in Christ's manner, on the familiar concerns of his contemporary country people. 'Redemption', for instance, explains the central Christian mystery in terms of tenancy and rent. Herbert is careful not to refer openly to his theological subject, but to bring home its implications under the disguise of a predicament familiar to an impoverished parishioner:

> Having been tenant long to a rich Lord,
> Not thriving, I resolved to be bold,
> And make a suit unto him, to afford
> A new small-rented lease, and cancel th' old.

# INTRODUCTION

The divine subject is only fleetingly admitted in the sonnet's second quatrain:

> In heaven at his manor I him sought:
>> They told me there, that he was lately gone
>> About some land, which he had dearly bought
> Long since on earth, to take possession.

However, the impercipient speaker remains unaware of his lord's nature. With worldly logic,

> I straight return'd, and knowing his great birth,
>> Sought him accordingly in great resorts;
>> In cities, theatres, gardens, parks, and courts ...

The climax of the story, stripped of familiarity, is turned into a shocking, inexplicable scene. The rich lord seems to have been caught up in a tavern brawl, and murdered:

> At length I heard a ragged noise and mirth
>> Of thieves and murderers: there I him espied
>> Who straight, *Your suit is granted*, said, and died.

The baffled reader is prompted to ask himself questions in much the same way as Herbert's catechist interrogated his parishioner on man's misery. Who is the rich lord? Christ. What has happened to him? He was killed. And how was Christ killed? He was crucified between two thieves. What did the speaker want of Christ? A new lease. And did he get it? Yes. How? Well, judging by the last line, he got it at and by Christ's death. How should that be? Presumably, because Christ's death changed the terms of the lease ... It isn't difficult to recognize the Crucifixion in its new disguise, but the unfamiliarity is crucial because it re-animates the extraordinary gulf between the greatness of this rich and powerful landlord, the appalling indignity of his end, and the mystery that such a profoundly debased death should bring about the salvation of mankind.

But the story also gently prompts more difficult questions. What was the old lease? The new, cheaper, 'small-rented' one? What is intended by Christ's expensive purchase of land on earth, long before this story took place?

The image of the two rents lightly evokes the distinction continually made in St. Paul's Epistles between the old covenant of works, whereby men hoped to merit salvation by obeying the Law, and the new covenant of grace bestowed by Christ:

For by grace are ye saved through faith; and that not of yourselves: it is the gift of God:
Not of works, lest any man should boast.

(Ephesians 2: 8–9)

Knowing that a man is not justified by the works of the law, but by the faith of Jesus Christ, even we have believed in Jesus Christ, that we might be justified by the faith of Christ, and not by the works of the law: for by the works of the law shall no flesh be justified.

(Galatians 2: 16)

The old rent was the laborious fulfilment of the Law; the new, the gift of grace. Finally, Christ's 'dearly bought' land is mankind itself, whose salvation was proposed before the creation:

... the power of God;
Who hath saved us, and called us with an holy calling, not according to our works, but according to his own purpose and grace, which was given us in Jesus Christ before the world began.

(II Timothy 1: 9)

The expense of the purchase was the price paid – the life of God's only son.

To paraphrase so laboriously may seem simplistic or impertinent to the reader. But it does bring home two things: how difficult it is to do so accurately and clearly; and that doing so entails a dogmatism about delicate questions of theology which Herbert eschews. He avoids the morass of doctrinaire debate, attempting instead to render comprehensible the fundamentals of Christianity, ironically remarking, in 'Divinity':

> *Love God, and love your neighbour. Watch and pray.*
> *Do as ye would be done unto.*
> O dark instructions; ev'n as dark as day!
> Who can these Gordian knots undo?

# INTRODUCTION

Many of Herbert's poems contain gunpowder-trails of significance like the one laid in 'Redemption'. Superficially, they appear to engage the reader in a gentle, sometimes even comic narrative. It takes firmness of purpose not to remain contented with the surface, but to worry at the details, to wheedle out the full meaning. Often a return to the title offers the initial nudge in the right direction. 'Redemption' clarifies itself by both title and position, since it is set in the run of poems opening *The Church*, which are all about the Crucifixion and Resurrection ('The Sacrifice', 'The Thanksgiving', 'The Reprisal', 'The Agony', 'The Sinner', 'Good Friday', 'Redemption', 'Sepulchre', 'Easter', 'Easter wings'). Significantly, too, Herbert changed the poem's title from its narrative subject, 'The Passion' to its spiritual result, the *redemption* of man by Christ.

As a comparable secular parable, consider the following animal fable in the manner of Aesop. It begins with a grand picture:

> I saw the Virtues sitting hand in hand
> In sev'ral ranks upon an azure throne,
> Where all the beasts and fowls by their command
> Presented tokens of submission.
> Humility, who sat the lowest there
>                 To execute their call,
> When by the beasts the presents tendred were,
>                 Gave them about to all.

The texture of significance begins to thicken almost immediately. In the next stanza each creature presents the token of its traditional attribute to the virtue opposed to it – anger to gentleness, timidity to fortitude, and so on. In this way the vices submit to their corresponding virtues:

> The angry Lion did present his paw,
> Which by consent was giv'n to Mansuetude.
> The fearful Hare her ears, which by the law
> Humility did reach to Fortitude.
> The jealous Turkey brought his coral-chain;
>                 That went to Temperance.
> On Justice was bestow'd the Fox's brain,
>                 Kill'd in the way by chance.

There is a nice appositeness in the turkey's gift of its lightly euphemized, enraged crimson wattle to temperance. And the fox clearly had no intention of giving its brain to anybody. Nor did its cunning save it from accidental death. The fact that Justice should be endowed with foxiness is even more double-edged. There is a dawning perception that the virtues may not be entirely above vice, which is intensified in the next stanza:

> At length the Crow bringing the Peacock's plume,
> (For he would not), as they beheld his grace
> Of that brave gift, each one began to fume,
> And challenge it, as proper to his place,
> Till they fell out: which when the beasts espied,
>> They leapt upon the throne;
> And if the Fox had liv'd to rule their side,
>> They had depos'd each one.

Typically, Herbert avoids glossing the emblem directly, the peacock's pride being implicit in his refusal to pay tribute ('For he would not'). The emblematic point of the next stanza is also left unspoken:

> Humility, who held the plume, at this
> Did weep so fast, that the tears trickling down
> Spoil'd all the train ...

According to the ritual of the assembly, the gift of pride should have been given to Humility, who is too humble even to think of claiming it. Appropriately, too, Humility's shame at the bad behaviour of the other virtues robs pride of all its splendour – not the single disputed feather, but all the peacock's train – and temporarily discomfits the virtues into rejecting all the vices whose tribute they were so eager to acquire:

> ... then saying, *Here it is*
> *For which ye wrangle*, made them turn their frown
> Against the beasts: so jointly bandying,
>> They drove them soon away.

Yet without Humility the enthroned virtues are incorrigible.

Their last imposition of a double fine on the beasts is indicative of nothing but pride, vanity and greed:

> And then amerc'd them, double gifts to bring
> At the next Session-day.

As the third stanza says, if the fox had been alive, its cunning could have united the vices and conquered the virtues. Equally, Humility is the unique guard against the pride of complete virtue. The quiet Cordelia of the poem, Humility's role is subordinate, its voice hardly heard. Only the poem's title, 'Humility', gives it pre-eminent authority.

Herbert's clarifying titles are another aspect of his predilection for accessibility. Dr. Johnson believed that the ideas of Christian theology were 'too simple for eloquence, too plain for fiction, and too majestic for ornament'. Herbert's sympathy with this position ('Who says that fictions only and false hair/Become a verse?') is evident in the Anglo-Saxon simplicity of his titles. They appear to have been consistently dignified by later editors and printers, who changed *The Church* to *The Temple*, *The Country Parson* to *A Priest to the Temple*, and *Outlandish Proverbs* to *Jacula Prudentum*.[12] It is noticeable that the sources of Herbert's imagery are nearly all scriptural or indigenous; apart from the ironic (and quasi-historic) Gordian knot quoted earlier, there is not an overtly evoked pagan myth or divinity, beloved of his Renaissance predecessors, in all his work. Carew's praise of Donne could be better applied to Herbert: 'the goodly exil'd train/Of gods and goddesses, which in thy just reign/Were banish'd nobler Poems ... '[13] In this context it is also interesting to compare Herbert to Wordsworth. Both authors changed the titles of their poems, but in opposite directions. With age, Wordsworth inclined to the ennobling moralization of his works and the altered titles betray the movement away from the particular and concrete to the abstract and general: from 'Old Man Travelling' to 'Animal Tranquillity and Decay'; from 'The Leech-Gatherer' to 'Resolution and Independence'. Herbert, on the contrary, clarifies by making concrete, and 'Perfection' becomes 'The Elixir', the alchemical substance that turns dross to gold, as doing drudgery for God makes it divine. Why should

GEORGE HERBERT

'The Pulley' be called that, when no pulley is mentioned in the body of the poem? It is another concretizing title, evoking a familiar mechanism we still see today in the double bucket system used by builders lowering rubble from the top of a house, the descent of the full bucket on one side of the pulley raising the empty bucket on the other side, to be filled in its turn. Shakespeare's Richard II uses the same image in his deposition speech, when he compares himself to a bucket full of grief down in the well, while Bolingbroke is the empty bucket, 'ever dancing in the air' in his rise to power.[14] In Herbert's poem, paradoxically, man is weighed down by his many blessings, which drag him away from God. The empty bucket of restlessness, ever dancing in the air, 'tosses' mankind up to God's breast. A commonplace artisan's tool is made to epitomize a central Herbertian theme – that suffering brings man to God.

Herbert, like Bunyan, uses the personifications of allegory to dramatize moral abstractions – his poem 'The Pilgrimage' is a miniature *Pilgrim's Progress* – and also draws on the popular fashion of his time for emblem books to literalize metaphor and agreeably puzzle the reader. Emblem books came from Europe to England with Witney's *Choice of Emblems* (1586), which derived from the Italian Alciati's *Emblematum Liber* of 1522. The basic ingredients were a picture – say, of Fortune standing blindfold on her turning wheel, or Opportunity, with her long forelock and otherwise bald head. The picture was furnished with a motto ('Catch opportunity by the forelock'), sometimes followed by a couplet or longer set of verses moralizing the illustration. Personified emblems jostle across the landscape of *The Faerie Queene*. Herbert draws on them as he does on proverbs, as concise, arresting metaphoric encapsulations of abstract ideas. 'The Church-floor' derives from this tradition, but his best-known emblem poem is 'Hope', in which a hand of familiar emblems is swiftly dealt out:

> I gave to Hope a watch of mine: but he
> An anchor gave to me.
> Then an old prayer-book I did present:
> And he an optic sent.

# INTRODUCTION

> With that I gave a vial full of tears:
> > But he a few green ears:
> Ah Loiterer! I'll no more, no more I'll bring:
> > I did expect a ring.

In *Seven Types of Ambiguity* Empson, Prospero-like, summons up a dark cloud of contradictory ambiguities to overcast the poem.[15] In effect, however, it is like the object-letter in Kipling's 'Beyond the Pale'. Trejago receives a packet containing a bit of broken glass bangle, a red *dhak* flower, a pinch of cattle food, and eleven cardamoms. They signify a widow (all Hindu widows have their glass bracelets broken) desiring (the *dhak* flower) an assignation at eleven o'clock at the house by the heap of cattle food. 'Hope' is comparably simple. In effect, it is a dialogue between the speaker of the poem, and Hope. The speaker begins by telling Hope, 'Look how long I've been waiting'. Hope's response is, predictably, 'Hang on a bit longer', be steadfast. The speaker protests, 'But I've been praying so long! My prayer-book's quite worn out'. Hope replies, 'Don't be so short-sighted' (an optic glass is a telescope). 'But I've suffered; look at my tears,' the speaker complains. 'The harvest's not yet ripe; wait a little longer,' Hope insists – at which the speaker flounces off impatiently: 'Layabout! Loiterer! And I thought there was a binding contract between us'. Yet, as so often in Herbert, the poem should not be read in isolation. 'Sin's round', which follows it, is an implicit continuation. The ring of the last line is not Hope's to offer. It is not a marriage ring, a piece of jewellery. It is a vicious circle that man must escape. While he is still caught up in his sinful whirl, his hopes of salvation can't be fulfilled.

> Sorry I am, my God, sorry I am,
> That my offences course it in a ring.
>
> ('Sin's round')

The modern reader may sometimes find Herbert's use of allegory, emblem and typology difficult to understand. Typology plays off Old Testament events against their New Testament pairings, Eva against Ave (Maria), the old Adam whose sin we inherit against the new Adam who redeemed us:

xxxvii

We think that Paradise and Calvary,
> Christ's Cross, and Adam's tree, stood in one place;
Look Lord, and find both Adams met in me;
> As the first Adam's sweat surrounds my face,
> May the last Adam's blood my soul embrace.
> > (Donne: 'Hymn to God my God, in my sickness')

Comparably, Herbert's crucified Christ links his trial to Noah's tribulations:

> Hark how they cry aloud still, *Crucify* ...

> My silence rather doth augment their cry;
> My dove doth back into my bosom fly,
> Because the raging waters still are high:
> > Was ever grief like mine?

> > ('The Sacrifice')

In 'The H. Scriptures II' Herbert praises the internal coherence of the Bible:

> Oh that I knew how all thy lights combine,
> > And the configurations of their glory!
> > Seeing not only how each verse doth shine,
> But all the constellations of the story.

> This verse marks that, and both do make a motion
> > Unto a third, that ten leaves off doth lie.

He could, in many ways, be describing his own methodology. *The Church* emulates a biblical density of texture. Innumerable repeated and modified images criss-cross it, a beautiful fan-vaulting, providing analogues and delayed glosses to earlier enigmas, resolutions to abandoned discontents.[16] 'Love (3)' is not only a supremely consoling poem on its own. Its position in the volume as the ultimate vision of heaven is further strengthened by a tracery of connections, from its expansion of the Church's mystical repast of 'Superliminare', and the banquet promised in 'Prayer', to its definitive answer to Herbert's earlier complaints:

> O that thou shouldst give dust a tongue
> > To cry to thee,
> And then not hear it crying!

> > ('Denial')

# INTRODUCTION

> Lord hear! *Shall he that made the ear,*
> > *Not hear?*
>
> ('Longing')
>
> I the unkind, ungrateful? Ah my dear,
> > I cannot look on thee.
> Love took my hand, and smiling did reply,
> > Who made the eyes but I?
>
> ('Love (3)')

Herbert also draws on natural rather than doctrinal typologies within particular poems. 'Mortification' does so through a series of parallel images, in which the several ages of man are matched with images of death, and this quietly remorseless pattern is sustained by a repeated, unobtrusive rhyme of 'breath' with 'death' straddling each stanza. Its effect is to create a refrain that has the untroubled, unnoticed regularity of your own breathing, but each breath brings you nearer to death:

> How soon doth man decay!
> When clothes are taken from a chest of sweets
> > To swaddle infants, whose young breath
> > Scarce knows the way;
> > Those clouts are little winding sheets,
> Which do consign and send them unto death.
>
> When boys go first to bed,
> They step into their voluntary graves,
> > Sleep binds them fast; only their breath
> > Makes them not dead;
> > Successive nights, like rolling waves,
> Convey them quickly, who are bound for death.

The doctrinal and technical may be occluded by time and waning faith; Herbert's personal voice is not. Above all, we respond immediately to his emotional intensity, his swings of mood from a lively relish of eye, ear and nose, to his frequent periods of affliction. 'The Flower' is one of Herbert's most attractive poems of spiritual recuperation, full of his gusto for life:

And now in age I bud again,
After so many deaths I live and write;
I once more smell the dew and rain,
And relish versing ...

His poetry is full of delicious natural observation. It is characteristic of him that one of the best examples should link earthly joys to heavenly ones:

Not, that he may not here
Taste of the cheer,
But as birds drink, and straight lift up their head,
So must he sip and think
Of better drink
He may attain to, after he is dead.

('Man's medley')

The whole of 'Providence' is a hymn of praise to divine household management:

Thy cupboard serves the world: the meat is set,
Where all may reach: no beast but knows his feed.
Birds teach us hawking; fishes have their net:
The great prey on the less, they on some weed.

Nothing engendred doth prevent his meat:
Flies have their table spread, ere they appear ...

Each creature hath a wisdom for his good.
The pigeons feed their tender off-spring, crying,
When they are callow; but withdraw their food
When they are fledge, that want may teach them flying ...
Sheep eat the grass, and dung the ground for more:
Trees after bearing drop their leaves for soil ...

Marianne Moore, a lover of Herbert, shares his *National Geographic* quality – a curious delight in natural history. Compare her celebration of the ant-eating Pangolin, 'This near artichoke with head and legs and grit-equipped gizzard ... on hind feet plantigrade', with Herbert's praise of the creator:

To show thou art not bound, as if thy lot
Were worse than ours, sometimes thou shiftest hands.

> Most things move th' under-jaw; the Crocodile not.
> Most things sleep lying; th' Elephant leans or stands.

He has a Keatsian sensuousness:

> How sweetly doth *My Master* sound! *My Master!*
> As Amber-grease leaves a rich scent,
> Unto the taster:
> So do these words a sweet content,
> An oriental fragrancy, *My Master*.

('The Odour')

His pleasure embraces a wide sense of humour, of which wit and ingenuity are only a part. Bunyan defended himself against the apparently worldly entertainment of *The Pilgrim's Progress* in a verse apology which could as well be applied to Herbert, since both write for the same audience and the same ends:

> You see the ways the Fisherman doth take
> To catch the Fish; what Engines doth he make?
> Behold how he engageth all his Wits,
> Also his Snares, Lines, Angles, Hooks and Nets.
> Yet Fish there be, that neither Hook, nor Line,
> Nor Snare, nor Net, nor Engine can make thine;
> They must be grop't for, and be tickled too,
> Or they will not be catcht, what e're you do.

Herbert isn't stuffy about jokes; in 'Perirrhanterium' he says 'All things are big with jest [i.e. pregnant with it]: nothing that's plain,/But may be witty, if thou hast the vein' – an aphorism later approvingly appropriated by Tristram Shandy's father. Herbert often tickles his readers by ridiculing objects of fear, particularly death. It is made to look rather silly:

> Death, thou wast once an uncouth hideous thing,
> Nothing but bones,
> The sad effect of sadder groans:
> Thy mouth was open, but thou couldst not sing.

('Death')

Resurrection is gloriously ordinary – like the Stanley Spencer

Resurrection where women on the graves' edges are brushing each other's hair:

> Come away,
> Make no delay,
> Summon all the dust to rise,
> Till it stir, and rub the eyes;
> While this member jogs the other,
> Each one whispring, *Live you brother?*

('Dooms-day')

Astrology becomes absurd:

> As men, for fear the stars should sleep and nod,
> And trip at night, have spheres supplied;
> As if a star were duller than a clod,
> Which knows his way without a guide.

('Divinity')

Even Christ's death is turned into something comfortably commonplace, in a poem attempting to jolly the grieving heart into joy at the Resurrection:

> Awake, sad heart, whom sorrow ever drowns ...
> Thy Saviour comes, and with him mirth ...
> Arise, arise;
> And with his burial-linen dry thine eyes:
> Christ left his grave-clothes that we might, when grief
> Draws tears, or blood, not want an handkerchief.

('The Dawning')

Ultimately it is Herbert's personality which wins the reader. His poems speak directly to us as love poems, whose subject is no less accessible because divine. They have all the absurd passion of, for instance, Yeats:

> My joy, my life, my crown!
> My heart was meaning all the day,
> Somewhat it fain would say:
> And still it runneth mutt'ring up and down
> With only this, *My joy, my life, my crown.*

('A true Hymn')

> She is foremost of those that I would hear praised.
> I have gone about the house, gone up and down

As a man does who has published a new book ...
And ... turned the talk by hook or crook
Until her praise should be the uppermost theme.

> (W. B. Yeats: 'Her Praise')

Sincerity, that elusive and unquantifiable quality – usually quite inappropriately sought for in Renaissance literature – is vibrant throughout Herbert's work. Yet again we find him putting into poetic practice his advice to the Parson preaching, 'dipping and seasoning all our words and sentences in our hearts before they come into our mouths, truly affecting and cordially expressing all that we say, so that the auditors may plainly perceive that every word is heart-deep' (ch.vii).

The hagiographical image of Herbert in Walton's *Life* evidently expresses genuine contemporary veneration. But the poems give a more complex picture of a man whose dualities are honestly summarized by his brother, Lord Herbert of Cherbury:[17]

his life was most holy and exemplary; insomuch, that about Salisbury, where he lived, beneficed for many years, he was little less than sainted. He was not exempt from passion and choler, being infirmities to which all our race is subject.

His quick spirit is evident in the spiritual autobiography of 'Affliction (1)', from the precipitancy of his original espousal of God:

> ... my sudden soul caught at the place,
> And made her youth and fierceness seek thy face

to his rebelliousness in adversity: 'I threatned oft the siege to raise/Not simpring all my age.' Walton's Herbert is, like Dyce's, regrettably, a bit of a simperer;[18] not so Herbert himself. His relationship with God is combative and difficult. 'Thou art my grief alone', he complains in 'Affliction (2)', ticking off God like a child: 'Thou Lord conceal it not: as thou art/All my delight, so all my smart.' This duality is encapsulated in 'Bitter-sweet':

> Ah my dear angry Lord,
> Since thou dost love, yet strike;
> Cast down, yet help afford;
> Sure I will do the like.

> I will complain, yet praise;
> I will bewail, approve:
> And all my sour-sweet days
> I will lament, and love.

The poems' diapason swings from rebellion, anger and depression to tenderness, delight and what Eliot calls 'joy in the convalescence of the spirit in surrender to God'. It is a common misapprehension, however, that Herbert's poems of suffering and revolt all end in relieved submission. Five times Herbert returns to 'Affliction'.[19] 'Sighs and Groans', 'Longing', 'Complaining', 'Grief', 'Misery' – none finds resolution. Herbert's relationship to God is most like that of Hopkins. Both are intense, childlike, passionately asexual (unlike the queasy Crashaw or desperately self-flagellatory Donne). Herbert, like Hopkins, knows the terrible clash of ungovernable feelings, and his cry to love God wholly or not at all – 'let me not love thee, if I love thee not' – is paralleled by the agonized internal conflict of Hopkins' 'Carrion Comfort': 'I wretch lay wrestling with (my God!) my God'. Both yearn to have some procreative function:

> Now I am here, what thou wilt do with me
>  None of my books will show:
> I read, and sigh, and wish I were a tree;
>  For sure I then should grow
> To fruit or shade: at least some bird would trust
> Her household to me, and I should be just.
>
> ('Affliction (1)')

>  ... See, banks and brakes
> Now, leavèd how thick! Lacèd they are again
> With fretty chervil, look, and fresh wind shakes
> Them; birds build – but not I build, no, but strain,
> Time's eunuch, and not breed one work that wakes.
> (G. M. Hopkins: 'Thou art indeed just, Lord')[20]

Both cling to God as a child reaches confidingly for its father's hand, and, given the context, Hopkins' line from 'The Wreck of the Deutschland', 'Over again I feel thy finger and find thee' must surely echo Herbert's tender image in 'Providence':

'Tempests are calm to thee; they know thy hand,/And hold it fast, as children do their father's,/Which cry and follow'.

Not surprising, then, that a state of submissive acceptance should be sought with such intensity, and accepted with such relief:

> O let me, when thy roof my soul hath hid,
> O let me roost and nestle there.

('The Temper (1)')

Yet even in adversity Herbert recognizes that suffering tempers him (hence the two poems with that title). 'We are the trees, whom shaking fastens more'.

Herbert's familiarity with a resisted, gradually dawning perception of affliction's spiritual function must lie behind a curious, but recurrent feature in his poems – the dramatic use of prolepsis. In several poems a positive aspect to negative experience is fleetingly evoked in mid-complaint, apparently without being registered by the speaker. It is an unacknow-ledged, unperceived hint of the resolution which is only openly understood and accepted at the poem's end. For instance, 'Affliction (4)' continues in unrelieved pain for four stanzas:

> My thoughts are all a case of knives,
> Wounding my heart
> With scatter'd smart,
> As watring pots give flowers their lives.
> Nothing their fury can control,
> While they do wound and prick my soul.

Resolution is only reached in the fifth and final stanza, with the realization that 'those powers, which work for grief,/Enter thy pay,/And ... Labour thy praise, and my relief'. But the lesson was offered proleptically in the image of the watering-can. Smuggled under the vividly observed battering, the 'scatter'd smart' a dousing drench from a watering-can gives delicate flowers, is the flip-side of invigorating refreshment: 'As watring pots give flowers their lives'. The single line is parenthetic, engulfed by the primary image of thoughts like knives dominating the stanza. The eye tends to slide over it without pause. The poem is thus mimetic of human response to suffering, our reluctance to look at it calmly, and see its curative function.

One of Herbert's most beautiful, apparently simplest poems, is built on the same principle:

### Virtue

Sweet day, so cool, so calm, so bright,
The bridal of the earth and sky;
The dew shall weep thy fall to night,
⠀⠀⠀⠀For thou must die.

Sweet rose, whose hue angry and brave
Bids the rash gazer wipe his eye:
Thy root is ever in its grave,
⠀⠀⠀⠀And thou must die.

Sweet spring, full of sweet days and roses,
A box where sweets compacted lie;
My music shows ye have your closes,
⠀⠀⠀⠀And all must die.

Only a sweet and virtuous soul,
Like season'd timber, never gives;
But though the whole world turn to coal,
⠀⠀⠀⠀Then chiefly lives.

Ostensibly, the first three stanzas are straightforward images of mortality, resolved finally by the promise of eternal life to the virtuous soul. Yet this very resolution is hidden, like the seeds in a windfall, in the first and second stanzas. The day that will turn to night is described in terms of a wedding, 'The bridal of the earth and sky', in which the day yields to night, her bridegroom. But the wedding-night will (as most marriages do) give birth – to another day. The same vegetative cycle, the natural image for regeneration, recurs in the next stanza. There the rose is painfully personified, flushed with defiance, 'angry and brave' in the face of decay, stinging the watcher to tears. And yet its root is buried in earth and it too will flower again. Images of mortality, 'if we could spell', are images of immortality.

'The Collar' is the most sustained poem in this vein. In it, as in many others (like 'Redemption' or 'Hope'), Herbert speaks through an unenlightened persona whose rebellious twists and turns he, as the Joyce-like artist, invisibly controls. The poem is riddled with *doubles entendres* of which the speaker is unaware. He merely rages against the constraints of his life:

> I struck the board, and cry'd, No more.
> I will abroad.
> What? shall I ever sigh and pine?
> My lines and life are free; free as the road,
> Loose as the wind, as large as store.

and complains about its sterility:

> Shall I be still in suit?
> Have I no harvest but a thorn
> To let me blood, and not restore
> What I have lost with cordial fruit?
> Sure there was wine
> Before my sighs did dry it: there was corn
> Before my tears did drown it.
> Is the year only lost to me?
> Have I no bays to crown it?
> No flowers, no garlands gay? all blasted?
> All wasted?

In his headlong rush, the speaker doesn't register the Christian connotations to his words. He can only think of real thorns, real wine and corn. He is blind to the spiritual dimension – Christ's crown of thorns, the blood he shed for man, the world Adam and Eve lost 'with cordial fruit', the bread and wine of Christ's Communion.[21] In our greater understanding of what the speaker misses, our hearts lift when he begins again:

> Not so, my heart: but there is fruit,
> And thou hast hands

only to sink as he takes another wrong turn into entrenched epicureanism:

> Recover all thy sigh-blown age
> On double pleasures: leave thy cold dispute
> Of what is fit, and not: forsake thy cage,
> Thy rope of sands.

By now the controlling intelligence of the poem has grown

clearer; its condemnation begins to sound audibly through the wild and whirling words of the speaker. In effect, the poem becomes a dialogue between the rebellious speaker, and his conscience, the controlling intelligence of the poem. The same words are spoken by both, to opposite effect. Everything the rebellious speaker says in rejection of an ordered life can be turned back on him, with greater justice. The speaker thinks he is attacking the tedious but easily broken restraints of a disciplined life, a rope of sand made of pettifogging scruples, 'petty thoughts', the 'cold dispute/Of what is fit, and not'. A sharper ear can hear, in the very same words, a reproof of his suicidal faith in a self-indulgent code of life whose support is no stronger than a rope made of sand:

> Thy rope of sands,
> Which petty thoughts have made, and made to thee
> Good cable, to enforce and draw,
> And be thy law,
> While thou didst wink and wouldst not see.

It is the rebellious speaker, not his conscience, that is wilfully blind. In a defiant flourish, he returns to his starting-point –

> Away; take heed:
> I will abroad.

defies death –

> Call in thy death's head there: tie up thy fears.

and resentfully defends his egocentricity –

> He that forbears
> To suit and serve his need,
> Deserves his load.

He does not take heed. He still doesn't see that the answer to a fear of death is not self-indulgence but faith; that with faith death is negligible, he will serve his own spiritual needs and lose the load of mortality. The final sudden repentant turn responds to all the arguments the poem has concealed. The rebellious speaker has been banging on, in order to deafen himself to the words which ultimately he cannot choose but hear:

> But as I rav'd and grew more fierce and wild
> At every word,
> Me thoughts I heard one calling, *Child*:
> And I reply'd, *My Lord*.

'The Collar' is fine poem in form as well as content, suiting one to the other more subtly than the triplets of 'Trinity Sunday' or even the convolutions of 'A Wreath'. The poem is a cry for liberty, and proclaims its form in its first lines: 'My lines and life are free ...' There is no regular, recurrent pattern to the rhymes, nor to the lines' length. Even the arrangement of the poem on the page is literally all over the place. Its final acceptance of restraint is marked by a gradual return to regularity, fully established in the last four lines, which make up a conventional four-line stanza with an abab rhyme-scheme. In fact, order begins to emerge with the turn after 'Thy rope of sands', in that the rhymes begin to settle down (abba cde ecd), although the verse line only gradually withdraws from its jerky alternation of long and short lines into the equilibrium of the last quatrain – a five-stress line followed by a two-stress line settling, like a spun coin coming to rest, in the traditional four-stress to three-stress regular iambic of

> Me thóughts Ĭ héard ŏne cálling, *Child*:
> Ănd Í replý'd, *My Lórd*.

Herbert makes and breaks form as his theme demands. 'Denial' is well-known for its final resolution of form in a manner comparable to, but cruder than 'The Collar'. 'Denial' consists of five-line stanzas, the last line being unrhymed:

> When my devotions could not pierce
> Thy silent ears;
> Then was my heart broken, as was my verse:
> My breast was full of fears
> And disorder.

Ultimately, an appeal for spiritual harmony is answered by stanzaic order, and the last line of the last verse joins the rhyme-scheme:

> O cheer and tune my heartless breast,
> Defer no time;

> That so thy favours granting my request,
>      They and my mind may chime,
>      And mend my rhyme.

In this relatively straightforward poem Herbert's formal effects are openly identified – not ony in the rhyme-scheme and content of the last line, but in the metre also. The metric pattern is firmly established in the poem's first two lines, and is the predictable iambic:

> When my devotions could not pierce
>      Thy silent ears ...

The pattern is promptly broken in the line telling us so (the disruptions are italicized):

> *Then was* my heart *broken*, as was my verse:
>      My breast was full of fears
>      *And disorder.*

In successive stanzas the broken-backed last line remains dislocated, only clicking back into an iambic dimeter in the last stanza.

Herbert's love of music is continually voiced in his poems, many of which, Walton tells us, he set to music, singing and accompanying them on his lute. He frequently uses metric harmony and disharmony to mirror spiritual states, as well as drawing on musical imagery for the same ends. Metric disruption is the finest final instance of his art. It is clear from the divergences between the two manuscript versions of his poems that, far from eradicating irregularity, he introduced it when appropriate. In 'The Thanksgiving' Herbert meditates on man's incapacity to deal with the death of Christ: 'Oh King of Wounds! how shall I grieve for thee,/Who in all grief prevent-est me?' In a bitter snapping of the iambic pattern set up at the poem's beginning, Herbert ironically asks whether he should turn the Crucifixion into something accessible and appealing:

> Shall I then sing, skipping, thy doleful story,
>      And side with thy triumphant glory?
> Shall thy strokes be my stroking? thorns, my flower?
>      Thy rod, my posy? cross, my bower?

Editors gloss 'skipping' as 'omitting', which is clearly one of its meanings here: should Herbert skip the pain of the Crucifixion and look only on the bright side of man's gain? But Herbert is also attacking the impulse to trivialize, changing the line from its original version, which was:[22]

> Shall I then sing, neglecting thy sad story.

'Skipping', the chosen replacement, is interesting for two reasons: because it introduces an image of jaunty triviality sustained in the next lines, and because it fractures the metre in a way 'neglecting' did not, reversing the sensitive third foot from an iamb to a trochee:

> Shall I then sing, skipping, thy doleful story.

The further change of 'sad' to 'doleful' throws the irregularity into higher relief. The third foot clashes with both its neighbours. Instead of the regular slack/stress alternation of both trochaic and iambic metres, stress is followed by stress, slack by slack ('sing, skipping, thy'). Had Herbert kept 'sad', he would simply have lost a slack in mid-line and the aberrant third foot would have gone unnoticed:

> Shall I then sing, skipping, thy sad story

The normal editorial excision of the first edition's comma after 'skipping' robs it of its light-hearted second sense, even though the metric fracture remains.

Similar effects recur elsewhere, often emphasized by some pointer to the broken harmony, as for instance in these lines from 'Affliction (2)':

> Kill me not ev'ry day,
> Thou Lord of life; since thy one death for me
> Is more than all my deaths can be,
> Though I in broken pay
> Die over each hour of Methusalem's stay.

The poem wobbles at the start with its reversed first foot ('Kill me'), to settle into a regular iambic beat thereafter, only breaking down again after the warning 'broken pay' of the penultimate line. The natural stresses, prompted by the sense

# GEORGE HERBERT

(and italicized below) fall quite differently from the expected iambic template (also marked below) – so that, in effect, the line can only be spoken (heavily) as prose:

*Die* over each *hour* of Methusalem's stay.

Though Herbert is a great poet, he is not without flaws. Extensive reading discloses intermittent faults, monotony being chief. His range of rhymes and vocabulary can become repetitive as he turns in his narrow pen of sighs and groans, afflictions and release. That delicate fan-vaulting of echoes, delayed resolutions to abandoned discontents, sometimes has a hollow sound. Poems on similar themes run into each other, and threadbare patches begin to show.

At the same time, with prolonged attention, richer colours emerge. Single images catch light and cast a glow, a dawning revelation. Immediate rewards are strewn among enigmas that can be returned to again and again, in the certainty that with the coming of understanding their secret charge will be released. Herbert's praise of the Bible can be aptly applied to his own *Church*:

> Oh Book! infinite sweetness! let my heart
> Suck ev'ry letter, and a honey gain.
>
> ('The H. Scriptures I')

Herbert died at forty, ready for his work to be destroyed. Had he lived longer, the collection might have been further shaped, the run of seventy-six new poems from the second manuscript carefully pruned. Many poems are what his first publisher rightly called private ejaculations. Herbert's modesty would have been surprised and maybe shocked to know that they have been read and loved for so long.

St Anne's College, Oxford, 1994          Ann Pasternak Slater

# NOTES TO INTRODUCTION

---

1. *George Herbert: The Critical Heritage*, ed. C. A. Patrides, 1983, pp. 89–90. Aubrey's anecdote is corroborated by Herbert's own recommendation to the parson in his home: 'Even the walls are not idle, but something is written or painted there which may excite the reader to a thought of piety', and in his church, 'that there be fit and proper texts of Scripture everywhere painted' (*The Country Parson*, chs. x, xiii, pp. 211, 216). 'Thou art my hiding place' comes from *Psalms* 32: 7 and 119: 114. For the verses referred to, see p. 82.

2. There are three major texts of *The Temple*. *W* is a manuscript arguably in the hand of a scribe but with corrections in Herbert's hand, and contains some 69 of *The Temple*'s 164 poems. It is reasonable to assume that this predates *B* which is also in the hand of a scribe and would appear to be a fair copy of the 'little book' Izaak Walton says Herbert gave Duncon on his death-bed (see p. 380 below). From it derives the First Edition of *1633*, the text used in this edition. See further, *Textual Note*, pp. lviff. The title *The Temple* is nowhere to be found in *W*, is introduced on the title page in *B* and repeated in *1633*. However, the title does not recur elsewhere in the texts of *B* and *1633*, and all three texts have headlines at the top of each page which divide the volume into three sections: (i) *The Church-porch* (containing 'Perirrhanterium'), (ii) *The Church* (containing all the poems from 'The Altar' to 'Love (3)'), and (iii) *The Church Militant* (containing the poem of that name). The title page may have been Herbert's own, or that of those responsible for *B*. But it is clear that all the poems contained in (ii) are thought – by Herbert – to make up *The Church*.

3. The poem is, in fact, a neat metaphorical transposition of Herbert's definition of the pastor, from the first chapter of *The Country Parson*: 'Out of this charter of the priesthood may be plainly gathered both the dignity thereof and the duty: the dignity [verse 2], in that a priest may do that which Christ did, and by his authority and as his vicegerent; the duty [verse 3], in that a priest is to do that which Christ did, and after his manner, both for doctrine and life' (p. 197).

4. 'Hell as the future abode of the damned, so thunderously present in the consciousness of Herbert's contemporaries, is completely bypassed in *The Temple*.' C. A. Patrides, *The English Poems of George Herbert*, 1974, p. 21. Not completely, however. Significantly it recurs frequently in early poems surviving only in *W*. See Appendix 2, pp. 331–7; also *Love I*, p. 51, l.12n and *The Priesthood*, p. 156, l.3n.

GEORGE HERBERT

5. 'Coloss. 3.3.' appears in *W* as well as *B*; i.e. it is among the first 69 poems Herbert thought of including in *The Church*. All generalizations are suspect, however; two other acrostic poems, 'Love-joy' and 'Jesu' only appear in *B*, and therefore arguably post-date *W*. And 'Love (3)', the acme of simplicity, first appears in *W*.

6. 'Heaven' is in *W*, 'Paradise' and 'The Pulley' are not.

7. Puttenham, *The Art of English Poesy*, 1589, II. xii: 'Of Proportion in Figure'. See *Elizabethan Critical Essays*, ed. G. Gregory Smith, repr. 1971, II. 95.

8. OED quotes a definition of 1678, as '(French) songs, or instrumental music, sung or played under anyone's chamber window in the morning'. The modern attribution of the term to 'the dawn song [that] expresses the regret of parting lovers at daybreak' (J. A. Cuddon, *The Penguin Dictionary of Literary Terms*) is an extension of its proper technical sense.

9. *George Herbert: The Critical Heritage*, p. 36, n. 2. Herbert also quotes Donne verbatim in *Perirrhanterium*; see p. 11, ll. 80, 83, nn.

10. Sir T. Browne, *Religio Medici*, ed. M. R. Ridley, 1965, p. 10.

11. *Note-Books and Papers of Gerard Manley Hopkins*, ed. H. House, 1937, pp. 304–5.

12. For *Outlandish Proverbs*, see F. E. Hutchinson, *The Works of George Herbert*, Oxford, 1941, pp. 572–3. The title, *A Priest to the Temple*, logically derives from *The Temple*, to which it was related by title in its first edition: *Herbert's Remains. Or, Sundry Pieces of that sweet Singer of the Temple, Mr. George Herbert* (1652); the Contents list it as *A Priest to the Temple, Or, The Country Parson. His Character, and Rule of Holy Life*. However, successive chapters are titled 'The Parson's Life', 'The Parson's Knowledge', and open correspondingly: 'The Country Parson is exceeding exact in his Life ...', 'The Country Parson is full of all knowledge ...', and so on. This pattern is sustained in each of the succeeding 33 chapters, with one minor modification in Chapter X, and the first two chapters as the only exceptions. The text therefore overwhelmingly indicates what we might in any case expect as the characteristic Herbertian preference, as do the headlines to *The Church Porch*, *The Church*, and *The Church Militant*.

13. 'An Elegy upon the death of Doctor Donne, Dean of Paul's, ll. 63–5.

14. *Richard II*, IV. i. 184ff.

15. W. Empson, *Seven Types of Ambiguity*, repr. 1953, pp. 118–19.

16. See n. 21 below.

17. *George Herbert: The Critical Heritage*, p. 66.

18. William Dyce's *George Herbert at Bemerton*, 1861, is in the Guildhall

Art Gallery, London, and is reproduced in, e.g., T. Hilton: *The Pre-Raphaelites*, 1970, p. 131. The face is closely modelled on the only drawing of Herbert, by Robert White (1645–1703), as it appears in the engraving for the first edition of Walton's *Life*, 1670. White's drawing is reproduced as the frontispiece to A. M. Charles: *A Life of George Herbert*, 1977.

19. The implication that Herbert intended this leitmotif is suggested by his changing the title of 'Temptation' in *W* to 'Affliction (4)' in *B*.

20. Hopkins annotates his poem: 'JUSTUS ES, &c. Jer. xii. 1 (for title)'. Herbert's last word and his imagery suggest the same derivation.

21. Patrides relates the solipsistic agonies of the speaker of 'The Collar' to Christ's words in 'The Sacrifice', in an excellent section on prevenient Grace, as defined by T. S. Eliot: 'The absolute paternal care/That will not leave us, but prevents us everywhere' ('East Coker', ll.160–61, and Patrides, op. cit., pp. 18–20). Prevenient Grace anticipates man's complaints and prayers. The recurrent motif of unapprehended prolepsis noted here is an enactment of this theme, as are the innumerable cross linkings between poems fortifying apparently worldly references with spiritual significance.

22. *W. B.* has no comma after 'skipping'.

# TEXTUAL NOTE

There are three major texts of Herbert's English poems.

*1. MS. Jones B 62 in Dr. Williams' Library, Gordon Square, London.* Known as *W*.

This has no title page and no author's name; the title, *The Temple*, is not to be found anywhere in the manuscript, the headlines being *The Church Porch*, *The Church*, and *The Church Militant*. The English poems are followed by two groups of Latin poems, titled *Passio Discerpta* and *Lucus*. These are agreed to be in Herbert's own hand; a pencilled note in an unknown hand further identifies them as 'supposed to be in Mr. Herbert's own Writing'. Amy M. Charles, Herbert's biographer, suggests a date around 1618 for this text. She also queries the assumption of Canon Hutchinson, the editor of Herbert's *Works*, that the English poems are in the hand of an amanuensis, suggesting that they are either in Herbert's own (secretary) hand, or copied under his supervision, because 'he apparently laid out the work with special care to accommodate his plan of order, working from front and back and completing his copying in the middle' (p. 80). Some 69 of the total 164 English poems (methods of counting vary) appear in this text, but apart from the opening and closing sequences their order differs from that of the two later texts. A complete breakdown is given in Appendix 1, pp. 328–30.

*2. MS. Tanner 307 in the Bodleian Library, Oxford.* Known as *B*.

This is titled *The Temple* on its title page, but without the author's name. The title does not recur and the headlines are as in *W*. It is identified on the first page as 'The Original of Mr. George Herbert's Temple; as it was first Licensed for the press'. The signatures of the licensers appear on the lower part of the title page. This is generally agreed to be a fair copy of the book Herbert entrusted to Duncon on his death-bed, made by members of Nicholas Ferrar's community at Little Gidding. Apart from the position of 'Anagram', the order of the complete run of poems is that of the next text.

3. *The Temple. Sacred Poems and Private Ejaculations. By Mr. George Herbert ... Cambridge: Printed by Thom. Buck, and Roger Daniel, printers to the University. 1633.* The first edition, referred to hereafter as *1633*.

There is general agreement that this text was set up from *B*, with the minor divergencies of spelling and punctuation common at this period. The care lavished on this edition created a text of 'unusual excellence ... The unusually good craftsmanship shown by the Cambridge printer in presenting Herbert's poems to the reader is too valuable to be sacrificed' (Hutchinson, pp. lxxiv–vi).

The present text is therefore that of *1633*, with the following editorial modifications. Spelling has been modernized throughout, except where abbreviated forms may indicate elisions which can affect the metre (e.g. 'oblig'd, 'stopt', 'sugred'), or when a particular form is required for a rhyme (see for instance 'Paradise', p. 129).[1] Punctuation in *W*, *B* and *1633* is fallible. It has been corrected in a small number of instances. This is most noteworthy in the addition of possessive apostrophes, which are rarely used in *1633* and whose omission creates some ambiguities. Major alterations of punctuation are recorded in the notes. The layout of the poems, which is of more than usual importance to Herbert, has been copied exactly, with a preference for *W* and/or *B* when they differ significantly from *1633* (such choices also recorded in the notes). The sonnets have been set solid, without spaces between the quatrains, following the general practice of *B*, but not *1633*. The two capital letters beginning each poem in *1633* have been replaced by one; otherwise all capitals are as in

1. Hutchinson points out that the preterite and participial *-ed* is always scanned as a separate syllable except where the abbreviation *'d* is found (a distinction observed 'almost always' in *W* and *B*, and always in *1633*). *Prayer* is always two syllables, *flower* and *power* one.

*1633*. Some poems with the same title were distinguished in *1633* by Roman numerals; for those that were not, arabic numerals have been added in parentheses. Herbert's other works are presented in modernized spelling and punctuation but his disinclination to capitalize divine pronouns and possessives ('thine', 'he', etc.) has been followed, as creating a greater informal intimacy of tone.

The intention of the present edition has been to bring the reader as close as possible to Herbert's works. His own advice seems clear in *Perirrhanterium*, ll.86–7: 'If studious, copy fair what time hath blurr'd;/Redeem truth from his jaws.' For many years I have seen students struggling to reproduce seventeenth-century spelling (followed in the previous major editions of Herbert's poems) when they were of questionable significance. This seemed pointless. On the other hand, I often found passages that were obscure to me, which Herbert's two best recent editors, Canon Hutchinson and C. A. Patrides, must have understood because they were passed over in silence. They also assumed a knowledge of the Bible well beyond my own. C. A. Patrides made his third editorial principle 'to avoid the impertinence of mere paraphrases' (p. 1). I hope the reader of this text will not mind ignoring unwanted impertinencies. I have drawn freely, with acknowledgement, on the notes of Hutchinson and Patrides. Where I have found further difficulties, I have tried to explain. Biblical quotations, taken from the Authorized Version and, for some allusions to the Psalms, from the Book of Common Prayer, are given quite fully on the assumption that many modern readers may not know their Bible well, and may be unable to chase up references for themselves. Where I have been thoroughly stumped, I have confessed it, in the hope that some readers may do better, and others be comforted.

# ABBREVIATIONS

BCP  The Book of Common Prayer.
*B*    MS. Tanner 307, Bodleian Library, Oxford.
H    F. E. Hutchinson, ed., *The Works of George Herbert*,
      Oxford, 1941.
P    C. A. Patrides, ed., *The English Poems of George Herbert*,
      London, 1974.
OED  The Oxford English Dictionary.
*W*    MS. Jones B 62, Dr. Williams' Library, London.

# SELECT BIBLIOGRAPHY

## BIOGRAPHY

AMY M. CHARLES, *A Life of George Herbert*, Ithaca and London, 1977.

## HERBERT'S LATIN POEMS AND ORATIONS

F. E. HUTCHINSON, ed., *The Works of George Herbert*, Oxford, 1941.
MARK MCCLOSKEY and PAUL R. MURPHY, trans., *The Latin Poetry of George Herbert: A Bilingual Edition*, Athens, Ohio, 1965.

## INTRODUCTORY ESSAYS

JOAN BENNETT, *Five Metaphysical Poets*, Cambridge, 1964, ch.iv.
T. S. ELIOT, 'George Herbert', *Writers and their Work*, No. 152, 1962.
ROSEMARY FREEMAN, *English Emblem Books*, 1948, ch.vi.
L. C. KNIGHTS, *Explorations*, 1946, pp. 112–30.
J. B. LEISHMAN, *The Metaphysical Poets*, 1934, pp. 99–144.
M. M. MAHOOD, 'Something Understood: The Nature of Herbert's Wit', in M. Bradbury and D. Palmer, eds, *Metaphysical Poetry*, *Stratford-upon-Avon Studies* xi, 1970, ch.v.
L. L. MARZ, *The Poetry of Meditation: A Study in English Religious Literature of the 17th Century*, New Haven, 1954, chs vii and viii.

## BOOK-LENGTH STUDIES

STANLEY E. FISH, *The Living Temple: George Herbert and Catechising*, Berkeley, 1978.
JOSEPH H. SUMMERS, *George Herbert: His Religion and Art*, Cambridge, Mass., 1954.
ROSEMOND TUVE, *A Reading of George Herbert*, Chicago, 1952.
H. VENDLER, *The Poetry of George Herbert*, Cambridge, Mass., 1975.

## SPECIALIZED ESSAYS

ELIZABETH COOK, *Seeing Through Words: The scope of late Renaissance Poetry*, New Haven and London, 1986, chs 2 and 3.
A. D. NUTTALL, *Overheard by God: Fiction and prayer in Herbert, Milton, Dante and St. John*, London and New York, 1980, Part 1, chs i–viii.
DOROTHY HUFF OBERHAUS, 'Herbert and Emily Dickinson: A Reading of Emily Dickinson'; ROBERT DI YANNI: 'Herbert and Hopkins: The Poetics of Devotion', both in Edmund Miller and Robert di Yanni, eds: *Like Season'd Timber: New Essays on George Herbert, Seventeenth Century Texts and Studies*, vol. 1, ed. Andrew Low, New York, 1987.

## CRITICAL TRADITION

C. A. PATRIDES, ed., *George Herbert: The Critical Heritage*, London, Boston, Melbourne and Henley, 1983.

## ANNOTATED BIBLIOGRAPHY

C. A. PATRIDES, ed., *The English Poems of George Herbert*, London and Vermont, 1974, pp. 214–38

## ON WALTON'S 'LIFE OF HERBERT'

JOHN BUTT, 'Izaak Walton's Methods in Biography', *Essays and Studies* XIX, 1934, pp. 67–84.

DAVID NOVARR, *The Making of Walton's 'Lives'*, Ithaca, 1958.

## REFERENCE

F. L. CROSS, ed., *The Oxford Dictionary of the Christian Church*, London, New York and Toronto, 1957.

JAMES HASTINGS, ed., *Dictionary of the Bible*, Edinburgh, 1909.

W. G. SMITH and J. E. HESELTINE, *The Oxford Dictionary of English Proverbs*, Oxford, 1963.

M. P. TILLEY, *A Dictionary of Proverbs in England in the Sixteenth and Seventeenth Centuries*, Michigan, 1950.

# CHRONOLOGY

---

| DATE | AUTHOR'S LIFE | LITERARY CONTEXT (Dates of publication) |
|---|---|---|
| 1593 | George Herbert born, 3 April, in Montgomery, Wales, the seventh child of Richard and Magdalene Herbert. Nicholas Ferrar, later his friend, is born the previous year. | Birth of Izaak Walton. Death of Marlowe. Shakespeare: *Venus and Adonis*. Nashe: *Christ's Tears over Jerusalem*. |
| 1594 | | Hooker: *Of the Laws of Ecclesiastical Polity*, Books i–iv. Marlowe: *Edward II*; *The Tragedy of Dido*. Shakespeare: *The Rape of Lucrece*; *Titus Andronicus*. |
| 1595 | | Death of Tasso, Thomas Kyd; execution of Robert Southwell. Sidney: *Apology for Poetry*. Spenser: *Amoretti*; *Epithalamion*; *Colin Clout's come home again*. Montaigne: *Essais* (final form). |
| 1596 | Herbert's father dies, survived by his wife and ten children. | Birth of Descartes. Ralegh: *Discovery of the Empire of Guiana*. Spenser: *Faerie Queene*, Books iv–vi; *Prothalamion*; *Four Hymns*. |
| 1597 | Magdalene Herbert and her children with Lady Newport at Eyton-upon-Severn (to 1599). | Bacon: *Essays*. Dowland: *First Book of Songs*. Shakespeare: *Richard II*, *Richard III*, *Romeo and Juliet*. |
| 1598 | | Hakluyt: *Principal Navigations, Voyages and Discoveries*. Chapman and Marlowe: *Hero and Leander*. Shakespeare: *1 Henry IV*, *Love's Labour's Lost*. |
| 1599 | Magdalene Herbert in Oxford (to 1601) where her friendship with Donne begins, according to Walton. | Death of Spenser. |

Henry of Navarre converts to Catholicism in order to unite France. In England, Conventicles Act passed: absentees from the Church of England to be punished in the last resort by exile or a felon's death. London theatres closed because of plague.

Henry of Navarre accepted as King in Paris. The London theatres re-open.

France declares war on Spain. Failure of the Indies voyage; death of Hawkins. Ralegh's first expedition to Guiana. Tyrone's rebellion in Ireland (to 1603).

England joins France in war against Spain. Death of Drake. Raid on Cadiz led by Essex. In the long-standing power struggle with Essex, Robert Cecil is appointed Secretary of State.

Islands Voyage led by Essex and Ralegh. Death of Philip II of Spain; succession of Philip III.

Edict of Nantes allows right of worship to French Protestants. Peace between France and Spain. Tyrone defeats the English on the Blackwater. Essex appointed Lord Deputy of Ireland. Death of William Cecil, Lord Burghley, Lord High Treasurer since 1572.

Failure of Essex's campaign in Ireland; after returning without permission to court he is arrested. The government suppresses satirical writings and burns pamphlets by Nashe and Harvey. Birth of Cromwell. Globe Theatre opened.

| DATE | AUTHOR'S LIFE | LITERARY CONTEXT |
|------|---------------|------------------|
| 1600 | | Death of Hooker. Birth of Calderón. Fairfax, tr. Tasso's *Gerusalemme Liberata*. Shakespeare: *2 Henry IV*, *Henry V*, *The Merchant of Venice*, *A Midsummer Night's Dream*, *Much Ado About Nothing*. |
| 1601 | Magdalene Herbert moves her family to London, establishing a household at Charing Cross. | Death of Nashe. Donne marries Anne More. |
| 1603 | | Daniel: *Defence of Rhyme*. Florio, tr. Montaigne's *Essays*. Shakespeare: *Hamlet*. |
| 1604 | Herbert probably a day student at Westminster School. | |
| 1605 | Herbert elected scholar at Westminster. Ferrar enters Clare Hall, Cambridge. | Birth of Sir Thomas Browne. Bacon: *Advancement of Learning*. Cervantes: *Don Quixote* (part 1). |
| 1606 | | Death of Lyly. Birth of Corneille. |
| 1607 | | Jonson: *Volpone*. Tourneur(?): *The Revenger's Tragedy*. |
| 1608 | | Birth of Milton. Shakespeare: *King Lear*. |
| 1609 | Magdalene Herbert marries Sir John Danvers. Herbert elected Scholar at Trinity College, Cambridge, and matriculates as pensioner. | Jonson: *Epicoene*. Shakespeare: *Sonnets*, *Troilus and Cressida*. |
| 1610 | Herbert sends two sonnets to his mother; mentions 'my late Ague'. Ferrar elected Fellow of Clare Hall, Cambridge. | |
| 1611 | | The Authorized Version of the Bible published. Chapman's translation of the *Iliad* completed. |
| 1612 | Herbert contributes two poems in Latin (*In Obitum Henrici Principis Walliae*), his first to be published, to a Cambridge | Birth of Samuel Butler. Jonson: *The Alchemist*. Webster: *The White Devil*. Drayton: *Poly-Olbion* (part 1). |

HISTORICAL EVENTS

Essex released but still in disgrace. East India Company founded. Giordano Bruno executed in Rome for his support of the Copernican theory of the universe.

Essex's Rebellion. Essex and Southampton arrested and the former executed. Spanish invasion of Ireland (repelled by English army under Mountjoy in 1602). Lancelot Andrewes appointed Dean of Westminster Abbey. Poor Law Act makes Justices of the Peace responsible for care of the poor in each parish. Monopolies debates in Parliament.
Death of Elizabeth I; accession of James I. Plague in London. Ralegh imprisoned in the Tower. Sir Thomas Bodley re-founds the library of Oxford University. Millenary Petition – Puritans demand reform of the Church of England.
The Hampton Court Conference (authorizing the King James, or Authorized Version of the Bible to be undertaken). Peace with Spain. Gunpowder Plot; severe laws passed against Roman Catholics.

English Parliament rejects union of England and Scotland. Bacon appointed Solicitor-General. Building of Hatfield House, Hertfordshire, for Robert Cecil (to 1672). First successful English colony founded in Virginia. Robert Cecil appointed Lord Treasurer. Plantation of Ulster by Protestant English and Scots begins.
Twelve-year truce between Spain and the Netherlands. Kepler draws up 'Laws of Planetary Motion'. Henry Hudson discovers the river named after him.

Assassination of Henry IV of France. Parliament submits the Petition of Grievances. Galileo reports on his telescopic view of the heavens. Printing of the Old Testament completes the Rheims and Douai Bible (English translation of the Latin Vulgate prepared by Roman Catholic scholars). The Inquisition in Rome begins investigating Galileo. Gustavus Adolphus King of Sweden. James I dissolves his first Parliament; introduces Order of Baronets as a means of raising money.

Death of Henry, Prince of Wales, and of Robert Cecil, Earl of Salisbury. Last recorded burning of heretics in England.

| DATE | AUTHOR'S LIFE | LITERARY CONTEXT |
|------|---------------|------------------|
| 1612 *cont.* | memorial volume (*Epicedium Cantabrigiense, In obitum immaturum Henrici, principis Walliae*) produced following the death of the heir apparent. | |
| 1613 | Herbert becomes Bachelor of Arts. Nicholas Ferrar visits the Continent (till 1618). | Birth of Crashaw. |
| 1614 | Herbert elected Minor Fellow at Trinity College. | Ralegh: *The History of the World*. |
| 1615 | | Cervantes: *Don Quixote* (part 2). Donne ordained. |
| 1616 | Herbert elected Major Fellow and Master of Arts at Trinity College. | Death of Shakespeare and Cervantes. Chapman: *Whole Works of Homer*. Jonson: *Works*. James I: *Works*. |
| 1617 | Herbert becomes sublector quartae classis at Trinity College. Deaths of two of Herbert's older brothers probably in this year. | Death of Donne's wife Anne. |
| 1618 | Herbert writes letter of congratulation to Buckingham for the University (January). Speaks of 'setting foot into Divinity' in a letter to his stepfather (March). Elected Praelector in Rhetoric, Cambridge University (December). Ferrar returns to England to take up employment with the Virginia Company. | Birth of Lovelace and Cowley. |
| 1619 | Herbert delivers oration in Latin for Cambridge University; appointed deputy for Sir Francis Nethersole, the University Orator (September–October); possibly visits Lancelot Andrewes late in the year. His oldest brother Edward appointed ambassador in Paris. | |
| 1620 | Herbert elected University Orator. | Death of Campion. Birth of Evelyn. Bacon: *Novum Organum*. |

# CHRONOLOGY

Marriage of Princess Elizabeth to Frederick Elector Palatine. The Globe Theatre burnt.

The second Globe built. Spilbergen sails round the world. Napier of Merchiston discovers logarithms.
Inquiry into the murder of Sir Thomas Overbury in the Tower implicates the wife of the King's favourite, Somerset.
Harvey expounds the theory of the circulation of the blood. Ralegh released from the Tower to lead an expedition to Guiana.

Inigo Jones begins the Queen's House at Greenwich.

Execution of Ralegh. George Villiers, royal favourite, created Marquess of Buckingham (and Duke in 1623). Bacon appointed Lord Chancellor. The Synod of Dort anathematizes Arminius' heresies. In Bohemia, Protestants rebel against Catholic Hapsburg authority; defenestration of Prague: Thirty Years War begins.

Lancelot Andrewes appointed Bishop of Winchester. Ferdinand II elected Holy Roman Emperor; rejected by Bohemia which offers the crown to the Calvinist Frederick, Elector Palatine. Inigo Jones commissioned to design the Whitehall Banqueting House (to 1622).

Spanish army invades the Palatinate; James I incenses public opinion by failing to intervene on behalf of his son-in-law and the Protestant cause. Settlement of Pilgrim Fathers at Plymouth, Massachusetts.

| DATE | AUTHOR'S LIFE | LITERARY CONTEXT |
|------|---------------|------------------|
| 1621 | | Birth of Marvell and La Fontaine. Donne appointed Dean of St. Paul's. Burton: *The Anatomy of Melancholy.* |
| 1622 | Herbert gravely ill and said to be 'at death's door' (February). Letter to his mother during her illness (May). *True Copies Of all the Latin Orations, made at Cambridge on the 25. and 27. of February last past 1622* published in London. Ferrar becomes Deputy-Treasurer of the Virginia Company. | Birth of Henry Vaughan and Molière. Hawkins: *Observations in His Voyage into the South Sea.* Drayton: *Poly-Olbion* (part 2). |
| 1623 | Herbert delivers farewell to James I (March) and oration to Prince Charles (October) on their visits to Cambridge (*Oratio Quam auspicatissimum Serenissimi Principis Caroli, Reditum ex Hispaniis celebravit Georgius Herbert Academiae Cantabrigiensis Orator*, published in Cambridge). Death of his elder sister Margaret. Named to Parliament for Montgomery borough (November). | Birth of Pascal. Daniel: *Whole Works.* Shakespeare's First Folio. |
| 1624 | Herbert's only service in Parliament probably during the session February–May. Ferrar also returned to Parliament. Herbert allowed six months' leave from university oratorship (June); dispensation by the Archbishop of Canterbury permitting him to be ordained deacon (November). Named comportioner to the rectory of Llandinam, Montgomeryshire (December). No evidence to show that he resumed his duties as orator or university life at Cambridge after the expiry of his leave on 11 December. | Edward Herbert: *De Veritate* published in Paris (with a part dedication to his brother, George). Donne: *Devotions upon Emergent Occasions.* |

# CHRONOLOGY

England in deep economic slump, blamed on James I for his interference in the wool trade and the use of monopolies. Bacon tried and impeached for accepting bribes as Lord Chancellor. Death of Philip III and accession of Philip IV of Spain; ascendancy of Olivarez begins.

James I's *Direction to Preachers* aims to suppress contentious (Calvinist) preaching. Growth of Arminianism within the Church of England.

Abortive expedition of Prince Charles and Buckingham to Spain to win the hand of the Infanta. Statute of Monopolies forbids royal granting of monopoly rights, but allows 14 year exclusive rights for new inventions, the beginning of patent laws.

Charter of the Virginia Company revoked. Birth of George Fox, founder of the Society of Friends, or Quakers. War declared against Spain. Cardinal Richelieu becomes chief minister of France. Peter Minuit, director of Dutch colonies in America, buys the island of Manhattan from the Indians for 24 dollars' worth of beads and ribbons.

| DATE | AUTHOR'S LIFE | LITERARY CONTEXT |
| --- | --- | --- |
| 1625 | Herbert and Donne at his mother's home in Chelsea (December). Ferrar settles at Little Gidding in Huntingdonshire and establishes a religious community of some thirty people. (Herbert does not deliver the Cambridge funeral oration for James I.) | Death of Lodge, Fletcher, Webster. Bacon dedicates his *Translations of Certain Psalms* to Herbert. Grotius: *De Jure belli et pacis*. |
| 1626 | Herbert installed by proxy as canon of Lincoln Cathedral and prebendary of Leighton Ecclesia; delivers oration at York House for Buckingham's installation as Chancellor of Cambridge University; installed at Leighton Bromswold (July). Contributes memorial poem in Latin on the death of Francis Bacon. Ferrar ordained deacon by Laud at Westminster Abbey. | Death of Bacon, Lancelot Andrewes, Tourneur. Birth of Aubrey. Donne: *Five Sermons*. |
| 1627 | Herbert's mother, Lady Magdalene Danvers, dies; Donne delivers memorial sermon at Chelsea; his sermon and Herbert's *Memoriae Matris Sacrum* (Latin poems) entered in the Stationers' Register in July (*A Sermon of Commemoration of the Lady Danvers. By John Donne. Together with other Commemorations of Her; by her Son G. Herbert*, London). | Bacon: *New Atlantis*. May, tr. Lucan's *Pharsalia*. |
| 1628 | Herbert's stepfather, Sir John Danvers, remarries. | Birth of Bunyan. Harvey: *De Motu Cordis*. Earle: *Microcosmographie*. |
| 1629 | Herbert marries his stepfather's cousin, Jane Danvers (March). His eldest brother becomes Lord Herbert of Cherbury. Herbert responsible for the preaching of a sermon at Lincoln Cathedral (May). | Lancelot Andrewes: *XCVI Sermons*. |
| 1631 | | Death of Donne. Birth of Dryden. |

# CHRONOLOGY

Death of James I. Accession of Charles I who marries Henrietta Maria of France. Buckingham's naval raid on Cadiz an expensive fiasco. Parliament dissolved, having refused Charles supplies for war with Spain. Plague in London. Imperial troops under Wallenstein defeat Protestant army of Mansfeld.

Charles I's second Parliament dissolved following attempt to impeach the Duke of Buckingham.

England at war with France. Failure of Buckingham's naval expedition for the relief of French Huguenots besieged at La Rochelle. Charles I raises money by forced loans; case of the Five Knights who unsuccessfully test the legality of imprisoning those who fail to contribute. Charles I buys great art collection of the Gonzaga Dukes of Mantua. Inigo Jones completes the Queen's Chapel at St. James's Palace.

Assassination of Buckingham. Laud is made Bishop of London. Parliament passes Petition of Right in protest against arbitrary taxation and church reform. The King counters with a Declaration to promote religious conformity.
Opposition leaders forcibly delay dissolution of Parliament and are imprisoned. Charles rules for eleven years without Parliament; Laud, effectively chief minister, relies upon the prerogative courts of the Star Chamber and High Commission to enforce policy. Great Puritan migration to New England begins. Massachusetts charter granted.

Magdeberg sacked by Imperial troops under Tilly, who is later defeated by Gustavus Adolphus at Breitenfeld.

| DATE | AUTHOR'S LIFE | LITERARY CONTEXT |
|------|---------------|------------------|
| 1632 | Ferrar's translation of Valdesso and Herbert's letter and notes sent to Ferrar. | Death of Dekker. Birth of Locke and Spinoza. |
| 1633 | Herbert's poems carried to Ferrar by Edmund Duncon (January or February); Herbert dictates his will (25 February); dies of consumption at Bemerton Rectory on 1 March; buried in St. Andrew's Church, Bemerton on 3 March. *The Temple: Sacred Poems and Private Ejaculations, by Mr. George Herbert* published in Cambridge. | Donne: *Poems*. Quarles: *Divine Poems*. Prynne: *Histrio-Mastix*. |
| 1634 | *A Treatise of Temperance and Sobriety: Written by Lud. Cornarus, Translated into English by Mr. George Herbert* (Cambridge). | |
| 1637 | Death of Ferrar. | Death of Jonson. Milton: *A Masque* [*Comus*]. |
| 1638 | *Brief Notes on Valdesso's Considerations* appended with a letter from Herbert to Nicholas Ferrar's translation of *The Hundred and Ten Considerations of Signior John Valdesso* (Oxford). | Cowley: *Loves Riddle* and *Naufragium Joculaire*. Suckling: *Aglaura*. Randolph: *Poems*. Milton: *Lycidas*. |
| 1640 | *Outlandish Proverbs, Selected by Mr. G. H.* (London). | Donne: *LXXX Sermons*, prefaced by Walton's *Life of Donne*. Carew: *Poems*. |
| 1642 | | |
| 1646 | Denunciation of the community at Little Gidding in a pamphlet titled *The Arminian Nunnery*; a Puritan raid destroys most of Ferrar's manuscripts and the community is dispersed. | |
| 1652 | *A Priest to the Temple, or the Country Parson, His Character, and Rule of Holy Life. The Author, Mr. G. H.*, in *Herbert's Remains. Or, Sundry Pieces of that sweet Singer of The Temple, Mr. George Herbert* ... (London). | |
| 1662 | *Georgii Herberti Angli Musae Responsoriae* (epigrams included in James Duport's *Ecclesiastes Solomonis*) (Cambridge). | |

# CHRONOLOGY

HISTORICAL EVENTS

John Eliot, one of the imprisoned Parliamentarians, dies in the Tower. Van Dyck court painter to Charles I. Swedish armies triumphant at Lech and Lützen, where Gustavus Adolphus is killed.

Charles I visits Little Gidding. Laud appointed Archbishop of Canterbury. Thomas Wentworth (later Earl of Strafford) Lord Deputy in Ireland where his policy of 'Thorough' creates efficient government but antagonizes Presbyterians in both Ireland and England. Condemnation of Galileo by the Inquisition for upholding the Copernican system. In France, the Abbé de St. Cyran appointed director of Port-Royal, which becomes a centre for Jansenism.

First writs for ship money on coastal counties, for naval defence of country. Increasing unpopularity of Laud, who suppresses conventicles and orders King James's Declaration of Sports to be revised and read in churches, implying condemnation of the Puritan sabbath.

Laud attempts to impose Book of Common Prayer on the Presbyterian Kirk; riots in St. Giles' Cathedral.

John Hampden fined for refusing to pay ship money. General Assembly of Church of Scotland organizes a Covenant against episcopacy. Prelude to the first Bishops' War in 1639.

Short Parliament (April–May). Scots defeat English at Newburn. Long Parliament (November). Root and Branch petition in London calls for abolition of episcopacy. Laud imprisoned.

Outbreak of Civil War.

King surrenders to Scots at Newark. Abolition of bishops.

# THE COMPLETE ENGLISH WORKS OF GEORGE HERBERT

with Izaak Walton's
*Life of Mr. George Herbert*

# THE TEMPLE.
## SACRED POEMS
### AND
### PRIVATE EJA-
### CULATIONS.

By Mr. GEORGE HERBERT,
late Oratour of the Universitie
of *Cambridge*.

PSAL. 29.

*In his Temple doth every
man speak of his honour.*

CAMBRIDGE:
Printed by *Thomas Buck*
and *Roger Daniel*:
¶ And are to be sold by *Francis
Green*, stationer in
*Cambridge*.

*Title page from the Bodleian Library copy of the first
edition, 1633.*

# The Dedication

Lord, my first fruits present themselves to thee;
Yet not mine neither: for from thee they came,
And must return. Accept of them and me,
And make us strive, who shall sing best thy name.
   Turn their eyes hither, who shall make a gain:     5
   Theirs, who shall hurt themselves or me, refrain.

Explanatory notes to the poems begin on page 387.

# The Printers to the Reader

The dedication of this work having been made by the Author to the *Divine Majesty* only, how should we now presume to interest any mortal man in the patronage of it? Much less think we it meet to seek the recommendation of the Muses, for that which himself was confident to have been 5 inspired by a diviner breath than flows from *Helicon*. The world therefore shall receive it in that naked simplicity, with which he left it, without any addition either of support or ornament, more than is included in it self. We leave it free and unforestalled to every man's judgement, and to the 10 benefit that he shall find by perusal. Only for the clearing of some passages, we have thought it not unfit to make the common Reader privy to some few particularities of the condition and disposition of the Person;

Being nobly born, and as eminently endued with gifts of 15 the mind, and having by industry and happy education perfected them to that great height of excellency, whereof his fellowship of Trinity College in Cambridge, and his Oratorship in the University, together with that knowledge which the King's Court had taken of him, could make relation far 20 above ordinary. Quitting both his deserts and all the opportunities that he had for worldly preferment, he betook himself to the Sanctuary and Temple of God, choosing rather to serve at God's Altar, than to seek the honour of State-employments. As for those inward enforcements to this 25 course (for outward there was none) which many of these ensuing verses bear witness of, they detract not from his freedom, but add to the honour of this resolution in him. As God had enabled him, so he accounted him meet not only to be called, but to be compelled to this service: Wherein his 30 faithful discharge was such, as may make him justly a companion to the primitive Saints, and a pattern or more for the age he lived in.

To testify his independency upon all others, and to

35 quicken his diligence in this kind, he used in his ordinary speech, when he made mention of the blessed name of our Lord and Saviour Jesus Christ, to add, *My Master*.

Next God, he loved that which God himself hath magnified above all things, that is, his Word: so as he hath been
40 heard to make solemn protestation, that he would not part with one leaf thereof for the whole world, if it were offered him in exchange.

His obedience and conformity to the Church and the discipline thereof was singularly remarkable. Though he
45 abounded in private devotions, yet went he every morning and evening with his family to the Church; and by his example, exhortations, and encouragements drew the greater part of his parishioners to accompany him daily in the public celebration of Divine Service.

50 As for worldly matters, his love and esteem to them was so little, as no man can more ambitiously seek, than he did earnestly endeavour the resignation of an Ecclesiastical dignity, which he was possessor of. But God permitted not the accomplishment of this desire, having ordained him his
55 instrument for reedifying of the Church belonging thereunto, that had lain ruinated almost twenty years. The reparation whereof, having been uneffectually attempted by public collections, was in the end by his own and some few others' private free-will offerings successfully effected. With
60 the remembrance whereof, as of an especial good work, when a friend went about to comfort him on his death-bed, he made answer, *It is a good work, if it be sprinkled with the blood of Christ*: otherwise than in this respect he could find nothing to glory or comfort himself with, neither in this, nor in any
65 other thing.

And these are but a few of many that might be said, which we have chosen to premise as a glance to some parts of the ensuing book, and for an example to the Reader. We conclude all with his own Motto, with which he used to conclude
70 all things that might seem to tend any way to his own honour;

*Less than the least of God's mercies.*

8

# The Church-porch

## Perirrhanterium

Thou, whose sweet youth and early hopes enhance
Thy rate and price, and mark thee for a treasure;
Harken unto a Verser, who may chance
Rhyme thee to good, and make a bait of pleasure.
 A verse may find him, who a sermon flies,     5
 And turn delight into a sacrifice.

Beware of lust: it doth pollute and foul
Whom God in Baptism washt with his own blood.
It blots thy lesson written in thy soul;
The holy lines cannot be understood.       10
 How dare those eyes upon a Bible look,
 Much less towards God, whose lust is all their book?

Abstain wholly, or wed. Thy bounteous Lord
Allows thee choice of paths: take no by-ways;
But gladly welcome what he doth afford;      15
Not grudging, that thy lust hath bounds and stays.
 Continence hath his joy: weigh both; and so
 If rottenness have more, let Heaven go.

If God had laid all common, certainly
Man would have been th' incloser: but since now   20
God hath impal'd us, on the contrary
Man breaks the fence, and every ground will plough.
 O what were man, might he himself misplace!
 Sure to be cross he would shift feet and face.

Drink not the third glass, which thou canst not tame,   25
When once it is within thee; but before
Mayst rule it, as thou list; and pour the shame,
Which it would pour on thee, upon the floor.
 It is most just to throw that on the ground,
 Which would throw me there, if I keep the round.   30

9

He that is drunken, may his mother kill
Big with his sister: he hath lost the reins,
Is outlawd by himself: all kind of ill
Did with his liquor slide into his veins.
    The drunkard forfeits Man, and doth devest    35
     All worldly right, save what he hath by beast.

Shall I, to please another's wine-sprung mind,
Lose all mine own? God hath giv'n me a measure
Short of his can, and body; must I find
A pain in that, wherein he finds a pleasure?    40
    Stay at the third glass: if thou lose thy hold,
     Then thou art modest, and the wine grows bold.

If reason move not Gallants, quit the room,
(All in a shipwreck shift their several way)
Let not a common ruin thee entomb:    45
Be not a beast in courtesy; but stay,
    Stay at the third cup, or forgo the place.
     Wine above all things doth God's stamp deface.

Yet, if thou sin in wine or wantonness,
Boast not thereof; nor make thy shame thy glory.    50
Frailty gets pardon by submissiveness;
But he that boasts, shuts that out of his story.
    He makes flat war with God, and doth defy
     With his poor clod of earth the spacious sky.

Take not his name, who made thy mouth, in vain:    55
It gets thee nothing, and hath no excuse.
Lust and wine plead a pleasure, avarice gain:
But the cheap swearer through his open sluice
    Lets his soul run for nought, as little fearing.
     Were I an *Epicure*, I could bate swearing.    60

When thou dost tell another's jest, therein
Omit the oaths, which true wit cannot need:
Pick out of tales the mirth, but not the sin.
He pares his apple, that will cleanly feed.
    Play not away the virtue of that name,    65
     Which is thy best stake, when griefs make thee tame.

The cheapest sins most dearly punisht are;
Because to shun them also is so cheap:
For we have wit to mark them, and to spare.
O crumble not away thy soul's fair heap.    70
  If thou wilt die, the gates of hell are broad:
  Pride and full sins have made the way a road.

Lie not; but let thy heart be true to God,
Thy mouth to it, thy actions to them both:
Cowards tell lies, and those that fear the rod;    75
The stormy working soul spits lies and froth.
  Dare to be true. Nothing can need a lie:
  A fault, which needs it most, grows two thereby.

Fly idleness, which yet thou canst not fly
By dressing, mistressing, and compliment.    80
If those take up thy day, the sun will cry
Against thee: for his light was only lent.
  God gave thy soul brave wings; put not those feathers
  Into a bed, to sleep out all ill weathers.

Art thou a Magistrate? then be severe:    85
If studious, copy fair, what time hath blurr'd;
Redeem truth from his jaws: if soldier,
Chase brave employments with a naked sword
  Throughout the world. Fool not: for all may have,
  If they dare try, a glorious life, or grave.    90

O England! full of sin, but most of sloth;
Spit out thy phlegm, and fill thy breast with glory:
Thy Gentry bleats, as if thy native cloth
Transfus'd a sheepishness into thy story:
  Not that they all are so; but that the most    95
  Are gone to grass, and in the pasture lost.

This loss springs chiefly from our education.
Some till their ground, but let weeds choke their son:
Some mark a partridge, never their child's fashion:
Some ship them over, and the thing is done.    100
  Study this art, and make it thy great design;
  And if God's image move thee not, let thine.

Some great estates provide, but do not breed
A mast'ring mind; so both are lost thereby:
Or else they breed them tender, make them need          105
All that they leave: this is flat poverty.
    For he, that needs five thousand pound to live,
    Is full as poor as he, that needs but five.

The way to make thy son rich, is to fill
His mind with rest, before his trunk with riches:          110
For wealth without contentment climbs a hill
To feel those tempests, which fly over ditches.
    But if thy son can make ten pound his measure,
    Then all thou addest may be call'd his treasure.

When thou dost purpose aught (within thy power)          115
Be sure to do it, though it be but small:
Constancy knits the bones, and makes us stour,
When wanton pleasures beckon us to thrall.
    Who breaks his own bond, forfeiteth himself:
    What nature made a ship, he makes a shelf.          120

Do all things like a man, not sneakingly:
Think the king sees thee still; for his King does.
Simpring is but a lay-hypocrisy:
Give it a corner, and the clue undoes.
    Who fears to do ill, sets himself to task:          125
    Who fears to do well, sure should wear a mask.

Look to thy mouth; diseases enter there.
Thou hast two sconces, if thy stomach call;
Carve, or discourse; do not a famine fear.
Who carves, is kind to two; who talks, to all.          130
    Look on meat, think it dirt, then eat a bit;
    And say withal, Earth to earth I commit.

Slight those who say amidst their sickly healths,
Thou liv'st by rule. What doth not so, but man?
Houses are built by rule, and common-wealths.          135
Entice the trusty sun, if that thou can,
    From his Ecliptic line: beckon the sky.
    Who lives by rule then, keeps good company.

12

Who keeps no guard upon himself, is slack,
And rots to nothing at the next great thaw.                    140
Man is a shop of rules, a well-truss'd pack,
Whose every parcel under-writes a law.
   Lose not thy self, nor give thy humours way:
   God gave them to thee under lock and key.

By all means use sometimes to be alone.                        145
Salute thy self: see what thy soul doth wear.
Dare to look in thy chest; for 'tis thine own:
And tumble up and down what thou find'st there.
   Who cannot rest till he good fellows find,
   He breaks up house, turns out of doors his mind.     150

Be thrifty, but not covetous: therefore give
Thy need, thine honour, and thy friend his due.
Never was scraper brave man. Get to live;
Then live, and use it: else, it is not true
   That thou hast gotten. Surely use alone                155
   Makes money not a contemptible stone.

Never exceed thy income. Youth may make
Ev'n with the year: but age, if it will hit,
Shoots a bow short, and lessens still his stake,
As the day lessens, and his life with it.                      160
   Thy children, kindred, friends upon thee call;
   Before thy journey fairly part with all.

Yet in thy thriving still misdoubt some evil;
Lest gaining gain on thee, and make thee dim
To all things else. Wealth is the conjuror's devil;           165
Whom when he thinks he hath, the devil hath him.
   Gold thou mayst safely touch, but if it stick
   Unto thy hands, it woundeth to the quick.

What skills it, if a bag of stones or gold
About thy neck do drown thee? raise thy head;                 170
Take stars for money; stars not to be told
By any art, yet to be purchased.
   None is so wasteful as the scraping dame.
   She loseth three for one; her soul, rest, fame.

By no means run in debt: take thine own measure.      175
Who cannot live on twenty pound a year
Cannot on forty: he's a man of pleasure,
A kind of thing that's for it self too dear.
   The curious unthrift makes his cloth too wide,
    And spares himself, but would his tailor chide.      180

Spend not on hopes. They that by pleading clothes
Do fortunes seek, when worth and service fail,
Would have their tale believed for their oaths,
And are like empty vessels under sail.
   Old courtiers know this; therefore set out so,      185
    As all the day thou mayst hold out to go.

In clothes, cheap handsomeness doth bear the bell.
Wisdom's a trimmer thing, than shop e're gave.
Say not then, This with that lace will do well;
But, This with my discretion will be brave.      190
   Much curiousness is a perpetual wooing
    Nothing with labour; folly long a doing.

Play not for gain, but sport. Who plays for more
Than he can lose with pleasure, stakes his heart;
Perhaps his wife's too, and whom she hath bore:      195
Servants and churches also play their part.
   Only a herald, who that way doth pass,
    Finds his crackt name at length in the church-glass.

If yet thou love game at so dear a rate,
Learn this, that hath old gamesters dearly cost:      200
Dost lose? rise up: dost win? rise in that state.
Who strive to sit out losing hands, are lost.
   Game is a civil gunpowder, in peace
    Blowing up houses with their whole increase.

In conversation boldness now bears sway.      205
But know, that nothing can so foolish be,
As empty boldness: therefore first assay
To stuff thy mind with solid bravery;
   Then march on gallant: get substantial worth.
    Boldness gilds finely, and will set it forth.      210

14

Be sweet to all. Is thy complexion sour?
Then keep such company; make them thy allay:
Get a sharp wife, a servant that will lour.
A stumbler stumbles least in rugged way.
    Command thy self in chief. He life's war knows,    215
    Whom all his passions follow, as he goes.

Catch not at quarrels. He that dares not speak
Plainly and home, is coward of the two.
Think not thy fame at ev'ry twitch will break:
By great deeds show, that thou canst little do;    220
    And do them not: that shall thy wisdom be;
    And change thy temperance into bravery.

If that thy fame with ev'ry toy be pos'd,
'Tis a thin web, which poisonous fancies make:
But the great soldier's honour was compos'd    225
Of thicker stuff, which would endure a shake.
    Wisdom picks friends; civility plays the rest.
    A toy shunn'd cleanly passeth with the best.

Laugh not too much: the witty man laughs least:
For wit is news only to ignorance.    230
Less at thine own things laugh; lest in the jest
Thy person share, and the conceit advance.
    Make not thy sport, abuses: for the fly
    That feeds on dung, is coloured thereby.

Pick out of mirth, like stones out of thy ground,    235
Profaneness, filthiness, abusiveness.
These are the scum, with which coarse wits abound.
The fine may spare these well, yet not go less.
    All things are big with jest: nothing that's plain,
    But may be witty, if thou hast the vein.    240

Wit's an unruly engine, wildly striking
Sometimes a friend, sometimes the engineer.
Hast thou the knack? pamper it not with liking:
But if thou want it, buy it not too dear.
    Many affecting wit beyond their power,    245
    Have got to be a dear fool for an hour.

A sad wise valour is the brave complexion,
That leads the van, and swallows up the cities.
The giggler is a milk-maid, whom infection,
Or a fir'd beacon frighteth from his ditties.            250
   Then he's the sport: the mirth then in him rests,
   And the sad man is cock of all his jests.

Towards great persons use respective boldness:
That temper gives them theirs, and yet doth take
Nothing from thine: in service, care, or coldness         255
Doth ratably thy fortunes mar or make.
   Feed no man in his sins: for adulation
   Doth make thee parcel-devil in damnation.

Envy not greatness: for thou mak'st thereby
Thy self the worse, and so the distance greater.          260
Be not thine own worm: yet such jealousy,
As hurts not others, but may make thee better,
   Is a good spur. Correct thy passions' spite;
   Then may the beasts draw thee to happy light.

When baseness is exalted, do not bate                     265
The place its honour, for the person's sake.
The shrine is that which thou dost venerate;
And not the beast, that bears it on his back.
   I care not though the cloth of state should be
   Not of rich arras, but mean tapestry.                270

Thy friend put in thy bosom: wear his eyes
Still in thy heart, that he may see what's there.
If cause require, thou art his sacrifice;
Thy drops of blood must pay down all his fear:
   But love is lost; the way of friendship's gone,      275
   Though *David* had his *Jonathan*, *Christ* his *John*.

Yet be not surety, if thou be a father.
Love is a personal debt. I cannot give
My children's right, nor ought he take it: rather
Both friends should die, than hinder them to live.        280
   Fathers first enter bonds to nature's ends;
   And are her sureties, ere they are a friend's.

If thou be single, all thy goods and ground
Submit to love; but yet not more than all.
Give one estate, as one life. None is bound          285
To work for two, who brought himself to thrall.
 God made me one man; love makes me no more,
 Till labour come, and make my weakness score.

In thy discourse, if thou desire to please
All such is courteous, useful, new, or witty:          290
Usefulness comes by labour, wit by ease;
Courtesy grows in court; news in the city.
 Get a good stock of these, then draw the card
 That suits him best, of whom thy speech is heard.

Entice all neatly to what they know best;          295
For so thou dost thy self and him a pleasure
(But a proud ignorance will lose his rest,
Rather than show his cards). Steal from his treasure
 What to ask further. Doubts well rais'd do lock
 The speaker to thee, and preserve thy stock.          300

If thou be Master-gunner, spend not all
That thou canst speak, at once; but husband it,
And give men turns of speech: do not forestall
By lavishness thine own, and others' wit,
 As if thou mad'st thy will. A civil guest          305
 Will no more talk all, than eat all the feast.

Be calm in arguing: for fierceness makes
Error a fault, and truth discourtesy.
Why should I feel another man's mistakes
More, than his sicknesses or poverty?          310
 In love I should: but anger is not love,
 Nor wisdom neither: therefore gently move.

Calmness is great advantage: he that lets
Another chafe, may warm him at his fire:
Mark all his wandrings, and enjoy his frets,          315
As cunning fencers suffer heat to tire.
 Truth dwells not in the clouds: the bow that's there,
 Doth often aim at, never hit the sphere.

Mark what another says: for many are
Full of themselves, and answer their own notion.    320
Take all into thee; then with equal care
Balance each dram of reason, like a potion.
  If truth be with thy friend, be with them both:
  Share in the conquest, and confess a troth.

Be useful where thou livest, that they may    325
Both want, and wish thy pleasing presence still.
Kindness, good parts, great places are the way
To compass this. Find out men's wants and will,
  And meet them there. All worldly joys go less
  To the one joy of doing kindnesses.    330

Pitch thy behaviour low, thy projects high;
So shalt thou humble and magnanimous be:
Sink not in spirit: who aimeth at the sky,
Shoots higher much than he that means a tree.
  A grain of glory mixt with humbleness    335
  Cures both a fever and lethargicness.

Let thy mind still be bent, still plotting where,
And when, and how the business may be done.
Slackness breeds worms; but the sure traveller,
Though he alight sometimes, still goeth on.    340
  Active and stirring spirits live alone.
  Write on the others, Here lies such a one.

Slight not the smallest loss, whether it be
In love or honour: take account of all;
Shine like the sun in every corner: see    345
Whether thy stock of credit swell, or fall.
  Who say, I care not, those I give for lost;
  And to instruct them, 'twill not quit the cost.

Scorn no man's love, though of a mean degree
(Love is a present for a mighty king),    350
Much less make any one thine enemy.
As guns destroy, so may a little sling.
  The cunning workman never doth refuse
  The meanest tool, that he may chance to use.

All foreign wisdom doth amount to this,                                          355
To take all that is given; whether wealth,
Or love, or language; nothing comes amiss:
A good digestion turneth all to health:
    And then as far as fair behaviour may,
      Strike off all scores; none are so clear as they.                     360

Keep all thy native good, and naturalize
All foreign of that name; but scorn their ill:
Embrace their activeness, not vanities.
Who follows all things, forfeiteth his will.
    If thou observest strangers in each fit,                               365
      In time they'll run thee out of all thy wit.

Affect in things about thee cleanliness,
That all may gladly board thee, as a flower.
Slovens take up their stock of noisomeness
Beforehand, and anticipate their last hour.                                      370
    Let thy mind's sweetness have his operation
      Upon thy body, clothes, and habitation.

In Alms regard thy means, and others' merit.
Think heav'n a better bargain, than to give
Only thy single market-money for it.                                             375
Join hands with God to make a man to live.
    Give to all something; to a good poor man,
      Till thou change names, and be where he began.

Man is God's image; but a poor man is
Christ's stamp to boot: both images regard.                                      380
God reckons for him, counts the favour his:
Write, So much giv'n to God; thou shalt be heard.
    Let thy alms go before, and keep heav'ns gate
      Open for thee; or both may come too late.

Restore to God his due in tithe and time:                                        385
A tithe purloin'd cankers the whole estate.
Sundays observe: think when the bells do chime,
'Tis angels' music; therefore come not late.
    God then deals blessings: If a king did so,
      Who would not haste, nay give, to see the show?                     390

Twice on the day his due is understood;
For all the week thy food so oft he gave thee.
Thy cheer is mended; bate not of the food,
Because 'tis better, and perhaps may save thee.
   Thwart not th' Almighty God: O be not cross.      395
   Fast when thou wilt but then: 'tis gain, not loss.

Though private prayer be a brave design,
Yet public hath more promises, more love:
And love's a weight to hearts, to eyes a sign.
We all are but cold suitors; let us move      400
   Where it is warmest. Leave thy six and seven;
   Pray with the most: for where most pray, is heaven.

When once thy foot enters the church, be bare.
God is more there, than thou: for thou art there
Only by his permission. Then beware,      405
And make thy self all reverence and fear.
   Kneeling ne're spoil'd silk stocking: quit thy state.
   All equal are within the church's gate.

Resort to sermons, but to prayers most:
Praying's the end of preaching. O be drest;      410
Stay not for th' other pin: why thou has lost
A joy for it worth worlds. Thus hell doth jest
   Away thy blessings, and extremely flout thee,
   Thy clothes being fast, but thy soul loose about thee.

In time of service seal up both thine eyes,      415
And send them to thine heart, that spying sin,
They may weep out the stains by them did rise:
Those doors being shut, all by the ear comes in.
   Who marks in church-time others' symmetry,
   Makes all their beauty his deformity.      420

Let vain or busy thoughts have there no part:
Bring not thy plough, thy plots, thy pleasures thither.
Christ purg'd his temple; so must thou thy heart.
All worldly thoughts are but thieves met together
   To cozen thee. Look to thy actions well:      425
   For churches are either our heav'n or hell.

Judge not the preacher; for he is thy Judge:
If thou mislike him, thou conceiv'st him not.
God calleth preaching folly. Do not grudge
To pick out treasures from an earthen pot.          430
   The worst speak something good: if all want sense,
   God takes a text, and preacheth patience.

He that gets patience, and the blessing which
Preachers conclude with, hath not lost his pains.
He that by being at church escapes the ditch,        435
Which he might fall in by companions, gains.
   He that loves God's abode, and to combine
   With saints on earth, shall one day with them shine.

Jest not at preachers' language, or expression:
How know'st thou, but thy sins made him miscarry?    440
Then turn thy faults and his into confession:
God sent him, whatsoe're he be: O tarry,
   And love him for his Master: his condition,
   Though it be ill makes him no ill Physician.

None shall in hell such bitter pangs endure,         445
As those who mock at God's way of salvation.
Whom oil and balsams kill, what salve can cure?
They drink with greediness a full damnation.
   The Jews refused thunder; and we, folly.
   Though God do hedge us in, yet who is holy?       450

Sum up at night, what thou hast done by day;
And in the morning, what thou hast to do.
Dress and undress thy soul: mark the decay
And growth of it: if with thy watch, that too
   Be down, then wind up both; since we shall be     455
   Most surely judg'd, make thy accounts agree.

In brief, acquit thee bravely; play the man.
Look not on pleasures as they come, but go.
Defer not the least virtue: life's poor span
Make not an ell, by trifling in thy woe.             460
   If thou do ill; the joy fades, not the pains:
   If well; the pain doth fade, the joy remains.

# Superliminare

Thou, whom the former precepts have
Sprinkled and taught, how to behave
Thyself in church; approach, and taste
The church's mystical repast.

Avoid, profaneness; come not here:      5
Nothing but holy, pure, and clear,
Or that which groaneth to be so,
May at his peril further go.

# The Altar

A broken A L T A R, Lord, thy servant rears,
Made of a heart, and cemented with tears:
    Whose parts are as thy hand did frame;
    No workman's tool hath touch'd the same.
        A H E A R T alone        5
        Is  such  a  stone,
        As   nothing  but
        Thy pow'r doth cut.
        Wherefore each part
        Of my hard heart        10
        Meets in this frame,
        To praise thy name.
    That if I chance to hold my peace,
    These stones to praise thee may not cease.
O let thy blessed S A C R I F I C E be mine,    15
And sanctify this A L T A R to be thine.

# The Sacrifice

*Oh all ye*, who pass by, whose eyes and mind
To worldly things are sharp, but to me blind;
To me, who took eyes that I might you find:
                Was ever grief like mine?

The Princes of my people make a head                5
Against their Maker: they do wish me dead,
Who cannot wish, except I give them bread:
                Was ever grief like mine?

Without me each one, who doth now me brave,
Had to this day been an Egyptian slave.                10
They use that power against me, which I gave:
                Was ever grief like mine?

Mine own Apostle, who the bag did bear,
Though he had all I had, did not forbear
To sell me also, and to put me there:                15
                Was ever grief, &c.

For thirty pence he did my death devise,
Who at three hundred did the ointment prize,
Not half so sweet as my sweet sacrifice:
                Was ever grief, &c.                20

Therefore my soul melts, and my heart's dear treasure
Drops blood (the only beads) my words to measure:
*O let this cup pass, if it be thy pleasure:*
                Was ever grief, &c.

These drops being temper'd with a sinner's tears,        25
A Balsam are for both the Hemispheres:
Curing all wounds but mine; all, but my fears:
                Was ever grief, &c.

Yet my Disciples sleep: I cannot gain
One hour of watching; but their drowsy brain          30
Comforts not me, and doth my doctrine stain:
    Was ever grief like mine?


Arise, arise, they come. Look how they run.
Alas! what haste they make to be undone!
How with their lanterns do they seek the sun!         35
    Was ever grief, &c.


With clubs and staves they seek me, as a thief,
Who am the way of truth, the true relief;
Most true to those, who are my greatest grief:
    Was ever grief, &c.                          40


*Judas,* dost thou betray me with a kiss?
Canst thou find hell about my lips? and miss
Of life, just at the gates of life and bliss?
    Was ever grief, &c.


See, they lay hold on me, not with the hands          45
Of faith, but fury: yet at their commands
I suffer binding, who have loos'd their bands:
    Was ever grief, &c.


All my Disciples fly; fear puts a bar
Betwixt my friends and me. They leave the star        50
That brought the wise men of the East from far.
    Was ever grief, &c.


Then from one ruler to another bound
They lead me; urging, that it was not sound
What I taught: Comments would the text confound.      55
    Was ever grief, &c.


The Priest and rulers all false witness seek
'Gainst him, who seeks not life, but is the meek
And ready Paschal Lamb of this great week:
    Was ever grief, &c.                          60

Then they accuse me of great blasphemy,
That I did thrust into the Deity,
Who never thought that any robbery:
           Was ever grief like mine?

Some said, that I the Temple to the floor    65
In three days raz'd, and raised as before.
Why, he that built the world can do much more:
           Was ever grief, &c.

Then they condemn me all with that same breath,
Which I do give them daily, unto death.    70
Thus *Adam* my first breathing rendereth:
           Was ever grief, &c.

They bind, and lead me unto *Herod:* he
Sends me to *Pilate*. This makes them agree;
But yet their friendship is my enmity:    75
           Was ever grief, &c.

*Herod* and all his bands do set me light,
Who teach all hands to war, fingers to fight,
And only am the Lord of hosts and might:
           Was ever grief, &c.    80

*Herod* in judgement sits while I do stand;
Examines me with a censorious hand:
I him obey, who all things else command:
           Was ever grief, &c.

The *Jews* accuse me with despitefulness;    85
And vying malice with my gentleness,
Pick quarrels with their only happiness:
           Was ever grief, &c.

I answer nothing, but with patience prove
If stony hearts will melt with gentle love.    90
But who does hawk at eagles with a dove?
           Was ever grief, &c.

My silence rather doth augment their cry;
My dove doth back into my bosom fly;
Because the raging waters still are high:                    95
          Was ever grief like mine?


Hark how they cry aloud still, *Crucify:*
*It is not fit he live a day*, they cry,
Who cannot live less than eternally:
          Was ever grief, &c.                    100


*Pilate* a stranger holdeth off; but they,
Mine own dear people, cry, *Away, away,*
With noises confused frighting the day:
          Was ever grief, &c.


Yet still they shout, and cry, and stop their ears,          105
Putting my life among their sins and fears,
And therefore wish *my blood on them and theirs:*
          Was ever grief, &c.


See how spite cankers things. These words aright
Used, and wished, are the whole world's light:              110
But honey is their gall, brightness their night:
          Was ever grief, &c.


They choose a murderer, and all agree
In him to do themselves a courtesy:
For it was their own cause who killed me:                   115
          Was ever grief, &c.


And a seditious murderer he was:
But I the Prince of peace; peace that doth pass
All understanding, more than heav'n doth glass:
          Was ever grief, &c.                    120


Why, Caesar is their only King, not I:
He clave the stony rock, when they were dry;
But surely not their hearts, as I well try:
          Was ever grief, &c.

Ah! how they scourge me! yet my tenderness     125
Doubles each lash: and yet their bitterness
Winds up my grief to a mysteriousness.
                Was ever grief like mine?


They buffet me, and box me as they list,
Who grasp the earth and heaven with my fist,     130
And never yet, whom I would punish, miss'd:
                Was ever grief, &c.


Behold, they spit on me in scornful wise,
Who by my spittle gave the blind man eyes,
Leaving his blindness to mine enemies:     135
                Was ever grief, &c.


My face they cover, though it be divine.
As *Moses'* face was veiled, so is mine,
Lest on their double-dark souls either shine:
                Was ever grief, &c.     140


Servants and abjects flout me; they are witty:
*Now prophesy who strikes thee,* is their ditty.
So they in me deny themselves all pity:
                Was ever grief, &c.


And now I am deliver'd unto death,     145
Which each one calls for so with utmost breath,
That he before me well nigh suffereth:
                Was ever grief, &c.


Weep not, dear friends, since I for both have wept
When all my tears were blood, the while you slept:     150
Your tears for your own fortunes should be kept:
                Was ever grief, &c.


The soldiers lead me to the common hall;
There they deride me, they abuse me all:
Yet for twelve heav'nly legions I could call:     155
                Was ever grief, &c.

Then with a scarlet robe they me array;
Which shows my blood to be the only way,
And cordial left to repair man's decay:
                    Was ever grief like mine?          160

Then on my head a crown of thorns I wear:
For these are all the grapes *Sion* doth bear,
Though I my vine planted and watred there:
                    Was ever grief, &c.

So sits the earth's great curse in *Adam's* fall          165
Upon my head: so I remove it all
From th' earth unto my brows, and bear the thrall:
                    Was ever grief, &c.

Then with the reed they gave to me before,
They strike my head, the rock from whence all store          170
Of heav'nly blessings issue evermore:
                    Was ever grief, &c.

They bow their knees to me, and cry, *Hail king:*
What ever scoffs or scornfulness can bring,
I am the floor, the sink, where they it fling:          175
                    Was ever grief, &c.

Yet since man's sceptres are as frail as reeds,
And thorny all their crowns, bloody their weeds;
I, who am Truth, turn into truth their deeds:
                    Was ever grief, &c.          180

The soldiers also spit upon that face,
Which Angels did desire to have the grace,
And Prophets once to see, but found no place:
                    Was ever grief, &c.

Thus trimmed forth they bring me to the rout,          185
Who *Crucify him,* cry with one strong shout.
God holds his peace at man, and man cries out:
                    Was ever grief, &c.

They lead me in once more, and putting then
Mine own clothes on, they lead me out again.      190
Whom devils fly, thus is he toss'd of men:
               Was ever grief like mine?

And now weary of sport, glad to engross
All spite in one, counting my life their loss,
They carry me to my most bitter cross:      195
               Was ever grief, &c.

My cross I bear my self, until I faint:
Then Simon bears it for me by constraint,
The decreed burden of each mortal Saint:
               Was ever grief, &c.      200

*O all ye who pass by, behold and see*;
Man stole the fruit, but I must climb the tree;
The tree of life to all, but only me:
               Was ever grief, &c.

Lo, here I hang, charg'd with a world of sin,      205
The greater world o'th' two; for that came in
By words, but this by sorrow I must win:
               Was ever grief, &c.

Such sorrow, as if sinful man could feel,
Or feel his part, he would not cease to kneel,      210
Till all were melted, though he were all steel:
               Was ever grief, &c.

But, *O my God, my God!* why leav'st thou me,
The son, in whom thou dost delight to be?
*My God, my God*————      215
               Never was grief like mine.

Shame tears my soul, my body many a wound;
Sharp nails pierce this, but sharper that confound;
Reproaches, which are free, while I am bound.
               Was ever grief, &c.      220

Now heal thy self, Physician; now come down.
Alas! I did so, when I left my crown
And father's smile for you, to feel his frown:
     Was ever grief like mine?

In healing not my self, there doth consist   225
All that salvation, which ye now resist;
Your safety in my sickness doth subsist:
     Was ever grief, &c.

Betwixt two thieves I spend my utmost breath,
As he that for some robbery suffereth.    230
Alas! what have I stolen from you? death:
     Was ever grief, &c.

A king my title is, prefixt on high;
Yet by my subjects am condemn'd to die
A servile death in servile company:    235
     Was ever grief, &c.

They gave me vinegar mingled with gall,
But more with malice: yet, when they did call,
With Manna, Angels' food, I fed them all:
     Was ever grief, &c.    240

They part my garments, and by lot dispose
My coat, the type of love, which once cur'd those
Who sought for help, never malicious foes:
     Was ever grief, &c.

Nay, after death their spite shall further go;  245
For they will pierce my side, I full well know;
That as sin came, so Sacraments might flow:
     Was ever grief, &c.

But now I die; now all is finished.
My woe, man's weal: and now I bow my head.  250
Only let others say, when I am dead,
     Never was grief like mine.

# The Thanksgiving

Oh King of grief! (a title strange, yet true,
    To thee of all kings only due)
Oh King of wounds! how shall I grieve for thee,
    Who in all grief preventest me?
Shall I weep blood? why thou hast wept such store    5
    That all thy body was one door.
Shall I be scourged, flouted, boxed, sold?
    'Tis but to tell the tale is told.
*My God, my God, why dost thou part from me?*
    Was such a grief as cannot be.    10
Shall I then sing, skipping, thy doleful story,
    And side with thy triumphant glory?
Shall thy strokes be my stroking? thorns, my flower?
    Thy rod, my posy? cross, my bower?
But how then shall I imitate thee, and    15
    Copy thy fair, though bloody hand?
Surely I will revenge me on thy love,
    And try who shall victorious prove.
If thou dost give me wealth, I will restore
    All back unto thee by the poor.    20
If thou dost give me honour, men shall see,
    The honour doth belong to thee.
I will not marry; or, if she be mine,
    She and her children shall be thine.
My bosom friend, if he blaspheme thy name,    25
    I will tear thence his love and fame.
One half of me being gone, the rest I give
    Unto some Chapel, die or live.
As for thy passion——But of that anon,
    When with the other I have done.    30
For thy predestination I'll contrive,
    That three years hence, if I survive,
I'll build a spittle, or mend common ways,
    But mend mine own without delays.
Then I will use the works of thy creation,    35
    As if I us'd them but for fashion.

32

The world and I will quarrel; and the year
    Shall not perceive, that I am here.
My music shall find thee, and ev'ry string
    Shall have his attribute to sing;        40
That all together may accord in thee,
    And prove one God, one harmony.
If thou shalt give me wit, it shall appear;
    If thou hast giv'n it me, 'tis here.
Nay, I will read thy book, and never move    45
    Till I have found therein thy love;
Thy art of love, which I'll turn back on thee,
    O my dear Saviour, Victory!
Then for thy passion——I will do for that——
    Alas, my God, I know not what.    50


# The Reprisal

I have consider'd it, and find
There is no dealing with thy mighty passion:
For though I die for thee, I am behind;
    My sins deserve the condemnation.


    O make me innocent, that I    5
May give a disentangled state and free:
And yet thy wounds still my attempts defy,
    For by thy death I die for thee.


    Ah! was it not enough that thou
By thy eternal glory didst outgo me?    10
Couldst thou not grief's sad conquests me allow,
    But in all vict'ries overthrow me?


    Yet by confession will I come
Into the conquest. Though I can do nought
Against thee, in thee will I overcome    15
    The man, who once against thee fought.

# The Agony

Philosophers have measur'd mountains,
Fathom'd the depths of seas, of states, and kings,
Walk'd with a staff to heav'n, and traced fountains:
　　But there are two vast, spacious things,
The which to measure it doth more behove:　　　5
Yet few there are that sound them; Sin and Love.

　　Who would know Sin, let him repair
Unto mount Olivet; there shall he see
A man so wrung with pains, that all his hair,
　　His skin, his garments bloody be.　　　10
Sin is that press and vice, which forceth pain
To hunt his cruel food through ev'ry vein.

　　Who knows not Love, let him assay
And taste that juice, which on the cross a pike
Did set again abroach, then let him say　　　15
　　If ever he did taste the like.
Love is that liquor sweet and most divine,
Which my God feels as blood; but I, as wine.

# The Sinner

Lord, how I am all ague, when I seek
    What I have treasur'd in my memory!
    Since, if my soul make even with the week,
Each seventh note by right is due to thee.
I find there quarries of pil'd vanities,           5
    But shreds of holiness, that dare not venture
    To show their face, since cross to thy decrees:
There the circumference earth is, heav'n the centre.
In so much dregs the quintessence is small:
    The spirit and good extract of my heart       10
    Comes to about the many hundredth part.
Yet Lord restore thine image, hear my call:
    And though my hard heart scarce to thee can groan,
    Remember that thou once didst write in stone.

# Good Friday

O my chief good,
How shall I measure out thy blood?
How shall I count what thee befell,
  And each grief tell?

  Shall I thy woes     5
Number according to thy foes?
Or, since one star show'd thy first breath,
  Shall all thy death?

  Or shall each leaf,
Which falls in Autumn, score a grief?  10
Or cannot leaves, but fruit, be sign
  Of the true vine?

  Then let each hour
Of my whole life one grief devour:
That thy distress through all may run,  15
  And be my sun.

  Or rather let
My several sins their sorrows get;
That as each beast his cure doth know,
  Each sin may so.     20

Since blood is fittest, Lord, to write
Thy sorrows in, and bloody fight;
My heart hath store, write there, where in
One box doth lie both ink and sin:

That when sin spies so many foes,          25
Thy whips, thy nails, thy wounds, thy woes
All come to lodge there, sin may say,
*No room for me*, and fly away.

Sin being gone, oh fill the place,
And keep possession with thy grace;       30
Lest sin take courage and return,
And all the writings blot or burn.

# Redemption

Having been tenant long to a rich Lord,
    Not thriving, I resolved to be bold,
    And make a suit unto him, to afford
A new small-rented lease, and cancel th' old.
In heaven at his manor I him sought:       5
    They told me there, that he was lately gone
    About some land, which he had dearly bought
Long since on earth, to take possession.
I straight return'd, and knowing his great birth,
    Sought him accordingly in great resorts;    10
    In cities, theatres, gardens, parks, and courts:
At length I heard a ragged noise and mirth
    Of thieves and murderers: there I him espied
    Who straight, *Your suit is granted,* said, and died.

# Sepulchre

O blessed body! Whither art thou thrown?
No lodging for thee, but a cold hard stone?
So many hearts on earth, and yet not one
      Receive thee?
Sure there is room within our hearts' good store;    5
For they can lodge transgressions by the score:
Thousands of toys dwell there, yet out of door
      They leave thee.
But that which shows them large, shows them unfit.
What ever sin did this pure rock commit,    10
Which holds thee now? Who hath indicted it
      Of murder?
Where our hard hearts have took up stones to brain thee,
And missing this, most falsely did arraign thee;
Only these stones in quiet entertain thee,    15
      And order.
And as of old, the law by heav'nly art
Was writ in stone; so thou, which also art
The letter of the word, find'st no fit heart
      To hold thee.    20
Yet do we still persist as we began,
And so should perish, but that nothing can,
Though it be cold, hard, foul, from loving man
      Withhold thee.

# Easter

Rise heart; thy Lord is risen. Sing his praise
    Without delays,
Who takes thee by the hand, that thou likewise
    With him mayst rise:
That, as his death calcined thee to dust,      5
His life may make thee gold, and much more just.

Awake, my lute, and struggle for thy part
    With all thy art.
The cross taught all wood to resound his name,
    Who bore the same.      10
His stretched sinews taught all strings, what key
Is best to celebrate this most high day.

Consort both heart and lute, and twist a song
    Pleasant and long:
Or since all music is but three parts vied     15
    And multiplied,
O let thy blessed Spirit bear a part,
And make up our defects with his sweet art.

I got me flowers to straw thy way;
I got me boughs off many a tree:      20
But thou wast up by break of day,
And brought'st thy sweets along with thee.

The Sun arising in the East,
Though he give light, and th' East perfume;
If they should offer to contest      25
With thy arising, they presume.

Can there be any day but this,
Though many suns to shine endeavour?
We count three hundred, but we miss:
There is but one, and that one ever.      30

# Easter wings (1)

Lord, who createdst man in wealth and store,
    Though foolishly he lost the same,
        Decaying more and more,
            Till he became
                Most poor:
                With thee
            O let me rise
        As larks, harmoniously,
    And sing this day thy victories:
Then shall the fall further the flight in me.

5

10

# Easter wings (2)

My tender age in sorrow did begin:
And still with sicknesses and shame
Thou didst so punish sin,
That I became
Most thin.
With thee
Let me combine,
And feel this day thy victory:
For, if I imp my wing on thine,
Affliction shall advance the flight in me.

5

10

# H. Baptism (1)

As he that sees a dark and shady grove,
      Stays not, but looks beyond it on the sky;
      So when I view my sins, mine eyes remove
More backward still, and to that water fly,
Which is above the heav'ns, whose spring and rent          5
      Is in my dear Redeemer's pierced side.
      O blessed streams! either ye do prevent
And stop our sins from growing thick and wide,
Or else give tears to drown them, as they grow.
      In you Redemption measures all my time,          10
      And spreads the plaster equal to the crime:
You taught the book of life my name, that so
      What ever future sins should me miscall,
      Your first acquaintance might discredit all.


# H. Baptism (2)

      Since, Lord, to thee
      A narrow way and little gate
Is all the passage, on my infancy
      Thou didst lay hold, and antedate
      My faith in me.          5


      O let me still
      Write thee great God, and me a child:
Let me be soft and supple to thy will,
      Small to my self, to others mild,
      Behither ill.          10


      Although by stealth
      My flesh get on, yet let her sister
My soul bid nothing, but preserve her wealth:
      The growth of flesh is but a blister;
      Childhood is health.          15

42

# Nature

Full of rebellion, I would die,
Or fight, or travel, or deny
That thou has aught to do with me.
                O tame my heart;
                It is thy highest art     5
To captivate strong holds to thee.

If thou shalt let this venom lurk,
And in suggestions fume and work,
My soul will turn to bubbles straight,
                And thence by kind     10
                Vanish into a wind,
Making thy workmanship deceit.

O smooth my rugged heart, and there
Engrave thy rev'rend law and fear;
Or make a new one, since the old     15
                Is sapless grown,
                And a much fitter stone
To hide my dust, than thee to hold.

# Sin (1)

Lord, with what care hast thou begirt us round!
  Parents first season us: then schoolmasters
  Deliver us to laws; they send us bound
To rules of reason, holy messengers,
Pulpits and sundays, sorrow dogging sin,     5
  Afflictions sorted, anguish of all sizes,
  Fine nets and stratagems to catch us in,
Bibles laid open, millions of surprises,

Blessings beforehand, ties of gratefulness,
   The sound of glory ringing in our ears.      10
   Without, our shame; within, our consciences;
Angels and grace, eternal hopes and fears.
   Yet all these fences and their whole array
   One cunning bosom-sin blows quite away.


# Affliction (1)

When first thou didst entice to thee my heart,
       I thought the service brave:
So many joys I writ down for my part,
       Besides what I might have
Out of my stock of natural delights,      5
Augmented with thy gracious benefits.

I looked on thy furniture so fine,
       And made it fine to me:
Thy glorious household-stuff did me entwine,
       And 'tice me unto thee.      10
Such stars I counted mine: both heav'n and earth
Paid me my wages in a world of mirth.

What pleasures could I want, whose King I served?
       Where joys my fellows were?
Thus argu'd into hopes, my thoughts reserved      15
       No place for grief or fear.
Therefore my sudden soul caught at the place,
And made her youth and fierceness seek thy face.

At first thou gav'st me milk and sweetnesses;
       I had my wish and way:      20
My days were straw'd with flow'rs and happiness;
       There was no month but May.
But with my years sorrow did twist and grow,
And made a party unawares for woe.

My flesh began unto my soul in pain,      25
         Sicknesses cleave my bones;
Consuming agues dwell in ev'ry vein,
         And tune my breath to groans.
Sorrow was all my soul; I scarce believed,
Till grief did tell me roundly, that I lived.      30

When I got health, thou took'st away my life,
         And more; for my friends die:
My mirth and edge was lost; a blunted knife
         Was of more use than I.
Thus thin and lean without a fence or friend,      35
I was blown through with ev'ry storm and wind.

Whereas my birth and spirit rather took
         The way that takes the town;
Thou didst betray me to a lingring book,
         And wrap me in a gown.      40
I was entangled in the world of strife,
Before I had the power to change my life.

Yet, for I threatned oft the siege to raise,
         Not simpring all mine age,
Thou often didst with Academic praise      45
         Melt and dissolve my rage.
I took thy sweetned pill, till I came where
I could not go away, nor persevere.

Yet lest perchance I should too happy be
         In my unhappiness,
Turning my purge to food, thou throwest me      50
         Into more sicknesses.
Thus doth thy power cross-bias me, not making
Thine own gift good, yet me from my ways taking.

Now I am here, what thou wilt do with me                55
          None of my books will show:
I read, and sigh, and wish I were a tree;
          For sure I then should grow
To fruit or shade: at least some bird would trust
Her household to me, and I should be just.                60

Yet, though thou troublest me, I must be meek;
          In weakness must be stout.
Well, I will change the service, and go seek
          Some other master out.
Ah my dear God! though I am clean forgot,                65
Let me not love thee, if I love thee not.

# Repentance

Lord, I confess my sin is great;
  Great is my sin. Oh! gently treat
With thy quick flow'r, thy momentany bloom;
         Whose life still pressing
         Is one undressing,                5
  A steady aiming at a tomb.

Man's age is two hours' work, or three:
  Each day doth round about us see.
Thus are we to delights: but we are all
         To sorrows old,
         If life be told                10
From what life feeleth, Adam's fall.

O let thy height of mercy then
  Compassionate short-breathed men.
Cut me not off for my most foul transgression:                15
         I do confess
         My foolishness;
  My God, accept of my confession.

Sweeten at length this bitter bowl,
  Which thou hast pour'd into my soul;      20
Thy wormwood turn to health, winds to fair weather:
        For if thou stay,
        I and this day,
As we did rise, we die together.

When thou for sin rebukest man,      25
  Forthwith he waxeth woe and wan:
Bitterness fills our bowels; all our hearts
        Pine, and decay,
        And drop away,
And carry with them th' other parts.      30

But thou wilt sin and grief destroy;
  That so the broken bones may joy,
And tune together in a well-set song,
        Full of his praises,
        Who dead men raises;      35
Fractures well cur'd make us more strong.

# Faith

Lord, how couldst thou so much appease
Thy wrath for sin, as when man's sight was dim,
And could see little, to regard his ease,
  And bring by Faith all things to him?

Hungry I was, and had no meat:      5
I did conceit a most delicious feast;
I had it straight, and did as truly eat,
  As ever did a welcome guest.

There is a rare outlandish root,
Which when I could not get, I thought it here:      10
That apprehension cur'd so well my foot,
  That I can walk to heav'n well near.

I owed thousands and much more.
I did believe that I did nothing owe,
And liv'd accordingly; my creditor                    15
    Believes so too, and lets me go.


Faith makes me any thing, or all
That I believe is in the sacred story:
And where sin placeth me in Adam's fall,
    Faith sets me higher in his glory.              20


If I go lower in the book,
What can be lower than the common manger?
Faith puts me there with him, who sweetly took
    Our flesh and frailty, death and danger.


If bliss had lien in art or strength,                 25
None but the wise or strong had gained it:
Where now by Faith all arms are of a length;
    One size doth all conditions fit.


A peasant may believe as much
As a great Clerk, and reach the highest stature.      30
Thus dost thou make proud knowledge bend and crouch
    While grace fills up uneven nature.


When creatures had no real light
Inherent in them, thou didst make the sun
Impute a lustre, and allow them bright;               35
    And in this show what Christ hath done.


That which before was darkned clean
With bushy groves, pricking the looker's eye,
Vanisht away, when Faith did change the scene:
    And then appear'd a glorious sky.               40


What though my body run to dust?
Faith cleaves unto it, counting ev'ry grain
With an exact and most particular trust,
    Reserving all for flesh again.

# Prayer (1)

Prayer the Church's banquet, Angels' age,
    God's breath in man returning to his birth,
    The soul in paraphrase, heart in pilgrimage,
The Christian plummet sounding heav'n and earth;
Engine against th' Almighty, sinners' tower,         5
    Reversed thunder, Christ-side-piercing spear,
    The six-days-world transposing in an hour,
A kind of tune, which all things hear and fear;
Softness, and peace, and joy, and love, and bliss,
    Exalted Manna, gladness of the best,         10
    Heaven in ordinary, man well drest,
The milky way, the bird of Paradise,
    Church-bells beyond the stars heard, the soul's blood,
    The land of spices; something understood.

# The H. Communion

Not in rich furniture, or fine array,
    Nor in a wedge of gold,
    Thou, who from me wast sold,
    To me dost now thy self convey;
For so thou should'st without me still have been,     5
    Leaving within me sin:

But by the way of nourishment and strength
    Thou creep'st into my breast;
    Making thy way my rest,
    And thy small quantities my length;         10
Which spread their forces into every part,
    Meeting sin's force and art.

Yet can these not get over to my soul,
    Leaping the wall that parts
    Our souls and fleshly hearts;
  But as th' outworks, they may control    15
My rebel-flesh, and carrying thy name,
    Affright both sin and shame.


Only thy grace, which with these elements comes,
    Knoweth the ready way,    20
    And hath the privy key,
  Op'ning the soul's most subtle rooms;
While those to spirits refin'd, at door attend
    Dispatches from their friend.


Give me my captive soul, or take    25
    My body also thither.
Another lift like this will make
    Them both to be together.


Before that sin turn'd flesh to stone,
    And all our lump to leaven,    30
A fervent sigh might well have blown
    Our innocent earth to heaven.


For sure when Adam did not know
    To sin, or sin to smother;
He might to heav'n from Paradise go,    35
    As from one room t'another.


Thou hast restor'd to us this ease
    By this thy heav'nly blood;
Which I can go to, when I please,
    And leave th' earth to their food.    40

# Antiphon (1)

*Cho.* Let all the world in ev'ry corner sing
　　　　*My God and King.*

　　*Vers.* The heav'ns are not too high,
　　　　His praise may thither fly:
　　　　The earth is not too low,　　　　　　　5
　　　　His praises there may grow.

*Cho.* Let all the world in ev'ry corner sing,
　　　　*My God and King.*

　　*Vers.* The church with psalms must shout
　　　　No door can keep them out:　　　　　10
　　　　But above all, the heart
　　　　Must bear the longest part.

*Cho.* Let all the world in ev'ry corner sing,
　　　　*My God and King.*


# Love I

Immortal Love, author of this great frame,
　　Sprung from that beauty which can never fade;
　　How hath man parcel'd out thy glorious name,
And thrown it on that dust which thou hast made,
While mortal love doth all the title gain!　　　　5
　　Which siding with invention, they together
　　Bear all the sway, possessing heart and brain,
(Thy workmanship) and give thee share in neither.
Wit fancies beauty, beauty raiseth wit:
　　The world is theirs; they two play out the game,　　10
　　Thou standing by: and though thy glorious name
Wrought our deliverance from the infernal pit,
　　Who sings thy praise? only a scarf or glove
　　Doth warm our hands, and make them write of love.

# Love II

Immortal Heat, O let thy greater flame
   Attract the lesser to it: let those fires,
   Which shall consume the world, first make it tame;
And kindle in our hearts such true desires,
As may consume our lusts, and make thee way.      5
   Then shall our hearts pant thee; then shall our brain
   All her invention on thine Altar lay,
And there in hymns send back thy fire again:
Our eyes shall see thee, which before saw dust;
   Dust blown by wit, till that they both were blind:    10
   Thou shalt recover all thy goods in kind,
Who wert disseized by usurping lust:
   All knees shall bow to thee; all wits shall rise,
   And praise him who did make and mend our eyes.

# The Temper (1)

How should I praise thee, Lord! how should my rhymes
   Gladly engrave thy love in steel,
   If what my soul doth feel sometimes,
     My soul might ever feel!

Although there were some forty heav'ns, or more,      5
   Sometimes I peer above them all;
   Sometimes I hardly reach a score,
     Sometimes to hell I fall.

O rack me not to such a vast extent;
   Those distances belong to thee:      10
   The world's too little for thy tent,
     A grave too big for me.

Wilt thou meet arms with man, that thou dost stretch
    A crumb of dust from heav'n to hell?
    Will great God measure with a wretch?         15
      Shall he thy stature spell?

O let me, when thy roof my soul hath hid,
    O let me roost and nestle there:
    Then of a sinner thou art rid,
      And I of hope and fear.         20

Yet take thy way; for sure thy way is best:
    Stretch or contract me, thy poor debtor:
    This is but tuning of my breast,
      To make the music better.

Whether I fly with angels, fall with dust,       25
    Thy hands made both, and I am there:
    Thy power and love, my love and trust
      Make one place ev'ry where.

# The Temper (2)

It cannot be. Where is that mighty joy,
    Which just now took up all my heart?
    Lord, if thou must needs use thy dart,
Save that, and me; or sin for both destroy.

The grosser world stands to thy word and art;     5
    But thy diviner world of grace
    Thou suddenly dost raise and race,
And ev'ry day a new Creator art.

O fix thy chair of grace, that all my powers
    May also fix their reverence:           10
    For when thou dost depart from hence,
They grow unruly, and sit in thy bowers.

Scatter, or bind them all to bend to thee:
    Though elements change, and heaven move,
    Let not thy higher Court remove,      15
But keep a standing Majesty in me.

# Jordan (1)

Who says that fictions only and false hair
Become a verse? Is there in truth no beauty?
Is all good structure in a winding stair?
May no lines pass, except they do their duty
    Not to a true, but painted chair?      5

Is it no verse, except enchanted groves
And sudden arbours shadow coarse-spun lines?
Must purling streams refresh a lover's loves?
Must all be veil'd, while he that reads, divines,
    Catching the sense at two removes?      10

Shepherds are honest people; let them sing:
Riddle who list, for me, and pull for Prime:
I envy no man's nightingale or spring;
Nor let them punish me with loss of rhyme,
    Who plainly say, *My God, My King*.      15

# Employment (1)

If as a flower doth spread and die,
  Thou wouldst extend me to some good,
Before I were by frost's extremity
                    Nipt in the bud;

The sweetness and the praise were thine;       5
  But the extension and the room,
Which in thy garland I should fill, were mine
                    At thy great doom.

For as thou dost impart thy grace,
  The greater shall our glory be.          10
The measure of our joys is in this place,
                    The stuff with thee.

Let me not languish then, and spend
  A life as barren to thy praise,
As is the dust, to which that life doth tend,     15
                    But with delays.

All things are busy; only I
  Neither bring honey with the bees,
Nor flowers to make that, nor the husbandry
                    To water these.      20

I am no link of thy great chain,
  But all my company is a weed.
Lord place me in thy consort; give one strain
                    To my poor reed.

# The H. Scriptures I

Oh Book! infinite sweetness! let my heart
    Suck ev'ry letter, and a honey gain,
    Precious for any grief in any part;
To clear the breast, to mollify all pain.
Thou art all health, health thriving, till it make      5
    A full eternity: thou art a mass
    Of strange delights, where we may wish and take.
Ladies, look here; this is the thankfull glass,
That mends the looker's eyes: this is the well
    That washes what it shows. Who can endear      10
    Thy praise too much? thou art heav'n's Lidger here,
Working against the states of death and hell.
    Thou art joy's handsel: heav'n lies flat in thee,
    Subject to ev'ry mounter's bended knee.

# II

Oh that I knew how all thy lights combine,
    And the configurations of their glory!
    Seeing not only how each verse doth shine,
But all the constellations of the story.
This verse marks that, and both do make a motion      5
    Unto a third, that ten leaves off doth lie:
    Then as dispersed herbs do watch a potion,
These three make up some Christian's destiny:
Such are thy secrets, which my life makes good,
    And comments on thee: for in ev'ry thing      10
    Thy words do find me out, and parallels bring,
And in another make me understood.
    Stars are poor books, and oftentimes do miss:
    This book of stars lights to eternal bliss.

# Whitsunday

Listen sweet Dove unto my song,
    And spread thy golden wings in me;
    Hatching my tender heart so long,
Till it get wing, and fly away with thee.

    Where is that fire which once descended    5
    On thy Apostles? thou didst then
    Keep open house, richly attended,
Feasting all comers by twelve chosen men.

    Such glorious gifts thou didst bestow,
    That th' earth did like a heav'n appear;    10
    The stars were coming down to know
If they might mend their wages, and serve here.

    The sun which once did shine alone,
    Hung down his head, and wisht for night,
    When he beheld twelve suns for one    15
Going about the world, and giving light.

    But since those pipes of gold, which brought
    That cordial water to our ground,
    Were cut and martyr'd by the fault
Of those, who did themselves through their side wound,    20

    Thou shutt'st the door, and keep'st within;
    Scarce a good joy creeps through the chink:
    And if the braves of conqu'ring sin
Did not excite thee, we should wholly sink.

    Lord, though we change, thou art the same;    25
    The same sweet God of love and light:
    Restore this day, for thy great name,
Unto his ancient and miraculous right.

# Grace

My stock lies dead and no increase
Doth my dull husbandry improve:
O let thy graces without cease
        Drop from above!

If still the sun should hide his face,        5
Thy house would but a dungeon prove,
Thy works, night's captives: O let grace
        Drop from above!

The dew doth ev'ry morning fall;
And shall the dew outstrip thy dove?        10
The dew, for which grass cannot call,
        Drop from above.

Death is still working like a mole,
And digs my grave at each remove:
Let grace work too, and on my soul        15
        Drop from above.

Sin is still hammering my heart
Unto a hardness, void of love:
Let suppling grace, to cross his art,
        Drop from above.        20

O come! for thou dost know the way.
Or if to me thou wilt not move,
Remove me, where I need not say,
        *Drop from above.*

# Praise (1)

To write a verse or two is all the praise
        That I can raise:
    Mend my estate in any ways,
        Thou shalt have more.

I go to Church; help me to wings, and I        5
        Will thither fly;
    Or, if I mount unto the sky,
        I will do more.

Man is all weakness; there is no such thing
        As Prince or King:        10
    His arm is short; yet with a sling
        He may do more.

An herb distill'd, and drunk, may dwell next door,
        On the same floor,
    To a brave soul: Exalt the poor,        15
        They can do more.

O raise me then! poor bees, that work all day,
        Sting my delay,
    Who have a work, as well as they,
        And much, much more.        20

# Affliction (2)

        Kill me not ev'ry day,
Thou Lord of life; since thy one death for me
    Is more than all my deaths can be,
        Though I in broken pay
Die over each hour of Methusalem's stay.        5

If all men's tears were let
Into one common sewer, sea, and brine;
What were they all, compar'd to thine?
Wherein if they were set,
They would discolour thy most bloody sweat.          10

Thou art my grief alone,
Thou Lord conceal it not: and as thou art
All my delight, so all my smart:
Thy cross took up in one,
By way of imprest, all my future moan.          15

# Mattins

I cannot ope mine eyes,
But thou art ready there to catch
My morning-soul and sacrifice:
Then we must needs for that day make a match.

My God, what is a heart?          5
Silver, or gold, or precious stone,
Or star, or rainbow, or a part
Of all these things or all of them in one?

My God, what is a heart,
That thou should'st it so eye, and woo,          10
Pouring upon it all thy art,
As if that thou hadst nothing else to do?

Indeed man's whole estate
Amounts (and richly) to serve thee:
He did not heav'n and earth create,          15
Yet studies them, not him by whom they be.

Teach me thy love to know;
That this new light, which now I see,
May both the work and workman show:
Then by a sun-beam I will climb to thee.          20

# Sin (2)

O that I could a sin once see!
    We paint the devil foul, yet he
    Hath some good in him, all agree.
Sin is flat opposite to th' Almighty, seeing
It wants the good of *virtue*, and of *being*.        5

    But God more care of us hath had:
    If apparitions make us sad,
    By sight of sin we should grow mad.
Yet as in sleep we see foul death, and live:
So devils are our sins in perspective.        10

# Even-song

    Blest be the God of love,
Who gave me eyes, and light, and power this day,
    Both to be busy, and to play.
    But much more blest be God above,
        Who gave me sight alone,        5
    Which to himself he did deny:
    For when he sees my ways, I die:
But I have got his son, and he hath none.

        What have I brought thee home
For this thy love? have I discharg'd the debt,    10
    Which this day's favour did beget?
    I ran; but all I brought, was foam.
        Thy diet, care, and cost
    Do end in bubbles, balls of wind;
    Of wind to thee whom I have crost,    15
But balls of wild-fire to my troubled mind.

Yet still thou goest on,
And now with darkness closest weary eyes,
  Saying to man, *It doth suffice:*
  *Henceforth repose; your work is done.*   20
    Thus in thy Ebony box
  Thou dost enclose us, till the day
  Put our amendment in our way,
And give new wheels to our disorder'd clocks.


   I muse, which shows more love,   25
The day or night: that is the gale, this th' harbour;
  That is the walk, and this the arbour;
  Or that the garden, this the grove.
    My God, thou art all love.
  Not one poor minute scapes thy breast,   30
  But brings a favour from above;
And in this love, more than in bed, I rest.


# Church-monuments

While that my soul repairs to her devotion,
Here I entomb my flesh, that it betimes
May take acquaintance of this heap of dust;
To which the blast of death's incessant motion,
Fed with the exhalation of our crimes,   5
Drives all at last. Therefore I gladly trust
My body to this school, that it may learn
To spell his elements, and find his birth
Written in dusty heraldry and lines;
Which dissolution sure doth best discern,   10
Comparing dust with dust, and earth with earth.
These laugh at Jet, and Marble put for signs,
To sever the good fellowship of dust,
And spoil the meeting. What shall point out them,
When they shall bow, and kneel, and fall down flat   15
To kiss those heaps, which now they have in trust?
Dear flesh, while I do pray, learn here thy stem

And true descent; that when thou shalt grow fat,
And wanton in thy cravings, thou mayst know,
That flesh is but the glass, which holds the dust            20
That measures all our time; which also shall
Be crumpled into dust. Mark here below
How tame these ashes are, how free from lust,
That thou mayst fit thy self against thy fall.


# Church-music

Sweetest of sweets, I thank you: when displeasure
        Did through my body wound my mind,
You took me thence, and in your house of pleasure
        A dainty lodging me assign'd.

Now I in you without a body move,                            5
        Rising and falling with your wings:
We both together sweetly live and love,
        Yet say sometimes, *God help poor Kings*.

Comfort, I'll die; for if you post from me,
        Sure I shall do so, and much more:                10
But if I travel in your company,
        You know the way to heaven's door.


# Church-lock and key

I know it is my sin, which locks thine ears,
        And binds thy hands;
Out-crying my requests, drowning my tears;
Or else the chillness of my faint demands.

But as cold hands are angry with the fire,                   5
        And mend it still;
So I do lay the want of my desire,
Not on my sins, or coldness, but thy will.

Yet hear, O God, only for his blood's sake
                Which pleads for me:     10
For though sins plead too, yet like stones they make
His blood's sweet current much more loud to be.

# The Church-floor

Mark you the floor? that square and speckled stone,
          Which looks so firm and strong,
                Is *Patience*:

And th' other black and grave, wherewith each one
          Is checker'd all along,           5
                *Humility*:

The gentle rising, which on either hand
          Leads to the Choir above,
                Is *Confidence*:

But the sweet cement, which in one sure band    10
          Ties the whole frame, is *Love*
                And *Charity*.

    Hither sometimes Sin steals, and stains
    The marble's neat and curious veins:
But all is cleansed when the marble weeps.     15
    Sometimes Death, puffing at the door,
    Blows all the dust about the floor:
But while he thinks to spoil the room, he sweeps.
    Blest be the *Architect*, whose art
    Could build so strong in a weak heart.     20

# The Windows

Lord, how can man preach thy eternal word?
          He is a brittle crazy glass:
Yet in thy temple thou dost him afford

This glorious and transcendent place,
To be a window, through thy grace.          5

But when thou dost anneal in glass thy story,
    Making thy life to shine within
The holy Preacher's; then the light and glory
    More rev'rend grows, and more doth win:
    Which else shows watrish, bleak, and thin.          10

Doctrine and life, colours and light, in one
    When they combine and mingle, bring
A strong regard and awe: but speech alone
    Doth vanish like a flaring thing,
    And in the ear, not conscience ring.          15

# Trinity Sunday

Lord, who hast form'd me out of mud,
    And hast redeem'd me through thy blood,
    And sanctifi'd me to do good;

Purge all my sins done heretofore:
    For I confess my heavy score,          5
    And I will strive to sin no more.

Enrich my heart, mouth, hands in me,
    With faith, with hope, with charity;
    That I may run, rise, rest with thee.

# Content

Peace mutt'ring thoughts, and do not grudge to keep
    Within the walls of your own breast:
Who cannot on his own bed sweetly sleep,
    Can on another's hardly rest.

Gad not abroad at ev'ry quest and call                                    5
     Of an untrained hope or passion.
To court each place or fortune that doth fall,
     Is wantonness in contemplation.

Mark how the fire in flints doth quiet lie,
     Content and warm t' it self alone:                          10
But when it would appear to others' eye,
     Without a knock it never shone.

Give me the pliant mind, whose gentle measure
     Complies and suits with all estates;
Which can let loose to a crown, and yet with pleasure         15
     Take up within a cloister's gates.

This soul doth span the world, and hang content
     From either pole unto the centre:
Where in each room of the well-furnisht tent
     He lies warm, and without adventure.                       20

The brags of life are but a nine days' wonder;
     And after death the fumes that spring
From private bodies, make as big a thunder,
     As those which rise from a huge King.

Only thy Chronicle is lost; and yet                                       25
     Better by worms be all once spent,
Than to have hellish moths still gnaw and fret
     Thy name in books, which may not rent:

When all thy deeds, whose brunt thou feel'st alone,
     Are chaw'd by others' pens and tongue;                     30
And as their wit is their digestion,
     Thy nourisht fame is weak or strong.

Then cease discoursing soul, till thine own ground,
     Do not thy self or friends importune.
He that by seeking hath himself once found,                       35
     Hath ever found a happy fortune.

# The Quiddity

My God, a verse is not a crown,
No point of honour, or gay suit,
No hawk, or banquet, or renown,
Nor a good sword, nor yet a lute:

It cannot vault, or dance, or play;                    5
It never was in *France* or *Spain*;
Nor can it entertain the day
With a great stable or domain:

It is no office, art, or news,
Nor the Exchange, or busy Hall;                        10
But it is that which while I use
I am with thee, and *Most take all*.

# Humility

I saw the Virtues sitting hand in hand
In sev'ral ranks upon an azure throne,
Where all the beasts and fowls by their command
Presented tokens of submission.
Humility, who sat the lowest there                     5
                    To execute their call,
When by the beasts the presents tendred were,
                    Gave them about to all.

The angry Lion did present his paw,
Which by consent was giv'n to Mansuetude.              10
The fearful Hare her ears, which by their law
Humility did reach to Fortitude.
The jealous Turkey brought his coral-chain;
                    That went to Temperance.
On Justice was bestow'd the Fox's brain,               15
                    Kill'd in the way by chance.

At length the Crow bringing the Peacock's plume
(For he would not), as they beheld his grace
Of that brave gift, each one began to fume,
And challenge it, as proper to his place,                    20
Till they fell out: which when the beasts espied,
        They leapt upon the throne;
And if the Fox had liv'd to rule their side,
        They had depos'd each one.

Humility, who held the plume, at this                        25
Did weep so fast, that the tears trickling down
Spoil'd all the train: then saying, *Here it is*
*For which ye wrangle*, made them turn their frown
Against the beasts: so jointly bandying,
        They drive them soon away;                          30
And then amerc'd them, double gifts to bring
        At the next Session-day.

# Frailty

Lord, in my silence how do I despise
        What upon trust
Is styled *honour*, *riches*, or *fair eyes*;
        But is *fair dust*!
I surname them *gilded clay*,                                5
        *Dear earth*, *fine grass* or *hay*;
In all, I think my foot doth ever tread
        Upon their head.

But when I view abroad both Regiments;
        The world's, and thine:                             10
Thine clad with simpleness, and sad events;
        The other fine,
        Full of glory and gay weeds,
        Brave language, braver deeds:
That which was dust before, doth quickly rise,               15
        And prick mine eyes.

O brook not this, lest if what even now
My foot did tread,
Affront those joys, wherewith thou didst endow,
And long since wed　　　　　　20
My poor soul, ev'n sick of love:
It may a Babel prove
Commodious to conquer heav'n and thee
Planted in me.

# Constancy

Who is the honest man?
He that doth still and strongly good pursue,
To God, his neighbour, and himself most true:
Whom neither force nor fawning can
Unpin, or wrench from giving all their due.　　　　5

Whose honesty is not
So loose or easy, that a ruffling wind
Can blow away, or glittering look it blind:
Who rides his sure and even trot,
While the world now rides by, now lags behind.　　　10

Who, when great trials come,
Nor seeks, nor shuns them; but doth calmly stay,
Till he the thing and the example weigh:
All being brought into a sum,
What place or person calls for, he doth pay.　　　15

Whom none can work or woo
To use in any thing a trick or sleight,
For above all things he abhors deceit:
His words and works and fashion too
All of a piece, and all are clear and straight.　　　20

69

Who never melts or thaws
At close temptations: when the day is done,
His goodness sets not, but in dark can run:
　　　The sun to others writeth laws,
And is their virtue; Virtue is his Sun.　　　　　25

　　　Who, when he is to treat
With sick folks, women, those whom passions sway,
Allows for that, and keeps his constant way:
　　　Whom others' faults do not defeat;
But though men fail him, yet his part doth play.　　30

　　　Whom nothing can procure,
When the wide world runs bias from his will,
To writhe his limbs, and share, not mend the ill.
　　　This is the Mark-man, safe and sure,
Who still is right, and prays to be so still.　　　35

# Affliction (3)

My heart did heave, and there came forth, *O God!*
By that I knew that thou wast in the grief,
To guide and govern it to my relief,
　　　Making a sceptre of the rod:
　　　　Hadst thou not had thy part,　　　5
Sure the unruly sigh had broke my heart.

But since thy breath gave me both life and shape,
Thou know'st my tallies; and when there's assigned
So much breath to a sigh, what's then behind?
　　　Or if some years with it escape,　　　10
　　　　The sigh then only is
A gale to bring me sooner to my bliss.

Thy life on earth was grief, and thou art still
Constant unto it, making it to be
A point of honour now to grieve in me,                     15
      And in thy members suffer ill.
        They who lament one cross,
Thou dying daily, praise thee to thy loss.

# The Star

Bright spark, shot from a brighter place,
    Where beams surround my Saviour's face,
      Canst thou be any where
        So well as there?

Yet, if thou wilt from thence depart,                     5
    Take a bad lodging in my heart;
      For thou canst make a debtor,
        And make it better.

First with thy fire-work burn to dust
    Folly, and worse than folly, lust:                     10
      Then with thy light refine,
        And make it shine:

So disengag'd from sin and sickness,
    Touch it with thy celestial quickness,
      That it may hang and move                     15
        After thy love.

Then with our trinity of light,
    Motion, and heat, let's take our flight
      Unto the place where thou
        Before didst bow.                     20

Get me a standing there, and place
    Among the beams which crown the face
      Of him, who dy'd to part
        Sin and my heart:

That so among the rest I may     25
  Glitter, and curl, and wind as they:
    That winding is their fashion
      Of adoration.

Sure thou wilt joy, by gaining me
  To fly home like a laden bee     30
    Unto that hive of beams
      And garland-streams.

# Sunday

O day most calm, most bright,
The fruit of this, the next world's bud,
Th' endorsement of supreme delight,
Writ by a friend, and with his blood;
The couch of time; care's balm and bay:     5
The week were dark, but for thy light:
    Thy torch doth show the way.

    The other days and thou
Make up one man; whose face thou art,
Knocking at heaven with thy brow:     10
The worky-days are the back-part;
The burden of the week lies there,
Making the whole to stoop and bow,
    Till thy release appear.

    Man had straight forward gone     15
To endless death: but thou dost pull
And turn us round to look on one,
Whom, if we were not very dull,
We could not choose but look on still;
Since there is no place so alone,     20
    The which he doth not fill.

Sundays the pillars are,
On which heav'n's palace arched lies:
The other days fill up the spare
And hollow room with vanities. 25
They are the fruitful beds and borders
In God's rich garden: that is bare,
    Which parts their ranks and orders.

    The Sundays of man's life,
Threaded together on time's string 30
Make bracelets to adorn the wife
Of the eternal glorious King.
On Sunday heaven's gate stands ope;
Blessings are plentiful and rife,
    More plentiful than hope. 35

    This day my Saviour rose,
And did enclose this light for his:
That as each beast his manger knows,
Man might not of his fodder miss.
Christ hath took in this piece of ground, 40
And made a garden there for those
    Who want herbs for their wound.

    The rest of our Creation
Our great Redeemer did remove
With the same shake, which at his passion 45
Did th' earth and all things with it move.
As Samson bore the doors away,
Christ's hands, though nail'd, wrought our salvation,
    And did unhinge that day.

    The brightness of that day 50
We sullied by our foul offence:
Wherefore that robe we cast away,
Having a new at his expence,
Whose drops of blood paid the full price,
That was requir'd to make us gay, 55
    And fit for Paradise.

Thou art a day of mirth:
And where the week-days trail on ground,
Thy flight is higher, as thy birth.
O let me take thee at the bound,                    60
Leaping with thee from sev'n to sev'n,
Till that we both, being toss'd from earth,
      Fly hand in hand to heav'n!


## Avarice

Money, thou bane of bliss, and source of woe,
  Whence com'st thou, that thou art so fresh and fine?
  I know thy parentage is base and low:
Man found thee poor and dirty in a mine.
Surely thou didst so little contribute              5
  To this great kingdom, which thou now hast got,
  That he was fain, when thou wert destitute,
To dig thee out of thy dark cave and grot:
Then forcing thee, by fire he made thee bright:
  Nay, thou hast got the face of man; for we        10
  Have with our stamp and seal transferr'd our right:
Thou art the man, and man but dross to thee.
  Man calleth thee his wealth, who made thee rich;
  And while he digs out thee, falls in the ditch.


## Anagram

How well her name an *Army* doth present,
In whom the *Lord of hosts* did pitch his tent!

# To all Angels and Saints

Oh glorious spirits, who after all your bands
See the smooth face of God, without a frown
      Or strict commands:
Where ev'ry one is king, and hath his crown,
If not upon his head, yet in his hands:       5

Not out of envy or maliciousness
Do I forbear to crave your special aid:
      I would address
My vows to thee most gladly, blessed Maid,
And Mother of my God, in my distress.      10

Thou art the holy mine, whence came the gold,
The great restorative for all decay
      In young and old;
Thou art the cabinet where the jewel lay:
Chiefly to thee would I my soul unfold:      15

But now (alas!) I dare not; for our King,
Whom we do all jointly adore and praise,
      Bids no such thing:
And where his pleasure no injunction lays,
('Tis your own case) ye never move a wing.      20

All worship is prerogative, and a flower
Of his rich crown, from whom lies no appeal
      At the last hour:
Therefore we dare not from his garland steal,
To make a posy for inferior power.      25

Although then others court you, if ye know
What's done on earth, we shall not fare the worse,
      Who do not so;
Since we are ever ready to disburse,
If any one our Master's hand can show.      30

# Employment (2)

He that is weary, let him sit.
          My soul would stir
And trade in courtesies and wit,
          Quitting the fur
To cold complexions needing it.      5

Man is no star, but a quick coal
          Of mortal fire:
Who blows it not, nor doth control
          A faint desire,
Lets his own ashes choke his soul.    10

When th' elements did for place contest
          With him, whose will
Ordain'd the highest to be best;
          The earth sat still,
And by the others is opprest.     15

Life is a business, not good cheer;
          Ever in wars.
The sun still shineth there or here,
          Whereas the stars
Watch an advantage to appear.    20

Oh that I were an Orange-tree,
          That busy plant!
Then should I ever laden be,
          And never want
Some fruit for him that dressed me.   25

But we are still too young or old;
          The man is gone,
Before we do our wares unfold:
          So we freeze on,
Until the grave increase our cold.   30

# Denial

When my devotions could not pierce
      Thy silent ears;
Then was my heart broken, as was my verse:
    My breast was full of fears
        And disorder:      5

My bent thoughts, like a brittle bow,
      Did fly asunder:
Each took his way; some would to pleasures go,
    Some to the wars and thunder
        Of alarms.      10

As good go any where, they say,
      As to benumb
Both knees and heart, in crying night and day,
    *Come, come, my God, O come,*
        But no hearing.      15

O that thou shouldst give dust a tongue
      To cry to thee,
And then not hear it crying! all day long
    My heart was in my knee,
        But no hearing.      20

Therefore my soul lay out of sight,
      Untun'd, unstrung:
My feeble spirit, unable to look right
    Like a nipt blossom, hung
        Discontented.      25

O cheer and tune my heartless breast,
      Defer no time;
That so thy favours granting my request,
    They and my mind may chime,
        And mend my rhyme.      30

# Christmas

All after pleasures as I rid one day,
      My horse and I, both tir'd, body and mind,
      With full cry of affections, quite astray,
I took up in the next inn I could find.
There when I came, whom found I but my dear,      5
      My dearest Lord, expecting till the grief
      Of pleasures brought me to him, ready there
To be all passengers' most sweet relief?
O Thou, whose glorious, yet contracted light,
      Wrapt in night's mantle, stole into a manger;      10
      Since my dark soul and brutish is thy right,
To Man of all beasts be not thou a stranger:
      Furnish and deck my soul, that thou mayst have
      A better lodging, than a rack, or grave.


The shepherds sing; and shall I silent be?      15
      My God, no hymn for thee?
My soul's a shepherd too; a flock it feeds
      Of thoughts, and words, and deeds,
The pasture is thy word: the streams, thy grace
      Enriching all the place.      20
Shepherd and flock shall sing, and all my powers
      Out-sing the day-light hours.
Then we will chide the sun for letting night
      Take up his place and right:
We sing one common Lord; wherefore he should      25
      Himself the candle hold.
I will go searching, till I find a sun
      Shall stay, till we have done;
A willing shiner, that shall shine as gladly,
      As frost-nipt suns look sadly.      30
Then we will sing, and shine all our own day,
      And one another pay:
His beams shall cheer my breast, and both so twine,
Till ev'n his beams sing, and my music shine.

# Ungratefulness

Lord, with what bounty and rare clemency
       Hast thou redeem'd us from the grave!
           If thou hadst let us run,
         Gladly had man ador'd the sun,
            And thought his god most brave;     5
Where now we shall be better gods than he.

Thou has but two rare cabinets full of treasure,
       The *Trinity,* and *Incarnation*:
           Thou hast unlockt them both,
         And made them jewels to betroth     10
           The work of thy creation
Unto thy self in everlasting pleasure.

The statelier cabinet is the *Trinity,*
       Whose sparkling light access denies:
           Therefore thou dost not show     15
         This fully to us, till death blow
           The dust into our eyes:
For by that powder thou wilt make us see.

But all thy sweets are packt up in the other;
       Thy mercies thither flock and flow:     20
           That as the first affrights,
         This may allure us with delights;
           Because this box we know;
For we have all of us just such another.

But man is close, reserv'd, and dark to thee:     25
       When thou demandest but a heart,
           He cavils instantly.
         In his poor cabinet of bone
           Sins have their box apart,
Defrauding thee, who gavest two for one.     30

# Sighs and Groans

O do not use me
After my sins! look not on my desert,
But on thy glory! then thou wilt reform
And not refuse me: for thou only art
The mighty God, but I a silly worm;                5
        O do not bruise me!


O do not urge me!
For what account can thy ill steward make?
I have abus'd thy stock, destroy'd thy woods,
Suckt all thy magazines: my head did ache,        10
Till it found out how to consume thy goods:
        O do not scourge me!


O do not blind me!
I have deserv'd that an Egyptian night
Should thicken all my powers, because my lust      15
Hath still sew'd fig-leaves to exclude thy light:
But I am frailty, and already dust;
        O do not grind me!


O do not fill me
With the turn'd vial of thy bitter wrath!           20
For thou hast other vessels full of blood,
A part whereof my Saviour empti'd hath,
Ev'n unto death: since he di'd for my good,
        O do not kill me!


But O reprieve me!                                  25
For thou hast *life* and *death* at thy command;
Thou art both *Judge* and *Saviour*, *feast* and *rod*,
*Cordial* and *Corrosive*: put not thy hand
Into the bitter box; but O my God,
        My God, relieve me!                       30

# The World

Love built a stately house, where *Fortune* came,
And spinning fancies, she was heard to say,
That her fine cobwebs did support the frame,
Whereas they were supported by the same:
But *Wisdom* quickly swept them all away.          5

Then *Pleasure* came, who liking not the fashion,
Began to make *Balconies, Terraces*,
Till she had weakned all by alteration:
But rev'rend *laws*, and many a *proclamation*
Reformed all at length with menaces.          10

Then enter'd *Sin*, and with that Sycomore,
Whose leaves first sheltred man from drought and dew,
Working and winding slily evermore,
The inward walls and Sommers cleft and tore:
But *Grace* shor'd these, and cut that as it grew.          15

Then *Sin* combin'd with *Death* in a firm band
To raze the building to the very floor:
Which they effected, none could them withstand.
But *Love* and *Grace* took *Glory* by the hand,
And built a braver Palace than before.          20

# Coloss. 3. 3.

### *Our life is hid with Christ in God.*

*My* words and thoughts do both express this notion,
That *Life* hath with the sun a double motion.
The first  *Is* straight, and our diurnal friend,
The  other   *Hid*, and doth obliquely bend.
One life is wrapt  *In* flesh, and tends to earth.          5
The other winds towards *Him*, whose happy birth
Taught  me  to  live  here  so,  *That* still one eye
Should aim and shoot at that which *Is* on high:
Quitting  with  daily  labour  all  *My* pleasure,
To  gain  at  harvest  an  eternal  *Treasure*.          10

# Vanity (1)

The fleet Astronomer can bore,
And thread the spheres with his quick-piercing mind:
He views their stations, walks from door to door,
      Surveys, as if he had design'd
To make a purchase there: he sees their dances,    5
        And knoweth long before
Both their full-ey'd aspects, and secret glances.

    The nimble Diver with his side
Cuts through the working waves, that he may fetch
His dearly-earned pearl, which God did hide    10
      On purpose from the ventrous wretch,
That he might save his life, and also hers,
        Who with excessive pride
Her own destruction and his danger wears.

    The subtle Chymick can devest    15
And strip the creature naked, till he find
The callow principles within their nest:
      There he imparts to them his mind,
Admitted to their bed-chamber, before
        They appear trim and drest    20
To ordinary suitors at the door.

    What hath not man sought out and found,
But his dear God? who yet his glorious law
Embosoms in us, mellowing the ground
      With showres and frosts, with love and awe,    25
So that we need not say, Where's this command?
        Poor man, thou searchest round
To find out *death*, but missest *life* at hand.

# Lent

Welcome dear feast of Lent: who loves not thee,
He loves not Temperance, or Authority,
　　　　But is compos'd of passion.
The Scriptures bid us *fast*; the Church says, *now*:
Give to thy Mother, what thou wouldst allow　　　　5
　　　　To ev'ry Corporation.

The humble soul compos'd of love and fear
Begins at home, and lays the burden there,
　　　　When doctrines disagree.
He says, in things which use hath justly got,　　　　10
I am a scandal to the Church, and not
　　　　The Church is so to me.

True Christians should be glad of an occasion
To use their temperance, seeking no evasion,
　　　　When good is seasonable;　　　　15
Unless Authority, which should increase
The obligation in us, make it less,
　　　　And Power itself disable.

Besides the cleanness of sweet abstinence,
Quick thoughts and motions at a small expense,　　　　20
　　　　A face not fearing light:
Whereas in fulness there are sluttish fumes,
Sour exhalations, and dishonest rheums,
　　　　Revenging the delight.

Then those same pendant profits, which the spring　　　　25
And Easter intimate, enlarge the thing,
　　　　And goodness of the deed.
Neither ought other men's abuse of Lent
Spoil the good use; lest by that argument
　　　　We forfeit all our Creed.　　　　30

It's true, we cannot reach Christ's forti'th day;
Yet to go part of that religious way,
        Is better than to rest:
We cannot reach our Saviour's purity;
Yet are we bid, *Be holy ev'n as he*.      35
        In both let's do our best.

Who goeth in the way which Christ hath gone,
Is much more sure to meet with him, than one
        That travelleth by-ways:
Perhaps my God, though he be far before,      40
May turn and take me by the hand, and more:
        May strengthen my decays.

Yet Lord instruct us to improve our fast
By starving sin and taking such repast,
        As may our faults control:      45
That ev'ry man may revel at his door,
Not in his parlour; banqueting the poor,
        And among those his soul.

# Virtue

Sweet day, so cool, so calm, so bright,
The bridal of the earth and sky;
The dew shall weep thy fall to night;
        For thou must die.

Sweet rose, whose hue angry and brave      5
Bids the rash gazer wipe his eye:
Thy root is ever in its grave,
        And thou must die.

Sweet spring, full of sweet days and roses,
A box where sweets compacted lie;
My music shows ye have your closes,      10
        And all must die.

Only a sweet and virtuous soul,
Like season'd timber, never gives;
But though the whole world turn to coal,                    15
        Then chiefly lives.

# The Pearl. *Matth. 13.*

I know the ways of learning; both the head
And pipes that feed the press, and make it run;
What reason hath from nature borrowed,
Or of it self, like a good housewife, spun
In laws and policy; what the stars conspire,                5
What willing nature speaks, what forc'd by fire;
Both th' old discoveries, and the new-found seas,
The stock and surplus, cause and history:
All these stand open, or I have the keys:
        Yet I love thee.                                   10

I know the ways of honour, what maintains
The quick returns of courtesy and wit:
In vies of favours whether party gains,
When glory swells the heart, and mouldeth it
To all expressions both of hand and eye,                    15
Which on the world a true-love-knot may tie,
And bear the bundle, wheresoe're it goes:
How many drams of spirit there must be
To sell my life unto my friends or foes:
        Yet I love thee.                                   20

I know the ways of pleasure, the sweet strains,
The lullings and the relishes of it;
The propositions of hot blood and brains;
What mirth and music mean; what love and wit
Have done these twenty hundred years, and more:            25
I know the projects of unbridled store:
My stuff is flesh, not brass; my senses live,
And grumble oft, that they have more in me
Than he that curbs them, being but one to five:
        Yet I love thee.                                   30

I know all these, and have them in my hand:
Therefore not seeled, but with open eyes
I fly to thee, and fully understand
Both the main sale, and the commodities;
And at what rate and price I have thy love;                    35
With all the circumstances that may move:
Yet through the labyrinths, not my grovelling wit,
But thy silk twist let down from heav'n to me,
Did both conduct and teach me, how by it
          To climb to thee.                              40


# Affliction (4)

Broken in pieces all asunder,
      Lord, hunt me not,
      A thing forgot,
Once a poor creature, now a wonder,
    A wonder tortur'd in the space                            5
    Betwixt this world and that of grace.


My thoughts are all a case of knives,
      Wounding my heart
      With scatter'd smart,
As watring pots give flowers their lives.                      10
    Nothing their fury can control,
    While they do wound and prick my soul.


All my attendants are at strife,
      Quitting their place
      Unto my face:                                            15
Nothing performs the task of life:
    The elements are let loose to fight,
    And while I live, try out their right.


87

Oh help, my God! let not their plot
      Kill them and me,          20
      And also thee,
Who art my life: dissolve the knot,
      As the sun scatters by his light
      All the rebellions of the night.

Then shall those powers, which work for grief,    25
      Enter thy pay,
      And day by day
Labour thy praise, and my relief;
      With care and courage building me,
      Till I reach heav'n, and much more, thee.    30

# Man

      My God, I heard this day,
That none doth build a stately habitation,
      But he that means to dwell therein.
      What house more stately hath there been,
Or can be, than is Man? to whose creation    5
      All things are in decay.

      For Man is ev'ry thing,
And more: He is a tree, yet bears more fruit;
      A beast, yet is, or should be more:
      Reason and speech we only bring.    10
Parrots may thank us, if they are not mute,
      They go upon the score.

      Man is all symmetry,
Full of proportions, one limb to another,
      And all to all the world besides:    15
      Each part may call the furthest, brother:
For head with foot hath private amity,
      And both with moon and tides.

Nothing hath got so far,
But Man hath caught and kept it, as his prey.    20
    His eyes dismount the highest star:
    He is in little all the sphere.
Herbs gladly cure our flesh, because that they
        Find their acquaintance there.

    For us the winds do blow,    25
The earth doth rest, heav'n move, and fountains flow.
    Nothing we see, but means our good,
    As our *delight*, or as our *treasure*:
The whole is, either our cupboard of *food*,
        Or cabinet of *pleasure*.    30

    The stars have us to bed;
Night draws the curtain, which the sun withdraws;
    Music and light attend our head.
    All things unto our *flesh* are kind
In their *descent* and *being*; to our *mind*    35
        In their *ascent* and *cause*.

    Each thing is full of duty:
Waters united are our navigation;
    Distinguished, our habitation;
    Below, our drink; above, our meat;    40
Both are our cleanliness. Hath one such beauty?
        Then how are all things neat?

    More servants wait on Man,
Than he'll take notice of: in ev'ry path
    He treads down that which doth befriend him,    45
    When sickness makes him pale and wan.
Oh mighty love! Man is one world, and hath
        Another to attend him.

    Since then, my God, thou hast
So brave a Palace built; O dwell in it,    50
    That it may dwell with thee at last!
    Till then, afford us so much wit;
That, as the world serves us, we may serve thee,
        And both thy servants be.

# Antiphon (2)

*Chor.* Praised be the God of love,
　　　　*Men.* Here below,
　　　　*Angels.* And here above:
*Cho.* 　Who hath dealt his mercies so,
　　　　*Ang.* To his friend,　　　　　　　　5
　　　　*Men.* And to his foe,

*Cho.* 　That both grace and glory tend
　　　　*Ang.* Us of old,
　　　　*Men.* And us in th' end.
*Cho.* 　The great shepherd of the fold　　　10
　　　　*Ang.* Us did make,
　　　　*Men.* For us was sold.

*Cho.* 　He our foes in pieces brake;
　　　　*Ang.* Him we touch;
　　　　*Men.* And him we take.　　　　　　15
*Cho.* 　Wherefore since that he is such,
　　　　*Ang.* We adore,
　　　　*Men.* And we do crouch.

*Cho.* 　Lord, thy praises should be more.
　　　　*Men.* We have none,　　　　　　　20
　　　　*Ang.* And we no store.
*Cho.* 　Praised be the God alone,
　　　　Who hath made of two folds one.

# Unkindness

Lord, make me coy and tender to offend:
In friendship first I think if that agree,
　　　　　Which I intend,
　　　Unto my friend's intent and end.
I would not use a friend, as I use Thee.　　　5

If any touch my friend, or his good name,
It is my honour and my love to free
        His blasted fame
    From the least spot or thought of blame.
I could not use a friend as I use Thee.        10

My friend may spit upon my curious floor:
Would he have gold? I lend it instantly;
        But let the poor,
    And thou within them starve at door.
I cannot use a friend, as I use Thee.        15

When that my friend pretendeth to a place,
I quit my interest, and leave it free:
        But when thy grace
    Sues for my heart, I thee displace,
Nor would I use a friend as I use Thee.        20

Yet can a friend what thou hast done fulfil?
O write in brass, *My God upon a tree*
        *His blood did spill*
    *Only to purchase my good-will:*
*Yet use I not my foes, as I use thee.*        25

# Life

I made a posy, while the day ran by:
Here will I smell my remnant out, and tie
        My life within this band.
But time did beckon to the flowers, and they
By noon most cunningly did steal away,        5
        And wither'd in my hand.

My hand was next to them, and then my heart:
I took, without more thinking, in good part
        Time's gentle admonition:
Who did so sweetly death's sad taste convey,        10
Making my mind to smell my fatal day;
        Yet sugring the suspicion.

Farewell dear flowers, sweetly your time ye spent,
Fit, while ye liv'd, for smell or ornament,
    And after death for cures.    15
I follow straight without complaints or grief,
Since if my scent be good, I care not if
    It be as short as yours.


# Submission

But that thou art my wisdom, Lord,
  And both mine eyes are thine,
My mind would be extremely stirr'd
  For missing my design.

Were it not better to bestow      5
  Some place and power on me?
Then should thy praises with me grow,
  And share in my degree.

But when I thus dispute and grieve,
  I do resume my sight,      10
And pilfring what I once did give,
  Disseize thee of thy right.

How know I, if thou shouldst me raise,
  That I should then raise thee?
Perhaps great places and the praise    15
  Do not so well agree.

Wherefore unto my gift I stand;
  I will no more advise:
Only do thou lend me a hand,
  Since thou hast both mine eyes.    20

# Justice (1)

I cannot skill of these thy ways.
*Lord, thou didst make me, yet thou woundest me;*
*Lord, thou dost wound me, yet thou dost relieve me:*
*Lord, thou relievest, yet I die by thee:*
*Lord, thou dost kill me, yet thou dost reprieve me.*     5
    But when I mark my life and praise,
    Thy justice me most fitly pays:
*For, I do praise thee, yet I praise thee not:*
*My prayers mean thee, yet my prayers stray:*
*I would do well, yet sin the hand hath got:*    10
*My soul doth love thee, yet it loves delay.*
    I cannot skill of these my ways.

# Charms and Knots

Who read a chapter when they rise,
Shall ne're be troubled with ill eyes.

A poor man's rod, when thou dost ride,
Is both a weapon and a guide.

Who shuts his hand, hath lost his gold:    5
Who opens it, hath it twice told.

Who goes to bed and doth not pray,
Maketh two nights to ev'ry day.

Who by aspersions throw a stone
At th' head of others, hit their own.    10

Who looks on ground with humble eyes,
Finds himself there, and seeks to rise.

When th' hair is sweet through pride or lust,
The powder doth forget the dust.

Take one from ten, and what remains?                     15
Ten still, if sermons go for gains.

In shallow waters, heav'n doth show;
But who drinks on, to hell may go.


# Affliction (5)

My God, I read this day,
That planted Paradise was not so firm,
As was and is thy floating Ark; whose stay
And anchor thou art only, to confirm
    And strengthen it in ev'ry age,                    5
    When waves do rise, and tempests rage.


At first we liv'd in pleasure;
Thine own delights thou didst to us impart:
When we grew wanton, thou didst use displeasure
To make us thine: yet that we might not part,          10
    As we at first did board with thee,
    Now thou wouldst taste our misery.


There is but joy and grief;
If either will convert us, we are thine:
Some Angels us'd the first; if our relief               15
Take up the second, then thy double line
    And sev'ral baits in either kind
    Furnish thy table to thy mind.


Affliction then is ours;
We are the trees, whom shaking fastens more,           20
While blustring winds destroy the wanton bowers,
And ruffle all their curious knots and store.
    My God, so temper joy and woe
    That thy bright beams may tame thy bow.

# Mortification

How soon doth man decay!
When clothes are taken from a chest of sweets
　　To swaddle infants, whose young breath
　　　　Scarce knows the way;
　　Those clouts are little winding sheets,　　　　　　5
Which do consign and send them unto death.


　　When boys go first to bed,
They step into their voluntary graves,
　　Sleep binds them fast; only their breath
　　　　Makes them not dead;　　　　　　10
　　Successive nights, like rolling waves,
Convey them quickly, who are bound for death.


　　When youth is frank and free,
And calls for music, while his veins do swell,
　　All day exchanging mirth and breath,　　　　　15
　　　　In company;
　　That music summons to the knell,
Which shall befriend him at the hour of death.


　　When man grows staid and wise,
Getting a house and home, where he may move　　20
　　Within the circle of his breath,
　　　　Schooling his eyes;
　　That dumb enclosure maketh love
Unto the coffin, that attends his death.


　　When age grows low and weak,　　　　　25
Marking his grave, and thawing ev'ry year,
　　Till all do melt, and drown his breath
　　　　When he would speak;
　　A chair or litter shows the bier,
Which shall convey him to the house of death.　　30

       Man, ere he is aware,
Hath put together a solemnity,
       And drest his hearse, while he has breath
               As yet to spare:
       Yet Lord, instruct us so to die,                    35
That all these dyings may be life in death.


# Decay

Sweet were the days, when thou didst lodge with Lot,
Struggle with Jacob, sit with Gideon,
Advise with Abraham, when thy power could not
Encounter Moses' strong complaints and moan:
       Thy words were then, *Let me alone*.              5

One might have sought and found thee presently
At some fair oak, or bush, or cave, or well:
Is my God this way? No, they would reply:
He is to Sinai gone, as we heard tell:
       List, ye may hear great Aaron's bell.             10

But now thou dost thy self immure and close
In some one corner of a feeble heart:
Where yet both Sin and Satan, thy old foes,
Do pinch and straiten thee, and use much art
       To gain thy thirds and little part.               15

I see the world grows old, when as the heat
Of thy great love once spread, as in an urn
Doth closet up it self, and still retreat,
Cold sin still forcing it, till it return,
       And calling Justice, all things burn.            20

# Misery

Lord, let the Angels praise thy name.
Man is a foolish thing, a foolish thing,
    Folly and Sin play all his game.
His house still burns, and yet he still doth sing,
        *Man is but grass,*         5
        *He knows it, fill the glass.*


How canst thou brook his foolishness?
Why he'll not lose a cup of drink for thee:
    Bid him but temper his excess;
Not he: he knows, where he can better be,     10
        As he will swear,
        Than to serve thee in fear.


What strange pollutions doth he wed,
And make his own? as if none knew, but he.
    No man shall beat into his head     15
That thou within his curtains drawn canst see:
        They are of cloth,
        Where never yet came moth.


The best of men, turn but thy hand
For one poor minute, stumble at a pin:     20
    They would not have their actions scann'd,
Nor any sorrow tell them that they sin,
        Though it be small,
        And measure not their fall.


They quarrel thee, and would give over     25
The bargain made to serve thee: but thy love
    Holds them unto it, and doth cover
Their follies with the wing of thy mild Dove,
        Not suff'ring those
        Who would, to be thy foes.     30

My God, Man cannot praise thy name:
Thou art all brightness, perfect purity;
   The sun holds down his head for shame,
Dead with eclipses, when we speak of thee:
         How shall infection      35
          Presume on thy perfection?

As dirty hands foul all they touch,
And those things most, which are most pure and fine:
   So our clay hearts, ev'n when we crouch
To sing thy praises, make them less divine.      40
         Yet either this,
          Or none thy portion is.

Man cannot serve thee; let him go,
And serve the swine: there, there is his delight:
   He doth not like this virtue, no;      45
Give him his dirt to wallow in all night:
         These Preachers make
         His head to shoot and ache.

Oh foolish man! where are thine eyes?
How hast thou lost them in a crowd of cares?      50
   Thou pull'st the rug, and wilt not rise,
No not to purchase the whole pack of stars:
         There let them shine,
         Thou must go sleep, or dine.

The bird that sees a dainty bower      55
Made in the tree, where she was wont to sit,
   Wonders and sings, but not his power
Who made the arbour: this exceeds her wit.
         But Man doth know
         The spring, whence all things flow:      60

And yet, as though he knew it not,
His knowledge winks, and lets his humours reign;
   They make his life a constant blot,
And all the blood of God to run in vain.
         Ah wretch! what verse      65
         Can thy strange ways rehearse?

Indeed at first Man was a treasure,
A box of jewels, shop of rarities,
   A ring, whose posy was, *My pleasure:*
He was a garden in a Paradise:         70
        Glory and grace
      Did crown his heart and face.

    But sin hath fool'd him. Now he is
A lump of flesh, without a foot or wing
To raise him to the glimpse of bliss:     75
A sick toss'd vessel, dashing on each thing;
        Nay, his own shelf:
      My God, I mean my self.

# Jordan (2)

When first my lines of heav'nly joys made mention,
Such was their lustre, they did so excel,
That I sought out quaint words, and trim invention:
My thoughts began to burnish, sprout, and swell,
Curling with metaphors a plain intention,    5
Decking the sense, as if it were to sell.

Thousands of notions in my brain did run,
Off'ring their service, if I were not sped:
I often blotted what I had begun;
This was not quick enough, and that was dead.    10
Nothing could seem too rich to clothe the sun,
Much less those joys which trample on his head.

As flames do work and wind, when they ascend,
So did I weave my self into the sense.
But while I bustled, I might hear a friend    15
Whisper, *How wide is all this long pretence!*
*There is in love a sweetness ready penn'd:*
*Copy out only that, and save expense.*

## Prayer (2)

Of what an easy quick access,
My blessed Lord, art thou! how suddenly
    May our requests thine ear invade!
To show that state dislikes not easiness.
If I but lift mine eyes, my suit is made:       5
Thou canst no more not hear, than thou canst die.

Of what supreme almighty power
Is thy great arm which spans the east and west,
    And tacks the centre to the sphere!
By it do all things live their measur'd hour:      10
We cannot ask the thing, which is not there,
Blaming the shallowness of our request.

Of what unmeasurable love
Art thou possest, who, when thou couldst not die,
    Wert fain to take our flesh and curse,      15
And for our sakes in person sin reprove,
That by destroying that which ty'd thy purse,
Thou mightst make way for liberality!

Since then these three wait on thy throne,
*Ease*, *Power*, and *Love*; I value prayer so,      20
    That were I to leave all but one,
Wealth, fame, endowments, virtues, all should go;
I and dear prayer would together dwell,
And quickly gain, for each inch lost, an ell.

## Obedience

My God, if writings may
Convey a Lordship any way
Whither the buyer and the seller please;
    Let it not thee displease,
If this poor paper do as much as they.      5

On it my heart doth bleed
As many lines, as there doth need
To pass it self and all it hath to thee,
To which I do agree,
And here present it as my special deed.                    10

If that hereafter Pleasure
Cavil, and claim her part and measure,
As if this passed with a reservation,
Or some such words in fashion;
I here exclude the wrangler from thy treasure.             15

O let thy sacred will
All thy delight in me fulfil!
Let me not think an action mine own way,
But as thy love shall sway,
Resigning up the rudder to thy skill.                     20

Lord, what is man to thee,
That thou shouldst mind a rotten tree?
Yet since thou canst not choose but see my actions;
So great are thy perfections,
Thou mayst as well my actions guide, as see.              25

Besides, thy death and blood
Show'd a strange love to all our good:
Thy sorrows were in earnest; no faint proffer,
Or superficial offer
Of what we might not take, or be withstood.               30

Wherefore I all forgo:
To one word only I say, No:
Where in the deed there was an intimation
Of a *gift* or *donation*,
Lord, let it now by way of *purchase* go.                 35

He that will pass his land,
As I have mine, may set his hand
And heart unto this deed, when he hath read;
And make the purchase spread
To both our goods, if he to it will stand.          40

How happy were my part,
If some kind man would thrust his heart
Into these lines; till in heav'n's court of rolls
They were by winged souls
Entred for both, far above their desert!          45

# Conscience

Peace prattler, do not lour:
Not a fair look, but thou dost call it foul:
Not a sweet dish, but thou dost call it sour:
Music to thee doth howl.
By listning to thy chatting fears          5
I have both lost mine eyes and ears.

Prattler, no more, I say:
My thoughts must work, but like a noiseless sphere:
Harmonious peace must rock them all the day:
No room for prattlers there.
If thou persistest, I will tell thee,          10
That I have physic to expel thee.

And the receipt shall be
My Saviour's blood: when ever at his board
I do but taste it, straight it cleanseth me,
And leaves thee not a word;          15
No, not a tooth or nail to scratch,
And at my actions carp, or catch.

        Yet if thou talkest still,
Besides my physic, know there's some for thee:
Some wood and nails to make a staff or bill          20
        For those that trouble me:
    The bloody cross of my dear Lord
    Is both my physic and my sword.


# Sion

*& allegan*

Lord, with what glory wast thou serv'd of old,
When Solomon's temple stood and flourished!
    Where most things were of purest gold;
    The wood was all embellished
With flowers and carvings, mystical and rare:          5
All show'd the builders', crav'd the seers', care.

Yet all this glory, all this pomp and state
Did not affect thee much, was not thy aim;
    Something there was, that sow'd debate:
    Wherefore thou quitt'st thy ancient claim:          10
And now thy Architecture meets with sin;
For all thy frame and fabric is within.

There thou art struggling with a peevish heart,
Which sometimes crosseth thee, thou sometimes it:
    The fight is hard on either part.          15
    Great God doth fight, he doth submit.
All Solomon's sea of brass and world of stone
Is not so dear to thee as one good groan.

And truly brass and stones are heavy things,
Tombs for the dead, not temples fit for thee:          20
    But groans are quick, and full of wings,
    And all their motions upward be;
And ever as they mount, like larks they sing;
The note is sad, yet music for a king.

103

# Home

Come Lord, my head doth burn, my heart is sick,
 While thou dost ever, ever stay:
Thy long deferrings wound me to the quick,
 My spirit gaspeth night and day.
  O show thy self to me,               5
  Or take me up to thee!


How canst thou stay, considering the pace
 The blood did make, which thou did'st waste?
When I behold it trickling down thy face,
 I never saw thing make such haste.    10
  O show thy, &c.


When man was lost, thy pity lookt about
 To see what help in th' earth or sky:
But there was none; at least no help without:  15
 The help did in thy bosom lie.
  O show thy, &c.


There lay thy son: and must he leave that nest,
 That hive of sweetness, to remove       20
Thraldom from those, who would not at a feast
 Leave one poor apple for thy love?
  O show thy, &c.


He did, he came: O my Redeemer dear,        25
 After all this canst thou be strange?
So many years baptiz'd, and not appear?
 As if thy love could fail or change.
  O show thy, &c.                           29


Yet if thou stayest still, why must I stay?
 My God, what is this world to me?
This world of woe? hence all ye clouds, away,
 Away; I must get up and see.
  O show thy, &c.                           35

What is this weary world; this meat and drink,
    That chains us by the teeth so fast?
What is this woman-kind, which I can wink
    Into a blackness and distaste?          40
        O show thy self to me,
        Or take me up to thee!

With one small sigh thou gav'st me th' other day
    I blasted all the joys about me:
And scowling on them as they pin'd away,         45
    Now come again, said I, and flout me.
        O show thy, &c.

Nothing but drought and dearth, but bush and brake,
    Which way so-e're I look, I see.         50
Some may dream merrily, but when they wake,
    They dress themselves and come to thee.
        O show thy, &c.

We talk of harvests; there are no such things,     55
    But when we leave our corn and hay:
There is no fruitful year, but that which brings
    The last and lov'd, though dreadful day.
        O show thy, &c.         59

Oh loose this frame, this knot of man untie!
    That my free soul may use her wing,
Which now is pinion'd with mortality,
    As an entangled, hamper'd thing.
        O show thy, &c.         65

What have I left, that I should stay and groan?
    The most of me to heav'n is fled:
My thoughts and joys are all packt up and gone,
    And for their old acquaintance plead.     70
        O show thy, &c.

Come dearest Lord, pass not this holy season,
   My flesh and bones and joints do pray:
And ev'n my verse, when by the rhyme and reason     75
   The word is, *Stay,* says ever, *Come.*
        O show thy self to me,
        Or take me up to thee!

# The British Church

I joy, dear Mother, when I view
Thy perfect lineaments, and hue
      Both sweet and bright.
Beauty in thee takes up her place,
And dates her letters from thy face,     5
      When she doth write.

A fine aspect in fit array,
Neither too mean, nor yet too gay,
      Shows who is best.
Outlandish looks may not compare:     10
For all they either painted are,
      Or else undrest.

She on the hills, which wantonly
Allureth all, in hope to be
      By her preferr'd,     15
Hath kiss'd so long her painted shrines,
That ev'n her face by kissing shines,
      For her reward.

She in the valley is so shy
Of dressing, that her hair doth lie     20
      About her ears:
While she avoids her neighbour's pride,
She wholly goes on th' other side,
      And nothing wears.

But dearest Mother, what those miss,                    25
The mean, thy praise and glory is,
          And long may be.
Blessed be God, whose love it was
To double-moat thee with his grace,
          And none but thee.

# The Quip

The merry world did on a day
With his train-bands and mates agree
To meet together, where I lay,
And all in sport to jeer at me.

First, Beauty crept into a rose,                    5
Which when I pluckt not, Sir, said she,
Tell me, I pray, Whose hands are those?
But thou shalt answer, Lord, for me.

Then Money came, and chinking still,
What tune is this, poor man? said he:                    10
I heard in Music you had skill.
But thou shalt answer, Lord, for me.

Then came brave Glory puffing by
In silks that whistled, who but he?
He scarce allow'd me half an eye.                    15
But thou shalt answer, Lord, for me.

Then came quick Wit and Conversation,
And he would needs a comfort be,
And, to be short, make an oration.
But thou shalt answer, Lord, for me.                    20

Yet when the hour of thy design
To answer these fine things shall come;
Speak not at large, say, I am thine:
And then they have their answer home.

## Vanity (2)

Poor silly soul, whose hope and head lies low;
Whose flat delights on earth do creep and grow;
To whom the stars shine not so fair, as eyes;
Nor solid work, as false embroideries;
Hark and beware, lest what you now do measure          5
And write for sweet, prove a most sour displeasure.

O hear betimes, lest thy relenting
      May come too late!
To purchase heaven for repenting,
      Is no hard rate.          10
If souls be made of earthly mould,
      Let them love gold;
      If born on high,
Let them unto their kindred fly:
For they can never be at rest,          15
  Till they regain their ancient nest.
Then silly soul take heed; for earthly joy
Is but a bubble, and makes thee a boy.

## The Dawning

Awake sad heart, whom sorrow ever drowns;
  Take up thine eyes, which feed on earth;
Unfold thy forehead gather'd into frowns:
  Thy Saviour comes, and with him mirth:
      Awake, awake;          5
And with a thankful heart his comforts take.
  But thou dost still lament, and pine, and cry;
  And feel his death, but not his victory.

Arise sad heart; if thou dost not withstand,
    Christ's resurrection thine may be:          10
Do not by hanging down break from the hand,
    Which as it riseth, raiseth thee:
                Arise, arise;
And with his burial-linen dry thine eyes:
    Christ left his grave-clothes, that we might, when grief   15
    Draws tears, or blood, not want an handkerchief.

# JESU

JESU is in my heart, his sacred name
Is deeply carved there: but th' other week
A great affliction broke the little frame,
Ev'n all to pieces, which I went to seek:
And first I found the corner, where was *J*,         5
After, where *E S*, and next where *U* was graved.
When I had got these parcels, instantly
I sat me down to spell them, and perceived
That to my broken heart he was *I ease you*,
          And to my whole is *J E S U*.         10

# Business

    Canst be idle? canst thou play,
    Foolish soul who sinn'd to day?

    Rivers run, and springs each one
    Know their home, and get them gone:
    Hast thou tears, or hast thou none?         5

    If, poor soul, thou hast no tears,
    Would thou hadst no faults or fears!
    Who hath these, those ill forbears.

Winds still work: it is their plot,
Be the season cold, or hot:                              10
Hast thou sighs, or hast thou not?

If thou hast no sighs or groans,
Would thou hadst no flesh and bones!
Lesser pains scape greater ones.

       But if yet thou idle be,                15
       Foolish soul, Who di'd for thee?

Who did leave his Father's throne
To assume thy flesh and bone;
Had he life, or had he none?

If he had not liv'd for thee,                            20
Thou hadst di'd most wretchedly;
And two deaths had been thy fee.

He so far thy good did plot,
That his own self he forgot.
Did he die, or did he not?                               25

If he had not di'd for thee,
Thou hadst liv'd in misery.
Two lives worse than ten deaths be.

       And hath any space of breath
       'Twixt his sins and Saviour's death?     30

He that loseth gold, though dross,
Tells to all he meets, his cross:
He that sins, hath he no loss?

He that finds a silver vein,
Thinks on it, and thinks again:                          35
Brings thy Saviour's death no gain?

       Who in heart not ever kneels
       Neither sin nor Saviour feels.

# Dialogue

Sweetest Saviour, if my soul
    Were but worth the having,
Quickly should I then control
    Any thought of waiving.
But when all my care and pains          5
Cannot give the name of gains
To thy wretch so full of stains,
What delight or hope remains?

*What (child) is the balance thine,*
    *Thine the poise and measure?*        10
*If I say, Thou shalt be mine,*
    *Finger not my treasure.*
*What the gains in having thee*
*Do amount to, only he,*
*Who for man was sold, can see;*        15
*That transferr'd th' accounts to me.*

But as I can see no merit,
    Leading to this favour:
So the way to fit me for it,
    Is beyond my savour.        20
As the reason then is thine,
So the way is none of mine:
I disclaim the whole design:
Sin disclaims and I resign.

*That is all, if that I could*        25
    *Get without repining;*
*And my clay, my creature, would*
    *Follow my resigning.*
*That as I did freely part*
*With my glory and desert,*        30
*Left all joys to feel all smart——*
    Ah! no more: thou break'st my heart.

# Dullness

Why do I languish thus, drooping and dull,
      As if I were all earth?
O give me quickness, that I may with mirth
      Praise thee brim-full!

The wanton lover in a curious strain             5
      Can praise his fairest fair;
And with quaint metaphors her curled hair
      Curl o're again.

Thou art my loveliness, my life, my light,
      Beauty alone to me:             10
Thy bloody death and undeserv'd, makes thee
      Pure red and white.

When all perfections as but one appear,
      That those thy form doth show,
The very dust, where thou dost tread and go,      15
      Makes beauties here.

Where are my lines then? my approaches? views?
      Where are my window songs?
Lovers are still pretending, and ev'n wrongs
      Sharpen their Muse:          20

But I am lost in flesh, whose sugred lies
      Still mock me, and grow bold:
Sure thou didst put a mind there, if I could
      Find where it lies.

Lord, clear thy gift, that with a constant wit     25
      I may but look towards thee:
*Look* only; for to *love* thee, who can be,
      What angel fit?

# Love-joy

As on a window late I cast mine eye,
I saw a vine drop grapes with *J* and *C*
Anneal'd on every bunch. One standing by
Ask'd what it meant. I (who am never loth
To spend my judgement) said, It seem'd to me          5
To be the body and the letters both
Of *Joy* and *Charity*. Sir, you have not miss'd,
The man reply'd; It figures *JESUS CHRIST*.

# Providence

O sacred Providence, who from end to end
Strongly and sweetly movest! shall I write,
And not of thee, through whom my fingers bend
To hold my quill? shall they not do thee right?

Of all the creatures both in sea and land          5
Only to Man thou hast made known thy ways,
And put the pen alone into his hand,
And made him Secretary of thy praise.

Beasts fain would sing; birds ditty to their notes;
Trees would be tuning on their native lute          10
To thy renown: but all their hands and throats
Are brought to Man, while they are lame and mute.

Man is the world's high Priest: he doth present
The sacrifice for all; while they below
Unto the service mutter an assent,          15
Such as springs use that fall, and winds that blow.

He that to praise and laud thee doth refrain,
Doth not refrain unto himself alone,
But robs a thousand who would praise thee fain,
And doth commit a world of sin in one.          20

The beasts say, Eat me: but, if beasts must teach,
The tongue is yours to eat, but mine to praise.
The trees say, Pull me: but the hand you stretch,
Is mine to write, as it is yours to raise.

Wherefore, most sacred Spirit, I here present          25
For me and all my fellows praise to thee:
And just it is that I should pay the rent,
Because the benefit accrues to me.

We all acknowledge both thy power and love
To be exact, transcendent, and divine;                 30
Who dost so strongly and so sweetly move,
While all things have their will, yet none but thine.

For either thy *command*, or thy *permission*
Lay hands on all: they are thy *right* and *left*.
The first puts on with speed and expedition;           35
The other curbs sin's stealing pace and theft.

Nothing escapes them both; all must appear,
And be dispos'd, and dress'd, and tun'd by thee,
Who sweetly temper'st all. If we could hear
Thy skill and art, what music would it be!             40

Thou art in small things great, nor small in any:
Thy even praise can neither rise, nor fall.
Thou art in all things one, in each thing many:
For thou art infinite in one and all.

Tempests are calm to thee; they know thy hand,         45
And hold it fast, as children do their father's,
Which cry and follow. Thou hast made poor sand
Check the proud sea, ev'n when it swells and gathers.

Thy cupboard serves the world: the meat is set,
Where all may reach: no beast but knows his feed.      50
Birds teach us hawking; fishes have their net:
The great prey on the less, they on some weed.

Nothing engendred doth prevent his meat:
Flies have their table spread, ere they appear.
Some creatures have in winter what to eat;            55
Others do sleep, and envy not their cheer.

How finely dost thou times and seasons spin,
And make a twist checker'd with night and day!
Which as it lengthens winds, and winds us in,
As bowls go on, but turning all the way.            60

Each creature hath a wisdom for his good.
The pigeons feed their tender off-spring, crying,
When they are callow; but withdraw their food
When they are fledge, that need may teach them flying.

Bees work for man; and yet they never bruise      65
Their master's flower, but leave it, having done,
As fair as ever, and as fit to use;
So both the flower doth stay, and honey run.

Sheep eat the grass, and dung the ground for more:
Trees after bearing drop their leaves for soil:      70
Springs vent their streams, and by expense get store:
Clouds cool by heat, and baths by cooling boil.

Who hath the virtue to express the rare
And curious virtues both of herbs and stones?
Is there an herb for that? O that thy care            75
Would show a root, that gives expressions!

And if an herb hath power, what have the stars?
A rose, besides his beauty, is a cure.
Doubtless our plagues and plenty, peace and wars
Are there much surer than our art is sure.            80

Thou hast hid metals: men may take them thence;
But at his peril: when he digs the place,
He makes a grave; as if the thing had sense,
And threatned man, that he should fill the space.

Ev'n poisons praise thee. Should a thing be lost?              85
Should creatures want, for want of heed, their due?
Since where are poisons, antidotes are most:
The help stands close, and keeps the fear in view.

The sea, which seems to stop the traveller,
Is by a ship the speedier passage made.                       90
The winds, who think they rule the mariner,
Are rul'd by him, and taught to serve his trade.

And as thy house is full, so I adore
Thy curious art in marshalling thy goods.
The hills with health abound; the vales with store;           95
The South with marble; North with furs and woods.

Hard things are glorious; easy things good cheap.
The common all men have; that which is rare,
Men therefore seek to have, and care to keep.
The healthy frosts with summer-fruits compare.                100

Light without wind is glass: warm without weight
Is wool and furs: cool without closeness, shade:
Speed without pains, a horse: tall without height,
A servile hawk: low without loss, a spade.

All countries have enough to serve their need:                105
If they seek fine things, thou dost make them run
For their offence; and then dost turn their speed
To be commerce and trade from sun to sun.

Nothing wears clothes, but Man; nothing doth need
But he to wear them. Nothing useth fire,                      110
But Man alone, to show his heav'nly breed:
And only he hath fuel in desire.

When th' earth was dry, thou mad'st a sea of wet:
When that lay gather'd, thou didst broach the mountains:
When yet some places could no moisture get,                   115
The winds grew gard'ners, and the clouds good fountains.

Rain, do not hurt my flowers; but gently spend
Your honey drops: press not to smell them here:
When they are ripe, their odour will ascend,
And at your lodging with their thanks appear.          120

How harsh are thorns to pears! and yet they make
A better hedge, and need less reparation.
How smooth are silks compared with a stake,
Or with a stone! yet make no good foundation.

Sometimes thou dost divide thy gifts to man,          125
Sometimes unite. The Indian nut alone
Is clothing, meat and trencher, drink and can,
Boat, cable, sail and needle, all in one.

Most herbs that grow in brooks, are hot and dry.
Cold fruits warm kernels help against the wind.       130
The lemon's juice and rind cure mutually.
The whey of milk doth loose, the milk doth bind.

Thy creatures leap not, but express a feast,
Where all the guests sit close, and nothing wants.
Frogs marry fish and flesh; bats, bird and beast;     135
Sponges, non-sense and sense; mines, th' earth and plants.

To show thou art not bound, as if thy lot
Were worse than ours, sometimes thou shiftest hands.
Most things move th' under-jaw; the Crocodile not.
Most things sleep lying; th' Elephant leans or stands. 140

But who hath praise enough? nay who hath any?
None can express thy works, but he that knows them:
And none can know thy works, which are so many,
And so complete, but only he that owes them.

All things that are, though they have sev'ral ways,   145
Yet in their being join with one advise
To honour thee: and so I give thee praise
In all my other hymns, but in this twice.

Each thing that is, although in use and name
It go for one, hath many ways in store                    150
To honour thee; and so each hymn thy fame
Extolleth many ways, yet this one more.


# Hope

I gave to Hope a watch of mine: but he
        An anchor gave to me.
Then an old prayer-book I did present:
        And he an optic sent.
With that I gave a vial full of tears:                    5
        But he a few green ears:
Ah Loiterer! I'll no more, no more I'll bring:
        I did expect a ring.


# Sin's round

Sorry I am, my God, sorry I am,
That my offences course it in a ring.
My thoughts are working like a busy flame,
Until their cockatrice they hatch and bring:
And when they once have perfected their draughts,        5
My words take fire from my inflamed thoughts.

My words take fire from my inflamed thoughts,
Which spit it forth like the Sicilian hill.
They vent the wares, and pass them with their faults
And by their breathing ventilate the ill.               10
But words suffice not, where are lewd intentions:
My hands do join to finish the inventions.

My hands do join to finish the inventions:
And so my sins ascend three storeys high,
As Babel grew, before there were dissensions.          15
Yet ill deeds loiter not: for they supply
New thoughts of sinning: wherefore, to my shame,
Sorry I am, my God, sorry I am.


# Time

Meeting with Time, slack thing, said I,
Thy scythe is dull; whet it for shame.
No marvel Sir, he did reply,
If it at length deserve some blame:
   But where one man would have me grind it,          5
   Twenty for one too sharp do find it.

Perhaps some such of old did pass,
Who above all things lov'd this life;
To whom thy scythe a hatchet was,
Which now is but a pruning-knife.          10
   Christ's coming hath made man thy debtor,
   Since by thy cutting he grows better.

And in his blessing thou art blest:
For where thou only wert before
An executioner at best;          15
Thou art a gard'ner now, and more,
   An usher to convey our souls
   Beyond the utmost stars and poles.

And this is that makes life so long,
While it detains us from our God.          20
Ev'n pleasures here increase the wrong,
And length of days lengthen the rod.
   Who wants the place, where God doth dwell,
   Partakes already half of hell.

Of what strange length must that needs be,                    25
Which ev'n eternity excludes!
Thus far Time heard me patiently:
Then chafing said, This man deludes:
   What do I here before his door?
   He doth not crave less time, but more.                 30


# Gratefulness

Thou that hast giv'n so much to me,
Give one thing more, a grateful heart.
See how thy beggar works on thee
      By art.

He makes thy gifts occasion more,                              5
And says, If he in this be crost,
All thou hast giv'n him heretofore
      Is lost.

But thou didst reckon, when at first
Thy word our hearts and hands did crave,                       10
What it would come to at the worst
      To save.

Perpetual knockings at thy door,
Tears sullying thy transparent rooms,
Gift upon gift, much would have more.                          15
      And comes.

This notwithstanding, thou wentst on,
And didst allow us all our noise:
Nay thou hast made a sigh and groan
      Thy joys.                                         20

Not that thou hast not still above
Much better tunes, than groans can make;
But that these country-airs thy love
      Did take.

Wherefore I cry, and cry again;                    25
And in no quiet canst thou be,
Till I a thankful heart obtain
   Of thee:

Not thankful, when it pleaseth me;
As if thy blessings had spare days:                30
But such a heart, whose pulse may be
   Thy praise.


# Peace

Sweet Peace, where dost thou dwell? I humbly crave,
   Let me once know.
  I sought thee in a secret cave,
  And ask'd, if Peace were there.
A hollow wind did seem to answer, No:             5
   Go seek elsewhere.

I did; and going did a rainbow note:
   Surely, thought I,
  This is the lace of Peace's coat:
  I will search out the matter.              10
But while I look't, the clouds immediately
   Did break and scatter.

Then went I to a garden, and did spy
   A gallant flower,
  The crown Imperial: Sure, said I,          15
  Peace at the root must dwell.
But when I digg'd, I saw a worm devour
   What show'd so well.

At length I met a rev'rend good old man,
   Whom when for Peace                   20
  I did demand; he thus began:
  There was a Prince of old
At Salem dwelt, who liv'd with good increase
   Of flock and fold.

He sweetly liv'd; yet sweetness did not save     25
       His life from foes.
   But after death out of his grave
     There sprang twelve stalks of wheat:
Which many wondring at, got some of those
       To plant and set.     30

It prosper'd strangely, and did soon disperse
     Through all the earth:
   For they that taste it do rehearse
     That virtue lies therein,
A secret virtue bringing peace and mirth     35
       By flight of sin.

Take of this grain, which in my garden grows,
     And grows for you;
   Make bread of it: and that repose
     And peace which ev'ry where     40
With so much earnestness you do pursue,
       Is only there.

# Confession

O what a cunning guest
Is this same grief! within my heart I made
   Closets; and in them many a chest;
     And like a master in my trade,
In those chests, boxes; in each box, a till:     5
Yet grief knows all, and enters when he will.

      No screw, no piercer can
Into a piece of timber work and wind,
   As God's afflictions into man,
     When he a torture hath design'd.     10
They are too subtle for the subtlest hearts;
And fall, like rheums, upon the tendrest parts.

We are the earth; and they,
Like moles within us, heave, and cast about:
    And till they foot and clutch their prey,        15
    They never cool, much less give out,
No smith can make such locks, but they have keys:
Closets are halls to them; and hearts, high-ways.

        Only an open breast
Doth shut them out, so that they cannot enter;    20
    Or, if they enter, cannot rest,
    But quickly seek some new adventure.
Smooth open hearts no fastning have; but fiction
Doth give a hold and handle to affliction.

        Wherefore my faults and sins,    25
Lord, I acknowledge; take thy plagues away:
    For since confession pardon wins,
    I challenge here the brightest day,
The clearest diamond: let them do their best,
They shall be thick and cloudy to my breast.    30

# Giddiness

Oh, what a thing is man! how far from power,
        From settled peace and rest!
He is some twenty sev'ral men at least
        Each sev'ral hour.

One while he counts of heav'n, as of his treasure:    5
        But then a thought creeps in,
And calls him coward, who for fear of sin
        Will lose a pleasure.

Now he will fight it out, and to the wars;
        Now eat his bread in peace,    10
And snudge in quiet: now he scorns increase;
        Now all day spares.

He builds a house, which quickly down must go,
      As if a whirlwind blew
And crusht the building: and it's partly true,    15
      His mind is so.

O what a sight were Man, if his attires
      Did alter with his mind;
And like a Dolphin's skin, his clothes combin'd
      With his desires!    20

Surely if each one saw another's heart,
      There would be no commerce,
No sale or bargain pass: all would disperse,
      And live apart.

Lord, mend or rather make us: one creation    25
      Will not suffice our turn:
Except thou make us daily, we shall spurn
      Our own Salvation.

# The bunch of grapes

Joy, I did lock thee up: but some bad man
      Hath let thee out again:
And now, me thinks, I am where I began
      Sev'n years ago: one vogue and vein,
      One air of thoughts usurps my brain.    5
I did toward Canaan draw; but now I am
Brought back to the Red sea, the sea of shame.

For as the Jews of old by God's command
      Travell'd, and saw no town:
So now each Christian hath his journeys spann'd:    10
      Their story pens and sets us down.
      A single deed is small renown.
God's works are wide, and let in future times;
His ancient justice overflows our crimes.

Then have we too our guardian fires and clouds;          15
        Our Scripture-dew drops fast:
We have our sands and serpents, tents and shrouds;
      Alas! our murmurings come not last.
      But where's the cluster? where's the taste
Of mine inheritance? Lord, if I must borrow,          20
Let me as well take up their joy, as sorrow.


But can he want the grape, who hath the wine?
        I have their fruit and more.
Blessed be God, who prosper'd *Noah's* vine,
      And made it bring forth grapes' good store.          25
      But much more him I must adore,
Who of the law's sour juice sweet wine did make,
Ev'n God himself, being pressed for my sake.


# Love unknown

Dear Friend, sit down, the tale is long and sad:
And in my faintings I presume your love
Will more comply, than help. A Lord I had,
And have, of whom some grounds which may improve,
I hold for two lives, and both lives in me.          5
To him I brought a dish of fruit one day,
And in the middle plac'd my heart. But he
           (I sigh to say)
Lookt on a servant, who did know his eye
Better than you know me, or (which is one)          10
Than I my self. The servant instantly
Quitting the fruit, seiz'd on my heart alone,
And threw it in a font, wherein did fall
A stream of blood, which issu'd from the side
Of a great rock: I well remember all,          15
And have good cause: there it was dipt and dy'd,
And washt, and wrung: the very wringing yet
Enforceth tears. *Your heart was foul, I fear.*
Indeed 'tis true. I did and do commit

Many a fault more than my lease will bear;                    20
Yet still askt pardon, and was not deni'd.
But you shall hear. After my heart was well,
And clean and fair, as I one even-tide
                    (I sigh to tell)
Walkt by my self abroad, I saw a large                    25
And spacious furnace flaming, and thereon
A boiling cauldron, round about whose verge
Was in great letters set *AFFLICTION*.
The greatness show'd the owner. So I went
To fetch a sacrifice out of my fold,                    30
Thinking with that, which I did thus present,
To warm his love, which I did fear grew cold.
But as my heart did tender it, the man
Who was to take it from me, slipt his hand,
And threw my heart into the scalding pan;                    35
My heart, that brought it (do you understand?)
The offerer's heart. *Your heart was hard, I fear.*
Indeed 'tis true. I found a callous matter
Began to spread and to expatiate there:
But with a richer drug than scalding water,                    40
I bath'd it often, ev'n with holy blood,
Which at a board, while many drunk bare wine,
A friend did steal into my cup for good,
Ev'n taken inwardly, and most divine
To supple hardnesses. But at the length                    45
Out of the cauldron getting, soon I fled
Unto my house, where to repair the strength
Which I had lost, I hasted to my bed.
But when I thought to sleep out all these faults
                    (I sigh to speak)                    50
I found that some had stuff'd the bed with thoughts,
I would say *thorns*. Dear, could my heart not break,
When with my pleasures ev'n my rest was gone?
Full well I understood, who had been there:
For I had giv'n the key to none, but one:                    55
It must be he. *Your heart was dull, I fear.*
Indeed a slack and sleepy state of mind
Did oft possess me, so that when I pray'd,

Though my lips went, my heart did stay behind.
But all my scores were by another paid,                    60
Who took the debt upon him. *Truly, Friend,*
*For aught I hear, your Master shows to you*
*More favour than you wot of. Mark the end.*
*The Font did only, what was old, renew:*
*The Cauldron suppled, what was grown too hard:*          65
*The Thorns did quicken, what was grown too dull:*
*All did but strive to mend, what you had marr'd.*
*Wherefore be cheer'd, and praise him to the full*
*Each day, each hour, each moment of the week,*
*Who fain would have you be new, tender, quick.*          70

# Man's medley

Hark, how the birds do sing,
            And woods do ring.
All creatures have their joy: and man hath his.
            Yet if we rightly measure,
                        Man's joy and pleasure            5
Rather hereafter, than in present, is.

            To this life things of sense
                        Make their pretence:
In th' other Angels have a right by birth:
            Man ties them both alone,
                        And makes them one,               10
With th' one hand touching heav'n, with th' other earth.

            In soul he mounts and flies,
                        In flesh he dies.
He wears a stuff whose thread is coarse and round,
            But trimm'd with curious lace,               15
                        And should take place
After the trimming, not the stuff and ground.

Not, that he may not here
        Taste of the cheer,       20
But as birds drink, and straight lift up their head,
        So must he sip and think
        Of better drink
He may attain to, after he is dead.

But as his joys are double;       25
        So is his trouble.
He hath two winters, other things but one:
        Both frosts and thoughts do nip,
        And bite his lip;
And he of all things fears two deaths alone.    30

Yet ev'n the greatest griefs
        May be reliefs,
Could he but take them right, and in their ways.
        Happy is he, whose heart
        Hath found the art    35
To turn his double pains to double praise.

# The Storm

If as the winds and waters here below
        Do fly and flow,
My sighs and tears as busy were above;
        Sure they would move
And much affect thee, as tempestuous times    5
Amaze poor mortals, and object their crimes.

Stars have their storms, ev'n in a high degree,
        As well as we.
A throbbing conscience spurred by remorse
        Hath a strange force:    10
It quits the earth, and mounting more and more,
Dares to assault thee, and besiege thy door.

There it stands knocking, to thy music's wrong,
              And drowns the song.
Glory and honour are set by till it            15
              An answer get.
Poets have wrong'd poor storms: such days are best;
They purge the air without, within the breast.


# Paradise

I bless thee, Lord, because I G R O W
Among thy trees, which in a R O W
To thee both fruit and order O W.

What open force, or hidden C H A R M
Can blast my fruit, or bring me H A R M,     5
While the enclosure is thine A R M?

Enclose me still for fear I S T A R T.
Be to me rather sharp and T A R T,
Than let me want thy hand and A R T.

When thou dost greater judgements S P A R E,     10
And with thy knife but prune and P A R E,
Ev'n fruitful trees more fruitful A R E.

Such sharpness shows the sweetest F R E N D:
Such cuttings rather heal than R E N D:
And such beginnings touch their E N D.     15

# The Method

Poor heart, lament.
For since thy God refuseth still,
There is some rub, some discontent,
    Which cools his will.

Thy Father *could*         5
Quickly effect, what thou dost move;
For he is *Power*: and sure he *would*;
    For he is *Love*.

Go search this thing,
Tumble thy breast, and turn thy book.    10
If thou hadst lost a glove or ring,
    Wouldst thou not look?

What do I see
Written above there? *Yesterday*
*I did behave me carelessly,*        15
    *When I did pray.*

And should God's ear
To such indifferents chained be,
Who do not their own motions hear?
    Is God less free?        20

But stay! what's there?
*Late when I would have something done,*
*I had a motion to forbear,*
    *Yet I went on.*

And should God's ear,        25
Which needs not man, be ti'd to those
Who hear not him, but quickly hear
    His utter foes?

Then once more pray:
Down with thy knees, up with thy voice.    30
Seek pardon first, and God will say,
    *Glad heart, rejoice.*

# Divinity

As men, for fear the stars should sleep and nod,
      And trip at night, have spheres suppli'd;
As if a star were duller than a clod,
      Which knows his way without a guide:

Just so the other heav'n they also serve,           5
      Divinity's transcendent sky:
Which with the edge of wit they cut and carve.
      Reason triumphs, and faith lies by.

Could not that wisdom, which first broacht the wine,
      Have thicken'd it with definitions?       10
And jagg'd his seamless coat, had that been fine,
      With curious questions and divisions?

But all the doctrine, which he taught and gave,
      Was clear as heav'n, from whence it came.
At least those beams of truth, which only save,      15
      Surpass in brightness any flame.

*Love God, and love your neighbour. Watch and pray.*
      *Do as ye would be done unto.*
O dark instructions; ev'n as dark as day!
      Who can these Gordian knots undo?       20

But he doth bid us take his blood for wine.
      Bid what he please; yet I am sure,
To take and taste what he doth there design,
      Is all that saves, and not obscure.

Then burn thy Epicycles, foolish man;       25
      Break all thy spheres, and save thy head.
Faith needs no staff of flesh, but stoutly can
      To heav'n alone both go, and lead.

# Ephes. 4. 30.
## *Grieve not the Holy Spirit, &c.*

And art thou grieved, sweet and sacred Dove,
   When I am sour,
   And cross thy love?
Grieved for me? the God of strength and power
  Griev'd for a worm, which when I tread,  5
  I pass away and leave it dead?

Then weep mine eyes, the God of love doth grieve:
   Weep foolish heart,
   And weeping live:
For death is dry as dust. Yet if ye part,  10
  End as the night, whose sable hue
  Your sins express; melt into dew.

When saucy mirth shall knock or call at door,
   Cry out, Get hence,
   Or cry no more.  15
Almighty God doth grieve, he puts on sense:
  I sin not to my grief alone,
  But to my God's too; he doth groan.

Oh take thy lute, and tune it to a strain,
   Which may with thee
   All day complain.  20
There can no discord but in ceasing be.
  Marbles can weep; and surely strings
  More bowels have, than such hard things.

Lord, I adjudge my self to tears and grief,  25
   Ev'n endless tears
   Without relief.
If a clear spring for me no time forbears,
  But runs, although I be not dry;
  I am no Crystal, what shall I?  30

Yet if I wail not still, since still to wail
      Nature denies;
        And flesh would fail,
If my deserts were masters of mine eyes:
      Lord, pardon, for thy son makes good     35
      My want of tears with store of blood.

# The Family

What doth this noise of thoughts within my heart,
      As if they had a part?
What do these loud complaints and puling fears,
    As if there were no rule or ears?

But, Lord, the house and family are thine,     5
      Though some of them repine.
Turn out these wranglers, which defile thy seat:
    For where thou dwellest all is neat.

First Peace and Silence all disputes control,
      Then Order plays the soul;     10
And giving all things their set forms and hours,
    Makes of wild woods sweet walks and bowers.

Humble Obedience near the door doth stand,
      Expecting a command:
Than whom in waiting nothing seems more slow,     15
    Nothing more quick when she doth go.

Joys oft are there, and griefs as oft as joys:
      But griefs without a noise:
Yet speak they louder than distemper'd fears.
    What is so shrill as silent tears?     20

This is thy house, with these it doth abound:
      And where these are not found,
Perhapst thou com'st sometimes, and for a day;
    But not to make a constant stay.

# The Size

Content thee, greedy heart.
Modest and moderate joys to those, that have
Title to more hereafter when they part,
            Are passing brave.
   Let th' upper springs into the low          5
   Descend and fall, and thou dost flow.

   What though some have a fraught
Of cloves and nutmegs, and in cinnamon sail;
If thou hast wherewithal to spice a draught,
            When griefs prevail,          10
   And for the future time art heir
   To th' Isle of spices, is't not fair?

   To be in both worlds full
Is more than God was, who was hungry here.
Wouldst thou his laws of fasting disannul?          15
            Enact good cheer?
   Lay out thy joy, yet hope to save it?
   Wouldst thou both eat thy cake, and have it?

   Great joys are all at once;
But little do reserve themselves for more:          20
Those have their hopes; these what they have renounce,
            And live on score:
   Those are at home; these journey still,
   And meet the rest on Sion's hill.

   Thy Saviour sentenc'd joy,          25
And in the flesh condemn'd it as unfit,
At least in lump: for such doth oft destroy;
            Whereas a bit
   Doth 'tice us on to hopes of more,
   And for the present health restore.          30

A Christian's state and case
Is not a corpulent, but a thin and spare,
Yet active strength: whose long and bony face
    Content and care
  Do seem to equally divide,         35
  Like a pretender, not a bride.

    Wherefore sit down, good heart;
Grasp not at much, for fear thou losest all.
If comforts fell according to desert,
    They would great frosts and snows destroy:     40
  For we should count, Since the last joy.

    Then close again the seam,
Which thou hast open'd: do not spread thy robe
In hope of great things. Call to mind thy dream,
    An earthly globe,         45
  On whose meridian was engraven,
  *These seas are tears, and heaven the haven.*

# Artillery

As I one ev'ning sat before my cell,
Me thoughts a star did shoot into my lap.
I rose, and shook my clothes, as knowing well,
That from small fires comes oft no small mishap.
    When suddenly I heard one say,     5
    *Do as thou usest, disobey,*
    *Expel good motions from thy breast,*
*Which have the face of fire, but end in rest.*

I, who had heard of music in the spheres,
But not of speech in stars, began to muse:     10
But turning to my God, whose ministers
The stars and all things are; If I refuse,
    Dread Lord, said I, so oft my good,
    Then I refuse not ev'n with blood
    To wash away my stubborn thought:     15
For I will do, or suffer what I ought.

But I have also stars and shooters too,
Born where thy servants both artilleries use.
My tears and prayers night and day do woo,
And work up to thee; yet thou dost refuse.          20
    Not, but I am (I must say still)
    Much more oblig'd to do thy will,
    Than thou to grant mine: but because
Thy promise now hath ev'n set thee thy laws.

Then we are shooters both, and thou dost deign       25
To enter combat with us, and contest
With thine own clay. But I would parley fain:
Shun not my arrows, and behold my breast.
    Yet if thou shunnest, I am thine:
    I must be so, if I am mine.                 30
    There is no articling with thee:
I am but finite, yet thine infinitely.

# Church-rents and schisms

Brave rose (alas!) where art thou? in the chair
Where thou didst lately so triumph and shine,
A worm doth sit, whose many feet and hair
Are the more foul, the more thou wert divine.
This, this hath done it, this did bite the root        5
And bottom of the leaves: which when the wind
Did once perceive, it blew them under foot,
Where rude unhallow'd steps do crush and grind
    Their beauteous glories. Only shreds of thee,
    And those all bitten, in thy chair I see.      10

Why doth my Mother blush? is she the rose,
And shows it so? Indeed Christ's precious blood
Gave you a colour once; which when your foes
Thought to let out, the bleeding did you good,
And made you look much fresher than before.            15
But when debates and fretting jealousies
Did worm and work within you more and more,
Your colour faded, and calamities
    Turned your ruddy into pale and bleak:
    Your health and beauty both began to break.       20

Then did your sev'ral parts unloose and start:
Which when your neighbours saw, like a north-wind,
They rushed in, and cast them in the dirt
Where Pagans tread. O Mother dear and kind,
Where shall I get me eyes enough to weep,             25
As many eyes as stars? since it is night,
And much of Asia and Europe fast asleep,
And ev'n all Africk; would at least I might
    With these two poor ones lick up all the dew,
    Which falls by night, and pour it out for you!    30

# Justice (2)

O dreadful Justice, what a fright and terror
        Wast thou of old,
        When sin and error
    Did show and shape thy looks to me,
    And through their glass discolour thee!          5
He that did but look up, was proud and bold.

The dishes of thy balance seem'd to gape,
        Like two great pits;
        The beam and scape
    Did like some tort'ring engine show:            10
    Thy hand above did burn and glow,
Daunting the stoutest hearts, the proudest wits.

But now that Christ's pure veil presents the sight,
   I see no fears:
     Thy hand is white,     15
   Thy scales like buckets, which attend
   And interchangeably descend,
Lifting to heaven from this well of tears.

For where before thou still didst call on me
     Now I still touch     20
     And harp on thee.
   God's promises have made thee mine;
   Why should I justice now decline?
Against me there is none, but for me much.


# The Pilgrimage

I travell'd on, seeing the hill, where lay
     My expectation.
   A long it was and weary way.
   The gloomy cave of Desperation
I left on th' one, and on the other side     5
     The rock of Pride.

And so I came to fancy's meadow strow'd
     With many a flower:
   Fain would I here have made abode,
   But I was quicken'd by my hour.     10
So to care's copse I came, and there got through
     With much ado.

That led me to the wild of passion, which
     Some call the wold;
   A wasted place, but sometimes rich.     15
   Here I was robb'd of all my gold,
Save one good Angel, which a friend had ti'd
     Close to my side.

138

At length I got unto the gladsome hill,
          Where lay my hope,       20
   Where lay my heart; and climbing still,
   When I had gain'd the brow and top,
A lake of brackish waters on the ground
          Was all I found.

With that abash'd and struck with many a sting     25
          Of swarming fears,
   I fell, and cry'd, Alas my King;
   Can both the way and end be tears?
Yet taking heart I rose, and then perceiv'd
          I was deceiv'd:       30

My hill was further: so I flung away,
          Yet heard a cry
   Just as I went, *None goes that way*
   *And lives*: If that be all, said I,
After so foul a journey death is fair,      35
          And but a chair.

# The Holdfast

I threatned to observe the strict decree
   Of my dear God with all my power and might.
   But I was told by one, it could not be;
Yet I might trust in God to be my light.
Then will I trust, said I, in him alone.      5
   Nay, ev'n to trust in him, was also his:
   We must confess, that nothing is our own.
Then I confess that he my succour is:
But to have nought is ours, not to confess
   That we have nought. I stood amaz'd at this,   10
   Much troubled, till I heard a friend express,
That all things were more ours by being his.
   What Adam had, and forfeited for all,
   Christ keepeth now, who cannot fail or fall.

# Complaining

Do not beguile my heart,
　　Because thou art
My power and wisdom. Put me not to shame,
　　Because I am
Thy clay that weeps, thy dust that calls.　　5

Thou art the Lord of glory;
　　The deed and story
Are both thy due: but I a silly fly,
　　That live or die
According as the weather falls.　　10

Art thou all justice, Lord?
　　Shows not thy word
More attributes? Am I all throat or eye,
　　To weep or cry?
Have I no parts but those of grief?　　15

Let not thy wrathful power
　　Afflict my hour,
My inch of life: or let thy gracious power
　　Contract my hour,
That I may climb and find relief.　　20

# The Discharge

Busy enquiring heart, what wouldst thou know?
　　　　　Why dost thou pry,
And turn, and leer, and with a licorous eye
　　　　　Look high and low;
　　　And in thy lookings stretch and grow?　　　　5

Hast thou not made thy counts, and summ'd up all?
　　　　　Did not thy heart
Give up the whole, and with the whole depart?
　　　　　Let what will fall:
　　　That which is past who can recall?　　　　10

Thy life is God's, thy time to come is gone,
　　　　　And is his right.
He is thy night at noon: he is at night
　　　　　Thy noon alone.
　　　The crop is his, for he hath sown.　　　　15

And well it was for thee, when this befell,
　　　　　That God did make
Thy business his, and in thy life partake:
　　　　　For thou canst tell,
　　　If it be his once, all is well.　　　　20

Only the present is thy part and fee.
　　　　　And happy thou,
If, though thou didst not beat thy future brow,
　　　　　Thou couldst well see
　　　What present things requir'd of thee.　　　　25

They ask enough; why shouldst thou further go?
　　　　　Raise not the mud
Of future depths, but drink the clear and good.
　　　　　Dig not for woe
　　　In times to come; for it will grow.　　　　30

Man and the present fit: if he provide,
   He breaks the square.
This hour is mine: if for the next I care,
   I grow too wide,
   And do encroach upon death's side.    35

For death each hour environs and surrounds.
   He that would know
And care for future chances, cannot go
   Unto those grounds,
   But through a Church-yard which them bounds.   40

Things present shrink and die: but they that spend
   Their thoughts and sense
On future grief, do not remove it thence,
   But it extend,
   And draw the bottom out an end.    45

God chains the dog till night: wilt loose the chain,
   And wake thy sorrow?
Wilt thou forestall it, and now grieve to morrow,
   And then again
   Grieve over freshly all thy pain?    50

Either grief will not come: or if it must,
   Do not forecast.
And while it cometh, it is almost past.
   Away distrust:
   My God hath promis'd, he is just.    55

## Praise (2)

King of Glory, King of Peace,
   I will love thee:
And that love may never cease,
   I will move thee.

Thou hast granted my request,       5
      Thou hast heard me:
Thou didst note my working breast,
      Thou hast spar'd me.

Wherefore with my utmost art
      I will sing thee,       10
And the cream of all my heart
      I will bring thee.

Though my sins against me cried,
      Thou didst clear me;
And alone, when they replied,       15
      Thou didst hear me.

Sev'n whole days, not one in seven,
      I will praise thee.
In my heart, though not in heaven,
      I can raise thee.       20

Thou grew'st soft and moist with tears,
      Thou relentedst:
And when Justice call'd for fears,
      Thou dissentedst.

Small it is, in this poor sort       25
      To enrol thee:
Ev'n eternity is too short
      To extol thee.

# An Offering

Come, bring thy gift. If blessings were as slow
As men's returns, what would become of fools?
What hast thou there? a heart? but is it pure?
Search well and see; for hearts have many holes.
Yet one pure heart is nothing to bestow:       5
In Christ two natures met to be thy cure.

O that within us hearts had propagation,
Since many gifts do challenge many hearts!
Yet one, if good, may title to a number;
And single things grow fruitful by deserts.                    10
In public judgements one may be a nation,
And fence a plague, while others sleep and slumber.

But all I fear is lest thy heart displease,
As neither good, nor one: so oft divisions
Thy lusts have made, and not thy lusts alone;                  15
Thy passions also have their set partitions.
These parcel out thy heart: recover these,
And thou mayst offer many gifts in one.

There is a balsam, or indeed a blood,
Dropping from heav'n, which doth both cleanse and close    20
All sorts of wounds; of such strange force it is.
Seek out this All-heal, and seek no repose,
Until thou find and use it to thy good:
Then bring thy gift; and let thy hymn be this;

        Since my sadness                    25
        Into gladness
Lord thou dost convert,
        O accept
        What thou hast kept,
As thy due desert.                    30

        Had I many,
        Had I any
(For this heart is none),
        All were thine
        And none of mine:                    35
Surely thine alone.

        Yet thy favour
        May give savour
To this poor oblation;
        And it raise                    40
        To be thy praise,
And be my salvation.

# Longing

With sick and famisht eyes,
With doubling knees and weary bones,
      To thee my cries,
      To thee my groans,
To thee my sighs, my tears ascend: 5
      No end?

      My throat, my soul is hoarse;
My heart is wither'd like a ground
        Which thou dost curse.
        My thoughts turn round, 10
And make me giddy; Lord, I fall,
        Yet call.

      From thee all pity flows.
Mothers are kind, because thou art,
        And dost dispose 15
        To them a part:
Their infants, them; and they suck thee
        More free.

      Bowels of pity, hear!
Lord of my soul, love of my mind, 20
        Bow down thine ear!
        Let not the wind
Scatter my words, and in the same
        Thy name!

      Look on my sorrows' round! 25
Mark well my furnace! O what flames,
        What heats abound!
        What griefs, what shames!
Consider, Lord; Lord, bow thine ear,
        And hear! 30

Lord Jesu, thou didst bow
Thy dying head upon the tree:
    O be not now
    More dead to me!
Lord hear! *Shall he that made the ear,*        35
        *Not hear?*


    Behold, thy dust doth stir,
It moves, it creeps, it aims at thee:
    Wilt thou defer
    To succour me,
Thy pile of dust, wherein each crumb        40
        Says, Come?


    To thee help appertains.
Hast thou left all things to their course,
    And laid the reins        45
    Upon the horse?
Is all lockt? hath a sinner's plea
        No key?


    Indeed the world's thy book,
Where all things have their leaf assign'd:        50
      Yet a meek look
      Hath interlin'd.
Thy board is full, yet humble guests
        Find nests.


    Thou tarriest, while I die,        55
And fall to nothing: thou dost reign,
      And rule on high,
      While I remain
In bitter grief: yet am I stil'd
        Thy child.        60

Lord, didst thou leave thy throne,
Not to relieve? how can it be,
That thou art grown
Thus hard to me?
Were sin alive, good cause there were 65
To bear.

But now both sin is dead,
And all thy promises live and bide.
That wants his head;
These speak and chide, 70
And in thy bosom pour my tears,
As theirs.

Lord JESU, hear my heart,
Which hath been broken now so long,
That ev'ry part 75
Hath got a tongue!
Thy beggars grow; rid them away
Today.

My love, my sweetness, hear!
By these thy feet, at which my heart 80
Lies all the year,
Pluck out thy dart,
And heal my troubled breast which cries,
Which dies.

# The Bag

Away despair; my gracious Lord doth hear.
Though winds and waves assault my keel,
He doth preserve it: he doth steer,
Ev'n when the boat seems most to reel.
Storms are the triumph of his art: 5
Well may he close his eyes, but not his heart.

Hast thou not heard, that my Lord JESUS di'd?
  Then let me tell thee a strange story.
  The God of power, as he did ride
  In his majestic robes of glory,     10
  Resolv'd to light; and so one day
He did descend, undressing all the way.

The stars his tire of light and rings obtain'd,
  The cloud his bow, the fire his spear,
  The sky his azure mantle gain'd.     15
  And when they ask'd, what he would wear;
  He smil'd and said as he did go,
He had new clothes a making here below.

When he was come, as travellers are wont,
  He did repair unto an inn.     20
  Both then, and after, many a brunt
  He did endure to cancel sin:
  And having giv'n the rest before,
Here he gave up his life to pay our score.

But as he was returning, there came one     25
  That ran upon him with a spear.
  He, who came hither all alone,
  Bringing nor man, nor arms, nor fear,
  Receiv'd the blow upon his side,
And straight he turn'd, and to his brethren cry'd,     30

If ye have any thing to send or write,
  (I have no bag, but here is room)
  Unto my father's hands and sight
  (Believe me) it shall safely come.
  That I shall mind what you impart,     35
Look, you may put it very near my heart.

Or if hereafter any of my friends
  Will use me in this kind, the door
  Shall still be open; what he sends
  I will present, and somewhat more,     40
  Not to his hurt. Sighs will convey
Any thing to me. Hark despair, away.

# The Jews

Poor nation, whose sweet sap, and juice
Our scions have purloin'd, and left you dry:
Whose streams we got by the Apostles' sluice,
And use in baptism, while ye pine and die:
Who by not keeping once, became a debtor;          5
    And now by keeping lose the letter:

Oh that my prayers! mine, alas!
Oh that some Angel might a trumpet sound;
At which the Church falling upon her face
Should cry so loud, until the trump were drown'd,          10
And by that cry of her dear Lord obtain,
    That your sweet sap might come again!

# The Collar

I struck the board, and cry'd, No more.
    I will abroad.
What? shall I ever sigh and pine?
My lines and life are free; free as the road,
  Loose as the wind, as large as store.          5
    Shall I be still in suit?
  Have I no harvest but a thorn
  To let me blood, and not restore
What I have lost with cordial fruit?
    Sure there was wine          10
  Before my sighs did dry it: there was corn
  Before my tears did drown it.
  Is the year only lost to me?
    Have I no bays to crown it?
No flowers, no garlands gay? all blasted?          15
    All wasted?
  Not so, my heart: but there is fruit,
    And thou hast hands.

Recover all thy sigh-blown age
On double pleasures: leave thy cold dispute　　　　20
Of what is fit, and not; forsake thy cage,
　　　　Thy rope of sands,
Which petty thoughts have made, and made to thee
　　Good cable, to enforce and draw,
　　　　And be thy law,　　　　25
　　While thou didst wink and wouldst not see.
　　　　Away; take heed:
　　　　I will abroad.
Call in thy death's head there: tie up thy fears.
　　　　He that forbears　　　　30
　　To suit and serve his need,
　　　　Deserves his load.
But as I rav'd and grew more fierce and wild
　　　　At every word,
　　Me thoughts I heard one calling, *Child*:　　　35
　　And I reply'd, *My Lord*.

# The Glimpse

Whither away delight?
Thou cam'st but now; wilt thou so soon depart,
　　And give me up to night?
For many weeks of lingring pain and smart
But one half hour of comfort for my heart?　　　5

　　Me thinks delight should have
More skill in music, and keep better time.
　　Wert thou a wind or wave,
They quickly go and come with lesser crime:
Flowers look about, and die not in their prime.　　　10

　　Thy short abode and stay
Feeds not, but adds to the desire of meat.
　　Lime begg'd of old (they say)
A neighbour spring to cool his inward heat;
Which by the spring's access grew much more great.　　　15

In hope of thee my heart
Pickt here and there a crumb, and would not die;
    But constant to his part
When as my fears foretold this, did reply,
A slender thread a gentle guest will tie.      20

    Yet if the heart that wept
Must let thee go, return when it doth knock.
    Although thy heap be kept
For future times, the droppings of the stock
May oft break forth, and never break the lock.    25

    If I have more to spin,
The wheel shall go, so that thy stay be short.
    Thou knowst how grief and sin
Disturb the work. O make me not their sport,
Who by thy coming may be made a court!    30

# Assurance

    O spiteful bitter thought!
Bitterly spiteful thought! Couldst thou invent
So high a torture? Is such poison bought?
Doubtless, but in the way of punishment,
    When wit contrives to meet with thee,    5
    No such rank poison can there be.

    Thou said'st but even now,
That all was not so fair, as I conceiv'd,
Betwixt my God and me; that I allow
And coin large hopes; but, that I was deceiv'd:    10
    Either the league was broke, or near it;
    And, that I had great cause to fear it.

And what to this? what more
Could poison, if it had a tongue, express?
What is thy aim? wouldst thou unlock the door                    15
To cold despairs, and gnawing pensiveness?
    Wouldst thou raise devils? I see, I know,
    I writ thy purpose long ago.

    But I will to my Father,
Who heard thee say it. O most gracious Lord,                     20
If all the hope and comfort that I gather,
Were from my self, I had not half a word,
    Not half a letter to oppose
    What is objected by my foes.

    But thou art my desert:                                 25
And in this league, which now my foes invade,
Thou art not only to perform thy part,
But also mine; as when the league was made
    Thou didst at once thy self indite,
    And hold my hand, while I did write.                   30

    Wherefore if thou canst fail,
Then can thy truth and I: but while rocks stand,
And rivers stir, thou canst not shrink or quail:
Yea, when both rocks and all things shall disband,
    Then shalt thou be my rock and tower,                  35
    And make their ruin praise thy power.

    Now foolish thought go on,
Spin out thy thread, and make thereof a coat
To hide thy shame: for thou hast cast a bone
Which bounds on thee, and will not down thy throat:             40
    What for it self love once began,
    Now love and truth will end in man.

# The Call

Come, my Way, my Truth, my Life:
Such a Way, as gives us breath:
Such a Truth, as ends all strife:
And such a Life, as killeth death.

Come, my Light, my Feast, my Strength:        5
Such a Light, as shows a feast:
Such a Feast, as mends in length:
Such a Strength, as makes his guest.

Come, my Joy, my Love, my Heart:
Such a Joy, as none can move:              10
Such a Love, as none can part:
Such a Heart, as joys in love.


# Clasping of hands

Lord, thou art mine, and I am thine,
If mine I am: and thine much more,
Than I or ought, or can be mine.
Yet to be thine, doth me restore;
So that again I now am mine,               5
And with advantage mine the more.
Since this being mine, brings with it thine,
And thou with me doth thee restore.
   If I without thee would be mine,
   I neither should be mine nor thine.     10

Lord, I am thine, and thou art mine:
So mine thou art, that something more
I may presume thee mine, than thine.
For thou didst suffer to restore
Not thee, but me, and to be mine:          15
And with advantage mine the more,

Since thou in death wast none of thine,
Yet then as mine didst me restore.
  O be mine still! still make me thine!
  Or rather make no Thine and Mine!  20

# Praise (3)

Lord, I will mean and speak thy praise,
  Thy praise alone.
My busy heart shall spin it all my days:
  And when it stops for want of store,
Then will I wring it with a sigh or groan,  5
  That thou mayst yet have more.

When thou dost favour any action,
  It runs, it flies:
All things concur to give it a perfection.
  That which had but two legs before,  10
When thou dost bless, hath twelve: one wheel doth rise
  To twenty then, or more.

But when thou dost on business blow,
  It hangs, it clogs:
Not all the teams of Albion in a row  15
  Can hale or draw it out of door.
Legs are but stumps, and Pharaoh's wheels but logs,
  And struggling hinders more.

Thousands of things do thee employ
  In ruling all
This spacious globe: Angels must have their joy,  20
  Devils their rod, the sea his shore,
The winds their stint: and yet when I did call,
  Thou heardst my call, and more.

I have not lost one single tear:            25
           But when mine eyes
Did weep to heav'n, they found a bottle there
    (As we have boxes for the poor)
Ready to take them in; yet of a size
          That would contain much more.      30

But after thou hadst slipt a drop
           From thy right eye,
(Which there did hang like streamers near the top
    Of some fair church to show the sore
And bloody battle which thou once didst try)     35
          The glass was full and more.

Wherefore I sing. Yet since my heart,
           Though press'd, runs thin;
O that I might some other hearts convert,
    And so take up at use good store:     40
That to thy chests there might be coming in
          Both all my praise, and more!

# Joseph's coat

Wounded I sing, tormented I indite,
    Thrown down I fall into a bed, and rest:
Sorrow hath chang'd its note: such is his will,
Who changeth all things, as him pleaseth best.
    For well he knows, if but one grief and smart     5
Among my many had his full career,
Sure it would carry with it ev'n my heart,
And both would run until they found a bier
    To fetch the body; both being due to grief.
But he hath spoil'd the race; and giv'n to anguish     10
One of Joy's coats, 'ticing it with relief
To linger in me, and together languish.
    I live to show his power, who once did bring
    My *joys* to *weep*, and now my *griefs* to *sing*.

# The Pulley

When God at first made man,
Having a glass of blessings standing by,
Let us (said he) pour on him all we can:
Let the world's riches, which dispersed lie,
        Contract into a span.      5

So strength first made a way;
Then beauty flow'd, then wisdom, honour, pleasure:
When almost all was out, God made a stay,
Perceiving that alone of all his treasure
        Rest in the bottom lay.      10

For if I should (said he)
Bestow this jewel also on my creature,
He would adore his gifts in stead of me,
And rest in Nature, not the God of Nature.
        So both should losers be.      15

Yet let him keep the rest,
But keep them with repining restlessness:
Let him be rich and weary, that at least,
If goodness lead him not, yet weariness
        May toss him to my breast.     20

# The Priesthood

Blest Order, which in power dost so excel,
That with th' one hand thou liftest to the sky,
And with the other throwest down to hell
In thy just censures; fain would I draw nigh,
Fain put thee on, exchanging my lay-sword     5
        For that of th' holy word.

But thou art fire, sacred and hallow'd fire;
And I but earth and clay: should I presume
To wear thy habit, the severe attire
My slender compositions might consume.                    10
I am both foul and brittle; much unfit
       To deal in holy Writ.

Yet have I often seen, by cunning hand
And force of fire, what curious things are made
Of wretched earth. Where once I scorn'd to stand,          15
That earth is fitted by the fire and trade
Of skilful artists, for the boards of those
      Who make the bravest shows.

But since those great ones, be they ne're so great,
Come from the earth, from whence those vessels come;       20
So that at once both feeder, dish, and meat
Have one beginning and one final sum:
I do not greatly wonder at the sight,
      If earth in earth delight.

But th' holy men of God such vessels are,                  25
As serve him up, who all the world commands:
When God vouchsafeth to become our fare,
Their hands convey him, who conveys their hands.
O what pure things, most pure must those things be,
      Who bring my God to me!                    30

Wherefore I dare not, I, put forth my hand
To hold the Ark, although it seem to shake
Through th' old sins and new doctrines of our land.
Only, since God doth often vessels make
Of lowly matter for high uses meet,                        35
      I throw me at his feet.

There will I lie, until my Maker seek
For some mean stuff whereon to show his skill:
Then is my time. The distance of the meek
Doth flatter power. Lest good come short of ill            40
In praising might, the poor do by submission
      What pride by opposition.

# The Search

Whither, O, whither art thou fled,
      My Lord, my Love?
My searches are my daily bread;
      Yet never prove.

My knees pierce th' earth, mine eyes the sky;    5
      And yet the sphere
And centre both to me deny
      That thou art there.

Yet can I mark how herbs below
      Grow green and gay,     10
As if to meet thee they did know,
      While I decay.

Yet can I mark how stars above
      Simper and shine,
As having keys unto thy love,     15
      While poor I pine.

I sent a sigh to seek thee out,
      Deep drawn in pain,
Wing'd like an arrow: but my scout
      Returns in vain.     20

I tun'd another (having store)
      Into a groan,
Because the search was dumb before:
      But all was one.

Lord, dost thou some new fabric mould     25
      Which favour wins,
And keeps thee present, leaving th' old
      Unto their sins?

Where is my God? what hidden place
        Conceals thee still?       30
What covert dare eclipse thy face?
        Is it thy will?

O let not that of any thing;
        Let rather brass,
Or steel, or mountains be thy ring,      35
        And I will pass.

Thy will such an entrenching is,
        As passeth thought:
To it all strength, all subtleties
        Are things of nought.      40

Thy will such a strange distance is,
        As that to it
East and West touch, the poles do kiss,
        And parallels meet.

Since then my grief must be as large,     45
        As is thy space,
Thy distance from me; see my charge,
        Lord, see my case.

O take these bars, these lengths away;
        Turn, and restore me:      50
Be not Almighty, let me say,
        Against, but for me.

When thou dost turn, and wilt be near;
        What edge so keen,
What point so piercing can appear      55
        To come between?

For as thy absence doth excel
        All distance known:
So doth thy nearness bear the bell,
        Making two one.      60

# Grief

O who will give me tears? Come all ye springs,
Dwell in my head and eyes: come clouds, and rain:
My grief hath need of all the watry things,
That nature hath produc'd. Let ev'ry vein
Suck up a river to supply mine eyes,                    5
My weary weeping eyes, too dry for me,
Unless they get new conduits, new supplies
To bear them out, and with my state agree.
What are two shallow fords, two little spouts
Of a less world? the greater is but small,             10
A narrow cupboard for my griefs and doubts,
Which want provision in the midst of all.
Verses, ye are too fine a thing, too wise
For my rough sorrows: cease, be dumb and mute,
Give up your feet and running to mine eyes,            15
And keep your measures for some lover's lute,
Whose grief allows him music and a rhyme:
For mine excludes both measure, tune, and time.
     Alas, my God!

# The Cross

 What is this strange and uncouth thing?
To make me sigh, and seek, and faint, and die,
Until I had some place, where I might sing,
 And serve thee; and not only I,
But all my wealth, and family might combine           5
To set thy honour up, as our design.

 And then when after much delay,
Much wrestling, many a combat, this dear end,
So much desir'd, is giv'n, to take away
 My power to serve thee; to unbend             10
All my abilities, my designs confound,
And lay my threatnings bleeding on the ground.

One ague dwelleth in my bones,
Another in my soul (the memory
What I would do for thee, if once my groans          15
    Could be allow'd for harmony)
I am in all a weak disabled thing:
Save in the sight thereof, where strength doth sting.

    Besides, things sort not to my will,
Ev'n when my will doth study thy renown:          20
Thou turnest th' edge of all things on me still,
    Taking me up to throw me down:
So that, ev'n when my hopes seem to be sped,
I am to grief alive, to them as dead.

    To have my aim, and yet to be          25
Farther from it than when I bent my bow;
To make my hopes my torture, and the fee
    Of all my woes another woe,
Is in the midst of delicates to need,
And ev'n in Paradise to be a weed.          30

    Ah my dear Father, ease my smart!
These contrarieties crush me: these cross actions
Do wind a rope about, and cut my heart:
    And yet since these thy contradictions
Are properly a cross felt by thy son,          35
With but four words, my words, *Thy will be done*.

# The Flower

How fresh, O Lord, how sweet and clean
Are thy returns! ev'n as the flowers in spring;
    To which, besides their own demean,
The late-past frosts tributes of pleasure bring.
        Grief melts away          5
        Like snow in May,
    As if there were no such cold thing.

Who would have thought my shrivel'd heart
Could have recover'd greenness? It was gone
    Quite under ground; as flowers depart       10
To see their mother-root, when they have blown;
        Where they together
        All the hard weather,
Dead to the world, keep house unknown.

These are thy wonders, Lord of power,       15
Killing and quickning, bringing down to hell
    And up to heaven in an hour;
Making a chiming of a passing-bell.
        We say amiss,
        This or that is:        20
Thy word is all, if we could spell.

O that I once past changing were,
Fast in thy Paradise, where no flower can wither!
    Many a spring I shoot up fair,
Offring at heav'n, growing and groaning thither:       25
        Nor doth my flower
        Want a spring-shower,
My sins and I joining together:

But while I grow in a straight line,
Still upwards bent, as if heav'n were mine own,       30
    Thy anger comes, and I decline:
What frost to that? what pole is not the zone,
        Where all things burn,
        When thou dost turn,
And the least frown of thine is shown?       35

And now in age I bud again,
After so many deaths I live and write;
    I once more smell the dew and rain,
And relish versing: O my only light,
        It cannot be       40
        That I am he
On whom thy tempests fell all night.

These are thy wonders, Lord of love,
To make us see we are but flowers that glide:
    Which when we once can find and prove,       45
Thou hast a garden for us, where to bide.
        Who would be more,
        Swelling through store,
Forfeit their Paradise by their pride.


# Dotage

False glozing pleasures, casks of happiness,
Foolish night-fires, women's and children's wishes,
Chases in Arras, gilded emptiness,
Shadows well mounted, dreams in a career,
Embroider'd lies, nothing between two dishes;     5
        These are the pleasures here.

True earnest sorrows, rooted miseries,
Anguish in grain, vexations ripe and blown,
Sure-footed griefs, solid calamities,
Plain demonstrations, evident and clear,     10
Fetching their proofs ev'n from the very bone;
        These are the sorrows here.

But oh the folly of distracted men,
Who griefs in earnest, joys in jest pursue;
Preferring, like brute beasts, a loathsome den     15
Before a court, ev'n that above so clear,
Where are no sorrows, but delights more true,
        Than miseries are here!

# The Son

Let foreign nations of their language boast,
What fine variety each tongue affords:
I like our language, as our men and coast:
Who cannot dress it well, want wit, not words.
How neatly do we give one only name                    5
To parents' issue and the sun's bright star!
A son is light and fruit; a fruitful flame
Chasing the father's dimness, carri'd far
From the first man in th' East, to fresh and new
Western discov'ries of posterity.                      10
So in one word our Lord's humility
We turn upon him in a sense most true:
    For what Christ once in humbleness began,
    We him in glory call, *The Son of Man.*

# A true Hymn

    My joy, my life, my crown!
   My heart was meaning all the day,
    Somewhat it fain would say:
And still it runneth mutt'ring up and down
With only this, *My joy, my life, my crown.*          5

    Yet slight not these few words:
   If truly said, they may take part
    Among the best in art.
The fineness which a hymn or psalm affords,
Is, when the soul unto the lines accords.              10

    He who craves all the mind,
   And all the soul, and strength, and time,
    If the words only rhyme,
Justly complains, that somewhat is behind
To make his verse, or write a hymn in kind.           15

Whereas if th' heart be moved,
Although the verse be somewhat scant,
God doth supply the want.
As when th' heart says (sighing to be approved)
O, *could I love!* and stops: God writeth, *Loved.*    20

# The Answer

My comforts drop and melt away like snow:
I shake my head, and all the thoughts and ends,
Which my fierce youth did bandy, fall and flow
Like leaves about me; or like summer friends,
Flies of estates and sun-shine. But to all,    5
Who think me eager, hot, and undertaking,
But in my prosecutions slack and small;
As a young exhalation, newly waking,
Scorns his first bed of dirt, and means the sky;
But cooling by the way, grows pursy and slow,    10
And settling to a cloud, doth live and die
In that dark state of tears: to all, that so
    Show me, and set me, I have one reply,
Which they that know the rest, know more than I.

# A Dialogue-Anthem
## *Christian. Death*

*Chr.*  Alas, poor Death, where is thy glory?
    Where is thy famous force, thy ancient sting?
*Dea.*  *Alas poor mortal, void of story,*
    *Go spell and read how I have kill'd thy King.*
*Chr.*  Poor death! and who was hurt thereby?    5
    Thy curse being laid on him, makes thee accurst.
*Dea.*  *Let losers talk: yet thou shalt die;*
    *These arms shall crush thee.*
*Chr.*                    Spare not, do thy worst.
    I shall be one day better than before:
    Thou so much worse, that thou shalt be no more.    10

# The Water-course

Thou who dost dwell and linger here below,
Since the condition of this world is frail,
Where of all plants afflictions soonest grow;
If troubles overtake thee, do not wail:

For who can look for less, that loveth $\begin{cases} \text{Life.} \\ \text{Strife.} \end{cases}$  5

But rather turn the pipe, and water's course
To serve thy sins, and furnish thee with store
Of sov'reign tears, springing from true remorse:
That so in pureness thou mayst him adore,

Who gives to man, as he sees fit $\begin{cases} \text{Salvation.} \\ \text{Damnation.} \end{cases}$  10

# Self-condemnation

Thou who condemnest Jewish hate,
For choosing Barrabas a murderer
    Before the Lord of glory;
  Look back upon thine own estate,
Call home thine eye (that busy wanderer);  5
    That choice may be thy story.

  He that doth love, and love amiss
This world's delights before true Christian joy,
    Hath made a Jewish choice:
  The world an ancient murderer is;  10
Thousands of souls it hath and doth destroy
    With her enchanting voice.

He that hath made a sorry wedding
Between his soul and gold, and hath preferr'd
    False gain before the true,         15
  Hath done what he condemns in reading:
For he hath sold for money his dear Lord,
    And is a Judas-Jew.

Thus we prevent the last great day,
And judge our selves. That light, which sin and passion    20
    Did before dim and choke,
  When once those snuffs are ta'ne away,
Shines bright and clear, ev'n unto condemnation,
    Without excuse or cloak.

## Bitter-sweet

    Ah my dear angry Lord,
    Since thou dost love, yet strike;
    Cast down, yet help afford;
    Sure I will do the like.

    I will complain, yet praise;         5
    I will bewail, approve:
    And all my sour-sweet days
    I will lament, and love.

## The Glance

  When first thy sweet and gracious eye
Vouchsaf'd ev'n in the midst of youth and night
To look upon me, who before did lie
      Weltring in sin;
  I felt a sugred strange delight,         5
Passing all cordials made by any art,
Bedew, embalm, and overrun my heart,
      And take it in.

Since that time many a bitter storm
My soul has felt, ev'n able to destroy,      10
Had the malicious and ill-meaning harm
        His swing and sway:
  But still thy sweet original joy
Sprung from thine eye, did work within my soul,
And surging griefs, when they grew bold, control,      15
        And got the day.

If thy first glance so powerful be,
A mirth but open'd and seal'd up again;
What wonders shall we feel, when we shall see
        Thy full-ey'd love!      20
  When thou shalt look us out of pain,
And one aspect of thine spend in delight
More than a thousand suns disburse in light,
        In heav'n above.

# The 23 Psalm

The God of love my shepherd is,
    And he that doth me feed:
While he is mine, and I am his,
    What can I want or need?

He leads me to the tender grass,      5
    Where I both feed and rest;
Then to the streams that gently pass:
    In both I have the best.

Or if I stray, he doth convert
    And bring my mind in frame:      10
And all this not for my desert,
    But for his holy name.

Yea, in death's shady black abode
    Well may I walk, not fear:
For thou art with me; and thy rod        15
    To guide, thy staff to bear.

Nay, thou dost make me sit and dine,
    Ev'n in my enemies' sight:
My head with oil, my cup with wine
    Runs over day and night.        20

Surely thy sweet and wondrous love
    Shall measure all my days;
And as it never shall remove,
    So neither shall my praise.

# Mary Magdalene

When blessed Mary wip'd her Saviour's feet
(Whose precepts she had trampled on before)
And wore them for a jewel on her head,
    Showing his steps should be the street,
    Wherein she henceforth evermore        5
With pensive humbleness would live and tread:

She being stain'd her self, why did she strive
To make him clean, who could not be defil'd?
Why kept she not her tears for her own faults,
    And not his feet? Though we could dive        10
    In tears like seas, our sins are pil'd
Deeper than they, in words, and works, and thoughts.

Dear soul, she knew who did vouchsafe and deign
To bear her filth; and that her sins did dash
Ev'n God himself: wherefore she was not loth,        15
    As she had brought wherewith to stain,
    So to bring in wherewith to wash:
And yet in washing one, she washed both.

# Aaron

Holiness on the head,
Light and perfections on the breast,
Harmonious bells below, raising the dead
To lead them unto life and rest.
Thus are true Aarons drest.                    5

Profaneness in my head,
Defects and darkness in my breast,
A noise of passions ringing me for dead
Unto a place where is no rest,
Poor priest thus am I drest.                    10

Only another head
I have, another heart and breast,
Another music, making live not dead,
Without whom I could have no rest:
In him I am well drest.                    15

Christ is my only head,
My alone only heart and breast,
My only music, striking me ev'n dead;
That to the old man I may rest,
And be in him new drest.                    20

So holy in my head,
Perfect and light in my dear breast,
My doctrine tun'd by Christ (who is not dead,
But lives in me while I do rest)
Come people; Aaron's drest.                    25

# The Odour, 2. *Cor.* 2

How sweetly doth *My Master* sound! *My Master!*
As Amber-grease leaves a rich scent
Unto the taster:
So do these words a sweet content,
An oriental fragrancy, *My Master*.                    5

With these all day I do perfume my mind,
  My mind ev'n thrust into them both:
    That I might find
  What cordials make this curious broth,
This broth of smells, that feeds and fats my mind.  10

*My Master*, shall I speak? O that to thee
  *My servant* were a little so,
    As flesh may be;
  That these two words might creep and grow
To some degree of spiciness to thee!  15

Then should the Pomander, which was before
  A speaking sweet, mend by reflection,
    And tell me more:
  For pardon of my imperfection,
Would warm and work it sweeter than before.  20

For when *My Master*, which alone is sweet,
  And ev'n in my unworthiness pleasing,
    Shall call and meet
  *My servant*, as thee not displeasing,
That call is but the breathing of the sweet.  25

This breathing would with gains by sweetning me
  (As sweet things traffic when they meet)
    Return to thee.
  And so this new commerce and sweet
Should all my life employ, and busy me.  30

# The Foil

If we could see below
The sphere of virtue, and each shining grace
  As plainly as that above doth show;
This were the better sky, the brighter place.

God hath made stars the foil 5
To set off virtues; griefs to set off sinning:
Yet in this wretched world we toil,
As if grief were not foul, nor virtue winning.

# The Forerunners

The harbingers are come. See, see their mark;
White is their colour, and behold my head.
But must they have my brain? must they dispark
Those sparkling notions, which therein were bred?
Must dullness turn me to a clod? 5
Yet have they left me, *Thou art still my God*.

Good men ye be, to leave me my best room,
Ev'n all my heart, and what is lodged there:
I pass not, I, what of the rest become,
So *Thou art still my God* be out of fear. 10
He will be pleased with that ditty;
And if I please him, I write fine and witty.

Farewell sweet phrases, lovely metaphors.
But will ye leave me thus? when ye before
Of stews and brothels only knew the doors, 15
Then did I wash you with my tears, and more
Brought you to Church well drest and clad:
My God must have my best, ev'n all I had.

Lovely enchanting language, sugar-cane,
Honey of roses, whither wilt thou fly? 20
Hath some fond lover 'tic'd thee to thy bane?
And wilt thou leave the Church, and love a sty?
Fie, thou wilt soil thy broider'd coat,
And hurt thy self, and him that sings the note.

172

Let foolish lovers, if they will love dung,                    25
With canvas, not with arras clothe their shame:
Let folly speak in her own native tongue.
True beauty dwells on high: ours is a flame
        But borrow'd thence to light us thither.
Beauty and beauteous words should go together.                 30

Yet if you go, I pass not; take your way:
For *Thou art still my God* is all that ye
Perhaps with more embellishment can say.
Go birds of spring: let winter have his fee,
        Let a bleak paleness chalk the door,          35
So all within be livelier than before.

# The Rose

Press me not to take more pleasure
        In this world of sugred lies,
And to use a larger measure
        Than my strict, yet welcome size.

First, there is no pleasure here:                              5
        Colour'd griefs indeed there are,
Blushing woes, that look as clear
        As if they could beauty spare.

Or if such deceits there be,
        Such delights I meant to say,             10
There are no such things to me,
        Who have pass'd my right away.

But I will not much oppose
        Unto what you now advise:
Only take this gentle rose,                                    15
        And therein my answer lies.

What is fairer than a rose?
    What is sweeter? yet it purgeth.
Purgings enmity disclose,
    Enmity forbearance urgeth. 20

If then all that worldlings prize
    Be contracted to a rose;
Sweetly there indeed it lies,
    But it biteth in the close.

So this flower doth judge and sentence 25
    Worldly joys to be a scourge:
For they all produce repentance,
    And repentance is a purge.

But I health, not physic choose:
    Only, though I you oppose, 30
Say that fairly I refuse,
    For my answer is a rose.

# Discipline

Throw away thy rod,
Throw away thy wrath:
    O my God,
Take the gentle path.

For my heart's desire 5
Unto thine is bent:
    I aspire
To a full consent.

Not a word or look
I affect to own, 10
    But by book,
And thy book alone.

Though I fail, I weep:
Though I halt in pace,
             Yet I creep      15
To the throne of grace.

Then let wrath remove;
Love will do the deed:
             For with love
Stony hearts will bleed.      20

Love is swift of foot;
Love's a man of war,
             And can shoot,
And can hit from far.

Who can scape his bow?      25
That which wrought on thee,
             Brought thee low,
Needs must work on me.

Throw away thy rod;
Though man frailties hath,      30
             Thou art God:
Throw away thy wrath.

# The Invitation

Come ye hither all, whose taste
             Is your waste;
Save your cost, and mend your fare.
God is here prepar'd and drest,
             And the feast,      5
God, in whom all dainties are.

Come ye hither all, whom wine
        Doth define,
Naming you not to your good:
Weep what ye have drunk amiss,         10
        And drink this,
Which before ye drink is blood.

Come ye hither all, whom pain
        Doth arraign,
Bringing all your sins to sight:         15
Taste and fear not: God is here
        In this cheer,
And on sin doth cast the fright.

Come ye hither all, whom joy
        Doth destroy,         20
While ye graze without your bounds:
Here is joy that drowneth quite
        Your delight,
As a flood the lower grounds.

Come ye hither all, whose love         25
        Is your dove,
And exalts you to the sky:
Here is love, which having breath
        Ev'n in death,
After death can never die.         30

Lord I have invited all,
        And I shall
Still invite, still call to thee.
For it seems but just and right
        In my sight,
Where is all, there all should be.        35

# The Banquet

Welcome sweet and sacred cheer,
   Welcome dear;
With me, in me, live and dwell:
For thy neatness passeth sight,
   Thy delight       5
Passeth tongue to taste or tell.

O what sweetness from the bowl
   Fills my soul,
Such as is, and makes divine!
Is some star (fled from the sphere)    10
   Melted there,
As we sugar melt in wine?

Or hath sweetness in the bread
   Made a head
To subdue the smell of sin;      15
Flowers, and gums, and powders giving
   All their living,
Lest the enemy should win?

Doubtless, neither star nor flower
   Hath the power      20
Such a sweetness to impart:
Only God, who gives perfumes,
   Flesh assumes,
And with it perfumes my heart.

But as Pomanders and wood     25
   Still are good,
Yet being bruis'd are better scented:
God, to show how far his love
   Could improve,
Here, as broken, is presented.     30

When I had forgot my birth,
                    And on earth
In delights of earth was drown'd;
God took blood, and needs would be
                    Spilt with me,                    35
And so found me on the ground.

Having rais'd me to look up,
                    In a cup
Sweetly he doth meet my taste.
But I still being low and short,                    40
                    Far from court,
Wine becomes a wing at last.

For with it alone I fly
                    To the sky
Where I wipe mine eyes, and see                    45
What I seek, for what I sue;
                    Him I view,
Who hath done so much for me.

Let the wonder of this pity
                    Be my ditty,                    50
And take up my lines and life:
Harken under pain of death,
                    Hands and breath;
Strive in this, and love the strife.

# The Posy

Let wits contest,
And with their words and posies windows fill:
        *Less than the least*
*Of all thy mercies*, is my posy still.


                    This on my ring,                    5
This by my picture, in my book I write:
                    Whether I sing,
Or say, or dictate, this is my delight.

Invention rest,
Comparisons go play, wit use thy will:          10
    *Less than the least*
*Of all God's mercies*, is my posy still.


# A Parody

Soul's joy, when thou art gone,
        And I alone,
        Which cannot be,
Because thou dost abide with me,
    And I depend on thee;          5

Yet when thou dost suppress
        The cheerfulness
        Of thy abode,
And in my powers not stir abroad,
    But leave me to my load:          10

O what a damp and shade
        Doth me invade!
        No stormy night
Can so afflict or so affright,
    As thy eclipsed light.          15

Ah Lord! do not withdraw,
        Lest want of awe
        Make Sin appear,
And when thou dost but shine less clear,
    Say, that thou art not here.          20

And then what life I have,
        While Sin doth rave,
        And falsely boast,
That I may seek, but thou art lost;
    Thou and alone thou know'st.          25

O what a deadly cold
    Doth me enfold!
    I half believe,
That Sin says true: but while I grieve
    Thou com'st and dost relieve.      30

# The Elixir

Teach me, my God and King,
    In all things thee to see,
And what I do in any thing,
    To do it as for thee:

    Not rudely, as a beast,      5
    To run into an action;
But still to make thee prepossest,
    And give it his perfection.

    A man that looks on glass,
    On it may stay his eye;      10
Or if he pleaseth, through it pass,
    And then the heav'n espy.

    All may of thee partake:
    Nothing can be so mean,
Which with his tincture (for thy sake)      15
    Will not grow bright and clean.

    A servant with this clause
    Makes drudgery divine:
Who sweeps a room, as for thy laws,
    Makes that and th' action fine.      20

    This is the famous stone
    That turneth all to gold:
For that which God doth touch and own
    Cannot for less be told.

# A Wreath

A wreathed garland of deserved praise,
Of praise deserved, unto thee I give,
I give to thee, who knowest all my ways,
My crooked winding ways, wherein I live,
Wherein I die, not live: for life is straight,          5
Straight as a line, and ever tends to thee,
To thee, who art more far above deceit,
Than deceit seems above simplicity.
Give me simplicity, that I may live,
So live and like, that I may know thy ways,          10
Know them and practise them: then shall I give
For this poor wreath, give thee a crown of praise.


# Death

Death, thou wast once an uncouth hideous thing,
               Nothing but bones,
          The sad effect of sadder groans:
Thy mouth was open, but thou couldst not sing.

For we consider'd thee as at some six          5
               Or ten years hence,
          After the loss of life and sense,
Flesh being turn'd to dust, and bones to sticks.

We lookt on this side of thee, shooting short,
               Where we did find          10
          The shells of fledge souls left behind,
Dry dust, which sheds no tears, but may extort.

But since our Saviour's death did put some blood
               Into thy face,
          Thou art grown fair and full of grace,          15
Much in request, much sought for, as a good.

For we do now behold thee gay and glad,
   As at dooms-day,
  When souls shall wear their new array,
And all thy bones with beauty shall be clad.    20

Therefore we can go die as sleep, and trust
   Half that we have
  Unto an honest faithful grave;
Making our pillows either down, or dust.


# Dooms-day

   Come away,
   Make no delay,
Summon all the dust to rise,
Till it stir, and rub the eyes;
While this member jogs the other,    5
Each one whispring, *Live you brother?*

   Come away,
   Make this the day.
Dust, alas, no music feels,
But thy trumpet: then it kneels,    10
As peculiar notes and strains
Cure Tarantula's raging pains.

   Come away,
   O make no stay!
Let the graves make their confession,    15
Lest at length they plead possession:
Flesh's stubbornness may have
Read that lesson to the grave.

   Come away,
   Thy flock doth stray.    20
Some to winds their body lend,
And in them may drown a friend:
Some in noisome vapours grow
To a plague and public woe.

Come away,                                          25
Help our decay,
Man is out of order hurl'd
Parcel'd out to all the world.
Lord, thy broken consort raise,
And the music shall be praise.                      30

## Judgement

Almighty Judge, how shall poor wretches brook
                    Thy dreadful look,
Able a heart of iron to appal,
                    When thou shalt call
      For ev'ry man's peculiar book?                  5

What others mean to do, I know not well;
                    Yet I hear tell,
That some will turn thee to some leaves therein
                    So void of sin,
      That they in merit shall excel.                10

But I resolve, when thou shalt call for mine,
                    That to decline,
And thrust a Testament into thy hand:
                    Let that be scann'd.
      There thou shalt find my faults are thine.     15

## Heaven

O who will show me those delights on high?
            *Echo.*          *I.*
Thou Echo, thou art mortal, all men know.
            *Echo.*          *No.*
Wert thou not born among the trees and leaves?        5
            *Echo.*          *Leaves.*

183

And are there any leaves, that still abide?
    *Echo.*    *Bide.*
What leaves are they? impart the matter wholly.
    *Echo.*    *Holy.*    10
Are holy leaves the Echo then of bliss?
    *Echo.*    *Yes.*
Then tell me, what is that supreme delight?
    *Echo.*    *Light.*
Light to the mind: what shall the will enjoy?    15
    *Echo.*    *Joy.*
But are there cares and business with the pleasure?
    *Echo.*    *Leisure.*
Light, joy, and leisure; but shall they persever?
    *Echo.*    *Ever.*    20

# Love (3)

Love bade me welcome: yet my soul drew back,
    Guilty of dust and sin.
But quick-ey'd Love, observing me grow slack
    From my first entrance in,
Drew nearer to me, sweetly questioning,    5
    If I lack'd any thing.

A guest, I answer'd, worthy to be here:
    Love said, you shall be he.
I the unkind, ungrateful? Ah my dear,
    I cannot look on thee.    10
Love took my hand, and smiling did reply,
    Who made the eyes but I?

Truth Lord, but I have marr'd them: let my shame
    Go where it doth deserve.
And know you not, says Love, who bore the blame?    15
    My dear, then I will serve.
You must sit down, says Love, and taste my meat:
    So I did sit and eat.

# FINIS

*Glory be to God on high, and on earth
peace, good will towards men.*

# The Church Militant

Almighty Lord, who from thy glorious throne
Seest and rulest all things ev'n as one:
The smallest ant or atom knows thy power,
Known also to each minute of an hour:
Much more do Common-weals acknowledge thee,                    5
And wrap their policies in thy decree,
Complying with thy counsels, doing nought
Which doth not meet with an eternal thought.
But above all, thy Church and Spouse doth prove
Not the decrees of power, but bands of love.                   10
Early didst thou arise to plant this vine,
Which might the more endear it to be thine.
Spices come from the East; so did thy Spouse,
Trim as the light, sweet as the laden boughs
Of *Noah's* shady vine, chaste as the dove;                    15
Prepar'd and fitted to receive thy love.
The course was westward, that the sun might light
As well our understanding as our sight.
Where th' Ark did rest, there *Abraham* began
To bring the other Ark from *Canaan*.                          20
*Moses* pursu'd this: but King *Solomon*
Finish'd and fixt the old religion.
When it grew loose, the Jews did hope in vain
By nailing Christ to fasten it again.
But to the Gentiles he bore cross and all,                     25
Rending with earthquakes the partition-wall:
Only whereas the Ark in glory shone,
Now with the cross, as with a staff, alone,
Religion, like a pilgrim, westward bent,
Knocking at all doors, ever as she went.                       30
Yet as the sun, though forward be his flight,
Listens behind him, and allows some light,
Till all depart: so went the Church her way,
Letting, while one foot stept, the other stay

Among the eastern nations for a time,                               35
Till both removed to the western clime.
To *Egypt* first she came, where they did prove
Wonders of anger once, but now of love.
The ten Commandments there did flourish more
Than the ten bitter plagues had done before.                       40
Holy *Macarius* and great *Anthony*
Made *Pharaoh Moses*, changing th' history.
*Goshen* was darkness, *Egypt* full of lights,
*Nilus* for monsters brought forth Israelites.
Such power hath mighty Baptism to produce                          45
For things misshapen, things of highest use.
*How dear to me, O God, thy counsels are!*
          *Who may with thee compare?*
Religion thence fled into *Greece*, where arts
Gave her the highest place in all men's hearts.                    50
Learning was pos'd, Philosophy was set,
Sophisters taken in a fisher's net.
*Plato* and *Aristotle* were at a loss,
And wheel'd about again to spell *Christ-Cross*.
Prayers chas'd syllogisms into their den,                          55
And *Ergo* was transform'd into *Amen*.
Though *Greece* took horse as soon as *Egypt* did,
And *Rome* as both; yet *Egypt* faster rid,
And spent her period and prefixed time
Before the other. *Greece* being past her prime,                   60
Religion went to *Rome*, subduing those,
Who, that they might subdue, made all their foes.
The Warrior his dear scars no more resounds,
But seems to yield Christ hath the greater wounds,
Wounds willingly endur'd to work his bliss,                        65
Who by an ambush lost his Paradise.
The great heart stoops, and taketh from the dust
A sad repentance, not the spoils of lust:
Quitting his spear, lest it should pierce again
Him in his members, who for him was slain.                         70
The Shepherd's hook grew to a sceptre here,
Giving new names and numbers to the year.
But th' Empire dwelt in *Greece*, to comfort them

Who were cut short in *Alexander's* stem.
In both of these Prowess and Arts did tame 75
And tune men's hearts against the Gospel came.
Which using, and not fearing skill in th' one,
Or strength in th' other, did erect her throne.
Many a rent and struggling th' Empire knew,
(As dying things are wont) until it flew 80
At length to *Germany*, still westward bending,
And there the Church's festival attending:
That as before Empire and Arts made way,
(For no less Harbingers would serve than they)
So they might still, and point us out the place 85
Where first the Church should raise her down-cast face.
Strength levels grounds, Art makes a garden there;
Then showers Religion, and makes all to bear.
*Spain* in the Empire shar'd with *Germany*,
But *England* in the higher victory: 90
Giving the Church a crown to keep her state,
And not go less than she had done of late.
*Constantine's* British line meant this of old,
And did this mystery wrap up and fold
Within a sheet of paper, which was rent 95
From time's great Chronicle, and hither sent.
Thus both the Church and Sun together ran
Unto the farthest old meridian.
*How dear to me, O God, thy counsels are!*
                *Who may with thee compare?* 100
Much about one and the same time and place,
Both where and when the Church began her race,
Sin did set out of Eastern *Babylon*,
And travell'd westward also: journeying on
He chid the Church away, where e're he came, 105
Breaking her peace, and tainting her good name.
At first he got to *Egypt*, and did sow
Gardens of gods, which ev'ry year did grow,
Fresh and fine deities. They were at great cost,
Who for a god clearly a sallet lost. 110
Ah, what a thing is man devoid of grace,
Adoring garlic with an humble face,

Begging his food of that which he may eat,
Starving the while he worshippeth his meat!
Who makes a root his god, how low is he,                    115
If God and man be sever'd infinitely!
What wretchedness can give him any room,
Whose house is foul, while he adores his broom?
None will believe this now, though money be
In us the same transplanted foolery.                         120
Thus Sin in *Egypt* sneaked for a while;
His highest was an ox or crocodile,
And such poor game. Thence he to *Greece* doth pass,
And being craftier much than Goodness was,
He left behind him garrisons of sins                         125
To make good that which ev'ry day he wins.
Here Sin took heart, and for a garden-bed
Rich shrines and oracles he purchased:
He grew a gallant, and would needs foretell
As well what should befall, as what befell.                  130
Nay, he became a poet, and would serve
His pills of sublimate in that conserve.
The world came both with hands and purses full
To this great lottery, and all would pull.
But all was glorious cheating, brave deceit,                 135
Where some poor truths were shuffled for a bait
To credit him, and to discredit those
Who after him should braver truths disclose.
From *Greece* he went to *Rome*: and as before
He was a God, now he's an Emperor.                           140
*Nero* and others lodg'd him bravely there,
Put him in trust to rule the Roman sphere.
Glory was his chief instrument of old:
Pleasure succeeded straight, when that grew cold.
Which soon was blown to such a mighty flame,                 145
That though our Saviour did destroy the game,
Disparking oracles, and all their treasure,
Setting affliction to encounter pleasure;
Yet did a rogue with hope of carnal joy
Cheat the most subtle nations. Who so coy,                   150
So trim, as *Greece* and *Egypt*? yet their hearts

Are given over, for their curious arts,
To such Mahometan stupidities,
As the old heathen would deem prodigies.
*How dear to me, O God, thy counsels are!*   155
    *Who may with thee compare?*
Only the West and *Rome* do keep them free
From this contagious infidelity.
And this is all the Rock, whereof they boast,
As *Rome* will one day find unto her cost.   160
Sin being not able to extirpate quite
The Churches here, bravely resolv'd one night
To be a Church-man too, and wear a Mitre:
The old debauched ruffian would turn writer.
I saw him in his study, where he sate   165
Busy in controversies sprung of late.
A gown and pen became him wondrous well:
His grave aspect had more of heav'n than hell:
Only there was a handsome picture by,
To which he lent a corner of his eye.   170
As Sin in *Greece* a Prophet was before,
And in old *Rome* a mighty Emperor;
So now being Priest he plainly did profess
To make a jest of Christ's three offices:
The rather since his scatter'd jugglings were   175
United now in one both time and sphere.
From *Egypt* he took petty deities,
From *Greece* oracular infallibilities,
And from old *Rome* the liberty of pleasure,
By free dispensings of the Church's treasure.   180
Then in memorial of his ancient throne
He did surname his palace, *Babylon*.
Yet that he might the better gain all nations,
And make that name good by their transmigrations,
From all these places, but at divers times,   185
He took fine vizards to conceal his crimes:
From *Egypt* Anchorism and retiredness,
Learning from *Greece*, from old *Rome* stateliness:
And blending these he carri'd all men's eyes,
While Truth sat by, counting his victories:   190

Whereby he grew apace and scorn'd to use
Such force as once did captivate the Jews;
But did bewitch, and finely work each nation
Into a voluntary transmigration.
All post to *Rome*: Princes submit their necks    195
Either t' his public foot or private tricks.
It did not fit his gravity to stir,
Nor his long journey, nor his gout and fur.
Therefore he sent out able ministers,
Statesmen within, without doors cloisterers:    200
Who without spear, or sword, or other drum
Than what was in their tongue, did overcome;
And having conquer'd, did so strangely rule,
That the whole world did seem but the Pope's mule.
As new and old *Rome* did one Empire twist;    205
So both together are one Antichrist,
Yet with two faces, as their *Janus* was;
Being in this their old crackt looking-glass.
*How dear to me, O God, thy counsels are!*
            *Who may with thee compare?*    210
Thus Sin triumphs in Western *Babylon*;
Yet not as Sin, but as Religion.
Of his two thrones he made the latter best,
And to defray his journey from the east.
Old and new *Babylon* are to hell and night,    215
As is the moon and sun to heav'n and light.
When th' one did set, the other did take place,
Confronting equally the law and grace.
They are hell's land-marks, Satan's double crest:
They are Sin's nipples, feeding th' east and west.    220
But as in vice the copy still exceeds
The pattern, but not so in virtuous deeds;
So though Sin made his latter feat the better,
The latter Church is to the first a debtor.
The second Temple could not reach the first:    225
And the late reformation never durst
Compare with ancient times and purer years;
But in the Jews and us deserveth tears.
Nay, it shall ev'ry year decrease and fade;

Till such a darkness do the world invade        230
At Christ's last coming, as his first did find:
Yet must there such proportions be assign'd
To these diminishings, as is between
The spacious world and *Jewry* to be seen.
Religion stands on tip-toe in our land,         235
Ready to pass to the *American* strand.
When height of malice, and prodigious lusts,
Impudent sinning, witchcrafts, and distrusts
(The mark of future bane) shall fill our cup
Up to the brim, and make our measure up;        240
When *Seine* shall swallow *Tiber*, and the *Thames*
By letting in them both, pollutes her streams:
When *Italy* of us shall have her will,
And all her calendar of sins fulfil;
Whereby one may foretell, what sins next year    245
Shall both in France and England domineer:
Then shall Religion to *America* flee:
They have their times of Gospel, ev'n as we.
My God, thou dost prepare for them a way
By carrying first their gold from them away:     250
For gold and grace did never yet agree:
Religion always sides with poverty.
We think we rob them, but we think amiss:
We are more poor, and they more rich by this.
Thou wilt revenge their quarrel, making grace    255
To pay our debts, and leave our ancient place
To go to them, while that which now their nation
But lends to us, shall be our desolation.
Yet as the Church shall thither westward fly,
So Sin shall trace and dog her instantly:        260
They have their period also and set times
Both for their virtuous actions and their crimes.
And where of old the Empire and the Arts
Usher'd the Gospel ever in men's hearts,
*Spain* hath done one; when Arts perform the other, 265
The Church shall come, and Sin the Church shall smother:
That when they have accomplished the round,
And met in th' east their first and ancient sound,

Judgement may meet them both and search them round.
Thus do both lights, as well in Church as Sun,    270
Light one another, and together run.
Thus also Sin and Darkness follow still
The Church and Sun with all their power and skill.
But as the Sun still goes both west and east;
So also did the Church by going west    275
Still eastward go; because it drew more near
To time and place, where judgement shall appear.
*How dear to me, O God, thy counsels are!*
          *Who may with thee compare?*


# L'Envoy

*K*ing *of glory, King of peace,*
With the one make war to cease;
With the other bless thy sheep,
Thee to love, in thee to sleep.
Let not Sin devour thy fold,    5
Bragging that thy blood is cold,
That thy death is also dead,
While his conquests daily spread;
That thy flesh hath lost his food,
And thy Cross is common wood.    10
Choke him, let him say no more,
But reserve his breath in store,
Till thy conquests and his fall
Make his sighs to use it all,
And then bargain with the wind    15
To discharge what is behind.


     *Blessed be God alone,*
     *Thrice blessed Three in One.*


## FINIS

# THE COUNTRY PARSON, HIS CHARACTER, AND RULE OF HOLY LIFE

# The Author to the Reader

BEING desirous (through the mercy of God) to please him, for whom I am and live, and who giveth me my desires and performances; and considering with myself that the way to please him is to feed my flock diligently and faithfully, since our Saviour hath made that the argument of a pastor's love, I have resolved to set down the form and character of a true pastor, that I may have a mark to aim at, which also I will set as high as I can, since he shoots higher that threatens the moon, than he that aims at a tree. Not that I think, if a man do not all which is here expressed, he presently sins and displeases God; but that it is a good strife to go as far as we can in pleasing of him who hath done so much for us. The Lord prosper the intention to myself and others, who may not despise my poor labours, but add to those points which I have observed, until the book grow to a complete pastoral.

1632                                          GEO. HERBERT

# CHAPTER I
## Of a Pastor

A PASTOR is the deputy of Christ, for the reducing of man to the obedience of God. This definition is evident, and contains the direct steps of pastoral duty and authority. For, first, man fell from God by disobedience; secondly, Christ is the glorious instrument of God for the revoking of man; thirdly, Christ being not to continue on earth, but after he had fulfilled the work of reconciliation, to be received up into heaven, he constituted deputies in his place, and these are priests. And therefore St. Paul, in the beginning of his Epistles, professeth this; and in the First to the Colossians[1] plainly avoucheth that he *fills up that which is behind of the afflictions of Christ in his flesh, for his body's sake, which is the Church,*[2] wherein is contained the complete definition of a minister. Out of this charter of the priesthood may be plainly gathered both the dignity thereof and the duty: the dignity, in that a priest may do that which Christ did, and by his authority and as his vicegerent; the duty, in that a priest is to do that which Christ did, and after his manner, both for doctrine and life.

# CHAPTER II
## Their Diversities

OF pastors (intending mine own nation only, and also therein setting aside the reverend prelates of the Church, to whom this discourse ariseth not) some live in the Universities, some in noble houses, some in parishes residing on their cures. Of those that live in the Universities, some live there in office, whose rule is that of the apostle, *Romans* 12: 6: *Having gifts differing according to the grace that is given to us, whether prophecy, let us prophesy according to*

---

1. *I Colossians* 1: 24.
2. The first edition uses italics for quotations and, apparently, for emphasis. They may also indicate authorial afterthoughts.

*the proportion of faith; or ministry, let us wait on our ministering; or he that teacheth, on teaching,* &c., *he that ruleth, let him do it with diligence,* &c. Some in a preparatory way, whose aim and labour must be not only to get knowledge, but to subdue and mortify all lusts and affections; and not to think that when they have read the fathers or schoolmen, a minister is made and the thing done. The greatest and hardest preparation is within; for *unto the ungodly saith God, why dost thou preach my laws, and takest my covenant in thy mouth? Psalm* 50: 16. Those that live in noble houses are called chaplains, whose duty and obligation being the same to the houses they live in, as a parson's to his parish, in describing the one (which is, indeed, the bent of my discourse) the other will be manifest. Let not chaplains think themselves so free *as many of them do,* and, because they have different names, think their office different. Doubtless they are parsons of the families they live in, and are entertained to that end either by an open or implicit covenant. Before they are in orders, they may be received for companions or discoursers; but after a man is once minister, he cannot agree to come into any house where he shall not exercise what he is, unless he forsake his plough and look back. Wherefore they are not to be over-submissive and base, but to keep up with the lord and lady of the house, and to preserve a boldness with them and all, even so far as reproof to their very face when occasion calls, but seasonably and discreetly. They who do not thus, while they remember their earthly lord, do much forget their heavenly; they wrong the priesthood, neglect their duty, and shall be so far from that which they seek with their over-submissiveness and cringings, that they shall ever be despised. They who for the hope of promotion neglect any necessary admonition or reproof, sell (with Judas) their Lord and Master.

# CHAPTER III
# The Parson's Life

THE Country Parson is exceeding exact in his life, being holy, just, prudent, temperate, bold, grave, in all his ways. And because the two highest points of life, wherein a Christian is most seen, are patience and mortification: patience in regard of afflictions – mortification in regard of lusts and affections, and the stupefying and deading of all the clamorous powers of the soul; therefore he hath thoroughly studied these, that he may be an absolute master and commander of himself, for all the purposes which God hath ordained him. Yet in these points he labours most in those things which are most apt to scandalize his parish. And, first, because country people live hardly, and therefore, as feeling their own sweat, and consequently knowing the price of money, are offended much with any who by hard usage increase their travail, the country parson is very circumspect in avoiding all covetousness, neither being greedy to get, nor niggardly to keep, nor troubled to lose any worldly wealth; but in all his words and actions slighting and disesteeming it, even to a wondering that the world should so much value wealth, which, in the day of wrath, hath not one dram of comfort for us. Secondly, because luxury is a very visible sin, the parson is very careful to avoid all the kinds thereof, but especially that of drinking, because it is the most popular vice; into which if he come, *he prostitutes himself* both to shame and sin, and by having *fellowship with the unfruitful works of darkness* he disableth himself of authority *to reprove them*; for sins make all equal whom they find together, and then they are worst who ought to be best. Neither is it for the servant of Christ to haunt inns, or taverns, or alehouses, *to the dishonour of his person and office*. The parson doth not so, but orders his life in such a fashion, that when death takes him, as the Jews and Judas did Christ, he may say as he did *I sat daily with you teaching in the Temple*. Thirdly, because country people (as indeed all honest men) do much esteem their word, it being the life of buying and selling and dealing in the world, therefore the parson is very strict in keeping his word, though it be to his own hindrance, as knowing that if he be not so, he will quickly be discovered and disregarded; neither will they believe him in the pulpit whom they cannot trust in his conversation. As for oaths and apparel, the disorders thereof are also very manifest. The parson's yea is yea, and nay, nay; and his apparel plain, but reverend and clean, without spots, or dust, or smell; the purity of his mind breaking out and dilating itself even to his body, clothes, and habitation.

# CHAPTER IV
## The Parson's Knowledge

THE Country Parson is full of all knowledge. They say it is an ill mason that refuseth any stone; and there is no knowledge, but in a skilful hand serves either positively as it is, or else to illustrate some other knowledge. He condescends even to the knowledge of tillage and pasturage, and makes great use of them in teaching, because people by what they understand are best led to what they understand not. But the chief and top of his knowledge consists in the book of books, the storehouse and magazine of life and comfort, the holy Scriptures. There he sucks and lives. In the Scriptures he finds four things: Precepts for life, Doctrines for knowledge, Examples for illustration, and Promises for comfort: these he hath digested severally. But for the understanding of these; the means he useth are, first, a holy life, remembering what his Master saith, that *if any do God's will, he shall know of the doctrine, John* 7; and assuring himself that wicked men, however learned, do not know the Scriptures, because they feel them not, and because they are not understood but with the same Spirit that writ them. The second means is prayer, which if it be necessary even in temporal things, how much more in things of another world, where the well is deep, and we have nothing of ourselves to draw with? Wherefore he ever begins the reading of the Scripture with some short inward ejaculation, as, *Lord, open mine eyes, that I may see the wondrous things of thy law*, &c. The third means is a diligent collation of Scripture with Scripture. For all truth being consonant to itself, and all being penned by one and the self-same Spirit, it cannot be but that an industrious and judicious comparing of place with place must be a singular help for the right understanding of the Scriptures. To this may be added the consideration of any text with the coherence thereof, touching what goes before and what follows after, as also the scope of the Holy Ghost. When the Apostles would have called down fire from heaven, they were reproved, as ignorant of what spirit they were. For the Law required one thing, and the Gospel another; yet as diverse, not as repugnant;

therefore the spirit of both is to be considered and weighed. The fourth means are commenters and fathers, who have handled the places controverted, which the parson by no means refuseth. As he doth not so study others as to neglect the grace of God in himself, and what the Holy Spirit teacheth him, so doth he assure himself that God in all ages hath had his servants, to whom he hath revealed his truth, as well as to him; and that as one country doth not bear all things that there may be a commerce,[1] so neither hath God opened or will open all to one, that there may be a traffic in knowledge between the servants of God for the planting both of love and humility. Wherefore he hath one comment at least upon every book of Scripture, and ploughing with this and his own meditations, he enters into the secrets of God treasured in the holy Scripture.

## CHAPTER V
# The Parson's Accessory Knowledges

THE Country Parson hath read the fathers also, and the schoolmen, and the later writers, or a good proportion of all, out of all which he hath compiled a book and body of divinity, which is the storehouse of his sermons, and which he preacheth all his life; but diversely clothed, illustrated and enlarged. For though the world is full of such composures, yet every man's own is fittest, readiest and most savoury to him. Besides, this being to be done in his younger and preparatory times, it is an honest joy ever after to look upon his well-spent hours. This body he made by way of expounding the Church Catechism, to which all divinity may easily be reduced. For it being indifferent in itself to choose any method, that is best to be chosen of which there is likeliest to be most use. Now, catechizing being a work of singular and admirable benefit to the Church of God, and a thing required under canonical obedience,[2] the expounding of our Catechism must needs be the most useful

1. Herbert praises commerce and traffic between nations in *Perirrhanterium*, p. 19, ll.355–66, and *Providence*, p. 116, ll.105–8.
2. Canon lix.

form. Yet hath the parson, besides this laborious work, a slighter form of catechizing, fitter for country people: according as his audience is, so he useth one or other, or sometimes both, if his audience be intermixed. He greatly esteems also of cases of conscience, wherein he is much versed. And, indeed, herein is the greatest ability of a parson, to lead his people exactly in the ways of truth, so that they neither decline to the right hand nor to the left. Neither let any think this a slight thing. For every one hath not digested when it is a sin to take something for money lent, or when not; when it is a fault to discover another's fault, or when not; *when the affections of the soul in desiring and procuring increase of means or honour be a sin of covetousness or ambition and when not; when the appetites of the body in eating, drinking, sleep, and the pleasure that comes with sleep, be sins of gluttony, drunkenness, sloth, lust, and when not*; and so in many circumstances of actions. Now, if a shepherd know not which grass will bane and which not, how is he fit to be a shepherd? Wherefore the parson hath thoroughly canvassed all the particulars of human actions, at least all those which he observeth are most incident to his parish.

## CHAPTER VI
# The Parson Praying

THE Country Parson when he is to read divine services composeth himself to all possible reverence, lifting up his heart and hands and eyes, and using all other gestures which may express a hearty and unfeigned devotion. This he doth, first, as being truly touched and amazed with the majesty of God, before whom he then presents himself; yet not as himself alone, but as presenting with himself the whole congregation, whose sins he then bears, and brings with his own to the heavenly altar to be bathed and washed in the sacred laver of Christ's blood. Secondly, as this is the true reason of his inward fear, so he is content to express this outwardly to the utmost of his power; that being first affected himself, he may affect also his people, knowing that no sermon moves them so much to a reverence, which they forget again when they come to pray, as a devout behaviour in the very act of praying. Accordingly his voice is humble, his words treatable and slow, yet not so slow neither as to let the fervency of the supplicant hang and die between speaking, but with a grave liveliness, between fear and zeal, pausing yet pressing, he performs his duty. Besides, his example, he having often instructed his people how to carry themselves in divine service, exacts of them all possible reverence, by no means enduring either talking or sleeping, or gazing, or leaning, or half-kneeling, or any undutiful behaviour in them, but causing them when they sit, or stand, or kneel, to do all in a straight and steady posture, as attending to what is done in the Church; and every one, man and child, answering aloud both Amen and all other answers which are on the clerk's and people's part to answer, which answers also are to be done not in a huddling or slubbering fashion, gaping, or scratching the head, or spitting even in the midst of their answer, but gently and pausably, thinking what they say, so that while they answer, *As it was in the beginning*, &c., they meditate as they speak, that God hath ever had his people that have glorified him as well as now, and that he shall have so for ever. And the like in other answers. This is that which the Apostle calls a reasonable service, *Romans* 12, when we speak not as parrots, without reason, or offer up such sacrifices as they did of old, which was of beasts devoid of reason; but when we use our reason, and apply our powers to the service of him that gives them. If there be any of the gentry or nobility of the parish, who sometimes make it a piece of state not to come at the beginning of service with their poor neighbours, but at mid-prayers, both to their own loss and of theirs also who gaze upon them when they come in, and neglect the present service of God, he by no means suffers it, but after divers gentle admonitions, if they persevere, he causes them to be presented; or if the poor churchwardens be affrighted with their greatness, notwithstanding his instruction that they ought not to be so, but even to let the world sink so they do their duty, he presents them himself, only protesting to them that not any ill-will draws him to it, but the debt and obligation of his calling being to obey God rather than men.

# CHAPTER VII
## The Parson Preaching

THE Country Parson preacheth constantly: the pulpit is his joy and his throne. If he at any time intermit, it is either for want of health, or against some great festival, that he may the better celebrate it, or for the variety of the hearers, that he may be heard at his return more attentively. When he intermits, he is ever very well supplied by some able man, who treads in his steps, and will not throw down what he hath built; whom also he entreats to press some point, that he himself hath often urged with no great success, that so, in the mouth of two or three witnesses, the truth may be more established. When he preacheth he procures attention by all possible art, both by earnestness of speech (it being natural to men to think that where is much earnestness there is somewhat worth hearing), and by a diligent and busy cast of his eye on his auditors, with letting them know that he observes who marks and who not; and with particularizing of his speech – now to the younger sort, then to the elder; now to the poor, and now to the rich. This is for you, and This is for you; for particulars ever touch and awake more than generals. Herein also he serves himself of the judgments of God, as those of ancient times, so especially of the late ones; and those most which are nearest to his parish; for people are very attentive at such discourses, and think it behoves them to be so, when God is so near them, and even over their heads. Sometimes he tells them stories and sayings of others, according as his text invites him; for them also men heed and remember better than exhortations, which though earnest, yet often die with the sermon, especially with country people, which are thick and heavy, and hard to raise to a point of zeal and fervency, and need a mountain of fire to kindle them; but stories and sayings they will well remember. He often tells them that sermons are dangerous things, that none goes out of the church as he came in, but either better or worse; that none is careless before his Judge, and that the Word of God shall judge us. By these and other means the parson procures attention; but the character of his sermon is holiness: he is not witty, or learned, or eloquent, but holy; a character that Hermogenes[1] never dreamed of, and therefore he could give no precepts thereof. But it is gained, first, by choosing texts of devotion, not controversy, moving and ravishing texts, whereof the Scriptures are full. Secondly, by dipping and seasoning all our words and sentences in our hearts before they come into our mouths, truly affecting and cordially expressing all that we say, so that the auditors may plainly perceive that every word is heart-deep. Thirdly, by turning often, and making many apostrophes to God, as Oh Lord, bless my people and teach them this point; or Oh my Master, on whose errand I come, let me hold my peace, and do thou speak thyself, for thou art Love, and when thou teachest all are scholars. Some such irradiations scatteringly in the sermon carry great holiness in them. The prophets are admirable in this. So *Isaiah* 64, *Oh that thou wouldst rend the heavens, that thou wouldst come down!* &c.; and *Jeremiah* 10, after he had complained of the desolation of Israel, turns to God suddenly, *Oh Lord, I know that the way of man is not in himself*, &c. Fourthly, by frequent wishes of the people's good, and joying therein, though he himself were with St. Paul even sacrificed upon the service of their faith; for there is no greater sign of holiness than the procuring and rejoicing in another's good. And herein St. Paul excelled in all his Epistles. How did he put the Romans in all his prayers? *Rom.* 1: 9; and ceased not to give thanks for the Ephesians, *Eph.* 1: 16; and for the Corinthians 1: 4; and for the Philippians made request with joy, 1: 4; and is in contention for them whether to live or die; be with them or Christ (verse 23); which, setting aside his care of his flock, were a madness to doubt of. What an admirable epistle is the second to the Corinthians! how full of affections! he joys and he is sorry, he grieves and he glories: never was there such care of a flock expressed, save in the great shepherd of the fold, who first shed tears over Jerusalem, and afterwards blood. Therefore this care may be learned there, and then woven into sermons, which will make them appear exceeding reverend and holy. Lastly, by an often urging of the presence and majesty of God, by these or suchlike speeches: Oh, let us all

1. Hermogenes was a Greek writer on Rhetoric, died 180 A.D.

take heed what we do. God sees us, he sees whether I speak as I ought, or you hear as you ought; he sees hearts as we see faces: he is among us; for if we be here, he must be here, since we are here by him, and without him could not be here. Then turning the discourse to his majesty, And he is a great God and terrible: as great in mercy, so great in judgment. There are but two devouring elements, fire and water: he hath both in him; *his voice is as the sound of many waters* (*Revelation* 1); and he himself *is a consuming fire* (*Hebrews* 12). Such discourses show very holy. The parson's method in handling of a text consists of two parts: first, a plain and evident declaration of the meaning of the text; and secondly, some choice observations drawn out of the whole text as it lies entire and unbroken in the Scripture itself. This he thinks natural, and sweet, and grave. Whereas the other way of crumbling a text into small parts, as, the person speaking or spoken to, the subject and object, and the like, hath neither in it sweetness, nor gravity, nor variety, since the words apart are not Scripture, but a dictionary, and may be considered alike in all the Scripture. The parson exceeds not an hour in preaching, because all ages have thought that a competency, and he that profits not in that time, will less afterwards, the same affection which made him not profit before making him then weary, and so he grows from not relishing to loathing.

## CHAPTER VIII
# The Parson on Sundays

THE Country Parson, as soon as he awakes on Sunday morning, presently falls to work, and seems to himself so as a market man is when the market day comes, or a shopkeeper when customers use to come in. His thoughts are full of making the best of the day, and contriving it to his best gains. To this end, besides his ordinary prayers, he makes a peculiar one for a blessing on the exercises of the day. That nothing befall him unworthy of that Majesty before which he is to present himself, but that all may be done with reverence to his glory, and with edification to his flock, humbly beseeching his Master that how or whenever he punish him, it may be not in his ministry; then he turns to request for his people that the Lord would be pleased to sanctify them all, that they may come with holy hearts and awful minds into the congregation, and that the good God would pardon all those who come with less prepared hearts than they ought. This done, he sets himself to the consideration of the duties of the day, and if there be any extraordinary addition to the customary exercises, either from the time of the year, or from the state, or from God by a child born, or dead, or any other accident, he contrives how and in what manner to induce it to the best advantage. Afterwards, when the hour calls, with his family attending him, he goes to church, at his first entrance *humbly adoring and worshipping the invisible majesty and presence of Almighty God*, and blessing the people, either openly or to himself. Then having read Divine Service twice fully, and preached in the morning, and catechized in the afternoon, he thinks he hath in some measure, according to poor and frail man, discharged the public duties of the congregation. The rest of the day he spends either in reconciling neighbours that are at variance, or in visiting the sick, or in exhortations to some of his flock by themselves, whom his sermons cannot or do not reach. And every one is more awaked when we come and say, *Thou are the man*. This way he finds exceeding useful and winning; and these exhortations he calls his privy purse, even as princes have theirs, besides their public disbursements. At night, he thinks it a very fit time, both suitable to the joy of the day and without hindrance to public duties, either to entertain some of his neighbours or to be entertained of them, where he takes occasion to discourse *of such things as are both profitable and pleasant, and to raise up their minds to apprehend God's good blessing to our Church and state – that order is kept in the one, and peace in the other, without disturbance or interruption of public divine offices*. As he opened the day with prayer, so he closeth it, humbly beseeching the Almighty to pardon and accept our poor services and to improve them, that we may grow therein, and that our feet may be like hinds' feet, ever climbing up higher and higher unto him.[1]

1. Cf. *Psalm* 18: 33 (H).

# CHAPTER IX
## The Parson's State of Life

THE Country Parson, considering that virginity is a higher state than matrimony, and that the ministry requires the best and highest things, is rather unmarried than married. But yet as the temper of his body may be, or as the temper of his parish may be, where he may have occasion to converse with women, and that among suspicious men, *and other like circumstances considered*, he is rather married than unmarried. Let him communicate the thing often by prayer unto God, and as his grace shall direct him, so let him proceed. If he be unmarried and keep house, he hath not a woman in his house, but finds opportunities of having his meat dressed and other services done by men-servants at home, and his linen washed abroad. If he be unmarried, and sojourn, he never talks with any woman alone, but in the audience of others, and that seldom, and then also in a serious manner, never jestingly or sportfully. *He is very circumspect in all companies, both of his behaviour, speech, and very looks, knowing himself to be both suspected and envied. If he stand steadfast in his heart, having no necessity, but hath power over his own will, and hath so decreed in his heart that he will keep himself a virgin, he spends his days in fasting and prayer, and blesseth God for the gift of continency, knowing that it can no way be preserved but only by those means by which at first it was obtained. He therefore thinks it not enough for him to observe the fasting days of the Church, and the daily prayers enjoined him by authority, which he observeth out of humble conformity and obedience, but adds to them, out of choice and devotion, some other days for fasting and hours for prayers; and by these he keeps his body tame, serviceable, and healthful, and his soul fervent, active, young, and lusty as an eagle. He often readeth the lives of the primitive monks, hermits, and virgins, and wondereth not so much at their patient suffering and cheerful dying under persecuting emperors (though that indeed be very admirable), as at their daily temperance, abstinence, watchings, and constant prayers and mortifications in the times of peace and prosperity. To put on the profound humility, and the exact temperature of our Lord Jesus, with other exemplary virtues of that sort, and to keep them on in the sunshine and noon of prosperity, he findeth to be as necessary, and as difficult at least, as to be clothed with perfect patience and Christian fortitude in the cold midnight storms of persecution and adversity. He keepeth his watch and ward night and day against the proper and peculiar temptations of his state of life, which are principally these two, spiritual pride and impurity of heart: against these ghostly enemies he girdeth up his loins, keeps the imagination from roving, puts on the whole armour of God, and, by the virtue of the shield of faith, he is not afraid of the pestilence that walketh in darkness [carnal impurity], nor of the sickness that destroyeth at noonday [ghostly pride and self-conceit]. Other temptations he hath, which, like mortal enemies, may sometimes disquiet him likewise; for the human soul being bounded and kept in, in her sensitive faculty, will run out more or less in her intellectual. Original concupiscence is such an active thing, by reason of continual inward or outward temptations, that it is ever attempting or doing one mischief or other. Ambition, or untimely desire of promotion to a higher state or place, under colour of accommodation or necessary provision, is a common temptation to men of any eminency, especially being single men. Curiosity in prying into high speculative and unprofitable questions is another great stumbling-block to the holiness of scholars. These and many other spiritual wickednesses in high places doth the parson fear, or experiment,[1] or both, and that much more being single than if he were married; for then commonly the stream of temptations is turned another way, – into covetousness, love of pleasure, or ease, or the like. If the parson be unmarried, and means to continue so, he doth at least as much as hath been said.* If he be married, the choice of his wife was made rather by his ear than his eye; his judgment, not his affection found out a fit wife for him, whose humble and liberal disposition he preferred before beauty, riches or honour. *He knew that (the good instrument of God to bring women to heaven) a wise and loving husband could, out of humility, produce any special grace of faith, patience, meekness, love, obedience, &c., and out of liberality make her fruitful in all good works.* As he is just in all things, so is he to his wife also, counting nothing so much his own as that he may be unjust unto it. Therefore he gives her respect both afore her servants and others, and half at least of the government of the house, reserving so much of the affairs as serve for a diversion for him; yet never so giving over the reins but that he sometimes looks how things go, demanding an account, but not by the way

1. Have experience of (a now obsolete sense).

of an account; and this must be done the oftener or the seldomer, according as he is satisfied of his wife's discretion.

## CHAPTER X
# The Parson in his House

THE Parson is very exact in the governing of his house, making it a copy and model for his parish. He knows the temper and pulse of every person in his house, and accordingly either meets with their vices or advanceth their virtues. His wife is either religious, or night and day he is winning her to it. Instead of the qualities of the world, he requires only three of her: first, a training up of her children and maids in the fear of God, with prayers, and catechizing, and all religious duties. Secondly, a curing and healing of all wounds and sores with her own hands, which skill either she brought with her, or he takes care she shall learn it of some religious neighbour. Thirdly, a providing for her family in such sort as that neither they want a competent sustenation nor her husband be brought in debt. His children he first makes Christians, and then commonwealth's men: the one he owes to his heavenly country, the other to his earthly, having no title to either, except he do good to both. Therefore, having seasoned them with all piety, not only words in praying and reading, but in actions, in visiting other sick children, and tending their wounds, and sending his charity by them to the poor, and sometimes giving them a little money to do it of themselves, that they get a delight in it, and enter favour with God, who weighs even children's actions, *I Kings* 14: 12, 13. He afterwards turns his care to fit all their dispositions with some calling, not sparing the eldest, but giving him the prerogative of his father's profession, which happily for his other children he is not able to do. Yet in binding them prentices (in case he think fit to do so) he takes care not to put them into vain trades, and unbefitting to the reverence of their father's calling, such as are taverns for men, and lace-making for women; because those trades, for the most part, serve but the vices and vanities of the world, which he is to deny and not augment. However, he resolves with himself never to omit any present good deed of charity in consideration of providing a stock for his children, but assures himself that money thus lent to God is placed surer for his children's advantage than if it were given to the Chamber of London. Good deeds and good breeding are his two great stocks for his children; if God give anything above those, and not spent in them, he blesseth God, and lays it out as he sees cause. His servants are all religious, and were it not his duty to have them so, it were his profit, for none are so well served as by religious servants, both because they do best and because what they do is blessed and prospers. After religion, he teacheth them that three things make a complete servant – Truth, and diligence, and neatness or cleanliness. Those that can read are allowed times for it, and those that cannot are taught, for all in his house are either teachers or learners, or both, so that his family is a school of religion, and they all account that to teach the ignorant is the greatest alms. Even the walls are not idle, but something is written or painted there which may excite the reader to a thought of piety, especially the 101 Psalm, which is expressed in a fair table, as being the rule of the family. And when they go abroad, his wife among her neighbours is the beginner of good discourses, his children among children, his servants among other servants, so that as in the house of those that are skilled in music all are musicians,[1] so in the house of a preacher all are preachers. He suffers not a lie or equivocation by any means in his house, but counts it the art and secret of governing to preserve a directness and open plainness in all things, so that all his house knows that there is no help for a fault done but confession. He *himself*, or his *wife*, takes account of sermons, and how every one profits, comparing this year with the last; and besides the common prayers of the family, he straightly requires of all to pray by themselves before they sleep at night and stir out in the morning, and knows what prayers they say, and till they have learned them makes them kneel by him, esteeming that this private praying is a more voluntary act in them than when they are called to others' prayers, and that which, when they leave the family, they carry with them. He keeps his servants between love and fear, according as he finds them, but generally he distributes

1. *Outlandish Proverbs*, no. 219.

it thus: to his children he shows more love than terror, to his servants more terror than love, but an old good servant boards a child.[1] The furniture of his house is very plain, but clean, whole, and sweet, as sweet as his garden can make; for he hath no money for such things, charity being his only perfume, which deserves cost when he can spare it. His fare is plain and common, but wholesome; what he hath is little, but very good; it consisteth most of mutton, beef, and veal; if he adds anything for a great day or a stranger, his garden or orchard supplies it, or his barn and back-side:[2] he goes no further for any entertainment lest he go into the world, esteeming it absurd that he should exceed who teacheth others temperance. But those which his home produceth he refuseth not, as coming cheap and easy, and arising from the improvement of things with otherwise would be lost. Wherein he admires and imitates the wonderful providence and thrift of the great householder of the world; for there being two things which as they are, are unuseful to man, – the one for smallness, as crumbs and scattered corn and the like, the other for the foulness, as wash and dirt, and things thereinto fallen, – God hath provided creatures for both: for the first, poultry; for the second, swine. These save man the labour, and doing that which either he could not do or was not fit for him to do, by taking both sorts of food into them, do as it were dress and prepare both for man in themselves by growing themselves fit for his table. The parson in his house observes fasting days, and particularly, as Sunday is his day of joy, so Friday his day of humiliation, which he celebrates not only with abstinence of diet, but also of company, recreation, and all outward contentments, and besides, with confession of sins and all acts of mortification. Now fasting days contain a treble obligation: First, of eating less that day than on other days; secondly of eating no pleasing or over-nourishing things, as the Israelites did eat sour herbs; thirdly, of eating no flesh, which is but the determination of the second rule by authority to this particular. The two former obligations are much more essential to a true fast than the third and last, and fasting days were fully performed by keeping of the two former,

1. Is like a child.
2. Backyard.

had not authority interposed; so that to eat little, and that unpleasant, is the natural rule of fasting, although it be flesh. For since fasting in Scripture language is an afflicting of our souls, if a piece of dry flesh at my table be more unpleasant to me than some fish there, certainly to eat the flesh, and not the fish, is to keep the fasting day naturally. And it is observable that the prohibiting of flesh came from hot countries, where both flesh alone, and much more with wine, is apt to nourish more than in cold regions, and where flesh may be much better spared and with more safety than elsewhere, where both the people and the drink being cold and phlegmatic, the eating of flesh is an antidote to both. For it is certain that a weak stomach being prepossessed with flesh shall much better brook and bear a draught of beer than if it had taken before either fish or roots, or such things, which will discover itself by spitting, and rheum, or phlegm. To conclude, the parson, if he be in full health, keeps the three obligations, eating fish or roots, and that for quantity little, for quality unpleasant. If his body be weak and obstructed, as most students are, he cannot keep the last obligation nor suffer others in his house that are so to keep it, but only the two former, which also in diseases of exinanition (as consumptions) must be broken, for meat was made for man, not man for meat. To all this may be added, not for emboldening the unruly, but for the comfort of the weak, that not only sickness breaks these obligations of fasting, but sickliness also. For it is as unnatural to do anything that leads me to a sickness to which I am inclined, as not to get out of that sickness, when I am in it, by any diet. One thing is evident, that an English body, and a student's body, are two great obstructed vessels, and there is nothing that is food, and not physic, which doth less obstruct than flesh moderately taken, as being immoderately taken it is exceeding obstructive. And obstructions are the cause of most diseases.

## CHAPTER XI
## The Parson's Courtesy

THE Country Parson owing a debt of charity to the poor and of courtesy to his other parishioners, he so distinguisheth, that he keeps his money for the poor, and his table for those that are above alms. Not but that the poor are welcome also to his table, whom he sometimes purposely takes home with him, setting them close by him, and carving for them, both for his own humility and their comfort, who are much cheered with such friendliness. But since both is to be done, the better sort invited, and meaner relieved, he chooseth rather to give the poor money, which they can better employ to their own advantage, and suitably to their needs, than so much given in meat at dinner. Having then invited some of his parish, he taketh his times to do the like to the rest; so that in the compass of the year he hath them all with him, because country people are very observant of such things, and will not be persuaded but, being not invited, they are hated. Which persuasion the parson by all means avoids, knowing that where there are such conceits there is no room for his doctrine to enter. Yet doth he oftenest invite those whom he sees take the best courses, that so both they may be encouraged to persevere, and others spurred to do well, that they may enjoy the like courtesy. For though he desire that all should live well and virtuously, not for any reward of his, but for virtue's sake; yet that will not be so; and therefore as God, although we should love him only for his own sake, yet out of his infinite pity hath set forth heaven for a reward to draw men to piety, and is content if at least so they will become good: so the country parson, who is a diligent observer and tracker of God's ways, sets up as many encouragements to goodness as he can, both in honour, and profit, and fame, that he may, if not the best way, yet any way, make his parish good.

## CHAPTER XII
# The Parson's Charity

THE Country Parson is full of charity; it is his predominant element. For many and wonderful things are spoken of thee, thou great virtue. To charity is given the covering of sins, *I Peter* 4: 8; and the forgiveness of sins, *Matthew* 6: 14, *Luke* 7: 47; the fulfilling of the law, *Romans* 13: 10; the life of faith, *James* 2: 26; the blessings of this life, *Proverbs* 22: 9, *Psalm* 41: 2; and the reward of the next, *Matthew* 25: 35. In brief, it is the body of religion (*John* 13: 35), and the top of Christian virtues (*I Corinthians* 13). Wherefore all his works relish of charity. When he riseth in the morning he bethinketh himself what good deeds he can do that day, and presently doth them; counting that day lost wherein he hath not exercised his charity. He first considers his own parish, and takes care that there be not a beggar or idle person in his parish, but that all be in a competent way of getting their living. This he effects either by bounty, or by persuasion, or by authority, making use of that excellent statute which binds all parishes to maintain their own. If his parish be rich, he exacts this of them; if poor, and he able, he easeth them therein. But he gives no set pension to any; for this in time will lose the name and effect of charity with the poor people, though not with God; for then they will reckon upon it as on a debt; and if it be taken away, though justly, they will murmur and repine as much as he that is disseized of his own inheritance. But the parson having a double aim, and making a hook of his charity, causeth them still to depend on him; and so by continual and fresh bounties, unexpected to them, but resolved to himself, he wins them to praise God more, to live more religiously, and to take more pains in their vocation, as not knowing when they shall be relieved; which otherwise they would reckon upon and turn to idleness. Besides this general provision, he hath other times of opening his hand; as at great festivals and communions; not suffering any that day that he receives to want a good meal suiting to the joy of the occasion. But specially at hard times and dearths, he even parts his living and life among them, giving some corn outright, and selling other at under rates; and when his own stock serves not, working those that are able to the same charity, still pressing it in the pulpit and out of the pulpit, and never leaving them till he obtain his desire. Yet in all his charity he distinguisheth, giving them most who live best, and take most pains, and are most charged; so is his charity in effect a sermon. After the consideration of his own parish, he enlargeth himself, if he be able, to the neighbourhood, for that also is some kind of obligation; so doth he also to those at his door, whom God puts in his way and makes his neighbours. But these he helps not without some testimony, except the evidence of the misery bring testimony with it. For though these testimonies also may be falsified, yet considering that the law allows these in case they be true, but allows by no means to give without testimony, as he obeys authority in the one, so that being once satisfied he allows his charity some blindness in the other; especially, since of the two commands we are more enjoined to be charitable than wise. But evident miseries have a natural privilege and exemption from all law. Whenever he gives anything, and sees them labour in thanking of him, he exacts of them to let him alone, and say rather, God be praised, God be glorified; that so the thanks may go the right way, and thither only where they are only due. So doth he also before giving make them say their prayers first, or the Creed, and ten Commandments, and as he finds them perfect, rewards them the more. For other givings are lay and secular, but this is to give like a priest.

## CHAPTER XIII
# The Parson's Church

THE Country Parson hath a special care of his church, that all things there be decent, and befitting his name by which it is called. Therefore, first, he takes order that all things be in good repair; as walls plastered, windows glazed, floor paved, seats whole, firm, and uniform, especially that the pulpit, and desk, and communion table, and font, be as they ought for those great duties that are performed in them. Secondly, that the church be swept and kept clean, without dust or cobwebs, and at great festivals strewed and stuck with boughs, and perfumed with incense. Thirdly, that there be fit and proper texts of Scripture everywhere painted, and that all the painting be grave and reverend, not with light colours or foolish antics. Fourthly, that all the books appointed by authority be there, and those not torn or fouled, but whole, and clean, and well bound; and that there be a fitting and sightly communion cloth *of fine linen, with a handsome and seemly carpet of good and costly stuff or cloth, and all kept sweet and clean, in a strong and decent chest, with a chalice and cover, and a stoup or flagon, and a basin for alms and offerings; besides which he hath a poor man's box conveniently seated to receive the charity of well-minded people, and to lay up treasure for the sick and needy.* And all this he doth, not as out of necessity, or as putting a holiness in the things, but as desiring to keep the middle way between superstition and slovenliness, and as following the Apostle's two great and admirable rules in things of this nature; the first whereof is, *Let all things be done decently and in order*; the second, *Let all things be done to edification, I Cor.* 14. For these two rules comprise and include the double object of our duty, God, – and our neighbour; the first being for the honour of God, the second for the benefit of our neighbour. So that they excellently score out the way, and fully and exactly contain, even in external and indifferent things, what course is to be taken, and put them to great shame who deny the Scripture to be perfect.

## CHAPTER XIV
# The Parson in Circuit

THE Country Parson upon the afternoons in the week-days takes occasion sometimes to visit in person, now one quarter of his parish, now another. For there he shall find his flock most naturally as they are, wallowing in the midst of their affairs; whereas on Sunday it is easy for them to compose themselves to order, which they put on as their holy-day clothes, and come to church in frame, but commonly the next day put off both. When he comes to any house, first he blesseth it, and then as he finds the persons of the house employed, so he forms his discourse. Those that he finds religiously employed he both commends them much, and furthers them when he is gone in their employment; as if he finds them reading, he furnisheth them with good books; if curing poor people, he supplies them with receipts, and instructs them further in that skill, showing them how acceptable such works are to God, and wishing them ever to do the cures with their own hands, and not to put them over to servants. Those that he finds busy in the works of their calling, he commendeth them also; for it is a good and just thing for every one to do their own business. But then he admonisheth them of two things: first, that they dive not too deep into worldly affairs, plunging themselves over head and ears into carking and caring; but that they so labour as neither to labour anxiously, nor distrustfully, nor profanely. Then they labour anxiously, when they overdo it, to the loss of their quiet and health; then distrustfully, when they doubt God's providence, thinking that their own labour is the cause of their thriving, as if it were in their own hands to thrive or not to thrive. *Then they labour profanely, when they set themselves to work like brute beasts, never raising their thoughts to God, nor sanctifying their labour with daily prayer; when on the Lord's day they do unnecessary servile work, or in time of divine service on other holy days, except in the cases of extreme poverty, and in the seasons of seedtime and harvest.* Secondly, he adviseth them so to labour for wealth and maintenance as that they make not that the end of their labour, but that they may have wherewithal to serve God the better, and to do good deeds. After these discourses, if they be poor and needy whom he thus finds labouring, he gives them somewhat; and opens not only his mouth, but his purse to their relief, that so they go on more cheerfully in their vocation, and himself be ever the more welcome to them. Those that the parson finds idle or ill employed he chides not at first, for that were neither civil nor profitable, but always in the close, before he departs from them; yet in this he distinguisheth; for if he be a plain countryman he reproves him plainly, for they are not sensible of fineness; if they be of higher quality they commonly are quick, and sensible, and very tender of reproof; and therefore he lays his discourse so that he comes to the point very leisurely, and oftentimes, as Nathan did, in the person of another, making them to reprove themselves. However, one way or other, he ever reproves them, that he may keep himself pure, and not be entangled in others' sins. Neither in this doth he forbear, though there be company by; for as when the offence is particular, and against me, I am to follow our Saviour's rule, and to take my brother aside and reprove him; so when the offence is public and against God, I am then to follow the Apostle's rule, *I Timothy* 5: 20, and to *rebuke openly* that which is done openly. Besides these occasional discourses, the parson questions what order is kept in the house, as about prayers morning and evening on their knees, reading of Scripture, catechizing, singing of psalms at their work and on holy days; who can read, who not; and sometimes he hears the children read himself, and blesseth them, encouraging also the servants to learn to read, and offering to have them taught on holy days by his servants. If the parson were ashamed of particularizing in these things he were not fit to be a parson; but he holds the rule that nothing is little in God's service: if it once have the honour of that name, it grows great instantly. Wherefore neither disdaineth he to enter into the poorest cottage, though he even creep into it, and though it smell never so loathsomely; for both God is there also, and those for whom God died. And so much the rather doth he so, as his access to the poor is more comfortable than to the rich, and in regard of himself it is more humiliation. These are the parson's general aims in his circuit; but with these he mingles other discourses for conversation sake, and to make his higher purposes slip the more easily.

## CHAPTER XV
# The Parson Comforting

THE Country Parson, when any of his cure is sick, or afflicted with loss of friend or estate, or any ways distressed, fails not to afford his best comforts, and rather goes to them than sends for the afflicted, though they can and otherwise ought to come to him. To this end he hath thoroughly digested all the points of consolation, as having continual use of them, such as are from God's general providence extended even to lilies; from his particular to his church; from his promises; from the examples of all saints that ever were; from Christ himself, perfecting our redemption no other way than by sorrow; from the benefit of affliction which softens and works the stubborn heart of man; from the certainty both of deliverance and reward if we faint not; from the miserable comparison of the moment of griefs here with the weight of joys hereafter. *Besides this, in his visiting the sick or otherwise afflicted, he followeth the Church's counsel, namely, in persuading them to particular confession; labouring to make them understand the great good use of this ancient and pious ordinance, and how necessary it is in some cases; he also urgeth them to do some pious charitable works as a necessary evidence and fruit of their faith at that time especially: the participation of the Holy Sacrament, how comfortable and sovereign a*

*medicine it is to all sin-sick souls; what strength, and joy, and peace it
administers against all temptations, even to death itself; he plainly and
generally intimateth all this to the disaffected or sick person, that so the
hunger and thirst after it may come rather from themselves than from his
persuasion.*

## CHAPTER XVI
## The Parson a Father

THE Country Parson is not only a father to his flock, but also
professeth himself thoroughly of the opinion, carrying it
about with him as fully as if he had begot his whole parish. And
of this he makes great use; for by this means, when any sins, he
hateth him not as an officer, but pities him as a father; and even
in those wrongs which, either in tithing or otherwise, are done to
his own person, he considers the offender as a child, and forgives,
so he may have any sign of amendment; so also when, after many
admonitions, any continues to be refractory, yet he gives him not
over, but is long before he proceed to disinheriting, or perhaps
never goes so far, knowing that some are called at the eleventh
hour; and therefore he still expects, and waits, lest he should
determine God's hour of coming, which, as he cannot, touching
the last day, so neither the intermediate days of conversion.

## CHAPTER XVII
## The Parson in Journey

THE Country Parson, when a just occasion calleth him out of
his parish (which he diligently and strictly weigheth, his
parish being all his joy and thought), leaveth not his ministry
behind him, but is himself wherever he is. Therefore those he
meets on the way he blesseth audibly, and with those he over-
takes or that overtake him, he begins good discourses such as
may edify, interposing sometimes some short and honest refresh-
ments which may make his other discourses more welcome and
less tedious. And when he comes to his inn he refuseth not to join,
that he may enlarge the glory of God to the company he is in, by

a due blessing of God for their safe arrival, and saying grace at meat, and at going to bed by giving the host notice that he will have prayers in the hall, wishing him to inform his guests thereof, that if any be willing to partake they may resort thither. The like he doth in the morning, using pleasantly the outlandish proverb, that *Prayers and Provender never hinder Journey*.[1] When he comes to any other house where his *kindred or other relations give him any authority over the family*, if he be to stay for a time, he considers diligently the state thereof to Godward, and that in two points: first, what disorders there are either in apparel, or diet, or too open a buttery, or reading vain books, or swearing, or breeding up children to no calling, but in idleness, or the like. Secondly, what means of piety, whether daily prayers be used, grace, reading of Scriptures, and other good books; how *Sundays, holy days, and fasting days* are kept. And accordingly, as he finds any defect in these, he first considers with himself what kind of remedy fits the temper of the house best, and then he faithfully and boldly applieth it, yet seasonably and discreetly, by taking aside the lord or lady, or *master* and *mistress* of the house, and showing them clearly that they respect them most who wish them best, and that not a desire to meddle with others' affairs, but the earnestness to do all the good he can, moves him to say thus and thus.

## CHAPTER XVIII
# The Parson in Sentinel

THE Country Parson, wherever he is, keeps God's watch; that is, there is nothing spoken of or done in the company where he is but comes under his test and censure: if it be well spoken or done, he takes occasion to commend and enlarge it; if ill, he presently lays hold of it, lest the poison steal into some young and unwary spirits, and possess them even before they themselves heed it. But this he doth discreetly, with mollifying and suppling words: This was not so well said as it might have been forborne; We cannot allow this. Or else, if the thing will admit

1. *Outlandish Proverbs*, no. 273.

interpretation, Your meaning is not thus, but thus; or, So far indeed what you say is true and well said; but this will not stand. This is called keeping God's watch, when the baits which the enemy lays in company are discovered and avoided; this is to be on God's side, and be true to his party. Besides, if he perceive in company any discourse tending to ill, either by the wickedness or quarrelsomeness thereof, he either prevents it judiciously, or breaks it off seasonably by some diversion. Wherein a pleasantness of disposition is of great use, men being willing to sell the interest and engagement of their discourses for no price sooner than that of mirth; whither the nature of man, loving refreshment, gladly betakes itself, even to the loss of honour.

## CHAPTER XIX
# The Parson in Reference

THE Country Parson is sincere and upright in all his relations. And, first, he is just to his country; as when he is set at an armour or horse, he borrows them not to serve the turn, nor provides slight and unuseful, but such as are every way fitting to do his country true and laudable service when occasion requires. To do otherwise is deceit, and therefore not for him, who is hearty and true in all his ways, as being the servant of him in whom there was no guile. Likewise in any other country duty, he considers what is the end of any command, and then he suits things faithfully according to that end. Secondly, he carries himself very respectively, as to all the fathers of the Church, so especially to his diocesan, honouring him both in word and behaviour, and resorting unto him in any difficulty either in his studies or in his parish. He observes visitations, and being there, makes due use of them, as of clergy councils, for the benefit of the diocese. And therefore, before he comes, having observed some defects in the ministry, he then, either in sermon, if he preach, or at some other time of the day, propounds among his brethren what were fitting to be done. Thirdly, he keeps good correspondence with all the neighbouring pastors round about him, performing for them any ministerial office, which is not to the prejudice of his own parish. Likewise he welcomes to his house any minister, how poor or mean soever, with as joyful a countenance as if he were to entertain some great lord. Fourthly, he fulfils the duty and debt of neighbourhood to all the parishes which are near him; for the Apostle's rule, *Philip* 4 being admirable and large, that *we should do whatsoever things are honest, or just, or pure, or lovely, or of good report, if there be any virtue or any praise.* And neighbourhood being ever reputed, even among the heathen, as an obligation to do good, rather than to those that are farther, where things are otherwise equal, therefore he satisfies this duty also. Especially if God have sent any calamity, either by fire or famine, to any neighbouring parish, then he expects no brief; but taking his parish together *the next Sunday*, or *holy day*, and exposing to them the uncertainty of human affairs, none knowing whose turn may be next; and then, when he hath affrighted them with this, exposing the obligation of charity and neighbourhood, he first gives himself liberally, and then incites them to give – making together a sum either to be sent, or, which were more comfortable, all together choosing some fit day to carry it themselves, and cheer the afflicted. So, if any neighbouring village be overburdened with poor, and his own less charged, he finds some way of relieving it, and reducing the manna and bread of charity to some equality, representing to his people that the blessing of God to them ought to make them the more charitable, and not the less, lest he cast their neighbours' poverty on them also.

## CHAPTER XX

# The Parson in God's Stead

THE Country Parson is in God's stead to his parish, and dischargeth God what he can of his promises. Wherefore there is nothing done either well or ill, whereof he is not the rewarder or punisher. If he chance to find any reading in another's Bible, he provides him one of his own. If he find another giving a poor man a penny, he gives him a tester[1] for it, if the giver be fit to receive it; or if he be of a condition above

1. Sixpence.

such gifts, he sends him a good book, or easeth him in his tithes, telling him when he hath forgotten it, This I do because at such and such a time you were charitable. This is in some sort a discharging of God, as concerning this life, who hath promised that godliness shall be gainful; but in the other, God is his own immediate paymaster, rewarding all good deeds to their full proportion. *The parson's punishing of sin and vice is rather by withdrawing his bounty and courtesy from the parties offending, or by private or public reproof, as the case requires, than by causing them to be presented or otherwise complained of. And yet, as the malice of the person or heinousness of the crime may be, he is careful to see condign punishment inflicted, and with truly godly zeal, without hatred to the person, hungereth and thirsteth after righteous punishment of unrighteousness. Thus, both in rewarding virtue and in punishing vice, the parson endeavoureth to be in God's stead, knowing that country people are drawn or led by sense more than by faith, by present rewards or punishments more than by future.*

## CHAPTER XXI
## The Parson Catechizing

THE Country Parson values catechizing highly, for there being three points of his duty – the one, to infuse a competent knowledge of salvation in every one of his flock; the other, to multiply and build up this knowledge to a spiritual temple; the third, to inflame this knowledge, to press and drive it to practice, turning it to reformation of life by pithy and lively exhortations. Catechizing is the first point, and but by catechizing the other cannot be attained. Besides, whereas in sermons there is a kind of state, in catechizing there is an humbleness very suitable to Christian regeneration, which exceedingly delights him as by way of exercise upon himself, and by way of preaching to himself, for the advancing of his own mortification; for in preaching to others he forgets not himself, but is first a sermon to himself, and then to others, growing with the growth of his parish. He useth and preferreth the ordinary Church Catechism, partly for obedience to authority, partly for uniformity sake, that the same common truths may be everywhere professed, especially since many remove from parish to parish, who, like Christian soldiers, are to give the word, and to satisfy the congregation by their catholic answers. He exacts of all the doctrine of the Catechism: of the younger sort the very words, of the elder the substance. Those he catechizeth publicly, these privately, giving age honour, according to the Apostle's rule, *I Tim.* 5: 1. He requires all to be present at catechizing. First for the authority of the work; secondly, that parents and masters, as they hear the answers prove, may when they come home either commend or reprove, either reward or punish; thirdly, that those of the elder sort who are not well grounded may then, by an honourable way, take occasion to be better instructed; fourthly, that those who are well grown in the knowledge of religion may examine their grounds, renew their vows, and, by occasion of both, enlarge their meditations. When once all have learned the words of the Catechism, he thinks it the most useful way that a pastor can take to go over the same, but in other words; for many say the Catechism by rote, as parrots, without ever piercing into the sense of it. In this course the order of the Catechism would be kept, but the rest varied, as thus, in the Creed: How came this world to be as it is? Was it made, or came it by chance? Who made it? Did you see God make it? Then are there some things to be believed that are not seen? Is this the nature of belief? Is not Christianity full of such things as are not to be seen but believed? You said God made the world. Who is God? And so forward, requiring answers to all these, and helping and cherishing the answerer by making the questions very plain with comparisons, and making much even of a word of truth from him. This order being used to one would be a little varied to another. And this is an admirable way of teaching, wherein the catechized will at length find delight, and by which the catechizer, if he once get the skill of it, will draw out of ignorant and silly souls even the dark and deep points of religion. Socrates did thus in philosophy, who held that the seeds of all truths lay in everybody, and accordingly, by questions well ordered, he found philosophy in silly tradesmen. That position will not hold in Christianity, because it contains things above nature; but after that the Catechism is once learned, that which nature is towards philosophy the Catechism is towards divinity. To this purpose some dialogues in Plato were worth the reading, where the singular dexterity of Socrates in this kind may be observed and imitated. Yet the skill consists but in these three points: First, an aim and mark of the whole discourse, whither to drive the answerer, which the questionist must have in his mind before any question be propounded, upon which and to which the questions are to be chained; secondly, a most plain and easy framing the question, even containing, in virtue, the answer also, especially to the more ignorant; thirdly, when the answerer sticks, an illustrating the thing by something else which he knows, making what he knows to serve him in that which he knows not; as, when the parson once demanded, after other questions about man's misery, since man is so miserable, what is to be done? And the answerer could not tell; he asked him again, what he would do if he were in a ditch? This familiar illustration made the answer so plain that he was even ashamed of his ignorance, for he could not but say he would haste out of it as fast as he could. Then he proceeded to ask whether he could get out of the ditch alone, or whether he needed a helper, and who was that helper? This is the skill, and doubtless the holy Scripture intends thus much when it condescends to the naming of a plough, a hatchet, a bushel, leaven, boys piping and dancing, showing that things of ordinary use are not only to serve in the way of drudgery, but to be washed and cleansed and serve for lights even of heavenly truths. This is the practice which the parson so much commends to all his fellow-labourers; the secret of whose good consists in this: that at sermons and prayers men may sleep or wander, but when one is asked a question he must discover what he is. This practice exceeds even sermons in teaching. But there being two things in sermons, the one informing, the other inflaming; as sermons come short of questions in the one, so they far exceed them in the other. For questions cannot inflame or ravish: that must be done by a set, and laboured, and continued speech.

## CHAPTER XXII
## The Parson in Sacraments

THE Country Parson being to administer the Sacraments, is at a stand with himself how or what behaviour to assume for so holy things. Especially at Communion times he is in a great confusion, as being not only to receive God, but to break and administer him. Neither finds he any issue in this but to throw himself down at the throne of grace, saying Lord, thou knowest what thou didst when thou appointedst it to be done thus; therefore do thou fulfil what thou dost appoint; for thou art not only the feast, but the way to it. At Baptism, being himself in white, he requires the presence of all, and baptizeth not willingly but on Sundays or great days. He admits no vain or idle names, but such as are usual and accustomed. He says that prayer with great devotion, where God is thanked for calling us to the knowledge of his grace, baptism being a blessing that the world hath not the like. He willingly and cheerfully crosseth the child, and thinketh the ceremony not only innocent but reverend. He instructeth the godfathers and godmothers that it is no complimental or light thing to sustain that place, but a great honour and no less burden, as being done both in the presence of God and his saints, and by way of undertaking for a Christian soul. He adviseth all to call to mind their baptism often; for if wise men have thought it the best way of preserving a state to reduce it to its principles by which it grew great, certainly it is the safest course for Christians also to meditate on their baptism often (being the first step into their great and glorious calling), and upon what terms and with what vows they were baptized. At the times of the Holy Communion he first takes order with the churchwardens that the elements be of the best, not cheap or coarse, much less ill tasted or unwholesome. Secondly, he considers and looks into the ignorance or carelessness of his flock, and accordingly applies himself with catechizings and lively exhortations, not on the Sunday of the Communion only (for then it is too late) but the Sunday or Sundays before the Communion, or on the eves of all those days. If there be any, who having not received yet, are to enter into this great work, he takes the more pains with them that he may lay the foundation of future blessings. The time of every one's first receiving is not so much by years as by understanding; particularly the rule may be this: When any one can distinguish the sacramental from common bread, knowing the institution and the difference, he ought to receive, of what age soever. Children and youths are usually deferred too long under pretence of devotion to the Sacrament, but it is for want of instruction; their understandings being ripe enough for ill things, and why not then for better? But parents and masters should make haste in this as to a great purchase for their children and servants, which, while they defer, both sides suffer; the one in wanting many excitings of grace; the other in being worse served and obeyed. The saying of the Catechism is necessary, but not enough; because to answer in form may still admit ignorance; but the questions must be propounded loosely and wildly, and then the answerer will discover what he is. Thirdly, for the manner of receiving, as the parson useth all reverence himself, so he administers to none but to the reverent. The feast indeed requires sitting, because it is a feast; but man's unpreparedness asks kneeling. He that comes to the Sacrament hath the confidence of a guest, and he that kneels confesseth himself an unworthy one, and therefore differs from other feasters; but he that sits or lies puts up to an Apostle: contentiousness in a feast of charity is more scandal than any posture. Fourthly, touching the frequency of the Communion, the parson celebrates it, if not duly once a month, yet at least five or six times in the year; as at Easter, Christmas, Whitsuntide, before and after Harvest, and the beginning of Lent. And this he doth not only for the benefit of the work, but also for the discharge of the churchwardens, who being to present all that receive not thrice a year, if there be but three Communions, neither can all the people so order their affairs as to receive just at those times, nor the churchwardens so well take notice who receive thrice, and who not.

## CHAPTER XXIII
## The Parson's Completeness

THE Country Parson desires to be all to his parish, and not only a pastor, but a lawyer also, and a physician. Therefore he endures not that any of his flock should go to law; but in any controversy, that they should resort to him as their judge. To this end he hath gotten to himself some insight in things ordinarily incident and controverted, by experience and by reading some initiatory treatises in the law, with Dalton's 'Justice of Peace',[1] and the abridgements of the statutes, as also by discourse with men of that profession, whom he hath ever some cases to ask when he meets with them – holding that rule that to put men to discourse of that wherein they are most eminent is the most gainful way of conversation. Yet, whenever any controversy is brought to him, he never decides it alone, but sends for three or four of the ablest of the parish to hear the cause with him, whom he makes to deliver their opinion first; out of which he gathers, in case he be ignorant himself, what to hold; and so the thing passeth with more authority and less envy. In judging, he follows that which is altogether right; so that if the poorest man of the parish detain but a pin unjustly from the richest, he absolutely restores it as a judge; but when he hath so done, then he assumes the parson, and exhorts to charity. Nevertheless, there may happen sometimes some cases wherein he chooseth to permit his parishioners rather to make use of the law than himself; as in cases of an obscure and dark nature not easily determinable by lawyers themselves; or in cases of high consequence, as establishing of inheritances; or, lastly, when the persons in difference are of a contentious disposition and cannot be gained, but that they still fall from all compromises that have been made. But then he shows them how to go to law, even as brethren, and not as enemies, neither avoiding therefore one another's company, much less defaming one another. Now, as the parson is in law, so he is in sickness also: if there be any of his flock sick, he is their physician, or at least his wife, of whom, instead of the qualities of the world, he asks no other but to have the skill of healing a wound or helping the sick. But if neither himself nor his wife have the skill, and his means serve, he keeps some young practitioner in his house for the benefit of his parish, whom yet he ever exhorts not to exceed his bounds, but in tickle cases to call in help. If all fail, then he keeps good correspondence with some neighbour physician, and entertains him for the cure of his parish. Yet it is easy for any scholar to attain to such a measure of physic as may be of much use to him both for himself and others.

1. Michael Dalton (1554–1620), a celebrated lawyer and author of *The Country Justice*, a standard legal work.

This is done by seeing one anatomy, reading one book of physic, having one herbal by him. And let Fernelius[1] be the physic author, for he writes briefly, neatly, and judiciously; especially let his method of physic be diligently perused, as being the practical part and of most use. Now, both the reading of him and the knowing of herbs may be done at such times as they may be an help and a recreation to more divine studies, Nature serving grace both in comfort of diversion and the benefit of application when need requires; as also by way of illustration, even as our Saviour made plants and seeds to teach the people; for he was the true householder, who bringeth out of his treasure things new and old – the old things of philosophy, and the new of grace – and maketh the one serve the other. And I conceive our Saviour did this for three reasons: First; that by familiar things he might make his doctrine slip the more easily into the hearts even of the meanest. Secondly, that labouring people (whom he chiefly considered) might have everywhere monuments of his doctrine, remembering in gardens, his mustard seed and lilies; in the field, his seed-corn and tares; and so not be drowned altogether in the works of their vocation, but sometimes lift up their minds to better things even in the midst of their pains. Thirdly, that he might set a copy for parsons. In the knowledge of simples, wherein the manifold wisdom of God is wonderfully to be seen, one thing would be carefully observed: which is, to know what herbs may be used instead of drugs of the same nature, and to make the garden the shop; for home-bred medicines are both more easy for the parson's purse, and more familiar for all men's bodies. So, where the apothecary useth either for loosing, rhubarb, or for binding, bolearmena, the parson useth damask or white roses for the one, and plantain, shepherd's-purse, knot-grass for the other, and that with better success. As for spices, he doth not only prefer home-bred things before them, but condemns them for vanities, and so shuts them out of his family, esteeming that there is no spice comparable for herbs to rosemary, thyme, savory, mints; and for seeds to fennel and caraway-seeds. Accordingly, for salves, his wife seeks not the

1. Jean Fernel (1497–1558), first physician to Henry II of France, and author of *Universa Medicina* (1586).

city, but prefers her garden and fields, before all outlandish gums. And surely hyssop, valerian, mercury, adder's-tongue, yarrow, melilot, and St. John's wort made into a salve, and elder, camomile, mallows, comphrey, and smallage made into a poultice, have done great and rare cures. In curing of any the parson and his family use to premise prayers, for this is to cure like a parson, and this raiseth the action from the shop to the church. But though the parson sets forward all charitable deeds, yet he looks not in this point of curing beyond his own parish, except the person be so poor that he is not able to reward the physician; for as he is charitable, so he is just also. Now, it is a justice and debt to the commonwealth he lives in not to encroach on others' professions, but to live on his own. And justice is the ground of charity.

## CHAPTER XXIV
## The Parson's Arguing

THE Country Parson, if there be any of his parish that hold strange doctrines, useth all possible diligence to reduce them to the common faith. The first means he useth is prayer, beseeching the Father of lights to open their eyes, and to give him power so to fit his discourse to them that it may effectually pierce their hearts and convert them. The second means is a very loving and sweet usage of them, both in going to and sending for them often, and in finding out courtesies to place on them, as in their tithes, or otherwise. The third means is the observation what is the main foundation and pillar of their cause whereon they rely; as, if he be a Papist, the Church is the hinge he turns on; if a schismatic, scandal. Wherefore the parson hath diligently examined these two with himself: as, What the Church is; how it began; how it proceeded; whether it be a rule to itself; whether it hath a rule; whether, having a rule, it ought not to be guided by it; whether any rule in the world be obscure; and how, then, should the best be so, at least, in fundamental things, the obscurity in some points being the exercise of the Church, the light in the foundations being the guide; the Church needing both an evidence and an exercise. So for scandal: What scandal is, when given or taken; whether, there being two precepts, one of obeying authority, the other of not giving scandal, that ought not to be preferred, especially since in disobeying there is scandal also; whether things once indifferent, being made by the precept of authority more than indifferent, it be in our power to omit or refuse them. These and the like points he hath accurately digested, having ever besides two great helps and powerful persuaders on his side: the one, a strict religious life; the other, an humble and ingenuous search of truth, being unmoved in arguing, and void of all contentiousness, which are two great lights able to dazzle the eyes of the misled, while they consider that God cannot be wanting to them in doctrine, to whom he is so gracious in life.

## CHAPTER XXV
## The Parson Punishing

WHENSOEVER the Country Parson proceeds so far as to call in authority, and to do such things of legal opposition either in the presenting or punishing of any, as the vulgar ever construes for signs of ill will, he forbears not in any wise to use the delinquent as before in his behaviour and carriage towards him, not avoiding his company, or doing anything of averseness, save in the very act of punishment; neither doth he esteem him for an enemy, but as a brother still, except some small and temporary estranging may corroborate the punishment to a better subduing and humbling of the delinquent, which, if it happily take effect, he then comes on the faster, and makes so much the more of him as before he alienated himself; doubling his regards, and showing by all means that the delinquent's return is to his advantage.

## CHAPTER XXVI
## The Parson's Eye

THE Country Parson at spare times from action, standing on a hill and considering his flock, discovers two sorts of vices and two sorts of vicious persons. There are some vices whose natures are always clear and evident, as adultery, murder, hatred, lying, &c. There are other vices, whose natures, at least in the beginning, are dark and obscure, as covetousness and gluttony. So likewise there are some persons who abstain not even from known sins; there are others, who when they know a sin evidently, they commit it not. It is true, indeed, they are long a-knowing it, being partial to themselves and witty to others who shall reprove them for it. A man may be both covetous and intemperate, and yet hear sermons against both, and himself condemn both in good earnest; and the reason hereof is, because the natures of these vices being not evidently discussed or known commonly, the beginnings of them are not easily observable; and the beginnings of them are not observed because of the sudden passing from that which was just now lawful, to that which is presently unlawful, even in one continued action. So a man dining, eats at first lawfully; but proceeding on, comes to do unlawfully, even before he is aware, not knowing the bounds of the action, nor when his eating begins to be unlawful. So a man storing up money for his necessary provisions, both in present for his family, and in future for his children, hardly perceives when his storing becomes unlawful; yet is there a period for his storing, and a point or centre when his storing, which was even now good, passeth from good to bad. Wherefore the parson being true to his business hath exactly sifted the definitions of all virtues and vices, especially canvassing those whose natures are most stealing, and beginnings uncertain: particularly concerning these two vices, not because they are all that are of this dark and creeping disposition, but for example sake, and because they are most common, he thus thinks: first, for covetousness, he lays this ground: Whosoever, when a just occasion calls, either spends not at all, or not in some proportion to God's blessing upon him, is covetous. The reason of the ground is manifest, because wealth is given to that end to supply our occasions. Now, if I do not give everything its end, I abuse the creature, I am false to my reason which should guide me, I offend the supreme Judge in perverting that order which he hath set both to things and to reason. The application of the ground would be infinite; but in brief, a poor man is an occasion, my country is an occasion, my friend is an occasion, my table is an occasion, my apparel is an occasion. If in all these, and those more which concern me, I either do nothing, or pinch and scrape, and squeeze blood indecently to the station where God hath placed me, I am covetous. More particularly, and to give one instance for all, if God have given me servants, and I either provide too little for them, or that which is unwholesome, being sometimes baned[1] meat, sometimes too salt, and so not competent nourishment, I am covetous. I bring this example, because men usually think that servants for their money are as other things that they buy, even as a piece of wood which they may cut, or hack, or throw into the fire, and so they pay them their wages all is well. Nay, to descend yet more particularly, if a man hath wherewithal to buy a spade, and yet he chooseth rather to use his neighbour's and wear out that, he is covetous. Nevertheless, few bring covetousness thus low, or consider it so narrowly, which yet ought to be done, since there is a justice in the least things, and for the least there shall be a judgment. Country people are full of these petty injustices, being cunning to make use of another and spare themselves; and scholars ought to be diligent in the observation of these, and driving of their general school rules ever to the smallest actions of life, which while they dwell in their books they will never find, but being seated in the country and doing their duty faithfully they will soon discover; especially if they carry their eyes ever open, and fix them on their charge, and not on their preferment. Secondly, for gluttony, the parson lays this ground: He that either for quantity eats more than his health or employments will bear or for quality is licorous after dainties, is a glutton, as he that eats more than his estate will bear is a prodigal; and he that eats offensively to the company, either in his order or length of eating, is scandalous and uncharitable. These three rules generally comprehend the faults of eating, and the truth of them needs no proof; so that men must eat neither to the disturbance of their health, nor of their affairs (which being over-burdened or studying dainties too much, they cannot well dispatch), nor of their estate, nor of their brethren. One act in these things is bad, but it is the custom and habit that names a glutton. Many think

1. Not good; diseased.

they are at more liberty than they are, as if they were masters of their health, and, so they will stand to the pain, all is well. But to eat to one's hurt comprehends, besides the hurt, an act against reason, because it is unnatural to hurt oneself, and this they are not masters of. Yet of hurtful things I am more bound to abstain from those which by mine own experience I have found hurtful, than from those which by a common tradition and vulgar knowledge are reputed to be so. That which is said of hurtful meats extends to hurtful drinks also. As for the quantity, touching our employments, none must eat so as to disable themselves from a fit discharging either of divine duties or duties of their calling. So that, if after dinner they are not fit (or unwieldy) either to pray or work, they are gluttons. Not that all must presently work after dinner (for they rather must not work, especially students, and those that are weakly); but that they must rise so, as that it is not meat nor drink that hinders them from working. To guide them in this there are three rules: first, the custom and knowledge of their own body, and what it can well digest; the second, the feeling of themselves in time of eating, which because it is deceitful (for one thinks in eating that he can eat more than he afterwards finds true); the third is the observation with what appetite they sit down. This last rule, joined with the first, never fails; for knowing what one usually can well digest and feeling when I go to meat in what disposition I am, either hungry or not, according as I feel myself, either I take my wonted proportion or diminish of it. Yet physicians bid those that would live in health not keep an uniform diet, but to feed variously, now more, now less; and Gerson,[1] a spiritual man, wisheth all to incline rather to too much than to too little; his reason is, because diseases of exinanition are more dangerous than diseases of repletion. But the parson distinguisheth according to his double aim, either of abstinence a moral virtue, or mortification a divine. When he deals with any that is heavy and carnal, he gives him those freer rules; but when he meets with a refined and heavenly disposition, he carries them higher, even

1. Jean Charlier de Gerson (1363–1429), author of *De Consolatione Theologiæ* and supposed by some to have been the author of the *Imitation of Jesus Christ*, generally attributed to Thomas à Kempis.

sometimes to a forgetting of themselves, knowing that there is one who, when they forget, remembers for them; as when the people hungered and thirsted after our Saviour's doctrine, and tarried so long at it that they would have fainted had they returned empty, he suffered it not, but rather made food miraculously than suffered so good desires to miscarry.

## CHAPTER XXVII
## The Parson in Mirth

THE Country Parson is generally sad, because he knows nothing but the Cross of Christ, his mind being defixed on it with those nails wherewith his Master was; or if he have any leisure to look off from thence, he meets continually with two most sad spectacles, Sin and Misery; God dishonoured every day, and man afflicted. Nevertheless, he sometimes refresheth himself, as knowing that nature will not bear everlasting droopings, and that pleasantness of disposition is a great key to do good; not only because all men shun the company of perpetual severity, but also for that when they are in company, instructions seasoned with pleasantness both enter sooner and root deeper. Wherefore he condescends to human frailties both in himself and others, and intermingles some mirth in his discourses occasionally, according to the pulse of the hearer.

## CHAPTER XXVIII
## The Parson in Contempt

THE Country Parson knows well that both for the general ignominy which is cast upon the profession, and much more for those rules which out of his choicest judgment he hath resolved to observe, and which are described in this book, he must be despised; because this hath been the portion of God his master, and of God's saints his brethren, and this is foretold that it shall be so still until things be no more. Nevertheless, according to the Apostle's rule, he endeavours that none shall despise him; especially in his own parish he suffers it not to his utmost power; for that where contempt is, there is no room for instruction. This he procures, First, by his holy and unblamable life, which carries a reverence with it, even above contempt. Secondly, by a courteous carriage and winning behaviour: he that will be respected must respect;[1] doing kindnesses, but receiving none, at least of those who are apt to despise; for this argues a height and eminency of mind which is not easily despised, except it degenerate to pride. Thirdly, by a bold and impartial reproof, even of the best in the parish, when occasion requires; for this may produce hatred in those that are reproved, but never contempt either in them or others. Lastly, if the contempt shall proceed so far as to do anything punishable by law, as contempt is apt to do if it be not thwarted, *the parson having a due respect both to the person and to the cause, referreth the whole matter to the examination and punishment of those which are in authority*; that so the sentence lighting upon one, the example may reach to all. But if the contempt be not punishable by law, or, being so, the parson think it in his discretion either unfit or bootless to contend, then when any despises him, he takes it either in an humble way, saying nothing at all; or else in a slighting way, showing that reproaches touch him no more than a stone thrown against heaven, where he is and lives; or in a sad way, grieved at his own and others' sins, which continually break God's laws, and dishonour him with those mouths which he continually fills and feeds; or else in a doctrinal way, saying to the contemner, Alas! why do you thus? you hurt yourself, not me: he that throws a stone at another hits himself; and so between gentle reasoning and pitying he overcomes the evil; or lastly, in a triumphant way, being glad and joyful, that he is made conformable to his Master; and being in the world as he was, hath this undoubted pledge of his salvation. These are the five shields wherewith the godly receive the darts of the wicked; leaving anger, and retorting, and revenge to the children of the world, whom another's ill mastereth, and leadeth captive without any resistance, even in resistance, to the same destruction. For while they resist the person that reviles, they resist not the evil which takes hold of them, and is far the worst enemy.

1. *Outlandish Proverbs,* no. 423.

# CHAPTER XXIX
## The Parson with his Churchwardens

THE Country Parson doth often, both publicly and privately, instruct his churchwardens what a great charge lies upon them, and that indeed the whole order and discipline of the parish is put into their hands. If himself reform anything, it is out of the overflowing of his conscience, whereas they are to do it by command and by oath. Neither hath the place its dignity from the ecclesiastical laws only, since even by the common statute law they are taken for a kind of corporation, as being parsons enabled by that name to take movable goods or chattels, and to sue and to be sued at the law concerning such goods for the use and profit of their parish; and by the same law they are to levy penalties for negligence in resorting to church, or for disorderly carriage in time of divine service. Wherefore the parson suffers not the place to be vilified or debased by being cast on the lower rank of people, but invites and urges the best unto it, showing that they do not lose or go less, but gain by it; it being the greatest honour of this world to do God and his chosen service; or as David says, to be even a door-keeper in the house of God. Now, the Canons being the churchwardens' rule, the parson adviseth them to read or hear them read often, as also the Visitation Articles, which are grounded upon the Canons, that so they may know their duty and keep their oath the better; in which regard, considering the great consequence of their place, and more of their oath, he wisheth them by no means to spare any, though never so great; but if after gentle and neighbourly admonitions they still persist in ill, to present them; yea, though they be tenants, or otherwise engaged to the delinquent; for their obligation to God and their own soul is above any temporal tie. Do well and right, and let the world sink.

# CHAPTER XXX
# The Parson's Consideration of Providence

THE Country Parson, considering the great aptness country people have to think that all things come by a kind of natural course, and that if they sow and soil their grounds they must have corn, if they keep and fodder well their cattle they must have milk and calves, labours to reduce them to see God's hand in all things, and to believe that things are not set in such an inevitable order, but that God often changeth it according as he sees fit, either for reward or punishment. To this end he represents to his flock that God hath and exerciseth a threefold power in everything which concerns man. The first is a sustaining power; the second, a governing power; the third, a spiritual power. By his sustaining power he preserves and actuates everything in his being; so that corn doth not grow by any other virtue than by that which he continually supplies as the corn needs it, without which supply the corn would instantly dry up, as a river would if the fountain were stopped. And it is observable that if anything could presume of an inevitable course and constancy in its operations, certainly it should be either the sun in heaven or the fire on earth, by reason of their fierce, strong, and violent natures; yet when God pleased, the sun stood still, the fire burned not.[1] By God's governing power he preserves and orders the references of things one to the other, so that though the corn do grow and be preserved in that act by his sustaining power, yet if he suit not other things to the growth, as seasons, and weather, and other accidents, by his governing power, the fairest harvests come to nothing. And it is observable that God delights to have men feel and acknowledge, and reverence his power, and therefore he often overturns things when they are thought past danger: that is his time of interposing. As when a merchant hath a ship come home after many a storm, which it hath escaped, he destroys it sometimes in the very haven; or if the goods be housed, a fire hath broken forth

1. *Joshua* 10: 12–14, *Exodus* 3: 2.

239

and suddenly consumed them. Now this he doth that men should perpetuate and not break off their acts of dependence, how fair soever the opportunities present themselves. So that if a farmer should depend upon God all the year, and being ready to put hand to sickle, shall then secure himself, and think all cock sure; then God sends such weather as lays the corn and destroys it; or if he depend on God further, even till he imbarn his corn, and then think all sure, God sends a fire and consumes all that he hath; for that he ought not to break off, but to continue his dependence on God, not only before the corn is inned, but after also; and, indeed, to depend and fear continually. The third power is spiritual, by which God turns all outward blessings to inward advantages. So that if a farmer hath both a fair harvest, and that also well inned and imbarned, and continuing safe there, yet if God give him not the grace to use and utter this well, all his advantages are to his loss. Better were his corn burnt than not spiritually improved. And it is observable in this, how God's goodness strives with man's refractoriness: man would sit down at this world; God bids him sell it and purchase a better; just as a father who hath in his hand an apple, and a piece of gold under it; the child comes, and with pulling gets the apple out of his father's hand; his father bids him throw it away, and he will give him the gold for it, which the child utterly refusing, eats it and is troubled with worms; so is the carnal and wilful man with the worm of the grave in this world, and the worm of conscience in the next.

# CHAPTER XXXI
## The Parson in Liberty

THE Country Parson observing the manifold wiles of Satan (who plays his part sometimes in drawing God's servants from him, sometimes in perplexing them in the service of God) stands fast in the liberty wherewith Christ hath made us free. This liberty he compasseth by one distinction, and that is, of what is necessary and what is additionary. As for example: it is necessary that all Christians should pray twice a day every day of the week, and four times on Sunday if they be well. This is so necessary and essential to a Christian that he cannot without this maintain himself in a Christian state. Besides this, the godly have ever added some hours of prayer, as at nine, or at three, or at midnight, or as they think fit and see cause, or rather as God's spirit leads them. But these prayers are not necessary, but additionary. Now it so happens that the godly petitioner upon some emergent interruption in the day, or by oversleeping himself at night, omits his additionary prayer. Upon this his mind begins to be perplexed and troubled, and Satan, who knows the exigent, blows the fire, endeavouring to disorder the Christian, and put him out of his station, and to enlarge the perplexity until it spread and taint his other duties of piety, which none can perform so well in trouble as in calmness. Here the parson interposeth with his distinction, and shows the perplexed Christian that his prayer being additionary, not necessary – taken in, not commanded – the omission thereof upon just occasion ought by no means to trouble him. God knows the occasion as well as he, and he is as a gracious Father, who more accepts a common course of devotion than dislikes an occasional interruption. And of this he is so to assure himself as to admit no scruple, but to go on as cheerfully as if he had not been interrupted. By this it is evident that the distinction is of singular use and comfort, especially to pious minds, which are ever tender and delicate. But here there are two cautions to be added. First, that this interruption proceed not out of slackness or coldness, which will appear if the pious soul foresee and prevent such interruptions, what he may, before they come, and when for all that they do come, he be a little affected therewith, but not afflicted or troubled; if he resent it to a mislike, but not a grief. Secondly, that this interruption proceed not out of shame. As for example: a godly man, not out of superstition, but of reverence to God's house, resolves whenever he enters into a church to kneel down and pray, either blessing God that he will be pleased to dwell among men, or beseeching him that when-ever he repairs to his house he may behave himself so as befits so great a presence, and this briefly. But it happens that near the place where he is to pray he spies some scoffing ruffian, who is likely to deride him for his pains: if he now shall, either for fear or shame, break his custom, he shall do passing ill: so much the rather ought he to proceed, as that by this he may take into his prayer humiliation also. On the other side, if I am to visit the sick in haste, and my nearest way lie through the church, I will not doubt to go without staying to pray there (but only, as I pass, in my heart), because this kind of prayer is additionary, not necessary, and the other duty overweighs it, so that if any scruple arise I will throw it away, and be most confident that God is not displeased. This distinction may run through all Christian duties, and it is a great stay and settling to religious souls.

## CHAPTER XXXII
## The Parson's Surveys

THE Country Parson hath not only taken a particular survey of the faults of his own parish, but a general also of the diseases of the time, that so, when his occasions carry him abroad, or bring strangers to him, he may be the better armed to encounter them. The great and national sin of this land he esteems to be idleness, great in itself and great in consequence; for when men have nothing to do then they fall to drink, to steal, to whore, to scoff, to revile, to all sorts of gamings. Come, they say, we have nothing to do, let's go to the tavern, or to the stews, or what not. Wherefore the parson strongly opposeth this sin wheresoever he goes. And because idleness is twofold, the one having no calling, the other in walking carelessly in our calling, he first represents to everybody the necessity of a vocation. The reason of this assertion is taken from the nature of man, wherein God hath placed two great instruments, reason in the soul and a hand in the body, as engagements of working, so that even in Paradise man had a calling, and how much more out of Paradise, when the evils which he is now subject unto may be prevented or diverted by reasonable employment. Besides, every gift or ability is a talent to be accounted for, and to be improved to our Master's advantage. Yet it is also a debt to our country to have a calling, and it concerns the commonwealth that none shall be idle, but all busied. Lastly, riches are the blessing of God, and the great instrument of doing admirable good; therefore all are to procure them honestly and seasonably when they are not better employed. Now this reason crosseth not our Saviour's precept of selling what we have, because when we have sold all, and given it to the poor, we must not be idle, but labour to get more, that we may give more, according to St. Paul's rule, *Ephesians* 4: 28, *I Thessalonians* 4: 11, 12. So that our Saviour's selling is so far from crossing St. Paul's working that it rather establisheth it, since they that have nothing are fittest to work. Now, because the only opposer to this doctrine is the gallant, who is witty enough to abuse both others and himself, and who is ready to ask if he shall mend shoes, or what he shall do? Therefore, the parson, unmoved, showeth that *ingenuous and fit* employment is never wanting to those that seek it. But if it should be, the assertion stands thus: All are either to have a calling, or prepare for it; he that hath or can have yet no employment, if he truly and seriously prepare for it, he is safe and within bounds. Wherefore all are either presently to enter into a calling, if they be fit for it and it for them, or else to examine with care, and advice, what they are fittest for, and to prepare for that with all diligence. But it will not be amiss in this exceeding useful point to descend to particulars, for exactness lies in particulars. Men are either single or married. The married and housekeeper hath his hands full if he do what he ought to do. For there are two branches of his affairs: first, the improvement of his family, by bringing them up in the fear and nurture of the Lord; and secondly, the improvement of his grounds, by drowning, or draining, or stocking, or fencing and ordering his land to the best advantage both of himself and his neighbours. The Italian says, none fouls his hands in his own business[1] and it is an honest and just care so it exceed not bounds, for every one to employ himself to the advancement of his affairs, that he may have wherewithal to do good. But his family is his best care, to labour Christian souls, and raise them to their height, even to heaven; to dress and prune them, and take as much joy in a straight-growing child or servant as a gardener doth in a choice tree. Could men find out this delight, they would seldom be from home, whereas now of any place they are least there. But if after all this care well dispatched the housekeeper's family be so small,

1. *Outlandish Proverbs*, no. 415.

and his dexterity so great, that he have leisure to look out, the village or parish which either he lives in, or is near unto it, is his employment. He considers every one there, and either helps them in particular or hath general propositions to the whole town or hamlet, of advancing the public stock, and managing commons or woods, according as the place suggests. But if he may be of the commission of peace, there is nothing to that: no commonwealth in the world hath a braver institution than that of justices of the peace, for it is both a security to the king, who hath so many dispersed officers at his beck throughout the kingdom accountable for the public good, and also an honourable employment of a gentle or nobleman in the country he lives in, enabling him with power to do good, and to restrain all those who else might both trouble him and the whole state. Wherefore it behoves all who are come to the gravity and ripeness of judgment for so excellent a place, not to refuse, but rather to procure it. And whereas there are usually three objections made against the place: the one, the abuse of it, by taking petty country bribes; the other, the casting of it on mean persons, especially in some shires; and lastly, the trouble of it, these are so far from deterring any good men from the place, that they kindle them rather to redeem the dignity either from true faults or unjust aspersions. Now, for single men, they are either heirs or younger brothers; the heirs are to prepare in all the forementioned points against the time of their practice. Therefore they are to mark their father's discretion in ordering his house and affairs, and also elsewhere when they see any remarkable point of education or good husbandry, and to transplant it in time to his own home, with the same care as others, when they meet with good fruit, get a graft of the tree, enriching their orchard and neglecting their house. Besides, they are to read books of law and justice, especially the statutes at large. As for better books of divinity, they are not in this consideration, because we are about a calling and a preparation thereunto. But chiefly and above all things they are to frequent sessions and sizes, for it is both an honour which they owe to the reverend judges and magistrates to attend them at least in their shire, and it is a great advantage to know the practice of the land, for our law is practice. Sometimes he may go to court, as the eminent place both of good and ill. At other times he is to travel over the king's dominions, cutting out the kingdom into portions, which every year he surveys piecemeal. When there is a parliament, he is to endeavour by all means to be a knight or burgess there, for there is no school to a parliament. And when he is there he must not only be a morning man, but at committees also, for there the particulars are exactly discussed which are brought from thence to the House but in general. When none of these occasions call him abroad, every morning that he is at home he must either ride the great horse or exercise some of his military gestures. For all gentlemen that are now weakened and disarmed with sedentary lives are to know the use of their arms; and as the husbandman labours for them, so must they fight for and defend them when occasion calls. This is the duty of each to other, which they ought to fulfil. And the parson is a lover of and exciter to justice in all things, even as John the Baptist squared out to every one (even to soldiers) what to do. As for younger brothers, those whom the parson finds loose, and not engaged in some profession by their parents, whose neglect in this point is intolerable, and a shameful wrong both to the commonwealth and their own house; to them, after he hath showed the unlawfulness of spending the day in dressing, complimenting, visiting, and sporting, he first commends the study of the civil law, as a brave and wise knowledge, the professors whereof were much employed by Queen Elizabeth, because it is the key of commerce, and discovers the rules of foreign nations. Secondly, he commends the mathematics as the only wonder-working knowledge, and therefore requiring the best spirits. After the several knowledge of these, he adviseth to insist and dwell chiefly on the two noble branches thereof, of fortification and navigation; the one being useful to all countries, and the other especially to islands. But if the young gallant think these courses dull and phlegmatic, where can he busy himself better than in those new plantations[1] and discoveries, which are not only a noble, but also, as they may be handled, a religious employment? Or let him travel into Germany and France, and observing the artifices and manufactures there, transplant them hither, as divers have done lately, to our country's advantage.

1. The new plantations in America.

## CHAPTER XXXIII

# The Parson's Library

THE Country Parson's library is a holy life; for (besides the blessing that that brings upon it, there being a promise that if the kingdom of God be first sought, all other things shall be added) even it self is a sermon. For the temptations with which a good man is beset, and the ways which he used to overcome them, being told to another, whether in private conference or in the church, are a sermon. He that hath considered how to carry himself at table about his appetite, if he tell this to another, preacheth, and much more feelingly and judiciously than he writes his rules of temperance out of books. So that the parson having studied and mastered all his lusts and affections within, and the whole army of temptations without, hath ever so many sermons ready penned as he hath victories. And it fares in this as it doth in physic: he that hath been sick of a consumption, and knows what recovered him, is a physician, so far as he meets with the same disease and temper, and can much better and particularly do it than he that is generally learned and was never sick. And if the same person had been sick of all diseases, and were recovered of by all things that he knew, there were no such physician as he both for skill and tenderness. Just so it is in divinity, and that not without manifest reason; for, though the temptations may be diverse in divers Christians, yet the victory is alike in all, being by the self-same Spirit. Neither is this true only in the military state of a Christian life, but even in the peaceable also, when the servant of God, freed for a while from temptation, in a quiet sweetness seeks how to please his God. Thus the parson, considering that repentance is the great virtue of the Gospel, and one of the first steps of pleasing God, having for his own use examined the nature of it, is able to explain it after to others. And particularly, having doubted sometimes whether his repentance were true, or at least in that degree it ought to be, since he found himself sometimes to weep more for the loss of some temporal things than for offending God, he came at length to this resolution, that repentance is an act of the mind, not of the body, even as the original signifies; and that the chief thing which God in Scriptures requires is the heart and the spirit, and to worship him in truth and spirit. Wherefore, in case a Christian endeavour to weep and cannot, since we are not masters of our bodies, this sufficeth. And consequently he found that the essence of repentance, that it may be alike in all God's children (which, as concerning weeping, it cannot be, some being of a more melting temper than others) consisteth in a true detestation of the soul, abhorring and renouncing sin, and turning unto God in truth of heart and newness of life, which acts of repentance are and must be found in all God's servants. Not that weeping is not useful where it can be, that so the body may join in the grief, as it did in the sin; but that, so the other acts be, that is not necessary; so that he as truly repents who performs the other acts of repentance when he cannot more, as he that weeps a flood of tears. This instruction and comfort the parson getting for himself, when he tells it to others, becomes a sermon. The like he doth in other Christian virtues, as of faith and love, and the cases of conscience belonging thereto, wherein (as St. Paul implies that he ought, *Romans* 2) he first preacheth to himself, and then to others.

## CHAPTER XXXIV
# The Parson's Dexterity in Applying of Remedies

THE Country Parson knows that there is a double state of a Christian even in this life: the one military, the other peaceable. The military is when we are assaulted with temptations, either from within or from without; the peaceable is when the devil for a time leaves us, as he did our Saviour, and the angels minister to us their own food, even joy, and peace, and comfort in the Holy Ghost. These two states were in our Saviour, not only in the beginning of his preaching, but afterwards also, as, *Matt.* 22: 35: He was tempted, and *Luke* 10: 21: He rejoiced in spirit; and they must be likewise in all that are his. Now the parson having a spiritual judgment, according as he discovers any of his flock to be in one or the other state, so he applies

247

himself to them. Those that he finds in the peaceable state, he adviseth to be very vigilant, and not to let go the reins as soon as the horse goes easy. Particularly he counselleth them to two things: First, to take heed lest their quiet betray them (as it is apt to do) to a coldness and carelessness in their devotions, but to labour still to be as fervent in Christian duties as they remember themselves were when affliction did blow the coals. Secondly, not to take the full compass and liberty of their peace: not to eat of all those dishes at table which even their present health otherwise admits; nor to store their house with all those furnitures which even their present plenty of wealth otherwise admits; nor when they are among them that are merry, to extend themselves to all that mirth which the present occasion of wit and company otherwise admits; but to put bounds and hoops to their joys; so will they last the longer, and, when they depart, return the sooner. If we would judge ourselves, we should not be judged; and if we would bound ourselves, we should not be bounded. But if they shall fear that at such or such a time their peace and mirth have carried them further than this moderation, then to take Job's admirable course, who sacrificed lest his children should have transgressed in their mirth; so let them go, and find some poor afflicted soul, and there be bountiful and liberal; for with such sacrifices God is well pleased. Those that the parson finds in the military state, he fortifies and strengthens with his utmost skill. Now, in those that are tempted, whatsoever is unruly falls upon two heads: either they think that there is none that can or will look after things, but all goes by chance or wit; or else, though there be a great Governor of all things, yet to them he is lost – as if they said, God doth forsake and persecute them, and there is none to deliver them. If the parson suspect the first, and find sparks of such thoughts now and then to break forth, then, without opposing directly (for disputation is no cure for atheism), he scatters in his discourse three sorts of arguments: the first taken from nature, the second from the law, the third from grace.

For nature, he sees not how a house could be either built without a builder, or kept in repair without a housekeeper. He conceives not possibly how the winds should blow so much as they can, and the sea rage so much as it can, and all things do what they can, and all, not only without dissolution of the whole, but also of any part, by taking away so much as the usual seasons of summer and winter, earing and harvest. Let the weather be what it will, still we have bread, though sometimes more, sometimes less; wherewith also a careful Joseph might meet. He conceives not possibly how he that would believe a divinity, if he had been at the creation of all things, should less believe it, seeing the preservation of all things; for preservation is a creation, and more, it is a continued creation, and a creation every moment.

Secondly, for the law: there may be so evident though unused a proof of divinity taken from thence, that the atheist or epicurean can have nothing to contradict. The Jews yet live and are known: they have their law and language bearing witness to them, and they to it; they are circumcised to this day, and expect the promises of the Scripture; their country also is known, the places and rivers travelled unto and frequented by others, but to them an unpenetrable rock, an inaccessible desert. Wherefore, if the Jews live, all the great wonders of old live in them, and then who can deny the stretched-out arm of a mighty God? especially since it may be a just doubt, whether considering the stubbornness of the nation, their living then in their country, under so many miracles, were a stranger thing than their present exile and disability to live in their country. And it is observable that this very thing was intended by God, that the Jews should be his proof and witnesses, as he calls them, *Isaiah* 43: 12. And their very dispersion in all lands was intended not only for a punishment to them, but for an exciting of others by their sight to the acknowledging of God, and his power, *Psalm* 59: 11. And therefore this kind of punishment was chosen rather than any other.

Thirdly, for grace: besides the continual succession (since the Gospel) of holy men, who have borne witness to the truth (there being no reason why any should distrust St. Luke, or Tertullian, or Chrysostom, more than Tully, Virgil, or Livy) there are two prophecies in the Gospel which evidently argue Christ's divinity by their success: the one concerning the woman that spent the ointment on our Saviour, for which he told that it should never be forgotten, but with the Gospel itself be preached to all ages, *Matthew* 26: 13; the other concerning the destruction of Jerusalem, of which our Saviour said that that generation should not pass till all were fulfilled, *Luke* 21: 32, which Josephus's History confirmeth, and the continuance of which verdict is yet evident. To these might be added the preaching of the Gospel in all nations, *Matthew* 24: 14, which we see even miraculously effected in these new discoveries, God turning men's covetousness and ambitions to the effecting of his word. Now, a prophecy is a wonder sent to posterity, lest they complain of want of wonders. It is a letter sealed and sent, which to the bearer is but paper, but to the receiver and opener is full of power. He that saw Christ open a blind man's eyes saw not more divinity than he that reads the woman's ointment in the Gospel or sees Jerusalem destroyed. With some of these heads enlarged, and woven into his discourse at several times and occasions, the parson settleth wavering minds. But if he sees them nearer desperation than atheism, not so much doubting a God, as that he is theirs, then he dives into the boundless ocean of God's love and the unspeakable riches of his loving-kindness. He hath one argument unanswerable. If God hate them, either he doth it as they are creatures, dust and ashes, or as they are sinful. As creatures, he must needs love them; for no perfect artist ever yet hated his own work. As sinful, he must much more love them; because, notwithstanding his infinite hate of sin, his love overcame that hate; and with an exceeding great victory; which in the creation needed not, gave them love for love, even the son of his love out of his bosom of love. So that man, which way soever he turns, hath two pledges of God's love, that in the mouth of two or three witnesses every word may be established: the one in his being, the other in his sinful being; and this as the more faulty in him, so the more glorious in God. And all may certainly conclude that God loves them, till either they despise that love or despair of his mercy; not any sin else but is within his love; but the despising of love must needs be without it. The thrusting away of his arm makes us only not embraced.

## CHAPTER XXXV
## The Parson's Condescending

THE Country Parson is a lover of old customs, if they be good and harmless; and the rather, because country people are much addicted to them, so that to favour them therein is to win their hearts, and to oppose them therein is to deject them. If there be any ill in the custom that may be severed from the good, he pares the apple, and gives them the clean to feed on. Particularly he loves procession,[1] and maintains it, because there are contained therein four manifest advantages: first, a blessing of God for the fruits of the field; secondly, justice in the preservation of bounds; thirdly, charity in loving walking and neighbourly accompanying one another, with reconciling of differences at that time, if there be any; fourthly, mercy in relieving the poor by a liberal distribution and largess, which at that time is or ought to be used. Wherefore he exacts of all to be present at the perambulation, and those that withdraw and sever themselves from it, he mislikes, and reproves as uncharitable and unneighbourly; and if they will not reform, presents them. Nay, he is so far from condemning such assemblies, that he rather procures them to be often, as knowing that absence breeds strangeness, but presence love. Now, love is his business and aim; wherefore he likes well that his parish at good times invite one another to their houses, and he urgeth them to it; and sometimes, where he knows there hath been, or is, a little difference, he takes one of the parties, and goes with him to the other, and all dine or sup together. There is much preaching in this friendliness. Another old custom there is of saying, when light is brought in, God send us the light of heaven. And the parson likes this very well; neither is he afraid of praising or praying to God at all times, but is rather glad of catching opportunities to do them. Light is a great blessing, and as great as food, for which we give thanks; and those that think this superstitious, neither know superstition nor themselves. As for those that are ashamed to use this form as being old and obsolete and not the fashion, he reforms and teaches them that at baptism they professed not to be ashamed of Christ's cross, or for any shame to leave that which is good. He that is ashamed in small things, will extend his pusillanimity to greater. Rather should a Christian soldier take such occasions to harden himself, and to further his exercises of mortification.

1. Beating the bounds, or walking in procession round the boundaries of a parish.

# CHAPTER XXXVI
## The Parson Blessing

THE Country Parson wonders that blessing the people is in so little use with his brethren, whereas he thinks it not only a grave and reverend thing, but a beneficial also. Those who use it not do so either out of niceness, because they like the salutations and compliments and forms of worldly language better – which conformity and fashionableness is so exceeding unbefitting a minister that it deserves reproof, not refutation – or else because they think it empty and superfluous. But that which the Apostles used so diligently in their writings, nay, which our Saviour himself used, *Mark* 10: 16, cannot be vain and superfluous. But this was not proper to Christ or the Apostles only, no more than to be a spiritual father was appropriated to them. And if temporal fathers bless their children, how much more may and ought spiritual fathers? Besides, the priests of the Old Testament were commanded to bless the people, and the form thereof is prescribed, *Numbers* 6. Now, as the Apostle argues in another case, if the ministration of condemnation did bless, how shall not the ministration of the Spirit exceed in blessing? The fruit of this blessing good Hannah found, and received with great joy, *I Samuel* 1: 18, though it came from a man disallowed by God, for it was not the person, but priesthood, that blessed, so that even ill priests may bless. Neither have the ministers power of blessing only, but also of cursing. So in the Old Testament, Elisha cursed the children, *2 Kings* 2: 24, which though our Saviour reproved as unfitting for his particular, who was to show all humility before his passion, yet he allows it in his Apostles. And therefore St. Peter used that fearful imprecation to Simon Magus, *Acts* 8, *Thy money perish with thee*, and the event confirmed it; so did St. Paul, *2 Timothy* 4: 14, and *I Timothy* 1: 20. Speaking of Alexander the coppersmith, who had withstood his preaching, *the Lord* (saith he) *reward him according to his works*. And again, of Hymeneus and Alexander, he saith he had *delivered them to Satan, that they might learn not to blaspheme*. The forms both of blessing and cursing are expounded in the Common Prayer Book, the one in The Grace of our Lord Jesus Christ, &c., and The Peace of God, &c., the other in general in the Commination. Now blessing differs from prayer, in assurance, because it is not performed by way of request, but of confidence and power, effectually applying God's favour to the blessed, by the interesting of that dignity wherewith God hath invested the priest, and engaging of God's own power and institution for a blessing. The neglect of this duty in ministers themselves hath made the people also neglect it, so that they are so far from craving this benefit from their ghostly father that they oftentimes go out of church before he hath blessed them. In the time of Popery, the priest's *Benedicite* and his holy water were over highly valued, and now we are fallen to the clean contrary, even from superstition to coldness and atheism. But the parson first values the gift in himself, and then teacheth his parish to value it. And it is observable that if a minister talk with a great man in the ordinary course of complimenting language, he shall be esteemed as ordinary complimenters; but if he often interpose a blessing, when the other gives him just opportunity, by speaking any good, this unusual form begets a reverence, and makes him esteemed according to his profession. The same is to be observed in writing letters also. To conclude, if all men are to bless upon occasion, as appears, *Romans* 12: 14, how much more those who are spiritual fathers?

## CHAPTER XXXVII
# Concerning Detraction

THE Country Parson perceiving that most, when they are at leisure, make others' faults their entertainment and discourse, and that even some good men think, so they speak truth, they may disclose another's fault, finds it somewhat difficult how to proceed in this point. For if he absolutely shut up men's mouths, and forbid all disclosing of faults, many an evil may not only be, but also spread in his parish, without any remedy (which cannot be applied without notice), to the dishonour of God, and the infection of his flock, and the discomfort, discredit, and hindrance of the pastor. On the other side, if it be unlawful to open faults, no benefit or advantage can make it lawful; for we must not do evil that good may come of it. Now the parson taking this point to task, which is so exceeding useful, and hath taken so deep root, that it seems the very life and substance of conversation, hath proceeded thus far in the discussing of it. Faults are either notorious or private. Again, notorious faults are either such as are made known by common fame (and of these, those that know them may talk, so they do it not with sport, but commiseration), or else such as have passed judgment, and been corrected either by whipping, or imprisoning, or the like. Of these also men may talk, and more, they may discover them to those that know them not; because infamy is a part of the sentence against malefactors, which the law intends, as is evident by those which are branded for rogues, that they may be known, or put into the stocks, that they may be looked upon. But some may say, though the law allow this, the Gospel doth not, which hath so much advanced charity, and ranked backbiters among the generation of the wicked, *Romans* 1: 30. But this is easily answered: as the executioner is not uncharitable that takes away the life of the condemned, except, besides his office, he add a tincture of private malice in the joy and haste of acting his part; so neither is he that defames him whom the law would have defamed, except he also do it out of rancour. For in infamy all are executioners, and the law gives a malefactor to all to be defamed. And as malefactors may lose and forfeit their goods or life, so may their good name and the possession thereof, which before their offence and judgment they had in all men's breasts; for all are honest till the contrary be proved. Besides, it concerns the commonwealth that rogues should be known, and charity to the public hath the precedence of private charity. So that it is so far from being a fault to discover such offenders, that it is a duty rather, which may do much good and save much harm. Nevertheless, if the punished delinquent shall be much troubled for his sins, and turn quite another man, doubtless then also men's affections and words must turn, and forbear to speak of that which even God himself hath forgotten.

# THE AUTHOR'S PRAYER
## BEFORE SERMON

O Almighty and ever-living Lord God! Majesty, and Power, and Brightness, and Glory! How shall we dare to appear before thy face, who are contrary to thee, in all we call thee? for we are darkness, and weakness, and filthiness, and shame. Misery and sin fill our days; yet art thou our Creator, and we thy work. Thy hands both made us, and also made us lords of all thy creatures, giving us one world in ourselves, and another to serve us; then didst thou place us in Paradise, and wert proceeding still on in thy favours, until we interrupted thy counsels, disappointed thy purposes, and sold our God, our glorious, our gracious God, for an apple. O write it! O brand it in our foreheads for ever: for an apple once we lost our God, and still lose him for no more – for money, for meat, for diet. But thou, Lord, art patience, and pity, and sweetness, and love, therefore we sons of men are not consumed. Thou hast exalted thy mercy above all things, and hast made our salvation, not our punishment, thy glory; so that then where sin abounded, not death but grace superabounded; accordingly, when we had sinned beyond any help in heaven or earth, then thou saidst, Lo, I come! then did the Lord of life, unable of himself to die, contrive to do it. He took flesh, he wept, he died; for his enemies he died, even for those that derided him then, and still despise him. Blessed Saviour! many waters could not quench thy love, nor no pit overwhelm it. But though the streams of thy blood were current through darkness, grave, and hell, yet by these thy conflicts and seemingly hazards didst thou arise triumphant and therein madest us victorious.

Neither doth thy love yet stay here! for this word of thy rich peace and reconciliation thou hast committed, not to thunder or angels, but to silly and sinful men; even to me, pardoning my sins, and bidding me go feed the people of thy love.

Blessed be the God of heaven and earth! who only doth wondrous things. Awake, therefore, my lute, and my viol! awake all my powers to glorify thee! We praise thee! we bless thee! we magnify thee for ever! And now, O Lord! in the power of thy victories, and in the ways of thy ordinances, and in the truth of thy love, lo, we stand here beseeching thee to bless thy word wherever spoken this day throughout the universal Church. O make it a word of power and peace to convert those who are not yet thine, and to confirm those that are; particularly, bless it in this thy own kingdom, which thou hast made a land of light, a storehouse of thy treasures and mercies. O let not our foolish and unworthy hearts rob us of the continuance of this thy sweet love; but pardon our sins, and perfect what thou hast begun. Ride on, Lord, because of the word of truth, and meekness, and righteousness, and thy right hand shall teach thee terrible things. Especially bless this portion here assembled together, with thy unworthy servant speaking unto them. Lord Jesu! teach thou me that I may teach them. Sanctify and enable all my powers, that in their full strength they may deliver thy message reverently, readily, faithfully, and fruitfully. O make thy word a swift word, passing from the ear to the heart, from the heart to the life and conversation; that as the rain returns not empty, so neither may thy word, but accomplish that for which it is given. O Lord, hear, O Lord forgive! O Lord, harken, and do so for thy blessed Son's sake, in whose sweet and pleasing words we say, *Our Father*, &c.

# A PRAYER AFTER SERMON

Blessed be God! and the Father of all mercy! who continueth to pour his benefits upon us. Thou hast elected us, thou hast called us, thou hast justified us, sanctified and glorified us, thou wast born for us, and thou livedst and diedst for us, thou hast given us the blessings of this life and of a better. O Lord, thy blessings hang in clusters, they come trooping upon us! they break forth like mighty waters on every side. And now, Lord, thou hast fed us with the bread of life; so man did eat angels' food. O Lord, bless it: O Lord, make it health and strength unto us, still striving and prospering so long within us, until our obedience reach the measure of thy love, who hast done for us as much as may be. Grant this, dear Father, for thy Son's sake, our only Saviour; to whom with thee and the Holy Ghost, three Persons, but one most glorious incomprehensible God, be ascribed all honour, and glory, and praise, ever. Amen.

# OUTLANDISH PROVERBS[1]

1. Man proposeth; God disposeth.
2. He begins to die that quits his desires.
3. A handful of good life is better than a bushel of learning.
4. He that studies his content, wants it.
5. Every day brings his bread with it.
6. Humble hearts have humble desires.
7. He that stumbles and falls not, mends his pace.
8. The house shows the owner.
9. He that gets out of debt, grows rich.
10. All is well with him who is beloved of his neighbours.
11. Building and marrying of children are great wasters.

---

1. The first collection of English proverbs was made by John Heywood: *A Dialogue containing the number in effect of all the proverbs in the English tongue* (1546). Their use was recommended in Thomas Wilson's *Art of Rhetoric* (1553), a popular textbook of the period. An interest in foreign proverbs had also been created by Erasmus's *Adagia* (1500), prompting several collections translating foreign proverbs: Sainlien's *French Littelton* (1566), Sandford's *Hours of Recreation* (1572), Minsheu's *Spanish Grammar* (1591), and Stepney's *Spanish Schoolmaster* (1591). In 1578 John Florio published what was, in effect, the first ever Italian–English phrasebook, *Florio his First Fruits: which yield familiar speech, merry proverbs, witty sentences, and golden sayings ...The like heretofore never by any man published*, which contained three hundred Italian proverbs in parallel text. It was followed by his *Second Fruits* (1591) which included a collection of six thousand untranslated Italian proverbs. Even though at least nine of Herbert's *Outlandish Proverbs* appear in Florio's *First Fruits* (nos 73, 215, 235, 302, 339, 447, 470, 759, 832 below) and H points out that all but two of the first ninety are also given in Cotgrave's *A Dictionary of the French and English Tongues* (1611), he will have got them from many sources, possibly including his contacts abroad – Nicholas Ferrar was travelling on the Continent 1613–18, his brother Henry spent all of 1618 in France, and his brother Edward was made Ambassador to France in 1619. This compilation puts into practice Herbert's own principle: *All foreign wisdom doth amount to this,| To take all that is given; whether wealth,| Or love, or language; nothing comes amiss* (*Perirrhanterium*, p.19, ll.355–7).

12. A good bargain is a pick-purse.
13. The scalded dog fears cold water.
14. Pleasing ware is half sold.
15. Light burdens, long borne, grow heavy.
16. The wolf knows what the ill beast thinks.
17. Who hath none to still him, may weep out his eyes.
18. When all sins grow old, covetousness is young.
19. If ye would know a knave, give him a staff.
20. You cannot know wine by the barrel.
21. A cool mouth and warm feet live long.
22. A horse made, and a man to make.
23. Look not for musk in a dog's kennel.
24. Not a long day, but a good heart, rids work.
25. He pulls with a long rope that waits for another's death.
26. Great strokes make not sweet music.
27. A cake and an ill custom must be broken.
28. A fat housekeeper makes lean executors.
29. Empty chambers make foolish maids.
30. The gentle hawk half mans herself.
31. The devil is not always at one door.
32. When a friend asks, there is no tomorrow.
33. God sends cold according to clothes.
34. One sound blow will serve to undo us all.
35. He loseth nothing that loseth not God.
36. The German's wit is in his fingers.
37. At dinner my man appears.
38. Who gives to all, denies all.
39. Quick believers need broad shoulders.
40. Who remove stones, bruise their fingers.
41. All came from and will go to others.
42. He that will take the bird must not scare it.
43. He lives unsafely that looks too near on things.
44. A gentle housewife mars the household.
45. A crooked log makes a strait fire.
46. He hath great need of a fool that plays the fool himself.
47. A merchant that gains not, loseth.
48. Let not him that fears feathers come among wild-fowl.
49. Love and a cough cannot be hid.
50. A dwarf on a giant's shoulder sees further of the two.

51. He that sends a fool, means to follow him.
52. Brabbling curs never want torn ears.
53. Better the feet slip than the tongue.
54. For washing his hands, none sells his lands.
55. A lion's skin is never cheap.
56. The goat must browse where she is tied.
57. Who hath a wolf for his mate, needs a dog for his man.
58. In a good house all is quickly ready.
59. A bad dog never sees the wolf.
60. God oft hath a great share in a little house.
61. Ill ware is never cheap.
62. A cheerful look makes a dish a feast.
63. If all fools had baubles we should want fuel.
64. Virtue never grows old.
65. Evening words are not like to morning.
66. Were there no fools bad ware would not pass.
67. Never had ill workman good tools.
68. He stands not surely that never slips.
69. Were there no hearers there would be no backbiters.
70. Everything is of use to a housekeeper.
71. When prayers are done my lady is ready.[1]
72. At length the fox turns monk.
73. Flies are busiest about lean horses.
74. Harken to reason, or she will be heard.
75. The bird loves her nest.
76. Everything new is fine.
77. When a dog is drowning every one offers him drink.
78. Better a bare foot than none.
79. Who is so deaf as he that will not hear?
80. He that is warm thinks all so.
81. At length the fox is brought to the furrier.
82. He that goes barefoot must not plant thorns.
83. They that are booted are not always ready.
84. He that will learn to pray, let him go to sea.
85. In spending lies the advantage.
86. He that lives well is learned enough.
87. Ill vessels seldom miscarry.

1. Cf. *Perirrhanterium*, p.20, l.411.

88. A full belly neither fights nor flies well.
89. All truths are not to be told.
90. An old wise man's shadow is better than a young buzzard's sword.
91. Noble housekeepers need no doors.
92. Every ill man hath his ill day.
93. Sleep without supping, and wake without owing.
94. I gave the mouse a hole, and she is become my heir.
95. Assail who will, the valiant attends.
96. Whither goest, grief? Where I am wont.
97. Praise day at night, and life at the end.
98. Whither shall the ox go where he shall not labour?
99. Where you think there is bacon there is no chimney.
100. Mend your clothes and you may hold out this year.
101. Dress a stick and it seems a youth.
102. The tongue walks where the teeth speed not.
103. A fair wife and a frontier castle breed quarrels.
104. Leave jesting while it pleaseth, lest it turn to earnest.
105. Deceive not thy physician, confessor, nor lawyer.
106. Ill natures, the more you ask them, the more they stick.
107. Virtue and a trade are the best portion for children.[1]
108. The chicken is the country's, but the city eats it.
109. He that gives thee a capon, give him the leg and the wing.
110. He that lives ill, fear follows him.
111. Give a clown your finger, and he will take your hand.
112. Good is to be sought out, and evil attended.
113. A good paymaster starts not at assurances.
114. No alchemy to saving.
115. To a grateful man give money when he asks.
116. Who would do ill ne're wants occasion.
117. To fine folks a little ill finely wrapt.
118. A child correct behind, and not before.
119. To a fair day open the window, but make you ready as to a foul.
120. Keep good men company, and you shall be of the number.
121. No love to a father's.
122. The mill gets by going.

1. Cf. *The Country Parson*, ch. xxxii, pp.242–3.

123. To a boiling pot flies come not.
124. Make haste to an ill way, that you may get out of it.
125. A snow year, a rich year.
126. Better to be blind than to see ill.
127. Learn weeping, and thou shalt laugh gaining.
128. Who hath no more bread than need must not keep a dog.
129. A garden must be looked unto and dressed, as the body.
130. The fox, when he cannot reach the grapes, says they are not ripe.
131. Water trotted is as good as oats.
132. Though the mastiff be gentle, yet bite him not by the lip.
133. Though a lie be well drest, it is ever overcome.
134. Though old and wise, yet still advise.
135. Three helping one another bear the burden of six.
136. Old wine and an old friend are good provisions.
137. Happy is he that chastens himself.
138. Well may he smell fire whose gown burns.
139. The wrongs of a husband or master are not reproached.
140. Welcome evil, if thou comest alone.
141. Love your neighbour, yet pull not down your hedge.
142. The bit that one eats, no friend makes.
143. A drunkard's purse is a bottle.
144. She spins well that breeds her children.
145. Good is the *mora* that makes all sure.
146. Play with a fool at home, and he will play with you in the market.
147. Every one stretcheth his legs according to his coverlet.
148. Autumnal agues are long or mortal.
149. Marry your son when you will; your daughter when you can.
150. Dally not with money or women.
151. Men speak of the fair as things went with them there.
152. The best remedy against an ill man is much ground between both.
153. The mill cannot grind with the water that's past.
154. Corn is cleaned with wind, and the soul with chastenings.
155. Good words are worth much and cost little.
156. To buy dear is not bounty.
157. Jest not with the eye or with religion.

158. The eye and religion can bear no jesting.
159. Without favour none will know you, and with it you will not know yourself.
160. Buy at a fair, but sell at home.
161. Cover yourself with your shield, and care not for cries.
162. A wicked man's gift hath a touch of his master.
163. None is a fool always; every one sometimes.
164. From a choleric man withdraw a little; from him that says nothing, for ever.
165. Debtors are liars.
166. Of all smells, bread; of all tastes, salt.
167. In a great river great fish are found; but take heed lest you be drowned.
168. Ever since we wear clothes we know not one another.
169. God heals, and the physician hath the thanks.
170. Hell is full of good meanings and wishings.
171. Take heed of still waters; the quick pass away.
172. After the house is finished, leave it.
173. Our own actions are our security, not others' judgments.
174. Think of ease, but work on.[1]
175. He that lies long abed, his estate feels it.
176. Whether you boil snow or pound it, you can have but water of it.
177. One stroke fells not an oak.
178. God complains not, but doth what is fitting.
179. A diligent scholar, and the master's paid.
180. Milk says to wine, 'Welcome, friend.'
181. They that know one another salute afar off.
182. Where there is no honour there is no grief.
183. Where the drink goes in, there the wit goes out.
184. He that stays does the business.
185. Alms never make poor. *Or thus:*
186. Great alms-giving lessens no man's living.
187. Giving much to the poor doth enrich a man's store.
188. It takes much from the account to which his sin doth amount.

1. Misnumbered from here onwards in the first edition, followed by H.

189. It adds to the glory both of soul and body.

190. Ill comes in by ells, and goes out by inches.

191. The smith and his penny both are black.

192. Whose house is of glass must not throw stones at another.

193. If the old dog bark, he gives counsel.

194. The tree that grows slowly keeps itself for another.

195. I wept when I was born, and every day shows why.

196. He that looks not before finds himself behind.

197. He that plays his money ought not to value it.

198. He that riseth first is first drest.

199. Diseases of the eye are to be cured with the elbow.

200. The hole calls the thief.

201. A gentleman's greyhound and a salt box, seek them at the fire.

202. A child's service is little, yet he is no little fool that despiseth it.

203. The river past, and God forgotten.

204. Evils have their comfort, good none can support (to wit – with a moderate and contented heart).

205. Who must account for himself and others must know both.

206. He that eats the hard shall eat the ripe.

207. The miserable man maketh a penny of a farthing, and the liberal of a farthing sixpence.

208. The honey is sweet, but the bee stings.

209. Weight and measure take away strife.

210. The son full and tattered, the daughter empty and fine.

211. Every path hath a puddle.

212. In good years corn is hay, in ill years straw is corn.

213. Send a wise man on an errand and say nothing unto him.

214. In life you loved me not, in death you bewail me.

215. Into a mouth shut flies fly not.

216. The heart's letter is read in the eyes.

217. The ill that comes out of our mouth falls into our bosom.

218. In great pedigrees there are governors and chandlers.

219. In the house of a fiddler, all fiddle.[1]

220. Sometimes the best gain is to lose.

221. Working and making a fire doth discretion require.

222. One grain fills not a sack, but helps his fellows.

---

1. Used in *The Country Parson*, ch.x, p.211.

223. It is a great victory that comes without blood.
224. In war, hunting, and love, men for one pleasure a thousand griefs prove.
225. Reckon right, and February hath one and thirty days.
226. Honour without profit is a ring on the finger.
227. Estate in two parishes is bread in two wallets.
228. Honour and profit lie not in one sack.
229. A naughty child is better sick than whole.
230. Truth and oil are ever above.
231. He that riseth betimes hath something in his head.
232. Advise none to marry or to go to war.
233. To steal the hog and give the feet for alms.
234. The thorn comes forth with his point forwards.
235. One hand washeth another, and both the face.
236. The fault of the horse is put on the saddle.
237. The corn hides itself in the snow as an old man in furs.
238. The Jews spend at Easter, the Moors at marriages, the Christians in suits.
239. Fine dressing is a foul house swept before the doors.
240. A woman and a glass are ever in danger.
241. An ill wound is cured, not an ill name.
242. The wise hand doth not all that the foolish mouth speaks.
243. On painting and fighting look aloof.
244. Knowledge is folly, except grace guide it.
245. Punishment is lame, but it comes.
246. The more women look in their glass the less they look to their house.
247. A long tongue is a sign of a short hand.
248. Marry a widow before she leave mourning.
249. The worst of law is that one suit breeds twenty.
250. Providence is better than a rent.
251. What your glass tells you will not be told by counsel.
252. There are more men threatened than stricken.
253. A fool knows more in his house than a wise man in another's.
254. I had rather ride on an ass that carries me than a horse that throws me.
255. The hard gives more than that he hath nothing.
256. The beast that goes always never wants blows.

257. Good cheap is dear.
258. It costs more to do ill than to do well.
259. Good words quench more than a bucket of water.
260. An ill agreement is better than a good judgment.
261. There is more talk than trouble.
262. Better spare to have of thine own than ask of other men.
263. Better good afar off than evil at hand.
264. Fear keeps the garden better than the gardener.
265. I had rather ask of my sire brown bread than borrow of my neighbour white.
266. Your pot broken seems better than my whole one.
267. Let an ill man lie in thy straw and he looks to be thy heir.
268. By suppers more have been killed than Galen ever cured.
269. While the discreet advise the fool doth his business.
270. A mountain and a river are good neighbours.
271. Gossips are frogs, they drink and talk.
272. Much spends the traveller, more than the abider.
273. Prayers and provender hinder no journey.[1]
274. A well-bred youth neither speaks of himself, nor being spoken to is silent.
275. A journeying woman speaks much of all and all of her.
276. The fox knows much, but more he that catcheth him.
277. Many friends in general, one in special.
278. The fool asks much, but he is more fool that grants it.
279. Many kiss the hand they wish cut off.
280. Neither bribe nor lose thy right.
281. In the world who knows not to swim goes to the bottom.
282. Choose not a house near an inn (viz. for noise) or in a corner (for filth).
283. He is a fool that thinks not that another thinks.
284. Neither eyes on letters nor hands in coffers.
285. The lion is not so fierce as they paint him.
286. Go not for every grief to the physician, nor for every quarrel to the lawyer, nor for every thirst to the pot.
287. Good service is a great enchantment.
288. There would be no great ones if there were no little ones.
289. It's no sure rule to fish with a cross-bow.

1. Used in *The Country Parson*, ch.xvii, p.221.

290. There were no ill language if it were not ill taken.
291. The groundsel speaks not save what it heard at the hinges.
292. The best mirror is an old friend.
293. Say no ill of the year till it be past.
294. A man's discontent is his worst evil.
295. Fear nothing but sin.
296. The child says nothing but what it heard by the fire.
297. Call me not an olive till thou see me gathered.
298. That is not good language which all understand not.
299. He that burns his house warms himself for once.
300. He will burn his house to warm his hands.
301. He will spend a whole year's rent at one meal's meat.
302. All is not gold that glisters.
303. A blustering night, a fair day.
304. Be not idle and you shall not be longing.
305. He is not poor that hath little, but he that desireth much.
306. Let none say, I will not drink water.
307. He wrongs not an old man that steals his supper from him.
308. The tongue talks at the head's cost.
309. He that strikes with his tongue must ward with his head.
310. Keep not ill men company, lest you increase the number.
311. God strikes not with both hands, for to the sea he made havens, and to rivers fords.
312. A rugged stone grows smooth from hand to hand.
313. No lock will hold against the power of gold.
314. The absent party is still faulty.
315. Peace, and patience, and death with repentance.
316. If you lose your time you cannot get money nor gain.
317. Be not a baker, if your head be of butter.
318. Ask much to have a little.
319. Little sticks kindle the fire, great ones put it out.
320. Another's bread costs dear.
321. Although it rain, throw not away thy watering-pot.
322. Although the sun shine, leave not thy cloak at home.
323. A little with quiet is the only diet.
324. In vain is the mill-clack, if the miller his hearing lack.
325. By the needle you shall draw the thread, and by that which

is past see how that which is to come will be drawn on.

326. Stay a little and news will find you.

327. Stay till the lame messenger come, if you will know the truth of the thing.

328. When God will, no wind but brings rain.

329. Though you rise early, yet the day comes at his time, and not till then.

330. Pull down your hat on the wind's side.

331. As the year is, your pot must seethe.

332. Since you know all, and I nothing, tell me what I dreamed last night.

333. When the fox preacheth, beware your geese.

334. When you are an anvil, hold you still; when you are a hammer, strike your fill.

335. Poor and liberal, rich and covetous.

336. He that makes his bed ill, lies there.

337. He that labours and thrives spins gold.

338. He that sows trusts in God.

339. He that lies with the dogs riseth with fleas.

340. He that repairs not a part, builds all.

341. A discontented man knows not where to sit easy.

342. Who spits against heaven, it falls in his face.

343. He that dines and leaves lays the cloth twice.

344. Who eats his cock alone must saddle his horse alone.

345. He that is not handsome at 20, nor strong at 30, nor rich at 40, nor wise at 50, will never be handsome, strong, rich or wise.

346. He that doth what he will, doth not what he ought.

347. He that will deceive the fox must rise betimes.

348. He that lives well sees afar off.

349. He that hath a mouth of his own must not say to another, Blow.

350. He that will be served must be patient.

351. He that gives thee a bone would not have thee die.

352. He that chastens one, chastens 20.

353. He that hath lost his credit is dead to the world.

354. He that hath no ill fortune is troubled with good.

355. He that demands, misseth not, unless his demands be foolish.

356. He that hath no honey in his pot, let him have it in his mouth.
357. He that takes not up a pin, slights his wife.
358. He that owes nothing, if he makes not mouths at us, is courteous.
359. He that loseth his due gets no thanks.
360. He that believeth all, misseth; he that believeth nothing, hits not.
361. Pardons and pleasantness are great revenges of slanders.
362. A married man turns his staff into a stake.
363. If you would know secrets, look them in grief or pleasure.
364. Serve a noble disposition; though poor, the time comes that he will repay thee.
365. The fault is as great as he that is faulty.
366. If folly were grief, every house would weep.
367. He that would be well old must be old betimes.
368. Sit in your place, and none can make you rise.
369. If you could run as you drink you might catch a hare.
370. Would you know what money is, go borrow some.
371. The morning sun never lasts a day.
372. Thou hast death in thy house, and dost bewail another's.
373. All griefs with bread are less.
374. All things require skill but an appetite.
375. All things have their place, knew we how to place them.
376. Little pitchers have wide ears.
377. We are fools to one another.
378. This world is nothing except it tend to another.
379. There are three ways – the universities, the sea, the court.
380. God comes to see without a bell.
381. Life without a friend is death without a witness.
382. Clothe thee in war, arm thee in peace.
383. The horse thinks one thing and he that saddles him another.
384. Mills and wives ever want.
385. The dog that licks ashes, trust not with meal.
386. The buyer needs a hundred eyes, the seller not one.
387. He carries well to whom it weighs not.
388. The comforter's head never aches.
389. Step after step the ladder is ascended.
390. Who likes not the drink, God deprives him of bread.
391. To a crazy ship all winds are contrary.

392. Justice pleaseth few in their own house.
393. In time comes he whom God sends.
394. Water afar off quencheth not fire.
395. In sports and journeys men are known.
396. An old friend, a new house.
397. Love is not found in the market.
398. Dry feet, warm head, bring safe to bed.
399. He is rich enough that wants nothing.
400. One father is enough to govern one hundred sons, but not a hundred sons one father.
401. Fair shooting never killed bird.
402. An upbraided morsel never choked any.
403. Dearths foreseen come not.
404. An ill labourer quarrels with his tools.
405. He that falls into the dirt, the longer he stays there the fouler he is.
406. He that blames would buy.
407. He that sings on Friday will weep on Sunday.
408. The charges of building and making of gardens are unknown.
409. My house, my house, though thou art small, thou art to me the Escurial.
410. A hundred load of thought will not pay one of debts.
411. He that comes of a hen must scrape.
412. He that seeks trouble never misses.
413. He that once deceives is ever suspected.
414. Being on sea sail, being on land settle.
415. Who doth his own business fouls not his hands.[1]
416. He that makes a good war makes a good peace.
417. He that works after his own manner, his head aches not at the matter.
418. Who hath bitter in his mouth spits not all sweet.
419. He that hath children, all his morsels are not his own.[2]
420. He that hath the spice may season as he list.
421. He that hath a head of wax must not walk in the sun.
422. He that hath love in his breast hath spurs in his sides.

1. Used in *The Country Parson*, ch.xxxii, p.243.
2. Cf. *Perirrhanterium*, p.16, ll.277–282.

423. He that respects not is not respected.[1]
424. He that hath a fox for his mate hath need of a net at his girdle.
425. He that hath right, fears; he that hath wrong, hopes.
426. He that hath patience hath fat thrushes for a farthing.
427. Never was strumpet fair.
428. He that measures not himself is measured.
429. He that hath one hog makes him fat, and he that hath one son makes him a fool.
430. Who lets his wife go to every feast, and his horse drink at every water, shall neither have good wife nor good horse.
431. He that speaks sows, and he that holds his peace gathers.
432. He that hath little is the less dirty.
433. He that lives most dies most.
434. He that hath one foot in the straw hath another in the spittle.
435. He that's fed at another's hand may stay long ere he be full.
436. He that makes a thing too fine breaks it.
437. He that bewails himself hath the cure in his hands.
438. He that would be well needs not go from his own house.
439. Counsel breaks not the head.
440. Fly the pleasure that bites tomorrow.
441. He that knows what may be gained in a day never steals.
442. Money refused loseth its brightness.
443. Health and money go far.
444. Where your will is ready your feet are light.
445. A great ship asks deep waters.
446. Woe to the house where there is no chiding.
447. Take heed of the vinegar of sweet wine.
448. Fools bite one another, but wise men agree together.
449. Trust not one night's ice.
450. Good is good, but better carries it.
451. To gain teacheth how to spend.
452. Good finds good.
453. The dog gnaws the bone because he cannot swallow it.
454. The crow bewails the sheep, and then eats it.
455. Building is a sweet impoverishing.

1. Used in *The Country Parson*, ch.xxviii, p.237.

456. The first degree of folly is to hold one's self wise, the second to profess it, the third to despise counsel.

457. The greatest step is that out of doors.

458. To weep for joy is a kind of manna.

459. The first service a child doth his father is to make him foolish.

460. The resolved mind hath no ears.

461. In the kingdom of a cheater the wallet is carried before.

462. The eye will have his part.

463. The good mother says not, Will you? but gives.

464. A house and a woman suit excellently.

465. In the kingdom of blind men the one-eyed is king.

466. A little kitchen makes a large house.

467. War makes thieves, and peace hangs them.

468. Poverty is the mother of health.

469. In the morning mountains, in the evening fountains.

470. The back door robs the house.

471. Wealth is like rheum, it falls on the weakest parts.[1]

472. The gown is his that wears it, and the world his that enjoys it.

473. Hope is the poor man's bread.

474. Virtue now is in herbs and stones and words only.

475. Fine words dress ill deeds.

476. Labour as long lived, pray as ever dying.

477. A poor beauty finds more lovers than husbands.

478. Discreet women have neither eyes nor ears.

479. Things well fitted abide.

480. Prettiness dies first.

481. Talking pays no toll.

482. The master's eye fattens the horse, and his foot the ground.

483. Disgraces are like cherries, one draws another.

484. Praise a hill, but keep below.

485. Praise the sea, but keep on land.

486. In choosing a wife and buying a sword we ought not to trust another.

487. The wearer knows where the shoe wrings.

488. Fair is not fair, but that which pleaseth.

489. There is no jollity but hath a smack of folly.

---

1. Used in *Confession*, p.122, l.12.

490. He that's long a-giving knows not how to give.
491. The filth under the white snow the sun discovers.
492. Every one fastens where there is gain.
493. All feet tread not in one shoe.
494. Patience, time, and money accommodate all things.
495. For want of a nail the shoe is lost, for want of a shoe the horse is lost, for want of a horse the rider is lost.
496. Weigh justly and sell dearly.
497. Little wealth, little care.
498. Little journeys and good cost bring safe home.
499. Gluttony kills more than the sword.
500. When children stand quiet they have done some ill.
501. A little and good fills the trencher.
502. A penny spared is twice got.
503. When a knave is in a plum-tree he hath neither friend nor kin.
504. Short boughs, long vintage.
505. Health without money is half an ague.
506. If the wise erred not it would go hard with fools.
507. Bear with evil and expect good.
508. He that tells a secret is another's servant.
509. If all fools wore white caps, we should seem a flock of geese.
510. Water, fire, and soldiers quickly make room.
511. Pension never enriched young man.
512. Under water, famine; under snow, bread.
513. The lame goes as far as your staggerer.
514. He that loseth is merchant as well as he that gains.
515. A jade eats as much as a good horse.
516. All things in their being are good for something.[1]
517. One flower makes no garland.
518. A fair death honours the whole life.
519. One enemy is too much.
520. Living well is the best revenge.
521. One fool makes a hundred.
522. One pair of ears draws dry a hundred tongues.
523. A fool may throw a stone into a well, which a hundred wise men cannot pull out.

1. Celebrated at length in *Providence*, pp.113ff.

524. One slumber finds another.

525. On a good bargain think twice.

526. To a good spender God is the treasurer.

527. A curst cow hath short horns.

528. Music helps not the toothache.

529. We cannot come to honour under a coverlet.

530. Great pains quickly find ease.

531. To the counsel of fools a wooden bell.

532. The choleric man never wants woe.

533. Help thyself, and God will help thee.

534. At the game's end we shall see who gains.

535. There are many ways to fame.

536. Love is the true price of love.

537. Love rules his kingdom without a sword.

538. Love makes all hard hearts gentle.

539. Love makes a good eye squint.

540. Love askes faith, and faith firmness.

541. A sceptre is one thing, and a ladle another.

542. Great trees are good for nothing but shade.

543. He commands enough that obeys a wise man.

544. Fair words make me look to my purse.

545. Though the fox run, the chicken hath wings.

546. He plays well that wins.

547. You must strike in measure, when there are many to strike on one anvil.

548. The shortest answer is doing.

549. It's a poor stake that cannot stand one year in the ground.

550. He that commits a fault thinks every one speaks of it.

551. He that's foolish in the fault, let him be wise in the punishment.

552. The blind eat many a fly.

553. He that can make a fire well can end a quarrel.

554. The toothache is more ease than to deal with ill people.

555. He that should have what he hath not, should do what he doth not.

556. He that hath no good trade, it is to his loss.

557. The offender never pardons.

558. He that lives not well one year, sorrows seven after.

559. He that hopes not for good fears not evil.

560. He that is angry at a feast is rude.
561. He that mocks a cripple, ought to be whole.
562. When the tree is fallen, all go with their hatchet.
563. He that hath horns in his bosom, let him not put them on his head.
564. He that burns most shines most.
565. He that trusts in a lie shall perish in truth.
566. He that blows in the dust fills his eyes with it.
567. Bells call others, but themselves enter not into the church.
568. Of fair things, the autumn is fair.
569. Giving is dead, restoring very sick.
570. A gift much expected is paid, not given.
571. Two ill meals make the third a glutton.
572. The royal crown cures not the headache.
573. 'Tis hard to be wretched, but worse to be known so.
574. A feather in hand is better than a bird in the air.
575. It's better to be the head of a lizard than the tail of a lion.
576. Good and quickly seldom meet.
577. Folly grows without watering.
578. Happier are the hands compassed with iron than a heart with thoughts.
579. If the staff be crooked the shadow cannot be straight.
580. To take the nuts from the fire with the dog's foot.
581. He is a fool that makes a wedge of his fist.
582. Valour that parleys is near yielding.
583. Thursday come, and the week's gone.
584. A flatterer's throat is an open sepulchre.
585. There is great force hidden in a sweet command.
586. The command of custom is great.
587. To have money is a fear, not to have it a grief.
588. The cat sees not the mouse ever.
589. Little dogs start the hare, the great get her.
590. Willows are weak, yet they bind other wood.
591. A good payer is master of another's purse.
592. The thread breaks where it is weakest.
593. Old men, when they scorn young, make much of death.
594. God is at the end, when we think he is farthest off it.
595. A good judge conceives quickly, judges slowly.

596. Rivers need a spring.
597. He that contemplates hath a day without night.
598. Give losers leave to talk.[1]
599. Loss embraceth shame.
600. Gaming, women, and wine, while they laugh they make men pine.
601. The fat man knoweth not what the lean thinketh.
602. Wood half burnt is easily kindled.
603. The fish adores the bait.
604. He that goeth far hath many encounters.
605. Every bee's honey is sweet.
606. The slothful is the servant of the counters.[2]
607. Wisdom hath one foot on land, and another on sea.
608. The thought hath good legs and the quill a good tongue.
609. A wise man needs not blush for changing his purpose.
610. The March sun raises, but dissolves not.
611. Time is the rider that breaks youth.
612. The wine in the bottle doth not quench thirst.
613. The sight of a man hath the force of a lion.
614. An examined enterprise goes on boldly.
615. In every art it is good to have a master.
616. In every country dogs bite.
617. In every country the sun rises in the morning.
618. A noble plant suits not with a stubborn ground.
619. You may bring a horse to the river, but he will drink when and what he pleaseth.
620. Before you make a friend eat a bushel of salt with him.
621. Speak fitly or be silent wisely.
622. Skill and confidence are an unconquered army.
623. I was taken by a morsel, says the fish.
624. A disarmed peace is weak.
625. The balance distinguisheth not between gold and lead.
626. The persuasion of the fortunate sways the doubtful.
627. To be beloved is above all bargains.
628. To deceive oneself is very easy.
629. The reasons of the poor weight not.

1. Used in *A Dialogue-Anthem*, p.165, l.7.
2. *Counters:* the sheriffs' prisons in London (H).

630. Perverseness makes one squint-eyed.

631. The evening praises the day, and the morning a host.

632. The table robs more than a thief.

633. When age is jocund it makes sport for death.

634. True praise roots and spreads.

635. Fears are divided in the midst.

636. The soul needs few things, the body many.

637. Astrology is true, but the astrologers cannot find it.

638. Tie it well and let it go.

639. Empty vessels sound most.

640. Send not a cat for lard.

641. Foolish tongues talk by the dozen.

642. Love makes one fit for any work.

643. A pitiful mother makes a scald head.

644. An old physician, and a young lawyer.

645. Talk much and err much, says the Spaniard.

646. Some make a conscience of spitting in the church, yet rob the altar.

647. An idle head is a box for the wind.

648. Show me a liar and I'll show thee a thief.

649. A bean in liberty is better than a comfit in prison.

650. None is born master.

651. Show a good man his error, and he turns it to a virtue; but an ill, it doubles his fault.

652. None is offended but by himself.

653. None says his garner is full.

654. In the husband wisdom, in the wife gentleness.

655. Nothing dries sooner than a tear.

656. In a leopard the spots are not observed.

657. Nothing lasts but the Church.

658. A wise man cares not for what he cannot have.

659. It's not good fishing before the net.

660. He cannot be virtuous that is not rigorous.

661. That which will not be spun, let it not come between the spindle and the distaff.

662. When my house burns, it's not good playing at chess.

663. No barber shaves so close but another finds work.

664. There's no great banquet but some fares ill.

665. A holy habit cleanseth not a foul soul.

666. Forbear not sowing because of birds.

667. Mention not a halter in the house of him that was hanged.

668. Speak not of a dead man at the table.

669. A hat is not made for one shower.

670. No sooner is a temple built to God but the devil builds a chapel hard by.[1]

671. Every one puts his fault on the times.

672. You cannot make a windmill go with a pair of bellows.

673. Pardon all but thyself.

674. Every one is weary: the poor in seeking, the rich in keeping, the good in learning.

675. The escaped mouse ever feels the taste of the bait.

676. A little wind kindles, much puts out the fire.

677. Dry bread at home is better than roast meat abroad.

678. More have repented speech than silence.

679. The covetous spends more than the liberal.

680. Divine ashes are better than earthly meal.

681. Beauty draws more than oxen.

682. One father is more than a hundred schoolmasters.

683. One eye of the master's sees more than ten of the servants'.

684. When God will punish, he will first take away the understanding.

685. A little labour, much health.

686. When it thunders the thief becomes honest.

687. The tree that God plants, no wind hurts it.

688. Knowledge is no burthen.

689. It is a bold mouse that nestles in the cat's ear.

690. Long jesting was never good.

691. If a good man thrive, all thrive with him.

692. If the mother had not been in the oven, she had never sought her daughter there.

693. If great men would have care of little ones, both would last long.

694. Though you see a churchman ill, yet continue in the Church still.

695. Old praise dies unless you feed it.

696. If things were to be done twice, all would be wise.

1. Cf. *The Church Militant*, p.192, ll.259–60.

697. Had you the world on your chess-board, you could not fit all to your mind.
698. Suffer and expect.
699. If fools should not fool it they should lose their season.
700. Love and business teach eloquence.
701. That which two will, takes effect.
702. He complains wrongfully of the sea that twice suffers shipwreck.
703. He is only bright that shines by himself.
704. A valiant man's look is more than a coward's sword.
705. The effect speaks, the tongue needs not.
706. Divine grace was never slow.
707. Reason lies between the spur and the bridle.
708. It's a proud horse that will not carry his own provender.
709. Three women make a market.
710. Three can hold their peace, if two be away.
711. It's an ill counsel that hath no escape.
712. All our pomp the earth covers.
713. To whirl the eyes too much shows a kite's brain.
714. Comparisons are odious.
715. All keys hang not on one girdle.
716. Great businesses turn on a little pin.
717. The wind in one's face makes one wise.
718. All the arms of England will not arm fear.
719. One sword keeps another in the sheath.
720. Be what thou wouldst seem to be.
721. Let all live as they would die.
722. A gentle heart is tied with an easy thread.[1]
723. Sweet discourse makes short days and nights.
724. God provides for him that trusteth.
725. He that will not have peace, God gives him war.
726. To him that will, ways are not wanting.
727. To a great light, a great lanthorn.
728. To a child all weather is cold.
729. Where there is peace, God is.
730. None is so wise, but the fool overtakes him.
731. Fools give to please all but their own.

1. Used in *The Glimpse*, p.151, l.20.

732. Prosperity lets go the bridle.
733. The friar preached against stealing, and had a goose in his sleeve.
734. To be too busy gets contempt.
735. February makes a bridge, and March breaks it.
736. A horse stumbles that hath four legs.
737. The best smell is bread, the best savour salt, the best love that of children.
738. That's the best gown that goes up and down the house.
739. The market is the best garden.
740. The first dish pleaseth all.
741. The higher the ape goes, the more he shows his tail.
742. Night is the mother of counsels.
743. God's mill grinds slow, but sure.
744. Every one thinks his sack heaviest.
745. Drought never brought dearth.
746. All complain.
747. Gamesters and race-horses never last long.
748. It's a poor sport that's not worth the candle.
749. He that is fallen cannot help him that is down.
750. Every one is witty for his own purpose.
751. A little let lets an ill workman.
752. Good workmen are seldom rich.
753. By doing nothing we learn to do ill.
754. A great dowry is a bed full of brabbles.
755. No profit to honour, no honour to religion.
756. Every sin brings its punishment with it.
757. Of him that speaks ill, consider the life more than the words.
758. You cannot hide an eel in a sack.
759. Give not St. Peter so much, to leave St. Paul nothing.
760. You cannot flea a stone.
761. The chief disease that reigns this year is folly.
762. A sleepy master makes his servant a lout.
763. Better speak truth rudely, than lie covertly.
764. He that fears leaves, let him go not into the wood.
765. One foot is better than two crutches.
766. Better suffer ill than do ill.
767. Neither praise nor dispraise thyself: thy actions serve the turn.

768. Soft and fair goes far.
769. The constancy of the benefits of the year in their seasons argues a Deity.
770. Praise none too much, for all are fickle.
771. It's absurd to warm one in his armour.
772. Lawsuits consume time, and money, and rest, and friends.
773. Nature draws more than ten teams.
774. He that hath a wife and children wants not business.
775. A ship and a woman are ever repairing.
776. He that fears death lives not.
777. He that pities another, remembers himself.
778. He that doth what he should not shall feel what he would not.
779. He that marries for wealth sells his liberty.
780. He that once hits is ever bending.
781. He that serves, must serve.
782. He that lends, gives.
783. He that preacheth giveth alms.
784. He that cockers his child provides for his enemy.
785. A pitiful look asks enough.
786. Who will sell the cow must say the word.
787. Service is no inheritance.
788. The faulty stands on his guard.
789. A kinsman, a friend, or whom you entreat, take not to serve you, if you will be served neatly.
790. At court, every one for himself.
791. To a crafty man a crafty and a half.
792. He that is thrown would ever wrestle.
793. He that serves well needs not ask his wages.
794. Fair language grates not the tongue.
795. A good heart cannot lie.
796. Good swimmers at length are drowned.
797. Good land, evil way.
798. In doing we learn.
799. It's good walking with a horse in one's hand.
800. God, and parents, and our master, can never be requited.
801. An ill deed cannot bring honour.
802. A small heart hath small desires.
803. All are not merry that dance lightly.

804. Courtesy on one side only lasts not long.
805. Wine-counsels seldom prosper.
806. Weening is not measure.
807. The best of the sport is to do the deed and say nothing.
808. If thou thyself canst do it, attend no other's help or hand.
809. Of a little thing a little displeaseth.
810. He warms too near that burns.
811. God keep me from four houses: a usurer's, a tavern, a spital, and a prison.
812. In an hundred ells of contention there is not an inch of love.
813. Do what thou oughtest, and come what come can.
814. Hunger makes dinners, pastime suppers.
815. In a long journey straw weighs.
816. Women laugh when they can and weep when they will.
817. War is death's feast.
818. Set good against evil.
819. He that brings good news knocks hard.
820. Beat the dog before the lion.
821. Haste comes not alone.
822. You must lose a fly to catch a trout.
823. Better a snotty child than his nose wiped off.
824. He is not free that draws his chain.
825. He goes not out of his way that goes to a good inn.
826. There comes nought out of the sack but what was there.
827. A little given seasonably excuses a great gift.
828. He looks not well to himself that looks not ever.
829. He thinks not well that thinks not again.
830. Religion, credit, and the eye are not to be touched.
831. The tongue is not steel, yet it cuts.
832. A white wall is the paper of a fool.
833. They talk of Christmas so long, that it comes.
834. That is gold which is worth gold.
835. It's good tying the sack before it be full.
836. Words are women, deeds are men.
837. Poverty is no sin.
838. A stone in a well is not lost.
839. He can give little to his servant, that licks his knife.
840. Promising is the eve of giving.
841. He that keeps his own makes war.

842. The wolf must die in his own skin.
843. Goods are theirs that enjoy them.
844. He that sends a fool expects one.
845. He that can stay obtains.
846. He that gains well and spends well needs no count-book.
847. He that endures is not overcome.
848. He that gives all before he dies provides to suffer.
849. He that talks much of his happiness summons grief.
850. He that loves the tree loves the branch.
851. Who hastens a glutton chokes him.
852. Who praiseth St. Peter doth not blame St. Paul.
853. He that hath not the craft, let him shut up shop.
854. He that knows nothing doubts nothing.
855. Green wood makes a hot fire.
856. He that marries late, marries ill.
857. He that passeth a winter's day escapes an enemy.
858. The rich knows not who is his friend.
859. A morning sun and a wine-bred child and a Latin-bred woman seldom end well.
860. To a close shorn sheep God gives wind by measure.
861. A pleasure long expected is dear enough sold.
862. A poor man's cow dies, a rich man's child.
863. The cow knows not what her tail is worth till she have lost it.
864. Choose a horse made and a wife to make.
865. It's an ill air where we gain nothing.
866. He hath not lived that lives not after death.
867. So many men in court and so many strangers.
868. He quits his place well that leaves his friend there.
869. That which sufficeth is not little.
870. Good news may be told at any time, but ill in the morning.
871. He that would be a gentleman, let him go to an assault.
872. Who pays the physician does the cure.
873. None knows the weight of another's burthen.
874. Every one hath a fool in his sleeve.
875. One hour's sleep before midnight is worth three after.
876. In a retreat the lame are foremost.
877. It's more pain to do nothing than something.

878. Amongst good men two men suffice.
879. There needs a long time to know the world's pulse.
880. The offspring of those that are very young or very old lasts not.
881. A tyrant is most tyrant to himself.
882. Too much taking heed is loss.
883. Craft against craft makes no living.
884. The reverend are ever before.
885. France is a meadow that cuts thrice a year.
886. It's easier to build two chimneys than to maintain one.
887. The court hath no almanac.
888. He that will enter into Paradise must have a good key.
889. When you enter into a house leave the anger ever at the door.
890. He hath no leisure who useth it not.
891. It's a wicked thing to make a dearth one's garner.
892. He that deals in the world needs four sieves.
893. Take heed of an ox before, of a horse behind, of a monk on all sides.
894. The year doth nothing else but open and shut.
895. The ignorant hath an eagle's wings and an owl's eyes.
896. There are more physicians in health than drunkards.
897. The wife is the key of the house.
898. The law is not the same at morning and at night.
899. War and physic are governed by the eye.
900. Half the world knows not how the other half lives.
901. Death keeps no calendar.
902. Ships fear fire more than water.
903. The least foolish is wise.
904. The chief box of health is time.
905. Silks and satins put out the fire in the chimney.
906. The first blow is as much as two.
907. The life of man is a winter way.
908. The way is an ill neighbour.
909. An old man's staff is the rapper of death's door.
910. Life is half spent before we know what it is.
911. The singing man keeps his shop in his throat.
912. The body is more dressed than the soul.
913. The body is sooner dressed than the soul.

914. The physician owes all to the patient, but the patient owes nothing to him but a little money.

915. The little cannot be great, unless he devour many.

916. Time undermines us.

917. The choleric drinks, the melancholic eats, the phlegmatic sleeps.

918. The apothecary's mortar spoils the luter's music.

919. Conversation makes one what he is.

920. The deaf gains the injury.

921. Years know more than books.

922. Wine is a turn-coat (first a friend, then an enemy).

923. Wine ever pays for his lodging.

924. Wine makes all sorts of creatures at table.

925. Wine that cost nothing is digested before it be drunk.

926. Trees eat but once.

927. Armour is light at table.

928. Good horses make short miles.

929. Castles are forests of stones.

930. The dainties of the great are the tears of the poor.

931. Parsons are souls' waggoners.

932. Children when they are little make parents fools, when they are great they make them mad.

933. The master absent, and the house dead.

934. Dogs are fine in the field.

935. Sins are not known till they be acted.

936. Thorns whiten yet do nothing.

937. All are presumed good till they are found in a fault.

938. The great put the little on the hook.

939. The great would have none great and the little all little.

940. The Italians are wise before the deed, the Germans in the deed, the French after the deed.

941. Every mile is two in winter.

942. Spectacles are death's harquebus.[1]

943. Lawyers' houses are built on the heads of fools.

944. The house is a fine house when good folk are within.

945. The best bred have the best portion.[2]

---

1. A portable gun.
2. Used in the *Letters*, p.297.

946. The first and last frosts are the worst.

947. Gifts enter everywhere without a wimble.

948. Princes have no way.

949. Knowledge makes one laugh, but wealth makes one dance.

950. The citizen is at his business before he rise.

951. The eyes have one language everywhere.

952. It is better to have wings than horns.

953. Better be a fool than a knave.

954. Count not four, except you have them in a wallet.

955. To live peaceably with all breeds good blood.

956. You may be on land, yet not in a garden.

957. You cannot make the fire so low but it will get out.

958. We know not who lives or dies.

959. An ox is taken by the horns, and a man by the tongue.

960. Many things are lost for want of asking.

961. No churchyard is so handsome that a man would desire straight to be buried there.

962. Cities are taken by the ears.

963. Once a year a man may say, On his conscience.

964. We leave more to do when we die than we have done.

965. With customs we live well, but laws undo us.

966. To speak of a usurer at the table mars the wine.

967. Pains to get, care to keep, fear to lose.

968. For a morning rain leave not your journey.

969. One fair day in winter makes not birds merry.

970. He that learns a trade hath a purchase made.

971. When all men have what belongs to them, it cannot be much.

972. Though God take the sun out of the heaven, yet we must have patience.

973. When a man sleeps his head is in his stomach.

974. When one is on horseback he knows all things.

975. When God is made master of a family, he orders the disorderly.

976. When a lackey comes to hell's door, the devils lock the gates.

977. He that is at ease seeks dainties.

978. He that hath charge of souls transports them not in bundles.

979. He that tells his wife news is but newly married.

980. He that is in a town in May loseth his spring.

981. He that is in a tavern thinks he is in a vine-garden.

982. He that praiseth himself spattereth himself.

983. He that is a master must serve (another).

984. He that is surprised with the first frost feels it all the winter after.

985. He a beast doth die, that hath done no good to his country.

986. He that follows the Lord hopes to go before.

987. He that dies without the company of good men puts not himself into a good way.

988. Who hath no head needs no hat.

989. Who hath no haste in his business, mountains to him seem valleys.

990. Speak not of my debts, unless you mean to pay them.

991. He that is not in the wars is not out of danger.

992. He that gives me small gifts would have me live.

993. He that is his own counsellor knows nothing sure but what he hath laid out.

994. He that hath lands hath quarrels.

995. He that goes to bed thirsty riseth healthy.

996. Who will make a door of gold must knock a nail every day.

997. A trade is better than service.

998. He that lives in hope danceth without music.

999. To review one's store is to mow twice.

1000. St. Luke was a saint and a physician, yet is dead.

1001. Without business, debauchery.

1002. Without danger we cannot get beyond danger.

1003. Health and sickness surely are men's double enemies.

1004. If gold knew what gold is, gold would get gold, I wis.

1005. Little losses amaze, great tame.

1006. Choose none for thy servant who have served thy betters.

1007. Service without reward is punishment.

1008. If the husband be not at home, there is nobody.

1009. An oath that is not to be made is not to be kept.

1010. The eye is bigger than the belly.

1011. If you would be at ease, all the world is not.

1012. Were it not for the bone in the leg, all the world would turn carpenters (to make them crutches).

1013. If you must fly, fly well.

1014. All that shakes falls not.
1015. All beasts of prey are strong or treacherous.
1016. If the brain sows not corn it plants thistles.
1017. A man well mounted is ever choleric.
1018. Every one is a master and servant.
1019. A piece of a churchyard fits everybody.
1020. One month doth nothing without another.
1021. A master of straw eats a servant of steel.
1022. An old cat sports not with her prey.
1023. A woman conceals what she knows not.
1024. He that wipes the child's nose kisseth the mother's cheek.

# LETTERS[1]

## *To Sir John Danvers.*

Sir,

Though I had the best wit in the World, yet it would easily tire me, to find out variety of thanks for the diversity of your favours, if I sought to do so, but I profess it not. And therefore let it be sufficient for me, that the same heart which you have won long since is still true to you, and hath nothing else to answer your infinite kindnesses but a constancy of obedience; only hereafter I will take heed how I propose my desires unto you, since I find you so willing to yield to my requests; for, since your favours come a Horse-back, there is reason, that my desires should go a-foot. Neither do I make any question, but that you have performed your kindness to the full, and that the Horse is every way fit for me, and I will strive to imitate the completeness of your love, with being in some proportion, and after my manner,

Your most obedient Servant,
GEORGE HERBERT.

[1617/18]

## *To the same.*

Sir,

I dare no longer be silent, lest while I think I am modest, I wrong both my self, and also the confidence my Friends have in me; wherefore I will open my case unto you, which I think deserves the reading at the least; and it is this. I want books extremely. You know Sir, how I am now setting foot into Divinity, to lay the platform of my future life, and shall I then be fain always to borrow books, and build on another's foundation?

---

1. For the provenance of these letters, see H, pp. 576–8. The two quoted in Walton's *Life* (pp. 344, 355–7) have been omitted here. Conjectured dates are from H.

What tradesman is there who will set up without his tools? Pardon my boldness Sir, it is a most serious case, nor can I write coldly in that, wherein consisteth the making good of my former education, of obeying that spirit which hath guided me hitherto, and of achieving my (I dare say) holy ends. This also is aggravated, in that I apprehend what my friends would have been forward to say, if I had taken ill courses, *Follow your book, and you shall want nothing.* You know Sir, it is their ordinary speech, and now let them make it good; for since I hope I have not deceived their expectation, let not them deceive mine. But perhaps they will say, you are sickly, you must not study too hard. It is true (God knows) I am weak, yet not so, but that every day, I may step one step towards my journey's end; and I love my friends so well, as that if all things proved not well, I had rather the fault should lie on me than on them. But they will object again, What becomes of your annuity? Sir, if there be any truth in me, I find it little enough to keep me in health. You know I was sick last vacation, neither am I yet recovered, so that I am fain ever and anon, to buy somewhat tending towards my health; for infirmities are both painful and costly. Now this Lent I am forbid utterly to eat any Fish, so that I am fain to diet in my Chamber at mine own cost; for in our public Halls, you know, is nothing but fish and Whit-meats. Out of Lent also, twice a week, on Fridays and Saturdays, I must do so, which yet sometimes I fast. Sometimes, also I ride to Newmarket and there lie a day or two for fresh air; all which tend to avoiding of costlier matters, if I should fall absolutely sick. I protest and vow, I even study thrift, and yet I am scarce able with much ado to make one half year's allowance shake hands with the other. And yet if a book of four or five shillings come in my way, I buy it, though I fast for it; yea, sometimes of ten shillings. But, alas Sir, what is that to those infinite volumes of divinity, which yet every day swell, and grow bigger. Noble Sir, pardon my boldness, and consider but these three things. First, the bulk of divinity. Secondly, the time when I desire this (which is now, when I must lay the foundation of my whole life). Thirdly, what I desire, and to what end, not vain pleasures, nor to a vain end. If then, Sir, there be any course, either by engaging my future annuity, or any other way, I desire you, Sir, to be my mediator to them in my behalf.

Now I write to you, Sir, because to you I have ever opened my heart; and have reason, by the patents of your perpetual favour to do so still, for I am sure you love

Your faithfullest Servant,

*March 18.* 1617. [i.e. 1617/18]     GEORGE HERBERT

Trin: Coll.

## To Mr. Henry Herbert.

BROTHER,

The disease which I am troubled with now is the shortness of time, for it hath been my fortune of late to have such sudden warning, that I have not leisure to impart unto you some of those observations which I have framed to myself in conversation; and whereof I would not have you ignorant. As I shall find occasion, you shall receive them by pieces; and if there be any such which you have found useful to yourself, communicate them to me. You live in a brave nation, where, except you wink, you cannot but see many brave examples. Be covetous, then, of all good which you see in Frenchmen, whether it be in knowledge, or in fashion, or in words; for I would have you, even in speeches, to observe so much, as when you meet with a witty French speech, try to speak the like in English: so shall you play a good merchant, by transporting French commodities to your own country. Let there be no kind of excellency which it is possible for you to attain to, which you seek not; and have a good conceit of your wit, mark what I say, have a good conceit of your wit; that is, be proud, not with a foolish vaunting of yourself when there is no cause, but by setting a just price of your qualities: and it is the part of a poor spirit to undervalue himself and blush. But I am out of my time: when I have more time, you shall hear more; and write you freely to me in your letters, for I am

your ever loving brother,

G. HERBERT

P.S. My brother is somewhat of the same temper, and perhaps a little more mild, but you will hardly perceive it.

To my dear brother,

Mr. Henry Herbert, at Paris.   [1618]

## *To the truly Noble Sir John Danvers.*

SIR,

I understand by a letter from my brother *Henry,* that he hath bought a parcel of books for me, and that they are coming over. Now though they have hitherto travelled upon your charge, yet if my sister were acquainted that they are ready, I dare say she would make good her promise of taking five or six pound upon her, which she hath hitherto deferred to do, not of her self, but upon the want of those books which were not to be got in England; for that which surmounts, though your noble disposition is infinitely free, yet I had rather fly to my old ward, that if any course could be taken of doubling my annuity now, upon condition that I should surcease from all title to it, after I enter'd into a benefice, I should be most glad to entertain it, and both pay for the surplusage of these books, and for ever after cease my clamorous and greedy bookish requests. It is high time now that I should be no more a burden to you, since I can never answer what I have already received; for your favours are so ancient, that they prevent my memory, and yet still grow upon

Your humblest Servant,

[1618]                                  GEORGE HERBERT

I remember my most humble duty to my Mother. I have wrote to my dear sick Sister this week already, and therefore now I hope may be excused.

I pray Sir, pardon my boldness of enclosing my brother's letter in yours, for it was because I know your lodging, but not his.

## *To Sir Robert Harley, at Brampton.*

Sʳ

This letter runs to you with much eagerness, for I am enjoined to write to you by Sʳ John Danvers, to which mine own obligations were occasion enough, and therefore I am not over much beholding to those businesses which justly excuse him from writing at this time, because my recompenses of your favours consist in this only. Now his desire is to acquaint you with those passages of news which this time affords; for though it is likely that the time after the holy day will be fruitfuller of novelties, yet his love expects them not but first certifies you that there are come agents hither from the low-Countries to treat of divers matters, as of certain injuries which they are thought to have offered to our Merchants at the Indies, wherein they have satisfied the King reasonably. But yet he will hear of no other affairs, until they have satisfied him also concerning the fishing which the Hollanders use in our coasts, which the King would so appropriate to himself, as that either his subjects only should practise it, or at least that the Hollanders should pay him tribute out of their fishing. Now to the answering of this demand of the King's these agents pretend they have no commission, and therefore defer it until they hear farther from the States. My Lord of Buckingham was observed on Christmas day to be so devout as to come to the Chapel an hour before prayers began, of which is doubted whether it have some further meaning. S$^r$ Charles Howard and his Lady are at much difference, and she being at London sent for him (as she says) to make peace with him, which he refusing to do hath given her occasion to protest she will never speak with him again, and to threaten him that if he will not give her half her estate to live on by herself (for she desires no more) she will find friends to compel him to it. There is a Spanish lawyer hath written a treatise concerning the lawfulness of kings resuming the donation of spiritual livings into their own hands, and taking it from the Popes: this passeth in Spain freely with consent of King and counsel. There is a Frenchman who writ a poem here in England and presented it to the King, who because of his importunities gave him a reward, but not so great as he expected and therefore he grumblingly said that if he had given it to the pope he should have had a greater reward. Upon this he was forbid Court and kingdom, yet was seen lately near the king, which some observing who heard the interdiction denounced to him, told the King and so he is committed to prison. These are the things I am to acquaint you with, of whose rude delivery my haste makes me ashamed, only my comfort is that this is but an occasion for you to amplify your favour to me in pardoning

Your most indebted kinsman

*Decemb*. 26. 1618.     GEORGE HERBERT
Charing Cross.

## To Sir John Danvers.

SIR,

This Week hath loaded me with your favours; I wish I could have come in person to thank you, but it is not possible. Presently after Michaelmas, I am to make an Oration to the whole University of an hour long in Latin, and my Lincoln journey hath set me much behind hand: neither can I so much as go to Bugden, and deliver your letter, yet have I sent it thither by a faithful messenger this day. I beseech you all, you and my dear mother and sister to pardon me, for my Cambridge necessities are stronger to tie me here, than yours to London. If I could possibly have come, none should have done my message to Sir Frances Nethersole for me; he and I are ancient acquaintance, and I have a strong opinion of him, that if he can do me a courtesy, he will of himself; yet your appearing in it, affects me strangely. I have sent you here enclosed a letter from our master in my behalf, which if you can send to Sir Francis before his departure, it will do well, for it expresseth the University's inclination to me; yet if you cannot send it with much convenience, it is no matter, for the gentleman needs no incitation to love me.

The orator's place (that you may understand what it is) is the finest place in the University, though not the gainfullest; yet that will be about 30 *l. per an.* but the commodiousness is beyond the revenue; for the orator writes all the university letters, makes all the orations, be it to King, prince, or whatever comes to the university; to requite these pains, he takes place next the doctors, is at all their assemblies and meetings, and sits above the proctors, is regent or non-regent at his pleasure, and such like gaynesses, which will please a young man well.

I long to hear from Sir Francis; I pray Sir send the letter you receive from him to me as soon as you can, that I may work the heads to my purpose. I hope I shall get this place without all your London helps, of which I am very proud, not but that I joy in your favours, but that you may see, that if all fail, yet I am able to stand on mine own legs. Noble Sir, I thank you for your infinite favours, I fear only that I have omitted some fitting circumstance, yet you will pardon my haste, which is very great, though never so, but that I have both time and work to be

[Sept. 1619]     Your extreme Servant, GEORGE HERBERT

## *To the same.*

Sir,

I understand by Sir Francis Nethersole's Letter, that he fears I have not fully resolved of the matter, since this place being civil may divert me too much from divinity, at which, not without cause, he thinks I aim; but I have wrote him back, that this dignity hath no such earthiness in it, but it may very well be joined with heaven; or if it had to others, yet to me it should not, for aught I yet knew; and therefore I desire him to send me a direct answer in his next letter. I pray Sir therefore, cause this enclosed to be carried to his brother's house of his own name (as I think) at the sign of the Pedler and the Pack on London-bridge, for there he assigns me. I cannot yet find leisure to write to my Lord, or Sir Benjamin Ruddyard; but I hope I shall shortly, though for the reckoning of your favours, I shall never find time and paper enough, yet am I

Your readiest Servant,

*Octob.* 6. 1619.                          George Herbert

Trin: Coll.

I remember my most humble duty to my mother, who cannot think me lazy, since I rode 200 mile to see a sister, in a way I knew not, in the midst of much business, and all in a Fortnight, not long since.

## *To the same.*

Sir,

I have received the things you sent me, safe; and now the only thing I long for, is to hear of my dear sick Sister; first, how her health fares, next, whether my peace be yet made with her concerning my unkind departure. Can I be so happy, as to hear of both these that they succeed well? Is it not too much for me? Good Sir, make it plain to her, that I loved her even in my departure, in looking to her son, and my charge. I suppose she is not disposed to spend her eye-sight on a piece of paper, or else I had wrote to her; when I shall understand that a letter will be seasonable, my pen is ready. Concerning the orator's place all goes well yet; the next Friday it is tried, and accordingly you shall hear. I have forty businesses in my hands, your Courtesy will pardon the haste of

Your humblest Servant,<br>GEORGE HERBERT

*Jan.* 19. 1619. [i.e. 1619/20]<br>Trin: Coll.

## *For my dear sick Sister.*

MOST DEAR SISTER,

Think not my silence forgetfulness; or that my love is as dumb as my papers; though businesses may stop my hand, yet my heart, a much better member, is always with you: and which is more, with our good and gracious God, incessantly begging some ease of your pains, with that earnestness, that becomes your griefs, and my love. God who knows and sees this writing, knows also that my soliciting him has been much, and my tears many for you; judge me then by those waters, and not by my ink, and then you shall justly value

Your most truly,<br>most heartily,<br>affectionate Brother,<br>and Servant,<br>GEORGE HERBERT

*Decem.* 6. 1620.<br>Trin: Coll.

## *To Sir Henry Herbert.*

DEAR BRO;

That you did not only entertain my proposals, but advance them, was lovingly done, and like a good brother. Yet truly it was none of my meaning, when I wrote, to put one of our nieces into your hands but barely what I wrote I meant, and no more; and am glad that although you offer more, yet you will do as you write, that also. I was desirous to put a good mind into the way of charity, and that was all I intended. For concerning your offer of receiving one, I will tell you what I wrote to our eldest brother, when he urged one upon me, and but one, and that at my choice. I wrote to him that I would have both or neither; and that upon this ground, because they were to come into an unknown country, tender in knowledge, sense, and age, and knew none but one who could be no company to them. Therefore I considered that if one only came, the comfort intended would prove a discomfort. Since that I have seen the fruit of my observation, for they have lived so lovingly, lying, eating, walking, praying, working, still together, that I take a comfort therein; and would not have to part them yet, till I take some opportunity to let them know your love, for which both they shall, and I do, thank you. It is true there is a third sister, whom to receive were the greatest charity of all, for she is youngest, and least looked unto; having none to do it but her school-mistress, and you know what those mercenary creatures are. Neither hath she any to repair unto at good times, as Christmas, etc. which, you know, is the encouragement of learning all the year after, except my cousin Bett take pity of her, which yet at that distance is some difficulty. If you could think of taking her, as once you did, surely it were a great good deed, and I would have her conveyed to you. But I judge you not: do that which God shall put into your heart, and the Lord bless all your purposes to his glory. Yet, truly if you take her not, I am thinking to do it, even beyond my strength;[1] especially at this time, being more beggarly now than I have been these many years, as having spent two hundred pounds in building; which to me that have nothing yet, is very much. But though I both consider this, and your observation also of the unthankfulness of kindred bred up (which generally is very true) yet I care not; I forget all things, so I may do them good who want it. So I do my part to them, let them think of me what they will or can. I have another judge, to whom I stand or fall. If I should regard such things, it were in another's power to defeat my charity, and evil should be stronger than good: but difficulties are so far from cooling christians, that they whet them. Truly it grieves me to think of the child, how destitute she is, and that in this necessary time of education. For the time of breeding is the time of doing children good; and not as many who think they have done fairly, if they leave them a good portion after their decease. But take this rule,

1. He did. See Walton, p. 371.

and it is an outlandish one, which I commend to you as being now a father, 'the best-bred child hath the best portion'.[1] Well; the good God bless you more and more; and all yours; and make your family a houseful of God's servants. So prays

Your ever loving brother,

My wife's and nieces' service. G. HERBERT

 To my very dear brother
 Sir Henry Herbert, at Court.
  [? Autumn, 1630]

## To the Right Honourable the Lady Anne, Countess of Pembroke and Montgomery at Court.

MADAM,

 What a trouble hath your Goodness brought on you, by admitting our poor services? now they creep in a vessel of Metheglin, and still they will be presenting or wishing to see, if at length they may find out some thing not unworthy of those hands at which they aim. In the mean time a priest's blessing, though it be none of the Court-style, yet doubtless Madam, can do you no hurt. Wherefore the Lord make good the blessing of your mother upon you, and cause all her wishes, diligence, prayers and tears, to bud, blow and bear fruit in your soul, to his glory, your own good, and the great joy of

Madam,
Your most faithful Servant
in Christ Jesu,

GEORGE HERBERT

*Dec.* 10. 1631.
 Bemerton.
Madam, Your poor
 Colony of Servants
 present their hum-
 ble duties.

---

1. *Outlandish Proverbs*, no. 945.

## *To Sir Henry Herbert.*

DEAR BRO;

I was glad of your Cambridge news, but you joyed me
exceedingly with your relation of my Lady Duchess's forward-
ness in our church building. I am glad I used you in it, and you
have no cause to be sorry, since it is God's business. If there fall
out yet any rub, you shall hear of me; and your offering of
yourself to move my Lords of Manchester and Bolingbroke is
very welcome to me. To show a forwardness in religious works is
a good testimony of a good spirit. The Lord bless you, and make
you abound in every good work to the joy of

your ever loving brother,

*March* 21, Bemerton. [1631/2]           G. HERBERT
    To my dear brother,
  Sir Henry Herbert, at Court.

## *To Mr. Nicholas Ferrar.*

MY EXCEEDING DEAR BROTHER.

Although you have a much better Paymaster than myself,
even him, whom we both serve: yet I shall ever put your care of
Leighton upon my account, and give you myself for it, to be
yours for ever. God knows, I have desired a long time to do the
place good, and have endeavoured many ways, to find out a
man for it. And now my gracious Lord God is pleased to give me
you for the man I desired, for which I humbly thank him, and
am so far from giving you cause to apology about your counsell-
ing me herein, that I take it exceeding kindly of you. I refuse not
advice from the meanest that creeps upon God's earth, no not
tho' the advice step so far, as to be reproof: much less can I
disesteem it from you, whom I esteem to be God's faithful and
diligent servant, not considering you any other ways, as neither I
my self desire to be considered. Particularly, I like all your
Addresses, and for aught I see, they are ever to be liked. [*So he*

*goes on in the discourse of the building the Church, in such & such a form as N.F. advised, & letting N.F. know, all he had, & would do, to get moneys to proceed in it. And concludes thus.*] You write very lovingly that all your things are mine. If so, let this of Leighton Church the care be amongst the chiefest also, so also have I required M<sup>r</sup> W. for his part. Now God the Father of our Lord Jesus Christ bless you more and more, and so turn you all, in your several ways, one to the other, that ye may be a heavenly comfort, to his praise and the great joy of

Your brother and Servant in Christ Jesus
GEORGE HERBERT

*Postscript.*

As I had written thus much, I received a letter from my brother, S<sup>r</sup> Henry H: of the blessed Success, that God had given us by moving the Duchess's heart to an exceeding cheerfulness, in signing 100 *lib.* with her own hands (and promising to get her son to do as much) with some little apology that she had done nothing in it (as my brother writes) hitherto. She referred it also to my brother, to name at first, what the sum should be, but he told her grace, that he would by no means do so, urging that charity must be free. She liked our book well, and has given order to the tenants at Leighton to make payment of it. God Almighty prosper the work, Amen.

[*March* 1631/2]

## *To the same.*

MY DEAR BROTHER

I thank you heartily for Leighton, your care, your counsel, your cost. And as I am glad for the thing, so no less glad for the heart that God has given you and yours, to pious works. Blessed be my God and dear Master, the spring and fountain of all goodness. As for my assistance, doubt not, through God's blessing, but it shall be to the full; and for my power, I have sent my letters to your brother, investing him, in all that I have. [*And so he goes on in his advice, for the ordering of things, to that business.*]

## To Sir Henry Herbert.

DEAR BRO;

It is so long since I heard from you, that I long to hear both how you and yours do: and also what becomes of you this summer. It is the whole amount of this letter, and therefore entertain it accordingly from

Your very affectionate bro:

7 *June*, Bemerton. [1631 or 1632]        G. HERBERT

My wife's and nieces' service to you.


## Reasons for Arthur Woodnoth's living with Sir John Danvers.

### In the name of God. Amen

1° Higher opportunities of doing good are to be preferred before lower, even where to continue in the lower is no sin by the Apostle's rule. *1 Cor.* 7: 21 and in the whole chapter therefore your choice at first was good.

2° yet are you now engaged. It is a different thing to advise you now, and before you took Sʳ John's affairs. You have been at charges: you have stocked the grounds: you have laid out thoughts and prayers[:] you have sowed. Therefore expect a harvest.

3° To change shows not well and you are by the Apostle's rule (*Philip* 4: 8) not only to pursue pure things, but things that are lovely, and of good report if there be any virtue or any praise. Now constancy is such and of great esteem with all. As in things inwardly good to have an eye to the world may be pharisaical: so in things naturally visible and apparent, as the course of our life and the changes thereof, we are to regard others, and neither to scandalize them nor wound our own reputation.

4° When two things dislike you: the one for the nature thereof (as your trade) the other only for the success (as assistance of Sʳ John) do as David did: put your self into the hands of God (whose the success of things is) and not into the hands of men or men's trades: especially no obligation lying upon you either for the execution or benefit of a trade, by the way of supporting either it (in regard of the city) or your self or your kindred.

5° Whereas you complain of want of success consider how long God knocks at our hearts, before he be heard, and yet desists not. To be without doors with him, is no ill company. If God had done that (which you are thinking to do) to blessed Mary Magdalene and Paul, heaven had wanted chief saints: therefore God is styled with that glorious title, long suffering.

6° you do not want all success. As God where he finds no room for his inclining grace, yet useth his restraining grace, even in the most wicked: so though you incline not, happily you restrain. Things may grow worse by your withdrawing which grow not better by your presence. And if upon your withdrawing it should do so, it would trouble your conscience.

7° Though you want all success either in inclining or restraining, to desire good and endeavour it when we can do no more, is to do it. Complain not of the want of success, when you have the fruit of it. In God's accepting you have done the good you intended, and whom serve you? or whom would you please? David built the temple as much as Solomon because he desired it and prepared for it. Do this and be a man as David, after God's heart.

For any scruple of leaving your trade, throw it away. When we exhort people to continue in their vocation, it is in opposition to idleness. Work rather than do nothing. But to choose a higher work, as God gives me higher thoughts, and to rise with his favours, can not but be not only allowable but commendable. The case of ministers and magistrates is another thing; the one are God's servants, the other the commonwealth's, and therefore not relinquishable without their masters' consent. But a trade having two things, the one employment, the other profit, the work I may change, the profit, I am master of.

[October, 1631]

# THE WILL OF GEORGE HERBERT

I George Herbert commending my soul and body to Almighty God that made them do thus dispose of my goods. I give all my goods both within doors and without doors both moneys and books and household stuff whether in my possession or out of my possession that properly belong to me unto my dear wife excepting only these legacies hereafter ensuing. First there is seven hundred pounds in Mr. Thomas Lawley's hands a merchant of London which fell to me by the death of my dear Niece Mrs. Dorothy Vaughan whereof two hundred pounds belongs to my two Nieces that survive and the rest unto my self, this whole sum of five hundred pounds I bequeath unto my Nieces equally to be divided between them excepting some legacies of my deceased Niece which are to be paid out of it unto some whose names shall be annexed unto this bill. Then I bequeath twenty pounds unto the poor of this parish to be divided according to my dear wife's discretion. Then I bequeath to Mr. Hays the Comment of Lucas Brugensis upon the Scripture and his half year's wages aforehand, then I bequeath to Mr. Bostocke St. Augustine's works and his half year's wages aforehand, then I leave to my servant Elizabeth her double wages given her, three pound more beside that which is due to her, to Ann I leave thirty shillings: to Margaret twenty shillings. To William twenty Nobles, to John twenty shillings, all these are over and above their wages. To Sara thirteen shillings four pence. Also my will and pleasure is that Mr. Woodnoth should be mine Executor to whom I bequeath twenty pound whereof fifteen pound shall be bestowed upon Leighton Church, the other five pound I give to himself. Lastly I beseech Sr John Danvers that he would be pleased to be Overseer of this Will.

George: Herbert
(testes Nathaniel Bostocke, Elizabeth Burden)

On the other side are the names of those to whom my deceased Niece left legacies.

All those that are crossed are discharged already; the rest are to be paid.

To Mrs. Magdalen Vaughan one hundred pound, to Mrs. Catharine Vaughan one hundred pound, to Mr. George Herbert one hundred pound ×. To Mrs. Beatrice Herbert forty pound ×, to Mrs. Jane Herbert ten pound ×, to Mrs. Danvers five pound ×, to Amy Danvers thirty shillings, to Mrs. Anne Danvers twenty shillings, to Mrs. Mary Danvers twenty shillings, to Mrs. Michel twenty shillings, to Mrs. Elizabeth Danvers, Mr. Henry Danvers' wife, twenty shillings; to the poor of the parish twenty pound ×. To my Lord of Cherbury ten pound, to Mr. Bostocke forty shillings ×. To Elizabeth Burthen thirty shillings ×. To Mary Gifford ten shillings ×. To Anne Hibbert ten shillings ×. To William Scuce twenty shillings ×. To Mrs. Judith Spencer five pound. To Mary Owens forty shillings. To Mrs. Mary Lawly fifty shillings ×. To Mr. Gardiner ten pound. MS. that the five pound due to Mrs. Judith Spenser is to be paid to Mrs. Mary Lawly at Chelsey. MS. that there are divers moneys of mine in Mr. Stephen's hands, stationer of London, having lately received an hundred and two pounds besides some remainders of moneys whereof he is to give as I know he will a Just account: if there be any body else that owe me any thing else of old debt I forgive them.

# A TREATISE OF
# TEMPERANCE AND SOBRIETY

WRITTEN BY LUD. CORNARUS,[1] TRANSLATED INTO ENGLISH
BY MR. GEORGE HERBERT

Having observed in my time many of my friends, of excellent wit and noble disposition, overthrown and undone by intemperance, who, if they had lived, would have been an ornament to the world and a comfort to their friends, I thought fit to discover in a short treatise that intemperance was not such an evil but it might easily be remedied, which I undertake the more willingly, because divers worthy young men have obliged me unto it. For when they saw their parents and kindred snatched away in the midst of their days, and me, contrariwise, at the age of eighty and one, strong and lusty, they had a great desire to know the way of my life, and how I came to be so. Wherefore, that I may satisfy their honest desire, and withal help many others, who will take this into consideration, I will declare the causes which moved me to forsake intemperance and live a sober life, expressing also the means which I have used therein. I say, therefore, that the infirmities, which did not only begin, but had already gone far in me, first caused me to leave intemperance, to which I was much addicted; for by it and my ill constitution (having a most cold and moist stomach), I fell into divers diseases, to wit, into the pain of the stomach, and often of the side, and the beginning of the gout, with almost a continual fever and thirst.

From this ill temper there remained little else to be expected of me than that after many troubles and griefs I should quickly come to an end; whereas my life seemed as far from it by nature as it was near it by intemperance. When therefore I was thus affected from the thirty-fifth year of my age to the fortieth, having tried all remedies fruitlessly, the physicians told me that

1. Luigi Cornaro (1468–1566). His treatise was written at the age of eighty-three, fifteen years before his death. Herbert abridges a Latin translation of the original Italian.

yet there was one help for me, if I could constantly pursue it, to wit, *a sober and orderly life*; for this had every way great force for the recovering and preserving of health, as a disorderly life to the overthrowing of it, as I too well by experience found. For temperance preserves even old men and sickly men sound, but intemperance destroys most healthy and flourishing constitutions, for contrary causes have contrary effects, and the faults of nature are often amended by art, as barren grounds are made fruitful by good husbandry. They added withal that unless I speedily used that remedy, within a few months I should be driven to that exigent, that there would be no help for me but death shortly to be expected.

Upon this, weighing their reasons with myself, and abhorring from so sudden an end, and finding myself continually oppressed with pain and sickness, I grew fully persuaded that all my griefs arose out of intemperance; and therefore, out of a hope of avoiding death and pain, I resolved to live a temperate life.

Whereupon, being directed by them in the way I ought to hold, I understood that the food I was to use was such as belonged to sickly constitutions, and that in a small quantity. This they had told me before; but I, then not liking that kind of diet, followed my appetite, and did eat meats pleasing to my taste; and when I felt inward heats, drank delightful wines, and that in great quantity, telling my physicians nothing thereof, as is the custom of sick people. But after I had resolved to follow temperance and reason, and saw that it was no hard thing to do so, but the proper duty of man, I so addicted myself to this course of life that I never went a foot out of the way. Upon this I found, within a few days, that I was exceedingly helped, and by continuance thereof, within less than one year (although it may seem to some incredible), I was perfectly cured of all my infirmities.

Being now sound and well, I began to consider the force of temperance, and to think thus with myself: If *temperance* had so much power as to bring me to health, how much more to preserve it! Wherefore I began to search out most diligently what meats were agreeable unto me, and what disagreeable; and I purposed to try whether those that pleased my taste brought me commodity or discommodity; and whether that proverb, wherewith gluttons used to defend themselves, to wit – *That which savours, is good and nourisheth* – be consonant to truth. This upon trial I found most false; for strong and very cool wines pleased my taste best, as also melons and other fruit; in like manner raw lettuce, fish, pork, sausages, pulse, and cake and piecrust, and the like; and yet all these I found hurtful.

Therefore, trusting on experience, I forsook all these kind of meats and drinks, and chose that wine that fitted my stomach, and in such measure as easily might be digested – above all, taking care never to rise with a full stomach, but so as I might well both eat and drink more. By this means, within less than a year, I was not only freed from all those evils which had so long beset me, and were almost become incurable; but also afterwards I fell not into that yearly disease, whereunto I was wont, when I pleased my sense and appetite: which benefits also still continue, because from that time that I was made whole, I never since departed from my settled course of *sobriety*, whose admirable power causeth that the meat and drink that is taken in fit measure gives true strength to the body, all superfluities passing away without difficulty, and no ill humours being engendered in the body.

Yet with this diet I avoided other hurtful things also, as too much heat and cold, weariness, watching, ill air, overmuch use of the benefit of marriage. For although the power of health consists most in the proportion of meat and drink, yet these forenamed things have also their force. I preserved me also, as much as I could, from hatred and melancholy, and other perturbations of the mind, which have a great power over our constitutions. Yet could I not so avoid all these, but that now and then I fell into them, which gained me this experience, that I perceived that they had no great power to hurt those bodies which were kept in good order by a moderate diet; so that I can truly say that they who in these two things that enter in at the mouth keep a fit proportion, shall receive little hurt from other excesses.

This *Galen* confirms when he says that immoderate heats and colds, and winds and labours, did little hurt him, because in his meats and drinks he kept a due moderation, and therefore never was sick by any of these inconveniences, except it were for one only day. But mine own experience confirmeth this more, as all that know me can testify; for having endured many heats and colds, and other like discommodities of the body and troubles of the mind, all these did hurt me little, whereas they hurt them very much who live intemperately. For when my brother and others of my kindred saw some great powerful men pick quarrels against me, fearing lest I should be overthrown, they were possessed with a deep melancholy (a thing usual to disorderly lives), which increased so much in them, that it brought them to a sudden end; but I, whom that matter ought to have affected most, received no inconvenience thereby, because that humour abounded not in me.

Nay, I began to persuade myself that this suit and contention was raised by the divine Providence, that I might know what great power a sober and temperate life hath over our bodies and minds, and that at length I should be a conqueror, as also a little after it came to pass; for in the end I got the victory, to my great honour and no less profit; whereupon also I joyed exceedingly, which excess of joy neither could do me any hurt; by which it is manifest that neither melancholy nor any other passion can hurt a temperate life.

Moreover, I say, that even bruises, and squats, and falls, which often kill others, can bring little grief or hurt to those that are temperate. This I found by experience when I was seventy years old; for, riding in a coach in great haste, it happened that the coach was overturned, and then was dragged for a good space by the fury of the horses, whereby my head and whole body was sore hurt, and also one of my arms and legs put out of joint. Being carried home, when the physicians saw in what case I was, they concluded that I would die within three days; nevertheless, at a venture, two remedies might be used – letting of blood and purging, that the store of humours and inflammation and fever (which was certainly expected) might be hindered.

But I, considering what an ordinary life I had led for many years together, which must needs so temper the humours of the body that they could not much be troubled or make a great concourse, refused both remedies, and only commanded that my arm and leg should be set, and my whole body anointed with oil;

and so without other remedy or inconvenience I recovered, which seemed as a miracle to the physicians; whence I conclude that they that live a temperate life can receive little hurt from other inconveniences.

But my experience taught me another thing also, to wit, that an orderly and regular life can hardly be altered without exceeding great danger.

About four years since I was led, by the advice of physicians and the daily importunity of my friends, to add something to my usual stint and measure. Divers reasons they brought, as, that old age could not be sustained with so little meat and drink, which yet needs not only to be sustained, but also to gather strength, which could not be but by meat and drink. On the other side, I argued that nature was contented with a little, and that I had for many years continued in good health with that little measure; that custom was turned into nature, and therefore it was agreeable to reason, that my years increasing and strength decreasing, my stint of meat and drink should be diminished rather than increased, that the patient might be proportionable to the agent, and especially since the power of my stomach every day decreased. To this agreed two Italian proverbs, the one whereof was, *He that will eat much, let him eat little*; because by eating little he prolongs his life;[1] the other proverb was, *The meat which remaineth profits more than that which is eaten*,[2] by which is intimated that the hurt of too much meat is greater than the commodity of meat taken in a moderate proportion.

But all these things could not defend me against their importunities. Therefore, to avoid obstinacy and gratify my friends, at length I yielded, and permitted the quantity of meat to be increased, yet but two ounces only; for, whereas before, the measure of my whole day's meat, viz., of my bread, and eggs, and flesh, and broth, was twelve ounces exactly weighed, I increased it to the quantity of two ounces more; and the measure of my drink, which before was fourteen ounces, I made now sixteen.

1. Mangierà più chi manco mangia. Ed e' contrario, Chi più mangia, manco mangia. Il senso è, Poco vive chi troppo sparechia.
2. Fa più pro quel' che si lascia sul' tondo, che Quel' che si mette nel ventre.

This addition, after ten days, wrought so much upon me, that of a cheerful and merry man I became melancholy and choleric, so that all things were troublesome to me; neither did I know well what I did or said. On the twelfth day a pain of the side took me, which held me two and twenty hours. Upon the neck of it came a terrible fever, which continued thirty-five days and nights, although after the fifteenth day it grew less and less; besides all this I could not sleep – no, not a quarter of an hour – whereupon all gave me for dead.

Nevertheless, I, by the grace of God, cured myself only with returning to my former course of diet, although I was now seventy-eight years old, and my body spent with extreme leanness, and the season of the year was winter and most cold air; and I am confident that, under God, nothing holp me but that exact rule which I had so long continued, in all which time I felt no grief, save now and then a little indisposition for a day or two.

For the temperance of so many years spent all ill humours, and suffered not any new of that kind to arise, neither the good humours to be corrupted or contract any ill quality, as usually happens in old men's bodies which live without rule; for there is no malignity of old age in the humours of my body which commonly kills men; and that new one which I contracted by breaking my diet, although it was a sore evil, yet had no power to kill me.

By this it may clearly be perceived how great is the power of order and disorder; whereof the one kept me well for many years, the other, though it was but a little excess, in a few days had so soon overthrown me. If the world consist of order, if our corporal life depend on the harmony of humours and elements, it is no wonder that order should preserve and disorder destroy. Order makes arts easy and armies victorious, and retains and confirms kingdoms, cities, and families in peace. Whence I conclude that an orderly life is the most sure way and ground of health and long days, and the true and only medicine of many diseases.

Neither can any man deny this who will narrowly consider it. Hence it comes that a physician, when he cometh to visit his patient, prescribes this physic first, that he use a moderate diet; and when he hath cured him commends this also to him, if he will live in health. Neither is it to be doubted but that he shall ever after live free from diseases if he will keep such a course of life, because this will cut off all causes of diseases, so that he shall need neither physic nor physician; yea, if he will give his mind to those things which he should, he will prove himself a physician, and that a very complete one, for indeed no man can be a perfect physician to another, but to himself only. The reason whereof is this: every one by long experience may know the qualities of his own nature, and what hidden properties it hath, what meat and drink agrees best with it, which things in others cannot be known without such observation as is not easily to be made upon others, especially since there is a greater diversity of tempers than of faces. Who would believe that old wine should hurt my stomach and new should help it, or that cinnamon should heat me more than pepper? What physician could have discovered these hidden qualities to me if I had not found them out by long experience? Wherefore one to another cannot be a perfect physician. Whereupon I conclude, since none can have a better physician than himself, nor better physic than a temperate life, temperance by all means is to be embraced.

Nevertheless, I deny not but that physicians are necessary, and greatly to be esteemed for the knowing and curing of diseases into which they often fall who live disorderly; for if a friend who visits thee in thy sickness, and only comforts and condoles, doth perform an acceptable thing to thee, how much more dearly should a physician be esteemed, who not only as a friend doth visit thee but help thee!

But that a man may preserve himself in health I advise that, instead of a physician, a regular life is to be embraced, which, as is manifest by experience, is a natural physic most agreeable to us, and also doth preserve even ill tempers in good health, and procure that they prolong their life even to a hundred years and more, and that at length they shut up their days like a lamp, only by pure consumption of the radical moisture, without grief or perturbation of humours. Many have thought that this could be done by *aurum potabile*, or the *Philosopher's Stone*, sought of many and found of few; but surely there is no such matter if temperance be wanting.

But sensual men (as most are), desiring to satisfy their appetite and pamper their belly, although they see themselves ill handled by their intemperance, yet shun a sober life, because they say it is better to please the appetite (though they live ten years less than otherwise they should do) than always to live under bit and bridle. But they consider not of how great moment ten years are in mature age, wherein wisdom and all kind of virtues is most vigorous; which, but in that age, can hardly be perfected. And that I may say nothing of other things, are not almost all the learned books that we have, written by their authors in that age, and those ten years which they set at nought in regard of their belly?

Besides, these belly-gods say that an orderly life is so hard a thing that it cannot be kept. To this I answer that *Galen* kept it, and held it for the best *physic*; so did *Plato* also, and *Isocrates*, and *Tully*, and many others of the ancients, and in our age *Paul III*, and Cardinal *Bembo*, who therefore lived so long; and among our dukes, *Landus* and *Donatus*, and many others of inferior condition, not only in the city, but also in villages and hamlets.

Wherefore, since many have observed a regular life, both of old times and later years, it is no such thing which may not be performed, especially since in observing it there needs not many and curious things, but only that a man should begin, and by little and little accustom himself unto it.

Neither doth it hinder, that *Plato* says, that they who are employed in the commonwealth cannot live regularly, because they must often endure heats, and colds, and winds, and showers, and divers labours which suit not with an orderly life; for I answer that those inconveniences are of no great moment (as I showed before) if a man be temperate in meat and drink, which is both easy for commonweal's-men and very convenient, both that they may preserve themselves from diseases which hinder public employment, as also that their mind, in all things wherein they deal, may be more lively and vigorous.

But some may say he which lives a regular life, eating always light meat and in a little quantity, what diet shall he use in diseases, which being in health he hath anticipated? I answer, first, nature, which endeavours to preserve a man as much as she can, teacheth us how to govern ourselves in sickness; for suddenly it takes away our appetite, so that we can eat but a very little, wherewith she is very well contented, so that a sick man, whether he hath lived heretofore orderly or disorderly, when he is sick ought not to eat but such meats as are agreeable to his disease, and that in much smaller quantity than when he was well. For if he should keep his former proportion, nature, which is already burdened with a disease, would be wholly oppressed. Secondly, I answer better, that he which lives a temperate life cannot fall into diseases, and but very seldom into indispositions, because temperance takes away the cause of diseases, and the cause being taken away there is no place for the effect.

Wherefore, since an orderly life is so profitable, so virtuous, so decent, and so holy, it is worthy by all means to be embraced, especially since it is easy and most agreeable to the nature of man. No man that follows it is bound to eat and drink so little as I; no man is forbidden to eat fruit or fish, which I eat not, for I eat little because a little sufficeth my weak stomach, and I abstain from fruit, and fish, and the like, because they hurt me. But they who find benefit in these meats may, yea, ought to use them; yet all must needs take heed lest they take a greater quantity of any meat or drink (though most agreeable to them) than their stomach can easily digest, so that he which is offended with no kind of meat and drink hath the *quantity* and not the *quality* for his rule, which is very easy to be observed.

Let no man here object unto me, that there are many who, though they live disorderly, yet continue in health to their lives' end; because, since this is at the best but uncertain, dangerous, and very rare, the presuming upon it ought not to lead us to a disorderly life.

It is not the part of a wise man to expose himself to so many dangers of diseases and death, only upon a hope of a happy issue, which yet befalls very few. An old man of an ill constitution, but living orderly, is more sure of life than the most strong young man who lives disorderly.

But some, too much given to appetite, object that a long life is no such desirable thing, because that after one is once sixty-five years old, all the time we live after is rather death than life; but these err greatly, as I will show by myself, recounting the delights and pleasures in this age of eighty-three, which now I take, and which are such as that men generally account me happy.

I am continually in health, and I am so nimble that I can easily get on horseback without the advantage of the ground, and sometimes I go up high stairs and hills on foot. Then I am ever cheerful, merry, and well contented, free from all troubles and troublesome thoughts, in whose place joy and peace have taken up their standing in my heart. I am not weary of life, which I pass with great delight. I confer often with worthy men excelling in wit, learning, behaviour, and other virtues. When I cannot have their company, I give myself to the reading of some learned book, and afterwards to writing; making it my aim in all things how I may help others to the furthest of my power.

All these things I do at my ease, and at fit seasons, and in mine own houses; which, besides that they are in the fairest place of this learned city of Padua, are very beautiful and convenient above most in this age, being so built by me according to the rules of architecture, that they are cool in summer and warm in winter.

I enjoy also my gardens, and those divers parted with rills of running water, which truly is very delightful. Some times of the year I enjoy the pleasure of the Euganean Hills, where also I have fountains and gardens, and a very convenient house. At other times I repair to a village of mine, seated in a valley; which is therefore very pleasant, because many ways thither are so ordered that they all meet and end in a fair plot of ground, in the midst whereof is a church suitable to the condition of the place. This place is washed with the river *Brenta*; on both sides whereof are great and fruitful fields, well manured and adorned with many habitations. In former time it was not so, because the place was moorish and unhealthy, fitter for beasts than men. But I drained the ground, and made the air good; whereupon men flocked thither, and built houses with happy success. By this means the place is come to that perfection we now see it is; so that I can truly say that I have both given God a temple and men to worship him in it, the memory whereof is exceeding delightful to me.

Sometimes I ride to some of the neighbour-cities, that I may enjoy the sight and communication of my friends, as also of excellent artificers in *architecture*, *painting*, *stone-cutting*, *music* and *husbandry*, whereof in this age there is great plenty. I view their pieces, I compare them with those of antiquity, and ever I learn somewhat which is worthy of my knowledge. I survey *palaces*, *gardens*, and *antiquities*, public *fabrics*, *temples*, and *fortifications*; neither omit I anything that may either teach or delight me. I am much pleased also in my travels with the beauty of the situation. Neither is this my pleasure made less by the decaying dulness of my senses, which are all in their perfect vigour, but especially my taste; so that any simple fare is more savoury to me now than heretofore, when I was given to disorder and all the delights that could be.

To change my bed troubles me not; I sleep well and quietly anywhere, and my dreams are fair and pleasant. But this chiefly delights me, that my advice hath taken effect in the reducing of many rude and untoiled places in my country to cultivation and good husbandry. I was one of those that was deputed for the managing of that work, and abode in those fenny places two whole months in the heat of summer (which in *Italy* is very great), receiving not any hurt or inconvenience thereby, so great is the power and efficacy of that *temperance* which ever accompanied me.

These are the delights and solaces of my old age, which is altogether to be preferred before others' youth; because that by *temperance* and the *grace of God* I feel not those perturbations of body and mind wherewith infinite both young and old are afflicted.

Moreover, by this also, in what estate I am, may be discovered, because at these years (viz., eighty-three), I have made a most pleasant comedy, full of honest wit and merriment; which kind of poems useth to be the child of youth, which it most suits withal for variety and pleasantness, as a tragedy with old age, by reason of the sad events which it contains. And if a *Greek poet* of old was praised that at the age of seventy-three years he writ a tragedy,[1] why should I be accounted less happy, or less myself, who being ten years older have made a comedy?

Now, lest there should be any delight wanting to my old age, I daily behold a kind of immortality in the succession of my posterity. For when I come home I find eleven grandchildren of

1. Euripides wrote his last play, *Orestes*, at this age (H).

mine, all the sons of one father and mother, all in perfect health; all as far as I can conjecture very apt and well given both for learning and behaviour. I am delighted with their music and fashion, and I myself also sing often, because I have now a clearer voice than ever I had in my life.

By which it is evident that the life which I live at this age is not a dead, dumpish, and sour life, but cheerful, lively, and pleasant. Neither if I had my wish would I change age and constitution with them who follow their youthful appetites, although they be of a most strong temper; because such are daily exposed to a thousand dangers and deaths, as daily experience showeth, and I also, when I was a young man, too well found. I know how inconsiderate that age is, and, though subject to death, yet continually afraid of it; for death to all young men is a terrible thing, as also to those that live in sin and follow their appetites; whereas I, by the experience of so many years, have learned to give way to reason, whence it seems to me not only a shameful thing to fear that which cannot be avoided; but also I hope, when I shall come to that point, I shall find no little comfort in the favour of Jesus Christ. Yet I am sure that my end is far from me; for I know that (setting casualties aside) I shall not die but by a pure resolution; because that by the regularity of my life I have shut out death all other ways, and that is a fair and desirable death which nature brings by way of resolution.

Since, therefore, a temperate life is so happy and pleasant a thing, what remains but that I should wish all who have the care of themselves to embrace it with open arms?

Many things more might be said in commendation hereof; but lest in anything I forsake that temperance which I have found so good, I here make an end.

# BRIEF NOTES ON
## VALDESSO'S *CONSIDERATIONS*

A copy of a letter written by Mr. George Herbert to his friend
the Translator of this Book.

My dear and deserving brother, – Your *Valdesso*[1] I now
return with many thanks, and some notes, in which,
perhaps, you will discover some care, which I forbear not in the
midst of my griefs; first for your sake, because I would do
nothing negligently that you commit unto me; secondly, for the
author's sake, whom I conceive to have been a true servant of
God, and to such and all that is theirs I owe diligence; thirdly for
the Church's sake, to whom by printing it, I would have you
consecrate it. You owe the Church a debt, and God hath put this
into your hands (as he sent the fish with money to St. Peter) to
discharge it; happily also with this (as his thoughts are fruitful),
intending the honour of his servant the author, who being
obscured in his own country, he would have to flourish in this
land of light and region of the Gospel among his chosen. It is true
there are some things which I like not in him, as my fragments
will express, when you read them; nevertheless I wish you by all
means to publish it, for these three eminent things observable
therein: First, that God in the midst of Popery should open the
eyes of one to understand and express so clearly and excellently
the intent of the Gospel in the acceptation of Christ's righteous-
ness (as he showeth through all his Considerations), a thing
strangely buried and darkened by the adversaries and their
great stumbling-block. Secondly, the great honour and rever-
ence which he everywhere bears towards our dear Master and
Lord, concluding every Consideration almost with his holy

1. Juán de Valdés, or Valdesso (1495–1541), was a Spaniard of great
learning and virtue, who sympathized with those who sought to
introduce the principles of the Reformation into Spain, and, falling
under the suspicion of the Inquisition, was obliged to retire to Naples.
Among his friends were Vittoria Colonna, and Julia Gonzala. They
used to read the Scriptures together on Sunday mornings at Juán's
country house. See further Walton, pp.379ff.

Name, and setting his merit forth so piously; for which I do so love him that, were there nothing else, I would print it, that with it the honour of my Lord might be published. Thirdly, the many pious rules of ordering our life about mortification and observation of God's kingdom within us, and the working thereof, of which he was a very diligent observer. These three things are very eminent in the author, and overweigh the defects, as I conceive, towards the publishing thereof.

Bemerton,
September 29, 1632.

# Brief notes relating to the dubious and offensive places in the following considerations

*To the Third Consideration upon these words: 'Not for thy speech! Other law and other doctrine have we.'*[1]

These words about the H. Scripture suit with what he writes elsewhere, especially Consideration Thirty-two. But I like none of it, for it slights the Scripture too much. Holy Scriptures have not only an elementary use, but a use of perfection and are able to make the man of God perfect. (*II Tim.* 3) And David (though David) studied all the day long in it; and Joshua was to meditate therein day and night. (*Josh.* 1)

*To the Third Consideration upon these words: 'As they also make use of the Scriptures to conserve the health of their minds.'*

All the saints of God may be said in some sense to have put confidence in Scripture; but not as a naked word severed from God, but as the Word of God; and in so doing they do not sever their trust from God. But by trusting in the Word of God, they trust in God. He that trusts in the king's word for anything, trusts in the king.

*To the Fifth Consideration upon these words: 'God regards not how pious or how impious we be.'*

This place, together with many others, as, namely, Consideration Seventy-one upon 'Our Father,' and Consideration Ninety-four upon these words, 'God doth not hold them for good or for evil for that they observe, or not observe,' &c., though it were the author's opinion, yet the truth of it would be examined. See the note upon Consideration Thirty-six.

1. For full citations of the passages in Valdesso, see H, pp. 306–20.

*To the Sixth Consideration on ' Two depravations of man: the one
natural, the other acquisite.'*

The doctrine of the last passage must be warily understood:
First, that it is not to be understood of actual sins, but habitual;
for I can no more free myself from actual sins after baptism, than
I could of original before, and without baptism. The exemption
from both is by the grace of God. Secondly, among habits some
oppose theological virtues, as uncharitableness opposes charity;
infidelity, faith; distrust, hope: of these none can free themselves
of themselves, but only by the grace of God. Other habits oppose
moral virtues, as prodigality opposes moderation, and pusillani-
mity magnanimity. Of these the heathen freed themselves only
by the general providence of God, as Socrates and Aristides, &c.
Where he says 'the inflammation of the natural,' he says aptly, so
it be understood with the former distinction; for *fomes* is not
taken away, but *accensio fomitis*, – the natural concupiscence is
not quite extinguished, but the heat of it assuaged.

*To the Tenth Consideration.*

He often useth this manner of speech, 'believing by revela-
tion, not by relation;' whereby I understand he meaneth only
the effectual operation or illumination of the holy spirit, testify-
ing and applying the revealed truth of the Gospel, and not any
private enthusiasms or revelations: as if he should say, a general
apprehension or assent to the promises of the Gospel by hearsay
or relation from others, is not that which filleth the heart with joy
and peace in believing; but the spirit's bearing witness with
our spirit, revealing and applying the general promises to every
one in particular, with such sincerity and efficacy, that it makes
him godly, righteous, and sober all his life long. This I call
believing by revelation, and not by relation.

*To the Thirty-second Consideration.*

I much mislike the comparison of images and H. Scripture, as
if they were both but alphabets, and after a time to be left. The
H. Scriptures (as I wrote before) have not only an elementary

319

use, but a use of perfection; neither can they ever be exhausted (as pictures may by a plenary circumspection), but still, even to the most learned and perfect in them, there is somewhat to be learned more; therefore David desireth God, in the 119th Psalm, to open his eyes, that he might see the wondrous things of his laws, and that he would make them his study; although, by other words of the same psalm, it is evident that he was not meanly conversant in them. Indeed, he that shall so attend to the bark of the letter as to neglect the consideration of God's work in his heart through the Word, doth amiss – both are to be done: the Scriptures still used, and God's work within us still observed, who works by his Word, and ever in the reading of it. As for that text, 'They shall be all taught of God,' it being Scripture, cannot be spoken to the disparagement of Scripture; but the meaning is this, that God in the days of the Gospel will not give an outward law of ceremonies as of old, but such a one as shall still have the assistance of the holy spirit applying it to our hearts, and ever outrunning the teacher, as it did when Peter taught Cornelius. There the case is plain: Cornelius had revelation, yet Peter was to be sent for; and those that have inspirations must still use Peter – God's Word: if we make another sense of the text, we shall overthrow all means save catechizing, and set up enthusiasms. *In the Scriptures are Doctrines, these ever teach more and more; Promises, these ever comfort more and more. (Rom.* 15: 4.)

### To the Thirty-third Consideration.

The doctrine of this Consideration cleareth that of the precedent; for as the servant leaves not the letter when he hath read it, but keeps it by him and reads it again and again, and the more promise is delayed the more he reads it and fortifies himself with it, so are we to do with the Scriptures, and this is the use of the promises of the Scriptures. But the use of the doctrinal part is more, in regard it presents us not with the same thing only when it is read, as the promises do, but enlightens us with new considerations the more we read it. Much more might be said, but this sufficeth. He himself allows it for a holy conversation and refreshment.

## To the Thirty-sixth Consideration.

All the discourse from this place to the end of the chapter may seem strange, but it is suitable to what the author holds elsewhere; for he maintains that it is faith and infidelity that shall judge us now since the Gospel, and that no other sin or virtue hath anything to do with us: if we believe, no sin shall hurt us; if we believe not, no virtue shall help us. Therefore he saith here we shall not be punished (which word I like here better than chastisement, because even the godly are chastised, but not punished) for evil doing, nor rewarded for well doing or living, for all the point lies in believing or not believing. And with this exposition the chapter is clear enough, but the truth of the doctrine would be examined, however it may pass for his opinion: in the Church of God there is one fundamental, but else variety.

## To the Forty-sixth Consideration.

He meaneth (I suppose) that a man presume not to merit – that is to oblige God – or justify himself before God, by any acts or exercises of religion, but that he ought to pray God affectionately and fervently to send him the light of his Spirit, which may be unto him as the sun to a traveller in his journey, he, in the meanwhile, applying himself to the unquestioned duties of true piety and sincere religion, such as are prayer, fasting, almsdeeds, &c., after the example of devout Cornelius.

## To the Forty-ninth Consideration.

In indifferent things there is room for motions, and expecting of them, but in things good, as to relieve my neighbour, God hath already revealed his will about it; therefore we ought to proceed, except there be a restraining motion (as St. Paul had, when he would have preached in Asia). And I conceive that restraining motions are much more frequent to the godly than inviting motions, because the Scripture invites enough, for it invites us to all good. According to that singular place (*Phil.* 4: 8), a man is to embrace all good; but because he cannot do all, God often chooseth which he shall do, and that by restraining him from what he would not have him do.

*To the same Consideration, &c.*

He means, a man's free will is only outward, not in spiritual things.

*To the same Consideration.*

This doctrine, howsoever it is true in substance, yet it requireth discreet and wary explaining.

*To the Fifty-eighth Consideration.*

By 'occasions' I suppose he meaneth the ordinary or necessary duties and occasions of our calling and condition of life, and not those which are in themselves occasions of sin, such as are all vain conversations; or as these, pious persons ought always to avoid them; but in those other occasions, God's Spirit will mortify and try them as gold in the fire.

*To the Fifty-ninth Consideration.*

To say our Saviour prayed with doubtfulness is more than I can or dare say; but with condition, or conditionally, he prayed as man, though, as God, he knew the event. Fear is given to Christ, but not doubt, and upon good ground.

*To the Sixty-second Consideration.*

This chapter is considerable. The intent of it, that the world pierceth not godly men's actions no more than God's, is in some sort true, because they are spiritually discerned (*I Cor.* 2: 14); so likewise are the godly in some sort exempt from laws, for *Lex iusto non est posita*. But when he enlargeth he goes too far; for, first, concerning Abraham and Sarah, I ever took that for a weakness in the great patriarch; and that the best of God's servants should have weaknesses is no way repugnant to the way of God's Spirit in them, or to the Scriptures, or to themselves, being still men, though godly men. Nay, they are purposely recorded in Holy Writ. Wherefore, as David's adultery cannot be excused, so need not Abraham's equivocation, nor Paul's neither, when he professed himself a Pharisee, which strictly he was not, though in the point of resurrection he agreed with them, and they with him. The reviling also of Ananias seems by his own recalling an oversight; yet I remember the fathers forbid us to judge of the doubtful actions of saints in the Scriptures, which is a modest admonition. But it is one thing not to judge, another to defend them. Secondly, when he useth the word 'jurisdiction,' allowing no jurisdiction over the godly, this cannot stand, and it is ill doctrine in a commonwealth. The godly are punishable as others when they do amiss, and they are to be judged according to the outward fact, unless it be evident to others as well as to themselves that God moved them; for otherwise any malefactor may pretend motions, which is insufferable in a commonwealth. Neither do I doubt but if Abraham had lived in our kingdom under government, and had killed his son Isaac, but he might have been justly put to death for it by the magistrate, unless he could have made it appear that it was done by God's immediate precept. He had done justly, and yet had been punished justly – that is, *In humano foro et secundum præsumptionem legalem* – according to the common and legal proceedings among men. So may a war be just on both sides, and was just in the Canaanites and Israelites both. How the godly are exempt from laws is a known point among divines; but when he says they are equally exempt with God, that is dangerous and too far.

The best salve for the whole chapter is to distinguish judgment. There is a judgment of authority (upon a fact), and there is a judgment of the learned; for as a magistrate judgeth in his tribunal, so a scholar judgeth in his study, and censureth this or that, whence come so many books of several men's opinions: perhaps he meant all of this latter, not of the former. Worldly learned men cannot judge spiritual men's actions; but the magistrate may.

### To the Sixty-third Consideration.

The author doth still discover too slight a regard of the Scripture, as if it were but children's meat, whereas there is not only milk there, *but strong meat also* (*Heb.* 5: 14): *things hard to be understood* (*II Peter* 3: 16); *things needing great consideration* (*Matt.* 24: 15). Besides he opposeth the teaching of the spirit to

the teaching of Scripture which the holy spirit wrote. Although
the holy spirit apply the Scripture, yet, what the Scripture
teacheth the spirit teacheth: the holy spirit, indeed, some time
doubly teaching, both in penning and in applying. I wonder
how this opinion could befall so good a man as it seems Valdesso
was, since the saints of God in all ages have ever held in so
precious esteem the word of God as their joy and crown, and
their treasure on earth. Yet his own practice seems to confute his
opinion; for the most of his considerations, being grounded upon
some text of Scripture, shows that he was continually conversant
in it, and not used it for a time only, and then cast it away, as he
says, strangely.

There is no more to be said of this chapter but that his opinion
of the Scripture is insufferable. As for the text of St. Peter (*II
Peter* 1: 19), which he makes the ground of this Consideration,
building it all upon the word *Until the day-star arise*, it is nothing.
How many places do the fathers bring about *until* against the
heretics who disputed against the virginity of the blessed Virgin,
out of that text *Matt.* 1: 25, where it is said, *Joseph knew her not
until she had brought forth her first-born son* – as if afterwards he had
known her; and, indeed, in common sense, if I bid a man stay in
a place until I come, I do not then bid him go away, but rather
stay longer, that I may speak with him, or do something else
when I do come. So St. Peter, bidding the dispersed Hebrews
attend to the Word till the day dawn, doth not bid them then
cast away the Word, or leave it off; but, however, he would have
them attend to it till that time, and then afterward they will
attend it of themselves without his exhortation. Nay, it is
observable that in that very place he prefers the word before the
sight of the transfiguration of Christ. So that the Word hath the
precedence even of revelation and visions. And so his whole
discourse and sevenfold observation falls to the ground.

### To the Sixty-ninth Consideration.

Divines hold that justifying faith and the faith of miracles are
divers gifts, and of a different nature, the one being *gratia gratis
data*, the other *gratia gratum faciens*, this being given only to the
godly, and the other sometimes to the wicked; yet doubtless the

best faith in us is defective, and arrives not to the point it should, which, if it did, it would do more than it does. And miracle-working, as it may be severed from justifying faith, so it may be a fruit of it, and an exaltation (*I John* 5: 14).

## To the Ninety-fourth Consideration.

By Hebrew piety he meaneth not the very ceremonies of the Jews, which no Christian observes now, but an analogate observation of ecclesiastical and canonical laws superinduced to the Scriptures, like to that of the Jews, which they added to their divine law; this being well weighed will make the Consideration easy and very observable, for at least some of the Papists are come now to what the Pharisees were come to in our Saviour's time.

# The Oration of Master George Herbert

Orator of the University of Cambridge, when the
Ambassadors[1] were made Masters of Arts. 27 Feb. 1622.

Most excellent and most magnificent Lords, – After many singular honours, remarkable commands, most noble ambassages, and other titles most pleasing, as well to us remembering as to you deserving them; we at last salute you Masters of Arts; yea, indeed of all, both courtly, military, academical. The accession of which new title to your Excellencies all the Muses and Graces congratulate; entreating that you would awhile lay aside those warlike looks with which you use to conquer your enemies, and assume more mild and gracious aspects; and we also putting off that countenance and gravity by which we well know how to convince the stern and more austere sort of philosophy, for respect to you, embrace all that is cheerful, joyous, pleasing. For what could have happened more pleasing to us than the access of the officers of the Catholic King? whose exceeding glory is equally round with the world itself; who tying, as with a knot, both Indias to his Spain, knows no limits of his praise; no, not as in past ages, those pillars of Hercules. Long since all we and our whole kingdom exult with joy to be united with that blood which useth to infuse so great and worthy spirits. And that which first deserveth our observation, to the end we might the more by love grow on, both the Spanish and British nation serve and worship James. James is the protecting saint unto us both, that you may well conceive your Excellencies to be more dear unto us, in that you are of the same order and habit, of which we all in this kingdom glory to be. The praises also and virtues of the most renowned Princess Isabel, passing daily our neighbouring sea, wondrously sound through all our coasts and ears. And necessarily must the felicity of so great princes redound also to those servants, in the choice of whom their

1. Don Carlos de Coloma, Spanish ambassador, and Ferdinand, Baron de Boyschot, ambassador of Isabella, Archduchess of Austria and sovereign ruler of Flanders. This may or may not be Herbert's own translation of the Latin oration.

judgment doth even now appear. Wherefore, most excellent, most illustrious Lords, since you are so great both in your princes and yourselves, we justly fear that there is nothing here answerable to the greatness of your presence. For amongst us what glorious show is there, either of garments or of anything else? what splendour? surely, since there is a twofold brightness which dazzleth the eyes of men, we have as much failed as your Excellencies do excel in both. But yet the arts in quietness and silence here are reverenced: here is tranquillity, repose, peace with all but book-worms, perpetual poverty, but when your Excellencies appear. Yet do not ye contemn these our slight glories, which we raise from books and painful industry: how could you be like great Alexander, unless history delivered his actions? Fame is sown in this age, that it may be reaped in the following; let the first be the care of your Excellencies; we for your gracious acceptance of these poor duties wish, and vow unto you of the last a plenteous harvest.

# APPENDIX I

*The order of poems in* W *and* B

Herbert had almost finalized the sequence opening and closing his collection by the time he had compiled *W*. Lines link the same poems (titles may differ). It begins:

| Only in W | W | B | Only in B |
|---|---|---|---|
| | The Dedication———— | The Dedication | |
| | The Church-porch——— | The Church-porch/ Perirrhanterium | |
| | Perirrhanterium————— | Superliminare (st.1) | |
| | Superliminare ———— | Superliminare (st.2) | |
| | The Altar————— | The Altar | |
| | The Sacrifice———— | The Sacrifice | |
| | The Thanks-giving——— | The Thanksgiving | |
| | The Second Thanks-giving ——— | The Reprisal | |
| | The Passion | The Sinner | The Agony |
| | The Passion | Good Friday (part 1) | |
| | Good Friday | Good Friday (part 2) | |
| | The Sinner | Redemption | |
| | Easter———— | Easter (part 1) | |
| | Easter———— | Easter (part 2) | |
| | Easter-wings (1 and 2)——— | Easter-wings (1 and 2) | |
| | H. Baptism (1 and 2)——— | H. Baptism (1 and 2) | |

The sequence ends with a run of seventy-six poems, from *Conscience* (p. 102) to *A Parody* (p. 179), which appear only in *B*, followed by:

| Only in W | W | B | Only in B |
|---|---|---|---|
| | Perfection———— | The Elixir | |
| The Knell Perseverance | | | |
| | | A Wreath | |
| | Death———— | Death | |
| | Dooms-day———— | Doomsday | |
| | Judgement———— | Judgement | |
| | Heaven———— | Heaven | |
| | Love———— | Love (3) | |
| | The Church Militant——— | The Church Militant | |
| | L'Envoy———— | L'Envoy | |

The central section shows much shuffling, settling into congruence towards the end. As in the table above, the same poems are linked with lines when reasonably close to each other; where they are too widely separated in the two manuscripts for linking here, and their titles differ, *B*'s title is also added in brackets on *W*'s list.

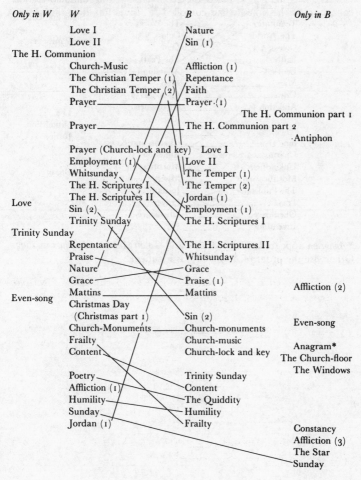

| *Only in W* | *W* | *B* | *Only in B* |
|---|---|---|---|
| | Love I | Nature | |
| | Love II | Sin (1) | |
| The H. Communion | | | |
| | Church-Music | Affliction (1) | |
| | The Christian Temper (1) | Repentance | |
| | The Christian Temper (2) | Faith | |
| | Prayer | Prayer (1) | |
| | | | The H. Communion part 1 |
| | Prayer | The H. Communion part 2 | |
| | | | Antiphon |
| | Prayer (Church-lock and key) | Love I | |
| | Employment (1) | Love II | |
| | Whitsunday | The Temper (1) | |
| | The H. Scriptures I | The Temper (2) | |
| | The H. Scriptures II | Jordan (1) | |
| Love | Sin (2) | Employment (1) | |
| | Trinity Sunday | The H. Scriptures I | |
| Trinity Sunday | | | |
| | Repentance | The H. Scriptures II | |
| | Praise | Whitsunday | |
| | Nature | Grace | |
| | Grace | Praise (1) | |
| Even-song | Mattins | Mattins | Affliction (2) |
| | Christmas Day (Christmas part 1) | Sin (2) | Even-song |
| | Church-Monuments | Church-monuments | |
| | Frailty | Church-music | Anagram* |
| | Content | Church-lock and key | The Church-floor |
| | | | The Windows |
| | Poetry | Trinity Sunday | |
| | Affliction (1) | Content | |
| | Humility | The Quiddity | |
| | Sunday | Humility | |
| | Jordan (1) | Frailty | |
| | | | Constancy |
| | | | Affliction (3) |
| | | | The Star |
| | | Sunday | |

329

| | | |
|---|---|---|
| Denial | | Avarice |
| Ungratefulness | To all Angels and Saints | |
| Employment (2) | Employment (2) | |
| A Wreath | Denial | |
| To all Angels and Saints | Christmas (part 1) | |
| | | Christmas (part 2) |
| | Ungratefulness | |
| The Pearl | | Sighs and Groans |
| Temptation | The World | |
| The World | Coloss. 3.3. | Vanity (1) |
| Coloss. 3.3. | Lent | Virtue |
| Faith | The Pearl | |
| Lent | Affliction (4) | |
| Man | Man | |
| Ode | Antiphon (2) | |
| Affliction (5) | Unkindness | |
| | | Life |
| | | Submission |
| Sin (1) | | Justice (1) |
| Charms and Knots | Charms and Knots | |
| Unkindness | Affliction (5) | |
| Mortification | Mortification | Decay |
| The Publican | Misery | |
| Prayer (2) | Jordan (2) | |
| Obedience | Prayer (2) | |
| Invention | Obedience | |

*Anagram appears between *Avarice* and *To all Angels and Saints* in *1633*. Otherwise the order of *B* and *1633* is identical.

# APPENDIX 2

*Poems found only in* W

## First version of 'H. Baptism (1)', opening lines

When backward on my sins I turn mine eyes
     And then beyond them all my Baptism view
     As he that Heaven beyond much thicket spies
I pass the shades, and fix upon the true
Waters above the Heavens. O sweet streams
     You do prevent most sins and for the rest
     You give us tears to wash them: let those beams
Which then join'd with you still meet in my breast
And mend as rising stars and rivers do.

## Rejected stanzas from 'Whitsunday'

But we are fall'n from Heaven to Earth,
     And if we can stay there, it's well.
     He that first fell from his great birth
Without thy help, leads us his way to Hell.

     Lord once more shake the Heaven and earth
     Lest want of Graces seem thy thrift:
     For sin would fain remove the dearth
And lay it on thy husbandry, for shift.

     Show that thy breasts cannot be dry,
     But that from them joys purle for ever,
     Melt into blessings all the sky,
So we may cease to suck: to praise thee, never.

331

# Rejected stanzas from 'Charms and Knots'

Who turns a trencher, setteth free
A prisoner crusht with gluttony.


The world thinks all things big and tall
Grace turns the Optick, then they fall.


A falling star has lost his place:
The Courtier has it, that has grace.


# Rejected stanzas from 'The Elixir'

(alternative stanza 1, a stanza falling between
stanzas 3 and 4, alternative last stanza)

Lord teach me to refer
All things I do to thee
That I not only may not err
But also pleasing be.


He that does aught for thee,
Marketh that deed for thine:
And when the Devil shakes the tree,
Thou saist, this fruit is mine.


But these are high perfections:
Happy are they that dare
Let in the Light to all their actions
And show them as they are.

# The H. Communion

O gracious Lord, how shall I know
Whether in these gifts thou be so
   As thou art everywhere;
Or rather so, as thou alone
Tak'st all the Lodging, leaving none     5
   For thy poor creature there?


First I am sure, whether bread stay
Or whether Bread do fly away
   Concerneth bread, not me.
But that both thou and all thy train     10
Be there, to thy truth, and my gain,
   Concerneth me and Thee.


And if in coming to thy foes
Thou dost come first to them, that shows
   The haste of thy good will.     15
Or if that thou two stations makest
In Bread and me, the way thou takest
   Is more, but for me still.


Then of this also I am sure
That thou didst all those pains endure     20
   To' abolish Sin, not Wheat.
Creatures are good, and have their place;
Sin only, which did all deface,
   Thou drivest from his seat.


I could believe an Impanation     25
At the rate of an Incarnation,
   If thou hadst died for Bread.
But that which made my soul to die,
My flesh, and fleshly villainy,
   That also made thee dead.     30

That flesh is there, mine eyes deny:
And what should flesh but flesh descry,
   The noblest sense of five?
If glorious bodies pass the sight,
Shall they be food and strength and might    35
   Even there, where they deceive?

Into my soul this cannot pass;
Flesh (though exalted) keeps his grass
   And cannot turn to soul.
Bodies and Minds are different Spheres,    40
Nor can they change their bounds and meres,
   But keep a constant Pole.

This gift of all gifts is the best,
Thy flesh the least that I request.
   Thou took'st that pledge from me:    45
Give me not that I had before,
Or give me that, so I have more;
   My God, give me all Thee.

# Love

Thou art too hard for me in Love:
There is no dealing with thee in that Art:
   That is thy Master-piece I see.
   When I contrive and plot to prove
Something that may be conquest on my part,    5
   Thou still, O Lord, outstrippest me.

   Sometimes, when as I wash, I say,
And shrewdly, as I think, Lord wash my soul
   More spotted than my flesh can be.
   But then there comes into my way    10
Thy ancient baptism, which when I was foul
   And knew it not, yet cleansed me.

I took a time when thou didst sleep,
Great waves of trouble combating my breast:
    I thought it brave to praise thee then,        15
    Yet then I found, that thou didst creep
Into my heart with joy, giving more rest
    Than flesh did lend thee back again.


Let me but once the conquest have
Upon the matter, 'twill thy conquest prove:     20
    If thou subdue mortality,
    Thou do'st no more than doth the grave:
Whereas if I orecome thee and thy Love,
    Hell, Death and Devil come short of me.

# Trinity Sunday

He that is one,
    Is none.
Two reacheth thee
    In some degree.
Nature and Grace        5
With Glory may attain thy Face.
    Steel and a flint strike fire,
        Wit and desire
    Never to thee aspire,
Except life catch and hold those fast.     10
    That which belief
Did not confess in the first Thief
    His fall can tell,
    From Heaven, through Earth, to Hell.
    Let two of those alone     15
        To them that fall,
Who God and Saints and Angels loose at last.
    He that has one,
        Has all.

# Even-song

The Day is spent, and hath his will on me:
   I and the Sun have run our races,
   I went the slower, yet more paces,
     For I decay, not he.

Lord make my Losses up, and set me free:        5
   That I who cannot now by day
   Look on his daring brightness, may
     Shine then more bright than he.

If thou defer this light, then shadow me:
   Lest that the Night, earth's gloomy shade,       10
   Fouling her nest, my earth invade,
     As if shades knew not Thee.

But thou art Light and darkness both together:
   If that be dark we can not see,
   The sun is darker than a Tree,       15
     And thou more dark than either.

Yet Thou art not so dark, since I know this,
   But that my darkness may touch thine,
   And hope, that may teach it to shine,
     Since Light thy Darkness is.       20

O let my Soul, whose keys I must deliver
   Into the hands of senseless Dreams
   Which know not thee, suck in thy beams
     And wake with thee for ever.

# The Knell

   The Bell doth toll:
Lord help thy servant whose perplexed Soul
   Doth wishly look

> On either hand
> And sometimes offers, sometimes makes a stand, 5
> > Struggling on th' hook.

> > Now is the season,
> Now the great combat of our flesh and reason:
> > O help, my God!
> > See, they break in, 10
> Disbanded humours, sorrows, troops of Sin,
> > Each with his rod.

> > Lord make thy Blood
> Convert and colour all the other flood
> > And streams of grief, 15
> > That they may be
> Juleps and Cordials when we call on thee
> > For some relief.

# Perseverance

My God, the poor expressions of my Love
Which warm these lines and serve them up to thee
Are so, as for the present I did move,
> Or rather as thou movedst me.

But what shall issue, whether these my words 5
Shall help another, but my judgment be,
As a burst fowling-piece doth save the birds
> But kill the man, is seal'd with thee.

For who can tell, though thou hast died to win
And wed my soul in glorious paradise, 10
Whether my many crimes and use of sin
> May yet forbid the banes and bliss?

Only my soul hangs on thy promises
With face and hands clinging unto thy breast,
Clinging and crying, crying without cease, 15
> Thou art my rock, thou art my rest.

# APPENDIX 3

## The Life of Mr. George Herbert

### BY IZAAK WALTON[1]

George Herbert was born the third day of April, in the year of our Redemption 1593. The place of his birth was near to the town of Montgomery, and in that castle that did then bear the name of that town and county. That castle was then a place of state and strength, and had been successively happy in the family of the Herberts, who had long possessed it; and with a plentiful estate, and hearts as liberal to their poor neighbours: a family that had been blessed with men of remarkable wisdom, and a willingness to serve their country, and indeed, to do good to all mankind ; for which they were eminent. But, alas! this family did in the late rebellion suffer extremely in their estates; and the heirs of that castle saw it laid level with that earth that was too good to bury those wretches that were the cause of it.

The father of our George was Richard Herbert, the son of Edward Herbert, Knight, the son of Richard Herbert, Knight, the son of the famous Sir Richard Herbert, of Colebrook, in the county of Monmouth, Banneret, who was the youngest brother of that memorable William Herbert, Earl of Pembroke, that lived in the reign of our King Edward IV.

His mother was Magdalen Newport, the youngest daughter of Sir Richard, and sister to Sir Francis Newport, of High Arkall, in the county of Salop, Knight, and grandfather of Francis, Lord Newport, now Comptroller of His Majesty's Household; a family

1. Walton's *Life of Herbert* was first published in 1670. In an Introduction he admits that 'though Mr. George Herbert ... were to me a stranger as to his person, for I have only seen him', yet 'many of his [friends] have been mine'. Although there are many factual inaccuracies in this biography, it is valuable because of its documentary material (ten of Herbert's seventeen extant letters were first published by Walton), anecdotal vitality, and proximity to its subject. For critical assessments, see Select Bibliography, p. lxi.

that for their loyalty have suffered much in their estates, and seen the ruin of that excellent structure where their ancestors have long lived and been memorable for their hospitality.

This mother of George Herbert (of whose person, wisdom, and virtue I intend to give a true account in a seasonable place) was the happy mother of seven sons and three daughters, which she would often say was Job's number and Job's distribution; and as often bless God that they were neither defective in their shapes or in their reason, and very often reprove them that did not praise God for so great a blessing. I shall give the reader a short account of their names, and not say much of their fortunes.

Edward, the eldest, was first made Knight of the Bath at that glorious time of our late Prince Henry's being installed Knight of the Garter, and after many years' useful travel, and the attainment of many languages, he was by King James sent Ambassador resident to the then French King Louis XIII. There he continued about two years; but he could not subject himself to a compliance with the humours of the Duke de Luines, who was then the great and powerful favourite at Court, so that, upon a complaint to our King, he was called back into England in some displeasure; but at his return he gave such an honourable account of his employment, and so justified his comportment to the Duke, and all the Court, that he was suddenly sent back upon the same embassy, from which he returned in the beginning of the reign of our good King Charles I, who made him first Baron of Castle Island, and not long after of Cherbury, in the county of Salop. He was a man of great learning and reason, as appears by his printed book *De Veritate*, and by his *History of the Reign of King Henry VIII*, and by several other tracts.

The second and third brothers were Richard and William, who ventured their lives to purchase honour in the wars of the Low Countries, and died officers in that employment. Charles was the fourth, and died Fellow of New College, in Oxford. Henry was the sixth, who became a menial servant to the Crown, in the days of King James, and continued to be so for fifty years, during all which time he hath been Master of the Revels, a place that requires a diligent wisdom, with which God hath blessed him. The seventh son was Thomas, who, being made captain of a ship in that fleet with which Sir Robert

Mansell was sent against Algiers, did there show a fortunate and true English valour. Of the three sisters I need not say more than that they were all married to persons of worth and plentiful fortunes, and lived to be examples of virtue, and to do good in their generations.

I now come to give my intended account of George, who was the fifth of those seven brothers.

George Herbert spent much of his childhood in a sweet content under the eye and care of his prudent mother, and the tuition of a chaplain or tutor to him, and two of his brothers, in her own family (for she was then a widow), where he continued till about the age of twelve years; and being at that time well instructed in the rules of grammar, he was not long after commended to the care of Dr. Neale, who was then Dean of Westminster, and by him to the care of Mr. Ireland, who was then chief master of that school; where the beauties of his pretty behaviour and wit shined and became so eminent and lovely in this his innocent age, that he seemed to be marked out for piety, and to become the care of Heaven, and of a particular good angel to guard and guide him. And thus he continued in that school till he came to be perfect in the learned languages, and especially in the Greek tongue, in which he after proved an excellent critic.

About the age of fifteen (he being then a King's scholar) he was elected out of that school for Trinity College in Cambridge, to which place he was transplanted about the year 1608; and his prudent mother, well knowing that he might easily lose or lessen that virtue and innocence which her advice and example had planted in his mind, did therefore procure the generous and liberal Dr. Nevil, who was then Dean of Canterbury, and Master of that college, to take him into his particular care, and provide him a tutor; which he did most gladly undertake; for he knew the excellences of his mother, and how to value such a friendship.

This was the method of his education, till he was settled in Cambridge, where we will leave him in his study till I have paid my promised account of his excellent mother, and I will endeavour to make it short.

I have told her birth, her marriage, and the number of her children, and have given some short account of them. I shall next tell the reader that her husband died when our George was about the age of four years. I am next to tell that she continued twelve years a widow; that she then married happily to a noble gentleman, the brother and heir of the Lord Danvers, Earl of Danby, who did highly value both her person and the most excellent endowments of her mind.

In this time of her widowhood, she being desirous to give Edward, her eldest son, such advantages of learning and other education as might suit his birth and fortune, and thereby make him the more fit for the service of his country, did, at his being of a fit age, remove from Montgomery Castle with him and some of her younger sons to Oxford; and having entered Edward into Queen's College, and provided him a fit tutor, she commended him to his care; yet she continued there with him, and still kept him in a moderate awe of herself, and so much under her own eye as to see and converse with him daily; but she managed this power over him without any such rigid sourness as might make her company a torment to her child; but with such a sweetness and compliance with the recreations and pleasures of youth, as did incline him willingly to spend much of his time in the company of his dear and careful mother; which was to her great content; for she would often say, 'That as our bodies take a nourishment suitable to the meat on which we feed, so our souls do as insensibly take in vice by the example or conversation with wicked company'. And would therefore as often say, 'That ignorance of vice was the best preservation of virtue; and that the very knowledge of wickedness was as tinder to inflame and kindle sin, and to keep it burning'. For these reasons she endeared him to her own company, and continued with him in Oxford four years; in which time her great and harmless wit, her cheerful gravity, and her obliging behaviour, gained her an acquaintance and friendship with most of any eminent worth or learning that were at that time in or near that university; and particularly with Mr. John Donne, who then came accidentally to that place in this time of her being there. It was that John Donne who was after Dr. Donne, and Dean of St. Paul's, London; and he, at his leaving Oxford, writ and left there in verse a character of the beauties of her body and mind. Of the first he says:

> No spring nor summer beauty has such grace
> As I have seen in an autumnal face.

Of the latter, he says:

> In all her words, to every hearer fit,
> You may at revels or at council sit.

The rest of her character may be read in his printed poems, in that elegy which bears the name of *The Autumnal Beauty*. For both he and she were then past the meridian of man's life.

This amity, begun at this time and place, was not an amity that polluted their souls, but an amity made up of a chain of suitable inclinations and virtues – an amity like that of St. Chrysostom's to his dear and virtuous Olympias, whom, in his letters, he calls his saint; or an amity, indeed, more like that of St. Hierome to his Paula, whose affection to her was such that he turned poet in his old age, and then made her epitaph: wishing all his body were turned into tongues, that he might declare her just praises to posterity. And this amity betwixt her and Mr. Donne was begun in a happy time for him, he being then near to the fortieth year of his age, which was some years before he entered into sacred orders – a time when his necessities needed a daily supply for the support of his wife, seven children, and a family; and in time she proved one of his most bountiful benefactors, and he as grateful an acknowledger of it. You may take one testimony for what I have said of these two worthy persons from this following letter and sonnet:

Madam,

Your favours to me are everywhere; I use them, and have them. I enjoy them at London, and leave them there; and yet find them at Micham. Such riddles as these become things inexpressible, and such is your goodness. I was almost sorry to find your servant here this day, because I was loth to have any witness of my not coming home last night, and indeed of my coming this morning; but my not coming was excusable, because earnest business detained me; and my coming this day is by the example of your St. Mary Magdalen, who rose early upon Sunday to seek that which she loved most; and so did I. And, from her and myself, I return such thanks as are due to one whom we owe all the good opinion that they whom we need most have of us. By this messenger, and on this good day, I commit the enclosed holy hymns and sonnets (which for the matter, not the workmanship, have yet escaped the fire) to your judgment, and to your protection too, if you think them worthy of it; and I have appointed this enclosed sonnet to usher them to your happy hand.

Your unworthiest servant,

Unless your accepting him to be so have mended him,

Jo. Donne.

Micham, July 11, 1607.

## To the Lady Magdalen Herbert, of St. Mary Magdalen.

Her of your name, whose fair inheritance
    Bethina was, and jointure Magdalo,
An active faith so highly did advance,
    That she once knew more than the Church did know, –
The resurrection; so much good there is
    Delivered of her, that some fathers be
Loth to believe one woman could do this,
    But think these Magdalens were two or three.
Increase their number, lady, and their fame:
    To their devotion add your innocence;
Take so much th' example as of the name;
    The latter half; and in some recompense
That they did harbour Christ Himself a guest,
Harbour these hymns to His dear name addrest.

J. D.

These hymns are now lost to us; but doubtless they were such as they two now sing in heaven.

There might be more demonstrations of the friendship and the many sacred endearments betwixt these two excellent persons (for I have many of their letters in my hand), and much more might be said of her great prudence and piety; but my design was not to write hers, but the life of her son, and therefore I shall only tell my reader that about that very day twenty years that this letter was dated, and sent her, I saw and heard this Mr. John Donne (who was then Dean of St. Paul's) weep, and preach her funeral sermon in the parish church of Chelsey, near London,

343

where she now rests in her quiet grave, and where we must now leave her, and return to her son George, whom we left in his study in Cambridge.

And in Cambridge we may find our George Herbert's behaviour to be such that we may conclude he consecrated the first-fruits of his early age to virtue and a serious study of learning. And that he did so, this following letter and sonnet, which were in the first year of his going to Cambridge, sent his dear mother for a New Year's gift, may appear to be some testimony:

————But I fear the heat of my late ague hath dried up those springs by which scholars say the Muses use to take up their habitations. However, I need not their help to reprove the vanity of those many love poems that are daily writ and consecrated to Venus, nor to bewail that so few are writ that look towards God and heaven. For my own part, my meaning, dear mother, is in these sonnets to declare my resolution to be that my poor abilities in poetry shall be all and ever consecrated to God's glory; and I beg you to receive this as one testimony:

My God, where is that ancient heat towards thee,
　　Wherewith whole shoals of martyrs once did burn,
Besides their other flames? Doth Poetry
　　Wear Venus' livery? only serve her turn?
Why are not sonnets made of thee, and lays
　　Upon thine altar burnt? Cannot thy love
Heighten a spirit to sound out thy praise
　　As well as any she? Cannot thy dove
Outstrip their Cupid easily in flight?
　　Or, since thy ways are deep, and still the same,
　　Will not a verse run smooth that bears thy name?
Why doth that fire, which by thy power and might
　　Each breast does feel, no braver fuel choose
　　Than that which one day worms may chance refuse?

Sure, Lord, there is enough in thee to dry
　　Oceans of ink; for, as the Deluge did
Cover the earth, so doth thy majesty;
　　Each cloud distils thy praise, and doth forbid

344

Poets to turn it to another use.
   Roses and lilies speak thee; and to make
A pair of cheeks of them is thy abuse:
   Why should I women's eyes for crystal take?
Such poor invention burns in their low mind,
   Whose fire is wild, and doth not upward go
   To praise, and on thee, Lord, some ink bestow.
Open the bones, and you shall nothing find
   In the best face but filth; when, Lord, in thee
   The beauty lies in the discovery.

G. H.

This was his resolution at the sending this letter to his dear mother, about which time he was in the seventeenth year of his age; and as he grew older, so he grew in learning, and more and more in favour both with God and man – insomuch, that in this morning of that short day of his life, he seemed to be marked out for virtue, and to become the care of Heaven; for God still kept his soul in so holy a frame, that he may and ought to be a pattern of virtue to all posterity, and especially to his brethren of the clergy, of which the reader may expect a more exact account in what will follow.

I need not declare that he was a strict student, because, that he was so, there will be many testimonies in the future part of his life. I shall therefore only tell that he was made Bachelor of Arts in the year 1611; Major Fellow of the College, March 15th, 1615; and that in that year he was also made Master of Arts, he being then in the twenty-second year of his age; during all which time all, or the greatest diversion from his study, was the practice of music, in which he became a great master, and of which he would say, that it did relieve his drooping spirits, compose his distracted thoughts, and raised his weary soul so far above the earth, that it gave him an earnest of the joys of heaven before he possessed them. And it may be noted, that from his first entrance into the college, the generous Dr. Nevil was a cherisher of his studies, and such a lover of his person, his behaviour, and the excellent endowments of his mind, that he took him often into his own company, by which he confirmed his native gentleness; and if during this time he expressed any error, it was that he kept himself too much retired, and at too great a distance with all his inferiors; and his clothes seemed to prove that he put too great a value on his parts and parentage.

This may be some account of his disposition, and of the employment of his time, till he was Master of Arts, which was anno 1615; and in the year 1619 he was chosen Orator for the university. His two precedent Orators were Sir Robert Naunton and Sir Francis Nethersole. The first was not long after made Secretary of State; and Sir Francis, not very long after his being orator, was made secretary to the Lady Elizabeth, Queen of Bohemia. In this place of orator our George Herbert continued eight years, and managed it with as becoming and grave a gaiety as any had ever before or since his time. For he had acquired great learning, and was blest with a high fancy, a civil and sharp wit, and with a natural elegance, both in his behaviour, his tongue, and his pen. Of all which there might be very many particular evidences, but I will limit myself to the mention of but three.

And the first notable occasion of showing his fitness for this employment of orator was manifested in a letter to King James upon the occasion of his sending that university his book, called *Basilicon Doron*; and their orator was to acknowledge this great honour, and return their gratitude to his Majesty for such a condescension, at the close of which letter he writ,

> Quid Vaticanam Bodleianamque objicis, hospes!
> Unicus est nobis Bibliotheca Liber.

This letter was writ in such excellent Latin, was so full of conceits, and all the expressions so suited to the genius of the King, that he inquired the orator's name, and then asked William, Earl of Pembroke, if he knew him; whose answer was, that he knew him very well, and that he was his kinsman; but he loved him more for his learning and virtue, than for that he was of his name and family. At which answer the King smiled, and asked the Earl leave that he might love him too; for he took him to be the jewel of that university.

The next occasion he had and took to show his great abilities was with them to show also his great affection to that Church in which he received his baptism, and of which he professed himself a member; and the occasion was this: There was one Andrew Melvin, a minister of the Scotch Church, and Rector of St. Andrew's, who, by a long and constant converse with a discontented part of that clergy which opposed episcopacy, became at last to be a chief leader of that faction; and had proudly appeared to be so to King James, when he was but King of that nation; who, the second year after his coronation in England, convened a part of the bishops and other learned divines of his Church, to attend him at Hampton Court, in order to a friendly conference with some dissenting brethren, both of this and the Church of Scotland; of which Scotch party Andrew Melvin was one; and he being a man of learning, and inclined to satirical poetry, had scattered many malicious bitter verses against our liturgy, our ceremonies, and our Church government; which were by some of that party so magnified for the wit, that they were therefore brought into Westminster School, where Mr. George Herbert then, and often after, made such answers to them, and such reflections on him and his kirk, as might unbeguile any man that was not too deeply pre-engaged in such a quarrel.

But to return to Mr. Melvin at Hampton Court conference: he there appeared to be a man of an unruly wit, of a strange confidence, of so furious a zeal, and of so ungoverned passions, that his insolence to the King and others at this conference lost him both his Rectorship of St. Andrew's and his liberty too. For his former verses and his present reproaches there used against the Church and State caused him to be committed prisoner to the Tower of London, where he remained very angry for three years. At which time of his commitment he found the Lady Arabella an innocent prisoner there; and he pleased himself much in sending the next day after his commitment these two verses to the good lady; which I will underwrite, because they may give the reader a taste of his others, which were like these:

Causa tibi mecum est communis, carceris, Ara-
Bella, tibi causa est, araque sacra mihi.

I shall not trouble my reader with an account of his enlargement from that prison, or his death; but tell him Mr. Herbert's verses were thought so worthy to be preserved, that Dr. Duport, the learned Dean of Peterborough, hath lately collected and caused many of them to be printed, as an honourable memorial of his friend, Mr. George Herbert, and the cause he undertook.

And in order to my third and last observation of his great abilities, it will be needful to declare that about this time King James came very often to hunt at Newmarket and Royston, and was almost as often invited to Cambridge, where his entertainment was comedies suited to his pleasant humour; and where Mr. George Herbert was to welcome him with gratulations and the applauses of an orator, which he always performed so well, that he still grew more into the King's favour, insomuch that he had a particular appointment to attend his Majesty at Royston; where, after a discourse with him, his Majesty declared to his kinsman, the Earl of Pembroke, That he found the orator's learning and wisdom much above his age or wit. The year following, the King appointed to end his progress at Cambridge, and to stay there certain days; at which time he was attended by the great secretary of nature and all learning, Sir Francis Bacon (Lord Verulam), and by the ever-memorable and learned Dr. Andrews, Bishop of Winchester, both which did at that time begin a desired friendship with our orator: upon whom the first put such a value on his judgment, that he usually desired his approbation before he would expose any of his books to be printed, and thought him so worthy of his friendship, that, having translated many of the prophet David's psalms into English verse, he made George Herbert his patron, by a public dedication[1] of them to him, as the best judge of divine poetry. And for the learned bishop, it is observable, that at that time there fell to be a modest debate betwixt them two about

1. Published in 1625. The dedication is: 'To his very good friend, Mr. George Herbert. The pains that it pleased you to take about some of my writings I cannot forget; which did put me in mind to dedicate to you this poor exercise of my sickness. Besides, it being my manner for dedications, to choose those that I hold most fit for the argument, I thought that in respect of divinity and poesy met (whereof the one is the matter, the other the style of this little writing), I could not make better choice. So, with signification of my love and acknowledgment, I ever rest,

Your affectionate friend,

FR. ST. ALBANS.'

predestination and sanctity of life; of both which the orator did, not long after, send the bishop some safe and useful aphorisms, in a long letter, written in Greek; which letter was so remarkable for the language and reason of it, that, after reading it, the bishop put it into his bosom, and did often show it to many scholars, both of this and foreign nations; but did always return it back to the place where he first lodged it, and continued it so near his heart till the last day of his life.

To these I might add the long and entire friendship betwixt him and Sir Henry Wotton, and Dr. Donne, but I have promised to contract myself, and shall therefore only add one testimony to what is also mentioned in the Life of Dr. Donne; namely, that a little before his death he caused many seals to be made, and in them to be engraven the figure of Christ crucified on an anchor (the emblem of hope), and of which Dr. Donne would often say, *crux mihi anchora*. These seals he gave or sent to most of those friends on which he put a value; and, at Mr. Herbert's death, these verses were found wrapped up with that seal which was by the doctor given to him:

> When my dear friend could write no more,
> He gave this seal, and so gave o'er.
>
> When winds and waves rise highest, I am sure,
> This anchor keeps my faith, that me, secure.[1]

1. In his *Life of Donne* (1658), where this episode is first recounted, Walton quotes a fragment of Herbert's Latin verse reply to Donne's gift, and his full English translation, of which the couplets given above appear to be a paraphrase. The poems first appeared in the 1650 edition of Donne's work (*Poems. By J.D.*). According to Donne's editor, Sir H. Grierson, ll. 11–18 are of uncertain authorship:

> Although the Cross could not Christ here detain,
> Though nail'd unto't, but he ascends again,
> Nor yet thy eloquence here keep him still,
> But only while thou speak'st; This Anchor will.
> Nor canst thou be content, unless thou to     5
> This certain Anchor add a Seal, and so
> The Water, and the Earth both unto thee
> Do owe the symbol of their certainty.
> Let the world reel, we and all ours stand sure,
> This holy Cable's of all storms secure.     10

(*footnote continued on next page*)

At the time of being orator, he had learnt to understand the Italian, Spanish, and French tongues very perfectly; hoping that, as his predecessors, so he might in time attain the place of a Secretary of State, he being at that time very high in the King's favour, and not meanly valued and loved by the most eminent and most powerful of the Court nobility. This and the love of a Court conversation, mixed with a laudable ambition to be something more than he then was, drew him often from Cambridge to attend the King wheresoever the Court was, who then gave him a sinecure, which fell into his Majesty's disposal, I think, by the death of the Bishop of St. Asaph. It was the same that Queen Elizabeth had formerly given to her favourite Sir Philip Sidney, and valued to be worth a hundred and twenty pounds per annum. With this and his annuity, and the advantage of his college and of his oratorship, he enjoyed his genteel humour for clothes and Court-like company, and seldom looked towards Cambridge unless the King were there, but then he never failed; and, at other times, left the manage of his orator's place to his learned friend Mr. Herbert Thorndike, who is now prebendary of Westminster.

I may not omit to tell that he had often designed to leave the university, and decline all study, which he thought did impair his health; for he had a body apt to a consumption, and to fevers, and other infirmities, which he judged were increased by his studies; for he would often say, He had too thoughtful a wit; a wit like a penknife in too narrow a sheath, too sharp for his body. But his mother would by no means allow him to leave the university or to travel; and though he inclined very much to both, yet he would by no means satisfy his own desires at so dear

---

*(footnote continued from previous page)*

> When Love being weary made an end
> Of kind Expressions to his friend,
> He writ; when 's hand could write no more,
> He gave the Seal, and so left o're.

How sweet a friend was he, who being griev'd 15
His letters were broke rudely up, believ'd
'Twas more secure in great Love's Common-weal
(Where nothing should be broke) to add a Seal.

a rate as to prove an undutiful son to so affectionate a mother; but did always submit to her wisdom. And what I have now said may partly appear in a copy of verses in his printed poems: it is one of those that bear the title of Affliction; and it appears to be a pious reflection on God's providence, and some passages of his life, in which he says:

> Whereas my birth and spirit rather took
> The way that takes the town;
> Thou didst betray me to a ling'ring book,
> And wrap me in a gown.
> I was entangled in a world of strife,
> Before I had the power to change my life.
>
> Yet, for I threaten'd oft the siege to raise,
> Not simp'ring all mine age,
> Thou often didst with academic praise
> Melt and dissolve my rage.
> I took thy sweeten'd pill, till I came where
> I could not go away, nor persevere.
>
> Yet, lest perchance I should too happy be
> In my unhappiness,
> Turning my purge to food, thou throwest me
> Into more sicknesses.
> Thus doth thy power cross-bias me, not making
> Thine own gifts good, yet me from my ways taking.
>
> Now I am here, what thou wilt do with me
> None of my books will show;
> I read, and sigh, and wish I were a tree;
> For then sure I should grow
> To fruit or shade; at least some bird would trust
> Her household to me, and I should be just.
>
> Yet, though thou troublest me, I must be meek,
> In weakness must be stout.
> Well, I will change the service, and go seek
> Some other master out.

Ah! my dear God, though I am clean forgot,
Let me not love thee, if I love thee not.

G. H.

In this time of Mr. Herbert's attendance and expectation of
some good occasion to remove from Cambridge to Court, God,
in whom there is an unseen change of causes, did, in a short time,
put an end to the lives of two of his most obliging and most
powerful friends, Lodowick, Duke of Richmond, and James,
Marquis of Hamilton; and not long after him, King James died
also, and with them all Mr. Herbert's Court hopes; so that he
presently betook himself to a retreat from London, to a friend in
Kent, where he lived very privately, and was such a lover of
solitariness, as was judged to impair his health more than his
study had done. In this time of retirement, he had many conflicts
with himself, whether he should return to the painted pleasures
of a Court life, or betake himself to a study of divinity, and enter
into sacred orders, to which his dear mother had often persuaded
him. These were such conflicts as they only can know that have
endured them; for ambitious desires, and the outward glory of
this world, are not easily laid aside; but at last God inclined him
to put on a resolution to serve at his altar.

He did at his return to London acquaint a Court friend with
his resolution to enter into sacred orders, who persuaded him to
alter it, as too mean an employment, and too much below his
birth and the excellent abilities and endowments of his mind. To
whom he replied, 'It hath been formerly adjudged that the
domestic servants of the King of heaven should be of the noblest
families on earth; and though the iniquity of the late times have
made clergymen meanly valued, and the sacred name of priest
contemptible, yet I will labour to make it honourable by
consecrating all my learning, and all my poor abilities, to
advance the glory of that God that gave them; knowing that I
can never do too much for him that hath done so much for me as
to make me a Christian. And I will labour to be like my Saviour,
by making humility lovely in the eyes of all men, and by
following the merciful and meek example of my dear Jesus.'

This was then his resolution, and the God of constancy, who
intended him for a great example of virtue, continued him in it;

for within that year he was made deacon, but the day when, or by whom, I cannot learn; but that he was about that time made deacon is most certain; for I find by the records of Lincoln that he was made prebendary of Layton Ecclesia, in the diocese of Lincoln, July 15th, 1626; and that this prebend was given him by John, then lord bishop of that See. And now he had a fit occasion to show that piety and bounty that was derived from his generous mother, and his other memorable ancestors, and the occasion was this:

This Layton Ecclesia is a village near to Spalden, in the county of Huntingdon, and the greatest part of the parish church was fallen down, and that of it which stood was so decayed, so little, and so useless, that the parishioners could not meet to perform their duty to God in public prayer and praises; and thus it had been for almost twenty years, in which time there had been some faint endeavours for a public collection, to enable the parishioners to rebuild it, but with no success, till Mr. Herbert undertook it; and he, by his own and the contribution of many of his kindred, and other noble friends, undertook the re-edification of it, and made it so much his whole business, that he became restless till he saw it finished as it now stands; being for the workmanship a costly mosaic; for the form an exact cross; and for the decency and beauty, I am assured, it is the most remarkable parish church that this nation affords. He lived to see it so wainscoted as to be exceeded by none; and by his order the reading pew and pulpit were a little distant from each other, and both of an equal height; for he would often say, They should neither have a precedency or priority of the other; but that prayer and preaching, being equally useful, might agree like brethren, and have an equal honour and estimation.

Before I proceed further, I must look back to the time of Mr. Herbert's being made prebendary, and tell the reader, that not long after, his mother, being informed of his intentions to rebuild that church, and apprehending the great trouble and charge that he was likely to draw upon himself, his relations, and friends, before it could be finished, sent for him from London to Chelsea (where she then dwelt), and at his coming said, 'George, I sent for you to persuade you to commit simony, by giving your patron as good a gift as he has given you; namely, that you give him back his prebend; for, George, it is not for your weak body and empty purse to undertake to build churches.' Of which he desired he might have a day's time to consider, and then make her an answer; and at his return to her the next day, when he had first desired her blessing, and she given it him, his next request was, That she would, at the age of thirty-three years, allow him to become an undutiful son; for he had made a vow to God that, if he were able, he would rebuild that church. And then showed her such reasons for his resolution that she presently subscribed to be one of his benefactors, and undertook to solicit William, Earl of Pembroke, to become another, who subscribed for fifty pounds; and not long after, by a witty and persuasive letter from Mr. Herbert, made it fifty pounds more. And in this nomination of some of his benefactors, James, Duke of Lennox, and his brother, Sir Henry Herbert, ought to be remembered; as also the bounty of Mr. Nicholas Ferrar and Mr. Arthur Woodnot; the one a gentleman in the neighbourhood of Layton, and the other a goldsmith in Foster Lane, London, ought not to be forgotten, for the memory of such men ought to outlive their lives. Of Mr. Ferrar I shall hereafter give an account in a more seasonable place; but before I proceed further, I will give this short account of Mr. Arthur Woodnot.

He was a man that had considered overgrown estates do often require more care and watchfulness to preserve than get them, and considered that there be many discontents that riches cure not, and did therefore set limits to himself as to the desire of wealth. And having attained so much as to be able to show some mercy to the poor and preserve a competence for himself, he dedicated the remaining part of his life to the service of God, and to be useful for his friends; and he proved to be so to Mr. Herbert, for, beside his own bounty, he collected and returned most of the money that was paid for the rebuilding of that church; he kept all account of the charges, and would often go down to state them, and see all the workmen paid. When I have said that this good man was an useful friend to Mr. Herbert's father and to his mother, and continued to be so to him, till he closed his eyes on his death-bed, I will forbear to say more, till I have the next fair occasion to mention the holy friendship that was betwixt him and Mr. Herbert. From whom Mr. Woodnot carried to his mother this following letter, and delivered it to her in a sickness, which was not long before that which proved to be her last:

### A letter of Mr. George Herbert to his Mother in her Sickness

MADAM,—

At my last parting from you, I was the better content because I was in hope I should myself carry all sickness out of your family; but since I know I did not, and that your share continues, or rather increaseth, I wish earnestly that I were again with you; and would quickly make good my wish, but that my employment does fix me here, it being now but a month to our commencement, wherein my absence by how much it naturally augmenteth suspicion, by so much shall it make my prayers the more constant and the more earnest for you to the God of all consolation. In the meantime, I beseech you to be cheerful, and comfort yourself in the God of all comfort, who is not willing to behold any sorrow but for sin. What hath affliction grievous in it more than for a moment? or why should our afflictions here have so much power or boldness as to oppose the hope of our joys hereafter? Madam, as the earth is but a point in respect of the heavens, so are earthly troubles compared to heavenly joys; therefore, if either age or sickness lead you to those joys, consider what advantage you have over youth and health, who are now so near those true comforts. Your last letter gave me earthly preferment, and I hope kept heavenly for yourself; but would you divide and choose too? Our college customs allow not that; and I should account myself most happy if I might change with you; for I have always observed the thread of life to be like other threads or skeins of silk, full of snarls and incumbrances. Happy is he whose bottom is wound up and laid ready for work in the New Jerusalem. For myself, dear mother, I always feared sickness more than death, because sickness hath made me unable to perform those offices for which I came into the world, and must yet be kept in it; but you are freed from that fear, who have already abundantly discharged that part, having both ordered your family and so brought up your children that they have attained to the years of discretion and competent maintenance.

So that now if they do not well, the fault cannot be charged on you, whose example and care of them will justify you both to the world and your own conscience; insomuch, that whether you turn your thoughts on the life past, or on the joys that are to come, you have strong preservatives against all disquiet. And for temporal afflictions, I beseech you consider all that can happen to you are either afflictions of estate, or body, or mind. For those of estate, of what poor regard ought they to be, since if we had riches, we are commanded to give them away? So that the best use of having them is, having, not to have them. But, perhaps, being above the common people, our credit and estimation call on us to live in a more splendid fashion; but, O God! how easily is that answered, when we consider that the blessings in the Holy Scripture are never given to the rich, but to the poor. I never find *Blessed be the rich*, or *Blessed be the noble*, but *Blessed be the meek*, and *Blessed be the poor*, and *Blessed be the mourners, for they shall be comforted*. And yet, O God! most carry themselves so, as if they not only not desired, but even feared to be blessed. And for afflictions of the body, dear madam, remember the holy martyrs of God, how they have been burnt by thousands, and have endured such other tortures as the very mention of them might beget amazement; but their fiery trials have had an end, and yours (which, praised be God, are less) are not like to continue long. I beseech you, let such thoughts as these moderate your present fear and sorrow; and know that if any of yours should prove a Goliath-like trouble, yet you may say with David, *That God, who delivered me out of the paws of the lion and bear, will also deliver me out of the hands of this uncircumcised Philistine*. Lastly, for those afflictions of the soul: consider that God intends that to be as a sacred temple for himself to dwell in, and will not allow any room there for such an inmate as grief, or allow that any sadness shall be his competitor. And, above all, if any care of future things molest you, remember those admirable words of the Psalmist: *Cast thy care on the Lord, and He shall nourish thee, Psal.* 55: 22. To which join that of St. Peter. *Casting all your care on the Lord, for He careth for you, I Pet.* 5: 7. What an admirable thing is this, that God puts his shoulder to our burden, and entertains our care for us, that we may the more quietly intend his service. To conclude, let me commend only one place more to you

(*Philip.* 4: 4): St. Paul saith there, *Rejoice in the Lord always; and again I say, rejoice.* He doubles it to take away the scruple of those that might say, What, shall we rejoice in affliction? Yes, I say again, rejoice; so that it is not left us to rejoice or not rejoice; but whatsoever befalls us, we must always, at all times, rejoice in the Lord, who taketh care of us. And it follows in the next verse: *Let your moderation appear unto all men: the Lord is at hand: be careful for nothing.* What can be said more comfortably? Trouble not yourselves, God is at hand to deliver us from all, or in all. Dear madam, pardon my boldness, and accept the good meaning of

Your most obedient son,

GEORGE HERBERT.

Trin. Coll. May 29, 1622.

About the year 1629, and the thirty-fourth of his age, Mr. Herbert was seized with a sharp quotidian ague, and thought to remove it by the change of air; to which end he went to Woodford in Essex, but thither more chiefly to enjoy the company of his beloved brother, Sir Henry Herbert, and other friends then of that family. In his house he remained about twelve months, and there became his own physician, and cured himself of his ague by forbearing drink, and not eating any meat, no, not mutton, nor a hen or pigeon, unless they were salted; and by such a constant diet he removed his ague, but with inconveniences that were worse; for he brought upon himself a disposition to rheums and other weaknesses, and a supposed consumption. And it is to be noted that in the sharpest of his extreme fits he would often say, 'Lord, abate my great affliction, or increase my patience; but, Lord, I repine not; I am dumb, Lord, before thee, because thou dost it.' By which, and a sanctified submission to the will of God, he showed he was inclinable to bear the sweet yoke of Christian discipline, both then and in the latter part of his life, of which there will be many true testimonies.

And now his care was to recover from his consumption by a change from Woodford into such an air as was most proper to that end. And his remove was to Dauntsey in Wiltshire, a noble house which stands in a choice air; the owner of it then was the Lord Danvers, Earl of Danby, who loved Mr. Herbert so very much, that he allowed him such an apartment in it as might best suit with his accommodation and liking. And in this place, by a spare diet, declining all perplexing studies, moderate exercise, and a cheerful conversation, his health was apparently improved to a good degree of strength and cheerfulness. And then he declared his resolution both to marry and to enter into the sacred orders of priesthood. These had long been the desire of his mother and other relations; but she lived not to see either, for she died in the year 1627. And though he was disobedient to her about Layton Church, yet in conformity to her will, he kept his Orator's place till after her death, and then presently declined it; and the more willingly that he might be succeeded by his friend Robert Creighton, who now is Dr. Creighton and the worthy Bishop of Wells.

I shall now proceed to his marriage; in order to which it will be convenient that I first give the reader a short view of his person, and then an account of his wife, and of some circumstances concerning both.

He was for his person of a stature inclining towards tallness; his body was very straight, and so far from being cumbered with too much flesh, that he was lean to an extremity. His aspect was cheerful, and his speech and motion did both declare him a gentleman; for they were all so meek and obliging, that they purchased love and respect from all that knew him.

These, and his other visible virtues, begot him much love from a gentleman of a noble fortune, and a near kinsman to his friend the Earl of Danby; namely, from Mr. Charles Danvers of Bainton, in the county of Wilts, Esq.; this Mr. Danvers having known him long and familiarly, did so much affect him, that he often and publicly declared a desire that Mr. Herbert would marry any of his nine daughters (for he had so many), but rather his daughter Jane than any other, because Jane was his beloved daughter. And he had often said the same to Mr. Herbert himself; and that if he could like her for a wife, and she him for a husband, Jane should have a double blessing; and Mr. Danvers had so often said the like to Jane, and so much commended Mr. Herbert to her, that Jane became so much a Platonic as to fall in love with Mr. Herbert unseen.

This was a fair preparation for a marriage; but, alas! her

father died before Mr. Herbert's retirement to Dauntsey; yet some friends to both parties procured their meeting; at which time a mutual affection entered into both their hearts, as a conqueror enters into a surprised city, and love having got such possession, governed and made there such laws and resolutions as neither party was able to resist; insomuch that she changed her name into Herbert the third day after this first interview.

This haste might in others be thought a love frenzy, or worse; but it was not, for they had wooed so like princes as to have select proxies; such as were true friends to both parties; such as well understood Mr. Herbert's and her temper of mind, and also their estates, so well before this interview, that the suddenness was justifiable by the strictest rules of prudence; and the more, because it proved so happy to both parties. For the eternal lover of mankind made them happy in each other's mutual and equal affections and compliance; indeed, so happy, that there never was any opposition betwixt them, unless it were a contest which should most incline to a compliance with the other's desires. And though this begot, and continued in them, such a mutual love, and joy, and content, as was in no way defective; yet this mutual content, and love, and joy, did receive a daily augmentation, by such daily obligingness to each other, as still added new affluences to the former fulness of these divine souls as was only improvable in heaven, where they now enjoy it.

About three months after his marriage, Dr. Curle, who was then rector of Bemerton in Wiltshire, was made Bishop of Bath and Wells, and not long after translated to Winchester, and by that means the presentation of a clerk to Bemerton did not fall to the Earl of Pembroke (who was the undoubted patron of it), but to the King, by reason of Dr. Curle's advancement. But Philip, then Earl of Pembroke (for William was lately dead), requested the King to bestow it on his kinsman, George Herbert; and the King said, 'Most willingly to Mr. Herbert, if it be worth his acceptance.' And the Earl as willingly and suddenly sent it to him without seeking. But though Mr. Herbert had formerly put on a resolution for the clergy, yet, at receiving this presentation, the apprehension of the last great account that he was to make for the cure of so many souls, made him fast and pray often, and consider for not less than a month; in which time he had some resolutions to decline both the priesthood and that living. And in this time of considering, he endured (as he would often say) such spiritual conflicts as none can think, but only those that have endured them.

In the midst of these conflicts, his old and dear friend, Mr. Arthur Woodnot, took a journey to salute him at Bainton (where he then was with his wife's friends and relations), and was joyful to be an eye-witness of his health and happy marriage. And after they had rejoiced together some few days, they took a journey to Wilton, the famous seat of the Earls of Pembroke; at which time the King, the Earl, and the whole Court were there, or at Salisbury, which is near to it. And at this time Mr. Herbert presented his thanks to the Earl for his presentation to Bemerton, but had not yet resolved to accept it, and told him the reason why; but that night the Earl acquainted Dr. Laud, then Bishop of London, and after Archbishop of Canterbury, with his kinsman's irresolution. And the Bishop did the next day so convince Mr. Herbert that the refusal of it was a sin, that a tailor was sent for to come speedily from Salisbury to Wilton to take measure, and make him canonical clothes against next day; which the tailor did; and Mr. Herbert being so habited, went with his presentation to the learned Dr. Davenant, who was then Bishop of Salisbury, and he gave him institution immediately (for Mr. Herbert had been made deacon some years before), and he was also the same day (which was April 26, 1630) inducted into the good and more pleasant than healthful parsonage of Bemerton, which is a mile from Salisbury.

I have now brought him to the parsonage of Bemerton, and to the thirty-sixth year of his age, and must stop here, and bespeak the reader to prepare for an almost incredible story of the great sanctity of the short remainder of his holy life; a life so full of charity, humility, and all Christian virtues, that it deserves the eloquence of St. Chrysostom to commend and declare it; a life, that if it were related by a pen like his, there would then be no need for this age to look back into times past for the examples of primitive piety, for they might be all found in the life of George Herbert. But now, alas! who is fit to undertake it? I confess I am not; and am not pleased with myself that I must; and profess myself amazed when I consider how few of the clergy lived like him then, and how many live so unlike him now. But it becomes not me to censure. My design is rather to assure the reader that I have used very great diligence to inform myself, that I might inform him of the truth of what follows; and though I cannot adorn it with eloquence, yet I will do it with sincerity.

When at his induction he was shut into Bemerton Church, being left there alone to toll the bell (as the law requires him),[1] he stayed so much longer than an ordinary time before he returned to those friends that stayed expecting him at the church door, that his friend Mr. Woodnot looked in at the church window, and saw him lie prostrate on the ground before the altar; at which time and place (as he after told Mr. Woodnot) he set some rules to himself for the future manage of his life, and then and there made a vow to labour to keep them.

And the same night that he had his induction, he said to Mr. Woodnot, 'I now look back upon my aspiring thoughts, and think myself more happy than if I had attained what then I so ambitiously thirsted for; and I can now behold the Court with an impartial eye, and see plainly that it is made up of fraud, and titles, and flattery, and many other such empty, imaginary, painted pleasures – pleasures that are so empty as not to satisfy when they are enjoyed. But in God and his service is a fulness of all joy and pleasure, and no satiety. And I will now use all my endeavours to bring my relations and dependants to a love and reliance on him, who never fails those that trust him. But, above all, I will be sure to live well, because the virtuous life of a clergyman is the most powerful eloquence to persuade all that see it to reverence and love, and at least to desire to live like him. And this I will do, because I know we live in an age that hath more need of good examples than precepts. And I beseech that God, who hath honoured me so much as to call me to serve him at his altar, that as by his special grace he hath put into my heart these good desires and resolutions; so he will, by his assisting grace, give me ghostly strength to bring the same to good effect. And I beseech him that my humble and charitable life may so win upon others as to bring glory to my Jesus, whom I have this day taken to be my Master and Governor; and I am so proud of

1. To make his induction known to the parishioners.

his service, that I will always observe, and obey, and do his will, and always call him Jesus, my Master; and I will always contemn my birth, or any title or dignity that can be conferred upon me, when I shall compare them with my title of being a priest, and serving at the altar of Jesus my Master.'

And that he did so may appear in many parts of his Book of *Sacred Poems*, especially in that which he calls 'The Odour' – in which he seems to rejoice in the thoughts of that word, Jesus, and say, that the adding these words, my Master, to it, and the often repetition of them, seemed to perfume his mind and leave an Oriental fragrancy in his very breath. And for his unforced choice to serve at God's altar, he seems in another place of his poems, 'The Pearl,' (*Matt.* 13: 45, 46) to rejoice, and say, 'he knew the ways of learning; knew what nature does willingly, and what, when it is forced by fire; knew the ways of honour, and when glory inclines the soul to noble expressions; knew the Court; knew the ways of pleasure, of love, of wit, of music, and upon what terms he declined all these for the service of his Master Jesus'; and then concludes, saying,

> That through these labyrinths, not my grovelling wit,
> But thy silk twist, let down from heaven to me,
> Did both conduct and teach me, how by it
> > To climb to thee.

The third day after he was made Rector of Bemerton, and had changed his sword and silk clothes into a canonical coat, he returned so habited with his friend Mr. Woodnot to Bainton; and immediately after he had seen and saluted his wife, he said to her, 'You are now a minister's wife, and must now so far forget your father's house, as not to claim a precedence of any of your parishioners; for you are to know that a priest's wife can challenge no precedence or place but that which she purchases by her obliging humility; and I am sure places so purchased do best become them. And let me tell you that I am so good a herald as to assure you that this is truth.' And she was so meek a wife as to assure him it was no vexing news to her, and that he should see her observe it with a cheerful willingness. And, indeed, her unforced humility – that humility that was in her so original as to be born with her – made her so happy as to do so; and her doing so begot her an unfeigned love and a serviceable respect from all that conversed with her; and this love followed her in all places as inseparably as shadows follow substances in sunshine.

It was not many days before he returned back to Bemerton, to view the church and repair the chancel, and, indeed, to rebuild almost three parts of his house, which was fallen down or decayed by reason of his predecessor's living at a better parsonage house, namely, at Minal, sixteen or twenty miles from this place. At which time of Mr. Herbert's coming alone to Bemerton, there came to him a poor old woman, with an intent to acquaint him with her necessitous condition, as also with some troubles of her mind; but after she had spoke some few words to him, she was surprised with a fear, and that begot a shortness of breath, so that her spirits and speech failed her, which he perceiving, did so compassionate her, and was so humble, that he took her by the hand, and said, 'Speak, good mother; be not afraid to speak to me, for I am a man that will hear you with patience, and will relieve your necessities too if I be able, and this I will do willingly; and therefore, mother, be not afraid to acquaint me with what you desire.' After which comfortable speech he again took her by the hand, made her sit down by him, and understanding she was of his parish, he told her, he would be acquainted with her, and take her into his care. And having with patience heard and understood her wants (and it is some relief for a poor body to be but heard with patience), he, like a Christian clergyman, comforted her by his meek behaviour and counsel; but because that cost him nothing, he relieved her with money too, and so sent her home with a cheerful heart, praising God and praying for him. Thus worthy, and (like David's blessed man) thus lowly, was Mr. George Herbert in his own eyes, and thus lovely in the eyes of others.

At his return that night to his wife in Bainton, he gave her an account of the passages betwixt him and the poor woman, with which she was so affected that she went next day to Salisbury, and there bought a pair of blankets, and sent them as a token of her love to the poor woman, and with a message that she would see and be acquainted with her when her house was built at Bemerton.

There be many such passages both of him and his wife, of

which some few will be related; but I shall first tell that he hasted
to get the parish church repaired; then to beautify the chapel
(which stands near his house), and that at his own great charge.
He then proceeded to rebuild the greatest part of the parsonage
house, which he did also very completely, and at his own charge;
and having done this good work, he caused these verses to be
writ upon, or engraven in, the mantel of the chimney in his hall:

To MY SUCCESSOR.

If thou chance for to find
A new house to thy mind,
    And built without thy cost;
Be good to the poor
As God gives thee store,
    And then my labour's not lost.

We will now, by the reader's favour, suppose him fixed at
Bemerton, and grant him to have seen the church repaired, and
the chapel belonging to it very decently adorned, at his own
great charge (which is a real truth), and having now fixed him
there, I shall proceed to give an account of the rest of his
behaviour both to his parishioners and those many others that
knew and conversed with him.

Doubtless Mr. Herbert had considered and given rules to
himself for his Christian carriage both to God and man before he
entered into holy orders. And it is not unlike but that he renewed
those resolutions at his prostration before the holy altar, at his
induction into the church of Bemerton; but as yet he was but a
deacon, and therefore longed for the next Ember Week, that he
might be ordained priest, and made capable of administering
both the sacraments. At which time the Rev. Dr. Humphrey
Henchman, now Lord Bishop of London (who does not mention
him but with some veneration for his life and excellent learn-
ing?), tells me, he laid his hand on Mr. Herbert's head, and, alas!
within less than three years lent his shoulder to carry his dear
friend to his grave.

And that Mr. Herbert might the better preserve those holy
rules which such a priest as he intended to be ought to observe;
and that time might not insensibly blot them out of his memory,
but that the next year might show him his variations from this
year's resolutions; he therefore did set down his rules, then

resolved upon, in that order as the world now sees them printed in a little book called *The Country Parson*, in which some of his rules are:

| | |
|---|---|
| *The Parson's knowledge.* | *The Parson arguing.* |
| *The Parson on Sundays.* | *The Parson condescending.* |
| *The Parson praying.* | *The Parson in his journey.* |
| *The Parson preaching.* | *The Parson in his mirth.* |
| *The Parson's charity.* | *The Parson with his Churchwardens.* |
| *The Parson comforting the sick.* | *The Parson blessing the people.* |

And his behaviour toward God and man may be said to be a practical comment on these and the other holy rules set down in that useful book; a book so full of plain, prudent, and useful rules, that that country parson, that can spare twelve pence and yet wants it, is scarce excusable; because it will both direct him what he ought to do, and convince him for not having done it.

At the death of Mr. Herbert this book fell into the hands of his friend Mr. Woodnot; and he commended it into the trusty hands of Mr. Barnabas Oley, who published it with a most conscientious and excellent preface; from which I have had some of the truths that are related in this life of Mr. Herbert. The text for his first sermon was taken out of Solomon's Proverbs, and the words were, 'Keep thy heart with all diligence.'[1] In which first sermon he gave his parishioners many necessary, holy, safe rules for the discharge of a good conscience both to God and man, and delivered his sermon after a most florid manner, both with great learning and eloquence. But, at the close of this sermon, told them, That should not be his constant way of preaching; for since Almighty God does not intend to lead men to heaven by hard questions, he would not therefore fill their heads with unnecessary notions; but that for their sakes his language and his expressions should be more plain and practical in his future sermons. And then he made it his humble request, that they would be constant to the afternoon's service and catechizing, and showed them convincing reasons why he desired it; and his obliging example and persuasions brought them to a willing conformity with his desires.

1. *Proverbs* 4: 23.

The texts for all his future sermons (which God knows were not many) were constantly taken out of the Gospel for the day; and he did as constantly declare why the Church did appoint that portion of Scripture to be that day read, and in what manner the collect for every Sunday does refer to the Gospel or to the Epistle then read to them; and, that they might pray with understanding, he did usually take occasion to explain, not only the collect for every particular Sunday, but the reasons of all the other collects and responses in our Church service; and made it appear to them that the whole service of the Church was a reasonable, and therefore an acceptable sacrifice to God; as, namely, that we begin with confession of ourselves to be vile, miserable sinners; and that we begin so because, till we have confessed ourselves to be such, we are not capable of that mercy which we acknowledge we need and pray for; but having, in the prayer of our Lord, begged pardon for those sins which we have confessed, and hoping that as the priest hath declared our absolution, so by our public confession and real repentance we have obtained that pardon; then we dare and do proceed to beg of the Lord to open our lips, that our mouths may show forth his praise; for, till then, we are neither able nor worthy to praise him. But this being supposed, we are then fit to say, 'Glory be to the Father, and to the Son, and to the Holy Ghost'; and fit to proceed to a further service of our God, in the collects, and psalms, and lauds that follow in the service.

And as to these psalms and lauds, he proceeded to inform them why they were so often, and some of them daily, repeated in our Church service, namely, the psalms every month, because they be an historical and thankful repetition of mercies past, and such a composition of prayers and praises as ought to be repeated often and publicly; for with such sacrifices God is honoured and well pleased. This for the psalms.

And for the hymns and lauds, appointed to be daily repeated or sung after the first and second lessons are read to the congregation, he proceeded to inform them that it was most reasonable, after they have heard the will and goodness of God declared or preached by the priest in his reading the two chapters, that it was then a seasonable duty to rise up and express their gratitude to Almighty God for those his mercies to them and to all mankind; and then to say with the blessed Virgin, that their souls do magnify the Lord, and that their spirits do also rejoice in God their Saviour. And that it was their duty also to rejoice with Simeon in his song, and say with him, that their eyes have also seen their salvation; for they have seen that salvation which was but prophesied till his time, and he then broke out into those expressions of joy that he did see it; but they live to see it daily in the history of it, and therefore ought daily to rejoice, and daily to offer up their sacrifice of praise to their God for that particular mercy – a service which is now the constant employment of that blessed Virgin, and Simeon, and all those blessed saints that are possessed of heaven, and where they are at this time interchangeably and constantly singing, 'Holy, holy, holy, Lord God, glory be to God on high, and on earth peace.' And he taught them that to do this was an acceptable service to God; because the prophet David says in his psalms, 'He that praiseth the Lord honoureth Him.'

He made them to understand how happy they be that are freed from the incumbrances of that law which our forefathers groaned under, namely, from the legal sacrifices and from the many ceremonies of the Levitical law – freed from circumcision, and from the strict observation of the Jewish Sabbath, and the like. And he made them to know that having received so many and so great blessings by being born since the days of our Saviour, it must be an acceptable sacrifice to Almighty God for them to acknowledge those blessings daily, and stand up and worship, and say as Zacharias did, 'Blessed be the Lord God of Israel, for he hath – in our days – visited and redeemed his people; and he hath – in our days – remembered and showed that mercy, which by the mouth of the prophets he promised to our forefathers; and this he hath done according to his holy covenant made with them.' And he made them to understand that we live to see and enjoy the benefit of it in his birth, his life, his passion, his resurrection, and ascension into heaven, where he now sits, sensible of all our temptations and infirmities, and where he is at this present time making intercession for us to his and our Father; and therefore they ought daily to express their public gratulations, and say daily with Zacharias, 'Blessed be the Lord God of Israel, that hath thus visited and thus redeemed his people.' These were some of the reasons by which Mr. Herbert instructed his congregation for the use of the psalms and the hymns appointed to be daily sung or said in the Church service.

He informed them also when the priest did pray only for the congregation and not for himself; and when they did only pray for him; as, namely, after the repetition of the creed, before he proceeds to pray the Lord's prayer, or any of the appointed collects, the priest is directed to kneel down and pray for them, saying, 'The Lord be with you;' and when they pray for him, saying 'And with thy spirit;' and then they join together in the following collects. And he assured them that when there is such mutual love, and such joint prayers offered for each other, then the holy angels look down from heaven, and are ready to carry such charitable desires to God Almighty, and he as ready to receive them; and that a Christian congregation calling thus upon God with one heart and one voice, and in one reverent and humble posture, look as beautiful as Jerusalem that is at peace with itself.

He instructed them also why the prayer of our Lord was prayed often in every full service of the Church, namely, at the conclusion of the several parts of that service; and prayed then, not only because it was composed and commanded by our Jesus that made it, but as a perfect pattern for our less perfect forms of prayer, and therefore fittest to sum up and conclude all our imperfect petitions.

He instructed them also that, as by the second commandment we are required not to bow down or worship an idol or false god, so, by the contrary rule, we are to bow down and kneel, or stand up, and worship the true God. And he instructed them why the Church required the congregation to stand up at the repetition of the creeds, namely, because they did thereby declare both their obedience to the Church, and an assent to that faith into which they had been baptized. And he taught them that in that shorter creed or doxology, so often repeated daily, they also stood up to testify their belief to be that the God that they trusted in was one God and three persons – the Father, the Son, and the Holy Ghost – to whom they and the priest gave glory. And because there had been heretics that had denied some of these three persons to be God, therefore the congregation stood up and honoured him by confessing, and saying, 'It was so in the beginning, is now so, and shall ever be so world without end.' And all gave their assent to this belief by standing up and saying, Amen.

He instructed them also what benefit they had by the Church's appointing the celebration of holy days, and the excellent use of them, namely, that they were set apart for particular commemorations of particular mercies received from Almighty God, and (as Reverend Mr. Hooker says) to be the landmarks to distinguish times; for by them we are taught to take notice how time passes by us, and that we ought not to let the year pass without a celebration of praise for those mercies which those days give us occasion to remember; and therefore they were to note that the year is appointed to begin the 25th day of March,[1] a day in which we commemorate the angel's appearing to the blessed Virgin, with the joyful tidings that she should conceive and bear a son that should be the Redeemer of mankind. And she did so forty weeks after this joyful salutation, namely, at our Christmas – a day in which we commemorate his birth with joy and praise; and that eight days after this happy birth we celebrate his circumcision, namely, in that which we call New Year's Day. And that, upon that day which we call Twelfth Day, we commemorate the manifestation of the unsearchable riches of Jesus to the Gentiles; and that that day we also celebrate the memory of his goodness in sending a star to guide the three wise men from the east to Bethlehem, that they might there worship and present him with their oblations of gold, frankincense, and myrrh. And he (Mr. Herbert) instructed them that Jesus was forty days after his birth presented by his blessed mother in the Temple, namely, on that day which we call The Purification of the Blessed Virgin St. Mary. And he instructed them that by the Lent fast we imitate and commemorate our Saviour's humiliation in fasting forty days, and that we ought to endeavour to be like him in purity. And that on Good Friday we commemorate and condole his crucifixion; and at Easter commemorate his glorious resurrection. And he taught

1. Lady Day. See *The British Church*, p. 106, l.5, n.

them that after Jesus had manifested himself to his disciples to be that Christ that was crucified, dead, and buried; and by his appearing and conversing with his disciples for the space of forty days after his resurrection, he then, and not till then, ascended into heaven in the sight of those disciples, namely, on that day which we call the Ascension, or Holy Thursday. And that we then celebrate the performance of the promise which he made to his disciples at or before his ascension, namely, that though he left them, yet he would send them the Holy Ghost to be their Comforter; and that he did so on that day which the Church calls Whitsunday. Thus the Church keeps an historical and circular commemoration of times as they pass by us – of such times as ought to incline us to occasional praises for the particular blessings which we do or might receive by those holy commemorations.

He made them know also why the Church hath appointed Ember Weeks; and to know the reason why the commandments, and the epistles, and gospels were to be read at the altar or communion table; why the priest was to pray the Litany kneeling, and why to pray some collects standing. And he gave them many other observations fit for his plain congregation, but not fit for me now to mention, for I must set limits to my pen, and not make that a treatise which I intended to be a much shorter account than I have made it: but I have done, when I have told the reader that he was constant in catechizing every Sunday in the afternoon, and that his catechizing was after his second lesson, and in the pulpit; and that he never exceeded his half-hour, and was always so happy as to have an obedient and full congregation.

And to this I must add that if he were at any time too zealous in his sermons, it was in reproving the indecencies of the people's behaviour in the time of divine service, and of those ministers that huddled up the Church prayers without a visible reverence and affection, namely, such as seemed to say the Lord's Prayer or collect in a breath; but for himself, his custom was to stop betwixt every collect, and give the people time to consider what they had prayed, and to force their desires affectionately to God before he engaged them into new petitions.

And by this account of his diligence to make his parishioners understand what they prayed, and why they praised and adored their Creator, I hope I shall the more easily obtain the reader's belief to the following account of Mr. Herbert's own practice, which was to appear constantly with his wife and three nieces (the daughters of a deceased sister) and his whole family twice every day at the church prayers in the chapel which does almost join to his parsonage house. And for the time of his appearing, it was strictly at the canonical hours of ten and four; and then and there he lifted up pure and charitable hands to God in the midst of the congregation. And he would joy to have spent that time in that place where the honour of his Master Jesus dwelleth; and there, by that inward devotion which he testified constantly by an humble behaviour and visible adoration, he, like Joshua, brought not only his own household thus to serve the Lord, but brought most of his parishioners and many gentlemen in the neighbourhood, constantly to make a part of his congregation twice a day; and some of the meaner sort of his parish did so love and reverence Mr. Herbert, that they would let their plough rest when Mr. Herbert's saints' bell rung to prayers, that they might also offer their devotions to God with him, and would then return back to their plough. And his most holy life was such, that it begot such reverence to God and to him, that they thought themselves the happier when they carried Mr. Herbert's blessing back with them to their labour. Thus powerful was his reason and example, to persuade others to a practical piety and devotion.

And his constant public prayers did never make him to neglect his own private devotions, nor those prayers that he thought himself bound to perform with his family, which always were a set form and not long; and he did always conclude them with that collect which the Church hath appointed for the day or week. Thus he made every day's sanctity a step towards that kingdom where impurity cannot enter.

His chiefest recreation was music, in which heavenly art he was a most excellent master, and did himself compose many divine hymns and anthems, which he set and sung to his lute or viol; and though he was a lover of retiredness, yet his love to music was such, that he went usually twice every week on certain appointed days to the cathedral church in Salisbury; and at his return would say, that his time spent in prayer and cathedral music elevated his soul, and was his heaven upon earth. But before his return thence to Bemerton, he would usually sing and play his part at an appointed private music meeting; and, to justify this practice, he would often say, religion does not banish mirth, but only moderates and sets rules to it.

And as his desire to enjoy his heaven upon earth drew him twice every week to Salisbury, so his walks thither were the occasion of many happy accidents to others, of which I will mention some few.

In one of his walks to Salisbury, he overtook a gentleman that is still living in that city, and in their walk together Mr. Herbert took a fair occasion to talk with him, and humbly begged to be excused if he asked him some account of his faith; and said, 'I do this the rather because though you are not of my parish, yet I receive tithe from you by the hand of your tenant; and, sir, I am the bolder to do it, because I know there be some sermon hearers that be like those fishes that always live in salt water, and yet are always fresh.' After which expression Mr. Herbert asked him some needful questions, and having received his answer, gave him such rules for the trial of his sincerity, and for a practical piety, and in so loving and meek a manner, that the gentleman did so fall in love with him and his discourse, that he would often contrive to meet him in his walk to Salisbury, or to attend him back to Bemerton, and still mentions the name of Mr. George Herbert with veneration, and still praiseth God for the occasion of knowing him.

In another of his Salisbury walks he met with a neighbour minister, and after some friendly discourse betwixt them, and some condolement for the decay of piety, and too general contempt of the clergy, Mr. Herbert took occasion to say, 'One cure for these distempers would be for the clergy themselves to keep the Ember Weeks strictly, and beg of their parishioners to join with them in fasting and prayers for a more religious clergy. And another cure would be for themselves to restore the great and neglected duty of catechizing,[1] on which the salvation of so many of the poor and ignorant lay people does depend; but

1. Cf. *The Country Parson*, ch. xxi, p. 224.

principally that the clergy themselves would be sure to live unblamably; and that the dignified clergy especially, which preach temperance, would avoid surfeiting, and take all occasions to express a visible humility and charity in their lives; for this would force a love and an imitation, and an unfeigned reverence from all that knew them to be such.' (And for proof of this we need no other testimony than the life and death of Dr. Lake, late Lord Bishop of Bath and Wells.) 'This,' said Mr. Herbert, 'would be a cure for the wickedness and growing atheism of our age. And, my dear brother, till this be done by us, and done in earnest, let no man expect a reformation of the manners of the laity; for it is not learning, but this, this only, that must do it; and till then the fault must lie at our doors.'

In another walk to Salisbury he saw a poor man with a poorer horse that was fallen under his load; they were both in distress, and needed present help, which Mr. Herbert perceiving, put off his canonical coat, and helped the poor man to unload, and after to load his horse. The poor man blessed him for it, and he blessed the poor man; and was so like the good Samaritan, that he gave him money to refresh both himself and his horse, and told him, that if he loved himself, he should be merciful to his beast. Thus he left the poor man, and at his coming to his musical friends at Salisbury, they began to wonder that Mr. George Herbert, who used to be so trim and clean, came into that company so soiled and discomposed; but he told them the occasion; and when one of the company told him he had disparaged himself by so dirty an employment, his answer was, that the thought of what he had done would prove music to him at midnight, and that the omission of it would have upbraided and made discord in his conscience, whensoever he should pass by that place. 'For if I be bound to pray for all that be in distress, I am sure that I am bound, so far as it is in my power, to practise what I pray for. And though I do not wish for the like occasion every day, yet let me tell you, I would not willingly pass one day of my life without comforting a sad soul, or showing mercy; and I praise God for this occasion. And now let's tune our instruments.'

Thus as our blessed Saviour, after his resurrection, did take occasion to interpret the Scripture to Cleopas and that other disciple which he met with and accompanied in their journey to

Emmaus; so Mr. Herbert, in his path toward heaven, did daily take any fair occasion to instruct the ignorant, or comfort any that were in affliction; and did always confirm his precepts by showing humility and mercy, and ministering grace to the hearers.

And he was most happy in his wife's unforced compliance with his acts of charity, whom he made his almoner, and paid constantly into her hand a tenth penny of what money he received for tithe, and gave her power to dispose that to the poor of his parish, and with it a power to dispose a tenth part of the corn that came yearly into his barn; which trust she did most faithfully perform, and would often offer to him an account of her stewardship, and as often beg an enlargement of his bounty; for she rejoiced in the employment; and this was usually laid out by her in blankets and shoes for some such poor people as she knew to stand in most need of them. This as to her charity. And for his own, he set no limits to it, nor did ever turn his face from any that he saw in want, but would relieve them, especially his poor neighbours; to the meanest of whose houses he would go, and inform himself of their wants, and relieve them cheerfully if they were in distress; and would always praise God as much for being willing as for being able to do it. And when he was advised by a friend to be more frugal, because he might have children, his answer was, 'he would not see the danger of want so far off; but being the Scripture does so commend charity as to tell us that charity is the top of Christian virtues, the covering of sins, the fulfilling of the law, the life of faith, and that charity hath a promise of the blessings of this life and of a reward in that life which is to come; being these and more excellent things are in Scripture spoken of thee, O Charity! and that being all my tithes and church-dues are a deodate[1] from thee, O my God, make me, O my God, so far to trust thy promise as to return them back to thee; and by thy grace I will do so, in distributing them to any of thy poor members that are in distress, or do but bear the image of Jesus my Master. Sir,' said he to his friend, 'my wife hath a competent maintenance secured her after my death, and therefore as this is my prayer, so this my resolution shall, by God's grace, be unalterable.'

1. A thing given to God.

This may be some account of the excellencies of the active part of his life; and thus he continued till a consumption so weakened him as to confine him to his house, or to the chapel which does almost join to it; in which he continued to read prayers constantly twice every day, though he were very weak; in one of which times of reading his wife observed him to read in pain, and told him so, and that it wasted his spirits and weakened him; and he confessed it did, but said, his life could not be better spent than in the service of his Master Jesus, who had done and suffered so much for him. 'But,' said he, 'I will not be wilful; for though my spirit be willing, yet I find my flesh is weak; and therefore Mr. Bostock shall be appointed to read prayers for me to-morrow and I will now be only a hearer of them, till this mortal shall put on immortality.' And Mr. Bostock did the next day undertake and continue this happy employment till Mr. Herbert's death. This Mr. Bostock was a learned and virtuous man, an old friend of Mr. Herbert's, and then his curate to the church of Fulston, which is a mile from Bemerton, to which church Bemerton is but a chapel of ease. And this Mr. Bostock did also constantly supply the church service for Mr. Herbert in that chapel, when the music meeting at Salisbury caused his absence from it.

About one month before his death, his friend Mr. Ferrar (for an account of whom I am by promise indebted to the reader, and intend to make him sudden payment) hearing of Mr. Herbert's sickness, sent Mr. Edmund Duncon (who is now Rector of Friar Barnet, in the county of Middlesex) from his house of Gidden Hall, which is near to Huntingdon, to see Mr. Herbert, and to assure him he wanted not his daily prayers for his recovery; and Mr. Duncon was to return back to Gidden with an account of Mr. Herbert's condition. Mr. Duncon found him weak, and at that time lying on his bed or on a pallet; but at his seeing Mr. Duncon, he raised himself vigorously, saluted him, and with some earnestness inquired the health of his brother Ferrar, of which Mr. Duncon satisfied him; and after some discourse of Mr. Ferrar's holy life, and the manner of his constant serving God, he said to Mr. Duncon, 'Sir, I see by your habit that you are a priest, and I desire you to pray with me;' which being granted, Mr. Duncon asked him, 'What prayers?'

to which Mr. Herbert's answer was, 'Oh, sir, the prayers of my mother, the Church of England. No other prayers are equal to them! – but, at this time, I beg of you to pray only the Litany, for I am weak and faint;' and Mr. Duncon did so. After which, and some other discourse of Mr. Ferrar, Mrs. Herbert provided Mr. Duncon a plain supper and a clean lodging, and he betook himself to rest. – This Mr. Duncon tells me; and tells me that at his first view of Mr. Herbert, he saw majesty and humility so reconciled in his looks and behaviour, as begot in him an awful reverence for his person, and says, 'his discourse was so pious, and his motion so genteel and meek, that after almost forty years, yet they remain still fresh in his memory.'

The next morning Mr. Duncon left him, and betook himself to a journey to Bath, but with a promise to return back to him within five days; and he did so. But before I shall say anything of what discourse then fell betwixt them two, I will pay my promised account of Mr. Ferrar.

Mr Nicholas Ferrar (who got the reputation of being called St. Nicholas at the age of six years) was born in London, and doubtless had good education in his youth; but certainly was at an early age made Fellow of Clare Hall in Cambridge, where he continued to be eminent for his piety, temperance, and learning. About the twenty-sixth year of his age he betook himself to travel, in which he added to his Latin and Greek a perfect knowledge of all the languages spoken in the western parts of our Christian world, and understood well the principles of their religion, and of their manner, and the reasons of their worship. In this his travel he met with many persuasions to come into a communion with that Church which calls itself Catholic; but he returned from his travels as he went, eminent for his obedience to his mother, the Church of England. In his absence from England, Mr. Ferrar's father (who was a merchant) allowed him a liberal maintenance; and, not long after his return into England, Mr. Ferrar had, by the death of his father, or an elder brother, or both, an estate left him, that enabled him to purchase land to the value of four or five hundred pounds a year, the greatest part of which land was at Little Gidden, four or six miles from Huntingdon, and about eighteen from Cambridge – which place he chose for the privacy of it, and for the hall, which had the parish church or chapel belonging and adjoining near to it; for Mr. Ferrar having seen the manners and vanities of the world, and found them to be, as Mr. Herbert says, 'a nothing between two dishes,' did so contemn it, that he resolved to spend the remainder of his life in mortifications, and in devotion, and charity, and to be always prepared for death; and his life was spent thus:

He and his family, which were like a little college, and about thirty in number, did most of them keep Lent and all Ember Weeks strictly, both in fasting and using all those mortifications and prayers that the Church hath appointed to be then used; and he and they did the like constantly on Fridays, and on the vigils or eves appointed to be fasted before the saints' days; and this frugality and abstinence turned to the relief of the poor; but this was but a part of his charity; none but God and he knew the rest.

This family, which I have said to be in number about thirty, were a part of them his kindred, and the rest chosen to be of a temper fit to be moulded into a devout life; and all of them were for their dispositions serviceable, and quiet, and humble, and free from scandal. Having thus fitted himself for his family, he did, about the year 1630, betake himself to a constant and methodical service of God, and it was in this manner: He, being accompanied with most of his family, did himself use to read the Common Prayers (for he was a deacon) every day at the appointed hours of ten and four, in the parish church, which was very near his house, and which he had both repaired and adorned, for it was fallen into a great ruin, by reason of a depopulation of the village before Mr. Ferrar bought the manor. And he did also constantly read the matins every morning at the hour of six, either in the church or in an oratory which was within his own house; and many of the family did there continue with him after the prayers were ended, and there they spent some hours in singing hymns or anthems, sometimes in the church, and often to an organ in the oratory. And there they sometimes betook themselves to meditate, or to pray privately, or to read a part of the New Testament to themselves, or to continue their praying or reading the psalms; and, in case the psalms were not always read in the day, then Mr. Ferrar, and others of the congregation, did at night, at the ring of a watch-bell, repair to the church or oratory, and there betake themselves to prayers and lauding God, and reading the psalms that had not been read in the day; and when these, or any part of the congregation, grew weary or faint, the watch-bell was rung, sometimes before and sometimes after midnight, and then another part of the family rose, and maintained the watch, sometimes by praying or singing lauds to God or reading the psalms; and when after some hours they also grew weary and faint, then they rung the watch-bell, and were also relieved by some of the former, or by a new part of the society, which continued their devotions (as hath been mentioned) until morning. And it is to be noted that in this continued serving of God, the psalter, or whole book of psalms, was, in every four-and-twenty hours, sung or read over from the first to the last verse; and this was done as constantly as the sun runs his circle every day about the world, and then begins again the same instant that it ended.

Thus did Mr. Ferrar and his happy family serve God day and night: thus did they always behave themselves as in his presence. And they did always eat and drink by the strictest rules of temperance; eat and drink so as to be ready to rise at midnight, or at the call of a watch-bell, and perform their devotions to God.

And 'tis fit to tell the reader that many of the clergy that were more inclined to practical piety and devotion than to doubtful and needless disputations, did often come to Gidden Hall, and make themselves a part of that happy society, and stay a week or more, and then join with Mr. Ferrar and the family in these devotions, and assist and ease him or them in the watch by night. And these various devotions had never less than two of the domestic family in the night; and the watch was always kept in the church or oratory, unless in extreme cold winter nights, and then it was maintained in a parlour which had a fire in it, and the parlour was fitted for that purpose. And this course of piety, and great liberality to his poor neighbours, Mr. Ferrar maintained till his death, which was in the year 1639.

Mr. Ferrar's and Mr. Herbert's devout lives were both so noted that the general report of their sanctity gave them occasion to renew that slight acquaintance which was begun at their being contemporaries in Cambridge; and this new holy friendship was long maintained without any interview, but only by loving and endearing letters. And one testimony of their friendship and pious designs may appear by Mr. Ferrar's commending 'The Considerations of John Valdesso' (a book which he had met with in his travels, and translated out of Spanish into English) to be examined and censured by Mr. Herbert before it was made public; which excellent book Mr. Herbert did read, and returned back with many marginal notes, as they be now printed with it; and with them Mr. Herbert's affectionate letter to Mr. Ferrar.

This John Valdesso was a Spaniard, and was for his learning and virtue much valued and loved by the great Emperor, Charles the Fifth, whom Valdesso had followed as a cavalier all the time of his long and dangerous wars; and when Valdesso grew old, and grew weary both of war and the world, he took his fair opportunity to declare to the Emperor that his resolution was to decline his Majesty's service, and betake himself to a quiet and contemplative life, because there ought to be a vacancy of time betwixt fighting and dying. The Emperor had himself, for the same or other like reasons, put on the same resolution; but God and himself did, till then, only know them; and he did therefore desire Valdesso to consider well of what he had said, and to keep his purpose within his own breast till they two might have a second opportunity of a friendly discourse, which Valdesso promised to do.

In the meantime the Emperor appoints privately a day for him and Valdesso to meet again, and after a pious and free discourse, they both agreed on a certain day to receive the blessed sacrament publicly, and appointed an eloquent and devout friar to preach a sermon of contempt of the world, and of the happiness and benefit of a contemplative life, which the friar did most affectionately. After which sermon the Emperor took occasion to declare openly, that the preacher had begot in him a resolution to lay down his dignities, and to forsake the world, and betake himself to a monastic life. And he pretended he had persuaded John Valdesso to do the like; but this is most certain, that after the Emperor had called his son Philip out of England,

and resigned to him all his kingdoms, that then the Emperor and John Valdesso did perform their resolutions.

This account of John Valdesso I received from a friend that had it from the mouth of Mr. Ferrar; and the reader may note that in this retirement John Valdesso wrote his *Hundred and Ten Considerations*, and many other treatises of worth, which want a second Mr. Ferrar to procure and translate them.

After this account of Mr. Ferrar and John Valdesso, I proceed to my account of Mr. Herbert and Mr. Duncon, who, according to his promise, returned from the Bath the fifth day, and then found Mr. Herbert much weaker than he left him; and therefore their discourse could not be long; but at Mr. Duncon's parting with him, Mr. Herbert spoke to this purpose: 'Sir, I pray give my brother Ferrar an account of the decaying condition of my body, and tell him I beg him to continue his daily prayers for me; and let him know that I have considered that God only is what he would be; and that I am, by his grace, become now so like him as to be pleased with what pleaseth him; and tell him that I do not repine, but am pleased with my want of health; and tell him my heart is fixed on that place where true joy is only to be found; and that I long to be there, and do wait for my appointed change with hope and patience.' Having said this, he did, with so sweet a humility as seemed to exalt him, bow down to Mr. Duncon, and, with a thoughtful and contented look, say to him, 'Sir, I pray deliver this little book to my dear brother Ferrar, and tell him he shall find in it a picture of the many spiritual conflicts that have passed betwixt God and my soul, before I could subject mine to the will of Jesus my Master; in whose service I have now found perfect freedom; desire him to read it; and then, if he can think it may turn to the advantage of any dejected poor soul, let it be made public; if not, let him burn it; for I and it are less than the least of God's mercies.' Thus meanly did this humble man think of this excellent book, which now bears the name of *The Temple; or, Sacred Poems and Private Ejaculations*; of which Mr. Ferrar would say, there was in it the picture of a divine soul in every page; and that the whole book was such a harmony of holy passions as would enrich the world with pleasure and piety. And it appears to have done so, for there have been more than twenty thousand of them sold since the first impression.

And this ought to be noted that when Mr. Ferrar sent this book to Cambridge to be licensed for the press, the Vice-Chancellor would by no means allow the two so much noted verses,

> Religion stands a tiptoe in our land,
> Ready to pass to the American strand,[1]

to be printed; and Mr. Ferrar would by no means allow the book to be printed and want them; but after some time, and some arguments for and against their being made public, the Vice-Chancellor said, 'I knew Mr. Herbert well, and know that he had many heavenly speculations, and was a divine poet; but I hope the world will not take him to be an inspired prophet, and therefore I license the whole book.' So that it came to be printed without the diminution or addition of a syllable since it was delivered into the hands of Mr. Duncon, save only that Mr. Ferrar hath added that excellent preface that is printed before it.

At the time of Mr. Duncon's leaving Mr. Herbert (which was about three weeks before his death), his old and dear friend Mr. Woodnot came from London to Bemerton, and never left him till he had seen him draw his last breath, and closed his eyes on his death-bed. In this time of his decay he was often visited and prayed for by all the clergy that lived near to him, especially by his friends the Bishop and Prebendaries of the cathedral church in Salisbury, but by none more devoutly than his wife, his three nieces (then a part of his family), and Mr. Woodnot, who were the sad witnesses of his daily decay, to whom he would often speak to this purpose: 'I now look back upon the pleasures of my life past, and see the content I have taken in beauty, in wit, and music, and pleasant conversation, are now all past by me like a dream, or as a shadow that returns not, and are now all become dead to me, or I to them; and I see that as my father and generation hath done before me, so I also shall now suddenly (with Job) make my bed also in the dark; and I praise God, I am prepared for it; and I praise him that I am not to learn patience now I stand in such need of it; and that I have practised mortification, and endeavoured to die daily that I might not die eternally; and my hope is that I shall shortly leave this valley of

1. *The Church Militant*, p. 192, ll.235–6.

tears, and be free from all fevers and pain; and which will be a more happy condition, I shall be free from sin, and all the temptations and anxieties that attend it; and this being past, I shall dwell in the new Jerusalem – dwell there with men made perfect; dwell where these eyes shall see my Master and Saviour Jesus, and with him see my dear mother, and all my relations and friends. But I must die, or not come to that happy place. And this is my content, that I am going daily towards it; and that every day which I have lived hath taken a part of my appointed time from me; and that I shall live the less time for having lived this and the day past.'

These and the like expressions, which he uttered often, may be said to be his enjoyment of heaven before he enjoyed it. The Sunday before his death, he rose suddenly from his bed or couch, called for one of his instruments, took it into his hand, and said,

> My God, my God!
> My music shall find thee,
>     And ev'ry string
> Shall have his attribute to sing.

And having tuned it, he played and sang:

> The Sundays of man's life,
>     Threaded together on time's string,
> Make bracelets to adorn the wife
>     Of the eternal glorious King.
> On Sundays heaven's door stands ope;
>     Blessings are plentiful and rife,
> More plentiful than hope.[1]

Thus he sang on earth such hymns and anthems as the angels, and he, and Mr. Ferrar now sing in heaven.

Thus he continued meditating, and praying, and rejoicing till the day of his death; and on that day said to Mr. Woodnot, 'My dear friend, I am sorry I have nothing to present to my merciful God but sin and misery; but the first is pardoned, and a few hours will now put a period to the latter, for I shall suddenly go hence, and be no more seen.' Upon which expression Mr. Woodnot took occasion to remember him of the re-edifying Layton Church, and his many acts of mercy; to which he made

1. *Sunday*, p. 73, ll.29–35.

answer, saying, 'They be good works if they be sprinkled with the blood of Christ, and not otherwise.'

After this discourse he became more restless, and his soul seemed to be weary of her earthly tabernacle; and this uneasiness became so visible, that his wife, his three nieces, and Mr. Woodnot stood constantly about his bed, beholding him with sorrow, and an unwillingness to lose the sight of him whom they could not hope to see much longer. As they stood thus beholding him, his wife observed him to breathe faintly and with much trouble; and observed him to fall into a sudden agony, which so surprised her, that she fell into a sudden passion, and required of him to know how he did; to which his answer was, 'That he had passed a conflict with his last enemy, and he had overcome him by the merits of his Master Jesus.' After which answer he looked up and saw his wife and nieces weeping to an extremity, and charged them, 'If they loved him, to withdraw to the next room, and there pray every one alone for him, for nothing but their lamentations could make his death uncomfortable.' To which request their sighs and tears would not suffer them to make any reply, but they yielded him a sad obedience, leaving only with him Mr. Woodnot and Mr. Bostock. Immediately after they had left him, he said to Mr. Bostock, 'Pray, sir, open that door; then look into that cabinet, in which you may easily find my last will, and give it into my hand:' which being done, Mr. Herbert delivered it into the hand of Mr. Woodnot, and said, 'My old friend, I here deliver you my last will, in which you will find that I have made you my sole executor for the good of my wife and nieces; and I desire you to show kindness to them, as they shall need it. I do not desire you to be just, for I know you will be so for your own sake; but I charge you, by the religion of our friendship, to be careful of them.' And having obtained Mr. Woodnot's promise to be so, he said 'I am now ready to die.' After which words he said, 'Lord, forsake me not, now my strength faileth me, but grant me mercy for the merits of my Jesus. And now, Lord – Lord, now receive my soul.' And with those words he breathed forth his divine soul without any apparent disturbance. Mr. Woodnot and Mr. Bostock attending his last breath, and closing his eyes.

Thus he lived, and thus he died like a saint, unspotted of the world, full of alms-deeds, full of humility, and all the examples of a virtuous life; which I cannot conclude better than with this borrowed observation:

> All must to their cold graves;
> But the religious actions of the just
> Smell sweet in death, and blossom in the dust.[1]

Mr. George Herbert's have done so to this, and will doubtless do so to succeeding generations. I have but this to say more of him, that if Andrew Melvin died before him, then George Herbert died without an enemy. I wish (if God shall be so pleased) that I may be so happy as to die like him.

Iz. Wa.

There is a debt justly due to the memory of Mr. Herbert's virtuous wife, a part of which I will endeavour to pay by a very short account of the remainder of her life, which shall follow.

She continued his disconsolate widow about six years, bemoaning herself and complaining that she had lost the delight of her eyes; but more, that she had lost the spiritual guide for her poor soul; and would often say, 'Oh that I had, like holy Mary, the mother of Jesus, treasured up all his sayings in my heart! but since I have not been able to do that, I will labour to live like him, that where he now is, I may be also.' And she would often say (as the prophet David for his son Absolom), 'O that I had died for him!' Thus she continued mourning, till time and conversation had so moderated her sorrows, that she became the happy wife of Sir Robert Cook, of Highnam, in the county of Gloucester, Knight; and though he put a high value on the excellent accomplishments of her mind and body, and was so like Mr. Herbert as not to govern like a master, but as an affectionate husband; yet she would, even to him, often take occasion to mention the name of Mr. George Herbert, and say, 'That name must live in her memory till she put off mortality.'

By Sir Robert she had only one child, a daughter, whose parts and plentiful estate make her happy in this world, and her well using of them gives a fair testimony that she will be so in that which is to come.

1. By James Shirley, dramatist (1596–1666).

Mrs. Herbert was the wife of Sir Robert eight years, and lived his widow about fifteen; all which time she took a pleasure in mentioning and commending the excellences of Mr. George Herbert. She died in the year 1663, and lies buried at Highnam; Mr. Herbert in his own church, under the altar, and covered with a gravestone without any inscription.

This Lady Cook had preserved many of Mr. Herbert's private writings, which she intended to make public; but they and Highnam House were burnt together by the late rebels, and so lost to posterity.

I. W.

# NOTES TO THE POEMS

**Title page to the First Edition**
**The Temple:** See Notes to Introduction, p. liii, n.2.
**Psal. 29:** 'The voice of the Lord maketh the hinds to bring forth young and discovereth the thick bushes: in his temple doth every man speak of his honour' (*Psalms* 29: 8). Quoted from the Psalter of the Great Bible of 1539, as used in BCP, rather than the Authorized Version of 1611.

**The Dedication** On the title page of *B*, and in isolation on the first written page of *W*, which has no title page. Placed after *The Printers to the Reader* in *1633* – an arrangement apparently forced by pressure of space in this tiny, closely printed volume. But the first sentence of *The Printers to the Reader* refers to the *Dedication* as precedent, which most probably was the author's intention. Modern editors (including H and P) tend to follow *1633*.
**5-6 Turn their eyes:** the injunction is addressed to God.
**Theirs:** their eyes.
**Who shall hurt themselves:** cf. *Perirrhanterium*, pp. 20–21, ll.425–7 and note.
**Refrain:** restrain.

**The Printers to the Reader** This is written by Nicholas Ferrar (1592–1637), Herbert's close friend and founder-leader of the religious community at Little Gidding. For Walton's description of Ferrar, and his account of Herbert sending Ferrar his 'little book' of poems from his death-bed, see pp. 376–80.
**6 Helicon:** home of the Greek Muses, on Mount Parnassos.
**37 My Master:** cf. *The Odour*, p. 170, and Walton, p. 362.
**39 his Word:** the Scriptures.
**52ff** i.e. Herbert had wanted to transfer the prebend at Leighton Bromswold to Nicholas Ferrar. Instead he was persuaded to restore Leighton Church (H, p. 584).
**62** See Walton, p. 383. *Sprinkled* acquires cumulative associations: see *Perirrhanterium* and *Superliminare*, p. 22, l.2.
**72** cf. *The Posy*, p. 178, and Walton, p. 380. 'I am not worthy of the least of all the mercies, and of all the truth, which thou hast showed unto thy servant' (*Genesis* 32: 10).

**The Church-porch** As the title suggests, the following poem forms an ante-chamber to the body of works making up *The Church*. See Introduction, p. xiv.

**Perirrhanterium:** an aspergil, an instrument for sprinkling holy water.

**2 Thy rate and price:** later echoed in *The Pearl*, p. 87, l.35: *I fly to thee, and fully understand | Both the main sale, and the commodities; | And at what rate and price I have thy love.* The Pearl refers to *Matthew* 13: 45–6: 'The kingdom of heaven is like unto a merchant man, seeking goodly pearls; Who, when he had found one pearl of great price, went and sold all that he had, and bought it.' Here Herbert reverses the metaphor: his young reader's soul is a pearl of great price.

**6 a sacrifice:** something consecrated by being offered to God. Also pointing forward to Christ's greater sacrifice, p. 24.

**9 thy lesson:** man, like a schoolboy, copies out God's lines in his soul but blots them with sin till they are illegible.

**12 whose lust is all their book:** i.e. when all those eyes want to study is lust.

**13 Abstain wholly, or wed:** see further *The Country Parson*, ch. ix, p. 208.

**16 stays:** restraints.

**18** If you prefer rottenness to continence, give up any idea of Heaven.

**19–24** Man is contrary. God made land common, now the landlords (of Herbert's time) enclose it; God made man monogamous (*impal'd us*: fenced us in) and we want free love. Herbert avoids making his land/sex parallel explicit, but the metaphor has common sexual connotations ('Is not your last act harsh, and violent, / As when a plough a stony ground doth rent?' Donne: *The Comparison*, ll.47–8; 'He ploughed her, and she cropp'd' *Antony and Cleopatra* II.ii.232).

**24 cross:** perverse. P makes a cross-reference to *The Cross*, p. 161, ll.32ff., where the word is used punningly.

**30 keep the round:** refill each time the bottle comes round.

**32 Big with:** pregnant with.

**35 devest:** make over a vested right.

**36 by beast:** as a beast.

**38–9 a measure / Short of his can:** a smaller capacity.

**41–2** If you give in and drink a third glass the wine will be emboldened by your pliability.

**46 a beast in courtesy:** cf. *Outlandish Proverbs* no. 924. 'Wine makes all sorts of creatures at table' (H).

**50** Cf. 'the enemies of the cross of Christ ... whose God is their belly, and whose glory is in their shame' (*Philippians* 3: 18–19) (H).

**53–4 poor clod of earth:** cf. 'Woe unto him that striveth with his Maker! ... Shall the clay say to him that fashioneth it, What makest thou?' (*Isaiah* 45: 9) (P).

**57 plead a pleasure:** have pleasure to be said for them.

**60 bate:** leave out.

**64 He pares his apple:** cf. 'The Country Parson is a lover of old customs ... If there be any ill in the custom that may be severed from the good, he pares the apple, and gives [his parishioners] the clean to feed on' (*The Country Parson*, ch. xxxv, pp. 250–51).

**65–6** There is a gaming motif here: 'When misfortunes get you down, don't gamble away your strongest stake, which is clean speech.'

**80 dressing, mistressing, and compliment:** quoted directly from Donne's *To Mr Tilman, after he had taken orders*, l.30 and repeated in *The Country Parson*, ch. xxxii, p. 245 (H).

**83 God gave thy soul brave wings:** cf. *Easter Wings* p. 40–41, and cf. Donne's *To Mr. Tilman* l.22: 'new feather'd with celestial love'.

**91 most of sloth:** cf. *The Country Parson* ch. xxxii, p. 242: 'the great and national sin of this land he esteems to be idleness' (H).

**92 phlegm:** one of the four humours, in excess tending to lethargy.

**93–6** Another dig at the wealth of the landowners deriving from the wool trade (*thy native cloth*), sheep farming (and hence enclosure). England's gentry have gone to grass and are good for nothing.

**99 mark:** used punningly (1) to aim at, (2) to notice.

**100** Some send their children abroad and have done with it.

**102** If you're not bothered about your child being brought up in God's image, look after him as an image of you.

**103–4** Some leave great estates to their children but don't teach them how to administer them properly, to the loss of both child and property.

**107–8** Cf. *Outlandish Proverbs* no. 305: 'He is not poor that hath little, but he that desireth much', and no. 399: 'He is rich enough that wants nothing' (H).

**111–12** Proverbial in sound, but Herbert's invention.

**117 stour:** sturdy.

**118 thrall:** thraldom, bondage.

**120 a shelf:** a reef. Cf. *Misery*, p. 99, ll.76–8: *Now* [*Man is*] ... *A sick toss'd vessel, dashing on each thing; | Nay, his own shelf: | My God, I mean my self.*

**123 Simpring is but a lay-hypocrisy:** i.e. the flatterer's phoney smile is a form of hypocrisy that works on earth but not in heaven: your *king* may be taken in by it, but not heaven's *King* (see l.122). *Lay* means worldly; it also implies the incompetence of the layman, the non-professional.

**124 Give it a corner, and the clue undoes:** the clue is the thread used to find one's way through a labyrinth, a very common metaphor (see OED *clew*). In a labyrinthine route it will snag on corners and the thread *undoes*, i.e. the twisty path of hypocrisy is hard to follow and full of hazards. (P and H gloss clue as 'a ball of thread' but leave the metaphor obscure.)

**125–6** The person who is afraid of doing evil (i.e. wants to be good) has a hard *task*; the one who is afraid of being good is being sneaky, and should wear a mask (which makes his dissimulation evident).

**128 sconces:** forts, defences. Greed (*thy mouth*) is a source of *dis-ease*, discomfort. The two defences are to carve for others, or to talk, rather than stuff yourself.

**132** Quoted from the Burial of the Dead.

**137 his Ecliptic line:** the apparent orbit of the Sun (H).

**142 under-writes:** subscribes to.

**147 chest:** punning on (1) coffer and (2) breast. For the image of this and the next line, cf. *The Method*, p. 130, l.10: *Tumble thy breast* (H).

**153 Never was scraper brave man:** cf. *The Country Parson*, ch. xxvi, p. 234: 'if ... I ... pinch and scrape ... I am covetous'.
**Get to live:** earn to live.

**157–60** Don't overshoot your income. In youth you can earn what's lost in a year; with age, the target has to be brought closer and closer. (An archery metaphor.)

**161–2** Herbert left a meticulous will, with six months' advance wages to his servants and numerous bequests, down to the settling of his deceased niece's legacies. See pp. 302–3.

**165–6** This evokes the Faustian predicament: just as the necromancer summons up a devil whom he thinks of as his servant, when actually the devil masters him, so wealth will overmaster you. *Conjuror* had more potent negative associations at this time, as one who conjures up spirits.

**169 What skills it:** what is the point.

**171 Take stars for money:** cf. *Affliction (1)*, p.44, ll.11–12: *Such stars I counted mine: both heav'n and earth/Paid me my wages*, and *Luke* 12: 33: 'provide yourselves bags that wax not old, a treasure in the heavens that faileth not' (H).
**Told:** counted.

**179–80** The overdressed spendthrift blames his tailor for his extravagant use of cloth, not himself.

**181–2 They that by pleading clothes/Do fortunes seek:** those who think fine clothes will persuade people to employ them.

**181–4** Herbert has three strands to his theme of display disguising worthlessness: fine clothes glossing over inadequate service is like swearing the truth of an unconvincing story or a sailing ship in full rig, with an empty hold.

**187 doth bear the bell:** is best.

**191–2 wooing/Nothing:** wooing of nothing.

**196 play their part:** i.e. can be lost at the gaming table.

**197–8** A potent image of bankruptcy and oblivion. If a man gambles his family wealth away, in the end his name will be his only memorial, engraved in the cracked church window. *Crackt name* implies (1) that the family honour is ruined, and (2) by transference, that the church itself is in decay, since the rich household that should have maintained it has been destroyed. A herald was meant to make his official Visitation about once every thirty years (H).

**199, 203 game:** gambling.

**204 increase:** progeny.

**212 allay:** alloy.

**220 that thou canst little do:** that you're capable of small deeds also.

**223** If your reputation is called into question by every trifle.

**224-6** H identifies Herbert's allusion to Bacon, who refers several times to the motto of a Spanish commander, that 'a Gentleman's honour should be, *De tela crassiore*, of a good strong warp or web that every little thing should not catch in it, when as now it seems they are but of cobweb lawn' (*Speech against Duels*, 1614, pp. 20–21).

**228** A trivial insult politely ignored will gain you credit among the best people.

**232 and the conceit advance:** and you become part of the joke.

**239-40** Echoed by Sterne: 'Everything in this world, said my father, is big with jest, – and has wit in it, and instruction too, – if we can but find it out' (*Tristram Shandy*, V.32) (P).

**247 sad:** sober.

**251** Then the giggler becomes the laughing-stock.

**253 respective:** respectful.

**255-6** Carefulness, or indifference, make or mar your fortunes accordingly.

**258 parcel-devil:** part devil (and partly responsible for his damnation).

**261 Be not thine own worm:** don't disparage yourself. Cf. Herbert's letter to his brother Henry, p. 290: 'have a good conceit of your wit ... it is the part of a poor spirit to undervalue himself and blush' (H).

**263-4** Restrain your passions and then they can be harnessed, like beasts, to your own advantage. The passions are also seen as beasts in the animal fable of *Humility*, p. 67.

**265 bate:** abate. This stanza draws on Aesop's fable of the ass who thought he was venerated, rather than the image he carried, or an emblem in Alciati's *Emblematum Liber* to the same effect.

**273-4** If necessary, sacrifice yourself for his sake; allay his fears with your blood. A clear lay parallel to Christ's sacrifice.

**275-6** We have lost the old biblical way of friendship.

**277 surety:** one who makes himself liable for another (financially and otherwise).

**280 them:** the children. Cf. *Outlandish Proverbs*, no. 419: 'He that hath children, all his morsels are not his own' (H).

**283-8** Coleridge wrote 'I do not understand this stanza' in his copy of *The Temple*. P passes over it in silence. Herbert is preaching the moderation recurrent in *The Country Parson*: don't overdo it. If you're

391

a single man, give everything you have to love, but not more than that: one estate, one life, not two ... Love can't make me more than the one man God created me, but hard work will multiply my weakness. Lines 285–6 would appear to refer to Adam's fall: he incurred the punishment of labouring, as did Eve, but no more than each was capable of.

**289–90** Another editorially unglossed enigma. *1633* has a colon after *please* and a full stop after *witty,* which would require two words to be understood (*In thy discourse ...* [use]/*All such* [as] *is courteous,*). Alternatively, *all such* is demonstrative, indicating the qualities listed in ll.291–2, with the punctuation emended as here. The erratic punctuation of the following lines is also suspect.

**293–8** Punctuation emended. *1633* has: *card: heard, pleasure: cards) steal.*

**295–6** Cf. *The Country Parson,* ch. xxiii, p. 229: 'to put men to discourse of that wherein they are most eminent is the most gainful way of conversation' (H).

**297 lose his rest:** lose his reserve stake (and so the game). An image taken from the card game of Primero (H).

**298 his treasure:** i.e. his stock of knowledge.

**317–18** The rainbow in the clouds never succeeds in making itself a circle, for all its trying. The clouds are another image of the stormy speaker of the preceding lines.

**323 them both:** your friend, and truth.

**324 a troth:** (1) a truth, (2) a bond.

**327 great places:** positions of consequence (H), i.e. patronage.

**333–4** Cf. *The Country Parson,* p. 196: 'he shoots higher that threatens the moon, than he that aims at a tree' (H).

**341 live alone:** are the only ones that are really alive.

**347–8** I consider the people who say 'I don't care' as lost; it's not even worth trying to teach them any better.

**352 a little sling:** like David's, killing Goliath (H).

**355–60** Cf. Herbert's letter to his brother Henry, p. 290: 'Be covetous ... of all good which you see in Frenchmen, whether it be in knowledge, or in fashion, or in words ... so shall you play a good merchant, by transporting French commodities to your own country' (H).

**360 clear:** obvious. The next two lines clarify this couplet: *fair behaviour* will *naturalize* your obvious debts (*scores*) of borrowed foreign manners.

**365 observest:** imitate.

**fit:** absurdity.

**368 board:** approach.

**372** Cf. *The Country Parson,* ch. iii, p. 199: 'The parson's ... apparel [is] plain, but reverend and clean, without spots, or dust, or smell; the purity of his mind breaking out and dilating itself even to his body,

392

clothes, and habitation' (H). Walton also notes Herbert's particularity, see pp. 346, 350.

**375 single market-money:** small change.

**376 Join hands with God:** cf. *Clasping of hands*, p. 153.

**377-8** [Give money] to a good, poor man till you swap roles, you becoming as good as he was to begin with.

**380 stamp:** image (stamped on a coin).

**383-4** Cf. *Acts* 10: 4: 'thine alms are come up for a memorial before God' (H).

**386 cankers:** corrupts.

**387-8 when the bells do chime,/'Tis angels' music:** cf. *Prayer (1)*, p. 49, l.13: *Church-bells beyond the stars heard*.

**391-6** Pay God his due twice on that day (Sunday), just as he gave you two mealtimes a day for the rest of the week. This is an improvement on your usual entertainment (*Thy cheer is mended*); don't hold back, because this food is better for you and can save your soul. Don't thwart God by being contrary; fast whenever you want but then, when the meal (of church service) is to your gain not loss. The metaphor of church as a *mystical repast* (*Superliminare*, p. 22, l.4) recurs throughout *The Church*. Punctuation emended at l.396; *wilt; but then 'tis* in *1633*.

**401 six and seven:** punning on a small company, and the gaming sense of hazarding a fortune (OED).

**403 bare:** bare-headed.

**410 the end:** the function, the point.

**411 Stay not for th' other pin:** cf. 'When prayers are done my lady is ready' (*Outlandish Proverbs*, no. 71). Herbert returns to the gentry's making it 'a piece of state' to be deliberately late for services in *The Country Parson*, ch. vi, p. 203.

**417 the stains:** 'that' should be understood: Close your eyes; send them down into your heart, so that they can see and weep clean the stains that they allowed to arise.

**423 Christ purg'd his temple:** see *Mark* 11: 15–17. He threw out the traders and money-lenders, saying, 'ye have made it a den of thieves' (H) (cf. ll.424–5).

**425-7** Cf. *The Country Parson*, ch. vii, p. 204: the parson tells his flock that 'sermons are dangerous things, that none goes out of the church as he came in, but either better or worse; that none is careless before his Judge, and that the Word of God shall judge us' (H).

**429 God calleth preaching folly:** *I Corinthians* 1: 20–21: 'Hath not God made foolish the wisdom of this world? For after that in the wisdom of God the world by wisdom knew not God, it pleased God by the foolishness of preaching to save them that believe' (H).

**430 treasures from an earthen pot:** *2 Corinthians* 4: 5–7. Paul is speaking of the preachers: 'we preach not ourselves ... For God, who

commanded the light to shine out of darkness, hath shined in our
hearts, to give the light of the knowledge of the glory of God ... But
we have this treasure in earthen vessels, that the excellency of the
power may be of God, and not of us' (H). The linking of this and the
two adjacent references (ll.429, 449) illustrates the observation made
in *The H. Scriptures II*, p. 56, ll.5–6: *This verse marks that, and both do
make a motion/Unto a third, that ten leaves off doth lie.*

**439–44** H identifies a Herbertian reproof of the gentry's social disdain
for the clergy. The jesting gallant may have ruined the preacher (*thy
sins made him miscarry*) by gambling (see ll.196–8 above). *Love him for
his Master:* cf. ll.265–8.

**449 The Jews refused thunder:** see *Exodus* 19: 16ff. God appeared on
Mount Sinai in thunder; the Jews later disobeyed the Ten Com-
mandments given by him to Moses.
**and we, folly:** we refuse the folly of preaching to the obdurate.
*1 Corinthians* 1: 18. 'For the preaching of the cross is to them that
perish foolishness' (H).

**450 Though God do hedge us in:** evoking two powerful protests
against the wrath of God: 'Why is light given to a man whose way is
hid, and whom God hath hedged in?' (*Job* 3: 23); 'He hath hedged
me about, that I cannot get out' (*Lamentations* 3: 7) (H).

**459–60 life's poor span/Make not an ell:** 'Behold, thou hast made
my days as an handbreadth' (*Psalms* 39: 5); *an ell:* 45 inches.

**461–2** A well-known secular aphorism.

**Superliminare:** The lintel over the threshold of the church. See
Introduction, p. xiv. In *W* the two stanzas are on separate pages, the
first titled *Perirrhanterium*, the second *Superliminare*. Neither page has a
headline. In *B* and *1633* the two stanzas are on a single page. *B* has
the headline *Superliminare* and no titles to the quatrains. *1633* has no
heading and titles the two quatrains *Superliminare*. This is thus a
threshold piece between *The Church-porch* and *The Church* proper.

**2 Sprinkled:** continuing the metaphor of *Perirrhanterium*. See note to
title, p. 388.

**4 mystical repast:** see Introduction, p. xvi.

**5 Avoid:** keep off. Comma added.

**The Altar:** see Introduction, p. xvi. In his *Art of English Poesy* Putten-
ham not only has a chapter devoted to poems in the shape of
geometrical figures (I.xii), but a highly relevant subsection on *The
Pillar, Pilaster or Cylinder:* 'The Pillar is a figure among all the rest of
the Geometrical most beautiful, in respect that he is tall and upright
and of one bigness from the bottom to the top. In Architecture he is
considered with two accessory parts, a pedestal or base, and a chapter
or head; the body is the shaft. By this figure is signified stay, support,

rest, state, and magnificence. Your ditty then being reduced into the
form of the Pillar, his base will require to bear the breadth of a metre
of six or seven or eight syllables; the shaft of four; the chapter egall
with the base' (Gregory Smith ed., *Elizabethan Critical Essays*, II.100-
101). Puttenham quotes two examples, one comparing the Queen to
a pillar, another a love poem. As often, Herbert converts a secular
tradition to holy ends, and appears to be following Puttenham's
recipe closely in form and content. His chapter and base consist of
two couplets, one decasyllabic, one octosyllabic; his shaft is tetrasylla-
bic; the *HEART* is located in the shaft or 'body' of the poem, whose
signification tallies with Puttenham's 'stay, support, rest, state, and
magnificence'. Later Herrick was to follow suit, syllable for syllable,
in a pedestrian poem which is titled, with disarming directness, *The
Pillar of Fame* (*Hesperides*, 1648, n. 1129). H and P both erroneously
relate *The Altar*'s shape to 'a classical altar', 'a pagan place of sacrifice
– here resolutely christianized' – an error initiated by editions from
1634 to 1809 which provided increasingly elaborate altars drawn
around or above the poem.

**4** God's instruction to Moses: 'And if thou wilt make me an altar of
stone, thou shalt not build it of hewn stone; for if thou lift up thy tool
upon it, thou hast polluted it' (*Exodus* 20: 25) (H). Hence *broken*, not
hewn, in l.1.

**5-6 A HEART alone/Is such a stone:** cf. *2 Corinthians* 3: 3: the
Christians are Christ's epistles 'written ... not in tables of stone, but
in fleshy tables of the heart' (P). A motif to recur in the following
poems.

**13-14** Evoking Christ's triumphal entry into Jerusalem, when he
answered the Pharisees' demand that he should rebuke his disciples
with: 'I tell you that, if these should hold their peace, the stones
would immediately cry out' (*Luke* 19: 40) (H).

**15-16** For the **mine/thine** interchange, cf. *Clasping of hands*, p. 153.
Line 15 points directly to *The Sacrifice*, where Herbert takes on the
persona of Christ, and undertakes the traditional Christian exercise
of reliving and illustrating his Passion (cf. *The Thanksgiving*, p. 32,
ll.15–16: *But how then shall I imitate thee, and/Copy thy fair, though bloody
hand?*)

**The Sacrifice:** Not Herbert's only dramatic monologue, but the only
one to be spoken in Christ's voice. The triple rhymes and refrain give
the poem a remorseless, driving intensity.

**1 Oh all ye, who pass by:** 'Is it nothing to you, all ye that pass by?
behold, and see if there be any sorrow like unto my sorrow'
(*Lamentations* 1: 12), echoed at the Crucifixion, *Matthew* 27: 39: 'And
they that passed by reviled him' (H). Here implicitly addressed to the
reader who has just entered *The Church*.

**3 who took eyes:** by the Incarnation. Picked up again in *Love (3)*, p. 184, l.12.

**5 make a head:** rise up.

**7 Who:** i.e. the Princes.

**10 Egyptian slave:** throughout this poem there are repeated links made between Moses' leading the Israelites out of Egypt, and Christ's salvation of man. See ll.122, 138, 170, 239 and notes.

**13 Mine own Apostle:** Judas, who was in charge of the Apostles' money. Cf. *Perirrhanterium*, l.171n (P).

**15 put me there:** in his *bag*. Judas pockets the cash given in exchange for his betrayal of Christ.

**17 For thirty pence:** 'Then one of the twelve, called Judas Iscariot, went unto the chief priests, And said unto them, What will ye give me, and I will deliver him unto you? And they covenanted with him for thirty pieces of silver' (*Matthew* 26: 14-15).

**18 at three hundred:** when Mary Magdalene anointed Christ with spikenard Judas protested, 'Why was not this ointment sold for three hundred pence, and given to the poor?' (*John* 12: 5) (P). But were 'pence' the same as 'pieces of silver'? Herbert appears to be heightening the contrast.

**22 Drops blood:** in the garden of Gethsemane, 'being in an agony he prayed more earnestly: and his sweat was as it were great drops of blood falling down to the ground' (*Luke* 22: 44).

**the only beads:** like a rosary.

**23 O let this cup pass:** 'And he said, Abba, Father, all things are possible unto thee; take away this cup from me: nevertheless not what I will, but what thou wilt' (*Mark* 14: 36).

**25-7** Christ's suffering together with man's remorse can cure (*A Balsam*) all the world – except the suffering of Christ. Comparable ironies riddles the rest of this poem.

**29-31** 'And he cometh unto the disciples, and findeth them asleep, and saith unto Peter, What, could ye not watch with me one hour? Watch and pray, that ye enter not into temptation: the spirit indeed is willing, but the flesh is weak' (*Matthew* 26: 40-41).

**33 Arise, arise, they come:** 'Then cometh he to his disciples, and saith to them ... Rise, rise, let us be going: behold, he is at hand that doth betray me' (*Matthew* 26: 45-6).

**35-7** 'Judas then, having received a band of men and officers from the chief priests and Pharisees, cometh thither with lanterns and torches and weapons' (*John* 18: 3). *With their lanterns do they seek the sun:* see Introduction, pp. xxviii–xxix.

**37 With clubs and staves they seek me, as a thief:** 'In that same hour said Jesus to the multitudes, Are ye come out as against a thief with swords and staves for to take me? I sat daily with you teaching in the temple, and ye laid no hold on me' (*Matthew* 26: 55).

**38 the way of truth:** cf. 'Jesus saith ... I am the way, the truth, and
the life: no man cometh unto the Father, but by me' (*John* 14: 6). *W*
and *B* both have *the Way and the Truth* (H). Cf. l.179: *I, who am Truth,*
and note.

**41** 'And he that was called Judas, one of the twelve, went before [the
multitude] and drew near unto Jesus to kiss him. But Jesus said unto
him, Judas, betrayest thou the Son of man with a kiss?' (*Luke*
22: 47–8).

**45-6 they lay hold on me, not with the hands/Of faith, but fury:**
a pointed ironic reversal of St. Paul's advice, 'Fight the good fight of
faith, lay hold on eternal life' (*1 Timothy* 6: 12) (H), and see quotation
for l.37.

**47 who have loos'd their bands:** 'They ... shall know that I am the
Lord, when I have broken the bands of their yoke' (*Ezekiel* 34: 27)
(H). *Bands:* bonds.

**49 All my Disciples fly:** 'Then all the disciples forsook him, and fled'
(*Matthew* 26: 56).

**50-51 the star/That brought the wise men:** see p. 406, *Good Friday*
l.8 n.

**53 from one ruler to another:** from Caiaphas, the high priest, to
Pontius Pilate, the Roman governor, to Herod, and back to Pilate
again. While Herbert conflates the movements of Christ's last two
days he vividly conveys the harrying to and fro: *They lead me in once
more ... they lead me out again./Whom devils fly, thus is he toss'd of men*
(ll.189–91).

**57 The Priest and rulers all false witness seek:** 'And the chief
priests and all the council sought for witness against Jesus to put him
to death; and found none. For many bare false witness against him,
but their witness agreed not together' (*Mark* 14: 55–6). *The Priest* is
Caiaphas.

**59 Paschal Lamb:** the lamb traditionally sacrificed and eaten
at Passover. 'For even Christ our passover is sacrificed for us'
(*1 Corinthians* 5: 7).

**61-2 they accuse me of great blasphemy,/That I did thrust into
the Deity:** see *John* 10: 30–33. Before the Passion week, when Christ
had answered the Jews' questioning with 'I and my Father are one',
they had wanted to stone him 'for blasphemy, and because that thou,
being a man, makest thyself God', but

**63** Christ, as St. Paul explained, 'being in the form of God, thought it
not robbery to be equal with God' (*Philippians* 2: 6) (P).

**65-7** 'At the last came two false witnesses, And said, This fellow said, I
am able to destroy the temple of God, and to build it in three days'
(*Matthew* 26: 60–61). Explained in *Mark* 14: 58: 'I will destroy this
temple that is made with hands, and within three days I will build
another made without hands' (i.e. by his Resurrection after three days).

397

**69–71** 'And the Lord God formed man of the dust of the ground, and breathed into his nostrils the breath of life; and man became a living soul' (*Genesis* 2: 7). Man (*Adam*) repays God by using that breath to condemn Christ to death. *Unto death* has a double function here: Christ gives man breath daily (1) till he dies; man uses it to condemn Christ (2) to death. For the *breath/death* rhyme see *Mortification* p. 95. For the proper rendering of breath see *Prayer (1)*, p. 49, l.2; prayer is *God's breath in man returning to his birth* i.e. its place of origin, God (H).

**73–5** 'And as soon as [Pilate] knew that [Jesus] belonged unto Herod's jurisdiction, he sent him to Herod ... And the same day Pilate and Herod were made friends together, for before they were at enmity between themselves' (*Luke* 23: 7, 12). (Herod was thought to be an Imperial spy; hence Pilate's enmity.)

**77** 'And Herod with his men of war set him at nought, and mocked him, ... and sent him again to Pilate' (*Luke* 23: 11).

**89 I answer nothing:** 'And the chief priests accused him of many things: but he answered nothing. And Pilate asked him again, saying, Answerest thou nothing? behold how many things they witness against thee. But Jesus yet answered nothing, so that Pilate marvelled' (*Mark* 15: 3–5).

**90 stony hearts:** ironically echoing *The Altar*, p. 23.

**94–5** A typological reference, recalling Noah's flood: after forty days the rains abated and Noah sent a raven and dove out of the ark, but the dove 'returned unto him into the ark, for the waters were on the face of the whole earth' (*Genesis* 8: 9) (P). Christ's dove-like behaviour increases the storm around him.

**96–106** 'And Pilate answered and said ... What will ye then that I shall do unto him whom ye call the King of the Jews? And they cried out again, Crucify him. Then Pilate said unto them, Why, what evil hath he done? And they cried out the more exceedingly, Crucify him' (*Mark* 15: 12–14). *Away, away:* 'But they cried out, Away with him, away with him, crucify him' (*John* 19: 15).

**103 Wíth nóisĕs cŏnfúsĕd fríghtĭng thĕ dáy:** an appropriately unmetrical line, breaking up the expected iambic pentameter (which could have been sustained in, e.g. 'With confus'd noises frightening the day').

**107 wish my blood on them and theirs:** when Pilate saw the crowd was immovable, he washed his hands, 'saying, I am innocent of the blood of this just person: see ye to it. Then answered all the people, and said, His blood be on us, and on our children' (*Matthew* 27: 24–5) (H).

**109–11 cankers:** corrupts. *These words aright/Used ... are the whole world's light:* because Christ's redemptive blood could save them. But they turn it into a curse.

**113, 117 a seditious murderer:** 'And they cried out all at once,

398

saying, Away with this man, and release unto us Barabbas: (Who for a certain sedition made in the city, and for murder, was cast into prison)' (*Luke* 23: 18–19).

**115 For it was their own cause who killed me:** W has *case* not *cause*; i.e. like to like – the murderers of Christ choose a murderer to be saved.

**118 peace:** 'the peace of God, which passeth all understanding' (*Philippians* 4: 7) (P).

**121 Caesar is their only King:** 'Pilate saith unto them, Shall I crucify your King? The chief priests answered, We have no King but Caesar' (*John* 19: 15) (P).

**122 He clave the stony rock:** an ironic reference to God's command to Moses, 'thou shalt smite the rock, and there shall come water out of it, that the people may drink' (*Exodus* 17: 6). Caesar is more likely to get water out of a rock than out of the stony hearts of Christ's accusers, as Christ knows from his own experience (*as I well try*). This also points forward to ll.170–71 (P) and 246–7.

**125-133 they scourge me ... They buffet me, and box me ... they spit on me:** 'Then did they spit on his face, and buffeted him; and others smote him with the palms of their hands' (*Matthew* 26: 67).

**127 mysteriousness:** a curious word in the present context, explained by the fact that in the Old Latin and Vulgate Versions 'sacrament' and, more often, 'mystery' were used interchangeably to render the Greek 'mysterion'. Christ's suffering is sacramental.

**129-31** In *W* and *B* this stanza switches to the third person: *They buffet him*, etc.

**130 Who grasp the earth and heaven with my fist:** cf. Donne: 'Could I behold those hands which span the Poles,/And turn all spheres at once, pierc'd with those holes?' (*Goodfriday, 1613, Riding Westward*, ll.21–2).

**134 Who by my spittle gave the blind man eyes:** 'he took the blind man by his hand ... and when he had spit in his eyes ... he asked him if he saw ought. And he looked up, and said, I see men as trees, walking' (*Mark* 8: 23ff.).

**137 My face they cover:** 'And some began to spit on him, and to cover his face' (*Mark* 14: 65).

**138 As Moses' face was veiled:** on Moses' descent from Mount Sinai with the tables of the law, his face shone and frightened the Israelites, so he veiled it (*Exodus* 34: 29–35). Moses' transfiguration is usually seen to prefigure Christ's when he talked with Moses and Elias (*Matthew* 17: 2). Herbert suggests another typology.

**141 abjects flout me:** evoking another parallel, to David's lamentation, which prefigures Christ's sufferings: 'False witnesses did rise up; they laid to my charge things that I knew not. They rewarded me evil for good to the spoiling of my soul ... in my adversity they rejoiced, and gathered themselves together, yea, the abjects gathered themselves together against me ... they did tear me, and ceased not' (*Psalm* 35: 11–15). *Abjects:* castaways, degraded people (OED), riff-raff.

**142 Now prophesy who strikes thee:** 'And the men that held Jesus mocked him, and smote him. And when they had blindfolded him, they struck him on the face, and asked him, saying, Prophesy, who is it that smote thee?' (*Luke* 22: 63–4).

**146–7** They all call for my death so vehemently (*with utmost breath*) that they almost die before me. The dying Christ will also spend his *utmost breath* at l.229; there is an ironic contrast here.

**149–51 Weep not, dear friends:** as Christ went to Calvary, a crowd of women followed him, weeping; 'But Jesus turning unto them said, Daughters of Jerusalem, weep not for me, but weep for yourselves, and for your children' (*Luke* 23: 28).

**for both:** for himself, and them.

**When all my tears were blood:** see l.22.

**153 The soldiers lead me to the common hall:** 'Then the soldiers of the governor took Jesus into the common hall, and gathered unto him the whole band of soldiers' (*Matthew* 27: 27).

**155 twelve heav'nly legions:** occurring earlier, in the Garden of Gethsemane, when Jesus rebuked one of the disciples for cutting off the ear of the high priest's servant, saying, 'Thinkest thou that I cannot now pray to my Father, and he shall presently give me more than twelve legions of angels?' (*Matthew* 26: 53) (P).

**157, 161, 169, 173 scarlet robe ... crown of thorns ... the reed ... Hail king:** 'And they stripped him, and put on him a scarlet robe. And when they had plaited a crown of thorns, they put it upon his head, and a reed in his right hand: and they bowed the knee before him, and mocked him, saying, Hail, King of the Jews!' (*Matthew* 27: 28–9).

**159 cordial:** (1) restorative, (2) deriving from the heart.

**161–3 thorns ... are all the grapes Sion doth bear:** referring to Isaiah's song of the much-tended vineyard that only brought forth wild grapes, so he laid it waste: 'it shall not be pruned, nor digged; but there shall come up briars and thorns ... For the vineyard of the Lord of hosts is the house of Israel, and the men of Judah his pleasant plant: and he looked for judgment, but behold oppression; for righteousness, but behold a cry' (*Isaiah* 5: 6–7) (H). It is easy to see this as a prophetic metaphor of Christ's disappointment in man.

**165 the earth's great curse:** God to Adam: 'cursed is the ground for thy sake; in sorrow shalt thou eat of it all the days of thy life; Thorns also and thistles shall it bring forth to thee' (*Genesis* 3: 17–18). Now Christ redeems Adam and wears the thorns in his crown.

**thrall:** bondage.

**169–70 with the reed … They strike my head:** 'And they smote him on the head with a reed, and did spit upon him, and bowing their knees worshipped him' (*Mark* 15: 19).

**170 my head, the rock:** Herbert is repeating the typological link made by St. Paul, between Moses' cleaving the rock to release water (see l.122n) and Christ: the Israelites 'were all baptized unto Moses in the cloud and in the sea; And did all eat the same spiritual meat; And did all drink the same spiritual drink: for they drank of that spiritual Rock that followed them: and that Rock was Christ' (*1 Corinthians* 10: 2–4) (P).

**177–9** In worldly terms, the trappings of Christ's Passion symbolize the guilt (*bloody weeds*), pain (*thorny crowns*) and feebleness (*sceptres frail as reeds*) of earthly power. Christ turns them into transcendental truths, as the preceding stanzas have shown: his scarlet robe symbolizes his redemptive blood; in the crown of thorns he takes on Adam's curse; his head struck with the reed is the source of all blessings.

**179 I, who am Truth:** cf. Pilate's interrogation of Christ, and his reply: 'for this cause came I into the world, that I should bear witness unto the truth. Every one that is of the truth heareth my voice. Pilate said unto him, What is truth?' (*John* 18: 37–8).

**183 Prophets … to see:** an earlier incident: 'he turned him unto his disciples, and said privately, Blessed are the eyes which see the things that ye see: For I tell you, that many prophets and kings have desired to see those things which ye see, and have not seen them' (*Luke* 10: 23–4) (P).

**185–6** 'Then came Jesus forth, wearing the crown of thorns, and the purple robe. And Pilate said unto them, Behold the man! When the chief priests … and officers saw him, they cried out, saying, Crucify him, crucify him' (*John* 19: 5–6).

**189–90** 'And after that they had mocked him, they took the robe off from him, and put his own raiment on him, and led him away to crucify him' (*Matthew* 27: 31).

**193 to engross:** to sum up.

**198 Simon:** 'And as they came out, they found a man of Cyrene, Simon by name: him they compelled to bear his cross' (*Matthew* 27: 32).

**199 The decreed burden of each mortal Saint:** another earlier episode: 'Then said Jesus unto his disciples, If any man will come after me, let him deny himself, and take up his cross, and follow me. For whosoever will save his life shall lose it: and whosoever will lose his life for my sake shall find it' (*Matthew* 16: 24–5) (P).

**201** See note to l.1.

**202 Man stole the fruit, but I must climb the tree:** Adam (and Eve) stole the apple from the tree of knowledge of good and evil (*Genesis* 2: 9, 3: 6); Christ redeems mankind by ascending the cross,

which corresponds to the other tree in the Garden of Eden, the tree of
life. Cf. Donne: 'We think that Paradise and Calvary,/Christ's Cross,
and Adam's tree, stood in one place' (*Hymn to God my God, in my
sickness*, ll.21–2).

**205-7** The world was created by God's word; the greater world of sin
must be redeemed by Christ's suffering.

**210-11 kneel,/Till all were melted, though he were all steel:** cf.
the guilty Claudius: 'Bow, stubborn knees; and heart, with strings of
steel,/Be soft as sinews of the new-born babe' (*Hamlet* III.iii.70–71).

**213 my God! why leav'st thou me:** 'And about the ninth hour Jesus
cried with a loud voice, saying, Eli, Eli, lama sabachthani? that is to
say, My God, my God, why hast thou forsaken me?' (*Matthew* 27: 46).

**215** Note the broken line, completed in *The Thanksgiving*, l.9, and
altered refrain.

**217-19** The sharper shame that tears his soul is at the reproaches
heaped on him.

**221** The proverb, 'Physician, heal thyself' was quoted by Christ early
in his ministry (*Luke* 4: 23). Conflated with: 'And they that passed by
railed on him, wagging their heads, and saying, Ah, thou that
destroyest the temple, and buildest it in three days, Save thyself and
come down from the cross' (*Mark* 15: 29–30).

**229 Betwixt two thieves:** 'And with him they crucify two thieves: the
one on his right hand, and the other on his left' (*Mark* 15: 27).

**231 what have I stolen from you? death:** Christ's death is an
expiatory sacrifice redeeming believers from the effects of sin: 'the
wages of sin is death; but the gift of God is eternal life through Jesus
Christ our Lord' (*Romans* 6: 23).

**233 A king my title is:** 'And a superscription also was written over
him in letters of Greek, and Latin, and Hebrew, THIS IS THE
KING OF THE JEWS' (*Luke* 23: 38).

**237 They gave me vinegar mingled with gall:** just before the
Crucifixion 'They gave him vinegar to drink mingled with gall: and
when he had tasted thereof, he would not drink' (*Matthew* 27: 34).
There is more *malice* than *gall* in the offered drink.

**239 With Manna, Angels' food, I fed them all:** see also note to
l.170. Referring once more to Moses leading the Israelites out of
Egypt, when God 'had rained down manna upon them to eat ...
Man did eat angels' food' (*Psalm* 78: 24–5). This Psalm also recalls
the smiting of the rock and the parting of the Red Sea, all well-
established prefigurations of Christ's salvation, and – appropriately
to the present context – all of them divine benefits slighted by man's
disobedience.

**241 They part my garments:** 'And they crucified him, and parted
his garments, casting lots' (*Matthew* 27: 35).

**242 My coat, the type of love:** because the diseased 'besought him that they might only touch the hem of his garment: and as many touched were made perfectly whole' (*Matthew* 14: 36) (H).

**246 they will pierce my side:** 'when they came to Jesus, and saw that he was dead ... one of the soldiers pierced his side, and forthwith came there out blood and water' (*John* 19: 34).

**247 as sin came:** when Eve was created from the side of Adam (*Genesis* 2: 21); it is redeemed by the sacrament of Christ's blood flowing from his side. Further elaborated in *The Agony*, p. 34 stanza 3. This moment is the heart of Herbert's faith and he is to return to it constantly in the rest of *The Church*.

**249 now all is finished:** 'he said, It is finished: and he bowed his head, and gave up the ghost' (*John* 19: 30).

**250 weal:** gain, benefit.

## The Thanksgiving

**4 preventest:** forestall and surpass.

**5 Shall I weep blood? why thou hast wept such store:** see *The Sacrifice*, pp. 24, 28, ll.22, 150.

**6 all thy body was one door:** H compares the assassination of Caesar; as Brutus withdrew his dagger, 'mark how the blood of Caesar follow'd it,/As rushing out of doors' (*Julius Caesar* III.ii.178–9).

**9 My God, my God, why dost thou part from me?:** completing *The Sacrifice*, l.215.

**11 Shall I then sing, skipping, thy doleful story:** see Introduction, pp. l–li.

**11–14** Shall I celebrate the triumph of the Passion, omitting all its pain?

**15 But how then shall I imitate thee:** as he did in the dramatic monologue of *The Sacrifice*.

**16 Copy thy fair, though bloody hand:** echoing the image of *Perirrhanterium*, p. 9, ll.8–10.

**19–20** 'He that hath pity upon the poor lendeth unto the Lord; and that which he hath given will he pay him again' (*Proverbs* 19: 17) (P).

**19, 21** Punctuation emended; *wealth;* and *honour;* in *1633*.

**26 thence:** from his bosom.

**31 predestination:** meaning, to match your predestination, I promise in my future to ... There is a distinct comic pathos in the speaker's attempt to match the eternity of divine providence by his short-winded promise to mend roads three years hence and to mend his own ways today. The whole poem dwells on the absurd imbalance between God's grace and man's meagre gratitude.

**33 spittle:** hospital.

**36 but for fashion:** i.e. as something wholly transitory (since he intends to renounce the world: *The world and I will quarrel*).

**44 'tis here:** any wit God has given him is in this book of poems.

**45 Nay, I will read thy book:** the boast of the preceding line is promptly abandoned as he turns to God's book, the Bible.

**47 Thy art of love:** as opposed to Ovid's carnal *Ars amatoria*.

**48 Victory!:** returning to ll.17–18: *Surely I will revenge me on thy love,/And try who shall victorious prove*. At the moment when he thinks he can match God's love, he remembers the Passion, for which he can offer no adequate equivalent.

**The Reprisal:** a continuation of the preceding poem, as its first lines and first title in *W* (*The Second Thanksgiving*) make clear. It is a reprise, a return to the original subject.

**3–4** Even if I die for you, I can't match you, because of my sins (Christ had none).

**6 disentangled state:** cf. *I was entangled in the world of strife* (*Affliction (1)*, p.45, l.41) (H). The implication may also be of an estate unencumbered by debt.

**8 For by thy death I die for thee:** it is only your death that gives me the strength to die for you (H).

**11 grief's sad conquests:** couldn't I have outdone you in grief, as you do me in glory?

**14 the conquest:** *W* and *B* both have *thy conquest*, which clarifies how the speaker finally resolves his duel with Christ. By confessing his sins, he will take part in Christ's victory over him, and, through Christ, overcome the man who vied with Christ. H points out the similarities to stanzas 1 and 4 of *W*'s *Love* (see Appendix 2, pp. 334–5).

**15–16 in thee I will overcome/The man:** referring to Jacob's wrestling with God, the turning point of his moral life: 'And Jacob was left alone; and there wrestled a man with him until the breaking of the day ... and he said, Let me go, for the day breaketh. And he [Jacob] said, I will not let thee go, except thou bless me ...' The man refused to give Jacob his name, but afterwards Jacob said 'I have seen God face to face' (*Genesis* 32: 24ff.).

**The Agony:** Not in *W*.

**4 two vast, spacious things:** see l.6 – *Sin and Love*.

**8 mount Olivet:** the mount of Olives, where the Garden of Gethsemane lay. This stanza is a description of the Agony in the Garden: 'And being in an agony he prayed more earnestly: and his sweat was as it were great drops of blood falling down to the ground' (*Luke* 22: 44).

**11 press and vice:** (1) instruments of torture which are also (2) evil. This poem reverses our expectations in that Christ's suffering for man's *vice* is presented in such violent terms that it suggests the Crucifixion. This misapprehension is corrected in the more tranquil

404

next stanza, which does describe the Crucifixion, when Christ's blood was released as the wine of the Eucharist. For such concealed positives clarified later in the same poem, see Introduction, pp. xlvff.

**13 assay:** test, as well as try.

**14–15 that juice, which on the cross a pike/Did set again abroach:** see p. 403: *The Sacrifice* l.246n. The image is of *broaching* (opening) a cask of wine and letting it run; *again* reaffirms that the blood had already flowed in the *press*ing of the preceding stanza.

**17 Love is that liquor:** The winepress derives from *Isaiah* 63, one of the liturgical epistles for Holy Week (H), which also draws on (1) Moses leading the Israelites out of Egypt, traditionally typologically linked with Christ's redemption of man (verses 11–14); (2) God's love (verses 7–9), and (3) his vengeance: 'Wherefore art thou red in thine apparel, and thy garments like him that treadeth in the winefat? I have trodden the winepress alone; and of the people there was none with me; for I will tread them in mine anger, and trample them in my fury; and their blood shall be sprinkled upon my garments' (*Isaiah* 63: 2–3). Herbert thus characteristically transfers the image of the winepress from God's anger, to Christ's love and suffering for our sins.

**The Sinner:** a sonnet.

**3–4 if my soul make even with the week:** if my soul were to follow the pattern of the week, a seventh part of it (like Sunday) would be devoted to God.

**5 I find there:** cf. *Perirrhanterium*, p. 21, ll.451ff., where the reader is urged to *Sum up at night, what thou hast done by day*. The speaker here is sickened by his weekly reckoning, which finds a mass of vanity, and minimal virtue.

**7 cross:** contrary.

**8 the circumference earth is:** the earth lies at the centre of the surrounding sky: in the soul's cosmography this is reversed.

**9–10 dregs ... quintessence:** a metaphor drawn from distilling. The *quintessence* (scanned quíntĕssénce) is the same as *The spirit and good extract*.

**12 Lord restore thine image:** 'God created man in his own image; in the image of God created he him' (*Genesis* 1: 27). The better we are, the more like God we become.

**14 Remember that thou once didst write in stone:** 'And he gave unto Moses, when he had made an end of communing with him upon Mount Sinai, two tables of testimony, tables of stone, written with the finger of God' (*Exodus* 31: 18) (P). The *hard heart* of l.13 redirects the reader to *The Altar*, whose *hard heart ... alone/Is such a stone,/As nothing but/Thy pow'r doth cut* (p. 23, ll.10, 5–8).

**Good Friday:** one of several two-part poems. Cf. *Easter*, p. 39, *The H.*

*Communion*, p. 49, *Christmas*, p. 78, *An Offering*, p. 143. In *W* the second half (ll.21–32) was a separate poem, entitled *The Passion*, following on what is now *The Reprisal*: a logical but more monotonous arrangement.

**5–6 Shall I thy woes/Number according to thy foes?** Christ's woes at the Passion were as innumerable as the *multitude, great companies*, the crowds of chief priests, scribes, soldiers, and ordinary people repeatedly referred to in the gospel accounts.

**8 Shall all:** shall all the stars of heaven show thy death? Cf. *The Sacrifice*, p. 25, ll.50–51: *They leave the star/That brought the wise men of the East from far*. These references to the nativity point to the last words of *The Church*, which complete its cyclic movement by heralding Christ's birth. See further, Introduction, p. xvi.

**12 the true vine:** maybe contrasting with *The Sacrifice*, p. 29, ll.161–3 and see note.

**13–16** Since your griefs are beyond computation, let my life be taken over by the single sorrow of your distress, running through my days like the sun.

**18 get:** beget.

**19 as each beast his cure doth know:** see further, *Humility*, p. 67.

**20 Each sin may so:** each individual sin can be cured by its particular sorrow.

**23 My heart hath store, write there:** continuing the image of *The Altar* and *The Sinner*, deriving from St. Paul's epistle: 'For as much as ye are manifestly declared to be the epistle of Christ ministered by us, written not with ink, but with the spirit of the living God; not in tables of stone, but in fleshy tables of the heart' (*2 Corinthians* 3: 3).

**24 ink:** i.e. his blood. But cf. the preceding note.

**31–2 sin ... all the writings blot:** cf. *Perirrhanterium*, p. 9, ll.7–10: *lust ... blots thy lesson written in thy soul;/The holy lines cannot be understood*.

**Redemption:** a sonnet. Titled *The Passion* in *W*. For an interpretation, see Introduction, pp. xxxff., and for the Christian's liberation from Levitical Law (i.e. the *old lease*), see further Walton, p. 367.

**Sepulchre:** layout as in *B*; four-line stanzas in *1633*. Joseph of Arimathaea took the body of Jesus, 'and wrapped it in linen, and laid it in a sepulchre that was hewn in stone, wherein never man before was laid' (*Luke* 23: 53). The poem develops further the hard heart–stone analogy of *The Altar* and *The Sinner*.

**5 store:** store-house.

**10 this pure rock:** pure partly because it was new, unused and therefore clean; more importantly, because, unlike man, it cannot sin; ultimately, *pure* because referring also to Christ, 'that spiritual Rock' (*1 Corinthians* 10: 4).

**11 indicted:** accused.

**13 our hard hearts have took up stones to brain thee:** an episode referred to in *The Sacrifice*, p. 26, l.61; see note. 'Then the Jews took up stones again to stone him. Jesus answered them, Many good works have I showed you from my Father: for which of those works do ye stone me? The Jews answered him, saying, For a good work we stone thee not: but for blasphemy' (*John* 10: 31–3).

**14 falsely did arraign thee:** the Jews' accusation was 'that thou, being a man, makest thyself God' (*John* 10: 33).

**17-18 the law by heav'nly art/Was writ in stone:** Moses' tables of the law; see *The Sinner*, p. 35, l.14 n.

**19 The letter of the word:** cf. 'In the beginning was the Word, and the Word was with God, and the Word was God' (*John* 1: 1); so Christ is the letter of the word of God.

**19-20 no fit heart/To hold thee:** reverting to *2 Corinthians* 3: 3, which lies behind *The Altar, The Sinner, Good Friday* also. See *Good Friday*, l.23n, p. 406.
**Though:** even though.

**23 cold, hard, foul:** attributes commonly expected of stones, which Herbert applies to our hearts.

**Easter:** one of several two-part poems. See *Good Friday*, p. 405, headnote.

**5 calcined:** burnt to ashes; in alchemical terms, reducing a mineral to its purest form by burning off impurities (P) – producing the *gold* of l.6.

**9-10** The cross, which bore Christ's name (in the superscription, 'This is the king of the Jews') has taught all wood to resound it.

**11-12** Christ's stretched sinews are compared to the taut catgut of stringed instruments. P points out that seventeenth-century church music reached a much higher pitch than that of madrigals and chamber music.

**13 Consort:** play together.

**15 three parts vied:** all music consists of the three notes (*parts*) of the common chord, multiplied by further additions (*vied*). The three parts are taken by the lute, heart, and Holy Spirit.

**19-30** These lines make up the song projected in the preceding stanzas. It is a religious transmutation of an aubade, or dawn song, sung by the lover to wake his beloved. Cf. *The Dawning*, p. 108, and see further Introduction, p. xxiii.

**19-20 I got me flowers to straw thy way:** linking the Resurrection with Christ's triumphal entry into Jerusalem: 'And many ... cut down branches off the trees, and strawed them in the way. And they that went before, and they that followed, cried, saying, Hosanna; Blessed is he that cometh in the name of the Lord' (*Mark* 11: 8–9).

**Straw:** strew.

**22 And brought'st thy sweets along with thee:** cf. 'And when the sabbath was past, Mary Magdalene, and Mary ... and Salome, had brought sweet spices, that they might come and anoint him. And very early in the morning the first day of the week, they came unto the sepulchre at the rising of the sun' (*Mark* 16: 1–2). But the risen Christ has no need of spices (*thy sweets*) to preserve his body.

**24-6** A variation on the theme of *The Reprisal*: there is no contest possible with God.

**29 We count three hundred:** an approximation of the year's 365 days.

**we miss:** we're mistaken.

**Easter wings:** set out, in *W*, *B*, and *1633*, as two separate poems, each with the same title, on two separate and adjacent pages. Also listed in *B* and *1633*'s indexes as two poems. In all modern editions set out as a single poem. But the first treats of man generically; the second is personal and autobiographical. The next two poems (*H. Baptism (1)* and *(2)*) form a comparable pair.

**Easter wings (1)**

**1-5** Summarizing the creation of man, when he was given dominion over all living things (*Genesis* 1: 26–8), his fall and God's punishment.

**6-7 With thee/O let me rise:** cf. *Easter: thy Lord ... Who takes thee by the hand, that thou likewise/With him mayst rise* (p. 39, ll.3–4), and *The Dawning*, p. 109, ll.11–12.

**7-8 rise/As larks:** cf. 'He giveth power to the faint; and to them that have no might he increaseth strength. Even the youths shall faint and be weary ... but they that wait upon the Lord shall renew their strength; they shall mount up with wings as eagles' (*Isaiah* 40: 29–31) and, more distantly, 'unto you that fear my name shall the Sun of righteousness arise with healing in his wings' (*Malachi* 4: 2) (P).

**9 victories:** to rhyme with *rise*. Also contrasting with *The Thanksgiving*, p. 33, l.48: *O my dear Saviour, Victory!*. The victory is God's, not man's – repeated again at the lift-off in *Easter wings (2)* l.8.

**10 Then shall the fall further the flight in me:** i.e. *Felix culpa*, the happy fall of man, happy because it was the cause of Christ's redemption of man.

**Easter wings (2)**

**1-5** Summarizing the autobiography detailed at greater length in *Affliction (1)*: *My flesh began unto my soul in pain,/Sicknesses cleave my bones ... Thus thin and lean without a fence or friend,/I was blown through with ev'ry storm and wind* (p. 45, ll.25–36).

**8 And feel this day thy victory:** one extra foot here. Otherwise both pairs of wings are made up of lines of 5, 4, 3, 2, 1, 1, 2, 3, 4, 5 iambic feet. The form is diagrammatized in Puttenham who says that the 'manner of proportion by situation of measures [i.e. metric shapes] giveth more efficacy to the matter often times than the [rhymes], and both proportions [metre and rhyme] concurring together as they needs must, it is of much more beauty and force to the hearer's mind' (*Art of English Poesy*, II.xi. 'Of Proportion by Situation', Gregory Smith, ed., *Elizabethan Critical Essays* II.94).

**9 imp:** 'to engraft feathers in a damaged wing, so as to restore or improve the powers of flight' (OED) i.e. *With thee/Let me combine*, and see *Easter wings (1)*, ll.6–7n.

**10 Affliction shall advance the flight in me:** a recurrent theme in Herbert; see Introduction, pp. xlivff. Though much derided by later critics (see *George Herbert: The Critical Heritage*, pp. 137, 149–50), the multiple appropriateness of visible shape to image and content make these poems more pleasing than *The Altar*. These three component parts are comparable to the lute, heart, and Spirit invoked in *Easter*, ll.13 ff. *Vied and multiplied* they *twist a song, pleasant* but not *long*.

**H. Baptism (1):** Much rewritten after *W*'s version; see Appendix 2, p. 331.

**1–4** An image which looks simpler than it is. For clarification, see *Faith*, p. 48, ll.37–40.

**5–6 spring and rent/Is in my dear Redeemer's pierced side:** see *The Sacrifice*, p. 31, ll.246–7, and *The Agony*, p. 34, stanza 3, and notes.

**10 measures:** keeps pace with.

**11 plaster:** like a modern medical plaster, but in those days often consisting of a curative substance *spread* on a tissue and then applied to the wound. Cf. *blister* in *H. Baptism (2)*, l.14.

**12 You:** i.e. baptism.

**the book of life:** the divine record of the righteous, often balanced in the Bible by the book of death for the damned (which Herbert avoids). It is characteristic that for Herbert the baptismal record of his name should *discredit* his subsequent sins: biblical references to the book of life are often less sanguine in both New and Old Testaments, e.g.: 'And the Lord said to Moses, Whoever hath sinned against me, him will I blot out of my book' (*Exodus* 32: 33); 'And if any man shall take away from the words of the book of this prophecy, God shall take away his part out of the book of life' (*Revelation* 22: 19).

**13 miscall:** malign.

**H. Baptism (2)**

**2 A narrow way and little gate:** quoting from the Sermon on the Mount: 'Enter ye in at the strait gate: for wide is the gate, and broad is the way, that leadeth to destruction, and many there be which go in thereat: Because strait is the gate, and narrow is the way, which leadeth unto life, and few there be that find it' (*Matthew* 7: 13–14).

**4 antedate:** forestall.

**10 Behither:** coming short of, avoiding.

**12 get on:** may get on (prosper).

**13 bid:** ask for, pray for, purchase.

    **preserve her wealth:** i.e. her primal, baptismal innocence.

### Nature

**1–3** One of many poems of restlessness and rebellion. Cf. *The Collar*, p. 149.

**6 strong holds:** strongholds, citadels. 'The weapons of our warfare are not carnal, but mighty through God to the pulling down of strong holds' (*2 Corinthians* 10: 4) (P).

**10 by kind:** according to its nature.

**12 making thy workmanship deceit:** i.e. deceiving thy workmanship, betraying it.

**13–14 there/Engrave thy rev'rend law:** 'Behold, the days come, saith the Lord, that I will make a new covenant with the house of Israel ... I will put my law in their inward parts, and write it in their hearts, and will be their God' (*Jeremiah* 31: 31–3) (P).

**15–17 make a new one, since the old ... Is ... stone:** 'Then will I sprinkle clean water upon you, and ye shall be clean ... A new heart also will I give you, and a new spirit will I put within you: and I will take away the stony heart out of your flesh, and I will give you an heart of flesh' (*Ezekiel* 36: 25–6) (P). I have quoted the neighbouring verses to the precise biblical reference because they relate to the poems on the baptism preceding this poem. Both Herbert's poems, and their allusions, need to be read in context to take account of their full significance. See *The H. Scriptures II*, p. 56, and Introduction, p. xxxviii. The final image of the stony heart also gestures back to *The Altar*, p. 23, *The Sinner*, p. 35, and particularly *Sepulchre*, p. 38 (cf. *stone/To hide my dust*); the *sapless* old *law* gestures forward to *The Jews*, p. 149, l.1.

### Sin (1):

A sonnet singled out for praise by Coleridge, 'for the purity of the language and the fulness of the sense', 'equally admirable for the weight, number, and expression of the thoughts, and for the simple dignity of the language' (*Biographia Literaria*, ch. xix) (H). Like *Prayer (1)*, p. 49, part of its strength lies in the sonnet's tight form holding together what is a list, and the great variety of tone within that list (e.g. the whisper of humour in l.8). Coleridge rightly draws attention to the metre ('number'): a large number of reversed first feet and strong caesuras break up the regular iambic pattern and create a naturally colloquial tone (e.g. *Púlpĭts ănd súndăys, Bíblĕs laĭd ópĕn, Bléssĭngs befórehănd, Ángĕls ănd grácĕ*).

**13 fences:** cf. *Affliction (1)*, p. 45, l.35.

**Affliction (1):** Herbert's fullest, most clearly autobiographical poem. It can be usefully read in conjunction with Ferrar's preface, pp. 7–8. In *The Country Parson*, ch. xv, p. 219, Herbert speaks of 'the benefit of affliction which softens and works the stubborn heart of man'.

**2 service:** like *household-stuff* and *furniture* below, suggesting religious service in terms of domestic service.
**brave** in this context would imply smart.

**6 gracious benefits:** in *W*, *gracious perquisites* – the same as the perks of modern employment.

**11 Such stars I counted mine:** cf. *Take stars for money; stars not to be told/By any art, yet to be purchased* (*Perirrhanterium*, p. 13, ll. 171–2).

**19 milk and sweetnesses:** the traditional food for babies.

**21 straw'd:** strewn. Cf. *I got me flowers to straw thy way* (*Easter*, p. 39, l. 19).

**24 a party:** a person.

**25 began:** i.e. said. The next three lines are spoken by the flesh.

**27 agues dwell in ev'ry vein:** pain is located in the veins in *The Agony*, p. 34, stanza 2, also.

**32 my friends die:** according to Walton, 'all Mr. Herbert's Court-hopes' died with the deaths of three patrons, the second Duke of Lennox and Richmond (1624), the second Marquis of Hamilton (1625), and King James I (1625). Bacon and Lancelot Andrewes died in 1626, and Herbert's mother in 1627 (H). A. M. Charles (op. cit., pp. 84–7) refers this poem to an earlier period, *c*. 1617, coinciding with the deaths of two of Herbert's brothers (*my friends* could mean my kinsmen). This dating creates problems at l. 45.

**38–40 The way that takes the town:** Herbert eschewed what Walton called 'the painted pleasures of a Court life', or the career of a Secretary of State (H) for the *lingring book* and *gown* of Cambridge.

**45 Academic praise:** A. M. Charles' dating of *c*. 1617 is early for this: see Chronology (p. lxvi). Herbert's academic successes fell at the end of 1617, 1618, 1619 and 1620.

**47 where:** *neare;* in *1633*, but *W* has *where* and *B* has *where* written above *neere*; furthermore it makes better sense.

**53 cross-bias:** a metaphor taken from bowls, meaning to deflect from a proper course.

**57–60** See Introduction, p. xliv, and *Employment (1)*, p. 55, l. 24n.

**62 In weakness must be stout:** H compares *Malachi* 3: 13: 'Your words have been stout against me, saith the Lord.' The following verses also reflect the concerns of this poem in its distinction between the complainers, and those who *serve* God: 'Ye have said, It is vain to serve God: and what profit is it that we have kept his ordinance, and that we have walked mournfully before the Lord of hosts? ... Then they that feared the Lord spoke often one to another, and the Lord hearkened, and heard it ... They shall be mine, saith the Lord of hosts, in that day when I make up my jewels; and I will spare them, as a man spareth his own son that serveth him' (*Malachi* 13: 14–17. The phrase evoked in *Easter Wings (1)*, p. 40, l.8, comes three verses later).

**63-4 I will change the service, and go seek/Some other master out:** cf. *The Odour*, p. 170, and Nicholas Ferrar: 'he used in his ordinary speech, when he made mention of the blessed name of our Lord and Saviour Jesus Christ, to add, *My Master*' (p. 8).

**63, 65** For these quick reversals, cf. the end of *The Collar*, p. 150.

**65 I am clean forgot:** could mean both I have forgotten myself, and God has forgotten me. It may feel like the latter, but it will be the former.

**66 Let me not love thee, if I love thee not:** if I can't love you properly, let me not love you at all.


**Repentance**

**2 treat/With:** come to terms with.

**3 quick:** alive, but also blooming (and dying) quickly.

**momentany:** *momentarie* in *B*, and meaning the same thing.

**4 pressing:** hurrying forward.

**5-6** For the sentiment, cf. *Mortification*, p. 95.

**7-12** A stanza not elucidated by the commentators. The gist of it is that our lives are transitory, our pleasures fleeting, but our sorrows as old as Adam's fall. *Each day doth round about us see*: i.e. our life is but a few hours of a day (*two hours' work, or three*).

**13 height of mercy:** contrasting with *short-breathed men*.

**14 compassionate:** (to rhyme with hate) take pity on.

**19-20 Sweeten at length this bitter bowl,/Which thou has pour'd into my soul:** cf. 'I am gall, I am heartburn. God's most deep decree/Bitter would have me taste: my taste was me' (G. M. Hopkins: *I wake and feel the fell of dark*).

**21 Thy wormwood:** with gall, wormwood is a recurrent biblical image of bitterness and suffering, e.g. 'He hath filled me with bitterness, he hath made me drunken with wormwood ... remembering mine affliction and my misery, the wormwood and the gall' (*Lamentations* 3: 15, 19). Such affliction points back to Christ's suffering (*They gave me vinegar mingled with gall*, *The Sacrifice*, p. 31, ll.237–8) and Herbert's *Affliction (1)*.

**22 stay:** delay, hold off.

**25 When thou for sin rebukest man:** 'When thou with rebukes dost chasten man for sin, thou makest his beauty to consume away' (*Psalm* 39: 12, BCP) (H).

**32 the broken bones may joy:** 'Make me to hear joy and gladness; that the bones which thou hast broken may rejoice' (*Psalm* 51: 8) (H) – a psalm all about repentance: 'For thou desirest not sacrifice; else would I give it; thou delightest not in burnt offering. The sacrifices of God are a broken spirit: a broken and contrite heart, O God, thou wilt not despise' (verses 16–17).

**33 well-set:** punning on setting bones, and a musical setting. P points out that *bones* were an 'early musical instrument', but they were pretty crude. They are called for in a telling original stage direction when Bottom asks for music in *A Midsummer Night's Dream*: 'I have a reasonable good ear in music. Let us have the tongs and the bones.' First Folio SD: *Music Tongs, Rural Music* (IV.i.27).

**36 Fractures well cur'd make us more strong:** cf. 'our peace will like a broken limb united,/Grow stronger for the breaking' (*2 Henry IV* IV.i.222–3) (H). Cf. the sentiment of *Easter Wings (1)* and *(2)*.

**Faith**

**2-3 when man's sight was dim,/And could see little:** in parenthesis.

**6 conceit:** imagine.

**feast:** see Introduction, p. xvi. The *mystical repast* of communion underlies the recurrent banquet images in *The Church*. See e.g. *Love (3)*, p. 184.

**9 rare outlandish root:** ostensibly evoking a literally rare foreign antidote, like the snake-root of Virginia (H), but really about faith, the cure to original sin, which is *outlandish* because unearthly, celestial.

**11 my foot:** referring to God's curse on the serpent: man 'shall bruise they head, and thou shalt bruise his heel' (*Genesis* 3: 15).

**19-20** Reverting to the theme of *Easter Wings (1)* and *(2)*.

**25 lien:** lain.

**29-30** Faith (rather than the usual death) is the Great Leveller.

**33-5** Just as (for instance) the moon looks bright by the light it receives from the sun, so Christ imparts his light to us, and makes us shine. Punctuation emended; *sun,* in *1633*.

**37-40** Appropriately, this stanza clarifies the obscurity of *H. Baptism (1)*, p. 42, ll. 1–4. By delaying this gloss, Herbert enacts the sudden understanding brought by Faith.

**44 Referring all for flesh again:** at the Resurrection.

**Prayer (1):** like *Sin (1)* (p. 43), a sonnet-list, and, like *Hope* (p. 118), having a riddling element. Many of the images convey the human-divine reciprocity (ll. 2, 4–7, 11), as in the *mine/thine* interchange closing *The Altar* and binding *Clasping of hands* (pp. 23, 153). Many are purely imagistic (ll. 12–14).

**1 the Church's banquet:** the feast of the Church. Add to the recurrent banquet–communion motif.

**Angels' age:** H compares with *Man's age* (*Repentance*, p. 46, l. 7);

prayer acquaints man with the angels' blessed, timeless existence.

**2 God's breath:** cf. *The Sacrifice*, p. 26, ll.69–71n.

**3 The soul in paraphrase:** cf. *the soul's blood*, l.13.

**4 plummet:** usually sounds the depth of water. Prayer is a reversed plummet measuring the distance from the earth up to heaven.

**5–6** A series of images for angry prayer, attacking God. Numerous subsequent poems in *The Church* will be of this kind. Cf. Donne: 'Earnest Prayer hath the nature of Importunity ... Prayer hath the nature of Impudency; We threaten God in Prayer ... And God suffers this impudency, and more. Prayer hath the nature of Violence ... we besiege God ... and we take God Prisoner ... and God is glad to be straitned by us in that siege' (Donne: *Sermons*, v, 364) (P). **Sinners' tower:** a scaling tower used against besieged cities (as *engine* is a military engine). Behind both images lies an implicit pun on suitor/shooter, made more obvious in *Artillery*, p. 136, ll.17–29.

**Christ-side-piercing spear:** cf. the original incident, described in *The Sacrifice*, p. 31, ll.246–7, reinterpreted in *The Agony*, p. 34, stanza 3.

**7 The six-days-world transposing in an hour:** (in *1633* world-transposing). Just as it took God six days to create the world so an hour of prayer reconverts the matter of the world into spirit. *Transpose* is a musical term: e.g. to translate a tune from one key to another.

**8 fear:** n.b., and contrast with l.9.

**10 Exalted Manna:** P suggests that just as Manna stood typologically for the Eucharist (God's body in earthly terms), so here the earthly is returned to heaven.

**12 Heaven in ordinary, man well drest:** see Introduction, pp. xxvi–xxvii.


**The H. Communion:** another two-part poem, cf. *Easter* and *Good Friday* (pp. 39, 36); *W* only has the second half, titled *Prayer*, and a different *The H. Communion* not included in *B* or *1633*; see Appendix 2, p. 333.

**1–4** God imparts himself to the speaker not in sumptuousness (H and P both identify a distinction between Catholic and Anglican worship here).

**2 a wedge of gold:** referring to Achan, who coveted and buried a rich booty, including 'a wedge of gold of fifty shekels weight', for which he and his family were stoned to death (*Joshua* 7: 21ff.). A covertly powerful condemnation of worldliness.

**3 from me:** *B: for me*. Referring to Judas' betrayal for thirty pieces of silver.

**5–6 without ... within:** i.e. outside me (and not possessing me) ... inside me.

**10 thy small quantities:** i.e. of regular communion.

**13-18** The image is of the soul like a besieged town threatened by the rebellious flesh surrounding it. Communion is like an outer rampart keeping back the flesh, but it can't reach the soul.

**19-22** Grace (which comes with communion) *can* reach the inner sanctum of the soul.

**23-4 those:** refers to *these elements* (l. 19), meaning the spiritual elements of communion, which wait at the door of *the soul's most subtle rooms* to receive dispatches from *their friend*, the soul (about how to control the rebellious flesh of the preceding stanza).

**25 my captive soul:** continuing the metaphor from above.

**26 thither:** to heaven.

**29 Before that:** before;

**sin turn'd flesh to stone:** sustaining the metaphor recurrent from *The Altar* onwards.

**30 all our lump to leaven:** not clarified by P or H. Referring to *1 Corinthians* 5: 6–8: 'Your glorying is not good. Know ye not that a little leaven leaveneth the whole lump? Purge out therefore the old leaven, that ye may be a new lump, as ye are unleavened. For even Christ our passover is sacrificed for us: Therefore let us keep the feast, not with old leaven, neither with the leaven of malice and wickedness, but with the unleavened bread of sincerity and truth.' (Unleavened bread is eaten at Passover.)

**40 And leave th' earth to their food:** the Communion wine is sufficient sustenance (*thy heav'nly blood*). Cf. 'his disciples prayed him, saying, Master, eat. But he said unto them, I have meat to eat of that ye know not of' (*John* 4: 31–2).

**Antiphon (1):** a composition sung alternately by two choirs in worship. Not in *W*.

**3-6** Cf. *Prayer (1)*.

**Love I:** one of many poems playing off divine against human love.

**1 this great frame:** i.e. 'this goodly frame, the earth' (*Hamlet* II.ii.300) (H).

**12 infernal pit:** this is the first of five overt references to hell in the final form of *The Church* (*hellish moths* in *Content*, p. 66, l. 27, hardly counts). See *The H. Scriptures I*, p. 56, l. 12; *Charms and Knots*, p. 94, l. 18; *Time*, p. 119, l. 24; *The Priesthood*, p. 156, l. 3 (and also, implicitly, *Business*, p. 110, ll. 13–14, 22, nn, and *Justice (2)*, p. 137, l. 8).

**Love II**

**6 pant thee:** P suggests 'pant after thee', comparing 'As the hart panteth after the water brooks, so panteth my soul after thee, O God' (*Psalm* 42: 1).

**11 in kind:** rightfully due to you: an obsolete but maybe legal sense.

**12 disseized:** wrongfully dispossessed by force.

**14 who did make and mend our eyes:** cf. *Love (3)*, *Who made the eyes but I?* (p. 184, l.12) (H).

**The Temper (1):** *W*'s title for this and the next poem, *The Christian Temper*, clarifies which kind of temper is primarily intended: the frame of mind. But the poem's content also evokes the extremes of heat and sousing used to temper steel (see l.2), and the slackening or tightening of a stringed instrument to temper or tune it.

**10 Those distances belong to thee:** cf. 'Could I behold that endless height which is/Zenith to us, and our Antipodes?' (Donne: *Goodfriday, 1613. Riding Westward*).

**13 meet arms with man:** H points out a pun on *mete* (measure), as duellists measure their foils to see they are of a length. The next lines suggest the arms of the body, rather than weapons: man is *rack*ed (l.9) to stretch *from heav'n to hell*, and in l.22 *stretch*ed and *contract*ed.

**18 roost and nestle:** 'Yea, the sparrow hath found an house, and the swallow a nest for herself, where she may lay her young, even thine altars, O Lord' (*Psalm* 84: 3) (H).

**28 Make one place ev'ry where:** see Introduction, pp. xxiii–xxiv.

**The Temper (2)**

**3–4 Save that, and me:** don't use your dart on my joy or me; or if you must, then use it to destroy sin for us.

**5 stands to:** stands in witness of. But see also ll.10–16, and note.

**7 race:** raze, demolish.

**16 standing Majesty:** stationary, not peripatetic. The OED example is apposite: 'that your Grace would settle a standing Mansion-house and Family, that Suitors may know whither to repair constantly' (*c.* 1645).

**Jordan (1):** the river in which John the Baptist baptized Christ; hence the waters of purification: God, 'by the Baptism of the well-beloved Son Jesus Christ, in the river Jordan, didst sanctify Water to the mystical washing away of sin' (from the BCP's Order of Baptism) (P). See Introduction, p. xxi.

**2 Become:** suit.

**5 chair:** i.e. throne – see *The Temper (2)*, l.9.

**9 Must all be veil'd:** one of Herbert's many pleas for simplicity.

**12 pull for Prime:** to draw for a winning hand in the card-game of Primero (P).

**Employment (1):** For Herbert's praise of employment, see *The Country Parson*, ch. xxxii, p. 242: 'even in Paradise man had a calling, and how much more out of Paradise, when the evils he is now subject unto may be prevented or diverted by reasonable employment'.

**2 extend:** stretch.

**5, 7 were:** would be.

**6 extension:** the space taken up by it (immediately paraphrased in *the room*).

**8 thy great doom:** the Day of Judgment.

**11-12** In the preceding two stanzas, there appears to be a sustained contrast between the mere *extension* of the man, or plant, employed by God, and its spiritual content, the *sweetness*, *praise* and *grace* divinely imparted to it. These lines summarize the contrast: the former, the container, is *the measure of our joys*, which is earthly (*in this place*), the latter, the essential content, is *The stuff* which is with God (*with thee*).

**17 All things are busy:** cf. 'All Nature seems at work. Slugs leave their lair – /The bees are stirring – birds are on the wing – ... And I the while, the sole unbusy thing,/Nor honey make, nor pair, nor build, nor sing' (S. T. Coleridge: *Work without Hope*, ll.1-6) (H).

**20 these:** the flowers.

**21 thy great chain:** the great chain of being, the ordered medieval and Renaissance hierarchy stretching from God to man and on down to animals, plants, and minerals.

**23 consort:** a group of instruments (or voices) playing harmoniously together.

**strain:** melody. Probably lying behind G. M. Hopkins: *Justus quidem es, Domine*, ll.12-14: 'birds build – but not I build; no, but *strain*,/ Time's eunuch, and not breed one work that wakes'. Both poems derive from *Jeremiah* 12: 1-2, Hopkins explicitly so in his title. 'Righteous art thou, O Lord, when I plead with thee: yet let me talk with thee of thy judgments: Wherefore doth the way of the wicked prosper? ... Thou has planted them, yea, they have taken root: they grow, yea, they bring forth fruit ...' See also *Affliction (1)*, p. 46, ll.57-60, and Introduction, p. xliv.

### The H. Scriptures I

**1-2 let my heart/Suck ev'ry letter, and a honey gain:** 'How sweet are thy words unto my taste! yea, sweeter than honey to my mouth!' (*Psalm* 119: 103) (H).

**8-10** This is the welcome mirror that improves the beholder's eyes. The initial sense of *mends*, to improve by making more beautiful, is corrected to a curative improvement by the next image: this is the well that washes what it reflects.

**10 endear:** make more precious, exalt.

**11 Lidger:** lieger, ambassador – in this case to the foreign *states of death and hell* (H).

**13 handsel:** first instalment, a pledge (H).

**14 Subject to ev'ry mounter's bended knee:** an unusually

417

paradoxical line for Herbert.

**The H. Scriptures II**

**1-4** Herbert's yearning to understand a divine cosmography in the Bible contrasts with his recurrent indifference to the contemporary advances in earthly astrology in, e.g. *The Agony, Divinity, Vanity (1)*.

**5-6** Herbert recommends the 'diligent collation of Scripture with Scripture' to his country parson. See ch. iv, p. 200. For links between biblical order and the order of Herbert's poems, see Introduction, p. xvi.

**7 as dispersed herbs do watch a potion:** are ready to make up a (curative) potion. (Each herb on its own may be inefficacious; it is the combination which is effective.)

**9-12** Lines about the links Herbert (and any reader) makes between what he reads in the Bible, and his own life. *And in another make me understood:* i.e. in another person's story I understand my own.

**13 Stars are poor books:** a sceptical reference to the art of astrology, or reading the future through the stars.

**Whitsunday:** the feast of the descent of the Holy Ghost upon the Apostles on the fiftieth day after Easter, which was Pentecost. See *Acts* 2. *W*'s version is considerably rewritten in *B*, and its last three stanzas replaced by four new ones. See Appendix 2, p. 331.

**5 Where is that fire:** 'There appeared unto them cloven tongues like as of fire, and it sat upon each of them. And they were filled with the Holy Ghost' (*Acts* 2: 3-4).

**8 Feasting all comers:** see *Acts* 2: 9-11 for a roll call of the many diverse races, from whom (verse 41) some three thousand souls were converted.

**13-14 The sun ... wisht for night:** maybe cf. Peter's promise at Pentecost of miracles to come: 'The sun shall be turned to darkness' (*Acts* 2: 20); see also *Misery*, p. 98, l.33n, p. 439.

**17 pipes of gold:** the Apostles, 'channels of Grace' (P). An irrigation metaphor, repeated in *The Jews*, p. 149, l.3.

**20 those, who did themselves through their side wound:** by martyring the Apostles, they hurt themselves more (the implicit parallel is with the martyrdom of Christ, wounded through the side as in *The Sacrifice*, p. 31, l.246, an act which ultimately harmed the perpetrators rather than their victim).

**23 braves:** taunts.

**28 his ancient and miraculous right:** see note to title.

**Grace**

**1 My stock:** referring to Job's lamentation over death: 'For there is hope of a tree, if it be cut down, that it will sprout again, and that the

tender branch thereof will not cease. Though the root thereof wax old
in the earth, and the *stock* thereof die in the ground: Yet through the
scent of water it will bud, and bring forth boughs like a plant: But
man dieth, and wasteth away: yea, man giveth up the ghost, and
where is he?' (*Job* 14: 7–10) (H).

**5 If still the sun should hide his face:** echoing *The sun . . . Hung down
his head* (*Whitsunday*, p. 57, l.14).

**7 Thy works, night's captives:** the works of Grace would be captives
of night.

**10** Can the dew do more than God's dove of grace?

**11–12** The grass can't ask for the dew, saying, *Drop from above.*

**19 to cross his heart:** to run athwart the hard heart created by sin.

## Praise (1)

**11 with a sling:** 'So David prevailed over the Philistine [Goliath] with
a sling and with a stone, and smote the Philistine, and slew him'
(*1 Samuel* 17: 50) (H).

**13–15 next door . . . To a brave soul:** H assumes the head is the seat
of the soul, and the effects of the potion rise to the brain; P tells us that
'the soul resides in the heart, *next door* to the stomach'. What matters is
that a humble herb can be distilled, drunk, and affect the spirit, just
like the poor, or short-armed man (in the preceding stanza) *may do
more* with God's help.

**17 poor bees:** returning to *Employment*, p. 55, ll.17ff. – a link created by
altering *W*'s last stanza:

> O raise me then: for if a Spider may
> > Spin all the day:
> > Not flies, but I shall be his prey
> > Who do no more.

**Affliction (2):** not in *W*.

**4–5** i.e. even if, in a staggered repayment, I were to die over every hour
of Methusalem's life (969 years). For the metre, see Introduction,
p. li.

**10 discolour:** spoil the colour of, adulterate.

**15 imprest:** payment in advance, the modern deposit. Each stanza
compares Christ's suffering with the vast inadequacy of the Chris-
tian's reciprocal grief.

**Mattins:** morning prayer.
**16 him by whom they be:** their creator, God: the *workman* of l.19.

**Sin (2):** This is one of only two poems in the final version of *The Church*
in which Herbert refers to the devil (*Decay* has Satan, as does *The
Church Militant*, an early poem). It is typical of Herbert that the devil

should be seen (a) positively, having *some good in him*, and (b) in human terms, as a way of clarifying our sins to ourselves. Sin is the real horror: *By sight of sin we should grow mad*. H comments: 'In *W* the earlier *Even-song* follows *Mattins*; it is not clear why in *B* and *1633 Sin* comes between *Mattins* and the new poem *Even-song*.' But the new arrangement makes the point that every day, between morning and evening prayers, sin intervenes.

**1–5** H points out the traditional nature of St. Augustine and Thomas Aquinas' doctrine that evil has no substance because it is a lack or corruption of good, just as the devil was a fallen angel (see ll.2–3). Since it is merely a defect it has no *being* and therefore can't be seen. He quotes Donne: 'You know, I presume, in what sense we say in the School, *Malum nihil*, and *Peccatum nihil*, that evil is nothing, sin is nothing; that is, it hath no reality, it is no created substance, it is but a privation.' But in another sermon Donne dismisses this as 'a school-shift', since we still fear death, damnation and sin (see H, p. 498). Herbert equally takes the argument further in his second stanza.

**10 devils are our sins in perspective:** devils are our sins, seen through a perspective glass (like a telescope or a microscope, an optic) – that is, they make clear to us the evil of our sins. For this now obsolete but then common sense of perspective, cf. the OED's citation from Sir T. Herbert (1634): 'Like an ill-sighted man, who sees with Spectacles or Perspectives.'

**Even-song:** set out as eight stanzas in *1633*. Replacing a different poem with the same title in *W*; see Appendix 2, p. 336.

**6–8** P and H don't explain how God denied himself sight. Presumably this is clarified in the next lines: in effect, God plays blind, because, when he sees the speaker's errant ways, he doesn't punish him, since he gave him his Son (punning with sun).

**15 crost:** thwarted.

**24 disorder'd clocks:** cf. Herbert's injunction to reassess the soul each night: *if with thy watch, that too/Be down, then wind up both* (*Perirrhanterium*, p. 21, ll.454–5).

**Church-monuments:** set out in six-line stanzas in *1633*; continuously, as here, in *B* and *W*. This poem is very unusual for Herbert in its long sentences, prosaic enjambement, heavy caesuras (ll.6, 14, 22), unobtrusive rhymes, and recurring stresses – on *dust* (recurring seven times), and *dust*-rhymes. Two of the three caesuras also fall on *dust* and *last* which sustains the leitmotif. See Appendix 1, p. 329, for Herbert's shuffling of poems to create this sequence of five church poems here.

**2 Here I entomb my flesh:** one needs to imagine the speaker prostrate on the church floor and its tombs as he meditates on the body being only dust. Walton describes Herbert lying prostrate

420

before the altar on the eve of his induction, p. 361.

**10 Which:** i.e. the body.

**dissolution:** the object of *discern*. The body can best see its own imminent dissolution by comparing dust to dust and earth to earth. Cf. God to Adam: 'out of [the ground] wast thou taken: for dust thou art, and unto dust shalt thou return' (*Genesis* 3: 19).

**12 These:** i.e. *dust* and *earth*. Funerary monuments vainly attempt to sever man's dust from the earth of its origin.

**14 point out:** distinguish (H).

**15 bow, and kneel, and fall down flat:** the ultimate decay of the tombs is described in terms of the speaker's prostration.

**16 those heaps:** i.e. of dust – the entombed dead.

**17 stem:** 'the stock of a family; the main line of descent from which the "branches" are offshoots' (OED).

**20 flesh is ... glass:** a surprise variation of the well-known 'The voice said Cry. And he said, what shall I cry? All flesh is grass' (*Isaiah* 40: 6). This *glass* is the hour-glass.

### Church-music

**1-2 displeasure/Did through my body wound my mind:** presumably referring to one of Herbert's many periods of sickness.

**6 Rising and falling with your wings:** cf. the movement of *Easter Wings (1)* and *(2)*.

**8** P and H suggest analogies, but the sentiment is commonplace.

**9 Comfort, I'll die:** H glosses this as 'take comfort', which seems inapposite (why should music wish for his death?). Perhaps he addresses music as *Comfort*. The exclamation, *I'll die*, appears initially as one of fear, but is quickly corrected. Certainly he will die, being mortal, but it would be much worse if he were deserted by music (*if you post from me*), whereas the comfort of music at his death will lead him to heaven. Walton tells us Herbert used to say that 'his time spent in prayer and cathedral music elevated his soul, and was his heaven upon earth', and that he sang to his lute on the Sunday before his death (pp. 371, 382).

**Church-lock and key:** originally titled *Prayer* in *W*, before it was much revised and *locks* in l.1 gave the title to fit it with this sequence.

**11-12** Sins plead in their own voice, but also, like stones making a fast stream turbulent, they make Christ's redemptive blood sound more loudly on their behalf.

**The Church-floor:** not in *W*. See Introduction, p. xiii, especially for elucidation of l.15. This poem has an unusual stanzaic pattern (abc abd efc efd ggh iih jj), creating a pleasant chequered effect as in the patterning of the floor.

**10 one sure band:** 'charity, which is the bond of perfectness' (*Colossians* 3: 14) (P).

**19 Blest be the Architect:** who also raised an Altar in men's hearts. This poem is in this sense a companion piece to *The Altar* (p. 23).

**The Windows:** not in *W*. See Introduction, p. xii, for an interpretation.

**6 anneal:** to burn in colours on glass: hence, describing the making of stained-glass windows.

**8 Preacher's:** there are no possessive apostrophes in *1633*, here or elsewhere. This could be a plural, but seems to make better sense meaning the Preacher's *life* (understood).

**9 rev'rend:** i.e. to be revered, honoured.

**Trinity Sunday:** appropriately written in three three-line stanzas. In *W* a second poem with the same title follows this: not in *B* or *1633*.

**7-9** Note the three sets of three words. Such a trope often also included parallelism between the separate parts of the lists, e.g. 'Hoo! hearts, tongues, figures, scribes, bards, poets, cannot/Think, speak, cast, write, sing, number – hoo! – /His love to Antony' (*Antony and Cleopatra* III.ii.16ff.). As this example shows, it was a rhetorical flourish ripe for ridicule, and Herbert avoids its potential for facile neatness.

**Content**

**15 let loose to:** aim at.

**16 Take up:** lodge. H refers to the Emperor Charles V who gave up his throne for the cloisters in 1556, and died in the monastery of Yuste in Estremadura.

**19 tent:** dwelling place (cf. *The Temper (1)*, p. 52, l.11).

**22-4 fumes ... which rise from a huge King:** H has an apposite reference to the burial of the corpulent William the Conqueror in a narrow coffin, releasing noxious gases.

**25-8** Continuing the argument of *The brags of life are but a nine days' wonder*. Death only means the lost record of your deeds: it's better to be consumed by worms and forgotten straight away than have your reputation chewed over by backbiters (the *moths* chewing your name in indestructible books). *May not rent:* will not tear.

**29-32** You bore the consequences of your deeds: but your reputation is at the mercy of other people's wit. *1633* has a comma after *is* in l.31.

**The Quiddity:** titled *Poetry* in *W*. The title is used punningly: its proper sense is the essence of a thing, but it was extended to mean a quibbling, oversubtle distinction (H). The latter sense persists through all the negations of the first ten lines; the true essence of a verse is described in the last two lines.

**12 Most take all:** a common proverb (cf. *winner takes all*). God is *Most*; everything returns to him, including Herbert's verse and all the things it isn't that are listed in the preceding lines.

**Humility:** for a reading of this poem, see Introduction, pp. xxxiiiff.
**7 tendred:** offered.
**10 Mansuetude:** gentleness.
**13-14 coral-chain:** i.e. his wattle. *Temperance:* moderation, restraint.
**17 Peacock's plume:** emblem of Pride.
**24 each one:** of the Virtues.
**31 amerc'd:** fined.

**Frailty**
**11 sad:** sober.
**13 weeds:** clothes (as in the still surviving 'widow's weeds'), but gesturing back to *fine grass* of l.6.
**14 Brave:** bold, glorious. This and the next two lines describe the same response as in *Virtue*, p. 85, ll.5–6: *Sweet rose, whose hue angry and brave/ Bids the rash gazer wipe his eye.* The futile combative boldness of mortality prompts his tears.
**16 And prick:** sting, *Troubling* (*W*).
**17 brook not this:** don't allow this (addressed to God).
**what even now/My foot did tread:** the honour, riches and beauty of stanza 1.
**19 Affront:** confront, defy.
**22 Babel:** 'And they said, Go to, let us build us a city and a tower, whose top may reach unto heaven ... And the Lord said, Behold, the people is one, and they have all one language; and this they have begun to do: and now nothing will be restrained from them, which they have imagined to do ... So the Lord scattered them abroad from thence upon the face of the earth, and they left off to build the city. Therefore is the name of it called Babel' (*Genesis* 11: 4–9). Herbert's reference does not touch on God's confounding of a common language, but stresses the frustrated hubris of a tower *Commodious to conquer heav'n.*

**Constancy:** not in *W*. H points out that this poem follows a contemporary fashion for Character poems and that Wordsworth's *Character of the Happy Warrior* 'owes something' to it. However, the similarities in spirit and stylistic directness are even closer to Kipling's *If* – ; by comparison, Wordsworth's poem is painfully pious and verbose.
**13 example:** a pattern or design to be copied (OED: a now obsolete sense but its two examples are biblical and of this date): i.e. the correct response.
**16-20** Cf. 'Or being lied about, don't deal in lies,/Or being hated, don't

give way to hating,/And yet don't look too good, nor talk too wise'
(*If* – , ll.16–19).

**24-5** Others regulate their life by the sun; the constant man governs his
life by Christ (the usual pun here on the Son of God), who is Virtue
itself.

**31-3** H quotes three splendid analogues that explain this image: 'like
an earnest bowler/He very passionately leans that way/He should
have his bowl run' (Webster: *The White Devil* I.ii); 'A Bowl-alley: No
antic screws men's bodies into such strange flexures' (J. Earle:
*Microcosmography* [1628]); 'See how their curved bodies wreath, and
screw/Such antic shapes as Proteus never knew' (Quarles: *Emblems*
I.x.13–14).

**34 Mark-man:** marksman, one skilled at shooting at a mark (and,
unlike those playing bowls, above, archers keep their bodies straight).

**Affliction (3):** not in *W*.

**7-12 breath ... tallies ... a gale:** tally sticks were a way of recording
debts. The stick was scored with horizontal notches equivalent to the
size of the debt, and then split lengthways, so the debtor and creditor
each kept an identical record. Here God is Herbert's creditor, giving
him breath, which Herbert, the debtor, returns in sighs (ll.7–9). Since
it was believed that sighs shortened a man's life, a deep sigh would
carry several years with it and bring Herbert back to God the quicker
(ll.10–12). H misinterprets *what's then behind* (l.9) to refer to the
remaining years of life but it means the sighs still owing to God.

**13-18** God's earthly life (in Christ) was one of suffering, and he
continues to suffer daily by sharing in man's grief (*to grieve in me,/And
in thy members suffer ill*). It is, then, inadequate to praise God for his
Crucifixion alone, since he still dies every day. *1633* has a comma after
*honour* in l.15.

**The Star:** not in *W*. One of Herbert's lighter, tenderer, more whimsical
poems.

**7-8** You can make my heart better, and so your debtor.

**16 After thy love:** in accordance with, following the movement of the
star's love.

**17-18 light,/Motion, and heat:** whose acquisition has been described
in the two preceding stanzas.

**21 standing:** a standing-place.

**30 like a laden bee:** a satisfactory conclusion to the bee images of
frustration in *Employment (1)*, p. 55, ll.18ff., and *Praise (1)*, p. 59,
ll.17ff.

**Sunday:** appropriately written in seven-line stanzas.

**1** Closely echoed in *Virtue*, p. 85, l.1: *Sweet day, so cool, so calm, so bright.*

**26-8** Cf. *W: They are the rows of fruitful trees/Parted with alleys or with grass/In God's rich Paradise.* The paradisal fruit-trees reappear, worked up, in *Paradise* (p. 129), a poem which must have been composed after *W*, since it doesn't appear in it. A. M. Charles' *Life of George Herbert*, pp. 61-4, quotes Aubrey's fascinating and meticulous description of the elaborate gardens at Herbert's maternal home in Chelsea: he was brought up to a love of formal gardens and artificial wildernesses.

**31 the wife:** *W: the spouse and wife*; i.e. the Church. Cf. 'Show me dear Christ, thy spouse, so bright and clear' (Donne: *Holy Sonnet* xviii, discussing the Catholic and Protestant churches).

**37 this light:** the light of this day (Sun/son-day).

**43-6** I.e. the day of rest, the seventh day of the Creation, was superseded by the Sabbath of Christ's Resurrection – a cataclysmic change comparable to the earthquake that accompanied the Crucifixion: 'Jesus, when he had cried again with a loud voice, yielded up the ghost. And, behold, the veil of the temple was rent in twain from the top to the bottom; and the earth did quake, and the rocks rent' (*Matthew* 27: 50–51).

**47 As Samson bore the doors away:** in his Latin poem, *Terraemotus*, Herbert also links the earthquake at the Crucifixion with Samson (l.2: *Samson vt ante fores*). This is mistranslated in the bilingual edition of Herbert's Latin poems 'As Samson moved the pillars long ago'. *Fores* are doors, or double-doors, but not pillars. It seems then that Herbert is referring in both poems to Samson's carrying away the gates of Gaza, where he was imprisoned: 'And Samson ... arose at midnight, and took the doors of the gate of the city, and the two posts, and went away with them, bar and all, and put them upon his shoulders, and carried them up to the top of an hill that is before Hebron' (*Judges* 16: 3). H assumes both poems to refer to Samson's more spectacular destruction of the Gaza temple and all its occupants, including himself, by pulling two of its pillars (no doors) down with his bare hands (*Judges* 16: 25–30). P corrects H with the right, though unexpected reference for this poem, but follows the incorrect reading of the Latin.

**48 Christ's hands, though nail'd:** unlike Samson's (understood). This link may suggest a conflation of Samson's two exploits, since stress is laid on his hands only in the destruction of the temple: 'And Samson took hold of the two middle pillars upon which the house stood ... of the one with his right hand, and of the other with his left' (*Judges* 16: 29). However, *did unhinge* is more like Samson's lifting Gaza gates (off their hinges).

**50 that day:** the original day of rest, sullied by Adam's fall.

**53 a new:** the finer robes of the Redemption.

**Avarice:** not in *W*.

**8 grot:** grotto.

**10 thou hast got the face of man:** since coins are stamped with the ruler's head.

**12 dross:** the scum and impurities rejected after the melting process described in l.9. There is thus a grotesque reversal of power between man and money.

**14 falls in the ditch:** cf. 'if the blind lead the blind, both shall fall into the ditch' (*Matthew* 15: 14) and *The Country Parson*, ch. xxi, p. 226: 'the parson once demanded, after other questions about man's misery, since man is so miserable, what is to be done? And the answerer could not tell; he asked him again, what would he do if he were in a ditch?' H links to *Providence*, p. 115, ll.81–4.

**Anagram:** not in *W*, and the only poem whose position is altered from *B*, where it falls between *Church-music* and *Church-lock and key*. Its link to the next poem, ll.9–15, is obvious. The title of this poem in *1633* is in a different type face from all the other titles in the collection. Listed in *B*'s index as *Anagr*; the game is given away in both:

*B*    Mary ⎱ Anagr:
       Army ⎰

*1633*   Ana- ⎱ MARY ⎱ gram
                 ⎰ ARMY ⎰

## To all Angels and Saints

**1 after all your bands:** either meaning in accordance with your ranks, or, more probably, *bands* is the old form of *bonds*, and refers to the saints, now free of earthly fetters.

**12 The great restorative:** gold was thought to be medicinal.

**14 the cabinet where the jewel lay:** Mary bore Christ in her womb: see *Anagram*.

**16–18** P: 'A tactful censure of Mariolatry, especially the Roman Catholic tendency to regard the Virgin as co-redemptrix with Christ.'

**29 disburse:** defray expenses or pay a charge. If the angels and saints can show God's corroboration for a demand (as earthly servants can show their master's signature: *our Master's hand*), then we will pay up. The coin envisaged is that of worship, which still goes to the *Master*, not the saints, angels, or Virgin.

**Employment (2):** The metre of this poem is interesting: the first lines of stanzas 1, 2, 4 and 5 are disrupted by an energetic reversed first foot and sometimes further disturbance of the iambic pattern (*He that is weary, let him sit . . . Man is no star, but a quick coal . . . Life is a business, not good cheer . . . Oh that I were an orange-tree*) to sink into deadened, flat regularity in the last stanza.

**4 fur:** worn by the elderly and infirm, who get cold easily. Cf. *The Church Militant*, p. 191, l.198.

**18-19 The sun ... the stars:** the sun is continually busy, lighting up one hemisphere or the other, whereas stars have to catch their opportunity at night.

**22 That busy plant!:** because its ungathered fruit still hang on its branches when it is in flower.

**25 dressed:** tended.

**27-8 The man is gone,/Before we do our wares unfold:** human development is out of sync; our physical, and mental or moral maturity don't coincide (like the blossom and fruit of the orange tree), and a long, chill senility precedes death. This unusually bitter, Hardyesque ending contrasts with the lighthearted dismissal of *cold complexions* at the beginning of the poem.

**Denial:** this is the third in a run of poems whose five-line stanzas begin with an open quatrain, rhyming abab. In the two preceding poems the fifth line satisfactorily closes the rhyme-scheme (ababa); here the fifth line is unrhymed till the last stanza, the preceding sequence setting up an expectation that is all the more rudely *broken* (l.3). The metre is also painfully disrupted; see further Introduction, pp. xlixff.

**2 silent ears:** a rhetorical piece of disorder to mirror the metrical and stanzaic. Ears are not silent; mouths are. Cf. 'Blind mouths! that scarce themselves know how to hold/A Sheep-hook' (Milton: *Lycidas*, ll.119-20 – another passage full of controlled stylistic harshness).

**15, 20 But no hearing:** the line is repeated because the speaker thinks God hasn't heard. Answered in *Prayer (2)*, p. 100, l.6: *Thou canst no more not hear, than thou canst die.*

**19 My heart was in my knee:** see note to l.2.

**21-2 out of sight,/Untun'd, unstrung:** like a neglected lute.

**26 my heartless breast:** because *My heart was in my knee*; and cf. *silent ears* in l.2.

**Christmas:** in *W* titled *Christmas-Day*, and the second part not in *W*. The first part is a sonnet.

**1 rid:** rode.

**3 full cry:** of hounds, is the metaphor understood: the affections bay man and rider off their proper course.

**6-7 till the grief/Of pleasures brought me to him:** an idea explored at greater length in *The Pulley*, p. 156 (H).

**11 my dark soul and brutish:** my bestial and dark soul.

**14 rack:** a manger (and proleptic of the Crucifixion).

**19-20** Reminiscent of *Psalm* 23: 1-3: 'The Lord is my shepherd; I shall not want. He maketh me to lie down in green pastures: he leadeth me

427

beside the still waters. He restoreth my soul.'

**30 frost-nipt suns:** picking up his *spirit* ... *Like a nipt blossom* in *Denial*, p. 77, l.24.

**33 cheer my breast:** also echoing *Denial*, l.26: *O cheer and tune my heartless breast.*

**twine:** so light and music are twisted in the last line, *beams sing* and *music shine*s – a rhetorical flourish comparable to the rhyme closing *Denial*.

## Ungratefulness

**6 Where now we shall be better gods than he:** cf. 'And they that be wise shall shine as the brightness of the firmament' (*Daniel* 12: 3); 'Then shall the righteous shine forth as the sun' (*Matthew* 13: 43) (H).

**7** The *two rare cabinets* are like a jewel case (the Trinity, *Whose sparkling light access denies*, l.14) and a box of pot pourri (*sweets*, l.19: cf. *Virtue*, p. 85, l.10: *A box where sweets compacted lie* – but see n.).

**16-17 till death blow/The dust into our eyes:** A recurrent image (cf. *Frailty*, p. 68, ll.15–16, *The Church-floor*, p. 64, ll.16–17), here extended into a medical (according to H, veterinary) practice.

**23-4 this box we know/For we have all of us just such another:** the Incarnation doesn't frighten us, because our bodies are like Christ's.

**25 close, reserv'd, and dark:** unlike God's two *unlockt* (l.9) cabinets, full of *sweets* and *sparkling light*.

**28 cabinet of bone:** the skeleton, or body.

**29 Sins have their box apart:** the heart.

**30 two for one:** God's two cabinets, the Trinity and the Incarnation, for our one sinful heart.

## Sighs and Groans: not in *W*.

**2 After:** in accordance with. Echoing *Psalm* 103, which assures the contrary: 'The Lord is merciful and gracious, slow to anger, and plenteous in mercy ... He hath not dealt with us after our sins, nor rewarded us according to our iniquities' (*Psalm* 103: 8, 10), an irony of unregistered allusion comparable to those in *The Collar*. See Introduction, p. xlvii.

**6 bruise me:** as Adam and his descendants were to *bruise* the serpent (*Genesis* 3: 15), so God could bruise the *silly* (innocent) *worm*, man.

**8 ill steward:** bad, inefficient steward.

**10 magazines:** store-houses.

**14 an Egyptian night/Should thicken:** the penultimate plague of Egypt: 'And the Lord said unto Moses, Stretch out thine hand toward heaven, that there may be darkness over the land of Egypt, even darkness which may be felt. And Moses stretched forth his hand toward heaven: and there was a *thick* darkness in all the land of Egypt three days' (*Exodus* 10: 21–2).

**15-16 lust ... fig-leaves:** recalling the Fall: 'And the eyes of them both were opened, and they knew that they were naked; and they sewed fig-leaves together, and made themselves aprons' (*Genesis* 3: 7).

**20 the turn'd vial of thy bitter wrath:** 'And one of the four beasts gave unto the seven angels seven golden vials full of the wrath of God ... And I heard a great voice out of the temple saying ... Go your ways, and pour out the vials of the wrath of God upon the earth' (*Revelation* 15: 7, 16: 1).

**28 Cordial and Corrosive:** both medicinal, but *Cordial* is used of medicines that cheer and restore the heart, often associated with sweetness; *Corrosive* is caustic, escharotic, and is a medicine to be found in the *bitter box* of l.29.

## The World

**1 a stately house:** this is mankind. *The World* of the title refers to the antagonistic forces (*Fortune, Pleasure, Sin* and *Death*) that are countered by the worldly forces of good (*Wisdom, Law*), and by divine *Love* and *Grace*, to bring man's soul to *Glory*.

**7 Balconies:** stress on second syllable.

**11 Sycomore:** P follows H in erroneously identifying a mistaken etymology linking the sycamore with a species of fig-tree. However, the sycomore is the *ficus sycamorus*, a fig-tree often 50 feet high, with an enormous trunk and leaves like a mulberry, frequently referred to in the Bible, and the fig whose leaves provided protective covering for Adam and Eve after the Fall (see l.12, and *Sighs and Groans*, p. 80, l.16). Hence it is an apt symbol for *Sin*.

**13 working and winding:** both words with negative associations for Herbert; cf. *Jordan (2)*, p. 99, l.13: *As flames do work and wind*.

**14 Sommers:** sommiers – bearing-beams in a house.

**15 these:** the inside walls and beams; *that:* the fig-tree.

**20 a braver Palace:** heaven, the abode of divine love, to which the human soul is welcomed after death in *Love (3)*.

**Coloss. 3. 3. Our life is hid with Christ in God.** The accurate biblical text differs only in the first word. The quotation comes from a passage exhorting a rejection of worldly things: 'Set your affections on things above, not on things on the earth. For ye are dead, and your life is hid with Christ in God' (*Colossians* 3: 2–3). See further, Introduction, pp. xi and xix.

**2-4 double motion ... straight ... obliquely bend:** in *A Wreath* (p. 181) Herbert improves on this poem. Here man's life on earth is straight, and his divine aspirations oblique: there the worldly is twisting and the divine straight. Kepler's observations of elliptical paths in the planets were a source of dismay to some contemporaries;

cf. Donne, who takes this to illustrate the world's *Disformity of parts*: 'nor can the Sun/Perfect a circle, or maintain his way/One inch direct; but where he rose today/He comes no more, but with a cozening line,/Steals by that point, and so is serpentine' (*The First Anniversary*, ll.268ff.). Herbert concurs with Sir Thomas Browne in seeing divine providence in every movement of the sun: *Pseudodoxia Epidemica* (1646) VI, v. is a hymn of praise in Herbertian mode to the obliquity of the ecliptic, and its 'dinetical illations' that ensure variety of seasons across the globe.

**6 winds:** cf. note to *The World*, p. 81, l.13.

**Vanity (1):** not in *W*.

**2 thread the spheres:** the spheres were the concentric hollow globes thought to revolve around the earth, carrying the heavenly bodies with them (P). This stanza clearly relates to the preceding poem.

**5 dances:** H quotes several contemporary usages of *dance* for the stars' movements.

**7 aspects:** stress on second syllable. A technical term for the stars' relative position to the earth, anthropomorphized by Herbert's *full-ey'd* and *secret glances*.

**15 Chymick:** chemist, or, more probably, alchemist.

**17 callow:** unfledged, i.e. very young, unformed. There is a growing stress on the impertinence of investigative science from the first to this stanza.

**23-4 his glorious law/Embosoms in us:** cf. 'I will put my law in their inward parts, and write it in their hearts' (*Jeremiah* 31: 33) (P).

**Lent:** for Herbert's sensible attitude to fasting, see *The Country Parson*, ch. x (p. 212), and his translation of Cornarus' *Treatise of Temperance and Sobriety* (p. 304). H quotes Oley mentioning Herbert's 'careful (not scrupulous) observation of appointed Fasts, Lents, and Embers' (p. 506).

**2 Temperance:** restraint.

**5 thy Mother:** the Church.

**6 Corporation:** a formal body of people – civil, municipal, ecclesiastical, etc.

**7-18** Stanzas 2 and 3 go together. The *humble* person blames himself when rival doctrines disagree about correct practice. In customs which have rightly evolved through common practice (*things which use hath justly got*, i.e. begot), he tends to think 'I'm a discredit to the Church', rather than vice versa, if he fails to follow them (understood). And indeed *True Christians* should be glad to fast when appropriate (*When good is reasonable*). But it's another matter when the rules are counter-productive (ll.16–18, and see note below). Herbert seems to be observing, rather than recommending, the self-castigation of the *humble soul*; his dislike of doctrinal controversy recurs throughout *The Church*.

**11 scandal:** a discredit, but also a stumbling-block – which implies, in l.12, either that the Church's laws of fasting can demand too much, or that they are simply confusing. In *The Country Parson* Herbert advises against sickly, as well as seriously sick people fasting to their physical detriment.

**16-18** Herbert criticized laws of fasting as counter-productive when they were (1) too strict, or (2) contradictory. For (1) see *The Country Parson*, ch. x, p. 213: excessive restraint debilitates, and 'it is as unnatural to do anything that leads me to a sickness to which I am inclined, as not to get out of that sickness, when I am in it, by any diet'. For (2), see ibid., p. 213, where he suggests that the two laws, eating nothing pleasing, and not eating meat, are either self dupli-cating, or self-defeating (nice fish being more pleasing than nasty meat). In this sense *Authority* (a word used in both texts) robs itself (*it-self disables*) of its own *Power* to *increase/The obligation in us* (to mortify our flesh).

**24 Revenging:** taking retribution on.

**25 pendant profits:** profits deriving from (abstinence). According to H and P *the spring* suggests an analogy with fruit, hanging (*pendant*) from the tree – yet spring is hardly the English season for fruit.

**31 we cannot reach Christ's forti'th day:** we can't emulate Christ's forty days' fast in the wilderness (*Matthew* 4: 2).

**35 Be holy ev'n as he:** 'Be ye therefore perfect, even as your Father which is in heaven is perfect' (*Matthew* 5: 48; part of the Sermon on the Mount) (P).

**44 such repast/As may our faults control:** i.e. *banqueting the poor ... at our door*. *Isaiah* 58: 3-7, distinguishing between false and godly fasting, lies behind this stanza and the whole poem's sentiments: 'Is it such a fast that I have chosen? a day for a man to afflict his soul? is it to bow down his head as a bulrush, and to spread sackcloth and ashes under him? wilt thou call this a fast, and an acceptable day to the Lord? ... Is it not to deal thy bread to the hungry, and that thou bring the poor that are cast out to thy house? when thou seest the naked, that thou cover him? ...' (H).

**Virtue:** not in *W*. See Introduction, p. xlvi, for a reading of this poem.

**5-7** An image of mortality containing the promise of regeneration, only made explicit in *The Flower*, p. 162, ll.8-14.

**10 A box where sweets compacted lie:** the obvious sense to us would be a box of sweet-meats; for Herbert *sweets* are more often used in the sense of fragrance (cf. a *chest of sweets*, *Mortification*, p. 95, l.2), so, a pot pourri; the musical image of l.11 might also suggest a musical box (whose music ends when it is closed, punning on *closes* which are .

properly musical cadences).

**14-16 season'd timber** does not warp (*never gives*) and burns long and steadily with a pure flame, leaving no clinkers (*coal*), only the silkiest ash – qualities perhaps imagined here in the Last Judgment (*the whole world turn to coal*), when the virtuous soul comes into its own.

**The Pearl. Matth. 13:** 'the kingdom of heaven is like unto a merchant man, seeking goodly pearls: Who, when he had found one pearl of great price, went and sold all that he had, and bought it' (*Matthew* 13: 45–6). The reference lies behind all the mercantile terminology and imagery dispersed through the poem: *stock and surplus* (l.8), *quick returns* (l.12), *bear the bundle* (l.17), *propositions* (l.23), *projects* (l.26), culminating in *main sale, commodities, rate and price* (ll.34–5).

**1-2 head/And pipes that feed the press:** in an olive or wine press.

**5 what the stars conspire:** the plots of the stars (i.e. either their preordained courses, the subject of contemporary investigation, as in *Vanity (1)*, p. 83, stanza 1, or what they predict).

**6 what forc'd by fire:** referring to elements released by heat, as in *Avarice*, p. 74, l.9.

**13 whether:** which.

**16-17** I.e. which may so captivate the world (*on the world a true-love knot may tie*), that it carries the world with it wherever it goes. *It* is the winning party in contests to win social favour (*vies of favours*) in l.13.

**18-19** Cf. *Perirrhanterium*, p. 10, ll.37–40: getting drunk (with *drams of spirit*) is a way of giving yourself up to others.

**29 one to five:** the five senses (touch, taste, hearing, smell, sight) resisting restraint from the one man they inhabit.

**32 seeled:** (*W*); spelt *sealed* in *1633*, but meaning the seeling or stitching up of the hawk's eyelids during training.

**34 main sale:** the purchase of God's love.

**commodities:** the items to be sold in order to raise the money for this purchase (as in *Matthew* 13: he 'sold all that he had').

**37 labyrinths:** it seems quite unnecessary to relate this to the myth of Theseus, as P does. (Theseus escaped from King Minos' labyrinth after killing the Minotaur, by following back the ball of thread Ariadne gave him to unroll as he went.) (a) Herbert's labyrinths are plural; (b) he avoids classical reference everywhere else in *The Church*; (c) there were plenty of other labyrinths: Pliny (in Holland's translation of 1601) lists three, in Crete, Egypt and Lemnos; while (d) garden labyrinths appear in literature from 1601 and (e) the *silk twist*, or thread guiding one out of a labyrinth was being used in non-classical and metaphorical contexts from 1387 (see OED *labyrinth* and *clew*), and is used in this sense in *Perirrhanterium*, p. 12, l.124.

**38 silk twist:** P's suggestion of a gold chain Zeus let down from

Heaven to earth (*Iliad* viii.19–27) is most unlikely. Jacob's ladder, also spanning heaven and earth (*Genesis* 28: 10–15) (H), too seems unlikely, given *silk twist* which is hardly a ladder. Most probably an image comparable to the *Christian plummet sounding heav'n and earth* of *Prayer (1)*, p. 49, l. 4. God's thread saves man from the worldly labyrinths of *learning*, *honour* and *pleasure* described in the preceding stanzas.

**Affliction (4):** titled *Tentation* (i.e. Temptation) in *W*.

**3 A thing forgot:** cf. 'I am forgotten as a dead man out of mind' (*Psalm* 31: 12) (H).

**4 now a wonder:** cf. 'I am as a wonder unto many; but thou art my strong refuge' (*Psalm* 71: 7) (H).

**7 My thoughts are all a case of knives:** H quotes Walton: 'he would often say, He had . . . a Wit like a penknife in too narrow a sheath, too sharp for his body' (see p. 350). A famous image, later echoed by Larkin: 'Your mind lay open like a drawer of knives' ('Deceptions', from *The Less Deceived*).

**10 As watring pots give flowers their lives:** the water batters the flowers, but also refreshes them – the positive aspect of this image pointing to the poem's resolution. See Introduction, p. xlv.

**12 prick:** in *W* and *B* pinke or pink, i.e. to prick or stab (as in fencing).

**13 my attendants:** metaphoric; his faculties, thoughts, etc.

**Man:** formally an unusual poem: each stanza, bar one, has a different arrangement of its three rhymes (abccba, abcabc, abcbac, etc.) till eight of the fourteen possible permutations have been covered by the end of the poem. See further Introduction, p. xvi.

**1–3** Possibly deriving from 'which of you, intending to build a tower, sitteth not down first, and counteth the cost, whether he have sufficient to finish it? Lest haply, after he hath laid the foundation, and is not able to finish it, all that behold it begin to mock him . . .' (*Luke* 14: 28–9) (H).

**stately habitation:** cf. *Love built a stately house* (*The World*, p. 81, l. 1) (H). For Herbert's knowledge of anatomy (l. 14) and herbs (ll. 23–4) see *The Country Parson*, ch. xxiii, p. 230.

**5 to:** compared to. Man alone has the gift of eternal life.

**8 more fruit:** (*W*); *no fruit* in *B* and *1633*. *W*'s reading makes better sense, since man exceeds other forms of nature elsewhere in this stanza and is *ev'ry thing/And more*. *W* has corrections in Herbert's hand and was therefore overseen by him; *B* does not (and *1633* derives from *B*). It may be that *B*'s scribe made an error here. Alternatively, *no* can at a pinch be paralleled by *Employment (2)*, p. 76, ll. 21–5 and *Affliction (1)*, p. 46, ll. 57–60, where Herbert laments his own sterility compared to fruit-bearing trees (Palmer), but this does

433

not make overall sense.

**12 They go upon the score:** they are in debt to us; possibly also they repeat the (musical) score composed by us (since they merely imitate our speech).

**13 Man is all symmetry:** cf. the Leonardo drawing of a man splayed within a circle, whose symmetry is obvious.

**15–18** P quotes literary analogues on these common beliefs.

**21 dismount:** bring down from a height.

**23–4 Herbs ... Find their acquaintance there:** another common belief in a sympathy between certain herbs and parts of the body.

**35–6 ascent:** 'A going back in time or in order of genealogical succession' (OED), and the opposite of *descent* (l.35). Herbert clarifies by the italicized alternatives: our bodies are comforted by living, material creation; our minds improved by the study of what caused them and whence they came.

**39 Distinguished:** separated; 'And God said, Let the waters under the heaven be gathered together unto one place, and let the dry land appear: and it was so. And God called the dry land Earth; and the gathering together of the waters called he Seas: and God saw that it was good' (*Genesis* 1: 9–10).

**40 above, our meat:** because rain feeds the earth, and we feed on its crops.

**43–8** This is the only verse to repeat the rhyme-scheme (of stanza 2). Perhaps the flaw is intended in a stanza lamenting man's failure to observe God's providence: so Herbert's miraculous order is also trodden down.

**53 as the world serves us:** cf. 'Thy hands both made us, and also made us lords of all thy creatures, giving us one world in our selves, and another to serve us' (*The Country Parson:* The Author's Prayer before Sermon, p. 255.) (P).

**Antiphon (2):** titled *Ode* in *W*. See note to *Antiphon (1)*, p. 415. The form of this poem is also ingenious. The fifth line of each stanza provides the first rhyme of the next (thus, stanza 1: ababcb; stanza 2: cdcded; stanza 3: efefgf). In the last stanza the aberrant fifth line is amalgamated with the sixth to create total harmony: ghghg. Metrically, this final line also amalgamates two expected short lines sung by *Men* and *Angels*, making *of two folds one*. (All the pairs of short lines scan ˘ ˘ ´ followed by ˘ ´ ˘ ´; l.23 combines the two, making ´ ˘ ´ ˘ ´ ˘ ´, the same metre as the majority of the Chorus's lines.)

**7 tend:** used punningly, meaning (1) look after (the angels are looked after by God) and (2) attend, or await man, who will enjoy God's grace and glory *in th' end*.

**15 him we take:** in the Eurcharist.

**18 crouch:** in homage and prayer.

**20-21** In *W* the parts were reversed here. But the order of *Men* and *Angels* singing the short lines depends not on a prearranged pattern but on content: a clear distinction is sustained throughout till the union of the last line.

**Unkindness**

**1 coy:** reluctant.

**tender:** 'solicitous or careful to avoid' (OED).

**2-6** *1633* has commas after *friendship*, *think*, and a semicolon after *name*.

**8 blasted fame:** sullied reputation.

**11 curious floor:** i.e. elaborately made (for instance, as with the patterning of *The Church-floor*, p. 64).

**16 pretendeth to a place:** has pretensions or aspirations to a position.

**17 interest:** i.e. vested interest, or aspirations of his own.

**22 a tree:** the cross.

**25** Not italicized in *W* and *B*.

**Life:** not in *W*.

**15 after death for cures:** many flowers and shrubs are medicinal; see *The Country Parson*, ch. xxiii, pp. 230–31.

**Submission:** not in *W*.

**1 But that:** if it weren't that …

**2 both mine eyes are thine:** i.e. he tries to see with God's eyes and his wisdom.

**4 missing my design:** failing to achieve what I intended.

**5-6** See the autobiography of *Affliction (1)* and Nicholas Ferrar's biographical note, *The Printers to the Reader* (p. 7).

**10 I do resume my sight:** I take back my sight, i.e. the speaker questions God's providence.

**12 Disseize:** dispossess (of a legal right). Eyesight, like life, is of course God's gift to us.

**15 the praise:** of God.

**17 unto my gift I stand:** I stand by my gift.

**19 lend me a hand:** to lead the sightless speaker.

**Justice (1):** not in *W*. Continuing the questioning of the preceding poem. Cf. *Sin's round*, p. 118, for the circular form.

**1 I cannot skill:** I don't understand.

**7 pays:** repays. God's apparent perversity justly matches that of the speaker.

**10 the hand:** the upper hand.

**Charms and Knots:** describing the poem's combination of rhyming moral aphorisms (*charm* without their negative, supernatural associations) and riddles (*knot* as an intricate figure and *knotty* problem). Compare with the *Outlandish Proverbs* (pp. 257ff.).

**1 Who:** those who.

**3-4** Elucidated by the earlier version in *W*: *A poor man's rod if thou wilt hire/Thy horse shall never fall or tire.* The poor man's rod is a staff, which can serve the walker as a weapon and helps him find his path. In *W*'s version it is recommended instead of a horse. *When thou dost ride* in the final version must be taken metaphorically (to *ride a poor man's rod* equals walking with a staff). The riddle is an exhortation to simple living and humility.

**5-6** I.e. the miser is a loser; the generous man gains twice what he gives. Cf. *Ecclesiastes* 11: 1: 'Cast your bread upon the waters, for thou shalt find it after many days.'

**8** Clarified in *W*: *Doubles the night, and trips by day.* The night is darker for his unabsolved sins.

**10** Cf. 'he that throws a stone at another, hits himself' (*The Country Parson*, ch. xxviii, p. 237), and *Assurance*, p. 152, ll.39-40 (H).

**12 Finds himself there:** i.e. in the dust. Man's spirit must *rise* beyond this. The next couplet clarifies: in *W* they appear in reverse order.

**13-14** Scented powders like that of orris-root were used to sweeten the hair, linen, etc. *Forget:* i.e. tries to ignore the malodorous mortality it disguises.

**15-16** I.e. if you pay your tithe (which was a tenth part of your produce), you gain the services (including *sermons*) of the parson (who was supported by everyone's tithes). *Go for:* count as. Ten minus one is then still ten.

**17-18** Against drunkenness (as repeatedly in *Perirrhanterium*). *Shallow waters* must refer to the sipped wine of communion. *W* has: *In small draughts Heav'en does shine and dwell;/Who dives on further may find Hell.* For three more rejected stanzas, see Appendix 2, p. 332.

### Affliction (5)

**2 planted Paradise:** 'And the Lord God planted a garden eastward in Eden; and there he put the man whom he had formed' (*Genesis* 2: 8). Paradise was not as firmly founded as the unsunk Ark because Adam and Eve fell there.

**5 it:** the Ark: but at this point its meaning transfers to the sacred ark in which the tables of the law were contained, and with which the presence of God was particularly associated. Hence in its widest connotations it is used typologically for the Church.

**7-9** Cf. 'then didst thou place us in Paradise, and wert proceeding still on in thy favours, until we interrupted thy counsels, disappointed thy purposes, and sold our God ... for an apple' (*The Country Parson, The Author's Prayer before Sermon*, p. 255).

**10 we might not part:** i.e. so that man and God would not part from

436

each other.

**11 board:** lodge. As man stayed with God in Paradise, so Christ came to us to see what our suffering was like.

**13 but:** only.

**15 Some Angels us'd the first:** cf. 'angels minister to us their own food, even *joy*, and peace, and comfort in the Holy Ghost' (*The Country Parson*, ch. xxxiv, p. 247) and *Praise (3)*, p. 154, l. 21, where *Angels must have their joy* in ruling the earth.

**15-16 if our relief/Take up the second:** if our conversion seizes on grief (as its impetus).

**16-18 double line:** there seems to be a fishing image here. Man is lured to God by the baits of joy, or of grief: between the two, all complexions are brought to him.

**Furnish thy table to thy mind:** so God's table is laid, as he wishes, with the souls he has won. Clearly the Apostles as the fishers of men lie behind this (*Mark* 1: 17).

**22 curious knots:** either the intricate lacery of the bowers, or knot-gardens (flower beds laid out in complex patterns).

**24 thy bow:** traditionally a weapon of God's wrath. But cf. *Who can scape his bow?* (*Discipline*, p. 175, l. 25), where it is paradoxically turned into an image of God's love. This paradox is central to Herbert (see Introduction, p. xlv) and is emphatic here: *We are the trees, whom shaking fastens more*. Affliction brings us to God, just as sunlight (*joy*) in rain (*woe*) created the rainbow of God's covenant with Noah: 'And God said ... I do set my *bow* in the cloud, and it shall be for a token of a covenant between me and the earth. And it shall come to pass, when I bring a cloud over the earth, that the *bow* shall be seen in the cloud' (*Genesis* 9: 12–14). The bow of wrath is turned by God's sunbeams into the rainbow of the covenant.

**Mortification:** probably meaning the deadening of vital qualities (OED 3, a now obsolete sense), i.e. the extended process of death, rather than our current sense, the taming of the flesh by abstinence and castigation (OED 1). For the form of this poem, see Introduction, p. xxxix.

**2 a chest of sweets:** sweet fragrances, or the herbs or dried flowers giving the scent.

**5 clouts:** the swaddling clothes. They were strips of linen bound around the baby from toe to armpit, fulfilling the function of nappies, and did indeed look like winding sheets. See, for instance, the Andrea della Robbia ceramics of swaddled babies on the Ospedale degli Innocenti, Piazza della Santissima Annunciata, Florence.

**17 the knell:** it was rung during death at this time, rather than after it. Donne's *Contemplation of our state in our death-bed* urges: 'Think that thou hear'st thy knell, and think no more,/But that, as Bells call'd

thee to Church before,/So this, to the Triumphant Church, calls thee'
(*The Second Anniversary*, ll.99ff.).

**18 hour:** *house* in *B* and *1633*, *houre* in *W*, which is preferable, *house of death* being more appropriate at l.30 (H).

**29 A chair or litter shows the bier:** a litter is a portable couch (sometimes curtained); *a chair* is a chair in which the aged can be carried (*convey*); e.g. in *1 Henry VI* III.ii, Bedford is '*brought in sick in a chair*' and at the end of the scene '*dies, and is carried in by two in his chair*' (authorial stage directions). Hence Shakespeare refers to old age as 'chair-days' (*2 Henry VI* V.ii.48) (H). Cf. also *The Pilgrimage*, p. 139, l.36: *death is ... but a chair*. Both chair and litter are prophetic of the bier on which the corpse in its turn is carried to burial.

**32 a solemnity:** a ceremony, or 'a ceremonial procession' (OED: a now obsolete sense current at this period).

**33 hearse:** a bier.

**Decay:** not in *W*. H points out the links with Donne's sermon for Whitsunday 1625, also on the world's decay: 'And the Angels of heaven, which did so familiarly converse with men in the beginning of the world ... seem so far to have deserted this world, as that they do not appear to us, as they did to those our Fathers.'

**1 lodge with Lot:** *Genesis* 19: 1ff.: two angels stayed in Lot's house in Sodom.

**2 Struggle with Jacob:** *Genesis* 33: 24ff: see *The Reprisal*, l.15n, p. 404.
**sit with Gideon:** 'And there came an angel of the Lord, and sat under an oak ... and the angel of the Lord appeared unto [Gideon]' (*Judges* 6: 11ff.) (P).

**3 Advise with Abraham:** in *Genesis* 18: 23-33 Abraham pleads with God not to destroy the people of Sodom.

**4-5** Herbert has slightly altered the course of events to give a new slant to God's words. In *Exodus* 32: 9-14 God says to Moses that his people are 'a stiff-necked people: Now therefore let me alone, that my wrath may wax hot against them'. Moses remonstrates, and then 'the Lord repented of the evil which he thought to do'. Herbert's version suggests that God's *Let me alone* was his response to Moses' remonstrations, and intensifies our sense of a real argument between the two – a colloquialism repeated at the end of the next stanza.

**7 fair oak:** see l.2n: 'And the angel of the Lord appeared unto [Moses] in a flame of fire out of the midst of a *bush*' (*Exodus* 3: 2); 'And [Elijah] came hither unto a *cave*, and lodged there; and, behold, the word of the Lord came to him, and he said unto him, What doest thou here, Elijah?' (*1 Kings* 19: 9); Abraham sent his servant to the *well* to find a wife for his son, saying 'The Lord will send his angel with thee, and prosper thy way', as indeed he did (*Genesis* 24: 7-51) (P).

**9-10 Sinai:** Mount Sinai, where God appeared to Moses. *Aaron* accompanied Moses (*Exodus* 19: 24, 24: 9). Later much space is devoted to his priestly robes. For his *bell*, see *Aaron*, p. 170, l.3n (pp. 478–9); in fact, the hem of his gown was fringed with many bells.

**14 straiten:** constrict, constrain.

**15 thy thirds:** a widow was legally entitled to a third of her husband's property; *thirds* is the legal term. Sin and Satan try to get even this meagre portion from God (H).

**16 when as:** seeing that (H).

**17 urn:** no comment from H and P. Herbert imagines the diminished love of God driven back by sin and kept, like glowing embers in a container (an image of the *feeble heart* of l.12) till it returns to God and he calls for the Last Judgment and general conflagration. The retreat of Christianity is powerfully outlined in the historic sweep of *The Church Militant* (pp. 186ff.). The majority of OED meanings for urn relate it to funerary urns or water vessels, but Cowley (1656) speaks of 'Tapers shut in ancient Urns'.

**Misery:** in *W* titled *The Publican* (i.e. tax-collector, repeatedly linked with sinner in the Bible).

**5** Cf. *Isaiah* 40: 6: 'All flesh is grass.'

**16 his curtains drawn:** H compares *Psalm* 139: 2: 'Thou art about my path, and about my bed: and spiest out all my ways' (BCP).

**17-18 They are of cloth:** this is man's foolish response. There are no moth-holes in his curtains, so how can God see him?

**19 turn but thy hand:** if you (God) let go of him.

**23 it:** the sorrow.

**24 And measure not their fall:** and not as big as their fall.

**25 quarrel:** dispute with.

**33 The sun holds down his head for shame:** eclipses as images of the sun's shame may also be evoked at *Whitsunday*, p. 57, l.14, and *Grace*, p. 58, l.5. The sun was eclipsed at the Crucifixion (*Matthew* 27: 45).

**35 infection:** that which is infected or corrupt.

**40 them:** God's praises, which are contaminated by our *clay hearts* (a biblical image first raised in *Perirrhanterium*, p. 21, l.430, and perfected in *The Priesthood*, pp. 156–7, ll.8–24).

**44 serve the swine:** like the Prodigal Son (*Luke* 15: 11–32). *W*'s version is equally wry: *Man cannot serve thee: let him go/And feed the swine, with all his mind and might:/For this he wondrous well doth know/They will be kind, and all his pain requite,/Making him free/Of that good company.*

**45, 47-8** all spoken in Man's voice.

**51 pull'st the rug:** *W* has *lyest warme*.

**52 purchase the ... stars:** cf. *Take stars for money; stars not to be told/By any art, yet to be purchased* (*Perirrhanterium*, p. 13, ll.171–2).

**62 winks:** shuts its eyes.

**69 posy:** motto.

**74 without a foot or wing:** cf. *Easter Wings (1)* and *(2)*, pp. 40–41.

**77 shelf:** sandbank (on which he founders). Cf. *Perirrhanterium*, p. 12, l.120: *What nature made a ship, he makes a shelf.*

**Jordan (2):** for title, see note to *Jordan (1)*, p. 416. *W* titled it *Invention*, as in l.3.

**4 burnish:** grow and spread. Often coupled with *spread*, as in *W* here (*sprout* in *1633*).

**10 quick:** alive, lively.

**11–12** Cf. *Misery*, p. 98, ll.33–4: *The sun holds down his head for shame,/... when we speak of thee.*

**15–16 a friend/Whisper:** cf. 'Fool, said my Muse to me, look in thy heart and write' (Sidney: *Astrophel and Stella* I, l.14) (H).

**Prayer (2)**

**4 state dislikes not easiness:** (God's) high estate doesn't mind familiarity.

**9 tacks the centre to the sphere:** just as God's arm can span the uttermost points of the compass, so it can link the centre of the universe to its outmost rim.

**11–12** i.e. we could not ask for anything you couldn't grant (*which is not there*), and this puts the shallowness of our requests to shame.

**15 curse:** i.e. death ('the wages of sin is death').

**17 destroying that which ty'd thy purse:** by destroying death. Man's mortality prevented God's supreme act of generosity (*ty'd thy purse*), the gift of eternal life, which Christ's death made possible, making *way for liberality*.

**20 Ease**, **Power and Love:** recapitulating the themes of stanzas 1, 2 and 3.

**24 ell:** 45 inches.

**Obedience:** a poem transferring the terms of a legal deed to a spiritual testament. For the use of legal technicalities, cf. *Dooms-day*, p. 182, ll.15–16, and *The Country Parson*, ch. xxiii, p. 228, where the parson is advised to acquire a grounding in law to assist his parishioners.

**2 Convey:** transfer from one person to another (as in modern conveyancing).

**Lordship:** probably not referring to the sale of office, even though James I and Charles I's governments assiduously sold off baronetcies and Irish peerages, but to the common sale of lordships of the manor. I am indebted to Dr. Heal for the following comment: 'The stanza would seem to refer to the ability of propertied men to convey and sell their lands, with all accompanying rights. Herbert appears to be using the precise language of these kinds of contracts in the rest of the poem. In this period landowners were particularly free of constraints in the ways in which they transmitted land, being bound neither by medieval forms of entail, nor by the strict settlement, which developed from the end of the sixteenth century as a way of protecting property transmission. Presumably Herbert is criticizing the general greed of property owners who neglected their duties as lords.' For various forms of irresponsibility of this kind, cf. also *Perirrhanterium*, pp. 11ff., ll.91–6, 193–6, 277–82.

**8 pass:** legally convey.

**12 Cavil:** quibble, raise frivolous objections.

**13 reservation:** a clause reserving rights or interests in the property being conveyed.

**15 wrangler:** an angry or noisy disputant (with strong negative associations). If Pleasure wants to keep back a part of the heart that is willing itself to God, then it will miss out on God's *treasure* (blessedness).

**16ff** Herbert's usual plea for reciprocity: *thy sacred will* is both God's wish or intention, and the divine deed or contract reciprocating his *special deed* (l.10). *Let me not think an action mine own way*: don't let me only think of this contract on my own terms, but submit to your love.

**23 actions:** here in the normal modern sense of what I do, but with the sense of legal action (as in l.18) still present.

**28 proffer:** a technical term: 'A provisional payment of estimated dues' (OED).

**30 or be withstood:** or (if we did try to take it) we would be withstood. God's love is not like some sham bargain (or modern 'free' offer) which turns out to be unattainable.

**33 intimation:** also technical: 'notification of a requirement made by law, coupled with an announcement of the penalty that will be incurred in case of default' (OED).

**33-5 intimation ... gift ... donation ... purchase:** there is a sequence of reversed expectations here: God's *gift* or *donation* of love is hedged with protective clauses, *intimations* of the penalties to be incurred if we refuse it, and in this inverted world of legal contracts the speaker then rejects God's deed of gift, replacing it by one of purchase, since he wants to give up all worldly things (the *land* of l.36) in return for God's love.

**36-40** He who, like me, wants to convey lands, can sign this deed and it will cover his property and mine – if he'll stand by his word.

**42 thrust his heart:** answered by Vaughan: 'Here I join hands, and thrust my stubborn heart/Into thy Deed' (*The Match*, ll.7–8) (H).

**43 heav'n's court of rolls:** the earthly court of the Master of the Rolls had custody of legal records.

**44-5 by winged souls/Entred:** registered by the recording angels (H).

**Conscience:** this, and the next seventy-five poems, are not in *W*.
**1 lour:** look threatening.
**13 at his board:** i.e. the altar, at communion.
**20–21 a staff .../For those that trouble me:** H identifies an echo of
*Psalm* 23: 4–5: 'thy rod and staff comfort me. Thou shalt prepare a
table before me against them that trouble me' (BCP).
**bill:** a halberd.

**Sion:** not in *W*. The poem is a comment on *Acts* 7: 46–8: '[David] found
favour before God, and desired to find a tabernacle for the God of
Jacob. But Solomon built him an house. Howbeit the most High
dwelleth not in temples made with hands' and *1 Corinthians* 3: 16:
'Know ye not that ye are the temple of God, and that the Spirit of
God dwelleth in you?' (H) as well as the texts lying behind *The Altar*.
**1–6** For an extended description of Solomon's supremely ornate temple
see *1 Kings* 6: 1–38, 7: 1–51. *Builders' ... seers': 1633* has few possessive
apostrophes; in this case, where none was provided, they could be
singular or plural. *Seers:* observers.
**9 Something there was, that sow'd debate:** probably a tactful
reference to Solomon's sharing in the idolatry of his many foreign
concubines, incurring God's rejection (see *1 Kings* 11: 1–13).
**11 thy Architecture meets with sin:** in man's heart. Cf. *the Architect,
whose art/Could build so strong in a weak heart* (*The Church-floor*, p. 64,
ll. 19–20).
**17 Solomon's sea of brass:** 'And he made a molten sea ... it
contained two thousand baths' (16,000 gallons) (*1 Kings* 7: 23–6)
contained in a vast basin of bronze.
**world of stone:** more directly hyperbolic, of the vast amount of
stone used in Solomon's temple.
**21, 23 full of wings ... like larks they sing:** cf. *Easter Wings (1)* and
*(2)*, pp. 40–41.

**Home:** not in *W*.
**2 stay:** stay away.
**8–10 The blood ... trickling down thy face:** referring to the Agony
in the Garden of Gethsemane (*Luke* 22: 44).
**15 But there was none:** 'and the [Lord] saw that there was no man,
and wondered that there was no intercessor' (*Isaiah* 59: 16) (H).
**19 There lay thy son:** in God's *bosom* (l. 16). H calls this 'a surprising
turn' since Christ is addressed in ll. 6–10, but Herbert often leaves it
indeterminate whether he is addressing God the Father, the Son, or
the Holy Ghost, and their unity is paramount. H notes a similar
change in *Ephes. 4. 30.*, pp. 132–3, ll. 1, 35 from addressing the Holy
Spirit to addressing God.
**20 That hive of sweetness:** cf. *The Star*, p. 72, ll. 30–31: heaven is *home*

442

*... that hive of beams.*

**21–2 feast ... apple:** the garden of Eden ... the Fall. Cf. *The Author's Prayer before Sermon, The Country Parson*, p. 255: 'O write it! O brand it in our foreheads for ever: for an apple once we lost our God.'

**27 So many years baptiz'd:** referring to the speaker, presumably.

**31** From this point onwards the poem turns into a rejection of the world and a straining to be lifted up to God, the *Home* of the poem's title.

**46 flout:** mock.

**51–2 Some may dream merrily:** i.e. some people may pass their lives in a frivolous dream but when they come to their senses (*wake*), they reform (*dress themselves*) and come to God.

**61 this knot of man untie!:** cf. 'this knot intrinsicate/Of life at once untie' (*Antony and Cleopatra* V.ii.302–3).

**63 pinion'd:** bound, which derives from cutting the *pinion* or terminal segment of a bird's wing to stop it flying away.

**73 this holy season:** H suggests that the references to the Day of Judgment (l.58) and Incarnation (l.19) suggest Advent, although ll.7–10 imply Passion-tide.

**76** The expected rhyme to *pray* is *Stay*. The breaking of form here is comparable to the mending of form in the last line of *Denial* (p. 77).

**The British Church:** not in *W*. One of Herbert's least interesting poems. The stanza arrangement is adopted from *B*; in *1633* it is set out in three-line stanzas. *B*'s arrangement tallies with the content (stanzas 1, 2 and 5 on the British Church, 3 on the Catholic, and 4 on the Calvinist). Herbert approves 'the middle way between superstition and slovenliness' in *The Country Parson*, ch. xiii, p. 217 (H).

**1 Mother:** the Church.

**5 dates her letters from thy face:** the Church of England reckoned the beginning of the year from Lady Day (the Feast of the Annunciation, 25 March); so did Herbert in his letters (H). See also Walton, p. 369.

**10 Outlandish:** foreign.

**11 painted:** Roman Catholic.

**12 undrest:** Genevan Calvinist.

**13 She on the hills:** the Catholic Church in Rome: 'She, which on the other shore/Goes richly painted' (Donne: *Holy Sonnet* xviii, ll.2–3).

**19 She in the valley:** Genevan Calvinism.

**25 what those miss:** in parenthesis in *1633*.

**26 The mean:** the Anglican Church's *via media*.

**29 double-moat:** the British Church is double-moated by God's grace and by being an island.

**The Quip:** not in *W*. The title means a sharp retort, also a verbal equivocation. The quip is withheld till l.23: *I am thine*. It is a pointedly

443

unquipping reply, not in the pert and witty world's mode at all. For
its delay, see the source of the refrain, *Psalm* 38: 12-14: 'They also
that sought after my life laid snares for me: and they that went about
to do me evil talked of wickedness, and imagined evil all day long. As
for me, I was like a deaf man, and heard not: and as one that is dumb,
who doth not open his mouth. I became even as a man who heareth
not: and in whose mouth are no reproofs' (BCP, and see l.8n below).

**2 train-bands:** i.e. trained bands – London's citizen soldiery.

**7 Whose hands are those?:** i.e. are those hands yours? why don't you
use them, to pick me? (with the usual connotations of 'Gather ye rose-
buds while ye may'). Of course the hands are ultimately God's, and
Beauty's cheeky question backfires.

**8 thou shalt answer:** 'For in thee, O Lord, have I put my trust: thou
shalt answer for me, O Lord my God' (*Psalm* 38: 15, BCP) (P).

**10 What tune is this?:** the speaker's music (the poem) seems to
Money to be a poor rival to the chinking of gold.

**18-19 he would needs a comfort be:** wonderfully ironic: Wit's *short
oration* promises to be no comfort at all.

**24 And then they have their answer home:** i.e. they are definitively
answered. The last word links this poem back to *Home*, especially,
p. 105, ll.44-6. The *joys* rejected there return here to *flout* the speaker.

**Vanity (2):** not in *W*.

**9 To purchase heaven for repenting:** as a reward for repentance.
This is not a *hard* price to pay (l.10).

**16 nest:** cf. *Home*, l.19, where God's breast is *that nest,/That hive of
sweetness*.

**18 bubble ... boy:** children chase bubbles. Cf. *Nature*, p. 43, l.9, and
*Even-song*, p. 61, l.14.

**The Dawning:** not in *W*. An Easter poem, and an aubade, or dawn
song, traditionally sung below the beloved's windows, calling on her
to get up. E.g. Cloten's aubade in *Cymbeline* (II.iii.19ff.): 'Hark, hark!
the lark at heaven's gate sings,/And Phoebus 'gins arise,/His steeds to
water at those springs/On chalic'd flow'rs that lies;/And winking
Mary-buds begin/To ope their golden eyes./With everything that
pretty bin,/My lady sweet, arise;/Arise; arise!'. Compare Shake-
speare's pastoral use of the church 'chalice' here, with Herbert's
sacred use of a profane form in this poem (see further, Introduction,
pp. xxiiff).

**2 Take up thine eyes:** a clear answer to the opening of the preceding
poem, ll.1-2.

**9 withstand:** resist.

**11-12 the hand,/Which as it riseth, raiseth thee:** cf. *thy Lord ...
takes thee by the hand, that thou likewise/With him mayst rise* (*Easter*, p. 39,

ll.1–4), and *Easter Wings (1)* and *(2)*: *With thee/O let me rise ... With thee/Let me combine* (p. 40–41, ll.6–7 in each case).

**15 Christ left his grave-clothes:** 'So they ran both together: and the other disciple did outrun Peter, and came first to the sepulchre. And he stooping down, and looking in, saw the linen clothes lying, yet went he not in. Then cometh Simon Peter following him, and went into the sepulchre, and seeth the linen clothes lie, And the napkin, that was about his head, not lying with the linen clothes, but wrapped together in a place by itself' (*John* 20: 4–7).

**16 not want an handkerchief:** not lack a hanky. There is a touch of rallying humour here, prepared for in l.4: *Thy Saviour comes, and with him mirth.* P states that *handkerchief* is used 'not in the modern but in the biblical sense of miraculous means of healing', quoting *Acts* 19: 11–12 where Paul heals the sick by 'handkerchiefs or aprons'. However, this is the unique use of the word in the Bible (which otherwise uses 'napkin'), and what P calls the 'modern' sense was in usage from 1530, predating the Geneva Bible's unique usage by twenty-seven years. A century later, it is most unlikely that Herbert intended only a rare biblical sense for his common reader. The two are not mutually exclusive. While the passage from *Acts* 19 may possibly add to the world's healing power, it is clear that it is there primarily to suggest wiping away the tears of grief in a comfortingly ordinary way. On several occasions Herbert attempts to diminish the fear of death; see Introduction, p. xli.

**JESU:** not in *W*. For the conceit of the fragmented heart, cf. Donne's *The broken heart:* 'what did become/Of my heart, when I first saw thee? ... Love, alas,/At one first blow did shiver it as glass ... my breast hath all/Those pieces still, though they be not unite;/And now as broken glasses show/A hundred lesser faces, so/My rags of heart can like, wish, and adore,/But after one such love, can love no more' (ll.17ff.). Another amorous commonplace transferred to the sacred from the profane.

**5 J:** J and I were incompletely differentiated at the time of writing.

**8 I sat me down to spell:** see *Love-joy*, p. 113, ll.4–5n, p. 448, and cf. *The Flower*, p. 162, l.21: *Thy word is all, if we could spell.*

**Business:** not in *W*. Another poem whose form repays analysis. It is written throughout in a remorselessly regular trochaic tetrameter catalectic ( ´ ˘ ´ ˘ ´ ˘ ´ ), falling into three clearly marked sections (one couplet and four tercets; the same again; couplet, two tercets and couplet). The driving *busyness* of the poem is intensified by the heavily stressed first syllable in each line, and the continual recurrence of repeated words, verbal patterns, and rhetorical questions, refusing to let the reader off the hook: *Hast thou tears, or hast thou none?/If, poor soul,*

445

*thou hast no tears ... Had he life or had he none?/If he had not liv'd for thee ...
Did he die, or did he not?/If he had not di'd for thee ...* Further patterns are
picked out below.

**1–2** Establishing the theme of the first section: *sin.*

**4–14 Rivers**, *springs* and *tears* are played off against *faults or fears*; then
*winds, sighs,* and *groans* against *flesh and bones*: their repetition creates
the leitmotif of this section.

**8 Who hath these, those ill forbears:** if you have faults or fears
(*these*), you're unlikely avoid tears (*those*).

**13–14** 'It were better to have no body to feel the pains of hell; these
however can be escaped by enduring the *Lesser pains* of a present
penitence' (H), i.e. *sighs* and *groans*. The oblique references to eternal
punishment here and in l.22 make this one of Herbert's most
emphatically admonitory poems.

**15–16** Establishing the theme of the second section: the Saviour's *death.*

**17–28** The key words repeated to create the leitmotif of this section are
*life, liv'd, di'd, two deaths,* and *die, di'd, liv'd, Two lives, ten deaths.* But it
also picks up *flesh and bones* (and associated rhymes) and *plot* (and
associated rhymes) from the preceding section, so that half this
section repeats the rhymes of the one before.

**22 two deaths:** the death of the body, and the 'second death'
(*Revelation* 20: 6–14, 21: 8) of eternal damnation (H).

**28 Two lives:** an earthly life of misery, and the life of eternal
damnation.

**29–30, 37–8** Recapitulating the themes of the first two sections, *sin* and
the *Saviour's death.*

**29 hath any space of breath:** does anyone have a breathing-space
between his sins and the redemption offered by Christ's death? The
implicit answer is, of course, no: man's idleness is sinful, his one
urgent business is to repent.

**34 a silver vein:** implies riches (as in the *gold dross* of the preceding
stanza) – a worldly interpretation overturned by the reference to
Christ's death. The reader must *think on it, and think again:* the silver
vein is not earthly, but spiritual, the vein of blood broached in
Christ's side, *That as sin came, so Sacraments might flow* (*The Sacrifice*,
p. 31, l.247).

**Dialogue:** not in *W.*

**4 waiving:** withholding the offer of my soul.

**6–7 Cannot give the name of gains/To thy wretch:** since all my
cares and pains can't make me worth having.

**8 What delight or hope remains?** This is a poem of despair: for all
his efforts at amendment, the speaker has no hope of ever being
worthy of salvation.

**15–16 sold ... accounts:** one of the many paradoxes of Christianity:

Christ was sold like a chattel (by Judas for thirty pieces of silver), and this gave him proprietorial rights over mankind. The image running through this stanza is, as it were, of Christ the grocer with his scales (*balance*) to weigh (*poise*) and *measure* mankind, and the impertinent speaker, like a *child*, fingering the wares (*Finger not my treasure*), and questioning the *accounts*.

**17 I can see no merit:** in himself.

**20 savour:** understanding (taste or perception).

**23-4 I disclaim ... Sin disclaims:** Herbert seems to be making a distinction between the transitive and intransitive use. *I disclaim the whole design* is transitive and means 'to repudiate a connexion with or concern in' (OED verse 3): the speaker has nothing to do with Christ's plan and *resigns* all responsibility for it. *Sin disclaims* is transitive and uses the verb in its prime, legal sense: 'to renounce or repudiate a legal claim' (OED verse 1); what sin renounces (judging by the next stanza) is its own rights of seigneury.

**25-6 if that I could/Get:** if I could get that resignation without your regretting it (*repining*).

**28 my resigning:** my resignation (or abdication) of divine status – the Incarnation is described in the next three lines.

**Dullness:** not in *W*. For the transference of traditional lovers' language to religion, see Introduction, pp. xxiiff.

**1 Why do I languish thus, drooping and dull:** an appropriately metrically broken line. The pattern later established is iambic pentameters in ll.1 and 3, trimeter in l.2 and dimeter in l.5. This line has its first and fourth feet reversed (*Whў dŏ Ĭ lănguĭsh thús, dróopĭng ănd dúll*).

**2 all earth:** the heaviest of the four elements of which man was supposed to be composed (the others being water, air and fire).

**12 Pure red and white:** the traditional lover's compliment transferred to Christ's blood, and light. P compares 'My beloved is white and ruddy' (*Song of Solomon* 5: 10).

**14 That:** So that (understood) i.e. when all perfections seem one perfection, so that all of them (*those*) are evident in you, Christ, then (understood) the very dust you trod (in your human incarnation) creates beauties in our world. There is a pun on *dust* and *dost*: by taking on the dust of earthly flesh, Christ makes all earthly things beautiful. *1633* has a semicolon after *here* in l.16.

**18 window songs:** not serenades, as H says (which are open-air evening songs and of which there are no instances in Herbert) but aubades as in *Easter* and *The Dawning*. See further, Introduction, p. liv, n.8.

**19 pretending:** pursuing, courting (H), but also lying (see l.21).

**23 there:** in the flesh.

**25 clear thy gift:** discharge the promised gift (of l.3: *give me quickness*)
(H).

**Love-joy:** not in *W*. See *John* 15: 1–16 for Christ's extended compari-
son of himself to the vine, and his disciples to its fruit. It ends with an
injunction to *joy* and love (which is *charity*), verses 9–13: 'I am the
vine, and my Father is the husbandman … As the Father hath loved
me, so have I loved you … These things have I spoken unto you, that
my joy might remain in you, and that your joy might be full.'

**2–3 grapes with J and C/Anneal'd on every bunch:** *anneal'd*
suggests that what the speaker sees is the image in a stained-glass
window; possibly the stem of each bunch suggested J and the grapes
the letter C. For Herbert's interpretative approach to church archi-
tecture, see the run of poems beginning *Church-monuments* (p. 62), and
Introduction, pp. xiff.

**4–5 I (who am never loth/To spend my judgement):** Herbert
pokes mild fun at his speaker's eager but naive ingenuity both here
(where *JC* prompts the association of Jesus Christ far more readily
than *Joy* and *Charity*) and in *Jesu*, p. 109, l.8, where *I sat me down to
spell* suggests a child settling down on the floor with spelling bricks.
Cf. also *The Quip* (pp. 443–4, headnote).

**6 body and letters both:** *body:* the substance – the eucharistic wine is
a symbol of God's love; *letters:* the two initials JC.

**providence:** not in *W*. P and H point to *Psalm* 104 and *Job* 38–9 as
biblical celebrations of God's providence. Herbert advises his
Country Parson to admire and imitate 'the wonderful providence
and thrift of the great householder of the world' (ch. x, p. 212) (P);
the poem's motto could be *Outlandish Proverbs* no. 516: 'All things in
their being are good for something.'

**1–2** Cf. 'Wisdom reacheth from one end to another mightily, and
sweetly doth she order all things' (*Wisdom of Solomon* 8: 1, from the
Apocrypha) (H).

**6 Only to Man thou hast made known thy ways:** contrasting
strongly with *Job* 38–9, where God accuses Job of ignorance: 'Where
wast thou when I laid the foundations of the earth? declare, if thou
hast understanding … Have the gates of death been opened to thee?
… Hast thou entered into the treasures of the snow?' etc.

**9 ditty:** to adapt words to music (OED; an obsolete sense). *Fain* **would**
is understood.

**17–20** to refrain from praising God is a double crime, on your own
behalf, and the world's which relies on Man to utter its praise for it.

**21–4** Continuing the argument of the preceding stanza: if the rest of
mankind is taught by nature to hunt and gather it for food, the
speaker is taught by it to praise God's bounty, on everyone's behalf.

**23 Pull:** pluck (fruit).

**33 permission:** 'an undogmatic affirmation of the permissive theory of evil so emphatically upheld in *Paradise Lost* I. 211ff.' (P).

**42 even:** regular, smooth.

**45-7** See Introduction, pp. xliv–xlv.

**47-8 Thou hast made poor sand/Check the proud sea:** cf. the Lord says, I 'have placed the sand for the bound of the sea by a perpetual decree, that it cannot pass it: and though the waves thereof toss themselves, yet can they not prevail; though they roar, yet can they not pass over it' (*Jeremiah* 5: 22) (H), and God 'said, hitherto shalt thou come, but no further: and here shall thy proud waves by stayed' (*Job* 38: 11) (P).

**49 Thy cupboard serves the world:** 'These wait all upon thee; that thou mayest give them their meat in due season. That thou givest them they gather: thou openest thine hand, they are filled with good' (*Psalm* 104: 27–8).

**51 fishes have their net:** their open mouths (P), or gills?

**53 prevent:** forestall; i.e. nothing was created before there was food for it.

**58 twist:** thread or cord composed of two or more fibres (OED). Compare ll.57–8 with G. M. Hopkins: 'let life wind/Off her once skeined stained veined variety upon, all on two spools ... black, white' (*Spelt from Sibyl's Leaves*, ll.10–12).

**63 callow:** young, unfledged.

**71-2** P and H do not suggest what processes Herbert has in mind. The two preceding lines describe self-refuelling cycles; on this analogy streams discharge (*vent*) their waters, and by pouring them out (*expense*) are refilled (*get store*) through evaporation (into clouds) and condensation (into rain). This also explains *Clouds cool by heat*, since the sun's heat evaporates the earth's moisture into cooling clouds. Herbert returns to this later: *When yet some places could no moisture get,/ The winds grew gard'ners, and the clouds good fountains* (ll.115–16). Herbert's understanding of the water cycle is clear from *The Answer*, p. 165, ll.8–11. P glosses *baths* as 'hot springs' which may be correct but is not obviously elucidatory. Any hot bath or spring cooling off, especially in a cold atmosphere, steams, which may be what Herbert intended by *boil*. Or: a cold bath makes the skin glow and feel warm. Cf. 'Surprise where driven sleet/had scalded to the bone' (W. H. Auden: *From scars where kestrels hover*, ll.11–12).

**73-4** A stanza about linguistic inadequacy, which is enacted in the lame repetition of *virtue, herb, express* and *expressions*. Herbert wishes for a herb endowing him with sufficient eloquence to describe the curative power of plants and minerals. H notes a pun on *expressions* as the expressed (squeezed out) juice from a root. For the idea, cf. Lear's 'Give me an ounce of civet, good apothecary, to sweeten my .

449

imagination' (IV.vi.130).

**77–80** The stars have power to predict our plagues and wars much more reliably than our art is able to interpret them. The comparison with the rose (whose curative powers recur in *The Country Parson*, ch. xxiii) implies that there is a benificent pattern to the cycles of *plagues and plenty, peace and wars* which lies beyond our understanding: we have got as far as understanding roses but not stars.

**81–4** Cf. *Avarice*, p. 74.

**85–8** Both P and H explain *Ev'n poisons praise thee* by pointing out that poisons have curative powers (cf. *Romeo and Juliet* II.iii.23–4: 'Within the infant rind of this weak flower/Poison hath residence, and medecine power'). However, this is not Herbert's point: poisons join the list of things praising God's providence because he has set their antidotes growing alongside them (we still look for dock-leaves near nettles) as both a cure and a warning.

**Should a thing be lost?:** Should anything be left out of this list, through our heedlessness?

**101–4** A beautiful, riddling stanza: by reversing the order to qualities first, then the thing that creates them, Herbert contrives a sense of wonder. Glass gives us light without draughts (*wind*); shade gives us coolness out of doors, without being enclosed (*without closeness*). The hawk flies high (*tall*) but obeys the hawker (so it is *servile*).

**105–8** Cf. 'one country doth not bear all things that there may be a commerce' (*The Country Parson*, ch. iv, p. 201) (H).

**112 in desire:** as much as he wants.

**117 Rain, do not hurt my flowers:** cf. *Affliction (4)*, p. 87, ll.9–10.

**126 The Indian nut:** the coconut.

**130 Cold fruits warm kernels:** *1633*'s lack of possessive apostrophes creates an ambiguity. Either: cold fruits help warm kernels act against flatulence (*wind*); or, more probably: the warm kernels of cold fruits (etc.). Presumably *warm* and *cold* in the sense of taste (as a peach could be called cold, and its kernel is hot and acrid).

**132 loose:** is laxative.

**bind:** vice versa.

**133 Thy creatures leap not:** there is a smooth sequence of transitions down the chain of being. 'Characteristically, Herbert transmutes the commonplace into an eucharistic *feast*' (P).

**134 nothing wants:** nothing's missing.

**135 marry:** combine.

**141–4** A turn to the position of *Job* 38–9.

**146 advise:** opinion (OED, now obsolete).

**148 twice:** on his own account, and on behalf of all creation: cf. *I here present/For me and all my fellows praise to thee* (l.25–6) (H).

**152 one more:** making the same point as the preceding stanza.

**Hope:** not in *W*. For an interpretation, see Introduction, pp. xxxvi–xxxvii.

**2 An anchor:** cf. 'hope we have as an anchor of the soul' (*Hebrews* 6: 19) (H). In his *Life of Donne* Walton reports that Donne had several seals engraved with '*Christ crucified* on an *Anchor*, which is the emblem of hope' which he sent to Herbert and other friends shortly before his death. For Herbert's poem on this, see p. 349, n.1.

**4 optic:** eyeglass, telescope.

**7 I'll no more, no more I'll bring:** initiating the circular form re-created in the next poem, a verbal *ring*.

**Sin's round:** not in *W*. A round was a dance in which the performers moved in a circule (cf. l.2: *my offences course it in a ring*). For the poem's relationship to *Hope*, see Introduction, p. xxxvii. The poem is an example of *carmina catenata*, where the last line of one stanza is the first of the next, and the last line is also the first. Cf. Donne's *Corona*, probably the 'Hymns' he dedicated to Herbert's mother.

**4 cockatrice:** a serpent identified with the basilisk, fabulously said to kill by its mere glance and to be hatched from a cock's egg. Cf. *Isaiah* 14: 29: 'out of the serpent's root shall come forth a cockatrice, and his fruit shall be a fiery flying serpent', and the evil 'hatch cockatrice's eggs' (*Isaiah* 59: 5).

**5 perfected:** stress on the first syllable. The speaker's thoughts make perfect his *draughts* (of flame) until his words catch fire also.

**8 the Sicilian hill:** the volcanic Mount Etna.

**9 vent the wares:** discharge the heat. H identifies a mercantile sense to *vent* (sell) prompted by *wares*.

**14 three storeys high:** like the poem's three stanzas, devoted to the speaker's fiery *thoughts*, *words* and *ill deeds*. The poem's form adds to this sense of the flames' spiralling growth. Cf. *As flames do work and wind, when they ascend* (*Jordan (2)*, p. 99, l.13).

**15 Babel:** see *Frailty*, l.22n, p. 423.

**Time:** not in *W*. H comments on 'the curiously light, bantering tone about his grave subject', but Herbert habitually and pointedly undermines the gravity of death by positivism and even humour (cf. *The Dawning*, p. 109, ll.15–16, or *Death*, p. 181, l.4).

**7–26** The speaker's reply to Time.

**7 pass:** die.

**10, 16 pruning-knife, gard'ner:** cf. *Paradise*, p. 129, l.11.

**23 wants:** lacks.

**25 that:** life without God. The seeming endlessness of life before death is *strange* because it seems, but is not, eternal.

**30** Time objects that though the speaker pretends to want less time (he asks Time to whet its scythe in l.2), all this argument is mere delay, a play for more time. H has a more complicated reading: that the speaker longs for the timeless life of eternity and in this sense *doth not crave less time, but more.*

**Gratefulness:** not in *W*. An appealing poem in which the speaker adopts the unflattering role of an importunate beggar in whom every indulgence only encourages further importunity.

**5 occasion:** prompt.

**9 thou didst reckon:** God had worked out the expenses he would incur in advance.

**15 much would have more:** proverbial (cf. 'Give him an inch and he takes a mile').

**16 And comes:** highly colloquial – picking up *What it would come to* of l.11.

**22-3 better tunes, than groans ... these country-airs:** cf. *Sion*, p. 103, ll.21ff.: *groans are quick, and full of wings ... like larks they sing; |The note is sad, yet music for a king. Country-airs:* folk tunes, i.e. not sophisticated court music.

**23-4 thy love/Did take:** appealed to your love.

**30-31** [Not] as if your blessings only had my gratitude on odd days, but the thankfulness of a heart whose every pulse-beat is praise of you. Rather engagingly, this last verse does just what the poem warned – as soon as God seems ready to grant the demand for a grateful heart, it is further escalated to a heart that is continuously grateful.

**Peace:** not in *W*.

**15 crown Imperial:** a kind of fritillary, but with clear emblematic associations with regal power, which is (ll.17–18) blighted by mortality and corruption. The emblematic nature of this stanza, however well disguised in the horticultural metaphor, suggests similar associations in stanzas 1 and 2 (*secret cave:* solitude; *rainbow ... lace:* society?).

**22-3 There was a Prince of old/At Salem dwelt:** i.e. Christ. In *Genesis* 14: 18 'Melchizedek King of Salem brought forth bread and wine' in blessing to Abraham; in *Hebrews* 7: 1–4 he is interpreted as a type of Christ: 'King of Salem, which is, King of Peace; without father, without mother, without descent, having neither beginnings of days, nor end of life; but made like unto the Son of God; abideth a priest continually'. *Salem:* Jerusalem.

**26 foes:** Christ died at the hands of his foes and Melchizedek had enemies for whose slaughter he blessed Abraham.

**28 twelve stalks of wheat:** the twelve apostles, who continued Melchizedek's priestly calling.

**33 rehearse:** repeat, recount.

**39 bread:** the bread of the Eucharist.

**Confession:** not in *W*.

**5 till:** a small box, casket or closed compartment within a larger box or cabinet (sometimes a drawer or a section that could be lifted out) for safe keeping of documents and valuables (OED, quoting this passage from Herbert. A now obsolete sense.)

**12 And fall, like rheums, upon the tendrest parts:** cf. 'Wealth is like rheum, it falls on the weakest parts' (*Outlandish Proverbs*, no. 471) (H).

**15 foot:** seize with the talons (usually of birds of prey). Not really appropriate to moles; Herbert has switched metaphors rather quickly.

**19 an open breast:** i.e. which has no secrets from God, but confesses its guilt.

**23 fiction:** usually used negatively by Herbert, as deceit (cf. *Jordan (1)*, p. 54, ll. 1–2: *Who says that fictions only and false hair|Become a verse?*).

**30 to:** in comparison with.

**Giddiness:** not in *W*.

**11 snudge:** stay snug and cosy (OED, citing this instance).
**scorns increase:** i.e. is improvident.

**12 spares:** saves.

**16 His mind is so:** like a whirlwind, in its quickly changing opinions (cf. *Lear* II.ii.74: flatterers 'turn their halcyon beaks/With every gale and vary of their masters').

**19 like a Dolphin's skin:** the dorado (H), a fish like the mackerel, popularly misnamed the dolphin, had a skin whose colours changed rapidly on being taken out of the water (which hardly related to its *desires*).

**21–4** There would be *no commerce* if we could see into each other's minds because we would realize how changeable and unreliable we all were.

**25–6 one creation/Will not suffice our turn:** cf. 'preservation is a creation, and more, it is a continued creation, and a creation every moment' (*The Country Parson*, ch. xxxiv, p. 249) (P). But Herbert is here thinking not merely of the eternal, sustained preservation of the world, but the need for man to be re-created and re-saved daily, because (as the rest of the poem has shown) he is so giddy and changeable: one day's salvation will not last to the next. A doubling motif recurs at the end of several poems hereabouts: *Providence*, pp. 117–18, ll. 148–52; *Time*, p. 120, l. 30; *Gratefulness*, p. 121, ll. 27–32; *Man's medley*, p. 128, ll. 34–6.

**The bunch of grapes:** not in *W*. The poem parallels the exodus of the Israelites out of Egypt, through the *Red sea* (l. 7) and towards the Promised Land (*Canaan*, l. 6) with the speaker's life and *each Christian*'s *journeys* (l. 10). Christ's links with Moses are one of the most familiar typological clusters in the Bible, expounded e.g. in *1 Corinthians*

10: 1–10: 'Moreover, brethren, I would not that ye should be
ignorant, how that all our fathers were under the cloud, and all
passed through the sea; And were all baptized unto Moses in the
cloud and in the sea; And did all eat the same spiritual meat; And did
all drink the same spiritual drink: for they drank of that spiritual
Rock that followed them: and that Rock was Christ ... Now these
things were our examples, to the intent we should not lust after evil
things, as they also lusted ... Neither murmur ye, as some of them
murmured ...'

**4 Sev'n years ago:** cf. the Israelites' forty years' wandering.

**vogue:** general course and tendency (OED, quoting this instance of a
now obsolete sense).

**11–14** I.e. the Jews' story prefigures our own; God's justice to them
covers our crimes as well. *Their story pens and sets us down:* meaning
both (1) their story is a record of our own, and consequently (2)
contains (*pens* in the sense of holding in a pen or fold, as well as
writing) our story too. 'Now all these things happened to them for
ensamples: and they are written for our admonition' (*1 Corinthians*
10: 11).

**15 our guardian fires and clouds:** we experience our own equiv-
alent of the flight from Egypt, when 'the Lord went before them by
day in a pillar of a cloud, to lead them the way; and by night in a
pillar of fire, to give them light' (*Exodus* 13: 21).

**16 Our Scripture-dew drops fast:** just as the Israelites were fed with
manna, so the Scriptures are our 'spiritual meat' (see head-note).
'And when the dew that lay was gone up, behold, upon the face of the
wilderness there lay a small round thing, as small as the hoar frost on
the ground. And when the children of Israel saw it, they said one to
another, It is manna: for they wist not what it was' (*Exodus*
16: 14–15).

**17 sands and serpents, tents and shrouds:** referring to the tents
and tabernacles of the Israelites' sojourn in the wilderness. When the
Israelites complained, 'the Lord sent fiery serpents among the people,
and they bit the people, and much people of Israel died' (*Numbers*
21: 6).

**18 our murmurings come not last:** we're not the last to complain.
*Murmurings* recurs repeatedly for the Israelite grumbling; see head-
note, and *Exodus* 16: 2–12, *Numbers* 14: 27.

**19–20 cluster ... inheritance:** the grapes were cut and brought back
to Moses and the Israelites by scouts as a symbol of the land's fertility:
'And they came unto the brook of Eshcol, and cut down from thence
a branch with one cluster of grapes, and they bare it between two
upon a staff ... And they returned from searching of the land after
forty days ... and said: We came unto the land whither thou sentest
us, and surely it floweth with milk and honey; and this is the fruit of

it' (*Numbers* 13: 23–7).

**22 who hath the wine:** Christ's blood is the wine, the Sacrament released at the Crucifixion (cf. *The Sacrifice*, p. 31, ll.246–7; *The Agony*, p. 34, ll.13ff.).

**24 Noah's vine:** 'And Noah began to be an husbandman, and he planted a vineyard' (*Genesis* 9: 20).

**28 pressed:** the image of *The Agony*, p. 34, ll.11ff. Note that Herbert uses *God* interchangeably for Christ.

**Love unknown:** not in *W*. Deriving from *Psalm* 51 (H), especially the following: 'Have mercy upon me, O God, according to thy loving kindness: according to the multitude of thy tender mercies blot out my transgressions. Wash me thoroughly from mine iniquity, and cleanse me from my sin ... Behold, thou desirest truth in the inward parts: and in the hidden part thou shalt make me to know wisdom. Purge me with hyssop, and I shall be clean: wash me, and I shall be whiter than snow ... Create in me a clean heart, O God; and renew a right spirit within me ... For thou desirest not sacrifice; else I would give it: thou delightest not in burnt offering. The sacrifices of God are a broken spirit: a broken and a contrite heart, O God, thou wilt not despise.' The un-dragoning of Eustace in C. S. Lewis's *The Voyage of the Dawn Treader*, ch. 7, has affinities with this poem and its biblical source. The poem's form is also unusual for Herbert; in spite of the regular abab rhyme-scheme, its plaintively monotonous spoken tone and continuous enjambement gives it the quality of blank verse.

**3 comply:** sympathize.

**4–5** Unconvoluted, the sense runs as follows: I have a Lord some of whose grounds I rent, in return for my two lives. The *two lives* are life on earth and life in the hereafter; the *grounds* belonging to the Lord are the speaker's soul, which *may improve* with the repentance about to be detailed.

**14–15 A stream of blood, which issu'd from the side/Of a great rock:** *see 1 Corinthians* 10: 1–4, quoted in the headnote to *The bunch of grapes*, pp. 453–4.

**20 my lease:** see ll.4–5 above, and cf. the sustained tenancy metaphor of *Redemption*, p. 37. A certain number of faults are accommodated by the lease: cf. *Psalm* 51: 5: 'Behold, I was shapen in iniquity; and in sin did my mother conceive me.'

**28 AFFLICTION:** the great leitmotif of Herbert's work.

**33 as my heart did tender it:** offer it; cf. l.70, where *tender* changes its meaning.

**36–7** lovely wounded incredulity here.

**42 at a board:** the table, or altar, at which Holy Communion is received.

**45 supple:** a verb; to make supple.

**51–2 thoughts ... thorns:** an assonantal half-pun.

**55 one:** God, the sole holder of the key to the speaker's heart. A variation on the imagery of *Confession*, pp. 122–3, ll. 1–6, 17.

**60–61 another .../Who took the debt upon him:** Christ.

**65 The Cauldron suppled, what was grown too hard:** cf. *Grace*, p. 58, ll. 17ff.: *Sin is still hammering my heart/Unto a hardness, void of love:/ Let suppling grace, to cross his art,/Drop from above.*

**Man's medley:** not in *W*. A medley is a mixture, and can be used of a musical mixture (suggested in stanza 1) and of cloth woven of different colours (suggested in stanza 3).

**8 Make their pretence:** have their pretensions.

**9 In th' other:** the joy of the *hereafter* (l.6).

**10 them both:** the joys of the *present* and *hereafter*.

**15 round:** a technical term for cloth made with thick thread (H).

**17 should take place:** take up a position (as at an assembly of God's creation).

**18 After:** in accordance with. I.e. man's status should be established by the *curious lace* of his spirit, not the *coarse* basic material (*stuff and ground*) of his flesh, on which it is a trimming.

**27 two winters:** of the body (*frosts*) and the mind (*thoughts*, the thorns of the preceding poem).

**30 two deaths:** of the flesh, and the spirit. Cf. *Business*, p. 110, l.22.

**The Storm:** not in *W*.

**6 Amaze:** *amuse* in *B*, presumably with the then obsolescent sense of to bemuse.

**object:** place before the mind, accuse (OED).

**7 Stars have their storms:** H suggests this means meteor-showers.

**12ff beseige thy door:** cf. *Perpetual knockings at thy door* (*Gratefulness*, p. 120, ll. 13ff.).

**18** Such storms purge the outside air and the breast within us.

**Paradise:** not in *W*. For the form of the poem, see Introduction, p. xx. The original spellings of the capitalized words have been preserved to heighten its visible pruning process. For the image, cf: 'his family is his best care, to labour Christian souls, and raise them to their height, even to heaven; to dress and prune them, and take as much joy in a straight-growing child or servant as a gardener doth in a choice tree' (*The Country Parson*, ch. xxxii, p. 243).

**10 When thou dost greater judgements SPARE:** i.e. when you spare us your more categorical judgment, and only make minor criticisms of us (*prune and PARE*).

**The Method:** not in *W*. The *Method* of self-improvement is

456

self-examination.

**3 rub:** impediment (a metaphor from bowls).

**6 move:** urge, request.

**10 Tumble thy breast, and turn thy book:** cf. *Perirrhanterium*, p. 21, l.451: *Sum up at night, what thou hast done by day*.

**14 Written above there:** in *thy book*, the speaker's spiritual diary.

**18 indifferents:** indifferent, unconcerned people who don't even hear what they are themselves asking for (*motions*).

**23 a motion to forbear:** an impulse to refrain. This *motion* is sent by God, and is ignored, pointedly linked with the ignored *motions* of l.19.

**32 Glad heart, rejoice:** reversing *Poor heart, lament* of l.1. This is a happy reversal, contrasting with the negative reversals, the *rubs*, of stanzas 4–7. (No comma in *1633*.)

**Divinity:** not in *W*. For the rejection of learning, cf. *The Agony*, stanza 1, p. 34, and *Vanity (1)*, p. 83.

**2 spheres:** globes showing the positions and courses of the heavenly bodies.

**4 Which:** i.e. when really they . . .

**5 the other heav'n:** God's heaven, *Divinity's transcendent sky*.

**8 faith lies by:** like an unused instrument (and cf. the poem's last line).

**9 that wisdom, which first broacht the wine:** heavily ironic: *that wisdom* was the malice of the soldiers who pierced Christ's side (*The Sacrifice*, p. 31, l.246), *the wine* is *that juice, which on the cross a pike/Did set again abroach* (*The Agony*, p. 34, ll.14–15).

**10–12 thicken'd . . . jagg'd:** Herbert introduces an ambiguity which is not resolved till the next stanza. God's *Wisdom* could have made things more complicated: he could have enriched (*thicken'd*) the wine of the Eucharist and decoratively pinked (*jagg'd*) Christ's seamless robe with intricate questions. The next stanza makes it clear that such complications are worldly, not divine: the wine is clouded (*thicken'd*) by unnecessary definitions, the robe tattered and torn (*jagg'd*) by dissensions and debate. Religious controversy despoils more than even Christ's executioners: 'Then the soldiers, when they had crucified Jesus, took his garments, and made four parts, to every soldier a part; and also his coat: now the coat was without seam, woven from the top throughout. They said therefore among themselves, Let us not rend it, but cast lots for it, whose it shall be' (*John* 19: 23–4).

**15 which only save:** which are the only thing that can save us.

**20 Gordian knots:** the unique overt classical reference in *The Church*. The knot bound the shepherd Gordius' chariot to its yoke. No man had ever been able to undo it, till it was simply cut by Alexander the Great (356–323 BC), so proving his destiny to rule Asia. Traditionally

457

used of any irresolvably tangled problem to which there is a
decisively simple answer. For another rejection of vexed questions of
divinity, see the dismissal of transubstantiation in *W*'s *The H.
Communion*, p. 333, ll. 7–9: *First I am sure, whether bread stay/Or whether
Bread do fly away/Concerneth bread, not me.*

**22 Bid what he please:** let him command what he likes.

**24 and not obscure:** and it isn't difficult to understand.

**25 Epicycles:** technical (the smaller circles described by each spinning
planet, as their centres move along a greater circle).

**Ephes 4.30. Grieve not the Holy Spirit, &c.:** Not in *W*. The relevant
part of the biblical reference is quoted in the title. The full verse runs:
'And grieve not the holy Spirit of God, whereby you are sealed unto
the day of redemption.'

**10 part:** die (of the eyes and heart). Cf. *The Size*, p. 134, l.3.

**16 puts on sense:** he assumes the feelings (of mankind, in grieving).

**22** The only discord is to be silent.

**23 Marbles can weep:** cf. *The Church-floor*, p. 64, l.15, and Introduc-
tion, p. xiii for an explanation.

**24 More bowels have:** bowels were thought to be the seat of tender
emotions ('Put on, therefore, as the elect of God, holy and beloved,
bowels of mercies, kindness, humbleness of mind, meekness, long-
suffering', *Colossians* 3: 12). Stringed instruments were strung with
gut, or literal bowels.

**25 adjudge my self to:** condemn myself to.

**28-30** If a clear spring goes on running without stopping, even though
I'm not thirsty, will I, who am no crystal (being stained with sin), do
any different?

**31-4** Nature stops me weeping endlessly, and my body could not
survive my weeping as much as my sins deserve.

**The Family:** not in *W*.

**3 puling:** (*B*) whining; *pulling* in *1633*.

**6 repine:** get discontented.

**10 plays:** P follows H in glossing this as to tune, a sense not given in
OED. To play on as an instrument, H's alternative, is marginally
preferable, but I do not see 'the many musical terms in this poem' H
refers to in its support. *Play* could mean to furnish with the means of
playing, to amuse (OED ll.b), a rare sense current at this time. The
image is, after all, of an unruly household where the wranglers are
sent outside, the quarrels quietened by Peace and Silence, and Order
brings congé, playtime, to the soul in the orderly routine of *set forms
and hours*.

**20 What is so shrill as silent tears?:** a commonplace. Of innumer-
able analogues, cf. Donne: 'great sorrow cannot speak ... Sad hearts,

the less they seem, the more they are' (*Elegy: Death*, ll.2ff.).

**The Size:** not in *W*. *Size:* a proper manner or method, a standard of action or conduct, a limit (OED sb.6: an obsolete sense whose last quoted example is dated 1574, but more appropriate than P's 'status or state'). However, the current sense of *size* is suggested by the *thin and spare, not ... corpulent* Christian of stanza 6, and his robe with its unextended seams of stanza 8.

**3 part:** die, as in *Ephes. 4.30.*, p. 132, l.10.

**4 passing brave:** sufficiently fine.

**5-6 springs:** metaphoric for springs of joy: let them fall from the *upper* reaches (heaven) to the *low* (earth), and you will *flow* with joy.

**7-12** If you have enough spices to put in your drink, and are heir to the Isle of spices (heaven), is that not fair enough for you? *1633* mispunctuates with a question mark after *spices*, and a semicolon after *prevail*.

**15-16 disannul ... Enact:** cancel ... decree. *B* has *exact* for *enact*, which makes just as good sense.

**18 Wouldst thou both eat thy cake, and have it?:** proverbial, and still current.

**19-24 Great joys ... Sion's hill:** *Those* (ll.21, 23) refers to the *Great joys* that are had and finished *all at once*; *these* (ll.21, 23) refers to the *little* joys that still keep back *more* to come. Great joys *have* all their *hopes* fulfilled immediately, little joys *renounce* their hopes and live on the credit (*on score*) of hopes to be fulfilled in the future, *the rest* that they will find waiting for them in heaven (*Sion's hill*).

**27 in lump:** i.e. *en masse*.

**36 pretender:** suitor. 'The suitor's mind is divided between happiness and anxiety before he has achieved his marriage' (H); Christians likewise have not yet achieved heaven.

**40 destroy:** outdo. If we received comfort according to our deserts, they would be even rarer than great frosts or snows and we would reckon events from *the last joy*. There is a short line missing between ll.39-40.

**42 close again the seam:** the addressee has (metaphorically) let out the seams of his clothes in expectation of a good blow-out.

**46 meridian:** the brass ring within which a globe is suspended and rotates.

**47 heaven the haven:** cf. G. M. Hopkins' beautiful poem, *Heaven-Haven*.

**Artillery:** not in *W*. The gist of the poem is that God shoots *good motions*, like stars, at us; we shoot back prayers and tears at him. For the military metaphor, cf. *Prayer (1)*, p. 49, l.5: prayer is an *Engine against th' Almighty, sinners' tower*; for stars as an acquirable emblem of virtue, cf. *Perirrhanterium*, p. 13, l.171: *Take stars for money*.

**2 a star did shoot into my lap:** landed suddenly in my lap. The secondary sense, 'fired into', emerges only at l.17.

**3-4** A pleasantly humorous, mundane introduction to a complex poem.

**8 Which have the face of fire:** punning on good impulses which (1) are fiery like stars, and (2) make you blush (*have the face of fire*) with guilt or shame.

**but end in rest:** but are ultimately curative.

**9 music in the spheres:** the traditional belief in a celestial music inaudible to mortal ears: 'There's not the smallest orb which thou behold'st/But in his motion like an angel sings,/Still quiring to the young-ey'd cherubins' (*Merchant of Venice* V.i.6off.).

**11-12 God, whose ministers/The stars and all things are:** God 'maketh his angels spirits; his ministers a flaming fire' (*Psalms* 104: 4) (H).

**12-13** If I refuse what is good for me so often . . .

**14-15** . . . then I still don't refuse to wash away my stubbornness with blood (i.e. suffering).

**17 stars and shooters:** H (and P following H) glosses *shooters* as shooting stars. However, OED gives no other example of this sense (which may therefore be the compiler's false conjecture). Herbert doesn't distinguish between the stars and shooting stars in stanza 1, and needs no such distinction here. The poem's argument pivots on a pun on *shooter* meaning (1) one who shoots, and (2) a suitor (similarly pronounced, as the forms 'shuter' and 'shewter', in the sixteenth century, show). The military sense is raised by the title, and sustained in stanza 4 (cf. *combat, parley, arrows, articling*); that of the wooing suitor predominates in stanza 3 (cf. *woo,/And work up to thee . . . thou dost refuse*). The suitor attacks God in his prayers as *Prayer (1)* also stresses.

**18 Born where thy servants both artilleries use:** i.e. heaven. *Prayer (1)* p.49, also stresses that prayers originate in heaven and return to it (*God's breath in man returning to his birth . . . Exalted Manna*, ll.2, 10).

**21-3 Not, but . . . but because:** i.e. [I assault you with prayers] because you are bound by your own promises – not that I don't recognize I'm more bound to obey you, than you are to indulge me.

**24 Thy promise now hath ev'n set thee thy laws:** ultimately referring to salvation through Christ; *now* suggests a promise made within the context of the poem, and can only be the promise of *rest* in l.8.

**29-30 I am thine . . . if I am mine:** cf. *The Altar*, p. 23, ll.15–16, and *Clasping of hands*, p. 153.

**32 infinitely:** powerfully extra-metric. What should have been an iambic pentameter fades away in a run of unstressed syllables: *I am but* *finite, yet thine infinitely* ... (cf. *The Church Militant*, p. 189, l.116).

**Church-rents and schisms:** (*or* in *B*). Not in *W*. The Greek word *schisma* means tear or rent, so explaining the *rents* of this title (which do not mean dues to be paid). It was often used for divisions within the Church, e.g. between Anglicanism, Roman Catholicism and Protestantism.

**1 Brave rose:** the Church, 'the rose of Sharon' (*Song of Solomon* 2: 1) in her *chair* (throne) of authority (H).

**3 A worm:** schisms; *debates and fretting jealousies* (l.16).

**9 shreds:** cf. title-note.

**11 Mother:** the Church. She shows herself to be a rose by her blushing (H).

**14–20** The opposition of *foes* was good for the Church, strengthening her as blood-letting was thought to do; internal dissension (*debates* ... *within*) have corrupted and rotted her from inside.

**21 start:** split apart.

**27–8** Herbert's disillusion with the Church in the Old World is deployed at length in *The Church Militant*.

**29 With these two poor ones:** with just the two eyes he has (cf. l.26). *Lick up all the dew:* P identifies a reference to Manna, which appeared at dawn with the dew, and could be thought to grow on, or *lick up*, the dew (see *The bunch of grapes*, l.16n, p. 454). Eyes can be thought to *pour out* dew but hardly to *lick* it *up*. With *The British Church*, this is one of Herbert's least satisfactory poems.

**Justice (2):** not in *W*.

**2 of old:** the poem is making a distinction between the retributive justice of the Old Testament, and the redemptive mercy of Christ. *To me*, however, l.4 also indicates a personal change of attitude. It is a change also registered by the difference between rejected poems from *W*, with their references to hell, and a markedly more benevolent image of God and divine mercy prevailing in the final form of *The Church*.

**3–5** I.e. when (my) sins and errors made me see you as something frightening.

**5 And through their glass discolour thee:** deriving from *1 Corinthians* 13: 12: 'For now we see through a glass, darkly; but then face to face.'

**6** Even not having your head bowed, but looking up, seemed a sign of excessive pride.

**7–9 dishes ... beam ... scape:** the old-fashioned scales had an upright shaft (*scape*) with a cross-*beam* from which were suspended two *dishes*, one containing the weights, the other the thing to be weighed.

461

**8 two great pits:** the nearest Herbert comes to suggesting hell, with *burn and glow* (l.11). Presumably sins of excess in the heavier scale, and omission in the lighter, condemned him both ways. See further *The Priesthood*, l.3n, p. 470.

**13 Christ's pure veil:** the distinction is between the discoloured, fearful vision of Justice in stanzas 1 and 2, which is that of the Old Testament, and the new purity of vision brought by Christ. This distinction derives from *2 Corinthians* 3: 7-18, which contrasts the Old Testament's Mosaic Law, 'the ministration of death' and 'of condemnation', to Christ's new 'ministration of the spirit' and 'of righteousness'. In this passage St. Paul explains how Moses hid his face in a veil because the children of Israel could not look upon him, but now '[this vail] is done away in Christ. But even unto this day, when Moses is read, the vail is upon their heart. Nevertheless when it shall turn to the Lord, the vail shall be taken away.' The passage ends by returning to the image of the darkened glass raised in *1 Corinthians* 13: 12 and this poem's line 5 (see above) in a transcendental reversal accurately followed in this poem: 'we all, with open face beholding as in a glass the glory of the Lord, are changed into the same image, from glory to glory, even as by the Spirit of the Lord' (*2 Corinthians* 3: 18). H's (and P's) preferred reference to *Hebrews* 10: 20, describing 'a new and living way, which [Christ] has consecrated for us, through the veil, that is to say, his flesh' is less helpful, and their other reference to a prosaic description of the veil in Solomon's temple (*2 Chronicles* 3: 14) is irrelevant.

**16 like buckets:** see Introduction, p. xx, on *The Pulley* (p. 156), which uses the same image. The scales are like two buckets in a well, one dropping down to scoop up water as the other rises with its freight, *interchangeably* (in turn). *B* and *1633* both have *attend*, though *ascend* is an attractive emendation (even if, as H says, a poor rhyme to *descend*).

**21 harp on:** dwell on, but with the musical metaphor heightened by *touch*.

**The Pilgrimage:** not in *W*. Another spiritual autobiography, detailing a comparable narrative to that of *Affliction (1)*. Clearly imitated in the extended allegory of Bunyan's *Pilgrim's Progress*.

**7 fancy's meadow:** evoking youth, love, and pastoral poetry.

**10 my hour:** cf. *my hour,/My inch of life* (*Complaining*, p. 140, ll.17-18) (H). Life doesn't allow him to dawdle.

**13-14 wild ... wold:** several puns here. *Passion* is of course *wild* and aptly imaged by a wilderness or wold (alternatively, weald, and surviving e.g. in the Cotswolds), which *B* spells *would*.

**15 sometimes rich:** because Herbert is well aware of the spiritual and artistic richness in passion, explored in so many of his poems.

**17 Angel:** also a coin.

**19 the gladsome hill:** cf. *Sion's hill* (*The Size*, p. 134, l.24).

**23 brackish waters:** i.e. the *tears* of l.28.

**25-6 sting/Of swarming fears:** Herbert lightly suggests the gnats and flies above the brackish water.

**36 a chair:** a portable chair (like a sedan-chair, and comparable to the modern wheel-chair), used for moving the elderly and dying. See *Mortification*, l.29n, p. 438.

**The Holdfast:** not in *W*. A holdfast is a staple, clamp or bolt securing a building or other structure. Probably also referring to *Psalm* 73: 27, BCP: 'it is good for me to hold fast by God; I have put my trust in the Lord God' (H). This sonnet is a dialogue partially in reported speech, with the different voices not marked by punctuation in *1633*.

**1 I threatned:** note the paradoxical absurdity of threatening to obey: it is not a threat except to someone sharing the repressive views of the poem's interlocutor.

**3 I was told by one:** the extreme position taken up by this *one* seems to be Calvinist in its denial of human will to salvation. The latter part of ll.3, 4, 6–7, and 9 to the first part of 10 are all spoken by this dour and joyless figure. He should not be associated with the *friend* of l.11, who is Christ, the decisive voice finally resolving many of Herbert's poems.

**8 Then I confess that he my succour is:** the speaker tries hard to think in the restrictive terms set by his interlocutor (his *confess* derives from *We must confess, that nothing is our own*), only to be driven back at each step to a more spiritually starved, supine position (human will diminishing from *threatned to observe* to *trust* to *confess*).

**9-10** I.e. (according to the extremist) our position is one of absolute absence of volition – we can only *have* nothing, not even say 'we have nothing'.

**13-14** Either spoken by the *friend* of l.11, or an impersonal final summing-up. The sonnet's last three lines reverse the interlocutor's extreme position by inviting mankind back into shared possession: *all things* are *more ours by being his* (Christ's). What Adam had, and forfeited for all mankind, is now in Christ's keeping – and Christ will not *fall* or *fail* us, as Adam did.

**Complaining:** not in *W*. For stanza 2, cf. Blake's *The Fly*, from *Songs of Experience*.

**5 thy dust that calls:** cf. *Denial*, p. 77, ll.16–18: *O that thou shouldst give dust a tongue/To cry to thee,/And then not hear it crying!* (H).

**The Discharge:** not in *W*. The poem *discharges* the heart from concern about the future, which lies with God. A discharge was a legal

463

document releasing the recipient from an obligation. An answer to the preceding poem.

**1 Busy enquiring heart:** an echo of Donne; see Introduction, p. xxiii.

**3 licorous:** lecherous, wanton.

**8 depart:** to *depart with* means to surrender.

**22–5** I.e. it's hard enough seeing what the present requires of you, let alone beating your head about the future.

**26 They:** present things.

**31 provide:** (for the future).

**32 breaks the square:** goes beyond what is required of him.

**45 And draw the bottom out an end:** unravel the skein of thread continuously. *An end* was sometimes hyphenated or written as one word; cf. 'A slave that still an end turns me to shame' (*The Two Gentlemen of Verona* IV.iv.68) (H).

**48 now grieve to morrow:** i.e. for tomorrow today (and then again tomorrow, ll.49–50).

**Praise (2):** not in *W*. A psalm of praise distantly deriving from *Psalm* 116 (P) 'I love the Lord, because he hath heard my voice and my supplications. Because he hath inclined his ear unto me, therefore will I call upon him as long as I live', etc.

**3–4 And that love may never cease,/I will move thee:** I will ask you for (my) love never to cease. The request is immediately granted in the next line.

**11 And the cream of all my heart/I will bring thee:** a beautiful example of Herbert's domestic concretization.

**23** Cf. *Justice (2)*, p. 137.

**26 enrol:** record in the roll of honour, celebrate.

**An Offering:** not in *W*. As in other poems where there may be more than one speaker, interpretation is complicated by the lack of inverted commas. In this case, the entire poem seems to be spoken by a single voice – that of the parson or poet to the contrite parishioner. For other two-part poems, see *Good Friday*, headnote, pp. 405–6.

**7–8** I.e. if only our hearts could multiply, since God's many gifts require a comparable repayment of many hearts.

**9 title:** OED cites this passage for an obsolete sense meaning to entitle. If the heart is good it can be thought of as a number of hearts, just as (l.10) single acts proliferate in their deserved consequences.

**11 one may be a nation:** one man may speak for and represent a nation.

**12 fence:** fence off. The reference is to David, who brought down a plague on Israel, and then begged God 'be on me, and on my father's house; but not on thy people, that they should be plagued' (*1 Chronicles* 21: 17) (P).

**17 parcel out:** divide into small portions (and distribute them).

**19 balsam ... blood:** Christ's redemptive blood.

**22 All-heal:** in the herbals of the late sixteenth century a number of plants (mistletoe, yarrow, valerian, woundwort) were called All-heal. Herbert transfers a mundane term to Christian significance.

**Longing:** not in *W*. One of Herbert's rare poems of unrelieved misery.

**8-9 ground/Which thou dost curse:** God's curse on Adam: 'cursed is the ground for thy sake' (*Genesis* 3: 17) (H).

**17 Their infants, them:** suck (understood).

**19 Bowels of pity:** see *Ephes. 4.30*., l.24n, p. 458.

**21, 29 Bow down thine ear:** 'Bow down thine ear, O Lord, hear me: for I am poor and needy' (*Psalm* 86: 1) (H).

**25 my sorrows' round:** cf. *Sin's round*, p. 118, with the same fire motif. *round:* coil or ring.

**31-2 thou didst bow/Thy dying head upon the tree:** 'he said, It is finished: and he bowed his head, and gave up the ghost' (*John* 19: 30).

**35-6 Shall he that made the ear,/Not hear?:** Significantly, this is taken from a Psalm attacking mankind for foolishness rather than God for indifference: 'Yet they say, the Lord shall not see it, neither shall the God of Jacob regard it. Understand, ye brutish among the people: and ye fools, when will ye be wise? He that planted the ear, shall he not hear? he that formed the eye, shall he not see?' (*Psalm* 94: 7-9). A hidden implicit reprimand of the speaker, as quite often in Herbert's use of allusion (cf. Introduction, p. xlvii, on *The Collar*).

**47-8 Is all lockt? hath a sinner's plea/No key?:** cf. *I know it is my sin, which locks thine ears* (*Church-lock and key*, p. 63, l.1).

**52 interlin'd:** written between the lines (of a book or manuscript). H quotes a comparable image from Donne, but the two passages also illustrate the difference between Herbert's humility (the *meek look* is that of God's *humble* guests) and Donne's retributive God: 'What place of Scripture soever thou pretend, that place is interlined – interlined by the Spirit of God Himself with conditions and limitations and provisions – "If thou return", "if thou repent", – and that interlining destroys the bill.' (*Sermon of 4 Feb 1625*).

**53 board:** supper table (and hence altar for Holy Communion). God the host has room for everybody.

**nests:** cf. *O let me, when thy roof my soul hath hid,/O let me roost and nestle there* (*The Temper (1)*, p. 53, ll.17-18).

**69 That:** sin.

**70 These:** *thy promises.*

**75-6** Cf. *Thy passions also have their set partitions./These parcel out thy heart* (*An Offering*, p. 144, ll.16-17).

**77-8 Thy beggars grow; rid them away:** picking up the

importunate beggar of *Gratefulness*, p. 120, ll.3ff.: *See how thy beggar works on thee/By art ... Perpetual knockings at thy door ... thou ... didst allow us all our noise*, etc. This poem is an example of all that noise, which is kindly answered in the next poem.

**The Bag:** not in *W*. Another pointedly prosaic, concretizing title. P quotes Tuve (see Bibliography) that a *saccus* was both a purse and a bag for straining wine, but the modern reader would probably better share Herbert's contemporaries' sense of shocked surprise if he thought of Christ in this poem as a kind of heavenly postman, his *bag* being the wound in his side.

**5 Storms are the triumph of his art:** cf. *Tempests are calm to thee; they know thy hand* (*Providence*, p. 114, l.45).

**6 close his eyes:** 'And behold, there arose a great tempest in the sea, insomuch that the ship was covered with the waves: but he was asleep. And his disciples came to him, and awoke him, saying, Lord, save us: we perish. And he saith unto them, Why are ye fearful, O ye of little faith? Then he arose, and rebuked the winds and the sea; and there was a great calm' (*Matthew* 8: 24–6) (H).

**11 light:** alight.

**13 tire:** either dress, apparel (attire), or more specifically, a headdress (cf. tiara).

**14 The cloud his bow:** Christ's bow becomes the rainbow in the clouds. Referring to God's covenant with Noah: 'I do set my bow in the cloud' (*Genesis* 9: 13 and see *Affliction (5)*, l.24n, p. 437).
**the fire:** i.e. the lightning.

**17 He smil'd and said:** cf. *Love took my hand, and smiling did reply* (*Love (3)*, p. 184, l.11) (H).

**18 new clothes:** i.e. human flesh.

**20 He did repair unto an inn:** or rather, Mary 'laid him in a manger, because there was no room for them in the inn' (*Luke* 2: 7).

**23 having giv'n the rest before:** i.e. his divinity, the disrobing of stanza 2.

**24 he gave up his life to pay our score:** Christ paid off our unpaid bill (sustaining the *inn* metaphor), redeeming mankind from the punishment incurred by Adam's fall.

**25–6** Referring to the wounding of Christ after his death: *The Sacrifice*, p. 31, ll.245–7: *after death their spite shall further go;/For they will pierce my side, I full well know;/That as sin came, so Sacraments might flow*. The moment Herbert repeatedly returns to.

**27–9 He, who came hither all alone ... Receiv'd the blow:** cf. *Redemption*, p. 37, whose narrative also defamiliarizes the Crucifixion and intensifies our sense of innocence waylaid and murdered.
**nor man:** i.e. servant.

**35–6 That I shall mind what you impart:** in proof that I will guard the message you want to send – look, you can put it right by my heart. (*1633* has a comma after *mind* and semicolon after *impart*.)

**38 in this kind:** as a messenger.

> **the door/Shall still be open:** cf. 'I am the door: by me if any man enter in, he shall be saved' (*John* 10: 9) (P).

**40 and somewhat more/Not to his hurt:** Christ will not only act as our messenger to God, but as our intermediary.

**The Jews:** not in *W*.

**2 scions:** a scion is a shoot or twig, and more particularly one cut off and used for grafting on to a different stock.

**3 sluice:** a water-gate, floodgate, or an overflow channel. See also *Whitsunday*, p. 57, ll. 17–19 for the same image.

**5 by not keeping once, became a debtor:** P and H assume *keeping* here means keeping the law, and refer to *Galatians* 5: 3: 'For I testify again to every man that is circumcised, that he is a debtor to do the whole law' (that is, by obeying the one law of circumcision, he is bound to obey all the Judaic laws). Tempting as this reference may be, it is contradicted by Herbert's wording, which speaks of *not keeping*, rather than keeping, and the law is not named at all. Since ll. 1–4 describe how the Jews failed to keep, or contain, the spiritual streams the Apostles deflected into Baptism, the implication of this line may be that *not keeping* them *once* has put the Jews into *debt* to Christianity, since now they can only be rejuvenated by Christ's spiritual sap (see ll. 11–12).

**6 And now by keeping lose the letter:** *the letter* inevitably evokes the Pauline distinction between Judaic obedience to the letter of the law, and Christ's liberation into its spirit (see *Romans* 7: 6). By keeping only the letter of the law, they lose it.

**7 mine, alas!:** a question mark might be more appropriate, since *mine* is corrected to *some Angel* in the next line. The speaker's prayers are inadequate; it needs an Angel for them to work.

**10 the trump:** the Last Trump. The conversion of the Jews was traditionally thought to precede the Last Judgment (P).

**The Collar:** not in *W*. For the form of this poem, and a commentary on its use of dramatic irony, see Introduction, pp. xlviff. *Collar* puns on choler (anger) and the collar used for restraint and discipline (e.g. of a dog); 'to slip the collar' was often used figuratively for evasion of restraint (H). Churchmen did not wear dog-collars, whose first appearance the OED dates in 1894.

**1 I struck the board:** prime sense, the table; vital subordinate sense, the altar or communion table. This is the first of a series of *doubles entendres* riddling the poem and explained in the Introduction. There is further paragrammatic play between *the board* and *abroad* in l. 2.

**4 road:** spelt *rode* in *1633*, and possibly also evoking the rood, or cross, which is of course what brings spiritual *free*dom.

**20 double pleasures:** ominously glossed in *Man's medley*, p. 128, ll. 25ff.: *But as his joys are double;/So is his trouble.*

**21** Semicolon provided.

**22 Thy rope of sands:** to twist a rope of sand was a proverbial image of futility (Erasmus: *Ex arena funiculum nectis*) – impossible to do, and useless, were it possible.

**The Glimpse:** not in *W*.

**13-15** Quicklime (calcium oxide: lime which has been burned and not yet slaked) combines readily with water to make slaked lime, releasing heat and vapour in the process.

**19 When as my fears foretold this:** *this* is the quick departure of delight.

**20 A slender thread a gentle guest will tie:** *Outlandish Proverbs*, no. 722 (H). The heart tentatively presses its gentle guest, delight, to stay a little longer.

**23-5** I.e. delight may keep back the bulk of its store for the future, but occasional droppings from the stock will not break the lock of the store-house and open it up to general depradation.

**26 more to spin:** i.e. more life to work through.

**27 The wheel shall go, so that thy stay be short:** the wheel will work so busily that your absence (*stay*: as in *Home*, p. 104, l. 2) will seem short.

**29-30** Don't leave me to be the plaything of grief and sin, when your presence can turn me into a court. *Court* is suggestive of heaven; cf. *Dotage*, p. 163, ll. 15-16; mankind prefers *a loathsome den/Before a court, ev'n that above.*

**Assurance:** not in *W*.

**2 thou:** the spiteful thought of l. 1.

**4-6** i.e. certainly there can be no comparable poison to the venom of wit and spite meeting together to concoct a punishment.

**9 allow:** allow myself.

**19 I will to my Father:** I will go to my Father, and say ... The childlike tone frequent in Herbert's relationship to God.

**29 at once:** at the same time. God the Father signed his half of the covenant, and helped the speaker sign his. Another version of the reciprocity explored e.g. in *Clasping of hands*.

**39-40 thou hast cast a bone/Which bounds on thee, and will not down thy throat:** to cast a bone between two people is proverbial for creating strife between them (H). Here the bone rebounds on the spiteful thought (cf. *Charms and Knots*, p. 93, ll. 9-10n, p. 436) and sticks in its throat – three colloquial or proverbial concepts in one.

**The Call:** not in *W*.

**2** Most journeys make us breathless; this gives us the breath of life (H).

**5 Feast:** communion.

**7 mends in length:** gets better as it goes on.

**8 Such a Strength, as makes his guest:** cf. 'He that comes to the Sacrament hath the confidence of a guest' (*The Country Parson*, ch. xxii, p. 228) (H).

**10 move:** remove.

**11 part:** separate from us.

**Clasping of hands:** not in *W*. The rhyme-words in both stanzas are identical, except that in stanza 1, lines 1, 3, 9, 10 they are *thine*, *mine*, *mine*, *thine*, and in stanza 2 they are reversed to *mine*, *thine*, *thine*, *mine*. See further Introduction, p. xvii. *Meum* and *tuum* was a popular phrase to express the laws of property (OED), overturned in this poem.

**6** This and l.16 are identical: the hub of the rotating *mine*s and *thine*s of the poem, as is the poem's only other rhyme: *restore/more*.

**12–13** I.e. you are mine so much, that I can think you more mine than your own.

**Praise (3):** not in *W*. Note the refrain-word, *more*, closing each stanza.

**3 spin:** echoing *The Glimpse*, p. 151, l.26.

**15 Albion:** England (a literary, rather un-Herbertian name).

**17 Pharaoh's wheels but logs:** as the Egyptians pursued the Israelites through the Red Sea, 'the Lord ... took off their chariot wheels, that they drave them heavily ... and the waters returned, and covered the chariots, and the horsemen, and all the host of Pharaoh' (*Exodus* 14: 25, 28) (H).

**19 do thee employ:** surprisingly, because one would expect 'thou dost employ'. But the angels, devils, etc., all employ attributes of God in controlling the world. His *Joy*, for instance, has been detailed in *The Call* just previously (and cf. *Thou heardst my call*, l.24) and is specifically associated with the angels: see *Affliction (5)*, l.15n, p. 436.

**22 the sea his shore:** see *Providence*, ll.47–8n, p. 449.

**23 their stint:** their allotted measure.

**27 a bottle:** cf. *Psalm* 56: 8: 'Thou tellest my wanderings: put thou my tears into thy bottle: are they not in thy book?' (H) and the Roman lachrymatories, or bottles, supposedly for the collection of mourners' tears for the dead.

**28 boxes for the poor:** H quotes Canon 84, which orders the provision of 'a strong Chest' (cf. l.41) in every church where alms for the poor can be collected. *The Country Parson*, ch. xiii, p. 216, lists *a poor man's box* among the church's necessary furnishings.

**33 streamers:** long narrow pointed flags or pennons.

**35 bloody battle:** the Crucifixion, in which Christ defeated death: the *bloody fight* of *Good Friday*, p. 36, l.22 (H).

**38 Though press'd, runs thin:** the speaker's heart is pressed like a wine press – an image evoking Christ's *Agony*, p. 34, ll.10ff. At this point the image is turning from tears, collected in bottles, to *praise* (l.42) collected in *chests* (l.41) or heavenly poor boxes.

**40 at use:** with interest.

**Joseph's coat:** not in *W*. A sonnet. 'Now Israel loved Joseph more than all his children, because he was the son of his old age: and he made him a coat of many colours. And when his brethren saw that their father loved him more than all his brethren, they hated him' (*Genesis* 37: 3–4). The many colours of Joseph's coat are paralleled by the mixed feelings of this poem (and indeed of Joseph's family).

**3 his will:** God's will.

**8 both:** the *one grief and smart* (singlular; *it* of l.7) and *my heart* (H).

**9 both:** *my heart* (l.7) and *body* (l.9).

**10 he:** God.

**11 'ticing:** enticing.

**with relief:** an abstract personification: Joy is tempted by God to *linger* in the speaker, languishing *together* with Relief.

**Joy's coats:** cf. Joseph's coat of the title.

**14 joys to weep ... griefs to sing:** a traditional Petrarchan lover's paradox. Cf. Surrey: 'I weep and sing/In joy and woe' (*Alas, so all things now do hold their peace*, ll.8–9), and *his beams sing ... my music shine* of *Christmas*, p. 78, l.34.

**The Pulley:** not in *W*. For an explanation of the title, and discussion of the poem, see Introduction, pp. xx, xxxvi. It is an ingenious familiarized inversion of the classical myth of Pandora, who was maliciously sent to mankind by Zeus with a jar, which she opened, releasing a multitude of ills, and shut in time to keep Hope in as a consolation to man. Post-classical myth turned the jar into a box, but Herbert's *glass of blessings* seems to evoke the original story.

**5 span:** a small unit of measurement; i.e. man.

**20** the *breast/rest* rhyme is also used in the poignant last stanza of *Perseverance*, a poem only appearing in *W*. See Appendix 2, p. 337.

**The Priesthood:** not in *W*.

**3 throwest down to hell:** one of the overt references to hell in the final form of *The Church* (and notably more in the few rejected poems from *W*, see Appendix 2, pp. 331ff.). See *Love 1*, l.12n, p. 415. It is clear from *Justice (2)*, p. 137, and this poem, that Herbert developed from a fear of hell to a faith in divine mercy.

**5 lay-sword:** the sword normally worn by a layman – a much less

470

effective weapon than God's word, as used by the priesthood, as ll.2–3 have shown.

**9 the severe attire:** detailed in *Aaron*, p. 170.

**10 slender compositions:** not merely thin in physical terms (though this recurs in *Affliction (1)*, p. 45, l.35: *Thus thin and lean ...*) but psychologically also of slender means.

**13–15** For the pottery metaphor, cf. 'O Lord, thou art our father; we are the clay, and thou our potter; and we all are the work of thy hand' (*Isaiah* 64: 8) (H).

**15 Where once I scorn'd to stand:** i.e. in the priesthood. There is a contrast between Herbert's offering himself up as a priest in his unrefined mortal self, which is *foul and brittle* like a vessel of dried but unfired *clay* (stanza 2), and his mortal self hardened by God's sacred fire (stanza 3). Now his wretched earth is transformed into fine china like that shaped and fired by *skilful artists* for the tables (*boards*) of the most exquisite households (*those/Who make the bravest shows*).

**19–24** Cf. God to Adam: 'In the sweat of thy face shalt thou eat bread, till thou return unto the ground; for out of it wast thou taken: for dust thou art, and unto dust shalt thou return' (*Genesis* 3: 19). Mankind, his food, and his dinner service, all come from the earth: no wonder then that one should delight in the other.

**26 As serve him up:** the priest serves up God in the Eucharist.

**31–3** Referring to the death of Uzzah: 'Uzzah put forth his hand to the ark of God, and took hold of it, for the oxen shook it. And the anger of the Lord was kindled against Uzzah; and God smote him there for his error; and there he died by the ark of God' (*2 Samuel* 6: 6–7) (H).

**35–8 lowly matter ... mean stuff:** Herbert's humility here can be read biographically as underlying his election of the extremely modest living at Bemerton where he chose to practise the priesthood.

**40 Lest good come short of ill/In praising might:** lest the good should be less effective than the bad in praising power...

**41–2** ... a person in power is as much lauded by the humility of the poor as by the rival displays of the proud. The last line of this compressed conclusion is a variation on the proverbial wisdom that imitation is the sincerest form of flattery. For the poor man's praise by submission, cf. *Outlandish Proverbs*, no. 484: 'Praise a hill, but keep below'.

**The Search:** not in *W*.

**3 My searches are my daily bread:** i.e. searching for you is a daily routine for me. P suggests a dramatic irony in bread, which points to the Eucharist, a redemptive sense unidentified by the speaker (cf. Introduction, pp. xlvff.).

**4 Yet never prove:** dough which does not *prove* has not risen: (a) the resulting bread will be heavy and sour (appropriately for the misery of the speaker); (b) the search does not reach its goal.

**6–7 sphere ... centre:** see *Prayer (2)*, p. 100, l.9.

**14 Simper:** glimmer, twinkle (an obsolete and rare sense), or smirk (a sense already used in *Perirrhanterium*, p. 12, l.123).

**19 Wing'd like an arrow:** cf. *Prayer (1)*, p. 49, l.5 and *Artillery*, p. 136, ll.17ff.

**23 dumb:** presumably because the *sigh* was more inaudible if no more articulate than the *groan*.

**25 new fabric:** a new world, or new race of men.

**31 What covert dare eclipse thy face?:** *covert* is either a straightforward covering (the sense identified by OED, which quotes this line), or, more specifically, a thicket in which wild game hide – a sense suggested by ll.29–30, and comparable to the *dark and shady grove* (which is sin) that hides heaven in *H. Baptism (1)*, p. 42, ll.1ff., and *Faith*, p. 48, ll.37–40, and see note. If the illuminating cross-reference Herbert celebrates in the Bible (*The H. Scriptures II*), p. 56, ll.1ff.) and displays in his own work (see Introduction, p. xxxviii) is operative here, then there is a potent irony in the speaker fearing it is God's will to be hidden, rather than recognizing that it is his own sins which obscure him.

**33 let not that:** *that* is God's will. The sentence is completed at l.35. Let it not be your will which rings you round ...

**36 pass:** pass through them.

**37 entrenching:** fortification by a trench.

**38 passeth:** surpasses, ironically countermanding *I will pass* of l.36.

**43 the poles do kiss:** north and south poles. Like East and West touching, and parallels meeting, for the poles to kiss is an impossibility except in the transcendent space spanned by God's will. Dylan Thomas may be echoing Herbert in *I see the boys of summer in their ruin*, which ends 'O see the poles are kissing as they cross.'

**47 my charge:** i.e. my load (of grief) (H).

**51–2** Let me say you are Almighty for me, rather than against me.

**56 between:** you and me (understood).

**59 bear the bell:** to take first place. A phrase originating with the bell worn by the leading cow or sheep of a flock (the bell-wether).

**Grief:** not in *W*.

**1–2** Cf. 'Oh that my head were waters, and mine eyes a fountain of tears, that I might weep day and night' (*Jeremiah* 9: 1) (P). A popular Renaissance trope; cf. the quickly parodied 'Oh eyes! no eyes, but fountains fraught with tears' of Kyd's *The Spanish Tragedy* III.ii.1.

**9 two shallow fords, two little spouts:** i.e. the weeping eyes of the speaker (who is *a lesser world*, or microcosm of *the greater* world in l.10).

**15 feet:** punning on metric feet.

**19 Alas, my God!:** a pointedly ametric, unrhymed line, fit for *rough*

472

*sorrows* in its complete freedom from art.

**The Cross:** not in *W*. The title puns on God's cross-biasing or frustration of the speaker, and Christ's Cross. It is a pun Herbert frequently taps: *Thus doth thy power cross-bias me* (*Affliction (1)*, p. 45, l. 53).

**5 all my wealth, and family:** see Walton's *Life of Herbert*, p. 371.

**8 this dear end:** the priesthood, described in one letter as 'my journey's end' (p. 289) (H).

**16 allow'd for:** accepted as.

**18 Save in the sight thereof, where strength doth sting:** except when contemplating the cross, whose strength stings me into action.

**19 things sort not to my will:** things don't come out the way I wanted.

**23 sped:** fulfilled.

**29 in the midst of delicates to need:** to feel need when surrounded by luxuries.

**32 these contrarieties:** cf. *The Temper (1)*, p. 52; a metrically uneasy line.

**36 my words:** the speaker stresses this, because he is adopting as his own Christ's words in the Garden of Gethsemane: 'Father, if thou be willing, remove this cup from me: nevertheless not my will, but thine, be done' (*Luke* 22: 42).

**The Flower:** not in *W*. Coleridge rightly called this 'a delicious poem'.

**3 demean:** demeanour, and demesne: so, both bearing, and estate (H).

**10–11 as flowers depart/To see their mother-root:** a regenerative cycle occluded in *Virtue*, p. 85, stanza 2: *Sweet rose ... Thy root is ever in its grave/And thou must die.*

**16 quickning:** bringing to life.

**18 passing-bell:** the bell rung as a person died (see *Mortification*, l. 17 n, pp. 437–8), which tolled, rather than chimed.

**22–3** Cf. 'Man that is born of woman hath but a short time to live, and is full of misery. He cometh up, and is cut down, like a flower; he fleeth as it were a shadow, and never continueth in one stay' (The Burial of the Dead, taken from *Job* 14: 1–2).

**25 Offring at:** aiming at.

**27 spring-shower:** of tears, remorse for his sins.

**32 the zone:** i.e. the torrid zone between the tropics, the hottest part of the earth.

**38 I once more smell the dew and rain:** cf. the continuation of Job's lament, quoted at l. 22 above: 'For there is hope of a tree, if it be cut down, that it will sprout again, and that the tender branch thereof will not cease. Though the root thereof wax old in the earth, and the stock thereof die in the ground; yet *through the scent of water* it will bud, and bring forth boughs like a plant' (*Job* 14: 7–9) (italics added).

**44 glide:** slip away.

**Dotage:** not in *W*. For the listing of stanzas 1 and 2, cf. *Prayer (1)* and *Sin (1)*, pp. 49, 43. The delayed definitions of ll.6 and 12 give a riddling suspense to these two stanzas wisely abandoned by stanza 3. Dotage is *the folly of distracted men* (l.13).

**1 glozing:** deceptive.

**casks of happiness:** *cask* here is either a barrel (as in wine-cask) or casket. In either case the point seems to be that it is empty of anything except happiness, which the subsequent lines show to be nothing.

**3-4 Chases in Arras:** hunting scenes woven in tapestries, i.e. unreal, leading to the increasing hyperbolic phantasmagoria of *Shadows well mounted* (on horseback), *dreams* running away with themselves (*in a career*).

**5 nothing between two dishes:** i.e. a Barmecidal banquet as in *Timon of Athens*, where the greedy guests gleefully note, 'All cover'd dishes!', 'Royal cheer, I warrant you', till *The dishes are uncovered and seen to be full of warm water* (III.vi.48, 85). H identifies this as a Spanish proverb. Misquoted by Walton, p. 377.

**7-8 rooted ... in grain ... ripe and blown:** all tree metaphors. H and P gloss *in grain* as fast dyed or ineradicable, but the adjacent metaphors suggest that Herbert is thinking of anguish being in the very grain of the tree.

**The Son:** not in *W*. A sonnet, exploring the common Son of God/Sun pun.

**3 coast:** country.

**7 A son is light and fruit:** *light* because of the pun on sun, and he brings light into the lives of his parents; *fruit* because he is the fruit of their union.

**8 Chasing the father's dimness:** the image is of the dawn of one day chasing away the dimness of the preceding day's dusk. Just as one day follows another, so generation follows on generation, an eternally repeated cycle sustained in the *East/West, first* (oldest) to the most recent (*fresh and new*) generations of ll.9–10.

**9 the first man in th' East:** Adam, whom God created and then put in 'a garden eastward in Eden' (*Genesis* 2: 8).

**10 Western discov'ries of posterity:** a riddling line whose sense only becomes apparent on a reading of *The Church Militant* (see p. 489, headnote). Herbert is referring to the dissemination of Christianity, from its beginnings in Adam and *Genesis*, to its most recent emigration from Europe westward to the *fresh and new* settlements in America, the

New World.

**13-14 in humbleness:** as mortal Son of Man.

**in glory:** as divine Sun of Man.


**A true Hymn:** not in *W*.

**11-15** I.e. if you demand the content of mind and soul from a poem which only provides the form of rhyme, you can justly complain that qualities are lacking which would make it *A true Hymn*.

**To make his verse:** to make it perfect, to complete it.

**in kind:** i.e. in all its qualities.

**17 Although the verse be somewhat scant:** even though the verse is poor (as for instance in stanza 1, where l.1 is rhymed in l.5 merely by verbatim repetition).

**18 God doth supply the want:** God completes this poem by the affirmative *Loved* (to rhyme with *moved* and *approved*). Herbert has many poems in which God supplies the missing rhyme (e.g. *The Method*, p. 130, *Denial*, p. 77) or the contrite speaker does so (*The Collar*, p. 149) or the lack is left painfully unresolved (*Grief*, p. 160, *Home*, p. 104).


**The Answer:** not in *W*. A sonnet. A teasingly titled poem: see note to ll.13–14.

**2 ends:** projects, ambitions.

**3 my fierce youth:** cf. the *youth and fierceness* of *my sudden soul* in *Affliction (1)*, p. 44, ll.17–18.

**bandy:** banded together, (as in *Humility*, p. 68, l.29: *so jointly bandying*): the integrated ambitions of his youth fall apart.

**4-5 leaves ... flies:** cf. Timon of Athens, who complains of his lost popularity in similar terms: 'the mouths, the tongues, the eyes, and hearts of men ... That numberless upon me stuck, as leaves/Do on the oak, have with one winter's brush/Fell from their boughs, and left me open, bare/For every storm that blows' (IV.iii.26off.).

**6 undertaking:** i.e. ready to undertake a lot.

**7 prosecutions:** the carrying through of an initiated action.

**8 exhalation:** a mist rising from the damp ground (*his bed of dirt*).

**9 means:** aims at.

**10-11** A demonstration that Herbert understood the water cycle (evaporation, transpiration, condensation, precipitation) probably lying behind *Providence*, p. 115, ll.71–2. H refers to one of Herbert's Latin epistles which draws on the same knowledge.

**pursy:** fat and shortwinded.

**12-13 so/Show me, and set me:** i.e. describe him in the terms outlined in ll.6–7.

**13-14 I have one reply,/Which they that know the rest, know more than I:** a deliberately elusive ending. H does not hazard an explanation. P offers *my answer is a rose* from *The Rose*, p. 174, l.32 – but that reply is completely irrelevant to this poem. Obviously, from the present context, the answer to the speaker's despair is God – as the preceding poem should have warned us. To make this sonnet a true poem *God* must *supply the want* of the missing answer. The tone of the final couplet is heavily ironic: The know-alls, the fair weather friends, *flies of estates and sun-shine*, who can tell the speaker so precisely what his shortcomings are, doubtless know his answer better than he does himself.

**A Dialogue-Anthem:** not in *W*.

**1–2** Cf. 'O death, where is thy sting? O grave, where is thy victory?' (*1 Corinthians* 15: 55: part of the Lesson in the BCP's Burial of the Dead).

**3 void of story:** i.e. with no reputation for heroism (unlike Death, who has killed Christian's King, Christ).

**7 Let losers talk:** *Outlandish Proverbs*, no. 598 (H).

**10 thou shalt be no more:** cf. Donne's sonnet, *Death be not proud*, which ends: 'One short sleep past, we wake eternally,/And death shall be no more; death, thou shalt die.' Both restate *1 Corinthians* 15: 26: 'the last enemy that shall be destroyed is death'. (Also part of the Lesson in the Burial of the Dead.)

**The Water-course:** not in *W*. The poem's form is identified by its title: each stanza closes with a choice between two alternative channels, the worldly and the divine, just as the two stanzas also embody the same distinction. The image of a watercourse has been used earlier, in *The Jews*, p. 149, ll.2–3.

**5** The person who loves (eternal) life is bound to find this worldly life full of trouble; and the person who loves the strife of worldly life is also bound to find it troubled.

**Self-condemnation:** not in *W*.

**2 Barrabas:** in *B* and elsewhere in Herbert, showing he stressed it ´ ´ ´ (H). *Barabbas* in *1633*.

**6 That choice may be thy story:** that choice (of championing evil rather than good) may be true of you too.

**10–12 The world ... doth destroy ... With her enchanting voice:** If this is a reference to the Sirens as a traditional Christian emblem of worldly lusts, as P suggests, then it is remarkably unspecific. Compare with Daniel's *Ulysses and the Sirens*.

**19 prevent:** forestall, anticipate.

**Bitter-sweet:** not in *W*.

**The Glance:** not in *W*.

**4 Weltring:** wallowing, rolling.

**8 take it in:** welcome it as a guest (cf. *Love (3)*, p. 184).

**10 ev'n able to destroy:** me (understood).

**11 Had:** if he had, had he but.

**12 His swing and sway:** his control. He is the *malicious . . . harm* of l.11.

**18 A mirth:** a diversion or entertainment – a now obsolete sense. The use of the indefinite article for *mirth* is undocumented by OED except in this sense (e.g. 'To give a Kingdom for a mirth', *Antony and Cleopatra* I.iv.18).

**20, 22 full-ey'd . . . aspect:** cf. *Vanity (1)*, l.7n, p. 430, on the stars' *full-ey'd aspects*.

**23 More than a thousand suns disburse in light:** more than the light shed by a thousand suns.

**The 23 Psalm:** not in *W*. The Psalm is quoted below, in the versions of the Authorized Version or the BCP (ll.9–12), as appropriate.

**1-4** 'The Lord is my shepherd; I shall not want.'

**5-8** 'He maketh me to lie down in green pastures: he leadeth me beside the still waters.'

**9-12** 'He shall convert my soul: and bring me forth in the paths of righteousness, for his Name's sake.'

**13-16** 'Yea, though I walk through the valley of the shadow of death, I will fear no evil: for thou art with me; thy rod and thy staff they comfort me.'

**17-20** 'Thou preparest a table before me in the presence of mine enemies: thou anointest my head with oil; my cup runneth over.'

**21-4** 'Surely goodness and mercy shall follow me all the days of my life: and I will dwell in the house of the Lord for ever.' Herbert adds his *praise* for God's love.

**Mary Magdalene:** not in *W*. 'And behold, a woman in the city, which was a sinner, when she knew that Jesus sat at meat in the Pharisee's house, brought an alabaster box of ointment. And stood at his feet behind him weeping, and began to wash his feet with tears, and did wipe them with the hairs of her head, and anointed them with the ointment . . . [And Jesus] turned to the woman, and said unto Simon, Seest thou this woman? I entered into thine house, thou gavest me no water for my feet: but she hath washed my feet with tears, and wiped them with the hairs of her head. Thou gavest me no kiss: but this woman since the time I came in hath not ceased to kiss my feet. *My head with oil thou didst not anoint:* but this woman hath anointed my feet with ointment. Wherefore I say unto thee, Her sins, which are many, are forgiven, for she loved much; but to whom little is forgiven, the same loveth little. And he said unto her, Thy sins are forgiven' (*Luke* 7: 37–48). The medieval Church identified this woman as

477

Mary Magdalene (H). The italicized passage links with *Psalm* 23 above, sustaining the submerged concatenation of these poems.

**4–6 Showing his steps would be the street/Wherein she ... would live and tread:** Re-creating Christ's metaphor: 'In my Father's house are many mansions ... I go to prepare a place for you ... whither I go ye know, and the way ye know. Thomas saith unto him, Lord, we know not whither thou goest: and how can we know the way? Jesus saith unto him, I am the way, the truth and the life: no man cometh unto the Father, but by me' (*John* 14: 2–6). Like *Psalm* 23, this points to the final welcome of *Love (3)*, with which Herbert's *Church* closes.

**14 dash:** splash, spatter (with dirt).

**18 she washed both:** because her tears of remorse made her clean.

**Aaron:** not in *W. Exodus* 28: 4–39 gives detailed specifications for Aaron's ornate and sumptuous priestly robes. Herbert selects and modifies the essentials in stanza 1, and reinterprets them in spiritual terms in the following stanzas. This poem is thus a companion piece to *The Priesthood*, pp. 156–7, ll.8–10: *should I presume/To wear thy [the Priesthood's] habit, the severe attire/My slender compositions might consume.* Aaron's elaborate dress is replaced by a simple trinity of qualities listed in ll.21–3. Grierson (quoted by H) notes a bell-like chiming to the repeated rhyme-words which are unchanged from stanza to stanza. Metrically the stanzas swell and die (going from lines of 3 to 4 to 5 to 4 to 3 stresses); each stanza's third line has a musical metaphor, modulating from death knell (stanza 2) to Herbert's recurrent resolution, harmony in Christ (stanza 5).

**1 Holiness on the head:** 'And thou shalt make a plate of pure gold, and grave upon it, like the engravings of a signet, HOLINESS TO THE LORD. And thou shalt put it on a blue lace, that it may be upon a mitre; upon the forefront of the mitre it shall be. And it shall be upon Aaron's forehead, that Aaron may bear the iniquity of the holy things' (*Exodus* 28: 36–8).

**2 Light and prefections on the breast:** 'And thou shalt put in the breastplate of judgment the Urim and the Thummim [identified in the marginal note of the Revised Version as 'the Lights and the Perfections']; and they shall be upon Aaron's heart, when he goeth in before the Lord: and Aaron shall bear the judgment of the children of Israel upon his heart before the Lord continually' (*Exodus* 28: 30). Like the labelled mitre, and the bells, this appears to have been talismanic and protective ornamentation.

**3 Harmonious bells below, raising the dead:** 'And beneath upon the hem of [the robe] thou shalt make pomegranates of blue, and of purple, and of scarlet, round about the hem thereof: and bells of gold between them round about: A golden bell and a pomegranate, upon the hem of the robe round about. And it shall be upon Aaron to minister: and his sound shall be heard when he goeth in unto the holy place before the Lord, and when he cometh out, *that he die not*' (Exodus 28: 33–5). Note the italicized divergence from l.3.

**17 My alone only heart and breast:** a striking line in metre as in meaning, with the emphatic tautology of *alone only*. Like ll.1–2, 11, and 16, it has to be scanned with a reversed first foot: *Mý ălŏne ónlỹ heárt ănd bréast*, giving *My alone* a particular weight.

**19-20 the old man ... new drest:** following St. Paul's distinction between the old, sinning self, and the new redeemed follower of Christ: 'Lie not to one another, seeing that ye have put off the old man with his deeds; And have put on the new man, which is renewed in knowledge after the image of him that created him' (*Colossians* 3: 9–10) (P).

**The Odour, 2 Cor. 2:** not in *W*. 'Now thanks be unto God, which always causeth us to triumph in Christ, and maketh manifest the savour of his knowledge by us in every place. For we are unto God a sweet savour of Christ, in them that are saved, and in them that perish: To the one we are the savour of death unto death; and to the other the savour of life unto life' (*2 Corinthians* 2: 14–16). Herbert moves from the first part of the metaphor, finding a sweetness in contemplation of *My Master* ('the savour of his knowledge'), to God finding 'a sweet savour' in man. This poem's form reverses *Aaron*'s (each stanza made up of lines of 5, 4, 2, 4, 5 stresses). Poetic exercises in sweetness recur in this period. Sidney satirized them in *Astrophel and Stella*: 'To some a sweetest plaint a sweetest style affords' (6, l.9); 'Sweet kiss, thy sweets I fain would sweetly indite/Which even of sweetness sweetest sweetener art' (79, ll.1–2, and see also 36, ll.9–11, 80). Shakespeare avoids cloying by scattering eight sweets and its derivatives over *The Merchant of Venice* V.i.1–100. Herbert equals his eight in this poem's thirty lines, but its rich vocabulary of perfume prevents monotomy.

**1** 'To testify his independency upon all others, and to quicken his diligence in this kind, he used in his ordinary speech, when he made mention of the blessed name of our Lord and Saviour Jesus Christ, to add, *My Master*' (Nicholas Ferrar: *The Printers to the Reader*, pp. 7–8).

**2 Amber-grease:** a waxy, ash-coloured secretion of the sperm whale, a costly spice used as a perfume and, surprisingly, in cookery (Macaulay says Charles II's favourite dish was eggs and ambergris). Hence perhaps the *broth* that *feeds and fats my mind* of ll.9–10.

**7 them both:** the two words, *My Master*.

**12 a little so:** spicy, pleasant-smelling.

**16 the Pomander:** an aromatic ball, releasing its scent when *warmed* and *worked* like wax (a metaphor recurring in *The Country Parson*: see

*Affliction (1)*, p. 411, headnote). Sometimes it was kept in a container, also so called (deriving from Old French pome d'embre, apple of amber).

**17 A speaking sweet:** because it communicates its scent (an idea repeated in l.25).

**mend by reflection:** not entirely clear. Presumably explained by the context of the preceding stanza, the next lines, and the next stanza: were God to reflect the speaker's homage, 'My master', with the reciprocal reply, 'My servant', that pardon would warm the speaker, like a pomander, to even greater fragrance.

**23** *1633* has a comma at the end of this line.

**25 the breathing of the sweet:** using breathe in a now obsolete, specific sense, to emit odour, to smell (OED 2).

**26–30** Drawing on the fact that scents combine to create an even richer complex – what Herbert has already called *this curious broth,/ This broth of smells*. Here Herbert runs his scent metaphor in tandem with one of prosperous trade: *with gains, traffic* (i.e. trade), *this new commerce, employ*. Trade with the East in spices (*An oriental fragrancy*) was booming at this time, and the trading metaphor recurs with positive connotations elsewhere: see *The Country Parson*, ch.iv, p. 201, and note.

**The Foil:** not in *W*. Foil has a number of widely divergent senses, of which the weapon (cited by P) is irrelevant. Herbert intends either the thin leaf of metal which was put under a precious stone to increase its brilliance, i.e. an intensifier (OED 5) or something that serves by contrast to adorn or set off another thing (OED 6). The first sense seems more appropriate to *stars* as *the foil* [to] ... *virtues*; the second is less likely because none of the foils Herbert suggests contrast, they all intensify.

**1–2** If we on earth *below* could see heaven (the *sphere of virtue*, and the *shining grace*s in that sphere) ...

**3** ... as clearly as we can see our sky (*that* sphere *above*) ...

**4** ... it would be the better sky of the two. I.e. mankind can't see heaven; if he could, he would see how much better it (*This* in l.4) is than our sky. But (as the next stanza shows) God has used our sky and stars, and our sufferings, as a foil to set off our virtues and our griefs – but we are fools enough to ignore it.

**6 griefs to set off sinning:** H points out that Herbert tends to use *grief* of physical pain, rather than sorrow: he is saying that suffering therefore heightens our sense of our sins.

**The Forerunners:** not in *W*. A forerunner was one who heralded the approach of a great one, or, more generally, a prognostic or sign of something to come. The specific sense is made even more specific in the metaphor of the harbingers in the first and last stanzas; the more general sense fills the body of the poem, where white hairs and failing invention are signs of senescence.

**1 The harbingers are come. See, see their mark:** Harbingers were forerunners sent ahead to procure lodgings for a prince's progress or an army: they chalked the doors of the chosen houses (l.35). One can easily imagine how unpopular such selection was, with all the expense and disorder of enforced hospitality (cf. *King Lear*). The speaker's white hairs mark him out for the *winter* of old age, the king descending on him and demanding his *fee* (l.34).

**3-4 dispark/Those sparkling notions:** H glosses dispark as disempark, to turn out of a park, i.e. the speaker's bright ideas are evicted from the park of his brain where they were bred. P concurs, but adds the alternative, to take the sparkle away, to dull. Curiously, OED identifies neither sense for dispark, which means to divest parkland of its character and convert it to other uses (*Richard II* III.i.23: 'You have fed upon my seignories, disparked my parks, and fell'd my forest woods') – the sense the OED identifies as metaphorically used here. Such a sense vividly conveys the ravages a seignory would suffer when acting unwilling host to a royal visitation, i.e. the brain is a park devastated, its bright notions laid waste. Another word, disparkle, meaning to scatter, may possibly also lie behind these lines.

**6 Thou art still my God:** 'But I trusted in thee, O LORD: I said, Thou art my God' (*Psalm* 31: 14) (H).

**7 Good men ye be, to leave me my best room:** the harbingers had to leave some apartments for the host-household to occupy; the speaker has been allowed his heart, even though his brain has been requisitioned.

**9 I pass not:** I don't care.

**10 be out of fear:** isn't at risk.

**11-12** An obviously artless, childlike couplet, the very reverse of *fine and witty*, whose rhyme has already been used ironically in *The Sacrifice*, p. 28, ll.141–2.

**13ff** see Introduction, p. xxii.

**26 With canvas, not with arras clothe their shame:** i.e. use plain language, rather than ornate, when writing about love. *Arras* was rich tapestry fabric (originating from Arras in France), disparaged in *Dotage*, p. 163, l.3.

**31-2 I pass not ... Thou are still my God:** repeating ll.6 and 9, a sure sign of lost inventiveness, departed *sparkling notions*.

**36 So all within be livelier than before:** beautifully evoking the bustle before the arrival of the royal guests.

**The Rose:** not in *W*.

**4 size:** portion. Cf. *The Size*, pp. 134–5, ll.1–2, 31–3: *Content thee, greedy heart./Modest and moderate joys ... A Christian's state ... Is not a corpulent,* *but a thin and spare,/Yet active strength.*

**6 Colour'd griefs:** griefs that are painted to look nice. The metaphor is of make-up: rouged. But they are also pink with shame, *Blushing woes* (l.7).

**8 As if they could beauty spare:** as if they had beauty and to spare.

**9–10** A Freudian slip: he miscalls *delights* what they really are, *deceits*. Cf. the *thoughts/thorns* slip in *Love unknown*, p. 126, ll.51–2.

**12 pass'd my right away:** conveyed my rights to someone else. Cf. *Obedience*, p. 101, ll.6–8.

**14 what you now advise:** *to take more pleasure/In this world.*

**18** In *The Country Parson*, ch.xxiii, p. 230, Herbert recommends 'damask or white roses' as a purgative. See also *Life*, p. 92, l.15: dead roses are used *for cures*.

**19–20 Purging enmity disclose,/Enmity forbearance urgeth:** in literal terms a purgative evacuates the food that was bad for you, encouraging you to avoid it in the future. In moral terms, a purgative cleanses the excesses of pleasure and encourages abstinence thereafter.

**22 Be contracted to a rose:** the rose is a traditional symbol of youth, love, beauty, pleasure (e.g. Herrick's 'Gather ye rose-buds while ye may'). For the speaker, this connotation is joined by the purgative function: hence the rose itself is his answer to the blandishments of pleasure.

**30–31** I.e. though I oppose you, only say ... *Fairly* is used in a double sense: (1) justly; (2) prettily.

**Discipline:** not in *W*. Metrically interesting, each stanza alternating between an urgent trochaic trimeter catalectic ( ´ ˘ ´ ˘ ´ ) in the long lines slowed by a molossus ( ´ ´ ´ ) in the short third line.

**22 Love's a man of war:** 'The Lord is a man of war' (*Exodus* 15: 3) (H). It is most unlikely that Herbert also intends Cupid with his bow, as P suggests: Herbert had repudiated him in his first recorded sonnet (see Walton's *Life*, p. 344).

**26–7 That which wrought on thee,/Brought thee low:** Christ died for love of mankind.

**The Invitation:** not in *W*. Reverting to the banquet motif (*The 23 Psalm*, p. 169, ll.17–20, and the source to *Mary Magdalene*, p 477, headnote) which comes to predominate in this last sequence and to climax in *Love (3)*.

**3 Save your cost, and mend your fare:** H quotes *Isaiah* 55: 1–2, which lies behind the whole poem: 'Ho, everyone that thirsteth, come ye to the waters, and he that hath no money; come ye, buy, and eat; yea, come, buy wine and milk without money and without price. Wherefore do ye spend money for that which is not bread? and your labour for that which satisfieth not? hearken diligently unto me, and eat ye that which is good, and let your soul delight itself in fatness.'

**7-8 wine/Doth define:** the tippler in the tavern calling for his ale is actually *Naming* (l.9) himself: he is defined by what he drinks.

**14 arraign:** call to account, indict. The same idea as in *The Foil*, p. 172, l.6.

**21 without:** beyond, outside. The speaker invites all the elements of a worldly feast (taste, wine, pain, joy, love) and transcends or annuls them in his divine banquet with God.

**The Banquet:** not in *W*. The same stanza form as in *The Invitation*.

**7 the bowl:** the wine-bowl.

**10 some star:** picking up the motif first raised in *Perrirhanterium*, p. 13, l.171 *Take stars for money*, and replayed frequently thereafter, most sustainedly in *Artillery*, p. 135.

**13-15** Picking up the motif of the leavened and unleavened bread first raised in *The H. Communion*, p. 50, l.29–30: *Before that sin turn'd flesh to stone,/And all our lump to leaven*, and see n. for the biblical source. The metaphor is reversed here: as in G.M. Hopkins: 'Selfyeast of spirit a dull dough sours' (*I wake and feel the fell of dark, not day*, l.12). The sinful flesh is sour, heavy, malodorous; the spirit, like yeast, raises and sweetens it (literally, since sugar is released through the action of the enzyme) – all the more so, when some sweetener is added, as here.

**14 Made a head:** i.e. risen. Suggesting (1) the forces of good rising in opposition *To subdue ... sin* and (2) the risen, leavened dough.

**16 gums:** i.e. aromatic gums.

**25 Pomanders:** see *The Odour*, l.16n, pp. 479–80. This poem clearly sustains *The Odour*'s motifs, especially in the aura of *sweet*ness, a word whose derivatives are repeated in the first line of three successive stanzas here, and twice more thereafter (ll.1, 7, 13, 21, 39).

**30 broken:** God's love on earth is presented as *broken* in the image of the crucified Christ (broken on the cross); like ground sandalwood, say, or a kneaded pomander, his love is mangled to release most fragrance.

**42 Wine becomes a wing:** cf. *Easter Wings (1)* and *(2)*, pp. 40–41, and the flight images recurring in subsequent poems.

**45 I wipe mine eyes:** echoing St. John's vision of heaven: 'They shall hunger no more, neither thirst any more; neither shall the sun light on them, nor any heat. For the Lamb which is in the midst of the throne shall feed them, and shall lead them unto living fountains of waters: and God shall wipe away all tears from their eyes', and again: 'And God shall wipe away all tears from their eyes; and there shall be no more death, neither sorrow, nor crying, neither shall there be any more pain: for the former things are passed away' (*Revelation* 7: 16–17, 21: 4).

**51  my lines and life:** answering *The Collar*'s rebellious *My lines and life are free* (p. 149, l.4).

**The Posy:** not in *W*. A posy was a rhyme or motto. Puttenham, whom Herbert certainly read (see *The Altar*, pp. 394–5, headnote), has a lengthy section on emblems and devices, ending with the anagrammatic motto, or what he calls the 'posy transposed' (Book II, ch. xii). He is eager to display his own ingenuity in what he still dismisses as a form of 'courtly trifles'. Herbert's posy is ostentatiously leaden-footed and unwitty by comparison. Its naive literalism recalls the earnest artlessness of his other motto: *Thou art still my God ... He will be pleased with that ditty;/And if I please him, I write fine and witty* (*The Forerunners*, p. 172, ll.10–13). But it has a point: see ll.3–4 n.

**2  windows fill:** words, names and mottoes were commonly inscribed on rings and windows (see for instance Donne's *Valediction, of my name, in the window*).

**3–4  Less than the least/Of all thy mercies:** Nicholas Ferrar corroborates this in 'The Printers to the Reader', p. 8, as does Walton, p. 380. For the motto's source, cf. *Genesis* 32: 10. 'I am not worthy of the least of all the mercies, and of all the truth, which thou hast showed unto thy servant' and *Ephesians* 3: 8: 'Unto me, who am less than the least of all saints, is this grace given, that I should preach among the gentiles the unsearchable riches of Christ' (H). Herbert's motto spans the beginning and end of the Bible. Cf. *The H. Scriptures II*, p. 56, ll.5–8: *This verse marks that, and both do make a motion/Unto a third ... These three make up some Christian's destiny* and indeed Herbert's own.

**8  dictate:** stressed on the first syllable at this time (H).

**A Parody:** not in *W*. H quotes (from OED) Dryden's definition of parody as 'Verses patch'd up from great Poets, and turn'd into another Sense than their Author intended them' (the 1693 *Dedication* to his translation of Juvenal), in an attempt to defend Herbert from the intention to travesty his original, only 'to convert the profane to sacred use'. However, OED's first usage of parody and its derivatives comes from 1598 – Ben Jonson's *Every Man in His Humour* V.v, when the town gull's verses (a clumsy theft of Daniel's *Delia*) are read to general derision: 'This is stol'n ... A parody! A parody! With a kind of miraculous gift, to make it absurder than it was.' This is closer in date to Herbert, and there is no doubt that, as so often in *The Church*, Herbert is critically reapplying the motifs of worldly love-poetry to their highest object, to make the original appear 'absurder than it was'. He also considerably clarifies the jerky, knotty syntax of his original, and rejects its cloying profanities ('lip-joying bliss'; 'our souls shall kiss' etc. from its second stanza, not quoted here). The

object of his parody is attributed to William Herbert, 3rd Earl of
Pembroke (literary patron and godfather of Herbert's nephew):

> Soul's joy, now I am gone,
>> And you alone,
>> (Which cannot be,
> Since I must leave my self with thee,
>> And carry thee with me)
> Yet when unto our eyes
>> Absence denies
>> Each other's sight,
> And makes to us a constant night,
>> When others change to light;
>>> *O give no way to grief*
>>> *But let belief*
>>>> *Of mutual love,*
>>> *This wonder to the vulgar prove:*
>>> *Our Bodies, not we move.*

**1 Soul's joy:** critically making literal the hyperbole of the amatory
original.

**3 Which cannot be:** I can't be alone, because you (God, my *soul's joy*)
are with me – even when (as in stanza 2) the cheerfulness of your
company deserts me.

**20** I.e. when God's presence is unperceived, and awe fades, sin takes its
chance to suggest that God is absent.

**The Elixir:** In *W* titled *Perfection*, with *The Elixir* added in Herbert's
hand. *W*'s title derives from the original last stanza (see Appendix 2,
p. 332). The elixir is the philosopher's stone, supposedly having the
power to turn base metals into gold: the subject of much futile, semi-
scientific research at this time (see Ben Jonson's *The Alchemist*).

**7 prepossest:** having prior possession. This stanza is not in *W*.

**9–12** Cf. St. Paul's image of ultimate understanding of God's will: 'For
we know in part, and we prophesy in part. But when that which is
*perfect* is come, then that which is in part shall be done away ... For
now we see through a glass, darkly; but then face to face' (*1 Corinthians*
13: 9–12).

**14 Nothing can be so mean:** the Country Parson 'holds the rule, that
nothing is little in God's service: if it once have the honour of that
name, it grows great instantly' (ch. xiv, p. 219) (H). See Introduc-
tion, p. xxx, for G.M. Hopkins' similar sentiments.

**15 tincture:** an alchemical term for 'a supposed spiritual principle or
immaterial substance whose character or quality may be infused into
material things' (OED). *For thy sake* is this spiritual principle.

**23 touch:** used not only in its simple, but also its technical sense, 'to
test the fineness of gold by rubbing it on a touchstone' (OED).

(Touchstone was a smooth, dark, fine grained variety of quartz or jasper: the purity of the gold or silver alloys rubbed on it was judged by the colour of the streak they left.) Once tested, metals were also touched, i.e. marked with their standard of purity. In effect then it means here touched, tried, tested, and accepted (*own*) by God: a beautiful premonition of the Judgment Day returned to later in this last sequence.

**A Wreath:** this and the run of the final six poems create a sequence taking the reader out of life, through death, and to heaven – a personal eschatology. For the form of this poem and a comparison with *Coloss. 3.3.*, see Introduction, pp. xviiff.

**Death**

**11 fledge:** fully plumed and able to fly.

**13-14** Cf. *Indeed Christ's precious blood/Gave you* [the Church] *a colour once* (*Church-rents and schisms*, p. 137, ll. 12–13) (H).

**17-18** H compares to *Home*, p. 105, l. 58: *This last and lov'd, though dreadful day*. As it approaches, however, Herbert is at pains to alleviate its dread: hence the gentle levity of stanzas 1 and 2.

**21, 24 we can go die as sleep**: we might as well die, as sleep – it is indifferent whether we find our rest on the *down* of pillows, or the *dust* of the grave. *Half that we have* is the half of life not spent asleep.

**Dooms-day:** P cites an anonymous aubade from *England's Helicon* (1600) which he believes is parodied here. Each stanza begins 'Come away, come sweet Love' (or 'my sweet Love') in what is otherwise a straightforward love-lyric with no other parallels to this poem. However, like *Easter* and *The Dawning* (pp. 39, 108), *Dooms-day* is an aubade transposed to its transcendental apogee, the Resurrection of the dead. As in *Death*, the first stanzas dispel some of the traditional horrors of the poem's subject.

**1 Come away:** i.e. God, the *Lord* of l. 29, to whom all the poem's imperatives are addressed.

**12 Tarantula's raging pains:** the wolf-spider, or tarantula, was erroneously thought to be highly poisonous, and the effects of its bite to be cured by music and dancing (hence the dance-music of the tarantella). Herbert uses the proper noun for its effect (correctly termed tarantism).

**15-18 confession ... possession ... lesson:** let the graves confess to their dead (by giving them up). Otherwise they may in the end plead possession of the dead, having learned a lesson from the stubbornness of the flesh (and also of the living). This legal metaphor turns on the distinction between actual and legal possession. OED cites a definition from 1579: 'Possession is said in two ways, either actual

486

possession, or possession in law. Actual possession is when a man entreth in deed into lands or tenements to him descended or otherwise. Possession in law is when lands or tenements are descended to a man, and he hath not as yet really, actually, and in deed entered into them.' The graves could plead actual but not legal possession of the dead if they hung on to them long enough. They could have learned this corrupt lesson both from the greed of the living (who are unwilling to hand over land held but not inherited by them), and from the stubbornness of the flesh, which possesses the body in life, but should not claim it as its own, as a mere corporeal entity whose resurrection is denied. See *1 Corinthians* 15: 35ff (the lesson at the Burial of the Dead): 'Some man will say, How are the dead raised up? And with what body do they come? Thou fool, that which thou sowest is not quickened, except it die ... So also is the resurrection of the dead: It is sown in corruption; it is raised in incorruption: It is sown in dishonour; it is raised in glory: It is sown in weakness; it is raised in power: It is sown a natural body; it is raised a spiritual body.' Thus the graves must release their dead.

**20-24 Thy flock doth stray:** cf. *Psalm* 49: 14: 'Like sheep they are laid in the grave; death shall feed on them'. The *flock* are the dead, some of whose dust may be blown by the wind in the eyes of their friends, drowning them in tears, while the corrupting flesh of others is a source of stench and disease. H explains ll.21-2 as follows: 'Bodies turning to dust may be scattered by winds which bring mortals to shipwreck', but unless there is a superstition to this effect (which he does not produce), it hardly makes sense. Eyes stung to tears by dust are common, on the other hand, as are eyes drowning in tears. For an analogue to both, cf. *Macbeth* I.vii.22ff.: 'the blast ... Shall blow the horrid deed in every eye,/That tears shall drown the wind'. See also *Frailty*, p. 68, ll.15-16, *The Church-floor*, p. 64, ll.16-17; *Ungratefulness*, p. 79, ll.16-17. For ll.23-4 cf. Milton's *Lycidas*: 'The hungry Sheep look up, and are not fed,/But swoln with wind, and the rank mist they draw,/Rot inwardly, and foul contagion spread' (ll.125-7). Herbert is evidently drawing on contemporary pastoral lore.

**27-8** An image of dispersal well paralleled by T.S. Eliot's image of death: 'De Bailhache, Fresca, Mrs. Cammel, whirled/Beyond the circuit of the shuddering Bear/In fractured atoms' (*Gerontion*, ll.77-9). For Herbert, however, there is no order in the world comparable to the harmony of God (ll.29-30).

**29 broken consort:** referring to the scattered limbs of the dead. But a broken consort is, technically, a group of instruments of mixed families (wind and string) playing together. In Renaissance literature it was often used to evoke moral inadequacy. See F.W. Sternfeld: *Music in Shakespearean Tragedy* (London 1963), pp. 206-7.

**Judgement:** cf. the *dies irae* (the thirteenth-century sequence in the Mass for the Dead): 'Liber scriptus proferetur/in quo totum continetur,/unde mundus judicetur . . Quid sum miser tunc dicturus? . . . Recordare, Jesu pie, quod sum causa tuae viae . . .' H points out that Herbert *declines* (l.12) the doctrine of *merit* (l.10), proposed by *some* in ll.8–10. His faith lies instead in the Pauline doctrine that Christ took men's sins upon himself (l.15). See further Introduction, p. xxxii, on *Redemption*.

**8 some leaves therein:** pages in *ev'ry man's peculiar book*, his record of his life.

**13 And thrust a Testament into thy hand:** the speaker is returning Christ's testament of the Last Supper to him: 'And he took the cup, and gave thanks, and gave it to them, saying, Drink ye all of it; For this is my blood of the new testament, which is shed for many for the remission of sins' (*Matthew* 26: 27–8).

**Heaven:** for the form of this poem and an analogue, see Introduction, p. xix. The traditional four last things were Death, Judgment, Heaven, Hell. For Herbert, Hell is conspicuously absent. See further Introduction, p. xv and n.4, p. liii.

**5-6 among the trees and leaves?/Echo. Leaves:** judging by the preceding and following lines, Echo is saying that, not being mortal (l.4), it is not born among earthly trees and their foliage (l.5), but the *holy* (l.10) *leaves* (l.6) – i.e. of the Bible – which suffer no autumn, but *abide*: they are the *Echo of bliss* (l.11) (because they give us spiritual instruction). Cf. *The H. Scriptures I*, p. 56, l.13: *heav'n lies flat in thee*, and *II*, l.14: *This book of stars lights to eternal bliss*.

**8 Bide:** wait.

**Love (3):** a poem partly in dialogue where the distribution of speakers is clear except at l.16, which is spoken by the first-person narrator. 'The poem celebrates not the sacrament in the visible Church but the final communion in Heaven when God "shall gird himself, and make them sit down to meat, and will come forth and serve them"' (*Luke* 12: 37) (P). It does so in the simplest and most familiar of earthly terms, and a translucent tone of chastened tenderness.

**7 A guest ... worthy to be here:** cf. 'He that comes to the Sacrament hath the confidence of a guest, and he that kneels confesseth himself an unworthy one' (*The Country Parson*, ch. xxii, p. 228).

**17 taste my meat:** 'And as they were eating, Jesus took bread, and blessed it, and brake it, and gave it to the disciples, and said, Take, eat: this is my body' (*Matthew* 26: 26).

**Glory be to God on high:** not in *W*, and on separate final page in *B*. Spoken to the shepherds at the Nativity: 'And suddenly there was with the angel a multitude of the heavenly host praising God and saying, Glory to God in the highest, and on earth peace, good will toward men' (*Luke* 2: 13-14). See Introduction, p. xvi.

**The Church Militant:** in *W* there are five blank pages between the ending of *The Church* and this poem, and one blank page in *B*. It is a separate and early work. Internal references complimentary to Spain (ll.89, 265) and deprecatory of France (ll.241-6), and to the evangelization of the American colonies point to a date between 1620 (the settlement of the first New England colony by the Pilgrim Fathers) and 1624 (the Virginia Company's loss of patent) or 1625 (the death of James I, and accession of Charles I, who married Henrietta Maria of France, abandoning courtship of the Infanta of Spain). Anti-Catholic sentiments and the poem's style support an early date (H). A.M. Charles (op. cit. p. 82) suggests a date before 1619, when Herbert's eldest brother became Ambassador to France and public anti-French sentiments would have been imprudent, but this seems rather too early. There is no indication that Herbert contemplated publication of his poem. The courtship of the Infanta was at its height in February 1622/3, when Charles and Buckingham travelled incognito to Madrid, and in Cambridge Herbert delivered his Oration admitting two representatives of Habsburg thrones as Masters of Arts (see p. 326). In this year his friend Nicholas Ferrar became Deputy Treasurer of the Virginia Company (see ll.235ff.). The theme is that the Christian Church's development followed the sun's course from its inception in the East to its imminent departure for the uttermost West, *the American strand* (l.236). The poem's 279 lines are thus summarized by *The Son*, p. 164, ll.8-10, where the fruitful flame of Christ the son/sun is *carri'd far/From the first man in th' East, to fresh and new/Western discov'ries of posterity.*

**9 prove:** experience.

**10 bands:** bonds.

**11 this vine:** in the Old Testament Israel is often compared to a vine, most notably in the extended description of the planting and nurturing of the vineyard in *Isaiah* 5: 1-7 ('For the vineyard of the Lord of hosts is the house of Israel, and the men of Judah his pleasant plant').

**13 thy Spouse:** the Church.

**14 Trim:** lovely (with the sense also of being in good trim).

**15 Noah's shady vine:** see *Genesis* 9: 20ff.

**19-22** Noah's ark came to rest on Mount Ararat. *The other Ark* is primarily used metaphorically for *the old* (i.e. Jewish) *religion* (l.22). It was carried by the first patriarch, Abraham, to the land of Canaan (contrary to P's assertion, attributing to him 'the sojourn toward Egypt with the Ark of the Covenant'. The actual Ark of the

Covenant, containing the stone tables of the ten commandments, was only made by Moses long after the death of Abraham.) The process was further *pursu'd* by Moses and *finished* and *fixt* by Solomon, in whose temple the actual Ark of the Covenant came to rest. *Canaan* is Palestine: Herbert probably speaks of bringing the Ark from Canaan in the sense of bringing Judaism from the East to the West, rather than having in mind the complex peregrinations of the Israelites into and out of Canaan in the Old Testament. For the contradictions inherent in a precise interpretation of *from Canaan*, see H. N.B. that *from* is *B*'s correction of *W*'s *to*, suggesting a conscious authorial departure from historical literalism (Abraham travelled *to* Canaan) to the poem's overriding theme of a westward drift away from Canaan and towards Europe.

**26 earthquakes:** referring to the earthquake at the Crucifixion (*Matthew* 27: 51): 'the earth did quake, and the rocks rent'; *the partition-wall*: 'he is our peace, who hath made both one, and hath broken down the middle wall of partition between us' (*Ephesians* 2: 14). The reference is precise: St. Paul is referring specifically to the union of the faithful at Ephesus, who were Gentiles, with Christ's Jewish followers; Herbert intends the broader confluence of Jews and Gentiles into Christianity.

**27 the Ark in glory shone:** in the Old Testament the ark is mainly associated with the operations of war: its presence on the battlefield guaranteed victory, as its absence explained defeat; it was even associated with the presence of God himself. It contrasts with the humble pilgrim persona of Christianity.

**36 both:** steps.

**40-42** St. Macarius of Egypt (*c*.AD 300-390) and the hermit St. Anthony of Egypt (AD 251?-356) reversed the Mosaic story by turning Egypt (*Pharaoh*) Christian (*Moses*).

**43-4** One of the plagues Moses brought on Egypt before Pharaoh agreed to the Israelites' exodus was darkness: 'there was a thick darkness in all the land of Egypt three days: They saw not one another ... but all the children of Israel had light in their dwellings' in the part of Egypt called Goshen (*Exodus* 10: 22-3, 8: 22, 9: 26). Another was the plague of frogs (*Exodus* 8: 6) (H). Both are now reversed in a looking-glass typology.

**44, 46 for:** instead of.

**47-8** 'How dear are thy counsels unto me, O God' (*Psalm* 139: 17) and 'For who is he among the clouds: that shall be compared unto the Lord' (*Psalm* 89: 6 – both from BCP).

**49 Religion thence fled into Greece:** Christianity was first preached in Greece in the first century, mainly by St. Paul, whose chief centre was Corinth. The next lines describe how the ancient Greek arts (principally of philosophy) were metaphorically taken back to school again to learn afresh by Christian lights.

**51 pos'd:** nonplussed.

**set:** stumped.

**52 Sophisters:** in Greece sophists were originally teachers: the emergent pejorative sense probably intended here was purveyors of fallacious arguments. The *net* they are caught in is that of Christ's teaching, since he and his disciples were 'fishers of men' (*Mark* 1: 17).

**54 Christ-Cross:** the criss-cross-row was the alphabet (H).

**58–60 Egypt ... spent her period:** the Coptic church in Egypt became increasingly isolated from AD 451 and fell under permanent Arab rule in AD 642.

**61–2 those/Who, that they might subdue:** the Roman Empire.

**63 resounds:** celebrates, boasts.

**65–6 bliss,/Who:** i.e. man's salvation, lost by Satan's *ambush* of Adam and Eve.

**70** Referring to the wounding of the dead Christ (see *The Sacrifice*, p. 31, l.246n, p. 403), and punning on the *members* of Christ's Church. Rome gave up persecution of the Christians beginning with Galerius' edict of toleration in AD 311.

**71 The Shepherd's hook grew to a sceptre here:** metaphoric for the evolution of the early Roman bishops and episcopal authority (the bishop's crosier imitates the form of a shepherd's crook). Between Victor I (*c.*AD 189) and 268 the Roman Church became highly organized, and the list of early Roman bishops is exceptionally well recorded.

**72 Giving new names and numbers to the year:** this cannot refer to Pope Gregory XIII's much later reform of the calendar in 1582. H (and P following him) suggest vaguely 'some event of the early Christian centuries' replacing pagan festivals by the Christian calendar. One of the early bishops, Anicetus (*c.*155–66) discussed the dating of Easter. Christmas was fixed in the fourth century to coincide with the pagan observance of the winter solstice, which, according to the Roman calendar, fell at that time on 25 December. In AD 321 the Emperor Constantine (see ll.73, 93 below) ordered that Sunday should become a public holiday. And in Rome in the sixth century Dionysius Exiguus proposed beginning the Christian Era (AD) with the date of the Incarnation. His reform was accepted in due course throughout Christendom and remains in force to this day.

**73 th' Empire dwelt in Greece:** The Roman Emperor Constantine the Great (274/288–337) united the Christian Church to the secular state and took his capital from Rome to Greece. Constantinople was founded on the site of Byzantium in AD 330.

**74 Alexander's stem:** the descendants of Alexander the Great (356–323 BC). Alexander extended Greek rule over Persia and as far as India: his vast conquests spread the Greek language and institutions over the eastern world. That empire declined; his descendants were to be comforted by Constantine's reinstitution of the Christian Empire in Greece.

**75-8 In both of these:** Greece, and Rome: Greece had the arts (or *skill*); Rome the power (*strength*).

**against:** before, in preparation for the time when.

**79 rent:** division, schism, as in *Church-rents and schisms*, p. 136.

**79-83 th' Empire ... flew ... At length to Germany:** Charlemagne, King of the Franks, was crowned the first Holy Roman Emperor on Christmas Day, AD 800. *Empire* and *Arts* prepared the way for Religion here, as in Greece and Italy, because Charlemagne was a great military leader, extending his kingdom from the Franks to Lombardy, Bavaria, the Avar kingdom, Pannonia and Spain. He also encouraged ecclesiastical reform and the patronage of letters, fostering what is justly known as the Carolingian Renaissance, centred on his court at Aachen. It is not likely that Herbert is referring to the much later works of Holbein and Dürer, known to him from Nicholas Ferrar's purchases abroad, as H suggests.

**89 Spain in the Empire shar'd with Germany:** Spain was reached by Christian missionaries very early, according to tradition by St. Paul and St. James. It was conquered by Muslim Moors in the eighth century; their advance was first checked at Tours by the Frankish Charles Martel, in 732, and Northern Spain was won by his grandson, Charlemagne. His victories culminated in the capture of Barcelona in 801, making it part of the Holy Roman Empire, although the Christian reconquest of Spain was only finally completed by the reduction of Granada in 1492.

**91-2** The Church won a greater victory in England because the Church was defended by the crown, whose royal protection gave *the Church a crown to keep her state.*

**93 Constantine's British line:** Constantine was the son of St. Helena, who was reputedly of English birth. He was proclaimed Emperor at York in AD 306: hence the particular British pride in descent from him. In his reign toleration and Imperial favour were granted to the Christian faith.

**95 a sheet of paper:** the Donation of Constantine, a document of considerable influence in the Middle Ages, in which the Emperor Constantine was purported to have bestowed extensive secular powers on the Pope. Herbert was either unaware of, or chose to ignore its exposure as a forgery in the fifteenth century.

**98 Unto the farthest old meridian:** the meridian is the point at which the sun or a star reaches its highest altitude, and thus also the point of highest perfection preceding decline in any metaphysical application. Herbert is contrasting the sun of Christianity's *old meridian*, passing through England, with the new, in the Americas, the projected future zenith of Christianity's course around the globe.

**103 Sin did set out of Eastern Babylon:** *Eastern Babylon* is the Tower of Babel (commonly associated with Babylon), an emblem of man's hubris ('a tower, whose top may reach unto heaven'), whose destruction initiated man's dispersal, linguistic diversity, and enmity (see *Genesis* 11: 1–9). From ll.140ff. this will be typologically linked with the Babylon frequently denounced in *Revelation* (imagined at 17: 4–6, 18 as a scarlet whore, a great city whose sin had brought it to imminent destruction) which is traditionally associated with Rome. Sin names the palace of the Roman Catholic Church *Babylon* at l.182, and it is definitively identified as *Western Babylon* at l.211.

**105 He:** Sin, distinguished from the Church, which is feminine.

**109 at great cost:** rephrased at ll.111–14. The Egyptians paid dearly for making their foods their gods; they lost the salad (*sallet*) for a useless deity.

**112 Adoring garlic with an humble face:** a nice touch of straight-faced Herbertian humour. Cf. Donne: 'But as the Heathen make them several gods,/Of all God's Benefits, and all his Rods,/(For as the Wine, and Corn, and Onions are/Gods unto them, so Agues be, and war)' (*The Second Anniversary*, ll.425–8) (H).

**120 the same transplanted foolery:** see *Avarice*, p. 74, ll.9–12 for man's self-abasing veneration of money.

**127 for:** instead of.

**132 pills of sublimate:** poisonous pills of mercuric chloride, concealed in sugar (*conserve*); the equivalent of hubristic prophecy dressed up in verse.

**134 all would pull:** draw from the lottery.

**135 brave deceit:** fine lies. The oracles were renowned for their ambiguity.

**141–5 Nero and others ... a mightly flame:** Nero's reign (AD 54–68) was notorious for its corruption and extravagance (*Pleasure*). His decline began with the fire that destroyed a large part of Rome (18–24 July AD 64), which he blamed on the Christians, persecuting them as incendiaries for their 'hatred of the human race' (*odium humani generis*).

**147 Disparking oracles:** see *The Forerunners*, ll.3–4n, p. 481.

**149 a rogue:** i.e. Sin. Not Mahomet, as H, and P following him, suggest. Herbert is talking of the religions of Egypt and Greece, with their expectations of an afterlife reiterating worldly *carnal joy*. This is a *Mahometan stupidity* because it is comparable to the Koran's promise of pleasures beyond death.

**158 infidelity:** i.e. paganism (from the world infidel), lack of faith.

**166 Busy in controversies:** cf. *Divinity*, p. 131, ll.9–12; *Church-rents and schisms*, p. 137, l.16, attacking *debates and fretting jealousies* in the Church.

**169 a handsome picture:** either an allusion to the patronage of secular art by some Popes of the Renaissance (H), or to the (in Anglican eyes) unwarrantably *handsome* images of the Virgin Mary and other female figures in Catholic art.

**174 Christ's three offices:** of prophet, emperor and priest. Summarized at ll.171–3, and simultaneously exemplified by the Roman Catholic Church in Rome in the following lines.

**177 petty deities:** i.e. the saints. Cf. *To all Angels and Saints*, p. 75: Herbert rejects the worship of the Virgin Mary or the saints rather than God.

**178 oracular infallibities:** Papal infallibility was only declared in the Vatican Council of 1870, but in Catholic Christianity it is commonly held that there is more than one organ through which the faith receives infallible expression.

**182 Babylon:** cf. l.103 n.

**186 vizards:** masks.

**187 Anchorism:** from the Greek, meaning to withdraw, so tautologous with *retiredness*. Technically anchorism covers the retired, ascetic and silent life of the solitary hermit, and the coenobitic or communal life of a number of such hermits each living in his own separate cell. St. Anthony of Egypt (see ll.40–42n), himself a hermit, created such a community. In general this way of life originated in the desert.

**192-4 captivate:** used punningly. In the past, Sin took the Israelites (*Jews*) captive and transported them to Babylon; now Sin, in the guise of the Roman Catholic Church, *captivates* and *bewitches* its willing dupes into a *voluntary* exile, or *transmigration* (a term used originally specifically of the Jews' Captivity).

**195 post:** travel (fast).

**196 his public foot:** the customary obeisance to the Pope was to kiss his foot, or slipper (*mule*, l.204) (H).

**198 Nor his long journey:** the long journey to other states would not have befitted the Pope; his gout and inactive infirmity further precluded movement on his part.
**fur:** cf. *Employment (2)*, p. 76 ll.1–5: *He that is weary, let him sit.|My soul would stir ... Quitting the fur|To cold complexions needing it.*

**200 cloisterers:** monks or nuns (who live in cloisters).

**205-6 new and old Rome ... both together are one Antichrist:** Herbert is combining two common identifications of the Antichrist with (1) the Roman Emperors, particularly Caligula and Nero (cf. *Nero and others*, l.141) and with (2) the Pope. The biblical authorities include *2 Thessalonians* 2: 3–4: 'that day shall not come, except there come a falling away first, and that man of sin be revealed, the son of perdition; Who opposeth and exalteth himself above all that is called God, or that is worshipped; so that he as God sitteth in the temple of God, showing himself that he is God.' The destruction of Babylon

494

prophesied in *Revelation* equally combines these two associations, the first being operative for the original authors, the second for their Renaissance interpreters.

**207 their Janus:** the Roman God Janus, the gatekeeper, who had two faces: one in front, one behind. There is a symmetry of corruption in this *old crackt looking glass*.

**211 Western Babylon:** Rome. ('Babylon' is a movable term of disparagement: Petrarch and others called the exile of the Popes at Avignon from 1309–77 the Babylonian Captivity, while in 1520 Martin Luther's treatise on the *Babylonish Captivity of the Church* was a sustained attack on the bondage in which the Church had been held by Roman Catholic rituals.)

**215-18** Just as the heavenly sky is always illuminated, the moon rising as the sun sets, so Babylon is a permanent infernal night, the decline of the Eastern Babylon coinciding with the rise of the Western (cf. Yeats' theories of the gyres of history in *A Vision*).

**219 double crest:** a person could bear the surname and arms of another family as well as his own, by special grant from the crown (H). Satan's two Babylons are his double crest. The frequent references to hell and Satan here distinguish this work from *The Church*, where Herbert tends to avoid such allusions and excises them from earlier drafts as recorded in *W* (see Appendix 2, p. 331).

**221-2** Virtue diminishes in subsequent copies of the original perfect pattern; vice refines on vice. So Sin's latest, Roman throne is his best so far, while the modern Church is inferior to the primitive (cf. *Decay*, p. 96).

**225** The *first* Temple dated from the reign of Solomon (see *Sion*, p. 103, and notes), and was destroyed by the Babylonians in 586 BC. It was rebuilt as the *second* Temple in 520 BC, but was inferior to its predecessor.

**228 in the Jews and us deserveth tears:** 'But many of the priests and Levites and chief of the fathers, who were ancient men, that had seen the first house, when the foundation of this house was laid before their eyes, wept with a loud voice' (*Ezra* 3: 12) (H). We should now weep over the comparable inadequacy of the *late reformation* (l.226. OED quotes instances of the word reformation being used specifically for the movement of religious reform from 1563).

**232-4** The decline (*diminishings*) of the Church from its domination of *The spacious world* to its decay will be in proportion to its rise from small beginnings in Old Testament *Jewry*.

**235-6** For the proposed omission of these lines from *1633* see Walton, p. 381. The idea may have been common at Herbert's time; H cites a letter of 1634 by a Dr. Twisse, 'considering our English plantations of late, and the opinion of many divines concerning the Gospel's fleeting westward'.

**239 bane:** destruction.

**250 their gold:** the New World, particularly South America, was a source of great mineral wealth, freely pillaged by the Spanish, Cortes taking Mexico in 1519 and Francesco Pizarro conquering the Inca Empire in the 1530s (his prisoner, the Inca Emperor Atahualpa offered, and was refused, a ransom of a room 22 feet long, 17 feet broad and 9 feet high, filled with gold). In 1595 Ralegh embarked on an expedition up the Orinoco in search of El Dorado, returning with specimens of gold. The London Company was fuelled by hopes of easy profits from mining which were to be sadly disappointed on their settlement (the first British settlement in America) in Jamestown in 1607. The London Company later became the Virginia Company, of which Herbert's friend Nicholas Ferrar was Deputy Treasurer in 1622, the approximate date of this poem.

**254 We are more poor, and they more rich by this:** Herbert was not to know that the import of gold and silver from the Spanish Americas drastically affected the economy of Europe. Spanish prices were 3.4 times as high from 1600–1610 as they had been in the preceding decade, and smaller but comparable price rises affected France and England also. In this sense l.258 is prophetic: in England the maximum increase was not felt till the Civil War.

**255-6** The gold pillaged from the Americas will be repaid by *grace*, which will take flight from England, its *ancient place*, to the New World.

**259-60** For the sentiment, cf. *Outlandish Proverbs*, no. 670: 'No sooner is a temple built to God but the devil builds a chapel hard by.'

**265 Spain hath done one:** throughout the poem Herbert traces the dissemination of the Gospel through *Empire* (the military power, e.g. of Rome) and the *Arts* (e.g. as exemplified by the Greeks at l.49). Germany combined the two (l.83). Spain spread the Gospel through *one*, only – *Empire*, the territories in South America taken by its conquistadors. When *Art* joins its forces, the cycle will be complete again for the *Church* to be established, and *Sin* to destroy it.

**268-9 sound:** a wide natural inlet creating a harbour. Herbert envisages a cyclic process which ends where it began, in the East. The following lines suggest a circular typology comparable to that evoked in Donne's *Hymn to God my God in my Sickness*: the garden of Eden (properly, the garden 'eastward in Eden' *Genesis* 2: 8) was the place of the first Judgment, and will be the place of the last.

**270 both lights:** of Church and sun.

**274 as the Sun still goes both west and east:** Donne: 'As West and East/In all flat Maps (and I am one) are one' (*Hymn to God my God, in my Sickness*, ll.13–14).

**L'Envoy:** *Moth:* 'Is not l'envoy a salve?' *Armado:* 'No, page; it is an

epilogue or discourse to make plain/Some obscure precedence that
hath tofore been sain' (*Love's Labour's Lost* III.i.75ff.).

**1 King of glory, King of peace:** the first line of *Praise (2)*, p. 142.

**2 make war to cease:** 'He maketh wars to cease unto the end of the
earth' (*Psalm* 46: 9) (H).

**9 thy flesh hath lost his food:** i.e. God's flesh has lost its capacity to
sustain us (referring to the Eucharist; 'Take, eat: this is my body',
*Matthew* 26: 26). This is one in a series of negative injunctions asking
God not to allow Sin to annul the effects of Christ's sacrifice.

**11-16** Let Sin hold his breath in silence, till God's victory and his fall
release it all in sighs. Even that will not be enough; Sin will have to
bargain with the wind to finish off his sighing for him.

# INDEX OF FIRST LINES

# INDEX OF TITLES

# ABOUT THE EDITOR

ANN PASTERNAK SLATER is a Fellow of St Anne's College, Oxford. She has written on Shakespeare (*Shakespeare the Director*) and translated the memoirs of Alexander Pasternak (*A Vanished Present*).

This book is set in BASKERVILLE. John
Baskerville of Birmingham formed his
ideas of letter-design during his
early career as a writing-master
and engraver of inscriptions.
He retired in middle age,
set up a press of his
own and produced
his first book
in 1757.